ST/ESA/STAT/SER.W/33

Department of Economic and Social Affairs
Statistics Division

2018 Energy Balances

United Nations
New York, 2020

Department of Economic and Social Affairs

The Department of Economic and Social Affairs of the United Nations Secretariat is a vital interface between global policies in the economic, social and environmental spheres and national action. The Department works in three main interlinked areas: (i) it compiles, generates and analyses a wide range of economic, social and environmental data and information on which States Members of the United Nations draw to review common problems and to take stock of policy options; (ii) it facilitates the negotiations of Member States in many intergovernmental bodies on joint courses of action to address ongoing or emerging global challenges; and (iii) it advises interested Governments on the ways and means of translating policy frameworks developed in United Nations conferences and summits into programmes at the country level and, through technical assistance, helps build national capacities.

Note

Symbols of United Nations documents are composed of capital letters combined with figures.

General Disclaimer

The designations employed and the presentation of material in this publication do not imply the expression of any opinion whatsoever on the part of the Secretariat of the United Nations concerning the legal status of any country, territory, city or area, or of its authorities, or concerning the delimitation of its frontiers or boundaries.

Where the designation "country or area" appears in this publication, it covers countries, territories, cities or areas. In previous issues of this publication, where the designation "country" appears in the headings of tables, it should be interpreted to cover countries, territories, cities or areas.

The Energy Balances is published by United Nations Publications, 405 East 42nd Street, S-09FW001, New York, NY 10017 USA, Email: publications@un.org, Website: shop.un.org.

ST/ESA/STAT/SER.W/33

Sales number: E.21.XVII.5

ISBN 978-92-1-259162-9
eISBN 978-92-1-005524-6
ISSN 1014-465X
online ISSN 2412-1037

CONTENTS

CONTENTS

Energy Balances (2017 - 2018) (continued)

CONTENTS

Energy Balances (2017 - 2018) (continued)

Statistics compiled as of December 2020

INTRODUCTION

The *Energy Balances 2018* presents energy data for countries and areas in a format which shows the overall picture of the production, trade, transformation and consumption of energy products utilized in the region, published by the United Nations Statistics Division (UNSD). Such a format is useful in assessing and analysing supply and consumption patterns across both products and countries in detail on an internationally comparable basis.

It is the seventh edition of *Energy Balances* as a stand-alone publication, whereas until the 2011 edition it was part of the series *Energy Balances and Electricity Profiles*. The series was split in two and in addition to the *Energy Balances* a sister publication, the *Electricity Profiles*, is released.

This is the seventh issue where the standards brought about by the *International Recommendations for Energy Statistics*[1] (IRES) have been incorporated. IRES, in its draft form, was endorsed in 2011 by the United Nations Statistical Commission.

The old and the new energy balance formats have a number of similarities, for example the matrix presentation which shows energy sources in the columns and energy flows in the rows, taking into account the need for disaggregation of certain energy industries and final consumption. At the same time, to take a few examples of differences in the new publication, Natural gas is now shown on a net calorific basis (90% of the gross value), a less detailed oil product breakdown is displayed, and a different accounting of primary energy from Nuclear, Solar thermal and Geothermal sources is employed.

The level of detail of this matrix structure is presented in two formats: a detailed one for most countries; and a simplified one for countries of smaller size and/or with few types of energy flows to display.

It should be noted that unlike national energy balances designed for individual countries' various specific needs, the energy balance formats of UNSD have to accommodate the whole spectrum of national energy data which are received from national statistical offices and through official national publications.

Basic world energy data are also published in their natural units in the *Energy Statistics Yearbook*, which contains annual data on production, trade, stock changes, bunkers and supply (apparent consumption) for individual commodities for over 220 countries and areas of the world. In contrast with the *Energy Balances*, where tables refer to countries and show all products at once (in groups), in the *Energy Statistics Yearbook* the tables in most cases refer to products, showing all countries side by side. As such, in that publication, data for individual products can be identified, whereas here in this publication the products of the same type are grouped to allow easy visualisation of the overall energy flows.

The information contained in this publication is also available in electronic format.[2] Requests for information should be directed to United Nations Publications at: order@un.org.

Acknowledgement is due to the following specialized and intergovernmental agencies whose publications have been utilized in supplementing our statistics: African Energy Commission (AFREC), Asia-Pacific Economic Cooperation (APEC), Food and Agriculture Organization of the United Nations (FAO), International Atomic Energy Agency (IAEA), International Energy Agency of the Organisation for Economic Cooperation and Development (IEA/OECD), International Renewable Energy Agency (IRENA), International Sugar Organization (ISO), Organization of Arab Petroleum Exporting Countries (OAPEC), Organization of the Petroleum Exporting Countries (OPEC), Organización Latinoamericana de Energía (OLADE), Statistical Office of the European Union (Eurostat), World Energy Council (WEC). Acknowledgement is also made to governmental, energy and statistical authorities of the Member States which have been cooperative in providing data.

The annual energy data are being collected and processed by the Energy Statistics Section of UNSD, headed by Mr. Leonardo Souza. The processing of the

[1] Available at unstats.un.org/unsd/energystats/methodology/ires/

[2] For details, see unstats.un.org/unsd/energystats/pubs/balance/

INTRODUCTION

energy data and preparation for publication were carried out by Ms. Agnieszka Koscielniak, Ms. Costanza Giovannelli, Ms. Peng Guo, Mr. Man Soni and Mr. Graham Osborn.

Enquiries, comments and suggestions for improving this publication are welcome and should be addressed to: energy_stat@un.org.

CONCEPTS AND DEFINITIONS

INTRODUCTION

Concept of energy balances. The energy balance is an accounting framework for compilation and reconciliation of data on all energy products entering, exiting and used within a country or area during a reference period (in this publication, a year). Such a balance must necessarily express all forms of energy in a common accounting unit, and show the relationship between the inputs to and the outputs from the energy transformation processes. Energy balances should be as complete as possible so that all energy flows are, in principle, accounted for.

Balances can be compiled also for any particular energy product (energy commodity) and, in these cases, they are referred to as (energy) commodity balances. Apart from a few presentational differences such as showing secondary production together with primary production, commodity balances follow the general structure of energy balances (for more details, see IRES[3] Chapter 6).

Purpose of energy balances. The energy balance is a multipurpose tool to:

(a) Enhance the relevance of energy statistics by providing comprehensive and reconciled data on the energy situation on a national territory basis;

(b) Provide comprehensive information on the energy supply and demand on the national territory in order to understand the energy security situation, the effective functioning of energy markets and other relevant policy goals, as well as to formulate energy policies;

(c) Serve as a quality tool to ensure completeness, consistency and comparability of basic statistics;

(d) Ensure comparability between different reference periods and between different countries;

(e) Provide data for estimation of CO_2 emissions with respect to the national territory;

(f) Provide the basis for indicators of each energy product's role in the country's economy;

(g) Calculate efficiencies of transformation processes occurring in the country (e.g., refining, electricity production by combustion of fuels, etc.);

(h) Calculate the relative shares of the supply/consumption of various products (including renewables versus non-renewables) of the country's total supply/consumption;

(i) Provide an input for modeling and forecasting.

The multipurpose nature of the energy balance can also be increased by the development of supplementary tables which combine information from the balance with additional information on particular issues that are not explicitly reflected in the balance itself, for example combining total energy supply with population or national income data to obtain energy indicators.

Detailed and aggregated energy balances. Energy balances can be presented in both detailed and aggregated formats. The degree of detail depends on the policy concern, data and resource availability, and the underlying classifications used. In this publication, the aggregated (or simplified) format is used for countries of small size and/or for which the types of energy flows are few and far between, and as a result can be summarised without much information loss.

SCOPE AND GENERAL PRINCIPLES OF ENERGY BALANCE COMPILATION

The scope of an energy balance. The scope of an energy balance is determined, inter alia, by the territory, product and flow boundaries (see IRES for details on these boundaries):

(a) Territory boundary – defined by the boundary of the national territory of the compiling

[3] Available at unstats.un.org/unsd/energystats/methodology/ires/

CONCEPTS AND DEFINITIONS

country or the equivalent concept for other areas that do not constitute a country;

(b) Product boundary – defined by the scope of all energy products shown in the balance columns (see pages xiii-xxi for details);

(c) Flow boundary – defined by the scope of energy flows shown in the balance rows (see pages ix-xiii for details).

The scope of an energy balance does not include:

(a) Passive energy such as the heat gain of buildings and solar energy falling on the land to grow crops, etc;

(b) Deposits of energy resources and reserves (which can be nevertheless considered in additional tables);

(c) Extraction of any materials not covered in primary energy production

(d) Peat, waste and biomass used for non-energy purposes.

When compiling an energy balance, some **general principles on the coverage and structure of the balance** should be taken into account. These principles are as follows:

(a) The energy balance is compiled with respect to a clearly defined reference period (this publication displays annual balances considering calendar years, unless otherwise specified).

(b) The energy balance is a matrix represented by rows and columns;

(c) Columns represent groups of energy products that are available for use in the national territory or equivalent area;

(d) The column "Total" contains cells which provide the sum of the data entries in the corresponding row; however, the meaning of the cells in the "Total" column is not the same for all rows of the balance (see below);

(e) Rows represent energy flows;

(f) A separate row is reserved for statistical difference, calculated as the numerical difference between the total supply of a fuel, electricity or heat and the total use of it;

(g) Rows and columns should contain homogeneous information (refer to the same products and flows as defined in their headers);

(h) The detailed energy balance should contain sufficient rows and columns to show clearly the relationship between the inputs to and outputs from transformation processes (production of secondary energy products);

(i) All entries should be expressed in one energy unit (here, Terajoules are used); the conversion between energy units should be through the application of appropriate conversion factors (see pages xxiii-xxxiv);

(j) Net calorific values should be used for measuring the energy content of energy products;

(k) Production of primary and secondary energy as well as external trade in energy products, stock changes, final energy consumption and non-energy use should be clearly separated to better reflect the structure and relationships between energy flows and to avoid double-counting.

(l) To give a primary energy equivalent to electricity produced from non-combustible energy sources the "physical energy content" method should be used. According to this method the normal physical energy value of the primary energy form is used for the production figure. This is in contrast to the "partial substitution method" which requires assigning to such electricity a primary energy value equal to the hypothetical amount of fuel required to generate an identical amount of electricity in a thermal power station using combustible fuels.

In the "physical energy content" method, the normal physical energy value of the primary energy form is used for the production figure. For primary electricity, this is simply the gross generation figure for the source. Care is needed when expressing the percentage contributions from the various sources of national electricity production. As there is no transformation process recognized within the balances for the production of primary electricity, the respective percentage contributions from thermal and primary electricity cannot be calculated using a "fuel input" basis. Instead, the various contributions should be calculated from the amounts of electricity generated from the power stations classified by energy source (coal, nuclear, hydro, etc.).

Which energy product is primary and which is secondary is determined by the principle of multiple uses: the primary energy form should be the first energy form downstream in the production process for which multiple energy uses are practical. For example, in the case of nuclear energy, the choice is between the energy content of the nuclear fuel, the heat generated in the reactors and the electricity produced. Nuclear fuels are outside the scope of energy balances, as they do not fit the multiple energy uses criterion. On the other hand, nuclear electricity is not primary because the nuclear heat from the atomic fission that moves the turbines can also be used as heat. As a result of this principle, nuclear heat is chosen as the primary form.

For electricity and heat, the application of this principle leads to the choice of the following primary energy forms:

- Heat for nuclear, geothermal and solar thermal;
- Electricity for hydro, wind, tide, wave and other marine, and solar photovoltaic.

In the case of electricity generation from primary heat (nuclear, geothermal and solar thermal), it can be difficult to obtain measurements of the heat flow to the turbines. As a result, an estimate of the heat input is often used based on an efficiency of 33% for nuclear and solar thermal, and 10% for geothermal. This means that, in the absence of measurements of heat input, the equivalent primary nuclear heat and solar thermal heat is estimated as 3 times the nuclear electricity and solar thermal electricity produced, respectively, and the equivalent geothermal heat is estimated as 10 times the geothermal electricity output.

Where there is direct use of geothermal heat, the primary energy is equivalent to the use; whereas heat coming from geothermal heat plants is considered the output of a conversion process with a 50% efficiency in relation to its geothermal heat input. This means that in the latter case the primary energy is equivalent to twice the heat produced. This stems from the generally low quality of the heat from geothermal sources.

DESCRIPTION OF THE ROWS OF THE ENERGY BALANCE

Top block – Energy supply

The top block of an energy balance – *Energy supply* – is intended to show flows representing energy entering the national territory for the first time, energy removed from the national territory and stock changes. The entering flows consist of production of primary energy products and imports of both primary and secondary energy products. The flows removing energy from the national territory are exports of primary and secondary energy products and international bunkers.

The balance item of the flows described above and the changes in stock represents the amount of energy which is available on the national territory during the reference period. This aggregate is named **Total energy supply**.

Primary production (row 1) refers to production of primary energy, which in turn is defined as the capture or extraction of fuels or energy from natural energy flows, the biosphere and natural reserves of fossil fuels within the national territory in a form suitable for use. Inert matter removed from the extracted fuels and quantities reinjected, flared or vented are not included. The resulting products are referred to as "primary" products.

Secondary production, that is, the manufacture of energy products through the process of transformation of primary fuels or energy, is not displayed under this item, but in Transformation.

Some conventions are used to account for

CONCEPTS AND DEFINITIONS

primary production of electricity and heat consistently with IRES, and are described in the previous section.

Production of **Biomass** and **wastes,** as well as **Peat**, includes only that portion used for energy purposes.

Imports (row 2) of energy products comprise all fuel and other energy products entering the national territory. Goods simply being transported through a country (goods in transit) and goods temporarily admitted are excluded but re-imports, which are domestic goods exported but subsequently readmitted, are included. The bunkering of fuel outside the reference territory by national merchant ships and civil aircraft engaged in international travel is excluded from imports.

Exports (row 3) of energy products comprise all fuel and other energy products leaving the national territory with the exception that exports exclude quantities of fuels delivered for use by merchant (including passenger) ships and civil aircraft, of all nationalities, during international transport of goods and passengers. Goods simply being transported through a country (goods in transit) and goods temporarily withdrawn are excluded but re-exports, foreign goods exported in the same state as previously imported, are included.

For electricity, trade data include "goods in transit", i.e. electricity transmitted through the country from one neighbour to another, as there is no practical way of discerning which quantities are re-exported and which are consumed by the transit country.

In the energy balance format, imports are positive numbers, while exports are negative numbers and carry a negative sign (-).

International marine bunkers (row 4) are quantities of fuels delivered to merchant (including passenger) ships, of any nationality, for consumption during international voyages transporting goods or passengers. International voyages take place when the ports of departure and arrival are in different national territories. Fuels delivered for consumption by ships during domestic transportation, fishing or military uses are not included here. For the purposes of energy statistics International Marine Bunkers are not included in exports. In the energy balance format, International Marine Bunkers are negative numbers and carry a negative sign (-).

International aviation bunkers (row 5) are quantities of fuels delivered to civil aircraft, of any nationality, for consumption during international flights transporting goods or passengers. International flights take place when the ports of departure and arrival are in different national territories. Fuels delivered for consumption by aircraft undertaking domestic or military flights are not included here. For the purposes of energy statistics International Aviation Bunkers are not included in exports. In the energy balance format, International Aviation Bunkers are negative numbers and carry a negative sign (-).

Stocks – For the purposes of energy statistics, stocks are quantities of energy products that are held on the national territory and can be used to: (a) maintain service under conditions where supply and demand are variable in their timing or amount due to normal market fluctuations, or (b) supplement supply in the case of a supply disruption. Stocks used to manage a supply disruption may be called "strategic" or "emergency" stocks and are often held separately from stocks designed to meet normal market fluctuations. **Stock changes** (row 6) are defined as the increase (stock build) or decrease (stock draw) in the quantity of stock over the reporting period and are thus calculated as the difference between the closing and opening stocks.

A positive number indicates a reduction in stocks and thus an increase in available energy; the negative sign (-) indicates a net increase in stocks and thus a decrease in energy available for consumption.

Total energy supply (row 7) reflects, for each group of products, the supply of energy embodied in the energy products included in that particular group. The total supply of energy on the national territory is shown under the column "Total".

It is computed as: Total energy supply = primary production (row 1) + imports (row 2) + exports (row 3) + international marine bunkers (row 4) + international aviation bunkers (row 5) + stock changes (row 6).[4]

[4] Because of the sign convention in energy balances, where quantities that contribute to the supply receive positive signs while

CONCEPTS AND DEFINITIONS

Statistical difference (row 8) in the energy balance is the numerical difference between the total supply of the group of energy products described by the respective column and the total use of it. It is calculated by subtracting latter from the former, as follows: Statistical difference = total energy supply (row 6) + transfers (row 9) + transformation (row 10) + energy industries own use + losses – final consumption.

The statistical difference is a discrepancy that arises from various practical limitations and problems related to the collection of the data which make up supply and demand. The data may be subject to sampling or other collection errors, and/or be taken from different data sources which use different time periods, different spatial coverage, different fuel specifications or different conversions from volume to mass or from mass to energy content in the supply and demand sides of the balance.

The middle block

The main purpose of the middle block of an energy balance is to show transfers, energy transformation, energy industries own use and losses.

Transfers (row 9) are essentially statistical devices to overcome practical classification and presentation issues resulting from changes in use or identity of a product. Transfers comprise products transferred and interproduct transfers. Products transferred refer to the reclassification (renaming) of products which is necessary when finished oil products are used as feedstock in refineries. Interproduct transfers refer to the movements of fuels between product categories because of reclassification of a product which no longer meets its original specification. The transferred product (negative sign) is often blended with its host (positive sign). Where a product belonging to a column group is transferred out (negative sign) and another belonging to the same column group receives transfers in (positive sign), the resulting net transfers are displayed.

Transformation (row 10) describes the processes that convert an energy product into another energy product which, in general, is more suitable for specific uses. It occurs when part or all of the energy content of a product entering a process moves from this product to one or more different products leaving the process (e.g., coking coal to coke, crude oil to oil products, and fuel oil to electricity).

Energy entering transformation processes are shown with a negative sign to represent the input and energy which is an output of transformation activities is shown as a positive number. The sum of cells in each row appearing in the column "Total" should therefore be negative as transformation always results in a certain loss of energy when expressed in energy units. Depending on the level of aggregation, there are instances when only a residual negative number is displayed, for example in the total coal column (of the simplified format) where both a negative coking coal input and a positive coke oven coke output are collated.

Transformation is broken down into 11 types of processes in the detailed energy balance format, whereas the simplified energy balance format displays a breakdown of just three types. These processes are described as follows:

- **Electricity plants** refer to plants producing only electricity. The electricity may be obtained directly from natural sources such as hydro, geothermal, wind, tidal, marine, solar energy or from fuel cells, or from the heat obtained from the combustion of fuels or nuclear reactions. For the simplified balance format, Electricity plants include CHP and Heat plants.

- **CHP plants** (Combined Heat and Power) refer to plants which produce both heat and electricity from at least one generating unit in the plant. They are sometimes referred to as "co-generation" plants.

- **Heat plants** refer to plants (including heat pumps and electric boilers) designed to produce heat only, for deliveries to third parties. Deliveries of fuels for heat generated by an autoproducer (which are enterprises whose principal activity is NOT heat production) for its own purposes are classified within the part of final consumption where they are consumed, and not as part of transformation.

---

those that are removed receive negative signs, these parts can be straightly added up.

CONCEPTS AND DEFINITIONS

• **Coke ovens** are large ovens within which coke oven coke, coke oven gas and coal tars are produced by high temperature carbonisation of coking coal.

• **Briquetting plants** comprise Patent fuel plants, Brown coal briquette plants and Peat briquette plants. **Patent fuel plants** are plants manufacturing patent fuels. **Brown coal briquette plants** are plants manufacturing brown coal briquettes (BKB). **Peat briquette plants** are plants manufacturing peat briquettes (included here are plants producing all kinds of peat products from primary peat).

• **Liquefaction plants** comprise Coal liquefaction plants and Gas to liquid (GTL) plants. **Coal liquefaction plants** are plants where coal is used as a feedstock to produce liquid fuels by hydrogenation or carbonisation. They are also known as coal-to-liquid (CTL) plants. **Gas-to-liquid (GTL) plants** are plants in which natural gas is used as a feedstock for the production of liquid fuels. The liquid fuels are usually used as vehicle fuels. Note that the gas-to-liquid plants are quite different from LNG plants which convert gaseous natural gas into liquid natural gas.

• **Gas works** (and other conversion to gases) are plants manufacturing gases for distribution to the public either directly or after blending with natural gas. Note that the gases are collectively referred to as "Gas Works Gas and other manufactured gases for distribution'; short name - gas works gas. Some gas works may produce coke as well as gas.

• **Blast furnaces** are furnaces which produce blast furnace gas as a by-product when making pig iron from iron ore. During the process, carbon, mainly in the form of coke, is added to the blast furnace to support and reduce the iron oxide charge and provide heat.

• **NGL plants and gas blending** comprise Natural gas liquids (NGL) separation plants and Natural gas blending plants. **Natural gas liquids (NGL) separation plants** are plants involved in the separation of water, impurities and natural gas liquids from natural gas. In addition, the activities of these plants may also involve fractionation of the recovered natural gas liquids. **Natural gas blending plants** are plants, separate from gas works, in which substitute natural gas (see gas works gas), petroleum gases or biogases are mixed with natural gas for distribution in the gas mains. Where blending of substitute natural gas with natural gas takes place within gas works the blending is considered part of the gas works process.

• **Oil refineries** are plants which transform crude oil and other hydrocarbons (together with additives, feedstocks and natural gas liquids) into finished oil products. Typical finished products are liquefied petroleum gases, naphtha, motor gasoline, gas oils, aviation fuels and other kerosene, and fuel oils.

• **Charcoal plants** are plants in which wood or other vegetal matter is carbonised through slow pyrolysis to produce charcoal. Charcoal plants are shown separately in the simplified balance format, but they are grouped with "Other transformation" in the detailed balance.

• **Other transformation**: In the detailed balance format, it comprises Charcoal plants, Petrochemical plants and Other transformation processes not elsewhere classified. In the simplified balance format, it comprises all transformation processes other than: Electricity plants, CHP plants, Heat plants and Charcoal plants. **Petrochemical plants** are plants which convert hydrocarbon feedstock into organic chemicals, intermediate compounds and finished products such as plastics, fibres, solvents and surfactants.

Energy industries own use refers to consumption of fuels and energy for the direct support of the production, and preparation for use of fuels and energy. Quantities of fuels which are transformed into other fuels or energy are not included here but within transformation. Neither are quantities which are used for transportation purposes in the energy industry. These quantities are reported within final consumption, more specifically in Transport. The negative sign is used for entries under this item.

Losses refer to losses during the transmission, distribution and transport of fuels, heat and electricity. Losses also include venting and flaring of manufactured gases, losses of geothermal heat after production and pilferage of fuels or electricity. Production of secondary gases includes quantities subsequently vented or flared. This ensures that a balance can be constructed between the use of the primary fuels from which the gases are derived and the production of the gases. The losses carry a negative sign.

CONCEPTS AND DEFINITIONS

The bottom block - Final consumption

The bottom block of an energy balance - *final consumption* - covers *final energy consumption*, as well as *non-energy use* of energy products. It excludes deliveries of fuel and other energy products for use in transformation processes (covered in the middle block) and the use of energy products for energy needs of the energy industries (also covered in the middle block).

Energy consumers are grouped into three main categories: (i) Manufacturing, construction and non-fuel mining industries, (ii) Transport and (iii) Other, and further disaggregated as applicable.

Final consumption refers to all fuel and energy that is delivered to users for both their energy and non-energy uses which do not involve a transformation process.

Final energy consumption refers to the consumption of primary and secondary energy by Manufacturing, construction and non-fuel mining, by Transport, and by Others (agriculture, forestry and fishing, commerce and public services, households, and other consumers).

Manufacturing, construction and mining refers to final energy consumption by manufacturing, construction and non-fuel mining industries. The final consumption recorded under this category covers the use of energy products for energy purposes by economic units belonging to the industry groups listed below (excluding the use of energy products for transport, which is recorded under Transport in its respective row).

- Iron and steel
- Chemical and petrochemical
- Non-ferrous metals
- Non-metallic minerals
- Transport equipment
- Machinery
- Mining and quarrying
- Food and tobacco
- Paper, pulp and print
- Wood and wood products (other than pulp and paper)
- Textile and leather
- Construction
- Industries, not elsewhere specified

The breakdown into these groups is available only for the detailed energy balance format.

Transport refers to the consumption of energy products by any economic entity to transport goods or persons between points of departure and destination within the national territory. Quantities of fuels delivered to merchant (including passenger) ships and civil aircraft, of any nationality, for consumption during international voyages transporting goods or passengers are not included here, but in international bunkers.

The category "transport" is subdivided into the following modes of transport:

- Road
- Rail
- Domestic aviation
- Domestic navigation
- Pipeline transport
- Transport not elsewhere specified

In the simplified energy balance format, Rail and Pipeline transport are grouped with Transport not elsewhere specified into the category "Other transport".

Energy used at compressor and/or pumping stations in pipeline transport (fuels and electricity) within the national territory or equivalent area is included in transport. However, it is recognized that some countries or areas with a large production of oil and gas find it difficult to split between energy for pipeline transport and other fuels consumed in the oil and gas extraction industries.

Other: This group consists of energy consumers not classified in Manufacturing, construction and non-fuel mining industries, and is subdivided into the following subgroups:

- Agriculture, Forestry, Fishing
- Commerce and public services
- Households
- Not elsewhere specified

Fuels used in tractors for the purpose of farming, transport by military vehicles and fishing are not considered, by convention, as fuels for transport purposes and are included here. Fuels and other energy products' consumption in fishing covers all fishing vessels, including those engaged in deep-sea fishing.

CONCEPTS AND DEFINITIONS

Non-Energy Use consists of the use of energy products as raw materials for the manufacture of products outside the scope of SIEC, as well as for direct uses that do not involve using the products as a source of energy, nor as a transformation input. Examples are lubrication, sealing, preservation, road surfacing, and use as a solvent.

DESCRIPTION OF THE COLUMNS OF THE ENERGY BALANCE

The description of the energy balance columns is done in two parts: first, for both energy balance formats the products grouped under each column are listed; then, the products themselves are defined.

Detailed energy balance format

Column 1 (Primary coal and peat) includes Hard coal, Brown coal, Peat and Oil shale.

Column 2 (Coal and peat products) includes Coal coke, Patent fuel, Brown coal briquettes (BKB), Coal tar, Coke oven gas, Gas works gas, Recovered gases, Other coal products and Peat products.

Column 3 (Primary oil) includes Conventional crude oil, Natural gas liquids (NGL), Additives and oxygenates, and Other hydrocarbons.

Column 4 (Oil products) includes Feedstocks, Refinery gas, Ethane, Liquefied petroleum gases (LPG), Naphtha, Aviation gasoline, Motor gasoline, Gasoline-type jet fuel, Kerosene-type jet fuel, Other kerosene, Gas oil/diesel oil, Fuel oil, White spirit and SBP industrial spirits, Lubricants, Paraffin waxes, Petroleum coke, Bitumen, and Other oil products n.e.c..

Column 5 (Natural gas) includes Natural gas. Other gases (e.g., Biogas, LPG or Manufactured gas) are included only when blended with Natural gas, their quantities appearing as outputs of the respective transformation process (or in the transfers row in some cases).

Column 6 (Biofuels and waste) includes Fuelwood, wood residues and by-products, Bagasse, Animal waste, Black liquor, Other vegetal material and residues, Charcoal, Biogasoline, Biodiesels, Bio jet kerosene, Other liquid biofuels, Biogases, Industrial waste, and Municipal waste.

Column 7 (Nuclear) includes Heat from nuclear sources as well as the primary heat equivalent of electricity production from nuclear sources.

Column 8 (Electricity) includes Electricity.

Column 9 (Heat) includes Heat produced for sale and the primary heat equivalent of electricity production from geothermal and solar thermal sources. It also includes direct use of solar thermal heat and geothermal heat.

For columns 7, 8 and 9, see pages viii and ix for the choice of the primary energy for each source and respective notional efficiencies used to back calculate this primary energy from electricity and heat generation. In the case of electricity sources whose primary energy equivalent is displayed under heat and nuclear, the electricity production is secondary and as such shown under transformation (electricity plants or CHP plants). The equivalent primary energy is shown as a transformation input (negative sign) on the same row under the appropriate column.

Nuclear is displayed separately from electricity and heat to distinguish it from the renewable primary energy production from other sources.

Column 10 (Total energy) aggregates columns 1 to 9, summarising, among other flows, Primary energy production, Energy imports and exports, Total energy supply, Transformation losses, and Final consumption.

Column 11 (of which: renewables) distinguishes the part of Total energy that comes from renewable sources as recommended in IRES. From Column 6, it includes Fuelwood, wood residues and by-products, Bagasse, Animal waste, Black liquor, Other vegetal material and residues, Charcoal, Biogasoline, Biodiesels, Bio jet kerosene, Other liquid biofuels, Biogases, and 50% of Municipal waste[5]. It does not include Industrial waste and 50% of Municipal waste. From Column 8, it includes all primary production of

[5] In the absence of details on what percentage of Municipal waste comes from biomass and what percentage does not (which is the criterion to distinguish between renewable and non-renewable Municipal waste defined in IRES), a 50-50 split is used.

CONCEPTS AND DEFINITIONS

Electricity, as well the secondary production when coming from solar thermal and geothermal sources (secondary production is shown in Transformation, according to energy balance conventions). From Column 9, it includes all primary production of Heat, including primary Heat calculated from geothermal and solar thermal electricity production based on notional efficiencies[6], as well as the direct use of geothermal and solar thermal heat.

Apart from Primary production, figures from Column 11 should be taken with caution. For electricity and heat, by the nature of these energy products, the percentage of renewable imports and exports can rarely be determined. The same happens with consumption/use when the production of electricity and heat from renewable sources is mixed with that from non-renewable sources (for example, if hydroelectricity and electricity from the combustion of coal are distributed through the same network). Because of these practical limitations, no attempt is made at determining the renewable share for these cases. As a result, no part of imports and exports of heat or electricity, nor their consumption, losses or own use, is considered as renewable in Column 11. The exception is Direct use of geothermal heat and solar thermal heat, for which data are available primarily on the consumption side and thus can be distinguished as renewable.

Simplified energy balance format

Column 1 (All coal) is an aggregation of columns 1 and 2 of the detailed format, including Hard coal, Brown coal, Peat, Oil shale, Coal coke, Patent fuel, Brown coal briquettes (BKB), Coal tar, Coke oven gas, Gas works gas, Recovered gases, Other coal products and Peat products.

Column 2 (All oil) is an aggregation of columns 3 and 4 of the detailed format, including Conventional crude oil, Natural gas liquids (NGL), Additives and oxygenates, Other hydrocarbons, Feedstocks, Refinery gas, Ethane, Liquefied petroleum gases (LPG), Naphtha, Aviation gasoline, Motor gasoline, Gasoline-type jet fuel, Kerosene-type jet fuel, Other kerosene, Gas oil/diesel oil, Fuel oil, White spirit and SBP industrial spirits, Lubricants, Paraffin waxes, Petroleum coke, Bitumen, and Other oil products n.e.c..

Column 3 (Natural gas) includes Natural gas. Other gases (e.g., Biogas, LPG or Manufactured gas) are included only when blended with Natural gas, their quantities appearing as outputs of the respective transformation process (or in the transfers row in some cases).

Column 4 (Primary biofuels / Waste) includes Fuelwood, wood residues and by-products, Bagasse, Animal waste, Black liquor, Other vegetal material and residues, Biogasoline, Biodiesels, Bio jet kerosene, Other liquid biofuels, Biogases, Industrial waste, and Municipal waste. It is similar to column 6 of the detailed format, the difference being that it does not include Charcoal (which is a secondary biofuel).

Column 5 (Charcoal) includes Charcoal.

Column 6 (Electricity) is an aggregation of columns 7, 8 and 9 of the detailed balance format, including Heat and Electricity, including from nuclear sources (see the explanation of those columns for reference). The countries and areas chosen to have their balances displayed in the simplified format in general do not have significant heat or nuclear production.

Column 7 (Total energy) aggregates columns 1 to 6, summarising, among other flows, Primary energy production, Energy imports and exports, Total energy supply, Transformation losses, and Final consumption. It includes the same products as column 10 of the detailed format.

Column 8 (of which: renewables) makes an attempt at distinguishing the part of Total energy that comes from renewable sources of energy, as recommended in IRES. It includes the same products as column 11 of the detailed format, as well as the same flows (but in less detail).

Product definitions

Hard coal – coals with a gross calorific value (moist, ash-free basis) which is not less than 24 MJ/kg or which is less than 24 MJ/kg provided that the coal

[6] This calculated primary Heat input to electricity production from geothermal and solar thermal sources appears with a positive sign in Primary production and with a negative sign in Transformation, so as to depict its conversion into electricity.

has a vitrinite mean random reflectance greater than or equal to 0.6 per cent. Hard coal comprises anthracite and bituminous coals.

Brown coal – coals with a gross calorific value (moist, ash-free basis) less than 24 MJ/ kg and a vitrinite mean random reflectance less than 0.6 per cent. Brown coal comprises sub-bituminous coal and lignite.

Peat – a solid fuel formed from the partial decomposition of dead vegetation under conditions of high humidity and limited air access (initial stage of coalification). It is available in two forms for use as a fuel, sod peat and milled peat. Only peat used as fuel is included.

Oil shale – A sedimentary rock which contains organic matter in the form of kerogen. Kerogen is a waxy hydrocarbon-rich material regarded as a precursor of petroleum. Oil shale may be burned directly or processed by heating to extract shale oil.

Coal coke – This group includes the solid, cellular, infusible material remaining after the carbonisation of certain coals. Various cokes are defined according to the type of coal carbonised and their conditions of carbonisation or use: coke oven coke, gas coke, coke breeze and semi cokes.

Patent fuel – A composition fuel made by moulding hard coal fines into briquette shapes with the addition of a binding agent such as pitch.

Brown coal briquettes (BKB) – A composition fuel made of brown coal produced by briquetting under high pressure with or without the addition of a binding agent. Either sub-bituminous coal or lignite may be used, including dried lignite fines and dust.

Coal tar – The liquid by-product of the carbonization of coal in coke ovens. Coal tar may be separated by distillation into several liquid products which may be used for pharmaceutical or wood preservative purposes.

Other coal products – coal products not elsewhere specified (if any).

Coke oven gas – A gas produced from coke ovens during the manufacture of coke oven coke.

Gas works gas (and other manufactured gases for distribution) – This includes gases obtained from the carbonisation or gasification of carbonaceous material of fossil or biomass origins in Gas Works. The gases comprise: (a) gases obtained from carbonisation or gasification of coals, cokes, biomass or waste; and (b) substitute natural gas (a methane-rich gas) made from synthesis gas[7].

Recovered gases – Combustible gases of solid carbonaceous origin recovered from manufacturing and chemical processes of which the principal purpose is other than the production of fuel. This includes gases containing carbon monoxide resulting from the partial oxidation of (a) carbon present as coke acting as a reductant in the process, (b) carbon anodes, or (c) carbon dissolved in iron. Examples are: Blast furnace gas (the by-product gas of blast furnace operation consisting mainly of nitrogen, carbon dioxide and carbon monoxide); Basic oxygen steel furnace gas (the by-product gas of the production of steel in a basic oxygen furnace); and Other recovered gases (combustible gases of solid carbonaceous origin recovered from manufacturing and chemical processes not elsewhere defined, such as from the production of zinc, tin, lead, ferroalloys, phosphorus and silicon carbide).

Other coal products – coal products not elsewhere classified

Peat products – This includes products such as peat briquettes derived directly or indirectly from sod peat and milled peat.

Conventional crude oil – A mineral oil of fossil origin extracted by conventional means from underground reservoirs, and comprises liquid or near-liquid hydrocarbons and associated impurities such as sulphur and metals. Conventional crude oil exists in the liquid phase under normal surface temperature and pressure, and usually flows to the surface under the pressure of the reservoir. This is termed "conventional" extraction. Crude oil includes

[7] Synthesis gas is a mixture of mainly hydrogen and carbon monoxide obtained by cracking hydrocarbons with high temperature steam.

condensate from condensate fields, and "field" or "lease" condensate extracted with the crude oil.

The various crude oils may be classified according to their sulphur content ("sweet" or "sour") and API gravity ("heavy" or "light"). There are no rigorous specifications for the classifications but a heavy crude oil may be assumed to have an API gravity of less than 20º and a sweet crude oil may be assumed to have less than 0.5% sulphur content.

Natural gas liquids (NGL) – Natural gas liquids are a mixture of ethane, propane, butane (normal and iso), (iso) pentane and a few higher alkanes collectively referred to as pentanes plus.

NGL are produced in association with oil or natural gas. They are removed in field facilities or gas separation plants before sale of the gas. All of the components of NGL except ethane are either liquid at the surface or are liquefied for disposal.

The definition given above is the most commonly used. However, there is some use of terms based on the vapour pressure of the components which are liquid at the surface or can be easily liquefied. The three resulting groups are in order of increasing vapour pressure: condensates, natural gasoline and liquefied petroleum gas.

NGL may be distilled with crude oil in refineries, blended with refined oil products or used directly. NGL differs from LNG (liquefied natural gas) which is obtained by liquefying natural gas from which the NGL has been removed.

Additives and oxygenates – Compounds added to or blended with oil products to modify their properties (octane, cetane, cold properties, etc.). Examples are: (a) oxygenates such as alcohols (methanol, ethanol) and ethers [MTBE (methyl tertiary butyl ether), ETBE (ethyl tertiary butyl ether), TAME (tertiary amyl methyl ether)]; (b) esters (e.g., rapeseed or dimethylester, etc.); and (c) chemical compounds (such as TML, TEL and detergents). Some additives/oxygenates may be derived from biomass while others may be of fossil hydrocarbon origin.

Other hydrocarbons – This includes non-conventional oils and hydrogen. Non-conventional oils refer to oils obtained by non-conventional production techniques, that is oils which are extracted from reservoirs containing extra heavy oils or oil sands which need heating or treatment (e.g., emulsification) in situ before they can be brought to the surface for refining/processing. They also include the oils extracted from oil sands, extra heavy oils, coal and oil shale which are at, or can be brought to, the surface without treatment and require processing after mining (ex situ processing). Non-conventional oils may also be produced from natural gas.

The oils may be divided into two groups: (i) oils for transformation (e.g., synthetic crudes extracted from extra heavy oils, oil sands, coal and oil shale); and (ii) oils for direct use (e.g., emulsified oils such as orimulsion and GTL liquids). Oil sands are also known as tar sands. Extra heavy oils are also known as bitumen. This is not the oil product of the same name which is made from vacuum distillation residue. Although not a hydrocarbon, hydrogen is included here unless it is a component of another gas.

Oil products – Products obtained from crude oil, non-conventional oils or gases from oil and gas fields. They may be produced through the refining of conventional crude and non-conventional oils or during the separation of natural gas from gases extracted from oil or gas fields. This category includes Feedstocks, Refinery gas, Ethane, Liquefied petroleum gases (LPG), Naphtha, Aviation gasoline, Motor gasoline, Gasoline-type jet fuel, Kerosene-type jet fuel, Other kerosene, Gas oil/diesel oil, Fuel oil, White spirit and SBP industrial spirits, Lubricants, Paraffin waxes, Petroleum coke, Bitumen, and Other oil products n.e.c.

Feedstocks – This includes refinery feedstocks, i.e. oils or gases from crude oil refining or the processing of hydrocarbons in the petrochemical industry which are destined for further processing in the refinery excluding blending. Typical feedstocks include naphthas, middle distillates, pyrolysis gasoline and heavy oils from vacuum distillation and petrochemical plants.

Refinery gas – Includes a mixture of non-condensable gases mainly consisting of hydrogen, methane, ethane and olefins obtained during distillation of crude oil or treatment of oil products

CONCEPTS AND DEFINITIONS

(e.g., cracking) in refineries or from nearby petrochemical plants. It is used mainly as a fuel within the refinery.

Ethane – A naturally straight-chain hydrocarbon (C_2H_6). Ethane is obtained at gas separation plants or from the refining of crude oil. It is a valuable feedstock for petrochemical manufacture.

Liquefied petroleum gases (LPG) – LPG refers to liquefied propane (C_3H_8) and butane (C_4H_{10}) or mixtures of both. Commercial grades are usually mixtures of the gases with small amounts of propylene, butylene, isobutene and isobutylene stored under pressure in containers.

The mixture of propane and butane used varies according to purpose and season of the year. The gases may be extracted from natural gas at gas separation plants or at plants re-gasifying imported liquefied natural gas. They are also obtained during the refining of crude oil. LPG may be used for heating and as a vehicle fuel.

See also the definition for natural gas liquids. Certain oil field practices also use the term LPG to describe the high vapour pressure components of natural gas liquids.

Naphtha – Light or medium oils distilling between 30ºC and 210ºC which do not meet the specification for motor gasoline. Different naphthas are distinguished by their density and the content of paraffins, isoparaffins, olefins, naphthenes and aromatics. The main uses for naphthas are as feedstock for high octane gasolines and the manufacture of olefins in the petrochemical industry.

Aviation gasoline – Gasoline prepared especially for aviation piston engines with additives which assure performance under flight conditions. Aviation gasolines are predominantly alkylates (obtained by combining C_4 and C_5 isoparaffins with C_3, C_4 and C_5 olefins) with the possible addition of more aromatic components including toluene. The distillation range is 25ºC to 170ºC.

Motor gasoline – A mixture of some aromatics (e.g., benzene and toluene) and aliphatic hydrocarbons in the C_5 to C_{12} range. The distillation range is 25ºC to 220ºC.

Additives are blended to improve octane rating, improve combustion performance, reduce oxidation during storage, maintain cleanliness of the engine and improve capture of pollutants by catalytic converters in the exhaust system. Motor gasoline may also contain biogasoline products when blended.

Gasoline-type jet fuel – Light hydrocarbons for use in aviation turbine power units, distilling between 100ºC and 250ºC. They are obtained by blending kerosene and gasoline or naphtha in such a way that the aromatic content does not exceed 25 per cent in volume, and the vapour pressure is between 13.7 kPa and 20.6 kPa. Gasoline-type jet fuel is also known as "aviation turbine fuel".

Kerosene – Mixtures of hydrocarbons in the range C_9 to C_{16} and distilling over the temperature interval 145ºC to 300°C, but not usually above 250ºC and with a flash point above 38ºC.

The chemical compositions of kerosenes depend on the nature of the crude oils from which they are derived and the refinery processes that they have undergone. Kerosenes obtained from crude oil by atmospheric distillation are known as straight-run kerosenes. Such streams may be treated by a variety of processes to produce kerosenes that are acceptable for blending as jet fuels. Kerosenes are primarily used as jet fuels. They are also used as domestic heating and cooking fuels, and as solvents. Kerosenes may include components or additives derived from biomass when blended.

Kerosene-type jet fuel – A blend of kerosenes suited to flight conditions with particular specifications, such as freezing point.

The specifications are set down by a small number of national standards committees, most notably ASTM (U.S.), MOD (UK), GOST (Russia).

Other kerosene – Kerosene which is used for heating, cooking, lighting, solvents and internal combustion engines. Other names for this product are burning oil, vaporizing oil, power kerosene and illuminating oil.

CONCEPTS AND DEFINITIONS

Gas oil/diesel oil – Gas oils are middle distillates, predominantly of carbon number range C_{11} to C_{25} and with a distillation range of 160ºC to 420°C. The principal marketed products are fuels for diesel engines (diesel oil), heating oils and marine fuel. Gas oils are also used as middle distillate feedstock for the petrochemical industry and as solvents. Also included here is heavy gasoil, which is a mixture of predominantly gas oil and fuel oil which distills in the range of approximately 380ºC to 540ºC.

Fuel oil – Comprises residual fuel oil and heavy fuel oil. Residual fuel oils have a distillation range of 350ºC to 650ºC and a kinematic viscosity in the range 6 to 55 cSt at 100ºC. Their flash point is always above 60ºC and their specific gravity is above 0.95. Heavy fuel oil is a general term describing a blended product based on the residues from various refinery processes. Other names commonly used to describe fuel oil include: bunker fuel, bunker C, fuel oil No. 6, industrial fuel oil, marine fuel oil and black oil.

Residual and heavy fuel oil are used in medium to large industrial plants, marine applications and power stations in combustion equipment such as boilers, furnaces and diesel engines. Residual fuel oil is also used as fuel within the refinery.

White spirit and SBP industrial spirits – White spirit and special boiling point industrial spirits (SBP) are refined distillate intermediates with a distillation in the naphtha/kerosene range. They are mainly used for non-fuel purposes and sub-divided as: (a) white spirit - an industrial spirit with a flash point above 30ºC and a distillation range of 135ºC to 200ºC; and (b) industrial spirit (SBP) - light oils distilling between 30ºC and 200ºC.

There are 7 or 8 grades of industrial spirits, depending on the position of the cut in the distillation range. The grades are defined according to the temperature difference between the 5 per cent and 90 per cent volume distillation points (which is not more than 60ºC). White spirit and Industrial spirits are mostly used as thinners and solvents.

Lubricants – Oils, produced from crude oil, for which the principal use is to reduce friction between sliding surfaces and during metal cutting operations.

Lubricant base stocks are obtained from vacuum distillates which result from further distillation of the residue from atmospheric distillation of crude oil. The lubricant base stocks are then further processed to produce lubricants with the desired properties.

Paraffin waxes – Residues extracted when dewaxing lubricant oils. The waxes have a crystalline structure which varies in fineness according to the grade, and are colourless, odourless and translucent, with a melting point above 45ºC.

Petroleum coke – Petroleum coke is a black solid obtained mainly by cracking and carbonizing heavy hydrocarbon oils, tars and pitches. It consists mainly of carbon (90 to 95 per cent) and has a low ash content.

The two most important categories are "green coke" and "calcined coke".

Green coke (raw coke) is the primary solid carbonization product from high boiling hydrocarbon fractions obtained at temperatures below 630ºC. It contains 4-15 per cent by weight of matter that can be released as volatiles during subsequent heat treatment at temperatures up to approximately 1330ºC.

Calcined coke is a petroleum coke or coal-derived pitch coke obtained by heat treatment of green coke to about 1330ºC. It will normally have a hydrogen content of less than 0.1 per cent by weight.

In many catalytic operations (e.g., catalytic cracking) carbon or catalytic coke is deposited on the catalyst, thus deactivating it. The catalyst is reactivated by burning off the coke which is used as a fuel in the refining process. The coke is not recoverable in a concentrated form.

Bitumen – A solid, semi-solid or viscous hydrocarbon with a colloidal structure, being brown to black in colour. It is obtained as a residue in the distillation of crude oil and by vacuum distillation of oil residues from atmospheric distillation. It should not be confused with the non-conventional primary extra heavy oils which may also be referred to as bitumen.

In addition to its major use for road pavements, bitumen is also used as an adhesive, a waterproofing agent for roof coverings and as a binder in the manufacture of patent fuel. It may also be used for electricity generation in specially designed power plants.

Bitumen is also known in some countries as asphalt but in others asphalt describes the mixture of bitumen and stone aggregate used for road pavements.

Other oil products n.e.c. – Products (including partly refined products) from the refining of crude oil and feedstocks which are not specified above. These products will include basic chemicals and organic chemicals destined for use within the refinery or for sale to or processing in the chemical industry such as propylene, benzene, toluene and xylene.

Natural gas – A mixture of gaseous hydrocarbons, primarily methane, but generally also including ethane, propane and higher hydrocarbons in much smaller amounts and some non-combustible gases such as nitrogen and carbon dioxide.

The majority of natural gas is separated from both "non-associated" gas originating from fields producing hydrocarbons only in gaseous form, and "associated" gas produced in association with crude oil.

The separation process produces natural gas by removing or reducing the hydrocarbons other than methane to levels which are acceptable in the marketable gas. The natural gas liquids (NGL) removed in the process are distributed separately.

Natural gas also includes methane recovered from coal mines (colliery gas) or from coal seams (coal seam gas) and shale gas. When distributed it may also contain methane from anaerobic fermentation or the methanation of biomass.

Natural gas may be liquefied (LNG) by reducing its temperature in order to simplify storage and transportation when production sites are remote from centres of consumption and pipeline transportation is not economically practicable.

Biofuels – Fuels derived directly or indirectly from biomass.

Fuels produced from animal fats, by-products and residues obtain their calorific value indirectly from the plants eaten by the animals.

Solid biofuels – Solid fuels derived from biomass.

Fuelwood, wood residues and by-products – Fuelwood or firewood (in log, brushwood, pellet or chip form) obtained from natural or managed forests or isolated trees. Also included are wood residues used as fuel and in which the original composition of wood is retained. Charcoal and black liquor are excluded.

Bagasse – The fuel obtained from the fibre which remains after juice extraction in sugar cane processing. It is often used as a fuel within the sugar milling industry.

Animal waste – Excreta of animals, meat and fish residues which, when dry, are used directly as a fuel.

This excludes waste used in anaerobic fermentation plants. Fuel gases from these plants are included under biogases.

Black liquor – The alkaline-spent liquor obtained from the digesters during the production of sulphate or soda pulp required for paper manufacture. The lignin contained in the liquor burns to release heat when the concentrated liquor is sprayed into a recovery furnace and heated with hot gases at 900ºC. Black liquor is used as a fuel in the pulping process.

Other vegetal material and residues – Refers to solid primary biofuels not specified elsewhere, including straw, vegetable husks, ground nut shells, pruning brushwood, olive pomace and other wastes arising from the maintenance, cropping and processing of plants.

Charcoal – The solid residue from the carbonisation of wood or other vegetal matter through slow pyrolysis.

Liquid biofuels – Liquids derived from biomass and used as fuels. Liquid biofuels comprise biogasoline, biodiesels, bio jet kerosene and other liquid biofuels. They are used for transport, electricity generation and stationary engines.

Biogasoline – Liquid fuels derived from biomass and used in spark-ignition internal combustion engines.

Common examples are: bioethanol (including both hydrous and anhydrous ethanol); biomethanol; biobutanol; bio ETBE (ethyl-tertio-butyl-ether); and bio MTBE (methyl-tertio-butyl-ether). Biogasoline may be blended with petroleum gasoline or used directly in engines. The blending may take place in refineries or at or near the point of sale.

Biodiesels – Liquid biofuels derived from biomass and used in diesel engines.

Biodiesels obtained by chemical modification are a linear alkyl ester made by transesterification of vegetable oils or animal fats with methanol. The transesterification distinguishes biodiesel from straight vegetable and waste oils. Biodiesel has a flash point of around 150°C and a density of about 0.88 kg/litre. Biological sources of biodiesel include, but are not limited to, vegetable oils made from canola (rapeseed), soybeans, corn, oil palm, peanut or sunflower. Some liquid biofuels (straight vegetable oils) may be used without chemical modification and their use usually requires modification of the engine.

A further category of diesel fuels can be produced by a range of thermal processes (including for example gasification followed by Fischer Tropsch synthesis, pyrolysis followed by hydrogenation, or conversion of sugar to hydrocarbons using microorganisms (e.g. yeast)). A wide range of biomass feedstocks, including cellulosic materials and algal biomass could be used in such processes.

Biodiesels may be blended with petroleum diesel or used directly in diesel engines.

Bio jet kerosene – Liquid biofuels derived from biomass and blended with or replacing jet kerosene. Bio jet kerosene can be produced by a range of thermal processes (including for example gasification followed by Fischer-Tropsch synthesis, pyrolysis followed by hydrogenation, or conversion of sugar to hydrocarbons using microorganisms (e.g. yeast). A wide range of biomass feedstocks, including cellulosic materials and algal biomass could be used in such processes.

Other liquid biofuels – Includes liquid biofuels not elsewhere specified.

Biogases – Gases arising from the anaerobic fermentation of biomass and the gasification of solid biomass (including biomass in wastes).

The biogases from anaerobic fermentation are composed principally of methane and carbon dioxide and comprise landfill gas, sewage sludge gas and other biogases from anaerobic fermentation.

Biogases can also be produced from thermal processes (by gasification or pyrolysis) of biomass and are mixtures containing hydrogen and carbon monoxide (usually known as syngas) along with other components. These gases may be further processed to modify their composition and can be further processed to produce substitute natural gas.

The gases are divided into two groups according to their production: biogases from anaerobic fermentation and biogases from thermal processes.

Biogases are used mainly as a fuel but can be used as a chemical feedstock.

Industrial waste – Non-renewable waste which is combusted with heat recovery in plants other than those used for the incineration of municipal waste.

Examples are used tires, specific residues from the chemical industry and hazardous wastes from health care. Combustion includes co-firing with other fuels.

The renewable portions of waste of industrial origin which are combusted with heat recovery are classified according to the biofuels which best describe them.

Municipal waste – Household waste and waste from companies and public services that resembles household waste and which is collected at installations specifically designed for the disposal of mixed wastes with recovery of combustible liquids, gases or heat.

Municipal wastes can be divided into renewable and non-renewable fractions.

Nuclear – refers to heat obtained from nuclear reactions, whether to produce Heat or Electricity as an energy product. If the output is Electricity, Nuclear refers to the theoretical primary heat input assuming a 33% efficiency from converting such primary nuclear heat into the secondary nuclear electricity. As such, the corresponding conversion is reflected in the transformation rows of the balance.

Electricity – The transfer of energy through the physical phenomena involving electric charges and their effects when at rest and in motion.

Electricity can be generated through different processes such as: the conversion of energy contained in falling or streaming water, wind or waves; the direct conversion of solar radiation through photovoltaic processes in semiconductor devices (solar cells); or by the combustion of fuels.

Electricity production in the energy balances refers to gross production, which is the sum of the electrical energy production by all the generating units/installations concerned (but excluding from pumped storage) measured at the output terminals of the main generators.

Primary electricity refers to electrical energy from hydro, solar photovoltaics, wind, tide, wave and ocean sources. Electricity production from these sources appears in the row Primary production.

Secondary electricity is defined as electricity derived from a product already accounted for within energy statistics. This includes electricity generated from combustible fuels, in addition to electricity coming from solar heat, nuclear heat, geothermal heat and heat from chemical sources. Electricity production from these sources appears in the same Transformation rows (Electricity Plants, CHP plants) as the transformation inputs (combustible fuels, nuclear heat or other types of heat).

Heat – The energy obtained from the translational, rotational and vibrational motion of the constituents of matter, as well as changes in its physical state.

Heat can be produced by different production processes, both primary and secondary. It is usually sold in the form of steam or hot water, and for the purposes of energy statistics it is important to note that heat only represents quantities of energy for sale (or generated and consumed directly by direct use of solar thermal or geothermal). This means that any quantities "generated" at an end-use site (for example through the combustion of coal to power a boiler, or an electric filament heating a kettle) are not considered within the scope of heat production.

ABBREVIATIONS AND SYMBOLS

The following abbreviations and symbols have been used in the publication:

cSt	centistoke
°C	degree Celsius
GCV	Gross Calorific Value
GJ	gigajoule (10^9 joules)
GWh	gigawatt-hour (10^6 kWh)
IRES	International Recommendations for Energy Statistics
kcal	kilocalorie
kg	kilogramme
kg/cm^2	kilogramme per square centimetre
kJ	kilojoule (10^3 joules)
kWh	kilowatt-hour
LPG	liquefied petroleum gas
mg/g	milligramme per gramme
MJ	megajoule (10^6 joules)
m^3	cubic metre.
NCV	Net Calorific Value
NGL	natural gas liquids
PJ	Petajoule (10^{15} joules)
SBP	Special Boiling Point
t	metric ton
TJ	terajoule (10^{12} joules)
*	estimate by the United Nations Statistics Division
..	data not applicable or not available

CONVERSION FACTORS

The data which have been supplied by the countries in original units are converted to the common unit, terajoules (TJ), by using standard conversion factors or, in the case of solids and liquids, specific factors, where available.

Standard conversion factors for liquid fuels are determined on the basis of the net calorific value for each product.

The conversion of fuelwood (solid volume, 9.135 GJ/m3) is based on an average 20-30% moisture content. When data on the transformation of fuelwood into charcoal are incomplete, estimations assume that it requires 6 cubic metres of fuelwood to produce 1 metric ton of charcoal, equivalent to an approximately 53% transformation efficiency on an energy basis.

For users wishing to convert the data from terajoules (TJ) to other common units: one thousand tons of coal equivalent (1,000 TCE) has traditionally been defined as comprising 29.3076 TJ, and one thousand tons of oil equivalent (1,000 TOE) as 42.6216 TJ. One calorie corresponds to 4.1868 joules and is the amount of energy which will raise the temperature of one gramme of water by one degree Celsius.

STANDARD NET CALORIFIC VALUES

(Terajoules per thousand metric tons, unless otherwise stated)

Hard coal	25.80
Brown coal	14.00
Peat	9.76
Oil shale	8.90
Coal coke	28.20
Patent fuel	20.70
Brown coal briquettes (BKB)	20.70
Coal tar	28.00
Coke-oven gas (original unit is TJ)	1.00
Gasworks gas (original unit is TJ)	1.00
Recovered gases (original unit is TJ)	1.00
Other coal products	20.00
Peat products	9.76
Conventional crude oil	42.30
Natural gas liquids	44.20
Additives and Oxygenates	30.00
Other hydrocarbons	36.00
Feedstocks	43.00
Refinery gas	49.50
Ethane	46.40
Liquefied petroleum gas	47.30
Naphtha	44.50
Aviation gasoline	44.30
Motor gasoline	44.30
Gasoline-type jet fuel	44.30
Kerosene-type jet fuel	44.10
Other kerosene	43.80
Gas-diesel oil	43.00
Fuel oil	40.40
White spirit and SBP industrial spirits	40.20
Lubricants	40.20
Paraffin waxes	40.20
Petroleum coke	32.50
Bitumen (asphalt)	40.20
Other oil products	40.20
Natural gas (original unit is TJ on a GCV basis)	0.90
Fuelwood, wood residues and by-products (10^3 m^3)	9.14
Bagasse	7.72
Animal waste (original unit is TJ)	1.00
Black liquor (original unit is TJ)	1.00
Other vegetal material and residues (original unit is TJ)	1.00
Biogasoline	26.80
Biodiesels	36.80
Bio jet kerosene	40.00

STANDARD NET CALORIFIC VALUES
(Terajoules per thousand metric tons, unless otherwise stated)

Other liquid biofuels	27.40
Biogases (original unit is TJ)	1.00
Industrial wastes (original unit is TJ)	1.00
Municipal wastes (original unit is TJ)	1.00
Charcoal	29.50
Nuclear heat (original unit is TJ)	1.00
Electricity (GWh)	3.60
Heat (original unit is TJ)	1.00

ENERGY BALANCES

Afghanistan

Terajoules

	Primary coal and peat	Coal and peat products	Primary Oil	Oil Products	Natural Gas	Biofuels and waste	Nuclear	Electricity	Heat	Total energy	of which: renewables
2017											
Primary production	56538	..	..	..	5482	16960	..	4478	..	83457	21437
Imports	..	*5713	..	46779	..	2	..	16601	..	69094	2
Exports	-26161	*-1889	..	..	..	0	..	..	..	-28051	0
International marine bunkers	..	..	..	..	..	..	..	..	..	..	..
International aviation bunkers	..	..	..	*-463	..	..	..	..	..	*-463	..
Stock changes	..	..	..	..	..	..	..	..	..	..	..
Total energy supply	30377	*3824	..	46316	5482	16961	..	21078	..	124038	21439
Statistical difference	0	0	..	0	0	0	..	1426	..	1426	4478
Transfers	..	..	..	..	..	..	..	..	..	..	..
Transformation	*-3720	*1889	..	*-900	..	*-3463	..	635	..	*-5560	*-3463
Electricity plants	*-1367	..	..	*-900	..	..	..	635	..	*-1633	..
CHP plants	..	..	..	..	..	..	..	..	..	..	..
Heat plants	..	..	..	..	..	..	..	..	..	..	..
Coke ovens	*-2353	*1889	..	..	..	..	..	..	..	*-464	..
Briquetting plants	..	..	..	..	..	..	..	..	..	..	..
Liquefaction plants	..	..	..	..	..	..	..	..	..	..	..
Gas works	..	..	..	..	..	..	..	..	..	..	..
Blast furnaces	..	..	..	..	..	..	..	..	..	..	..
NGL plants & gas blending	..	..	..	..	..	..	..	..	..	..	..
Oil refineries	..	..	..	..	..	..	..	..	..	..	..
Other transformation	..	..	..	..	..	*-3463	..	..	..	*-3463	*-3463
Energy industries own use	..	..	..	..	..	..	..	*-1476	..	*-1476	..
Losses	..	..	..	..	..	..	..	*-2556	..	*-2556	..
Final consumption	*26657	*5713	..	*45415	*5482	*13498	..	*16255	..	*113020	*13498
Final energy consumption	*26657	*5713	..	*42971	*5482	*13498	..	*16255	..	*110576	*13498
Manufacturing, const., mining	*26657	*5713	..	..	*5482	..	..	*3402	..	*41254	..
Iron and steel	..	..	..	..	..	..	..	..	..	..	..
Chemical and petrochemical	..	..	..	..	..	..	..	..	..	..	..
Non-ferrous metals	..	..	..	..	..	..	..	..	..	..	..
Non-metallic minerals	..	..	..	..	..	..	..	..	..	..	..
Transport equipment	..	..	..	..	..	..	..	..	..	..	..
Machinery	..	..	..	..	..	..	..	..	..	..	..
Mining and quarrying	..	..	..	..	..	..	..	..	..	..	..
Food and tobacco	..	..	..	..	..	..	..	..	..	..	..
Paper, pulp and printing	..	..	..	..	..	..	..	..	..	..	..
Wood and wood products	..	..	..	..	..	..	..	..	..	..	..
Textile and leather	..	..	..	..	..	..	..	..	..	..	..
Construction	..	..	..	..	..	..	..	..	..	..	..
Industries n.e.s	*26657	*5713	..	..	*5482	..	..	*3402	..	*41254	..
Transport	..	..	..	*41403	..	..	..	..	..	*41403	..
Road	..	..	..	*38902	..	..	..	..	..	*38902	..
Rail	..	..	..	..	..	..	..	..	..	..	..
Domestic aviation	..	..	..	*2500	..	..	..	..	..	*2500	..
Domestic navigation	..	..	..	..	..	..	..	..	..	..	..
Pipeline transport	..	..	..	..	..	..	..	..	..	..	..
Transport, n.e.s	..	..	..	..	..	..	..	..	..	..	..
Other	..	..	..	1568	..	*13498	..	*12853	..	*27919	*13498
Agriculture, forestry, fishing	..	..	..	..	..	..	..	*394	..	*394	..
Commerce, public services	..	..	..	..	..	..	..	*1126	..	*1126	..
Households	..	..	..	1568	..	*13498	..	*10122	..	*25188	*13498
Other consumers	..	..	..	..	..	..	..	*1211	..	*1211	..
Non-energy use	..	..	..	*2444	..	..	..	..	..	*2444	..

Afghanistan

Terajoules

2018	Primary coal and peat	Coal and peat products	Primary Oil	Oil Products	Natural Gas	Biofuels and waste	Nuclear	Electricity	Heat	Total energy	of which: renewables
Primary production	63081	..	..	..	5380	16960	..	3837	..	89258	20797
Imports	..	*5713	..	60629	..	2	..	17950	..	84294	2
Exports	-28819	*-1889	..	..	..	0	..	..	..	-30708	0
International marine bunkers	..	..	..	..	..	..	..	..	..	..	..
International aviation bunkers	..	..	..	*-463	..	..	..	..	..	*-463	..
Stock changes	..	..	..	..	..	..	..	..	..	..	..
Total energy supply	34262	*3824	..	60166	5380	16961	..	21786	..	142381	20798
Statistical difference	0	0	..	0	0	0	..	1566	..	1566	3837
Transfers	..	..	..	..	..	..	..	..	..	..	..
Transformation	*-3767	*1889	..	*-1442	..	*-3463	..	720	..	*-6063	*-3463
Electricity plants	*-1445	..	..	*-1442	..	..	..	720	..	*-2167	..
CHP plants	..	..	..	..	..	..	..	..	..	..	..
Heat plants	..	..	..	..	..	..	..	..	..	..	..
Coke ovens	*-2322	*1889	..	..	..	..	..	..	..	*-433	..
Briquetting plants	..	..	..	..	..	..	..	..	..	..	..
Liquefaction plants	..	..	..	..	..	..	..	..	..	..	..
Gas works	..	..	..	..	..	..	..	..	..	..	..
Blast furnaces	..	..	..	..	..	..	..	..	..	..	..
NGL plants & gas blending	..	..	..	..	..	..	..	..	..	..	..
Oil refineries	..	..	..	..	..	..	..	..	..	..	..
Other transformation	..	..	..	..	..	*-3463	..	..	..	*-3463	*-3463
Energy industries own use	..	..	..	..	..	..	..	*-1032	..	*-1032	..
Losses	..	..	..	..	..	..	..	*-2844	..	*-2844	..
Final consumption	*30496	*5713	..	*58724	*5380	*13498	..	*17064	..	*130875	*13498
Final energy consumption	*30496	*5713	..	*57928	*5380	*13498	..	*17064	..	*130079	*13498
Manufacturing, const., mining	*30496	*5713	..	..	*5380	..	..	*3571	..	*45160	..
Iron and steel	..	..	..	..	..	..	..	..	..	..	..
Chemical and petrochemical	..	..	..	..	..	..	..	..	..	..	..
Non-ferrous metals	..	..	..	..	..	..	..	..	..	..	..
Non-metallic minerals	..	..	..	..	..	..	..	..	..	..	..
Transport equipment	..	..	..	..	..	..	..	..	..	..	..
Machinery	..	..	..	..	..	..	..	..	..	..	..
Mining and quarrying	..	..	..	..	..	..	..	..	..	..	..
Food and tobacco	..	..	..	..	..	..	..	..	..	..	..
Paper, pulp and printing	..	..	..	..	..	..	..	..	..	..	..
Wood and wood products	..	..	..	..	..	..	..	..	..	..	..
Textile and leather	..	..	..	..	..	..	..	..	..	..	..
Construction	..	..	..	..	..	..	..	..	..	..	..
Industries n.e.s	*30496	*5713	..	..	*5380	..	..	*3571	..	*45160	..
Transport	..	..	..	*57407	..	..	..	..	..	*57407	..
Road	..	..	..	*54906	..	..	..	..	..	*54906	..
Rail	..	..	..	..	..	..	..	..	..	..	..
Domestic aviation	..	..	..	*2500	..	..	..	..	..	*2500	..
Domestic navigation	..	..	..	..	..	..	..	..	..	..	..
Pipeline transport	..	..	..	..	..	..	..	..	..	..	..
Transport, n.e.s	..	..	..	..	..	..	..	..	..	..	..
Other	..	..	..	521	..	*13498	..	*13493	..	*27512	*13498
Agriculture, forestry, fishing	..	..	..	..	..	..	..	*414	..	*414	..
Commerce, public services	..	..	..	..	..	..	..	*1181	..	*1181	..
Households	..	..	..	521	..	*13498	..	*10627	..	*24646	*13498
Other consumers	..	..	..	..	..	..	..	*1271	..	*1271	..
Non-energy use	..	..	..	*796	..	..	..	..	..	*796	..

Albania

Terajoules

2017	Primary coal and peat	Coal and peat products	Primary Oil	Oil Products	Natural Gas	Biofuels and waste	Nuclear	Electricity	Heat	Total energy	of which: renewables
Primary production	934	..	40563	..	3080	6959	..	16294	553	68383	23805
Imports	2697	..	..	50129	..	3811	..	10493	..	67130	3811
Exports	-611	..	-20642	-6176	..	-714	..	0	..	-28143	-714
International marine bunkers	..	..	..	-1548	..	..	..	..	..	-1548	..
International aviation bunkers	..	..	..	*-265	..	..	..	..	..	*-265	..
Stock changes	..	..	1785	-7713	..	..	..	..	..	-5928	..
Total energy supply	3020	..	21706	34427	3080	10056	..	26787	553	99629	26903
Statistical difference	178	..	-2	285	0	0	..	4	0	466	16294
Transfers	..	..	..	..	..	..	..	..	..	..	..
Transformation	..	..	-21707	19232	..	..	..	..	113	-2363	..
Electricity plants	..	..	..	..	..	..	..	..	..	..	..
CHP plants	..	..	..	..	..	..	..	..	..	..	..
Heat plants	..	..	..	-955	..	..	..	..	113	-842	..
Coke ovens	..	..	..	..	..	..	..	..	..	..	..
Briquetting plants	..	..	..	..	..	..	..	..	..	..	..
Liquefaction plants	..	..	..	..	..	..	..	..	..	..	..
Gas works	..	..	..	..	..	..	..	..	..	..	..
Blast furnaces	..	..	..	..	..	..	..	..	..	..	..
NGL plants & gas blending	..	..	..	..	..	..	..	..	..	..	..
Oil refineries	..	..	-21707	20203	..	..	..	..	..	-1504	..
Other transformation	..	..	..	-16	..	..	..	..	..	-16	..
Energy industries own use	..	..	..	-1595	-1044	..	..	-746	-40	-3425	..
Losses	..	..	..	..	..	..	..	-4594	..	-4594	..
Final consumption	2842	..	..	51779	2036	10056	..	21443	626	88782	10609
Final energy consumption	2842	..	..	49936	523	10056	..	21443	626	85426	10609
Manufacturing, const., mining	2725	..	..	6584	523	290	..	4518	103	14743	320
Iron and steel	..	..	..	179	..	..	..	641	..	819	..
Chemical and petrochemical	..	..	..	325	..	..	..	325	..	650	..
Non-ferrous metals	1014	..	..	13	..	..	..	283	..	1311	..
Non-metallic minerals	1710	..	..	95	..	..	..	360	..	2165	..
Transport equipment	..	..	..	..	..	..	..	..	..	..	..
Machinery	..	..	..	..	..	..	..	..	..	..	..
Mining and quarrying	..	..	..	0	..	..	..	396	..	396	..
Food and tobacco	..	..	..	823	271	..	..	1044	103	2241	30
Paper, pulp and printing	..	..	..	59	..	..	..	428	..	488	..
Wood and wood products	..	..	..	..	..	..	..	36	..	36	..
Textile and leather	..	..	..	90	..	..	..	516	..	606	..
Construction	..	..	..	50	..	..	..	306	..	356	..
Industries n.e.s	0	..	..	4951	251	290	..	182	0	5674	290
Transport	..	..	..	32260	..	3234	..	..	..	35494	3234
Road	..	..	..	30619	..	3234	..	..	..	33852	3234
Rail	..	..	..	90	..	..	..	..	..	90	..
Domestic aviation	..	..	..	*44	..	..	..	..	..	*44	..
Domestic navigation	..	..	..	1507	..	..	..	..	..	1507	..
Pipeline transport	..	..	..	..	..	..	..	..	..	..	..
Transport, n.e.s	..	..	..	..	..	..	..	..	..	..	..
Other	117	..	..	11091	..	6532	..	16925	523	35189	7055
Agriculture, forestry, fishing	..	..	..	4056	..	651	..	277	..	4983	651
Commerce, public services	117	..	..	2542	..	497	..	5245	209	8610	706
Households	..	..	..	4494	..	5385	..	10564	314	20756	5699
Other consumers	..	..	..	..	..	..	..	839	..	839	..
Non-energy use	..	..	..	1843	1514	..	..	..	..	3356	..

Albania

Terajoules

2018	Primary coal and peat	Coal and peat products	Primary Oil	Oil Products	Natural Gas	Biofuels and waste	Nuclear	Electricity	Heat	Total energy	of which: renewables
Primary production	1991	..	38521	..	2768	6710	..	30788	564	81342	38062
Imports	3242	..	..	42271	..	5177	..	3062	..	53752	5177
Exports	-44	..	-24652	-5838	..	-714	..	-6350	..	-37597	-714
International marine bunkers	..	..	..	-1333	..	..	..	..	..	-1333	..
International aviation bunkers	..	..	..	-251	..	..	..	..	..	-251	..
Stock changes	..	..	-1264	-3748	..	..	..	..	..	-5012	..
Total energy supply	5189	..	12605	31101	2768	11174	..	27500	564	90901	42525
Statistical difference	284	..	0	778	0	0	..	859	0	1921	30788
Transfers	..	..	..	..	..	..	..	..	..	..	..
Transformation	..	..	-12605	11325	..	..	..	..	122	-1159	..
Electricity plants	..	..	..	..	..	..	..	..	..	..	..
CHP plants	..	..	..	..	..	..	..	..	..	..	..
Heat plants	..	..	..	-421	..	..	..	..	122	-299	..
Coke ovens	..	..	..	..	..	..	..	..	..	..	..
Briquetting plants	..	..	..	..	..	..	..	..	..	..	..
Liquefaction plants	..	..	..	..	..	..	..	..	..	..	..
Gas works	..	..	..	..	..	..	..	..	..	..	..
Blast furnaces	..	..	..	..	..	..	..	..	..	..	..
NGL plants & gas blending	..	..	..	..	..	..	..	..	..	..	..
Oil refineries	..	..	-12605	11746	..	..	..	..	..	-860	..
Other transformation	..	..	..	..	..	..	..	..	..	..	..
Energy industries own use	..	..	..	-247	-1044	..	..	-575	-50	-1917	..
Losses	..	..	..	..	..	..	..	-4161	..	-4161	..
Final consumption	4905	..	..	41400	1724	11174	..	21906	635	81744	11738
Final energy consumption	4905	..	..	40597	307	11174	..	21906	635	79523	11738
Manufacturing, const., mining	4789	..	..	3296	307	315	..	4738	113	13557	356
Iron and steel	..	..	..	176	..	..	..	1007	..	1184	..
Chemical and petrochemical	..	..	..	321	..	..	..	323	..	645	..
Non-ferrous metals	2134	..	..	0	..	..	..	247	..	2381	..
Non-metallic minerals	2655	..	..	96	..	..	..	396	..	3147	..
Transport equipment	..	..	..	..	..	..	..	..	..	..	..
Machinery	..	..	..	..	..	..	..	..	..	..	..
Mining and quarrying	..	..	..	..	..	..	..	444	..	444	..
Food and tobacco	..	..	..	280	271	..	..	804	113	1468	41
Paper, pulp and printing	..	..	..	73	..	..	..	288	..	361	..
Wood and wood products	..	..	..	..	..	..	..	40	..	40	..
Textile and leather	..	..	..	82	..	..	..	490	..	571	..
Construction	..	..	..	67	..	..	..	434	..	501	..
Industries n.e.s	0	..	..	2199	35	315	..	265	0	2815	315
Transport	..	..	..	25734	..	4600	..	..	..	30334	4600
Road	..	..	..	24020	..	4600	..	..	..	28620	4600
Rail	..	..	..	90	..	..	..	..	..	90	..
Domestic aviation	..	..	..	44	..	..	..	..	..	44	..
Domestic navigation	..	..	..	1581	..	..	..	..	..	1581	..
Pipeline transport	..	..	..	..	..	..	..	..	..	..	..
Transport, n.e.s	..	..	..	..	..	..	..	..	..	..	..
Other	116	..	..	11566	..	6259	..	17168	523	35632	6782
Agriculture, forestry, fishing	..	..	..	4162	..	547	..	457	..	5165	547
Commerce, public services	116	..	..	2817	..	535	..	5382	205	9054	740
Households	..	..	..	4588	..	5178	..	11329	318	21412	5495
Other consumers	..	..	..	..	..	..	..	..	..	..	..
Non-energy use	..	..	..	803	1418	..	..	..	..	2221	..

Algeria

Terajoules

2017	Primary coal and peat	Coal and peat products	Primary Oil	Oil Products	Natural Gas	Biofuels and waste	Nuclear	Electricity	Heat	Total energy	of which: renewables
Primary production	..	..	2876781	..	3405831	484	..	*2286	..	6285383	*2770
Imports	0	8488	9391	149135	..	..	..	1933	..	168947	..
Exports	..	..	-1229477	-999985	-1896561	..	..	-3168	..	-4129191	..
International marine bunkers	..	..	..	-9701	..	..	..	..	..	-9701	..
International aviation bunkers	..	..	..	*-15656	..	..	..	..	..	*-15656	..
Stock changes	141	733	-16074	5758	-2599	..	..	..	..	-12041	..
Total energy supply	141	9221	1640621	-870448	1506671	484	..	1051	..	2287742	*2770
Statistical difference	0	-56	6022	6807	26691	0	..	0	..	39463	*2286
Transfers	..	..	..	0	..	..	..	..	..	0	..
Transformation	-141	-3972	-1592050	1613498	-650683	..	..	271379	..	-361968	..
Electricity plants	..	..	..	-9761	-650683	..	..	271379	..	-389065	..
CHP plants	..	..	..	..	..	..	..	..	..	..	..
Heat plants	..	..	..	..	..	..	..	..	..	..	..
Coke ovens	..	..	..	..	..	..	..	..	..	..	..
Briquetting plants	..	..	..	..	..	..	..	..	..	..	..
Liquefaction plants	..	..	..	..	..	..	..	..	..	..	..
Gas works	..	..	..	..	..	..	..	..	..	..	..
Blast furnaces	-141	-3972	..	..	..	..	..	..	..	-4113	..
NGL plants & gas blending	..	..	-376805	402916	..	..	..	..	..	26111	..
Oil refineries	..	..	-1215245	1220343	..	..	..	..	..	5099	..
Other transformation	..	..	..	..	..	..	..	..	..	..	..
Energy industries own use	..	..	-19120	-615	-138333	..	..	-30348	..	-188415	..
Losses	..	-2470	-23430	-1223	-40597	..	..	-39128	..	-106849	..
Final consumption	..	2836	..	734405	650367	484	..	202954	..	1591046	484
Final energy consumption	..	2836	..	713622	538619	484	..	202954	..	1458515	484
Manufacturing, const., mining	..	2836	..	31401	162706	329	..	72652	..	269924	329
Iron and steel	..	2836	..	..	9588	..	..	1577	..	14001	..
Chemical and petrochemical	..	..	..	1056	1791	..	..	3974	..	6822	..
Non-ferrous metals	..	..	..	..	..	..	..	..	..	..	..
Non-metallic minerals	..	..	..	..	*76549	..	..	*10289	..	*86837	..
Transport equipment	..	..	..	..	..	..	..	..	..	..	..
Machinery	..	..	..	..	..	..	..	..	..	..	..
Mining and quarrying	..	..	..	..	..	..	..	..	..	..	..
Food and tobacco	..	..	..	..	20509	..	..	7006	..	27515	..
Paper, pulp and printing	..	..	..	..	..	..	..	..	..	..	..
Wood and wood products	..	..	..	..	..	..	..	..	..	..	..
Textile and leather	..	..	..	..	1300	..	..	1354	..	2653	..
Construction	..	..	..	14792	*47948	..	..	*6311	..	*69050	..
Industries n.e.s	..	0	..	15553	5022	329	..	42142	..	63046	329
Transport	..	..	..	590585	31116	..	..	3848	..	625549	..
Road	..	..	..	581120	..	..	..	..	..	581120	..
Rail	..	..	..	0	..	..	..	3848	..	3848	..
Domestic aviation	..	..	..	*5204	..	..	..	..	..	*5204	..
Domestic navigation	..	..	..	..	..	..	..	..	..	..	..
Pipeline transport	..	..	..	..	31116	..	..	0	..	31116	..
Transport, n.e.s	..	..	..	*4261	..	..	..	..	..	*4261	..
Other	..	..	..	91636	344797	155	..	126454	..	563042	155
Agriculture, forestry, fishing	..	..	..	1307	1861	..	..	5476	..	8644	..
Commerce, public services	..	..	..	1085	..	..	..	..	..	1085	..
Households	..	..	..	66882	304972	155	..	78394	..	450403	155
Other consumers	..	..	..	22361	37964	..	..	42584	..	102910	..
Non-energy use	..	..	..	*20783	111749	..	..	..	..	132532	..

Algeria

Terajoules

2018	Primary coal and peat	Coal and peat products	Primary Oil	Oil Products	Natural Gas	Biofuels and waste	Nuclear	Electricity	Heat	Total energy	of which: renewables
Primary production	..	..	2816396	..	3433926	1032	..	*2822	..	6254177	*3855
Imports	338	14100	8629	34996	..	..	..	1822	..	59885	..
Exports	..	..	-1106513	-931006	-1805849	..	..	-2149	..	-3845517	..
International marine bunkers	..	..	..	-8796	..	..	..	..	..	-8796	..
International aviation bunkers	..	..	..	*-19139	..	..	..	..	..	*-19139	..
Stock changes	-113	1354	11199	-22280	-1861	..	..	..	..	-11701	..
Total energy supply	226	15454	1729712	-946226	1626215	1032	..	2495	..	2428908	*3855
Statistical difference	0	56	2535	-43290	21983	0	..	4	..	-18711	*2822
Transfers	..	..	..	0	..	..	..	..	..	0	..
Transformation	-226	-6508	-1681913	1678397	-666803	..	..	273168	..	-403884	..
Electricity plants	..	..	..	-9469	-666803	..	..	273168	..	-403103	..
CHP plants	..	..	..	..	..	..	..	..	..	..	..
Heat plants	..	..	..	..	..	..	..	..	..	..	..
Coke ovens	..	..	..	..	..	..	..	..	..	..	..
Briquetting plants	..	..	..	..	..	..	..	..	..	..	..
Liquefaction plants	..	..	..	..	..	..	..	..	..	..	..
Gas works	..	..	..	..	..	..	..	..	..	..	..
Blast furnaces	-226	-6508	..	..	..	..	..	..	..	-6733	..
NGL plants & gas blending	..	..	-371059	396857	..	..	..	..	..	25798	..
Oil refineries	..	..	-1310854	1291008	..	..	..	..	..	-19845	..
Other transformation	..	..	..	..	..	..	..	..	..	..	..
Energy industries own use	..	..	-21488	-1466	-128149	..	..	-30654	..	-181758	..
Losses	..	-4012	-23776	-3732	-18999	..	..	-35654	..	-86173	..
Final consumption	..	4878	..	770263	790281	1032	..	209351	..	1775804	1032
Final energy consumption	..	4878	..	728090	623431	1032	..	209351	..	1566782	1032
Manufacturing, const., mining	..	4878	..	24394	179282	703	..	74408	..	283665	703
Iron and steel	..	4878	..	..	16857	..	..	162	..	21897	..
Chemical and petrochemical	..	..	..	1019	2318	..	..	6797	..	10133	..
Non-ferrous metals	..	..	..	..	..	..	..	..	..	..	..
Non-metallic minerals	..	..	..	..	*82013	..	..	*10663	..	*92676	..
Transport equipment	..	..	..	..	..	..	..	..	..	..	..
Machinery	..	..	..	..	..	..	..	..	..	..	..
Mining and quarrying	..	..	..	..	..	..	..	..	..	..	..
Food and tobacco	..	..	..	..	19526	..	..	7258	..	26784	..
Paper, pulp and printing	..	..	..	..	..	..	..	..	..	..	..
Wood and wood products	..	..	..	..	..	..	..	..	..	..	..
Textile and leather	..	..	..	..	1300	..	..	1141	..	2441	..
Construction	..	..	..	16636	*51369	..	..	*6538	..	*74543	..
Industries n.e.s	..	0	..	6738	5900	703	..	41850	..	55191	703
Transport	..	..	..	601600	28341	..	..	4223	..	634164	..
Road	..	..	..	589109	..	..	..	..	..	589109	..
Rail	..	..	..	1634	..	..	..	4223	..	5857	..
Domestic aviation	..	..	..	*6395	..	..	..	..	..	*6395	..
Domestic navigation	..	..	..	..	..	..	..	..	..	..	..
Pipeline transport	..	..	..	..	28341	..	..	0	..	28341	..
Transport, n.e.s	..	..	..	*4462	..	..	..	..	..	*4462	..
Other	..	..	..	102097	415808	329	..	130720	..	648953	329
Agriculture, forestry, fishing	..	..	..	1539	1335	..	..	4334	..	7209	..
Commerce, public services	..	..	..	1487	..	..	..	..	..	1487	..
Households	..	..	..	67024	372998	329	..	89014	..	529364	329
Other consumers	..	..	..	32046	41476	..	..	37372	..	110893	..
Non-energy use	..	..	..	*42172	166850	..	..	..	..	209022	..

Andorra

Terajoules

	All Coal	All Oil	Natural Gas	Primary biofuels / Waste	Charcoal	Electricity	Total energy	of which: renewables
2017								
Primary production	..	..	..	*306	..	*319	*625	*472
Imports	*3	6633	..	28	1	1692	8358	29
Exports	..	..	..	0	..	0	0	0
International marine bunkers	..	..	..	..	..	..	..	..
International aviation bunkers	..	*-5	..	..	..	..	*-5	..
Stock changes	..	..	..	..	..	..	..	..
Total energy supply	*3	6628	..	*334	1	2011	8977	*501
Statistical Difference	0	-190	..	0	0	65	-124	*319
Transfers	..	..	..	..	..	..	..	..
Transformation	..	..	..	*-306	..	61	*-245	*-153
Electricity plants	..	..	..	*-306	..	61	*-245	*-153
Charcoal plants	..	..	..	..	..	..	..	..
Other transformation	..	..	..	0	..	..	0	0
Energy industries own use	..	..	..	..	..	0	0	..
Losses	..	..	..	..	..	-242	-242	..
Final consumption	3	6818	..	*28	1	1766	8615	*29
Final energy consumption	3	6810	..	*28	1	1766	8608	*29
Manufacturing, const., mining	3	..	..	..	..	29	32	..
Transport	..	4733	..	..	..	..	4733	..
Road	..	4733	..	..	..	..	4733	..
Domestic aviation	..	..	..	..	..	..	..	..
Domestic navigation	..	..	..	..	..	..	..	..
Other transport	..	..	..	..	..	..	..	..
Other	..	2078	..	*28	1	1737	3843	*29
Agriculture, forestry, fishing	..	..	..	..	..	..	..	..
Commerce and public services	..	..	..	..	..	1376	1376	..
Households	..	2078	..	*28	1	361	2468	*29
Other consumers	..	..	..	..	..	..	..	..
Non-energy use	..	*7	..	..	..	..	*7	..
2018								
Primary production	..	..	..	*366	..	*429	*795	*612
Imports	*3	7001	..	31	1	1581	8617	32
Exports	..	..	..	0	..	0	0	0
International marine bunkers	..	..	..	..	..	..	..	..
International aviation bunkers	..	*-7	..	..	..	..	*-7	..
Stock changes	..	..	..	..	..	..	..	..
Total energy supply	*3	6994	..	*398	1	2009	9404	*644
Statistical Difference	0	-200	..	0	0	67	-133	*429
Transfers	..	..	..	..	..	..	..	..
Transformation	..	..	..	*-366	..	73	*-293	*-183
Electricity plants	..	..	..	*-366	..	73	*-293	*-183
Charcoal plants	..	..	..	..	..	..	..	..
Other transformation	..	..	..	0	..	..	0	0
Energy industries own use	..	..	..	..	..	0	0	..
Losses	..	..	..	..	..	-243	-243	..
Final consumption	3	7195	..	*31	1	1772	9001	*32
Final energy consumption	3	7187	..	*31	1	1772	8994	*32
Manufacturing, const., mining	3	..	..	..	..	38	40	..
Transport	..	4968	..	..	..	..	4968	..
Road	..	4968	..	..	..	..	4968	..
Domestic aviation	..	..	..	..	..	..	..	..
Domestic navigation	..	..	..	..	..	..	..	..
Other transport	..	..	..	..	..	..	..	..
Other	..	2219	..	*31	1	1734	3985	*32
Agriculture, forestry, fishing	..	..	..	..	..	..	..	..
Commerce and public services	..	..	..	..	..	1349	1349	..
Households	..	2219	..	*31	1	385	2636	*32
Other consumers	..	..	..	..	..	..	..	..
Non-energy use	..	*7	..	..	..	..	*7	..

Angola

Terajoules

	Primary coal and peat	Coal and peat products	Primary Oil	Oil Products	Natural Gas	Biofuels and waste	Nuclear	Electricity	Heat	Total energy	of which: renewables
2017											
Primary production	..	..	3594767	..	198360	266729	..	27616	..	4087472	294345
Imports	..	..	..	151986	..	..	..	..	..	151986	..
Exports	..	..	-3471244	-86752	-169632	..	..	..	..	-3727629	..
International marine bunkers	..	..	..	-15666	..	..	..	..	..	-15666	..
International aviation bunkers	..	..	..	*-10502	..	..	..	..	..	*-10502	..
Stock changes	..	..	*18527	*784	..	..	..	..	..	*19311	..
Total energy supply	..	..	142050	39850	28728	266729	..	27616	..	504972	294345
Statistical difference	..	..	-7388	11611	0	0	..	0	..	4223	27616
Transfers	..	..	*1172	*31	..	..	..	..	..	*1203	..
Transformation	..	..	-150610	125553	..	*-67461	..	11038	..	-81480	*-67461
Electricity plants	..	..	..	*-29485	..	*-2402	..	11038	..	*-20849	*-2402
CHP plants	..	..	..	..	..	..	..	..	..	..	..
Heat plants	..	..	..	..	..	..	..	..	..	..	..
Coke ovens	..	..	..	..	..	..	..	..	..	..	..
Briquetting plants	..	..	..	..	..	..	..	..	..	..	..
Liquefaction plants	..	..	..	..	..	..	..	..	..	..	..
Gas works	..	..	..	..	..	..	..	..	..	..	..
Blast furnaces	..	..	..	..	..	..	..	..	..	..	..
NGL plants & gas blending	..	..	-41592	44509	..	..	..	..	..	2917	..
Oil refineries	..	..	-109018	108078	..	..	..	..	..	-940	..
Other transformation	..	..	..	..	..	*-65059	..	..	..	*-65059	*-65059
Energy industries own use	..	..	..	-3663	-14751	..	..	-1019	..	-19433	..
Losses	..	..	..	..	..	..	..	-4345	..	-4345	..
Final consumption	..	..	..	*150160	13977	*199269	..	33289	..	*396695	*199269
Final energy consumption	..	..	..	*146059	13977	*199269	..	33289	..	*392594	*199269
Manufacturing, const., mining	..	..	..	*10168	13977	*5866	..	11221	..	41232	*5866
Iron and steel	..	..	..	..	..	..	..	..	..	..	..
Chemical and petrochemical	..	..	..	..	..	..	..	..	..	..	..
Non-ferrous metals	..	..	..	..	..	..	..	..	..	..	..
Non-metallic minerals	..	..	..	*1293	..	..	..	..	..	*1293	..
Transport equipment	..	..	..	..	..	..	..	..	..	..	..
Machinery	..	..	..	..	..	..	..	..	..	..	..
Mining and quarrying	..	..	..	..	..	..	..	..	..	..	..
Food and tobacco	..	..	..	..	..	*1218	..	..	..	*1218	*1218
Paper, pulp and printing	..	..	..	..	..	..	..	..	..	..	..
Wood and wood products	..	..	..	..	..	..	..	..	..	..	..
Textile and leather	..	..	..	..	..	..	..	..	..	..	..
Construction	..	..	..	*5601	..	..	..	..	..	*5601	..
Industries n.e.s	..	..	..	*3274	13977	*4648	..	11221	..	33120	*4648
Transport	..	..	..	*74031	..	..	..	..	..	*74031	..
Road	..	..	..	*71899	..	..	..	..	..	*71899	..
Rail	..	..	..	..	..	..	..	..	..	..	..
Domestic aviation	..	..	..	*1400	..	..	..	..	..	*1400	..
Domestic navigation	..	..	..	*731	..	..	..	..	..	*731	..
Pipeline transport	..	..	..	..	..	..	..	..	..	..	..
Transport, n.e.s	..	..	..	..	..	..	..	..	..	..	..
Other	..	..	..	*61860	..	*193403	..	22068	..	*277331	*193403
Agriculture, forestry, fishing	..	..	..	*387	..	..	..	..	..	*387	..
Commerce, public services	..	..	..	*34793	..	..	..	..	..	*34793	..
Households	..	..	..	26548	..	*193403	..	22068	..	*242019	*193403
Other consumers	..	..	..	*132	..	..	..	..	..	*132	..
Non-energy use	..	..	..	4101	..	..	..	..	..	4101	..

Angola

Terajoules

2018	Primary coal and peat	Coal and peat products	Primary Oil	Oil Products	Natural Gas	Biofuels and waste	Nuclear	Electricity	Heat	Total energy	of which: renewables
Primary production	..	..	3279086	..	211698	270287	..	31507	..	3792578	301795
Imports	..	..	..	147859	..	..	..	..	..	147859	..
Exports	..	..	-3178516	-79066	-182286	..	..	..	..	-3439869	..
International marine bunkers	..	..	..	-10166	..	..	..	..	..	-10166	..
International aviation bunkers	..	..	..	*-10340	..	..	..	..	..	*-10340	..
Stock changes	..	..	8629	*25738	..	..	..	..	..	*34367	..
Total energy supply	..	..	109199	74025	29412	270287	..	31507	..	514430	301795
Statistical difference	..	..	-3559	34527	0	*-2	..	-4	..	30962	31506
Transfers	..	..	*1883	*43	..	..	..	..	..	*1926	..
Transformation	..	..	-114641	90247	..	*-68282	..	10804	..	-81872	*-68282
Electricity plants	..	..	..	*-29653	..	*-2402	..	10804	..	*-21251	*-2402
CHP plants	..	..	..	..	..	..	..	..	..	..	..
Heat plants	..	..	..	..	..	..	..	..	..	..	..
Coke ovens	..	..	..	..	..	..	..	..	..	..	..
Briquetting plants	..	..	..	..	..	..	..	..	..	..	..
Liquefaction plants	..	..	..	..	..	..	..	..	..	..	..
Gas works	..	..	..	..	..	..	..	..	..	..	..
Blast furnaces	..	..	..	..	..	..	..	..	..	..	..
NGL plants & gas blending	..	..	-36321	38868	..	..	..	..	..	2547	..
Oil refineries	..	..	-78320	78538	..	..	..	..	..	218	..
Other transformation	..	..	..	..	..	*-65881	..	..	..	*-65881	*-65881
Energy industries own use	..	..	..	-2624	-15851	..	..	-1109	..	-19583	..
Losses	..	..	..	..	..	..	..	-4759	..	-4759	..
Final consumption	..	..	..	*127165	13561	*202007	..	36446	..	*379180	*202007
Final energy consumption	..	..	..	*124066	13561	*202007	..	36446	..	*376081	*202007
Manufacturing, const., mining	..	..	..	*9821	13561	*5950	..	12287	..	41619	*5950
Iron and steel	..	..	..	..	..	..	..	..	..	..	..
Chemical and petrochemical	..	..	..	..	..	..	..	..	..	..	..
Non-ferrous metals	..	..	..	..	..	..	..	..	..	..	..
Non-metallic minerals	..	..	..	*2141	..	..	..	..	..	*2141	..
Transport equipment	..	..	..	..	..	..	..	..	..	..	..
Machinery	..	..	..	..	..	..	..	..	..	..	..
Mining and quarrying	..	..	..	..	..	..	..	..	..	..	..
Food and tobacco	..	..	..	..	..	*1239	..	..	..	*1239	*1239
Paper, pulp and printing	..	..	..	..	..	..	..	..	..	..	..
Wood and wood products	..	..	..	..	..	..	..	..	..	..	..
Textile and leather	..	..	..	..	..	..	..	..	..	..	..
Construction	..	..	..	*4864	..	..	..	..	..	*4864	..
Industries n.e.s	..	..	..	*2816	13561	*4711	..	12287	..	33375	*4711
Transport	..	..	..	*63799	..	..	..	..	..	*63799	..
Road	..	..	..	*61868	..	..	..	..	..	*61868	..
Rail	..	..	..	..	..	..	..	..	..	..	..
Domestic aviation	..	..	..	*1372	..	..	..	..	..	*1372	..
Domestic navigation	..	..	..	*559	..	..	..	..	..	*559	..
Pipeline transport	..	..	..	..	..	..	..	..	..	..	..
Transport, n.e.s	..	..	..	..	..	..	..	..	..	..	..
Other	..	..	..	*50446	..	*196057	..	24160	..	*270663	*196057
Agriculture, forestry, fishing	..	..	..	*301	..	..	..	..	..	*301	..
Commerce, public services	..	..	..	*27596	..	..	..	..	..	*27596	..
Households	..	..	..	*22373	..	*196057	..	24160	..	*242590	*196057
Other consumers	..	..	..	*176	..	..	..	..	..	*176	..
Non-energy use	..	..	..	3099	..	..	..	..	..	3099	..

Anguilla

Terajoules

	All Coal	All Oil	Natural Gas	Primary biofuels / Waste	Charcoal	Electricity	Total energy	of which: renewables
2017								
Primary production	..	..	..	*2	..	*1	*3	*3
Imports	..	*2019	..	..	..	..	*2019	..
Exports	..	..	..	..	..	..	..	..
International marine bunkers	..	..	..	..	..	..	..	..
International aviation bunkers	..	..	..	..	..	..	..	..
Stock changes	..	..	..	..	..	..	..	..
Total energy supply	..	*2019	..	*2	..	*1	*2022	*3
Statistical Difference	..	0	..	0	..	0	0	*1
Transfers	..	..	..	..	..	..	..	..
Transformation	..	*-808	..	..	..	287	*-522	..
Electricity plants	..	*-808	..	..	..	287	*-522	..
Charcoal plants	..	..	..	..	..	..	..	..
Other transformation	..	0	..	..	..	..	0	..
Energy industries own use	..	..	..	..	..	-9	-9	..
Losses	..	..	..	..	..	*-32	*-32	..
Final consumption	..	*1210	..	*2	..	*246	*1458	*2
Final energy consumption	..	*1210	..	*2	..	*246	*1458	*2
Manufacturing, const., mining	..	..	..	..	..	..	..	..
Transport	..	*804	..	..	..	..	*804	..
Road	..	*279	..	..	..	..	*279	..
Domestic aviation	..	..	..	..	..	..	..	..
Domestic navigation	..	..	..	..	..	..	..	..
Other transport	..	*525	..	..	..	..	*525	..
Other	..	*407	..	*2	..	*246	*654	*2
Agriculture, forestry, fishing	..	..	..	..	..	..	..	..
Commerce and public services	..	..	..	..	..	*171	*171	..
Households	..	*407	..	*2	..	*75	*484	*2
Other consumers	..	..	..	..	..	..	..	..
Non-energy use	..	..	..	..	..	..	..	..
2018								
Primary production	..	..	..	*2	..	*1	*3	*3
Imports	..	*2071	..	..	..	..	*2071	..
Exports	..	..	..	..	..	..	..	..
International marine bunkers	..	..	..	..	..	..	..	..
International aviation bunkers	..	..	..	..	..	..	..	..
Stock changes	..	..	..	..	..	..	..	..
Total energy supply	..	*2071	..	*2	..	*1	*2074	*3
Statistical Difference	..	0	..	0	..	0	0	*1
Transfers	..	..	..	..	..	..	..	..
Transformation	..	*-839	..	..	..	312	*-526	..
Electricity plants	..	*-839	..	..	..	312	*-526	..
Charcoal plants	..	..	..	..	..	..	..	..
Other transformation	..	0	..	..	..	..	0	..
Energy industries own use	..	..	..	..	..	-11	-11	..
Losses	..	..	..	..	..	*-36	*-36	..
Final consumption	..	*1233	..	*2	..	266	*1501	*2
Final energy consumption	..	*1233	..	*2	..	266	*1501	*2
Manufacturing, const., mining	..	..	..	..	..	..	..	..
Transport	..	*821	..	..	..	..	*821	..
Road	..	*284	..	..	..	..	*284	..
Domestic aviation	..	..	..	..	..	..	..	..
Domestic navigation	..	..	..	..	..	..	..	..
Other transport	..	*538	..	..	..	..	*538	..
Other	..	*412	..	*2	..	266	*680	*2
Agriculture, forestry, fishing	..	..	..	..	..	..	..	..
Commerce and public services	..	..	..	..	..	180	180	..
Households	..	*412	..	*2	..	*86	*500	*2
Other consumers	..	..	..	..	..	..	..	..
Non-energy use	..	..	..	..	..	..	..	..

Antigua and Barbuda

Terajoules

	All Coal	All Oil	Natural Gas	Primary biofuels / Waste	Charcoal	Electricity	Total energy	of which: renewables
2017								
Primary production	..	..	..	..	..	32	32	32
Imports	..	*10241	..	0	..	..	*10241	0
Exports	..	*-176	..	..	..	..	*-176	..
International marine bunkers	..	*-162	..	..	..	..	*-162	..
International aviation bunkers	..	*-2867	..	..	..	..	*-2867	..
Stock changes	..	..	..	..	..	..	..	..
Total energy supply	..	*7037	..	0	..	32	*7069	32
Statistical Difference	..	0	..	0	..	0	0	32
Transfers	..	..	..	..	..	..	..	..
Transformation	..	*-3860	..	..	..	*1238	*-2621	..
Electricity plants	..	*-3860	..	..	..	*1238	*-2621	..
Charcoal plants	..	..	..	..	..	..	..	..
Other transformation	..	0	..	..	..	..	0	..
Energy industries own use	..	..	..	..	..	*-29	*-29	..
Losses	..	..	..	..	..	*-324	*-324	..
Final consumption	..	*3177	..	0	..	*918	*4095	0
Final energy consumption	..	*2976	..	0	..	*918	*3894	0
Manufacturing, const., mining	..	..	..	..	..	*43	*43	..
Transport	..	*2806	..	..	..	..	*2806	..
Road	..	*1816	..	..	..	..	*1816	..
Domestic aviation	..	*516	..	..	..	..	*516	..
Domestic navigation	..	..	..	..	..	..	..	..
Other transport	..	*473	..	..	..	..	*473	..
Other	..	*170	..	0	..	*875	*1045	0
Agriculture, forestry, fishing	..	..	..	..	..	..	..	..
Commerce and public services	..	..	..	..	..	*504	*504	..
Households	..	*170	..	0	..	*371	*541	0
Other consumers	..	..	..	..	..	..	..	..
Non-energy use	..	*201	..	..	..	..	*201	..
2018								
Primary production	..	..	..	..	..	47	47	47
Imports	..	*10422	..	0	..	..	*10422	0
Exports	..	*-176	..	..	..	..	*-176	..
International marine bunkers	..	*-162	..	..	..	..	*-162	..
International aviation bunkers	..	*-2911	..	..	..	..	*-2911	..
Stock changes	..	..	..	..	..	..	..	..
Total energy supply	..	*7174	..	0	..	47	*7220	47
Statistical Difference	..	0	..	0	..	-25	*-25	47
Transfers	..	..	..	..	..	..	..	..
Transformation	..	*-3900	..	..	..	1256	*-2644	..
Electricity plants	..	*-3900	..	..	..	1256	*-2644	..
Charcoal plants	..	..	..	..	..	..	..	..
Other transformation	..	0	..	..	..	..	0	..
Energy industries own use	..	..	..	..	..	-97	-97	..
Losses	..	..	..	..	..	*-198	*-198	..
Final consumption	..	*3273	..	0	..	*1033	*4307	0
Final energy consumption	..	*3072	..	0	..	*1033	*4106	0
Manufacturing, const., mining	..	..	..	..	..	*47	*47	..
Transport	..	*2897	..	..	..	..	*2897	..
Road	..	*1861	..	..	..	..	*1861	..
Domestic aviation	..	*521	..	..	..	..	*521	..
Domestic navigation	..	..	..	..	..	..	..	..
Other transport	..	*516	..	..	..	..	*516	..
Other	..	*175	..	0	..	*986	*1161	0
Agriculture, forestry, fishing	..	..	..	..	..	..	..	..
Commerce and public services	..	..	..	..	..	*576	*576	..
Households	..	*175	..	0	..	*410	*585	0
Other consumers	..	..	..	..	..	..	..	..
Non-energy use	..	*201	..	..	..	..	*201	..

Argentina

Terajoules

	Primary coal and peat	Coal and peat products	Primary Oil	Oil Products	Natural Gas	Biofuels and waste	Nuclear	Electricity	Heat	Total energy	of which: renewables
2017											
Primary production	494	..	1199429	..	1405278	213498	65750	150739	..	3035188	364237
Imports	43545	..	47249	159626	361242	..	..	37904	..	649566	..
Exports	0	..	-73962	-82015	-2396	-60720	..	-248	..	-219341	-60720
International marine bunkers	..	..	..	-32700	..	..	..	..	..	-32700	..
International aviation bunkers	..	..	..	-43306	..	..	..	..	..	-43306	..
Stock changes	3236	..	-3299	-4337	315	..	..	..	..	-4086	..
Total energy supply	47275	..	1169417	-2733	1764439	152778	65750	188395	..	3385322	303517
Statistical difference	-500	0	-30371	-23224	95191	2306	0	-4	..	43397	153045
Transfers	..	..	..	..	..	..	..	..	..	..	..
Transformation	-46826	9808	-1195178	1076646	-629717	-19809	-65750	372042	..	-498784	-19809
Electricity plants	-19386	-2603	..	-114811	-629717	-14189	-65750	372042	..	-474414	-14189
CHP plants	..	..	..	..	..	..	..	..	..	..	..
Heat plants	..	..	..	..	..	..	..	..	..	..	..
Coke ovens	-27440	24688	..	..	..	..	..	..	..	-2752	..
Briquetting plants	..	..	..	..	..	..	..	..	..	..	..
Liquefaction plants	..	..	..	..	..	..	..	..	..	..	..
Gas works	..	..	..	..	..	..	..	..	..	..	..
Blast furnaces	..	-12277	..	-32175	..	..	..	..	..	-44452	..
NGL plants & gas blending	..	..	-112843	119875	..	..	..	..	..	7032	..
Oil refineries	..	..	-1082335	1103757	..	..	..	..	..	21422	..
Other transformation	..	..	..	..	..	-5620	..	..	..	-5620	-5620
Energy industries own use	..	-9808	-4611	-64146	-197537	..	..	-13306	..	-289407	..
Losses	..	..	..	..	-75348	..	..	-82732	..	-158080	..
Final consumption	949	..	..	1032991	766647	130664	..	464404	..	2395655	130664
Final energy consumption	949	..	..	940385	766647	130664	..	464404	..	2303048	130664
Manufacturing, const., mining	949	..	..	30113	265577	47312	..	181346	..	525297	47312
Iron and steel	..	..	..	..	..	..	..	..	..	..	..
Chemical and petrochemical	..	..	..	..	..	..	..	..	..	..	..
Non-ferrous metals	..	..	..	..	..	..	..	..	..	..	..
Non-metallic minerals	..	..	..	..	..	..	..	..	..	..	..
Transport equipment	..	..	..	..	..	..	..	..	..	..	..
Machinery	..	..	..	..	..	..	..	..	..	..	..
Mining and quarrying	..	..	..	..	..	..	..	..	..	..	..
Food and tobacco	..	..	..	..	..	43730	..	..	..	43730	43730
Paper, pulp and printing	..	..	..	..	..	3582	..	..	..	3582	3582
Wood and wood products	..	..	..	..	..	..	..	..	..	..	..
Textile and leather	..	..	..	..	..	..	..	..	..	..	..
Construction	..	..	..	..	..	..	..	..	..	..	..
Industries n.e.s	949	..	..	30113	265577	0	..	181346	..	477985	0
Transport	..	..	..	677988	111038	66000	..	2376	..	857402	66000
Road	..	..	..	653945	80388	66000	..	..	..	800333	66000
Rail	..	..	..	..	..	..	..	2376	..	2376	..
Domestic aviation	..	..	..	23639	..	..	..	..	..	23639	..
Domestic navigation	..	..	..	404	..	..	..	..	..	404	..
Pipeline transport	..	..	..	..	30650	..	..	..	..	30650	..
Transport, n.e.s	..	..	..	..	..	..	..	..	..	..	..
Other	..	..	..	232283	390033	17352	..	280681	..	920349	17352
Agriculture, forestry, fishing	..	..	..	162161	..	..	..	3388	..	165549	..
Commerce, public services	..	..	..	14444	53645	6572	..	116122	..	190783	6572
Households	..	..	..	55677	336389	10780	..	161172	..	564018	10780
Other consumers	..	..	..	..	..	..	..	..	..	..	..
Non-energy use	..	..	..	92607	..	..	..	..	..	92607	..

Argentina

Terajoules

2018	Primary coal and peat	Coal and peat products	Primary Oil	Oil Products	Natural Gas	Biofuels and waste	Nuclear	Electricity	Heat	Total energy	of which: renewables
Primary production	1482	..	1239954	..	1480011	207212	69692	153180	..	3151531	360392
Imports	48818	..	16751	168299	292255	..	..	36108	..	562231	..
Exports	-49	..	-146858	-142481	-13361	-51557	..	-1008	..	-355314	-51557
International marine bunkers	..	..	..	-29638	..	..	..	..	..	-29638	..
International aviation bunkers	..	..	..	-39381	..	..	..	..	..	-39381	..
Stock changes	-2124	..	-1311	2331	-287	..	..	..	..	-1391	..
Total energy supply	48126	..	1108536	-40871	1758619	155655	69692	188280	..	3288037	308835
Statistical difference	-3770	14	-41666	-19624	165810	-1541	0	18864	..	118088	151639
Transfers	..	..	..	..	..	..	..	..	..	..	..
Transformation	-49919	10769	-1146014	1067162	-593430	-21774	-69692	393383	..	-409515	-21774
Electricity plants	-19658	-2605	..	-66625	-593430	-12792	-69692	393383	..	-371419	-12792
CHP plants	..	..	..	..	..	..	..	..	..	..	..
Heat plants	..	..	..	..	..	..	..	..	..	..	..
Coke ovens	-30261	27327	..	..	..	..	..	..	..	-2934	..
Briquetting plants	..	..	..	..	..	..	..	..	..	..	..
Liquefaction plants	..	..	..	..	..	..	..	..	..	..	..
Gas works	..	..	..	..	..	..	..	..	..	..	..
Blast furnaces	..	-13953	..	-32923	..	..	..	..	..	-46876	..
NGL plants & gas blending	..	..	-125926	133766	..	..	..	..	..	7840	..
Oil refineries	..	..	-1020088	1032944	..	..	..	..	..	12856	..
Other transformation	..	..	..	..	..	-8982	..	..	..	-8982	-8982
Energy industries own use	..	-10755	-4188	-65906	-185512	..	..	-14101	..	-280461	..
Losses	..	..	..	..	-87784	..	..	-85219	..	-173003	..
Final consumption	1977	..	..	980010	726083	135422	..	463478	..	2306970	135422
Final energy consumption	1977	..	..	890888	726083	135422	..	463478	..	2217848	135422
Manufacturing, const., mining	1977	..	..	27420	263528	53632	..	182704	..	529261	53632
Iron and steel	..	..	..	..	..	..	..	..	..	..	..
Chemical and petrochemical	..	..	..	..	..	..	..	..	..	..	..
Non-ferrous metals	..	..	..	..	..	..	..	..	..	..	..
Non-metallic minerals	..	..	..	..	..	..	..	..	..	..	..
Transport equipment	..	..	..	..	..	..	..	..	..	..	..
Machinery	..	..	..	..	..	..	..	..	..	..	..
Mining and quarrying	..	..	..	..	..	..	..	..	..	..	..
Food and tobacco	..	..	..	..	..	49082	..	..	..	49082	49082
Paper, pulp and printing	..	..	..	..	..	*4550	..	..	..	*4550	*4550
Wood and wood products	..	..	..	..	..	..	..	..	..	..	..
Textile and leather	..	..	..	..	..	..	..	..	..	..	..
Construction	..	..	..	..	..	..	..	..	..	..	..
Industries n.e.s	1977	..	..	27420	263528	0	..	182704	..	475629	0
Transport	..	..	..	638045	96833	62972	..	1958	..	799808	62972
Road	..	..	..	614951	71353	62972	..	..	..	749276	62972
Rail	..	..	..	..	..	..	..	1958	..	1958	..
Domestic aviation	..	..	..	21478	..	..	..	..	..	21478	..
Domestic navigation	..	..	..	1616	..	..	..	..	..	1616	..
Pipeline transport	..	..	..	..	25479	..	..	..	..	25479	..
Transport, n.e.s	..	..	..	..	..	..	..	..	..	..	..
Other	..	..	..	225423	365722	18818	..	278816	..	888779	18818
Agriculture, forestry, fishing	..	..	..	158502	..	..	..	3298	..	161800	..
Commerce, public services	..	..	..	14598	50184	7079	..	115445	..	187306	7079
Households	..	..	..	52323	315538	11739	..	160074	..	539674	11739
Other consumers	..	..	..	..	..	..	..	..	..	..	..
Non-energy use	..	..	..	89122	..	..	..	..	..	89122	..

Armenia

Terajoules

2017	Primary coal and peat	Coal and peat products	Primary Oil	Oil Products	Natural Gas	Biofuels and waste	Nuclear	Electricity	Heat	Total energy	of which: renewables
Primary production	..	..	..	..	..	8510	28292	8186	223	45211	16919
Imports	14	23	..	16637	82399	359	..	1150	..	100582	359
Exports	..	..	..	-13	..	-2	..	-5183	..	-5197	-2
International marine bunkers	..	..	..	..	..	..	..	..	..	..	..
International aviation bunkers	..	..	..	-2399	..	..	..	..	..	-2399	..
Stock changes	..	..	..	-528	-814	-10	..	..	..	-1352	-10
Total energy supply	14	23	..	13698	81585	8857	28292	4154	223	136844	17266
Statistical difference	0	0	..	0	-4	0	0	0	0	-4	8186
Transfers	..	..	..	..	..	..	..	..	..	..	..
Transformation	..	..	..	..	-22084	..	-28292	19769	31	-30576	..
Electricity plants	..	..	..	..	-21907	..	-28292	19702	..	-30497	..
CHP plants	..	..	..	..	-176	..	..	67	31	-79	..
Heat plants	..	..	..	..	..	..	..	..	0	0	..
Coke ovens	..	..	..	..	..	..	..	..	..	..	..
Briquetting plants	..	..	..	..	..	..	..	..	..	..	..
Liquefaction plants	..	..	..	..	..	..	..	..	..	..	..
Gas works	..	..	..	..	..	..	..	..	..	..	..
Blast furnaces	..	..	..	..	..	..	..	..	..	..	..
NGL plants & gas blending	..	..	..	..	..	..	..	..	..	..	..
Oil refineries	..	..	..	..	..	..	..	..	..	..	..
Other transformation	..	..	..	..	..	..	..	..	..	..	..
Energy industries own use	..	..	..	..	-288	..	..	-1273	-2	-1562	..
Losses	..	..	..	..	-5161	..	..	-2406	-20	-7588	..
Final consumption	14	23	..	13698	54056	8857	..	20243	232	97122	9080
Final energy consumption	14	23	..	12380	54056	8857	..	20243	232	95805	9080
Manufacturing, const., mining	..	..	..	844	6935	3	..	5957	112	13851	115
Iron and steel	..	..	..	1	497	..	..	256	..	754	..
Chemical and petrochemical	..	..	..	1	88	..	..	48	..	136	..
Non-ferrous metals	..	..	..	192	843	3	..	885	..	1922	3
Non-metallic minerals	..	..	..	21	2999	..	..	490	..	3510	..
Transport equipment	..	..	..	..	..	..	..	..	..	..	..
Machinery	..	..	..	2	33	0	..	72	..	107	0
Mining and quarrying	..	..	..	606	283	..	..	2868	..	3757	..
Food and tobacco	..	..	..	3	1842	..	..	932	..	2777	..
Paper, pulp and printing	..	..	..	..	148	..	..	75	..	223	..
Wood and wood products	..	..	..	..	2	0	..	4	..	6	0
Textile and leather	..	..	..	..	18	..	..	45	..	63	..
Construction	..	..	..	18	141	..	..	113	..	272	..
Industries n.e.s	..	..	..	1	42	0	..	170	112	324	112
Transport	..	..	..	10588	16541	..	..	366	..	27494	..
Road	..	..	..	10588	16541	..	..	22	..	27150	..
Rail	..	..	..	..	..	..	..	241	..	241	..
Domestic aviation	..	..	..	..	..	..	..	..	..	..	..
Domestic navigation	..	..	..	..	..	..	..	..	..	..	..
Pipeline transport	..	..	..	..	..	..	..	..	..	..	..
Transport, n.e.s	..	..	..	..	..	..	..	103	..	103	..
Other	14	23	..	948	30580	8854	..	13920	120	54460	8965
Agriculture, forestry, fishing	..	..	..	866	..	..	..	570	..	1436	..
Commerce, public services	11	..	..	42	1947	..	..	845	56	2901	56
Households	3	23	..	40	21529	8854	..	6867	65	37380	8910
Other consumers	..	..	..	..	7105	..	..	5638	..	12743	..
Non-energy use	..	..	..	1317	..	..	..	..	..	1317	..

Armenia

Terajoules

2018	Primary coal and peat	Coal and peat products	Primary Oil	Oil Products	Natural Gas	Biofuels and waste	Nuclear	Electricity	Heat	Total energy	of which: renewables
Primary production	..	..	..	..	..	5637	22422	8422	432	36913	14491
Imports	21	23	..	16766	84855	467	..	734	..	102866	467
Exports	..	..	..	0	..	-45	..	-5858	..	-5903	-45
International marine bunkers	..	..	..	..	..	..	..	..	..	..	..
International aviation bunkers	..	..	..	-2729	..	..	..	..	..	-2729	
Stock changes	..	..	..	-565	716	29	..	..	..	181	29
Total energy supply	21	23	..	13473	85572	6088	22422	3298	432	131327	14942
Statistical difference	0	0	..	0	2	0	0	0	0	2	8422
Transfers	..	..	..	..	..	..	..	..	..	..	..
Transformation	..	..	..	..	-26452	..	-22422	19626	24	-29223	..
Electricity plants	..	..	..	..	-26306	..	-22422	19571	..	-29157	..
CHP plants	..	..	..	..	-146	..	..	55	24	-67	..
Heat plants	..	..	..	..	..	..	..	..	0	0	..
Coke ovens	..	..	..	..	..	..	..	..	..	..	..
Briquetting plants	..	..	..	..	..	..	..	..	..	..	..
Liquefaction plants	..	..	..	..	..	..	..	..	..	..	..
Gas works	..	..	..	..	..	..	..	..	..	..	..
Blast furnaces	..	..	..	..	..	..	..	..	..	..	..
NGL plants & gas blending	..	..	..	..	..	..	..	..	..	..	..
Oil refineries	..	..	..	..	..	..	..	..	..	..	..
Other transformation	..	..	..	..	..	..	..	..	..	..	..
Energy industries own use	..	..	..	..	-207	..	..	-1274	-2	-1482	..
Losses	..	..	..	..	-4292	..	..	-2201	-14	-6507	..
Final consumption	21	23	..	13473	54619	6088	..	19449	440	94113	6520
Final energy consumption	21	23	..	11825	54619	6088	..	19449	440	92465	6520
Manufacturing, const., mining	..	..	..	297	7799	1	..	5368	216	13681	217
Iron and steel	..	..	..	..	553	..	..	255	..	808	..
Chemical and petrochemical	..	..	..	14	83	..	..	48	..	145	..
Non-ferrous metals	..	..	..	1	387	0	..	798	..	1185	0
Non-metallic minerals	..	..	..	16	3401	0	..	544	..	3961	0
Transport equipment	..	..	..	..	1	..	..	1	..	2	..
Machinery	..	..	..	2	29	0	..	78	..	109	0
Mining and quarrying	..	..	..	233	320	..	..	2302	..	2855	..
Food and tobacco	..	..	..	9	2698	..	..	895	..	3603	..
Paper, pulp and printing	..	..	..	..	158	..	..	80	..	238	..
Wood and wood products	..	..	..	..	1	0	..	4	..	6	0
Textile and leather	..	..	..	..	18	0	..	50	..	69	0
Construction	..	..	..	13	101	..	..	118	..	231	..
Industries n.e.s	..	..	..	9	48	0	..	196	216	469	216
Transport	..	..	..	10647	19038	..	..	346	..	30031	..
Road	..	..	..	10647	19038	..	..	21	..	29706	..
Rail	..	..	..	..	..	..	..	231	..	231	..
Domestic aviation	..	..	..	..	..	..	..	..	..	..	..
Domestic navigation	..	..	..	..	..	..	..	..	..	..	..
Pipeline transport	..	..	..	..	..	..	..	..	..	..	..
Transport, n.e.s	..	..	..	..	..	..	..	94	..	94	..
Other	21	23	..	882	27781	6087	..	13735	224	48752	6303
Agriculture, forestry, fishing	..	..	..	709	..	..	..	613	..	1322	..
Commerce, public services	17	..	..	113	1509	..	..	1059	108	2805	108
Households	4	23	..	60	19087	6087	..	6586	116	31963	6195
Other consumers	..	..	..	0	7186	..	..	5476	..	12662	..
Non-energy use	..	..	..	1648	..	..	..	..	..	1648	..

Aruba

Terajoules

	All Coal	All Oil	Natural Gas	Primary biofuels / Waste	Charcoal	Electricity	Total energy	of which: renewables
2017								
Primary production	..	..	..	20	..	*518	*538	*538
Imports	..	*16452	..	0	8	..	*16460	8
Exports	..	..	..	..	..	..	..	..
International marine bunkers	..	*-444	..	..	..	..	*-444	..
International aviation bunkers	..	*-3881	..	..	..	..	*-3881	..
Stock changes	..	..	..	..	..	..	..	..
Total energy supply	..	*12126	..	20	8	*518	*12672	*546
Statistical Difference	..	0	..	0	0	0	0	*518
Transfers	..	..	..	..	..	..	..	..
Transformation	..	*-8278	..	*-13	7	*3005	*-5279	*-6
Electricity plants	..	*-8278	..	..	..	*3005	*-5273	..
Charcoal plants	..	..	..	*-13	7	..	*-6	*-6
Other transformation	..	0	..	0	..	..	0	0
Energy industries own use	..	..	..	..	..	0	0	..
Losses	..	..	..	..	..	*-594	*-594	..
Final consumption	..	*3849	..	*8	*15	*2928	*6799	*22
Final energy consumption	..	*3808	..	*8	*15	*2928	*6759	*22
Manufacturing, const., mining	..	..	..	..	..	..	..	..
Transport	..	*3288	..	..	..	..	*3288	..
Road	..	*3288	..	..	..	..	*3288	..
Domestic aviation	..	..	..	..	..	..	..	..
Domestic navigation	..	..	..	..	..	..	..	..
Other transport	..	..	..	..	..	..	..	..
Other	..	*520	..	*8	*15	*2928	*3471	*22
Agriculture, forestry, fishing	..	..	..	..	..	..	..	..
Commerce and public services	..	..	..	..	..	*1854	*1854	..
Households	..	*158	..	*8	*15	*1074	*1255	*22
Other consumers	..	*362	..	..	..	..	*362	..
Non-energy use	..	*40	..	..	..	..	*40	..
2018								
Primary production	..	..	..	21	..	*630	*651	*651
Imports	..	*16264	..	0	8	..	*16272	8
Exports	..	..	..	..	..	..	..	..
International marine bunkers	..	*-465	..	..	..	..	*-465	..
International aviation bunkers	..	*-3916	..	..	..	..	*-3916	..
Stock changes	..	..	..	..	..	..	..	..
Total energy supply	..	*11884	..	21	8	*630	*12542	*659
Statistical Difference	..	0	..	0	0	0	0	*630
Transfers	..	..	..	..	..	..	..	..
Transformation	..	*-8000	..	*-13	7	*2908	*-5097	*-6
Electricity plants	..	*-8000	..	..	..	*2908	*-5091	..
Charcoal plants	..	..	..	*-13	7	..	*-6	*-6
Other transformation	..	0	..	0	..	..	0	0
Energy industries own use	..	..	..	..	..	0	0	..
Losses	..	..	..	..	..	*-598	*-598	..
Final consumption	..	*3884	..	*8	*15	*2940	*6848	*23
Final energy consumption	..	*3844	..	*8	*15	*2940	*6807	*23
Manufacturing, const., mining	..	..	..	..	..	..	..	..
Transport	..	*3319	..	..	..	..	*3319	..
Road	..	*3319	..	..	..	..	*3319	..
Domestic aviation	..	..	..	..	..	..	..	..
Domestic navigation	..	..	..	..	..	..	..	..
Other transport	..	..	..	..	..	..	..	..
Other	..	*525	..	*8	*15	*2940	*3488	*23
Agriculture, forestry, fishing	..	..	..	..	..	..	..	..
Commerce and public services	..	..	..	..	..	*1861	*1861	..
Households	..	*160	..	*8	*15	*1079	*1262	*23
Other consumers	..	*365	..	..	..	..	*365	..
Non-energy use	..	*40	..	..	..	..	*40	..

Australia

Terajoules

2017	Primary coal and peat	Coal and peat products	Primary Oil	Oil Products	Natural Gas	Biofuels and waste	Nuclear	Electricity	Heat	Total energy	of which: renewables
Primary production	12265227	..	641247	..	3696081	228418	..	132131	15756	16978860	372534
Imports	2895	5022	680731	1216410	185867	..	..	..	..	2090925	..
Exports	-10224012	-12771	-426567	-117383	-2572196	..	..	..	..	-13352929	..
International marine bunkers	..	..	..	-22302	..	..	..	..	..	-22302	..
International aviation bunkers	..	..	..	-185749	..	..	..	..	..	-185749	..
Stock changes	-150903	210	2947	12635	..	..	..	..	..	-135111	..
Total energy supply	1893206	-7539	898358	903611	1309752	228418	..	132131	15756	5373694	372534
Statistical difference	9797	0	-85118	-76211	-24321	0	..	0	0	-175853	132142
Transfers	..	..	67693	73208	..	..	..	..	..	140901	..
Transformation	-1805676	69796	-1048096	945274	-502705	*-47916	..	795845	-58	-1593536	*-47963
Electricity plants	-1663791	-168	..	-49793	-400684	-17682	..	743526	-58	-1388649	-17729
CHP plants	-21523	..	..	-1327	-101981	*-30234	..	52319	..	-102745	*-30234
Heat plants	..	..	..	..	..	..	..	..	..	..	..
Coke ovens	-118608	96976	..	..	..	..	..	..	..	-21632	..
Briquetting plants	..	..	..	..	..	..	..	..	..	..	..
Liquefaction plants	..	..	0	..	..	..	..	..	..	0	..
Gas works	..	..	..	..	-41	..	..	..	..	-41	..
Blast furnaces	-1754	-27057	..	..	..	..	..	..	..	-28811	..
NGL plants & gas blending	..	45	-69750	72653	..	..	..	..	..	2948	..
Oil refineries	..	..	-978346	923740	..	..	..	..	..	-54606	..
Other transformation	..	..	..	..	0	..	..	..	..	0	..
Energy industries own use	..	-40701	-2467	-169331	-297659	..	..	-120496	..	-630653	..
Losses	..	..	..	..	..	..	..	-47596	..	-47596	..
Final consumption	77734	21556	606	1828973	533709	*180502	..	759884	15698	3418662	*192429
Final energy consumption	77734	21556	606	1659219	479939	*180502	..	759884	15698	3195139	*192429
Manufacturing, const., mining	77134	21490	606	150170	260267	*136662	..	269813	..	916141	*132891
Iron and steel	540	9614	..	802	7885	..	..	12298	..	31138	..
Chemical and petrochemical	6179	469	..	4379	36130	4033	..	14526	..	65715	*445
Non-ferrous metals	44341	6292	..	10910	115035	*2674	..	115376	..	294629	*2674
Non-metallic minerals	13626	108	..	6449	45380	*2074	..	16384	..	84020	*2074
Transport equipment	..	..	..	..	..	..	..	..	..	..	..
Machinery	..	..	..	939	2145	..	..	3092	..	6176	..
Mining and quarrying	1752	1458	..	100014	5377	*8	..	67522	..	176130	*8
Food and tobacco	7753	21	130	4428	30044	*107058	..	20815	..	*170249	*106875
Paper, pulp and printing	1273	..	..	2201	8602	*7853	..	14422	..	34350	*7853
Wood and wood products	162	..	..	421	2319	*12956	..	2714	..	*18572	*12956
Textile and leather	459	..	476	313	4634	..	..	1786	..	7667	..
Construction	..	..	..	19132	2623	..	..	828	..	22582	..
Industries n.e.s	1052	3528	0	182	94	*6	..	50	..	4912	*6
Transport	..	..	..	1357888	15607	4167	..	21179	..	1398841	4167
Road	..	..	..	1150014	3508	4167	..	..	..	1157690	4167
Rail	..	..	..	47178	..	..	..	11693	..	58871	..
Domestic aviation	..	..	..	128561	..	..	..	..	..	128561	..
Domestic navigation	..	..	..	24171	..	..	..	..	..	24171	..
Pipeline transport	..	..	..	..	11529	..	..	104	..	11633	..
Transport, n.e.s	..	..	..	7964	570	..	..	9382	..	17915	..
Other	599	66	..	151161	204066	*39673	..	468893	15698	880156	*55371
Agriculture, forestry, fishing	..	..	..	101977	1022	..	..	7099	..	110098	..
Commerce, public services	599	45	..	34474	53871	*914	..	248551	423	338878	1337
Households	..	21	..	14710	149172	*8587	..	213242	15275	401008	23862
Other consumers	..	..	..	..	..	*30172	..	..	..	*30172	*30172
Non-energy use	..	..	..	169754	53770	..	..	..	..	223524	..

Australia

Terajoules

2018	Primary coal and peat	Coal and peat products	Primary Oil	Oil Products	Natural Gas	Biofuels and waste	Nuclear	Electricity	Heat	Total energy	of which: renewables
Primary production	12034609	..	576244	..	4236881	219163	..	147316	16592	17230804	379286
Imports	6369	6367	753884	1295731	167864	..	..	..	..	2230214	..
Exports	-10282696	-15525	-430701	-121692	-3041874	..	..	..	..	-13892488	..
International marine bunkers	..	..	..	-22684	..	..	..	..	..	-22684	..
International aviation bunkers	..	..	..	-197700	..	..	..	..	..	-197700	..
Stock changes	75570	..	5234	-35839	..	..	..	..	..	44965	..
Total energy supply	1833851	-9158	904662	917816	1362870	219163	..	147316	16592	5393111	379286
Statistical difference	8478	0	-95624	-115385	-15112	0	..	0	0	-217643	147326
Transfers	..	..	84486	55177	..	..	..	..	..	139663	..
Transformation	-1736372	68751	-1082089	959528	-515086	*-48423	..	791593	-32	-1562131	*-48445
Electricity plants	-1600481	..	..	-47071	-407738	-18051	..	736114	-32	-1337260	-18073
CHP plants	-20095	..	..	-925	-107314	*-30372	..	55480	..	-103227	*-30372
Heat plants	..	..	..	..	..	..	..	..	..	..	..
Coke ovens	-114154	93289	..	..	..	..	..	..	..	-20865	..
Briquetting plants	..	..	..	..	..	..	..	..	..	..	..
Liquefaction plants	..	..	0	..	..	..	..	..	..	0	..
Gas works	..	..	..	..	-34	..	..	..	..	-34	..
Blast furnaces	-1642	-24576	..	..	..	..	..	..	..	-26218	..
NGL plants & gas blending	..	38	-40551	42239	..	..	..	..	..	1726	..
Oil refineries	..	..	-1041538	965284	..	..	..	..	..	-76254	..
Other transformation	..	..	..	..	0	..	..	..	..	0	..
Energy industries own use	..	-38123	-1991	-176516	-326915	..	..	-122576	..	-666121	..
Losses	..	..	..	..	..	..	..	-48298	..	-48298	..
Final consumption	89001	21470	693	1871389	535981	*170740	..	768035	16560	3473868	*183515
Final energy consumption	89001	21470	693	1700372	479690	*170740	..	768035	16560	3246560	*183515
Manufacturing, const., mining	88409	21410	693	162900	257748	*126418	..	273146	..	930724	*122633
Iron and steel	646	12773	..	802	8606	..	..	12852	..	35679	..
Chemical and petrochemical	6246	469	..	4422	34598	4068	..	14162	..	63965	*453
Non-ferrous metals	48443	3646	..	12745	112629	*1894	..	117418	..	296775	*1894
Non-metallic minerals	18129	108	..	6716	46083	*2707	..	16502	..	90245	*2707
Transport equipment	..	..	..	..	..	..	..	..	..	..	..
Machinery	..	..	..	843	1000	..	..	1868	..	3711	..
Mining and quarrying	2996	1026	..	109110	4702	*15	..	69736	..	187584	*15
Food and tobacco	7173	..	173	4731	30317	*96796	..	20671	..	*159862	*96626
Paper, pulp and printing	1598	..	..	2364	9574	*7658	..	14040	..	35235	*7658
Wood and wood products	162	..	..	384	2219	*13282	..	3157	..	*19204	*13282
Textile and leather	538	..	519	313	4933	..	..	1685	..	7989	..
Construction	..	..	..	20164	2993	..	..	997	..	24154	..
Industries n.e.s	2477	3388	0	306	95	*-2	..	58	..	6321	*-2
Transport	..	..	..	1382911	17285	5022	..	21463	..	1426680	5022
Road	..	..	..	1170301	3263	5022	..	..	..	1178586	5022
Rail	..	..	..	48210	..	..	..	11642	..	59852	..
Domestic aviation	..	..	..	131824	..	..	..	..	..	131824	..
Domestic navigation	..	..	..	24814	..	..	..	..	..	24814	..
Pipeline transport	..	..	..	..	13420	..	..	227	..	13647	..
Transport, n.e.s	..	..	..	7761	601	..	..	9594	..	17957	..
Other	592	60	..	154561	204657	*39300	..	473425	16560	889156	*55860
Agriculture, forestry, fishing	..	..	..	102686	1046	..	..	7636	..	111368	..
Commerce, public services	592	38	..	36981	54534	*1106	..	252468	451	346170	1557
Households	..	22	..	14805	149078	*8236	..	213322	16109	401571	24345
Other consumers	..	..	..	89	..	*29958	..	..	..	*30047	*29958
Non-energy use	..	..	..	171017	56291	..	..	..	..	227308	..

Austria

Terajoules

2017	Primary coal and peat	Coal and peat products	Primary Oil	Oil Products	Natural Gas	Biofuels and waste	Nuclear	Electricity	Heat	Total energy	of which: renewables
Primary production	..	..	31238	..	43664	265566	..	166082	9428	515978	415138
Imports	97552	33737	306808	286676	483179	35694	..	105703	..	1349347	35080
Exports	-28	-1120	..	-114757	-189434	-25989	..	-82141	..	-413469	-25989
International marine bunkers	..	..	..	-903	..	..	..	..	..	-903	..
International aviation bunkers	..	..	..	-31443	..	..	..	..	..	-31443	..
Stock changes	-312	257	6290	2542	-11825	*-299	..	..	..	-3347	*-299
Total energy supply	97212	32874	344335	142115	325584	274972	..	189644	9428	1416164	423930
Statistical difference	-28	2	43	-2557	1	114	..	-14	1	-2439	166878
Transfers	..	..	23132	-23050	..	..	..	..	..	82	..
Transformation	-90339	458	-367424	353026	-102388	*-103176	..	76712	87205	-145926	*-90028
Electricity plants	-10293	-18699	..	-1306	-41356	-29713	..	42080	-89	-59375	-24047
CHP plants	-6266	-1718	..	-12448	-48827	*-43928	..	34632	52361	-26194	*-37125
Heat plants	..	..	..	-1050	-12205	*-29476	..	..	34933	-7799	*-28798
Coke ovens	-50018	50036	..	..	..	..	..	..	..	17	..
Briquetting plants	..	..	..	..	..	..	..	..	..	..	..
Liquefaction plants	..	..	..	..	..	..	..	..	..	..	..
Gas works	..	..	..	..	..	..	..	..	..	..	..
Blast furnaces	-23761	-33478	..	..	..	..	..	..	..	-57239	..
NGL plants & gas blending	..	..	..	..	..	..	..	..	..	..	..
Oil refineries	..	..	-367424	367830	..	..	..	..	..	405	..
Other transformation	..	4317	..	..	..	*-59	..	..	..	4258	*-59
Energy industries own use	..	-19305	..	-11305	-8736	-1646	..	-27508	1	-68499	..
Losses	..	-810	..	..	-113	..	..	-12452	-13147	-26522	..
Final consumption	6901	13215	..	463342	214347	*170036	..	226411	83486	1177738	*167024
Final energy consumption	6816	11729	..	410471	200498	*170036	..	226411	83486	1109447	*167024
Manufacturing, const., mining	6549	11014	..	14882	111339	*63999	..	101696	10483	319961	*52923
Iron and steel	..	10728	..	83	17648	23	..	9288	317	38088	23
Chemical and petrochemical	1077	..	..	686	19121	3276	..	17050	2677	43887	760
Non-ferrous metals	..	86	..	40	4801	198	..	3766	65	8955	8
Non-metallic minerals	2125	..	..	2289	15404	7745	..	8618	54	36235	26
Transport equipment	..	..	..	171	1664	3	..	3488	772	6098	3
Machinery	..	..	..	1225	5987	26	..	13270	931	21439	25
Mining and quarrying	..	29	..	433	7238	10	..	7142	2	14854	10
Food and tobacco	..	171	..	636	12135	154	..	7225	1212	21533	154
Paper, pulp and printing	3346	..	..	162	20648	*30422	..	17140	794	72511	*30271
Wood and wood products	..	..	..	419	2457	415	..	6685	3005	12981	5
Textile and leather	..	..	..	40	1365	3	..	1253	19	2681	3
Construction	..	..	..	8574	1208	485	..	2038	194	12498	480
Industries n.e.s	0	0	..	124	1664	*21238	..	4734	441	28201	*21154
Transport	..	..	..	333446	12167	19733	..	11740	..	377086	19733
Road	..	..	..	330605	716	19660	..	50	..	351032	19660
Rail	..	..	..	1431	..	74	..	7344	..	8849	74
Domestic aviation	..	..	..	1235	..	..	..	..	..	1235	..
Domestic navigation	..	..	..	175	..	..	..	..	..	175	..
Pipeline transport	..	..	..	..	11451	..	..	799	..	12250	..
Transport, n.e.s	..	..	..	..	..	..	..	3546	..	3546	..
Other	267	715	..	62143	76991	*86304	..	112975	73003	412399	*94368
Agriculture, forestry, fishing	..	20	..	9518	1013	*7969	..	4270	552	23342	*8033
Commerce, public services	..	..	..	9027	14462	*3493	..	43974	32809	103766	6400
Households	267	696	..	43598	61516	*74842	..	64732	39642	285292	*79935
Other consumers	..	..	..	..	..	..	..	..	..	..	..
Non-energy use	85	1485	..	52871	13849	..	..	..	..	68291	..

Austria

Terajoules

2018	Primary coal and peat	Coal and peat products	Primary Oil	Oil Products	Natural Gas	Biofuels and waste	Nuclear	Electricity	Heat	Total energy	of which: renewables
Primary production	..	..	29240	..	35968	250996	..	162382	9303	487889	397538
Imports	89459	24063	354153	273195	453060	38446	..	101074	..	1333450	38446
Exports	-85	-1148	..	-132778	-181300	-31475	..	-68864	..	-415650	-31475
International marine bunkers	..	..	..	-559	..	..	..	..	..	-559	..
International aviation bunkers	..	..	..	-35412	..	..	..	..	..	-35412	..
Stock changes	3725	-1534	-1445	3831	1872	586	..	..	..	7035	586
Total energy supply	93099	21381	381948	108277	309600	258554	..	194591	9303	1376752	405095
Statistical difference	-50	27	-43	-2881	0	66	..	4	0	-2877	163110
Transfers	..	..	12278	-12491	..	..	..	..	..	-213	..
Transformation	-86493	8265	-394268	383273	-91224	*-97549	..	71687	81678	-124631	*-85131
Electricity plants	-11970	-16532	..	-5627	-31275	-26480	..	36965	-93	-55012	-21375
CHP plants	-5687	-1106	..	-7835	-50409	*-43264	..	34722	49477	-24102	*-36599
Heat plants	..	..	..	-929	-9540	*-27735	..	..	32294	-5911	*-27087
Coke ovens	-49616	48235	..	..	..	..	..	..	..	-1381	..
Briquetting plants	..	..	..	..	..	..	..	..	..	..	..
Liquefaction plants	..	..	..	..	..	..	..	..	..	..	..
Gas works	..	..	..	..	..	..	..	..	..	..	..
Blast furnaces	-19221	-25725	..	..	..	..	..	..	..	-44946	..
NGL plants & gas blending	..	..	..	..	..	..	..	..	..	..	..
Oil refineries	..	..	-394268	397665	..	..	..	..	..	3397	..
Other transformation	..	3393	..	..	..	*-70	..	..	..	3324	*-70
Energy industries own use	..	-16622	..	-11493	-9166	-597	..	-26755	1	-64631	..
Losses	..	-737	..	..	-106	..	..	-12452	-12281	-25577	..
Final consumption	6655	12260	..	470448	209104	*160342	..	227066	78701	1164577	*156854
Final energy consumption	6570	11311	..	408173	197535	*160342	..	227066	78701	1089699	*156854
Manufacturing, const., mining	6272	10733	..	14327	115585	*62286	..	103212	11043	323457	*50827
Iron and steel	..	9676	..	83	18005	50	..	9000	298	37112	50
Chemical and petrochemical	938	..	..	363	18548	2933	..	16686	2575	42044	289
Non-ferrous metals	..	112	..	95	5629	13	..	3816	85	9749	9
Non-metallic minerals	2433	..	..	1976	15548	7861	..	8831	55	36704	35
Transport equipment	..	..	..	171	1751	4	..	3460	820	6205	4
Machinery	..	..	..	1113	6873	58	..	14864	1289	24197	57
Mining and quarrying	..	..	..	393	7466	20	..	7153	..	15032	20
Food and tobacco	..	139	..	434	12053	138	..	7445	1292	21501	134
Paper, pulp and printing	2900	806	..	121	22540	*31033	..	17381	774	75555	*30836
Wood and wood products	..	..	..	257	2592	692	..	6559	3121	13221	4
Textile and leather	..	..	..	40	1425	3	..	1130	21	2620	3
Construction	..	..	..	9109	1454	488	..	1944	207	13202	482
Industries n.e.s	0	0	..	171	1703	*18992	..	4943	506	26315	*18903
Transport	..	..	..	337115	11301	19486	..	11783	..	379685	19486
Road	..	..	..	334271	697	19413	..	54	..	354435	19413
Rail	..	..	..	1345	..	74	..	7276	..	8695	74
Domestic aviation	..	..	..	1323	..	..	..	..	..	1323	..
Domestic navigation	..	..	..	175	..	..	..	..	..	175	..
Pipeline transport	..	..	..	..	10605	..	..	875	..	11480	..
Transport, n.e.s	..	..	..	..	..	..	..	3578	..	3578	..
Other	298	579	..	56732	70648	*78570	..	112072	67658	386556	*86541
Agriculture, forestry, fishing	..	20	..	9474	913	*7269	..	4198	507	22380	*7324
Commerce, public services	..	..	..	7969	13161	*3184	..	44114	30501	98929	6457
Households	298	559	..	39289	56575	*68118	..	63760	36650	265248	*72761
Other consumers	..	..	..	..	..	..	..	..	..	..	..
Non-energy use	85	948	..	62275	11570	..	..	..	..	74878	..

Azerbaijan

Terajoules

2017	Primary coal and peat	Coal and peat products	Primary Oil	Oil Products	Natural Gas	Biofuels and waste	Nuclear	Electricity	Heat	Total energy	of which: renewables
Primary production	..	..	1658080	..	639311	4162	..	6498	..	2308051	9270
Imports	55	..	2698	19618	74171	..	..	388	..	96931	..
Exports	..	..	-1406192	-48223	-311355	..	..	-4617	..	-1770387	..
International marine bunkers	..	..	..	-1892	..	..	..	..	..	-1892	..
International aviation bunkers	..	..	..	-7012	..	..	..	..	..	-7012	..
Stock changes	0	..	991	-2320	-19929	-12	..	..	..	-21269	-12
Total energy supply	55	..	255578	-39828	382198	4151	..	2269	..	604423	9258
Statistical difference	0	..	-17	1541	1062	2	..	112	0	2700	6500
Transfers	..	..	..	-2	..	..	..	..	..	-2	..
Transformation	..	..	-253397	227124	-199056	-2790	..	81055	6580	-140484	-1399
Electricity plants	..	..	..	-1238	-115133	-2782	..	49217	..	-69936	-1391
CHP plants	..	..	..	-11797	-76826	..	..	31838	598	-56186	..
Heat plants	..	..	..	0	-7098	..	..	..	5982	-1116	..
Coke ovens	..	..	..	..	..	..	..	..	..	..	..
Briquetting plants	..	..	..	..	..	..	..	..	..	..	..
Liquefaction plants	..	..	..	..	..	..	..	..	..	..	..
Gas works	..	..	..	..	..	..	..	..	..	..	..
Blast furnaces	..	..	..	..	..	..	..	..	..	..	..
NGL plants & gas blending	..	..	-1251	1458	..	..	..	..	..	206	..
Oil refineries	..	..	-252146	238702	..	..	..	..	..	-13444	..
Other transformation	..	..	..	..	..	-8	..	..	..	-8	-8
Energy industries own use	..	..	-431	-16112	-17419	..	..	-13604	-43	-47609	..
Losses	..	..	-1767	..	-27033	..	..	-8102	-795	-37697	..
Final consumption	55	..	..	169640	137628	1359	..	61506	5742	375930	1359
Final energy consumption	55	..	..	125032	136728	1359	..	61506	5742	330422	1359
Manufacturing, const., mining	..	..	..	3607	26355	55	..	13000	..	43017	55
Iron and steel	..	..	..	..	1104	..	..	1283	..	2387	..
Chemical and petrochemical	..	..	..	80	6162	..	..	1031	..	7274	..
Non-ferrous metals	..	..	..	..	28	..	..	2678	..	2706	..
Non-metallic minerals	..	..	..	105	10708	..	..	1304	..	12118	..
Transport equipment	..	..	..	..	7	..	..	58	..	65	..
Machinery	..	..	..	81	457	..	..	675	..	1212	..
Mining and quarrying	..	..	..	129	285	..	..	351	..	764	..
Food and tobacco	..	..	..	429	5990	53	..	2138	..	8610	53
Paper, pulp and printing	..	..	..	..	14	..	..	174	..	188	..
Wood and wood products	..	..	..	..	4	2	..	184	..	189	2
Textile and leather	..	..	..	0	299	..	..	566	..	864	..
Construction	..	..	..	2769	882	..	..	2188	..	5839	..
Industries n.e.s	..	..	..	13	415	0	..	373	..	801	0
Transport	55	..	..	107794	42	..	..	1430	..	109322	..
Road	..	..	..	91142	..	..	..	..	..	91142	..
Rail	55	..	..	387	..	..	..	1168	..	1611	..
Domestic aviation	..	..	..	14244	..	..	..	..	..	14244	..
Domestic navigation	..	..	..	2021	..	..	..	..	..	2021	..
Pipeline transport	..	..	..	..	42	..	..	262	..	304	..
Transport, n.e.s	..	..	..	..	..	..	..	..	..	..	..
Other	..	..	..	13631	110331	1304	..	47076	5742	178084	1304
Agriculture, forestry, fishing	..	..	..	12564	2137	65	..	3695	..	18461	65
Commerce, public services	..	..	..	391	8831	737	..	17697	1010	28664	737
Households	..	..	..	676	99363	502	..	25685	4733	130959	502
Other consumers	..	..	..	..	..	..	..	..	..	..	..
Non-energy use	..	..	..	44608	900	..	..	..	..	45508	..

Azerbaijan

Terajoules

2018	Primary coal and peat	Coal and peat products	Primary Oil	Oil Products	Natural Gas	Biofuels and waste	Nuclear	Electricity	Heat	Total energy	of which: renewables
Primary production	..	..	1662579	..	675206	4313	..	6804	..	2348903	9634
Imports	28	..	..	13971	63214	..	..	472	..	77685	..
Exports	..	..	-1397230	-55096	-348439	..	..	-5203	..	-1805968	..
International marine bunkers	..	..	..	-1849	..	..	..	..	..	-1849	..
International aviation bunkers	..	..	..	-4789	..	..	..	..	..	-4789	..
Stock changes	..	..	664	-7127	-612	-2	..	..	..	-7076	-2
Total energy supply	28	..	266013	-54891	389369	4311	..	2074	..	606904	9632
Statistical difference	0	..	0	1241	1160	4	..	81	0	2485	6808
Transfers	..	..	..	..	..	..	..	..	..	..	..
Transformation	..	..	-262224	257079	-216584	-2968	..	84021	12239	-128438	-1485
Electricity plants	..	..	..	-546	-121988	-2966	..	55001	..	-70499	-1483
CHP plants	..	..	..	..	-87199	..	..	29020	5951	-52229	..
Heat plants	..	..	..	-12	-7396	..	..	..	6291	-1118	..
Coke ovens	..	..	..	..	..	..	..	..	..	..	..
Briquetting plants	..	..	..	..	..	..	..	..	..	..	..
Liquefaction plants	..	..	..	..	..	..	..	..	..	..	..
Gas works	..	..	..	..	..	..	..	..	..	..	..
Blast furnaces	..	..	..	..	..	..	..	..	..	..	..
NGL plants & gas blending	..	..	-1239	1443	..	..	..	..	..	203	..
Oil refineries	..	..	-260985	256182	..	..	..	..	..	-4803	..
Other transformation	..	..	..	..	..	-3	..	..	..	-3	-3
Energy industries own use	..	..	-478	-13295	-16979	..	..	-13901	-14	-44667	..
Losses	..	..	-3310	..	-20417	..	..	-7991	-819	-32538	..
Final consumption	28	..	..	187653	134229	1339	..	64121	11406	398776	1339
Final energy consumption	28	..	..	137099	132977	1339	..	64121	11406	346971	1339
Manufacturing, const., mining	..	..	..	4053	18614	23	..	13406	5374	41469	23
Iron and steel	..	..	..	..	1262	..	..	1168	..	2430	..
Chemical and petrochemical	..	..	..	..	1424	..	..	987	5374	7785	..
Non-ferrous metals	..	..	..	40	77	..	..	3050	..	3168	..
Non-metallic minerals	..	..	..	13	8954	..	..	1548	..	10514	..
Transport equipment	..	..	..	26	4	..	..	13	..	43	..
Machinery	..	..	..	91	380	..	..	633	..	1104	..
Mining and quarrying	..	..	..	482	362	..	..	341	..	1185	..
Food and tobacco	..	..	..	421	4025	..	..	2290	..	6736	..
Paper, pulp and printing	..	..	..	..	77	..	..	157	..	235	..
Wood and wood products	..	..	..	..	4	23	..	116	..	142	23
Textile and leather	..	..	..	5	366	..	..	591	..	961	..
Construction	..	..	..	2928	1438	..	..	2096	..	6462	..
Industries n.e.s	..	..	..	47	243	0	..	414	0	704	0
Transport	28	..	..	118871	39	..	..	1383	..	120320	..
Road	..	..	..	99808	..	..	..	..	..	99808	..
Rail	28	..	..	270	..	..	..	1122	..	1420	..
Domestic aviation	..	..	..	16944	..	..	..	..	..	16944	..
Domestic navigation	..	..	..	1849	..	..	..	..	..	1849	..
Pipeline transport	..	..	..	..	39	..	..	261	..	299	..
Transport, n.e.s	..	..	..	..	..	..	..	..	..	..	..
Other	..	..	..	14175	114324	1317	..	49333	6032	185181	1317
Agriculture, forestry, fishing	..	..	..	13428	2869	12	..	4023	..	20331	12
Commerce, public services	..	..	..	107	4046	878	..	21193	981	27206	878
Households	..	..	..	640	107410	427	..	24117	5051	137645	427
Other consumers	..	..	..	..	..	..	..	..	..	..	..
Non-energy use	..	..	..	50553	1251	..	..	..	..	51805	..

Bahamas

Terajoules

	All Coal	All Oil	Natural Gas	Primary biofuels / Waste	Charcoal	Electricity	Total energy	of which: renewables
2017								
Primary production	..	..	..	309	..	..	309	309
Imports	*41	27902	..	1	1	..	27945	2
Exports	..	*-24	..	0	-1	..	*-25	-1
International marine bunkers	..	*-2852	..	..	..	..	*-2852	..
International aviation bunkers	..	*-1278	..	..	..	..	*-1278	..
Stock changes	..	*6173	..	..	..	..	*6173	..
Total energy supply	*41	29921	..	309	0	..	30271	310
Statistical Difference	0	*-44	..	0	0	*180	*136	0
Transfers	..	..	..	..	..	..	..	..
Transformation	..	*-17114	..	*-62	34	*7153	*-9990	*-29
Electricity plants	..	*-17114	..	..	..	*7153	*-9961	..
Charcoal plants	..	..	..	*-62	34	..	*-29	*-29
Other transformation	..	0	..	0	..	..	0	0
Energy industries own use	..	..	..	..	..	*-313	*-313	..
Losses	..	..	..	..	..	*-32	*-32	..
Final consumption	*41	*12851	..	*247	*34	*6628	*19801	*281
Final energy consumption	*41	*12497	..	*247	*34	*6628	*19447	*281
Manufacturing, const., mining	*41	*2630	..	..	..	*3931	*6602	..
Transport	..	*5607	..	..	..	..	*5607	..
Road	..	*5556	..	..	..	..	*5556	..
Domestic aviation	..	*51	..	..	..	..	*51	..
Domestic navigation	..	..	..	..	..	..	..	..
Other transport	..	..	..	..	..	..	..	..
Other	..	*4260	..	*247	*34	*2696	*7237	*281
Agriculture, forestry, fishing	..	..	..	..	..	..	..	..
Commerce and public services	..	*3218	..	..	..	*68	*3286	..
Households	..	*599	..	..	..	*2628	*3227	..
Other consumers	..	*443	..	*247	*34	..	*724	*281
Non-energy use	..	*354	..	..	..	..	*354	..
2018								
Primary production	..	..	..	309	..	..	309	309
Imports	*41	37624	..	..	2	..	37667	2
Exports	..	..	..	..	-1	..	-1	-1
International marine bunkers	..	*-2415	..	..	..	..	*-2415	..
International aviation bunkers	..	*-1715	..	..	..	..	*-1715	..
Stock changes	..	*5044	..	..	..	..	*5044	..
Total energy supply	*41	38538	..	309	2	..	38890	311
Statistical Difference	0	*-16	..	0	0	*-66	*-81	0
Transfers	..	..	..	..	..	..	..	..
Transformation	..	*-18920	..	*-63	34	*8208	*-10741	*-29
Electricity plants	..	*-18920	..	..	..	*8208	*-10712	..
Charcoal plants	..	..	..	*-63	34	..	*-29	*-29
Other transformation	..	0	..	0	..	..	0	0
Energy industries own use	..	..	..	..	..	*-288	*-288	..
Losses	..	..	..	..	..	*-33	*-33	..
Final consumption	*41	*19634	..	*246	*35	*7952	*27909	*282
Final energy consumption	*41	*19351	..	*246	*35	*7952	*27627	*282
Manufacturing, const., mining	*41	*3562	..	..	..	*4716	*8320	..
Transport	..	*9755	..	..	..	..	*9755	..
Road	..	*9631	..	..	..	..	*9631	..
Domestic aviation	..	*123	..	..	..	..	*123	..
Domestic navigation	..	..	..	..	..	..	..	..
Other transport	..	..	..	..	..	..	..	..
Other	..	*6035	..	*246	*35	*3236	*9553	*282
Agriculture, forestry, fishing	..	..	..	..	..	..	..	..
Commerce and public services	..	*4487	..	..	..	*83	*4570	..
Households	..	*750	..	..	..	*3154	*3904	..
Other consumers	..	*797	..	*246	*35	..	*1079	*282
Non-energy use	..	*282	..	..	..	..	*282	..

Bahrain

Terajoules

2017	Primary coal and peat	Coal and peat products	Primary Oil	Oil Products	Natural Gas	Biofuels and waste	Nuclear	Electricity	Heat	Total energy	of which: renewables
Primary production	..	..	430704	..	511523	66	..	*36	..	942329	102
Imports	..	..	463312	*19630	..	189	..	947	..	484078	189
Exports	..	..	-335445	-507437	..	-99	..	-936	..	-843918	-99
International marine bunkers	..	..	..	..	..	..	..	..	..	..	..
International aviation bunkers	..	..	..	-19713	..	..	..	..	..	-19713	..
Stock changes	..	..	*-972	16158	572	..	..	..	..	15758	..
Total energy supply	..	..	557599	-491362	512096	156	..	47	..	578535	192
Statistical difference	..	..	0	-84	38554	0	..	2732	..	41202	36
Transfers	..	..	..	..	..	..	..	..	..	..	..
Transformation	..	..	-557599	569731	-332053	*-29	..	105059	..	-214892	*-29
Electricity plants	..	..	..	..	-332053	..	..	82555	..	-249498	..
CHP plants	..	..	..	..	..	..	..	22504	..	22504	..
Heat plants	..	..	..	..	..	..	..	..	..	..	..
Coke ovens	..	..	..	..	..	..	..	..	..	..	..
Briquetting plants	..	..	..	..	..	..	..	..	..	..	..
Liquefaction plants	..	..	..	..	..	..	..	..	..	..	..
Gas works	..	..	..	..	..	..	..	..	..	..	..
Blast furnaces	..	..	..	..	..	..	..	..	..	..	..
NGL plants & gas blending	..	..	..	..	..	..	..	..	..	..	..
Oil refineries	..	..	-557599	569731	..	..	..	..	..	12132	..
Other transformation	..	..	..	..	..	*-29	..	..	..	*-29	*-29
Energy industries own use	..	..	..	*-5200	-53137	..	..	-144	..	-58481	..
Losses	..	..	..	..	..	..	..	-2275	..	-2275	..
Final consumption	..	..	..	73253	88351	*126	..	99954	..	261685	*126
Final energy consumption	..	..	..	56934	34669	*126	..	99954	..	191683	*126
Manufacturing, const., mining	..	..	..	788	34669	..	..	50000	..	85458	..
Iron and steel	..	..	..	788	16719	..	..	..	..	17508	..
Chemical and petrochemical	..	..	..	..	..	..	..	..	..	..	..
Non-ferrous metals	..	..	..	..	..	..	..	40244	..	40244	..
Non-metallic minerals	..	..	..	..	..	..	..	..	..	..	..
Transport equipment	..	..	..	..	..	..	..	..	..	..	..
Machinery	..	..	..	..	..	..	..	..	..	..	..
Mining and quarrying	..	..	..	..	..	..	..	..	..	..	..
Food and tobacco	..	..	..	..	..	..	..	..	..	..	..
Paper, pulp and printing	..	..	..	..	..	..	..	..	..	..	..
Wood and wood products	..	..	..	..	..	..	..	..	..	..	..
Textile and leather	..	..	..	..	..	..	..	..	..	..	..
Construction	..	..	..	..	..	..	..	..	..	..	..
Industries n.e.s	..	..	..	0	17950	..	..	9756	..	27706	..
Transport	..	..	..	52882	..	..	..	..	..	52882	..
Road	..	..	..	51647	..	..	..	..	..	51647	..
Rail	..	..	..	..	..	..	..	..	..	..	..
Domestic aviation	..	..	..	1235	..	..	..	..	..	1235	..
Domestic navigation	..	..	..	..	..	..	..	..	..	..	..
Pipeline transport	..	..	..	..	..	..	..	..	..	..	..
Transport, n.e.s	..	..	..	..	..	..	..	..	..	..	..
Other	..	..	..	3264	..	*126	..	49954	..	53344	*126
Agriculture, forestry, fishing	..	..	..	..	..	..	..	212	..	212	..
Commerce, public services	..	..	..	..	..	..	..	18922	..	18922	..
Households	..	..	..	3264	..	*40	..	30820	..	34123	*40
Other consumers	..	..	..	..	..	*86	..	..	..	*86	*86
Non-energy use	..	..	..	16319	53682	..	..	..	..	70002	..

Bahrain

Terajoules

2018	Primary coal and peat	Coal and peat products	Primary Oil	Oil Products	Natural Gas	Biofuels and waste	Nuclear	Electricity	Heat	Total energy	of which: renewables
Primary production	..	..	426566	..	519712	66	..	*36	..	946379	102
Imports	..	..	463227	*19890	..	189	..	1613	..	484919	189
Exports	..	..	-341547	-492837	..	-99	..	-655	..	-835138	-99
International marine bunkers	..	..	..	..	..	..	..	..	..	..	..
International aviation bunkers	..	..	..	-21300	..	..	..	..	..	-21300	..
Stock changes	..	..	*-884	7941	-1	..	..	..	..	7056	..
Total energy supply	..	..	547362	-486306	519711	156	..	994	..	581916	192
Statistical difference	..	..	0	-43	43593	0	..	922	..	44472	36
Transfers	..	..	..	..	..	..	..	..	..	..	..
Transformation	..	..	-547362	567163	-329032	*-29	..	106225	..	-203035	*-29
Electricity plants	..	..	..	..	-329032	..	..	81371	..	-247661	..
CHP plants	..	..	..	..	..	..	..	24851	..	24851	..
Heat plants	..	..	..	..	..	..	..	..	..	..	..
Coke ovens	..	..	..	..	..	..	..	..	..	..	..
Briquetting plants	..	..	..	..	..	..	..	..	..	..	..
Liquefaction plants	..	..	..	..	..	..	..	..	..	..	..
Gas works	..	..	..	..	..	..	..	..	..	..	..
Blast furnaces	..	..	..	..	..	..	..	..	..	..	..
NGL plants & gas blending	..	..	..	..	..	..	..	..	..	..	..
Oil refineries	..	..	-547362	567163	..	..	..	..	..	19801	..
Other transformation	..	..	..	..	..	*-29	..	..	..	*-29	*-29
Energy industries own use	..	..	..	*-5200	-52984	..	..	0	..	-58184	..
Losses	..	..	..	..	..	..	..	-1944	..	-1944	..
Final consumption	..	..	..	75700	94102	*126	..	104353	..	274282	*126
Final energy consumption	..	..	..	58518	38755	*126	..	104353	..	201752	*126
Manufacturing, const., mining	..	..	..	701	38755	..	..	52240	..	91695	..
Iron and steel	..	..	..	701	20449	..	..	..	..	21150	..
Chemical and petrochemical	..	..	..	..	..	..	..	..	..	..	..
Non-ferrous metals	..	..	..	..	..	..	..	42282	..	42282	..
Non-metallic minerals	..	..	..	..	..	..	..	..	..	..	..
Transport equipment	..	..	..	..	..	..	..	..	..	..	..
Machinery	..	..	..	..	..	..	..	..	..	..	..
Mining and quarrying	..	..	..	..	..	..	..	..	..	..	..
Food and tobacco	..	..	..	..	..	..	..	..	..	..	..
Paper, pulp and printing	..	..	..	..	..	..	..	..	..	..	..
Wood and wood products	..	..	..	..	..	..	..	..	..	..	..
Textile and leather	..	..	..	..	..	..	..	..	..	..	..
Construction	..	..	..	..	..	..	..	..	..	..	..
Industries n.e.s	..	..	..	0	18306	..	..	9958	..	28264	..
Transport	..	..	..	54411	..	..	..	..	..	54411	..
Road	..	..	..	52824	..	..	..	..	..	52824	..
Rail	..	..	..	..	..	..	..	..	..	..	..
Domestic aviation	..	..	..	1588	..	..	..	..	..	1588	..
Domestic navigation	..	..	..	..	..	..	..	..	..	..	..
Pipeline transport	..	..	..	..	..	..	..	..	..	..	..
Transport, n.e.s	..	..	..	..	..	..	..	..	..	..	..
Other	..	..	..	3406	..	*126	..	52114	..	55645	*126
Agriculture, forestry, fishing	..	..	..	..	..	..	..	220	..	220	..
Commerce, public services	..	..	..	..	..	..	..	21899	..	21899	..
Households	..	..	..	3406	..	*40	..	29995	..	33441	*40
Other consumers	..	..	..	..	..	*86	..	..	..	*86	*86
Non-energy use	..	..	..	17182	55347	..	..	..	..	72530	..

Bangladesh

Terajoules

2017	Primary coal and peat	Coal and peat products	Primary Oil	Oil Products	Natural Gas	Biofuels and waste	Nuclear	Electricity	Heat	Total energy	of which: renewables
Primary production	24289	..	18078	..	963851	594527	..	4735	..	1605479	599262
Imports	54701	..	71356	199674	..	1	..	17767	..	343498	1
Exports	..	..	..	-1780	..	-222	..	..	..	-2002	-222
International marine bunkers	..	..	..	-4929	..	..	..	..	..	-4929	..
International aviation bunkers	..	..	..	-16626	..	..	..	..	..	-16626	..
Stock changes	..	..	..	..	17970	..	..	..	..	17970	..
Total energy supply	78989	..	89434	176339	981821	594305	..	22502	..	1943391	599040
Statistical difference	-4087	..	13616	-5525	-53691	0	..	1770	..	-47917	4735
Transfers	..	..	-442	438	..	..	..	..	..	-4	..
Transformation	-11321	..	-75375	10097	-594746	-8556	..	258963	..	-420939	-8556
Electricity plants	-11321	..	..	-56951	-594746	..	..	258963	..	-404056	..
CHP plants	..	..	..	..	..	..	..	..	..	..	..
Heat plants	..	..	..	..	..	..	..	..	..	..	..
Coke ovens	..	..	..	..	..	..	..	..	..	..	..
Briquetting plants	..	..	..	..	..	..	..	..	..	..	..
Liquefaction plants	..	..	..	..	..	..	..	..	..	..	..
Gas works	..	..	..	..	..	..	..	..	..	..	..
Blast furnaces	..	..	..	..	..	..	..	..	..	..	..
NGL plants & gas blending	..	..	-6321	6339	..	..	..	..	..	18	..
Oil refineries	..	..	-69055	60709	..	..	..	..	..	-8346	..
Other transformation	..	..	..	..	..	-8556	..	..	..	-8556	-8556
Energy industries own use	-502	..	..	-2125	..	..	..	-14815	..	-17443	..
Losses	..	..	..	..	-19884	..	..	-27780	..	-47663	..
Final consumption	*71253	..	..	190274	420882	585750	..	237099	..	1505258	585750
Final energy consumption	*71253	..	..	185370	372049	585750	..	237099	..	1451521	585750
Manufacturing, const., mining	*71253	..	..	13603	162217	*1753	..	129098	..	377924	*1753
Iron and steel	..	..	..	..	..	..	..	..	..	..	..
Chemical and petrochemical	..	..	..	..	..	..	..	..	..	..	..
Non-ferrous metals	..	..	..	..	..	..	..	..	..	..	..
Non-metallic minerals	19400	..	..	..	..	..	..	..	..	19400	..
Transport equipment	..	..	..	..	..	..	..	..	..	..	..
Machinery	..	..	..	..	..	..	..	..	..	..	..
Mining and quarrying	..	..	..	..	..	..	..	..	..	..	..
Food and tobacco	..	..	..	..	..	..	..	..	..	..	..
Paper, pulp and printing	..	..	..	..	..	..	..	..	..	..	..
Wood and wood products	..	..	..	..	..	..	..	..	..	..	..
Textile and leather	..	..	..	..	..	..	..	..	..	..	..
Construction	..	..	..	..	..	..	..	..	..	..	..
Industries n.e.s	*51853	..	..	13603	162217	*1753	..	129098	..	358524	*1753
Transport	..	..	..	112687	46697	..	..	..	..	159384	..
Road	..	..	..	78760	46697	..	..	..	..	125457	..
Rail	..	..	..	14233	..	..	..	..	..	14233	..
Domestic aviation	..	..	..	..	..	..	..	..	..	..	..
Domestic navigation	..	..	..	19694	..	..	..	..	..	19694	..
Pipeline transport	..	..	..	..	..	..	..	..	..	..	..
Transport, n.e.s	..	..	..	0	..	..	..	..	..	0	..
Other	..	..	..	59080	163136	583997	..	108001	..	914213	583997
Agriculture, forestry, fishing	..	..	..	45021	967	..	..	2062	..	48050	..
Commerce, public services	..	..	..	..	8608	..	..	18120	..	26728	..
Households	..	..	..	8674	153560	574246	..	82817	..	819297	574246
Other consumers	..	..	..	5385	..	*9751	..	5002	..	20137	*9751
Non-energy use	..	..	..	4904	48833	..	..	..	..	53737	..

Bangladesh

Terajoules

2018	Primary coal and peat	Coal and peat products	Primary Oil	Oil Products	Natural Gas	Biofuels and waste	Nuclear	Electricity	Heat	Total energy	of which: renewables
Primary production	19321	..	17994	..	963311	596107	..	4979	..	1601712	601086
Imports	71037	..	51128	195449	..	0	..	18251	..	335866	0
Exports	..	..	..	-98	..	-17	..	..	..	-114	-17
International marine bunkers	..	..	..	-4880	..	..	..	..	..	-4880	..
International aviation bunkers	..	..	..	-18006	..	..	..	..	..	-18006	..
Stock changes	..	..	..	35746	13220	..	..	..	..	48966	..
Total energy supply	90358	..	69122	208211	976531	596091	..	23230	..	1963542	601070
Statistical difference	0	..	537	-16819	-51317	0	..	1472	..	-66128	4979
Transfers	..	..	-455	451	..	..	..	..	..	-4	..
Transformation	-16471	..	-68129	-18186	-587504	*-8578	..	278024	..	-420844	*-8578
Electricity plants	-16471	..	..	-78078	-587504	..	..	278024	..	-404029	..
CHP plants	..	..	..	..	..	..	..	..	..	..	..
Heat plants	..	..	..	..	..	..	..	..	..	..	..
Coke ovens	..	..	..	..	..	..	..	..	..	..	..
Briquetting plants	..	..	..	..	..	..	..	..	..	..	..
Liquefaction plants	..	..	..	..	..	..	..	..	..	..	..
Gas works	..	..	..	..	..	..	..	..	..	..	..
Blast furnaces	..	..	..	..	..	..	..	..	..	..	..
NGL plants & gas blending	..	..	-6798	6768	..	..	..	..	..	-30	..
Oil refineries	..	..	-61331	53124	..	..	..	..	..	-8208	..
Other transformation	..	..	..	..	..	*-8578	..	..	..	*-8578	*-8578
Energy industries own use	-806	..	..	-1861	..	..	..	-15900	..	-18567	..
Losses	..	..	..	..	-19892	..	..	-30410	..	-50302	..
Final consumption	*73082	..	..	205433	420453	587513	..	253472	..	1539953	587513
Final energy consumption	*73082	..	..	201083	377711	587513	..	253472	..	1492862	587513
Manufacturing, const., mining	*73082	..	..	12969	165633	*1771	..	135162	..	388617	*1771
Iron and steel	..	..	..	..	..	..	..	..	..	..	..
Chemical and petrochemical	..	..	..	..	..	..	..	..	..	..	..
Non-ferrous metals	..	..	..	..	..	..	..	..	..	..	..
Non-metallic minerals	22880	..	..	..	..	..	..	..	..	22880	..
Transport equipment	..	..	..	..	..	..	..	..	..	..	..
Machinery	..	..	..	..	..	..	..	..	..	..	..
Mining and quarrying	..	..	..	..	..	..	..	..	..	..	..
Food and tobacco	..	..	..	..	..	..	..	..	..	..	..
Paper, pulp and printing	..	..	..	..	..	..	..	..	..	..	..
Wood and wood products	..	..	..	..	..	..	..	..	..	..	..
Textile and leather	..	..	..	..	..	..	..	..	..	..	..
Construction	..	..	..	..	..	..	..	..	..	..	..
Industries n.e.s	*50201	..	..	12969	165633	*1771	..	135162	..	365736	*1771
Transport	..	..	..	127722	45941	..	..	..	..	173662	..
Road	..	..	..	86293	45941	..	..	..	..	132234	..
Rail	..	..	..	17183	..	..	..	..	..	17183	..
Domestic aviation	..	..	..	..	..	..	..	..	..	..	..
Domestic navigation	..	..	..	23813	..	..	..	..	..	23813	..
Pipeline transport	..	..	..	..	..	..	..	..	..	..	..
Transport, n.e.s	..	..	..	432	..	..	..	..	..	432	..
Other	..	..	..	60393	166137	585742	..	118311	..	930583	585742
Agriculture, forestry, fishing	..	..	..	46797	935	..	..	2219	..	49951	..
Commerce, public services	..	..	..	..	8124	..	..	19752	..	27877	..
Households	..	..	..	9196	157078	575761	..	90855	..	832889	575761
Other consumers	..	..	..	*4400	..	*9981	..	5485	..	*19866	*9981
Non-energy use	..	..	..	4350	42741	..	..	..	..	47091	..

Barbados

Terajoules

	All Coal	All Oil	Natural Gas	Primary biofuels / Waste	Charcoal	Electricity	Total energy	of which: renewables
2017								
Primary production	..	1358	411	522	..	136	2426	658
Imports	..	20987	*199	0	1	..	21187	1
Exports	..	-1354	..	0	..	..	-1355	0
International marine bunkers	..	..	..	..	..	..	..	..
International aviation bunkers	..	*-5849	..	..	..	..	*-5849	..
Stock changes	..	-531	..	-8	..	..	-539	-8
Total energy supply	..	14611	610	513	1	136	15871	650
Statistical Difference	..	-9	-10	0	0	-9	-28	136
Transfers	..	..	..	..	..	..	..	..
Transformation	..	-6996	-158	-41	9	3633	-3553	-33
Electricity plants	..	-6996	-158	-25	..	3633	-3546	-25
Charcoal plants	..	..	..	*-16	9	..	*-7	*-7
Other transformation	..	0	0	0	..	..	0	0
Energy industries own use	..	..	-42	..	..	-196	-238	..
Losses	..	..	-9	..	..	-76	-85	..
Final consumption	..	7623	411	472	*10	3507	12022	482
Final energy consumption	..	7623	411	472	*10	3507	12022	482
Manufacturing, const., mining	..	734	22	445	..	422	1624	445
Transport	..	5982	..	..	..	..	5982	..
Road	..	5982	..	..	..	..	5982	..
Domestic aviation	..	..	..	..	..	..	..	..
Domestic navigation	..	..	..	..	..	..	..	..
Other transport	..	..	..	..	..	..	..	..
Other	..	907	388	*27	*10	3084	4417	*37
Agriculture, forestry, fishing	..	..	..	..	..	..	..	..
Commerce and public services	..	534	303	..	..	1486	2322	..
Households	..	339	86	..	*10	*1205	*1639	*10
Other consumers	..	34	..	*27	..	394	456	*27
Non-energy use	..	..	..	..	..	..	..	..
2018								
Primary production	..	1262	902	582	..	159	2904	741
Imports	..	19875	..	..	1	..	19876	1
Exports	..	-1189	..	..	..	..	-1189	..
International marine bunkers	..	..	..	..	..	..	..	..
International aviation bunkers	..	*-4841	..	..	..	..	*-4841	..
Stock changes	..	143	..	-1	..	..	142	-1
Total energy supply	..	15249	902	581	1	159	16892	741
Statistical Difference	..	-8	9	0	0	271	272	159
Transfers	..	..	..	..	..	..	..	..
Transformation	..	-7713	-235	-44	9	3641	-4342	-35
Electricity plants	..	-7713	-235	-28	..	3641	-4334	-28
Charcoal plants	..	..	..	*-16	9	..	*-7	*-7
Other transformation	..	0	0	0	..	..	0	0
Energy industries own use	..	..	-175	..	..	-63	-237	..
Losses	..	..	-9	..	..	-73	-82	..
Final consumption	..	7544	474	537	*10	3393	11959	547
Final energy consumption	..	7544	474	537	*10	3393	11959	547
Manufacturing, const., mining	..	769	23	510	..	422	1724	510
Transport	..	5851	..	..	..	..	5851	..
Road	..	5851	..	..	..	..	5851	..
Domestic aviation	..	..	..	..	..	..	..	..
Domestic navigation	..	..	..	..	..	..	..	..
Other transport	..	..	..	..	..	..	..	..
Other	..	924	452	*27	*10	2971	4384	*37
Agriculture, forestry, fishing	..	..	..	..	..	..	..	..
Commerce and public services	..	540	367	..	..	1483	2391	..
Households	..	348	85	..	*10	1095	1538	*10
Other consumers	..	35	..	*27	..	393	456	*27
Non-energy use	..	..	..	..	..	..	..	..

Belarus

Terajoules

2017	Primary coal and peat	Coal and peat products	Primary Oil	Oil Products	Natural Gas	Biofuels and waste	Nuclear	Electricity	Heat	Total energy	of which: renewables
Primary production	19178	..	73066	..	5214	80182	..	2128	..	179767	81123
Imports	18690	1654	766899	76660	660923	37	..	21571	..	1546433	37
Exports	-4096	-1064	-68568	-549606	..	-4896	..	-12265	..	-640496	-4896
International marine bunkers	..	..	..	..	..	..	..	..	..	..	..
International aviation bunkers	..	..	..	-5557	..	..	..	..	..	-5557	..
Stock changes	1464	-177	1311	-10020	8099	..	..	..	..	678	..
Total energy supply	35236	413	772708	-488522	674236	75322	..	11434	..	1080826	76263
Statistical difference	0	0	1227	824	0	0	..	0	0	2050	2128
Transfers	..	..	20895	-20687	..	..	..	..	..	208	..
Transformation	-17383	8491	-780871	776853	-476245	-44047	..	122126	253365	-157709	-42892
Electricity plants	..	..	..	0	-107964	-61	..	48323	..	-59702	-61
CHP plants	-835	-400	..	-5113	-286560	-8135	..	73804	157597	-69642	-7460
Heat plants	-1966	-634	..	-4477	-81721	-35574	..	..	95768	-28604	-35094
Coke ovens	..	..	..	..	..	..	..	..	..	..	..
Briquetting plants	-14583	9526	..	..	..	..	..	..	..	-5057	..
Liquefaction plants	..	..	..	..	..	..	..	..	..	..	..
Gas works	..	..	..	..	..	..	..	..	..	..	..
Blast furnaces	..	..	..	..	..	..	..	..	..	..	..
NGL plants & gas blending	..	..	..	..	..	..	..	..	..	..	..
Oil refineries	..	..	-781471	786443	..	..	..	..	..	4973	..
Other transformation	..	..	600	..	..	-277	..	..	..	323	-277
Energy industries own use	-366	..	..	-37960	-9510	-1051	..	-15394	-21913	-86193	-1051
Losses	-863	..	-11506	-47	-1947	..	..	-10339	-19548	-44250	..
Final consumption	16624	8904	..	228813	186534	30225	..	107827	211904	790832	30193
Final energy consumption	15668	8353	..	181619	130675	30225	..	107827	211904	686270	30193
Manufacturing, const., mining	15235	3980	..	6612	37976	4289	..	45209	59385	172686	4257
Iron and steel	..	348	..	169	5109	9	..	6952	310	12898	9
Chemical and petrochemical	..	..	..	421	7704	33	..	12996	21743	42897	33
Non-ferrous metals	..	..	..	..	311	..	..	108	18	437	..
Non-metallic minerals	15235	3100	..	212	14981	114	..	4572	2501	40716	82
Transport equipment	..	145	..	129	706	37	..	1440	1525	3981	37
Machinery	..	358	..	347	2912	210	..	5116	3560	12502	210
Mining and quarrying	..	..	..	133	422	9	..	760	141	1465	9
Food and tobacco	..	10	..	721	3754	241	..	5897	18506	29128	241
Paper, pulp and printing	..	..	..	43	246	9	..	1120	2171	3588	9
Wood and wood products	..	..	..	173	627	2439	..	2142	3538	8920	2439
Textile and leather	..	0	..	172	243	27	..	1328	2340	4111	27
Construction	..	20	..	3962	765	658	..	914	..	6318	658
Industries n.e.s	0	0	..	129	195	502	..	1865	3032	5724	502
Transport	196	39	..	142772	18770	110	..	4403	..	166291	110
Road	..	..	..	134148	278	110	..	576	..	135112	110
Rail	196	39	..	7611	..	..	..	2232	..	10078	..
Domestic aviation	..	..	..	970	..	..	..	..	..	970	..
Domestic navigation	..	..	..	43	..	..	..	..	..	43	..
Pipeline transport	..	..	..	..	18492	..	..	1595	..	20087	..
Transport, n.e.s	..	..	..	..	..	..	..	..	..	..	..
Other	237	4333	..	32234	73929	25826	..	58216	152519	347294	25826
Agriculture, forestry, fishing	9	59	..	27831	4164	4627	..	5695	7224	49609	4627
Commerce, public services	203	693	..	1849	2087	3060	..	28789	47721	84403	3060
Households	25	3582	..	2554	67677	18139	..	23731	97574	213282	18139
Other consumers	..	..	..	..	..	..	..	..	..	..	..
Non-energy use	957	551	..	47195	55859	..	..	..	..	104562	..

Belarus

Terajoules

2018	Primary coal and peat	Coal and peat products	Primary Oil	Oil Products	Natural Gas	Biofuels and waste	Nuclear	Electricity	Heat	Total energy	of which: renewables
Primary production	23842	..	75044	..	5353	64908	..	1948	..	171095	65537
Imports	37756	1613	771738	54647	706667	..	..	11725	..	1584146	..
Exports	-19570	-1585	-69351	-482800	..	..	..	-15293	..	-588599	..
International marine bunkers	..	..	..	..	..	..	..	..	..	..	..
International aviation bunkers	..	..	..	-6350	..	..	..	..	..	-6350	..
Stock changes	-4848	-376	-296	-19321	3198	..	..	..	..	-21645	..
Total energy supply	37180	-348	777135	-453825	715217	64908	..	-1620	..	1138647	65537
Statistical difference	-1	-87	30	898	0	-3	..	1	0	838	1945
Transfers	..	..	29335	-29046	..	..	..	..	..	289	..
Transformation	-20184	9410	-794846	793535	-514307	-34530	..	138190	261356	-161377	-33358
Electricity plants	..	..	..	-654	-124024	-54	..	55458	..	-69274	-54
CHP plants	-816	-367	..	-4848	-307311	-6491	..	82732	164316	-72786	-5817
Heat plants	-2475	-522	..	-4512	-82972	-27709	..	..	97040	-21151	-27211
Coke ovens	..	..	..	..	..	..	..	..	..	..	..
Briquetting plants	-16892	10299	..	..	..	..	..	..	..	-6593	..
Liquefaction plants	..	..	..	..	..	..	..	..	..	..	..
Gas works	..	..	..	..	..	..	..	..	..	..	..
Blast furnaces	..	..	..	..	..	..	..	..	..	..	..
NGL plants & gas blending	..	..	..	..	..	..	..	..	..	..	..
Oil refineries	..	..	-794846	803550	..	..	..	..	..	8703	..
Other transformation	..	..	..	..	..	-277	..	..	..	-277	-277
Energy industries own use	-423	..	..	-42160	-8300	-947	..	-15984	*-25277	-93091	-947
Losses	-1058	..	-11594	0	-1807	..	..	-10206	-19367	-44033	..
Final consumption	15516	9148	..	267606	190804	29433	..	110379	216712	839597	29286
Final energy consumption	14468	8710	..	202843	132825	29433	..	110379	216712	715370	29286
Manufacturing, const., mining	13999	4383	..	7967	39635	4079	..	50704	64908	185675	3932
Iron and steel	..	322	..	169	5286	9	..	*8075	570	*14431	9
Chemical and petrochemical	..	..	..	212	7865	*50	..	*14134	*24200	*46461	*50
Non-ferrous metals	..	..	..	..	278	..	..	*108	..	386	..
Non-metallic minerals	13999	3474	..	318	15222	220	..	5831	2511	41575	73
Transport equipment	..	148	..	194	880	37	..	1553	1846	4657	37
Machinery	..	342	..	288	3293	192	..	3340	4174	11629	192
Mining and quarrying	..	..	..	641	414	9	..	1875	159	3098	9
Food and tobacco	..	20	..	1790	4219	237	..	5977	18313	30556	237
Paper, pulp and printing	..	..	..	..	286	9	..	1490	3758	5544	9
Wood and wood products	..	..	..	224	679	2229	..	3838	4132	11101	2229
Textile and leather	..	..	..	194	237	27	..	1319	2344	4121	27
Construction	..	20	..	3860	765	603	..	908	..	6155	603
Industries n.e.s	0	58	..	77	212	457	..	2256	2901	5960	457
Transport	199	39	..	160778	18840	74	..	4411	..	184341	74
Road	..	..	..	151535	243	74	..	572	..	152424	74
Rail	199	39	..	8480	..	..	..	2227	..	10945	..
Domestic aviation	..	..	..	763	..	..	..	..	..	763	..
Domestic navigation	..	..	..	..	..	..	..	..	..	..	..
Pipeline transport	..	..	..	..	18597	..	..	1612	..	20209	..
Transport, n.e.s	..	..	..	..	..	..	..	..	..	..	..
Other	270	4289	..	34099	74350	25280	..	55263	151804	345354	25280
Agriculture, forestry, fishing	10	58	..	29798	4081	2660	..	5714	7384	49703	2660
Commerce, public services	232	637	..	1888	2134	2149	..	25901	46441	79381	2149
Households	28	3594	..	2412	68135	20472	..	23648	97979	216270	20472
Other consumers	..	..	..	..	..	..	..	..	..	..	..
Non-energy use	1048	438	..	64762	57979	..	..	..	..	124227	..

Belgium

Terajoules

2017	Primary coal and peat	Coal and peat products	Primary Oil	Oil Products	Natural Gas	Biofuels and waste	Nuclear	Electricity	Heat	Total energy	of which: renewables
Primary production	2086	..	..	..	..	118963	456052	36324	12436	625861	128885
Imports	101137	22503	1440485	1226779	622315	46843	..	51080	..	3511142	46807
Exports	-2535	-532	..	-1436538	-26419	-9698	..	-29405	..	-1505126	-9698
International marine bunkers	..	..	..	-316565	-253	..	..	..	..	-316818	..
International aviation bunkers	..	..	..	-67914	..	..	..	..	..	-67914	..
Stock changes	6002	-1	-1266	38123	9737	..	..	..	..	52595	..
Total energy supply	106689	21969	1439219	-556115	605381	156109	456052	58000	12436	2299740	165995
Statistical difference	431	-2100	-112	6698	-3588	62	0	-220	36	1208	36439
Transfers	..	..	58914	-54710	..	..	..	..	..	4204	..
Transformation	-81968	20707	-1498245	1499066	-150615	-75569	-456052	272009	10787	-459880	-54019
Electricity plants	0	-19780	..	-218	-78064	*-41043	-456052	216846	-11272	-389583	*-33107
CHP plants	-412	0	..	-1272	-72551	-34517	..	55163	22101	-31487	-20857
Heat plants	..	..	..	..	0	-10	..	..	-42	-52	-56
Coke ovens	-47293	46232	..	..	..	..	..	..	..	-1061	..
Briquetting plants	..	..	..	..	..	..	..	..	..	..	..
Liquefaction plants	..	..	..	..	..	..	..	..	..	..	..
Gas works	..	..	..	..	..	..	..	..	..	..	..
Blast furnaces	-34264	-9510	..	..	..	..	..	..	..	-43774	..
NGL plants & gas blending	..	..	..	..	..	..	..	..	..	..	..
Oil refineries	..	..	-1498245	1503795	..	..	..	..	..	5550	..
Other transformation	..	3765	..	-3239	..	..	..	..	..	526	..
Energy industries own use	..	-11242	..	-54159	-16791	..	..	-20171	-4540	-106903	..
Losses	..	..	..	..	-1224	-24	..	-13856	-266	-15370	-24
Final consumption	24289	33534	..	827385	440339	*80454	..	296201	18381	1720583	*75513
Final energy consumption	24289	25610	..	566078	395018	*80454	..	296201	18381	1406032	*75513
Manufacturing, const., mining	20642	25446	..	59937	167385	*33766	..	139360	14660	461196	*29102
Iron and steel	10000	17540	..	511	20547	67	..	15930	..	64594	..
Chemical and petrochemical	..	376	..	49934	58753	455	..	53500	11750	174768	334
Non-ferrous metals	..	372	..	40	5580	1	..	7178	..	13172	..
Non-metallic minerals	8260	6751	..	1719	21826	*8911	..	8719	..	56186	*5160
Transport equipment	..	..	..	172	1987	..	..	2920	2	5081	..
Machinery	..	..	..	685	4800	51	..	6606	..	12143	50
Mining and quarrying	..	..	..	..	515	..	..	1627	..	2142	..
Food and tobacco	1147	117	..	343	35828	*3357	..	21420	1692	63904	*3357
Paper, pulp and printing	1235	165	..	373	5668	*13235	..	6721	1194	28593	*12538
Wood and wood products	..	..	..	..	848	*7589	..	1404	..	*9841	*7589
Textile and leather	..	..	..	43	3822	37	..	3852	21	7775	10
Construction	..	..	..	3087	2254	..	..	3143	..	8483	..
Industries n.e.s	0	124	..	3029	4957	*63	..	6340	1	14514	*64
Transport	..	..	..	351341	1566	19355	..	5875	..	378138	19355
Road	..	..	..	344116	369	19355	..	162	..	364002	19355
Rail	..	..	..	903	..	..	..	5677	..	6580	..
Domestic aviation	..	..	..	133	..	..	..	..	..	133	..
Domestic navigation	..	..	..	6190	..	..	..	..	..	6190	..
Pipeline transport	..	..	..	..	1197	..	..	29	..	1226	..
Transport, n.e.s	..	..	..	..	..	..	..	7	..	7	..
Other	3647	164	..	154800	226067	*27333	..	150966	3721	566698	*27056
Agriculture, forestry, fishing	382	..	..	13864	11028	1883	..	5760	189	33106	1885
Commerce, public services	..	..	..	32709	75834	3382	..	78361	2230	192515	2090
Households	3265	164	..	106334	139206	*22069	..	66845	1302	339184	*23082
Other consumers	..	..	..	1893	..	..	..	..	..	1893	..
Non-energy use	..	7924	..	261307	45320	..	..	..	..	314551	..

Belgium

Terajoules

2018	Primary coal and peat	Coal and peat products	Primary Oil	Oil Products	Natural Gas	Biofuels and waste	Nuclear	Electricity	Heat	Total energy	of which: renewables
Primary production	2748	..	..	..	..	118911	308848	42052	11548	484106	133929
Imports	112675	22383	1392253	1346900	675445	47214	..	77890	..	3674758	47199
Exports	-1374	-853	..	-1381972	-47444	-11506	..	-15509	..	-1458658	-11506
International marine bunkers	..	..	..	-392139	-369	..	..	..	..	-392508	..
International aviation bunkers	..	..	..	-72412	..	..	..	..	..	-72412	..
Stock changes	-6779	-117	295	-10577	-3472	..	..	..	..	-20651	..
Total energy supply	107269	21412	1392548	-510200	624160	154619	308848	104432	11548	2214636	169622
Statistical difference	-147	-947	-84	-30	-3721	100	0	-796	108	-5516	42205
Transfers	..	..	53157	-48806	..	..	..	..	..	4351	..
Transformation	-82163	22139	-1445789	1450577	-158441	-72563	-308848	224636	11888	-358563	-51424
Electricity plants	..	-19230	..	-174	-80933	*-37612	-308848	167756	-10288	-289327	*-29804
CHP plants	-441	..	..	-1117	-77510	-34939	..	56880	22221	-34906	-21560
Heat plants	..	..	..	..	..	-10	..	..	-45	-55	-58
Coke ovens	-47811	46659	..	..	..	..	..	..	..	-1152	..
Briquetting plants	..	..	..	..	..	..	..	..	..	..	..
Liquefaction plants	..	..	0	..	..	..	..	..	..	0	..
Gas works	..	..	..	..	..	..	..	..	..	..	..
Blast furnaces	-33911	-8954	..	..	..	..	..	..	..	-42866	..
NGL plants & gas blending	..	..	..	..	2	-2	..	..	..	0	-2
Oil refineries	..	..	-1449868	1454387	..	..	..	..	..	4519	..
Other transformation	..	3665	4079	-2519	..	..	..	..	..	5224	..
Energy industries own use	..	-10940	..	-48536	-26697	..	..	-18274	-4949	-109395	..
Losses	..	..	..	..	-1191	-23	..	-13673	-285	-15172	-23
Final consumption	25253	33558	..	843066	441553	*81932	..	297918	18094	1741374	*75971
Final energy consumption	25253	25634	..	566418	397887	*81932	..	297918	18094	1413138	*75971
Manufacturing, const., mining	21991	25521	..	62878	168889	*37791	..	140033	14092	471195	*31950
Iron and steel	9932	17272	..	511	21648	67	..	15685	..	65116	..
Chemical and petrochemical	..	347	..	52987	58288	510	..	52841	10678	175650	408
Non-ferrous metals	..	352	..	..	5745	..	..	7636	..	13732	..
Non-metallic minerals	9443	7268	..	1807	21628	*10682	..	8777	174	59779	*5762
Transport equipment	..	..	..	172	2038	..	..	2891	1	5101	..
Machinery	..	..	..	645	4847	*80	..	6617	..	12190	*80
Mining and quarrying	..	..	..	..	555	..	..	1638	..	2193	..
Food and tobacco	1322	117	..	390	37635	*3274	..	21744	1905	66388	*3274
Paper, pulp and printing	1293	165	..	454	5598	*15446	..	6732	1321	31009	*14722
Wood and wood products	..	..	..	..	768	*7560	..	1469	..	*9797	*7560
Textile and leather	..	..	..	43	3836	115	..	3938	12	7944	86
Construction	..	..	..	3092	2161	..	..	3344	..	8597	..
Industries n.e.s	0	0	..	2777	4143	*57	..	6721	1	13699	*58
Transport	..	..	..	352765	2435	19229	..	5965	..	380393	19229
Road	..	..	..	345754	636	19229	..	209	..	365828	19229
Rail	..	..	..	903	..	..	..	5713	..	6616	..
Domestic aviation	..	..	..	133	..	..	..	..	..	133	..
Domestic navigation	..	..	..	5975	..	..	..	..	..	5975	..
Pipeline transport	..	..	..	..	1798	..	..	36	..	1834	..
Transport, n.e.s	..	..	..	..	..	..	..	7	..	7	..
Other	3262	113	..	150776	226564	*24913	..	151920	4002	561550	*24792
Agriculture, forestry, fishing	382	..	..	13176	11568	1810	..	6160	210	33305	1812
Commerce, public services	..	..	..	31935	75985	3251	..	79373	2052	192595	2029
Households	2880	113	..	103727	139011	*19852	..	66388	1740	333712	*20951
Other consumers	..	..	..	1937	..	..	..	..	..	1937	..
Non-energy use	..	7924	..	276647	43665	..	..	..	..	328237	..

Belize

Terajoules

	All Coal	All Oil	Natural Gas	Primary biofuels / Waste	Charcoal	Electricity	Total energy	of which: renewables
2017								
Primary production	..	2277	57	5421	..	974	8729	6395
Imports	..	8889	..	0	0	829	9718	0
Exports	..	-1653	..	..	-1	..	-1654	-1
International marine bunkers	..	..	..	..	..	..	..	..
International aviation bunkers	..	-651	..	..	..	..	-651	..
Stock changes	..	-2	*18	..	..	..	*16	..
Total energy supply	..	8861	74	5421	0	1803	16158	6395
Statistical Difference	..	0	0	0	0	0	0	974
Transfers	..	..	..	..	..	..	..	..
Transformation	..	-398	*-74	-1884	23	*1315	-1018	-1861
Electricity plants	..	-398	*-46	-1841	..	*1315	-970	-1841
Charcoal plants	..	..	..	*-43	23	..	*-20	*-20
Other transformation	..	0	*-28	0	..	..	*-28	0
Energy industries own use	..	..	..	..	..	-94	-94	..
Losses	..	..	..	..	..	-282	-282	..
Final consumption	..	8462	..	3537	*23	2741	14764	3560
Final energy consumption	..	8361	..	3537	*23	2741	14662	3560
Manufacturing, const., mining	..	726	..	2429	..	621	3776	2429
Transport	..	6502	..	..	..	..	6502	..
Road	..	6127	..	..	..	..	6127	..
Domestic aviation	..	*19	..	..	..	..	*19	..
Domestic navigation	..	..	..	..	..	..	..	..
Other transport	..	*355	..	..	..	..	*355	..
Other	..	1132	..	*1108	*23	2121	4384	*1131
Agriculture, forestry, fishing	..	..	..	..	..	58	58	..
Commerce and public services	..	125	..	..	..	837	961	..
Households	..	1007	..	..	*23	1227	2256	*23
Other consumers	..	..	..	*1108	..	..	*1108	*1108
Non-energy use	..	*102	..	..	..	..	*102	..
2018								
Primary production	..	1910	46	5446	..	899	8302	6345
Imports	..	8800	..	0	0	846	9647	0
Exports	..	-1236	..	..	-1	..	-1236	-1
International marine bunkers	..	..	..	..	..	..	..	..
International aviation bunkers	..	-624	..	..	..	..	-624	..
Stock changes	..	-132	*3	..	..	..	-129	..
Total energy supply	..	8719	49	5446	0	1745	15959	6345
Statistical Difference	..	0	0	0	0	0	0	899
Transfers	..	..	..	..	..	..	..	..
Transformation	..	-520	*-49	-2394	24	*1445	-1494	-2371
Electricity plants	..	-520	*-29	-2350	..	*1445	-1454	-2350
Charcoal plants	..	..	..	*-44	24	..	*-20	*-20
Other transformation	..	0	*-20	0	..	..	*-20	0
Energy industries own use	..	..	..	..	..	-96	-96	..
Losses	..	..	..	..	..	-289	-289	..
Final consumption	..	8199	..	3052	*23	2805	14079	3075
Final energy consumption	..	8098	..	3052	*23	2805	13979	3075
Manufacturing, const., mining	..	630	..	1945	..	635	3210	1945
Transport	..	6268	..	..	..	..	6268	..
Road	..	5923	..	..	..	..	5923	..
Domestic aviation	..	*19	..	..	..	..	*19	..
Domestic navigation	..	..	..	..	..	..	..	..
Other transport	..	*326	..	..	..	..	*326	..
Other	..	1201	..	*1107	*23	2170	4501	*1130
Agriculture, forestry, fishing	..	..	..	..	..	59	59	..
Commerce and public services	..	133	..	..	..	856	989	..
Households	..	1068	..	..	*23	1255	2346	*23
Other consumers	..	..	..	*1107	..	..	*1107	*1107
Non-energy use	..	*101	..	..	..	..	*101	..

Benin

Terajoules

	Primary coal and peat	Coal and peat products	Primary Oil	Oil Products	Natural Gas	Biofuels and waste	Nuclear	Electricity	Heat	Total energy	of which: renewables
2017											
Primary production	..	..	..	..	..	114430	..	22	..	114452	114452
Imports	3277	..	..	89620	1373	..	..	4000	..	98270	..
Exports	..	..	..	..	..	..	..	..	..	..	..
International marine bunkers	..	..	..	-40	..	..	..	..	..	-40	..
International aviation bunkers	..	..	..	-1279	..	..	..	..	..	-1279	..
Stock changes	..	..	..	1516	..	..	..	..	..	1516	..
Total energy supply	3277	..	..	89817	1373	114430	..	4021	..	212918	114452
Statistical difference	0	..	..	1273	0	0	..	22	..	1295	22
Transfers	..	..	..	..	..	..	..	..	..	..	..
Transformation	..	..	..	-1678	-1373	*-29268	..	1170	..	*-31150	*-29268
Electricity plants	..	..	..	-1678	-1373	..	..	1170	..	-1882	..
CHP plants	..	..	..	..	..	..	..	..	..	..	..
Heat plants	..	..	..	..	..	..	..	..	..	..	..
Coke ovens	..	..	..	..	..	..	..	..	..	..	..
Briquetting plants	..	..	..	..	..	..	..	..	..	..	..
Liquefaction plants	..	..	..	..	..	..	..	..	..	..	..
Gas works	..	..	..	..	..	..	..	..	..	..	..
Blast furnaces	..	..	..	..	..	..	..	..	..	..	..
NGL plants & gas blending	..	..	..	..	..	..	..	..	..	..	..
Oil refineries	..	..	..	..	..	..	..	..	..	..	..
Other transformation	..	..	..	..	..	*-29268	..	..	..	*-29268	*-29268
Energy industries own use	..	..	..	..	..	..	..	0	..	0	..
Losses	..	..	..	..	..	..	..	-1069	..	-1069	..
Final consumption	3277	..	..	86865	..	*85162	..	4100	..	*179403	*85162
Final energy consumption	3277	..	..	86865	..	*85162	..	4100	..	*179403	*85162
Manufacturing, const., mining	3277	..	..	1336	..	*634	..	922	..	6168	*634
Iron and steel	..	..	..	..	..	..	..	..	..	..	..
Chemical and petrochemical	..	..	..	..	..	..	..	..	..	..	..
Non-ferrous metals	..	..	..	..	..	..	..	..	..	..	..
Non-metallic minerals	..	..	..	999	..	..	..	504	..	1503	..
Transport equipment	..	..	..	..	..	..	..	..	..	..	..
Machinery	..	..	..	..	..	..	..	..	..	..	..
Mining and quarrying	..	..	..	..	..	..	..	..	..	..	..
Food and tobacco	..	..	..	121	..	..	..	72	..	193	..
Paper, pulp and printing	..	..	..	..	..	..	..	..	..	..	..
Wood and wood products	..	..	..	..	..	..	..	..	..	..	..
Textile and leather	..	..	..	..	..	..	..	..	..	..	..
Construction	..	..	..	..	..	..	..	..	..	..	..
Industries n.e.s	3277	..	..	216	..	*634	..	346	..	4472	*634
Transport	..	..	..	83522	..	..	..	..	..	83522	..
Road	..	..	..	83479	..	..	..	..	..	83479	..
Rail	..	..	..	43	..	..	..	..	..	43	..
Domestic aviation	..	..	..	..	..	..	..	..	..	..	..
Domestic navigation	..	..	..	..	..	..	..	..	..	..	..
Pipeline transport	..	..	..	..	..	..	..	..	..	..	..
Transport, n.e.s	..	..	..	..	..	..	..	..	..	..	..
Other	..	..	..	2007	..	*84528	..	3179	..	*89714	*84528
Agriculture, forestry, fishing	..	..	..	560	..	..	..	43	..	603	..
Commerce, public services	..	..	..	95	..	*13997	..	1782	..	*15874	*13997
Households	..	..	..	1353	..	*70531	..	1354	..	*73237	*70531
Other consumers	..	..	..	..	..	..	..	..	..	..	..
Non-energy use	..	..	..	..	..	..	..	..	..	..	..

Benin

Terajoules

	Primary coal and peat	Coal and peat products	Primary Oil	Oil Products	Natural Gas	Biofuels and waste	Nuclear	Electricity	Heat	Total energy	of which: renewables
2018											
Primary production	..	..	..	..	..	113495	..	18	..	113513	113513
Imports	3096	..	..	100796	675	..	..	4655	..	109222	..
Exports	..	..	..	..	..	..	..	..	..	..	..
International marine bunkers	..	..	..	..	..	..	..	..	..	..	..
International aviation bunkers	..	..	..	-1323	..	..	..	..	..	-1323	..
Stock changes	-3096	..	..	514	..	..	..	..	..	-2582	..
Total energy supply	0	..	..	99987	675	113495	..	4673	..	218830	113513
Statistical difference	0	..	..	180	0	0	..	68	..	248	18
Transfers	..	..	..	..	..	..	..	..	..	..	..
Transformation	..	..	..	-1668	-675	*-33023	..	709	..	*-34656	*-33023
Electricity plants	..	..	..	-1668	-675	..	..	709	..	-1634	..
CHP plants	..	..	..	..	..	..	..	..	..	..	..
Heat plants	..	..	..	..	..	..	..	..	..	..	..
Coke ovens	..	..	..	..	..	..	..	..	..	..	..
Briquetting plants	..	..	..	..	..	..	..	..	..	..	..
Liquefaction plants	..	..	..	..	..	..	..	..	..	..	..
Gas works	..	..	..	..	..	..	..	..	..	..	..
Blast furnaces	..	..	..	..	..	..	..	..	..	..	..
NGL plants & gas blending	..	..	..	..	..	..	..	..	..	..	..
Oil refineries	..	..	..	..	..	..	..	..	..	..	..
Other transformation	..	..	..	..	..	*-33023	..	..	..	*-33023	*-33023
Energy industries own use	..	..	..	..	..	..	..	0	..	0	..
Losses	..	..	..	..	..	..	..	-1062	..	-1062	..
Final consumption	..	..	..	98140	..	*80472	..	4252	..	182863	*80472
Final energy consumption	..	..	..	98140	..	*80472	..	4252	..	182863	*80472
Manufacturing, const., mining	..	..	..	1598	..	*695	..	1030	..	3322	*695
Iron and steel	..	..	..	..	..	..	..	..	..	..	..
Chemical and petrochemical	..	..	..	..	..	..	..	..	..	..	..
Non-ferrous metals	..	..	..	..	..	..	..	..	..	..	..
Non-metallic minerals	..	..	..	1307	..	..	..	583	..	1890	..
Transport equipment	..	..	..	..	..	..	..	..	..	..	..
Machinery	..	..	..	..	..	..	..	..	..	..	..
Mining and quarrying	..	..	..	..	..	..	..	..	..	..	..
Food and tobacco	..	..	..	121	..	..	..	76	..	197	..
Paper, pulp and printing	..	..	..	..	..	..	..	..	..	..	..
Wood and wood products	..	..	..	..	..	..	..	..	..	..	..
Textile and leather	..	..	..	..	..	..	..	25	..	25	..
Construction	..	..	..	..	..	..	..	4	..	4	..
Industries n.e.s	..	..	..	169	..	*695	..	342	..	1206	*695
Transport	..	..	..	93984	..	..	..	..	..	93984	..
Road	..	..	..	93984	..	..	..	..	..	93984	..
Rail	..	..	..	..	..	..	..	..	..	..	..
Domestic aviation	..	..	..	..	..	..	..	..	..	..	..
Domestic navigation	..	..	..	..	..	..	..	..	..	..	..
Pipeline transport	..	..	..	..	..	..	..	..	..	..	..
Transport, n.e.s	..	..	..	..	..	..	..	..	..	..	..
Other	..	..	..	2558	..	*79778	..	3222	..	*85558	*79778
Agriculture, forestry, fishing	..	..	..	689	..	..	..	137	..	826	..
Commerce, public services	..	..	..	142	..	*13257	..	1732	..	*15131	*13257
Households	..	..	..	1727	..	*66521	..	1354	..	*69602	*66521
Other consumers	..	..	..	..	..	..	..	..	..	..	..
Non-energy use	..	..	..	..	..	..	..	..	..	..	..

Bermuda

Terajoules

	All Coal	All Oil	Natural Gas	Primary biofuels / Waste	Charcoal	Electricity	Total energy	of which: renewables
2017								
Primary production	..	..	..	*590	..	..	*590	*295
Imports	8	10414	..	3	0	..	10426	4
Exports	..	..	..	..	..	..	..	..
International marine bunkers	..	*-424	..	..	..	..	*-424	..
International aviation bunkers	..	*-679	..	..	..	..	*-679	..
Stock changes	..	*-645	..	..	..	..	*-645	..
Total energy supply	8	8666	..	*593	0	..	9267	*299
Statistical Difference	0	731	..	0	0	0	*731	0
Transfers	..	..	..	..	..	..	..	..
Transformation	..	*-5367	..	*-590	..	2431	*-3526	*-295
Electricity plants	..	*-5367	..	*-590	..	2431	*-3526	*-295
Charcoal plants	..	..	..	..	..	..	..	..
Other transformation	..	0	..	0	..	..	0	0
Energy industries own use	..	..	..	..	..	-166	-166	..
Losses	..	..	..	..	..	*-161	*-161	..
Final consumption	*8	*2567	..	*3	0	2104	*4683	*4
Final energy consumption	*8	*2536	..	*3	0	2104	*4652	*4
Manufacturing, const., mining	*8	*75	..	0	..	..	*83	0
Transport	..	*1579	..	*1	..	..	*1580	*1
Road	..	*1320	..	*1	..	..	*1320	*1
Domestic aviation	..	..	..	..	..	..	..	..
Domestic navigation	..	*259	..	..	..	..	*259	..
Other transport	..	..	..	..	..	..	..	..
Other	..	*881	..	*3	0	2104	2989	*3
Agriculture, forestry, fishing	..	..	..	..	..	..	..	..
Commerce and public services	..	..	..	..	..	1026	1026	..
Households	..	*881	..	*3	0	882	*1767	*3
Other consumers	..	..	..	..	..	196	196	..
Non-energy use	..	*32	..	..	..	..	*32	..
2018								
Primary production	..	..	..	*600	..	..	*600	*300
Imports	82	10778	..	3	0	..	10864	3
Exports	..	..	..	..	..	..	..	..
International marine bunkers	..	*-444	..	..	..	..	*-444	..
International aviation bunkers	..	*-684	..	..	..	..	*-684	..
Stock changes	..	0	..	..	..	..	0	..
Total energy supply	82	9650	..	*603	0	..	10336	*303
Statistical Difference	0	*-4	..	0	0	0	*-4	0
Transfers	..	..	..	..	..	..	..	..
Transformation	..	*-5861	..	*-600	..	2313	*-4148	*-300
Electricity plants	..	*-5861	..	*-600	..	2313	*-4148	*-300
Charcoal plants	..	..	..	..	..	..	..	..
Other transformation	..	0	..	0	..	..	0	0
Energy industries own use	..	..	..	..	..	-134	-134	..
Losses	..	..	..	..	..	*-135	*-135	..
Final consumption	*82	*3794	..	*3	0	2044	*5923	*3
Final energy consumption	*82	*3763	..	*3	0	2044	*5892	*3
Manufacturing, const., mining	*82	*32	..	0	..	..	*114	0
Transport	..	*1675	..	*1	..	..	*1676	*1
Road	..	*1372	..	*1	..	..	*1373	*1
Domestic aviation	..	..	..	..	..	..	..	..
Domestic navigation	..	*302	..	..	..	..	*302	..
Other transport	..	..	..	..	..	..	..	..
Other	..	*2056	..	*2	0	2044	*4103	*3
Agriculture, forestry, fishing	..	..	..	..	..	..	..	..
Commerce and public services	..	..	..	..	..	989	989	..
Households	..	*2056	..	*2	0	865	*2924	*3
Other consumers	..	..	..	..	..	190	190	..
Non-energy use	..	*31	..	..	..	..	*31	..

Bhutan

Terajoules

	All Coal	All Oil	Natural Gas	Primary biofuels / Waste	Charcoal	Electricity	Total energy	of which: renewables
2017								
Primary production	4167	..	..	47457	..	27829	79453	75286
Imports	..	8233	..	1	150	331	8715	151
Exports	-488	..	..	0	0	-20524	-21013	-1
International marine bunkers	..	..	..	..	..	..	..	..
International aviation bunkers	..	*-142	..	..	..	..	*-142	..
Stock changes	..	..	..	..	..	..	..	..
Total energy supply	3679	8091	..	47458	149	7636	67014	75436
Statistical Difference	0	148	..	0	0	-444	-296	27829
Transfers	..	..	..	..	..	..	..	..
Transformation	..	*-3	..	*-384	207	1	*-179	*-177
Electricity plants	..	*-3	..	..	..	1	*-2	..
Charcoal plants	..	..	..	*-384	207	..	*-177	*-177
Other transformation	..	0	..	0	..	..	0	0
Energy industries own use	..	..	..	..	..	-3	-3	..
Losses	..	..	..	..	..	-209	-209	..
Final consumption	3679	7940	..	*47075	*356	7869	*66918	*47430
Final energy consumption	3679	7204	..	*47075	*356	7869	*66182	*47430
Manufacturing, const., mining	3679	*70	..	..	..	5755	9503	..
Transport	..	6541	..	..	..	..	6541	..
Road	..	1278	..	..	..	..	1278	..
Domestic aviation	..	..	..	..	..	..	..	..
Domestic navigation	..	..	..	..	..	..	..	..
Other transport	..	5263	..	..	..	..	5263	..
Other	..	594	..	*47075	*356	2114	*50138	*47430
Agriculture, forestry, fishing	..	..	..	..	..	8	8	..
Commerce and public services	..	..	..	..	..	249	249	..
Households	..	594	..	*47002	*356	871	*48822	*47357
Other consumers	..	..	..	*73	..	986	1059	*73
Non-energy use	..	*736	..	..	..	..	*736	..
2018								
Primary production	4167	..	..	47457	..	25058	76682	72515
Imports	*653	9585	..	1	150	482	10871	151
Exports	..	..	..	0	0	-16491	-16492	-1
International marine bunkers	..	..	..	..	..	..	..	..
International aviation bunkers	..	*-174	..	..	..	..	*-174	..
Stock changes	..	..	..	..	..	..	..	..
Total energy supply	4820	9411	..	47458	149	9049	70887	72665
Statistical Difference	0	176	..	0	0	182	358	25058
Transfers	..	..	..	..	..	..	..	..
Transformation	..	0	..	*-384	207	0	*-177	*-177
Electricity plants	..	0	..	..	..	0	0	..
Charcoal plants	..	..	..	*-384	207	..	*-177	*-177
Other transformation	..	0	..	0	..	..	0	0
Energy industries own use	..	..	..	..	..	-1	-1	..
Losses	..	..	..	..	..	-997	-997	..
Final consumption	4820	9234	..	*47075	*356	7869	*69353	*47430
Final energy consumption	4820	8072	..	*47075	*356	7869	*68192	*47430
Manufacturing, const., mining	4820	*131	..	..	..	6532	11484	..
Transport	..	7408	..	..	..	..	7408	..
Road	..	1539	..	..	..	..	1539	..
Domestic aviation	..	..	..	..	..	..	..	..
Domestic navigation	..	..	..	..	..	..	..	..
Other transport	..	5869	..	..	..	..	5869	..
Other	..	534	..	*47075	*356	1336	*49300	*47430
Agriculture, forestry, fishing	..	..	..	..	..	8	8	..
Commerce and public services	..	..	..	..	..	243	243	..
Households	..	534	..	*47002	*356	871	*48762	*47357
Other consumers	..	..	..	*73	..	215	288	*73
Non-energy use	..	*1162	..	..	..	..	*1162	..

Bolivia (Plur. State of)

Terajoules

2017	Primary coal and peat	Coal and peat products	Primary Oil	Oil Products	Natural Gas	Biofuels and waste	Nuclear	Electricity	Heat	Total energy	of which: renewables
Primary production	..	..	135972	..	703282	39552	..	8280	..	887086	47832
Imports	258	..	..	52234	..	0	..	..	..	52493	0
Exports	..	..	0	-19012	-534568	-13	..	..	..	-553592	-13
International marine bunkers	..	..	..	..	..	..	..	..	..	..	..
International aviation bunkers	..	..	..	-3484	..	..	..	..	..	-3484	..
Stock changes	..	..	1692	13646	..	..	..	..	..	15338	..
Total energy supply	258	..	137664	43385	168714	39540	..	8280	..	397840	47820
Statistical difference	0	..	443	4963	-2824	-12	..	104	..	2674	8268
Transfers	..	..	..	23	..	..	..	..	..	23	..
Transformation	..	..	-137222	118582	-70891	*-9889	..	26377	..	-73043	*-9889
Electricity plants	..	..	..	-2666	-70891	*-6439	..	26377	..	-53619	*-6439
CHP plants	..	..	..	..	..	..	..	..	..	..	..
Heat plants	..	..	..	..	..	..	..	..	..	..	..
Coke ovens	..	..	..	..	..	..	..	..	..	..	..
Briquetting plants	..	..	..	..	..	..	..	..	..	..	..
Liquefaction plants	..	..	..	..	..	..	..	..	..	..	..
Gas works	..	..	..	..	..	..	..	..	..	..	..
Blast furnaces	..	..	..	..	..	..	..	..	..	..	..
NGL plants & gas blending	..	..	-21923	22907	..	..	..	..	..	984	..
Oil refineries	..	..	-115299	98341	..	..	..	..	..	-16958	..
Other transformation	..	..	..	..	..	*-3450	..	..	..	*-3450	*-3450
Energy industries own use	..	..	..	-1502	-31119	*-1579	..	-662	..	-34863	*-1579
Losses	..	..	..	-3839	-1155	..	..	-3740	..	-8734	..
Final consumption	258	..	..	151685	68373	*28084	..	30150	..	278550	*28084
Final energy consumption	258	..	..	149755	68373	*28084	..	30150	..	276620	*28084
Manufacturing, const., mining	258	..	..	5015	34927	*26668	..	7747	..	74615	*26668
Iron and steel	..	..	..	..	..	..	..	..	..	..	..
Chemical and petrochemical	..	..	..	..	..	..	..	..	..	..	..
Non-ferrous metals	258	..	..	..	..	..	..	..	..	258	..
Non-metallic minerals	..	..	..	..	..	..	..	..	..	..	..
Transport equipment	..	..	..	..	..	..	..	..	..	..	..
Machinery	..	..	..	..	..	..	..	..	..	..	..
Mining and quarrying	..	..	..	..	..	..	..	..	..	..	..
Food and tobacco	..	..	..	..	..	..	..	..	..	..	..
Paper, pulp and printing	..	..	..	..	..	..	..	..	..	..	..
Wood and wood products	..	..	..	..	..	..	..	..	..	..	..
Textile and leather	..	..	..	..	..	..	..	..	..	..	..
Construction	..	..	..	3440	..	..	..	..	..	3440	..
Industries n.e.s	0	..	..	1575	34927	*26668	..	7747	..	70917	*26668
Transport	..	..	..	119184	25839	..	..	..	..	145023	..
Road	..	..	..	114817	25839	..	..	..	..	140656	..
Rail	..	..	..	..	..	..	..	..	..	..	..
Domestic aviation	..	..	..	4367	..	..	..	..	..	4367	..
Domestic navigation	..	..	..	..	..	..	..	..	..	..	..
Pipeline transport	..	..	..	..	..	..	..	..	..	..	..
Transport, n.e.s	..	..	..	..	..	..	..	..	..	..	..
Other	..	..	..	25557	7607	1416	..	22403	..	56983	1416
Agriculture, forestry, fishing	..	..	..	5246	..	..	..	3247	..	8493	..
Commerce, public services	..	..	..	550	2047	..	..	7542	..	10139	..
Households	..	..	..	19761	5560	1416	..	11614	..	38351	1416
Other consumers	..	..	..	..	..	..	..	..	..	..	..
Non-energy use	..	..	..	1930	..	..	..	..	..	1930	..

Bolivia (Plur. State of)

Terajoules

2018	Primary coal and peat	Coal and peat products	Primary Oil	Oil Products	Natural Gas	Biofuels and waste	Nuclear	Electricity	Heat	Total energy	of which: renewables
Primary production	..	..	128819	..	656202	*39793	..	10076	..	834890	*49870
Imports	206	..	..	60887	..	0	..	..	..	61093	0
Exports	..	..	..	-12413	-485158	-30	..	..	..	-497601	-30
International marine bunkers	..	..	..	..	..	..	..	..	..	..	..
International aviation bunkers	..	..	..	-3396	..	..	..	..	..	-3396	..
Stock changes	..	..	3088	5893	..	..	..	..	..	8981	..
Total energy supply	206	..	131906	50971	171044	*39764	..	10076	..	403968	*49840
Statistical difference	0	..	590	4152	-1455	0	..	-140	..	3147	*10076
Transfers	..	..	..	22	..	..	..	..	..	22	..
Transformation	..	..	-131316	113698	-64756	*-10401	..	25502	..	-67273	*-10401
Electricity plants	..	..	..	-2838	-64756	*-6879	..	25502	..	-48970	*-6879
CHP plants	..	..	..	..	..	..	..	..	..	..	..
Heat plants	..	..	..	..	..	..	..	..	..	..	..
Coke ovens	..	..	..	..	..	..	..	..	..	..	..
Briquetting plants	..	..	..	..	..	..	..	..	..	..	..
Liquefaction plants	..	..	..	..	..	..	..	..	..	..	..
Gas works	..	..	..	..	..	..	..	..	..	..	..
Blast furnaces	..	..	..	..	..	..	..	..	..	..	..
NGL plants & gas blending	..	..	-22365	23487	..	..	..	..	..	1121	..
Oil refineries	..	..	-108951	93049	..	..	..	..	..	-15902	..
Other transformation	..	..	..	..	..	*-3522	..	..	..	*-3522	*-3522
Energy industries own use	..	..	..	-771	-36023	*-1583	..	-1357	..	-39735	*-1583
Losses	..	..	..	-1940	-1036	..	..	-3942	..	-6918	..
Final consumption	206	..	..	157827	70684	*27780	..	30420	..	286917	*27780
Final energy consumption	206	..	..	155937	70684	*27780	..	30420	..	285028	*27780
Manufacturing, const., mining	206	..	..	5135	35416	*26364	..	7456	..	74577	*26364
Iron and steel	..	..	..	..	..	..	..	..	..	..	..
Chemical and petrochemical	..	..	..	..	..	..	..	..	..	..	..
Non-ferrous metals	206	..	..	..	..	..	..	..	..	206	..
Non-metallic minerals	..	..	..	..	..	..	..	..	..	..	..
Transport equipment	..	..	..	..	..	..	..	..	..	..	..
Machinery	..	..	..	..	..	..	..	..	..	..	..
Mining and quarrying	..	..	..	..	..	..	..	..	..	..	..
Food and tobacco	..	..	..	..	..	..	..	..	..	..	..
Paper, pulp and printing	..	..	..	..	..	..	..	..	..	..	..
Wood and wood products	..	..	..	..	..	..	..	..	..	..	..
Textile and leather	..	..	..	..	..	..	..	..	..	..	..
Construction	..	..	..	3612	..	..	..	..	..	3612	..
Industries n.e.s	0	..	..	1523	35416	*26364	..	7456	..	70759	*26364
Transport	..	..	..	124230	27385	..	..	..	..	151615	..
Road	..	..	..	119819	27385	..	..	..	..	147204	..
Rail	..	..	..	..	..	..	..	..	..	..	..
Domestic aviation	..	..	..	4411	..	..	..	..	..	4411	..
Domestic navigation	..	..	..	..	..	..	..	..	..	..	..
Pipeline transport	..	..	..	..	..	..	..	..	..	..	..
Transport, n.e.s	..	..	..	..	..	..	..	..	..	..	..
Other	..	..	..	26572	7883	1416	..	22964	..	58836	1416
Agriculture, forestry, fishing	..	..	..	5504	..	..	..	3096	..	8600	..
Commerce, public services	..	..	..	598	2187	..	..	7916	..	10701	..
Households	..	..	..	20470	5696	1416	..	11952	..	39535	1416
Other consumers	..	..	..	..	..	..	..	..	..	..	..
Non-energy use	..	..	..	1889	..	..	..	..	..	1889	..

Bonaire, St Eustatius, Saba

Terajoules

	All Coal	All Oil	Natural Gas	Primary biofuels / Waste	Charcoal	Electricity	Total energy	of which: renewables
2017								
Primary production	..	..	..	..	..	145	145	145
Imports	..	*14824	..	*1	*3	..	*14828	*4
Exports	..	..	..	..	..	..	..	..
International marine bunkers	..	*-9042	..	..	..	..	*-9042	..
International aviation bunkers	..	*-348	..	..	..	..	*-348	..
Stock changes	..	..	..	..	..	..	..	..
Total energy supply	..	*5434	..	*1	*3	145	*5582	149
Statistical Difference	..	*-16	..	0	0	0	*-16	145
Transfers	..	..	..	..	..	..	..	..
Transformation	..	*-1228	..	..	..	365	*-863	..
Electricity plants	..	*-1228	..	..	..	365	*-863	..
Charcoal plants	..	..	..	..	..	..	..	..
Other transformation	..	0	..	..	..	..	0	..
Energy industries own use	..	..	..	..	..	-61	-61	..
Losses	..	..	..	..	..	*-76	*-76	..
Final consumption	..	*4222	..	*1	*3	*373	*4598	*4
Final energy consumption	..	*3586	..	*1	*3	*373	*3963	*4
Manufacturing, const., mining	..	*905	..	..	..	*191	*1096	..
Transport	..	*2279	..	..	..	..	*2279	..
Road	..	*2279	..	..	..	..	*2279	..
Domestic aviation	..	..	..	..	..	..	..	..
Domestic navigation	..	..	..	..	..	..	..	..
Other transport	..	..	..	..	..	..	..	..
Other	..	*402	..	*1	*3	*182	*588	*4
Agriculture, forestry, fishing	..	..	..	..	..	..	..	..
Commerce and public services	..	..	..	..	..	..	..	..
Households	..	*402	..	*1	*3	..	*406	*4
Other consumers	..	..	..	..	..	*182	*182	..
Non-energy use	..	*635	..	..	..	..	*635	..
2018								
Primary production	..	..	..	..	..	*173	*173	*173
Imports	..	*14891	..	*1	*3	..	*14895	*4
Exports	..	..	..	..	..	..	..	..
International marine bunkers	..	*-9079	..	..	..	..	*-9079	..
International aviation bunkers	..	*-353	..	..	..	..	*-353	..
Stock changes	..	..	..	..	..	..	..	..
Total energy supply	..	*5459	..	*1	*3	*173	*5636	*177
Statistical Difference	..	0	..	0	0	0	0	*173
Transfers	..	..	..	..	..	..	..	..
Transformation	..	*-1151	..	..	..	*342	*-809	..
Electricity plants	..	*-1151	..	..	..	*342	*-809	..
Charcoal plants	..	..	..	..	..	..	..	..
Other transformation	..	0	..	..	..	..	0	..
Energy industries own use	..	..	..	..	..	*-65	*-65	..
Losses	..	..	..	..	..	*-72	*-72	..
Final consumption	..	*4308	..	*1	*3	*378	*4690	*4
Final energy consumption	..	*3665	..	*1	*3	*378	*4046	*4
Manufacturing, const., mining	..	*929	..	..	..	*194	*1124	..
Transport	..	*2310	..	..	..	..	*2310	..
Road	..	*2310	..	..	..	..	*2310	..
Domestic aviation	..	..	..	..	..	..	..	..
Domestic navigation	..	..	..	..	..	..	..	..
Other transport	..	..	..	..	..	..	..	..
Other	..	*426	..	*1	*3	*184	*613	*4
Agriculture, forestry, fishing	..	..	..	..	..	..	..	..
Commerce and public services	..	..	..	..	..	..	..	..
Households	..	*426	..	*1	*3	..	*430	*4
Other consumers	..	..	..	..	..	*184	*184	..
Non-energy use	..	*643	..	..	..	..	*643	..

Bosnia and Herzegovina

Terajoules

2017	Primary coal and peat	Coal and peat products	Primary Oil	Oil Products	Natural Gas	Biofuels and waste	Nuclear	Electricity	Heat	Total energy	of which: renewables
Primary production	151220	..	..	..	..	28596	..	14429	..	194245	43025
Imports	40610	1655	35744	47224	8363	265	..	12046	..	145906	265
Exports	-2566	-8733	..	-11242	..	-9486	..	-18673	..	-50700	-9486
International marine bunkers	..	..	..	..	..	..	..	..	..	..	..
International aviation bunkers	..	..	..	-441	..	..	..	..	..	-441	..
Stock changes	-648	-6165	-3257	-1168	..	..	..	..	..	-11237	..
Total energy supply	188616	-13243	32486	34374	8363	19375	..	7801	..	277772	33804
Statistical difference	0	0	0	142	0	0	..	47	0	188	14428
Transfers	..	..	..	..	..	..	..	..	..	..	..
Transformation	-177243	23995	-32486	35224	-2104	-2568	..	44752	5793	-104638	-2568
Electricity plants	-136897	..	..	-646	-267	..	..	43927	..	-93883	..
CHP plants	-3672	..	..	..	..	-196	..	824	1817	-1227	-196
Heat plants	-2319	..	..	-606	-1837	-622	..	..	3976	-1408	-622
Coke ovens	-34355	30929	..	..	..	..	..	..	..	-3426	..
Briquetting plants	..	..	..	..	..	..	..	..	..	..	..
Liquefaction plants	..	..	..	..	..	..	..	..	..	..	..
Gas works	..	..	..	..	..	..	..	..	..	..	..
Blast furnaces	..	-6934	..	..	..	..	..	..	..	-6934	..
NGL plants & gas blending	..	..	..	..	..	..	..	..	..	..	..
Oil refineries	..	..	-32486	36476	..	..	..	..	..	3990	..
Other transformation	..	..	..	..	..	-1750	..	..	..	-1750	-1750
Energy industries own use	-118	-6527	..	-4696	..	..	..	-6624	-27	-17992	..
Losses	-193	..	..	..	-19	..	..	-4849	-438	-5499	..
Final consumption	11061	4226	..	64760	6240	16808	..	41033	5328	149455	16808
Final energy consumption	11061	4226	..	62107	6240	16808	..	41033	5328	146802	16808
Manufacturing, const., mining	4791	4226	..	5667	3585	720	..	15638	21	34647	720
Iron and steel	..	4197	..	1212	732	..	..	2952	..	9093	..
Chemical and petrochemical	..	..	..	90	50	..	..	490	..	630	..
Non-ferrous metals	1449	..	..	47	2342	..	..	6221	..	10059	..
Non-metallic minerals	2990	29	..	215	51	..	..	605	..	3890	..
Transport equipment	..	..	..	95	6	..	..	191	..	292	..
Machinery	61	..	..	310	8	..	..	1044	..	1423	..
Mining and quarrying	32	..	..	1075	1	..	..	331	..	1439	..
Food and tobacco	193	..	..	628	284	..	..	950	..	2056	..
Paper, pulp and printing	..	..	..	90	19	..	..	824	..	934	..
Wood and wood products	..	..	..	258	35	..	..	644	..	938	..
Textile and leather	54	..	..	138	51	..	..	626	..	869	..
Construction	..	..	..	1419	..	..	..	227	..	1646	..
Industries n.e.s	11	0	..	90	5	720	..	533	21	1379	720
Transport	..	..	..	52223	46	..	..	274	..	52542	..
Road	..	..	..	52223	46	..	..	..	..	52269	..
Rail	..	..	..	..	..	..	..	274	..	274	..
Domestic aviation	..	..	..	..	..	..	..	..	..	..	..
Domestic navigation	..	..	..	..	..	..	..	..	..	..	..
Pipeline transport	..	..	..	..	..	..	..	..	..	..	..
Transport, n.e.s	..	..	..	..	..	..	..	..	..	..	..
Other	6270	..	..	4217	2609	16088	..	25121	5307	59613	16088
Agriculture, forestry, fishing	11	..	..	608	..	..	..	173	..	791	..
Commerce, public services	..	..	..	1359	1028	1248	..	7826	1310	12771	1248
Households	4370	..	..	1888	1581	14840	..	17122	3997	43798	14840
Other consumers	1890	..	..	363	..	..	..	..	..	2253	..
Non-energy use	..	..	..	2653	..	..	..	..	..	2653	..

Bosnia and Herzegovina

Terajoules

2018	Primary coal and peat	Coal and peat products	Primary Oil	Oil Products	Natural Gas	Biofuels and waste	Nuclear	Electricity	Heat	Total energy	of which: renewables
Primary production	153187	..	..	..	..	60650	..	23915	..	237752	84565
Imports	43467	1085	28891	48881	8335	241	..	11131	..	142030	241
Exports	-2059	-16154	..	-10065	..	-11105	..	-27713	..	-67097	-11105
International marine bunkers	..	..	..	..	..	..	..	..	..	..	..
International aviation bunkers	..	..	..	-309	..	..	..	..	..	-309	..
Stock changes	-2767	342	592	1527	-1	..	..	..	..	-306	..
Total energy supply	191828	-14727	29483	40034	8334	49785	..	7333	..	312070	73700
Statistical difference	0	0	0	-1137	0	2	..	0	0	-1135	23917
Transfers	..	..	..	..	..	..	..	..	..	..	..
Transformation	-180034	26973	-29483	29025	-2102	-2604	..	45061	5759	-107404	-2604
Electricity plants	-135846	..	..	-444	-260	..	..	44276	..	-92274	..
CHP plants	-3496	..	..	..	..	-198	..	785	1757	-1152	-198
Heat plants	-2345	..	..	-323	-1841	-1093	..	..	4002	-1600	-1093
Coke ovens	-38337	34602	..	..	..	..	..	..	..	-3734	..
Briquetting plants	..	..	..	..	..	..	..	..	..	..	..
Liquefaction plants	..	..	..	..	..	..	..	..	..	..	..
Gas works	..	..	..	..	..	..	..	..	..	..	..
Blast furnaces	..	-7630	..	..	..	..	..	..	..	-7630	..
NGL plants & gas blending	..	..	..	..	..	..	..	..	..	..	..
Oil refineries	..	..	-29483	29793	..	..	..	..	..	310	..
Other transformation	..	..	..	..	..	-1313	..	..	..	-1313	-1313
Energy industries own use	-116	-7632	..	-4414	..	..	..	-6296	-21	-18479	..
Losses	0	..	..	..	-33	..	..	-4856	-425	-5315	..
Final consumption	11678	4614	..	65782	6199	47180	..	41242	5313	182008	47180
Final energy consumption	11678	4614	..	61602	6199	47180	..	41242	5313	177827	47180
Manufacturing, const., mining	6387	4614	..	6077	3645	721	..	15721	22	37187	721
Iron and steel	610	4614	..	1013	770	..	..	2948	..	9956	..
Chemical and petrochemical	..	..	..	131	58	..	..	504	..	692	..
Non-ferrous metals	1584	..	..	47	2389	..	..	6422	..	10442	..
Non-metallic minerals	3857	..	..	420	48	..	..	439	..	4764	..
Transport equipment	..	..	..	95	2	..	..	270	..	366	..
Machinery	61	..	..	413	7	..	..	994	..	1474	..
Mining and quarrying	32	..	..	1072	..	..	..	270	..	1374	..
Food and tobacco	180	..	..	788	275	..	..	958	..	2201	..
Paper, pulp and printing	..	..	..	535	12	..	..	796	..	1342	..
Wood and wood products	..	..	..	129	32	..	..	680	..	841	..
Textile and leather	53	..	..	225	49	..	..	673	..	1000	..
Construction	..	..	..	1076	..	..	..	227	..	1303	..
Industries n.e.s	11	0	..	133	5	721	..	540	22	1431	721
Transport	..	..	..	51801	86	..	..	212	..	52099	..
Road	..	..	..	51801	86	..	..	..	..	51887	..
Rail	..	..	..	..	..	..	..	212	..	212	..
Domestic aviation	..	..	..	..	..	..	..	..	..	..	..
Domestic navigation	..	..	..	..	..	..	..	..	..	..	..
Pipeline transport	..	..	..	..	..	..	..	..	..	..	..
Transport, n.e.s	..	..	..	..	..	..	..	..	..	..	..
Other	5291	..	..	3724	2469	46459	..	25308	5291	88541	46459
Agriculture, forestry, fishing	11	..	..	1561	..	..	..	223	..	1794	..
Commerce, public services	..	..	..	701	962	1127	..	8219	1327	12336	1127
Households	3211	..	..	1140	1507	45332	..	16866	3964	72019	45332
Other consumers	2070	..	..	323	..	..	..	..	..	2393	..
Non-energy use	..	..	..	4181	..	..	..	..	..	4181	..

Botswana

Terajoules

2017	Primary coal and peat	Coal and peat products	Primary Oil	Oil Products	Natural Gas	Biofuels and waste	Nuclear	Electricity	Heat	Total energy	of which: renewables
Primary production	52385	..	..	..	..	6388	..	7	..	58781	6395
Imports	..	..	..	41222	..	1	..	4637	..	45860	1
Exports	-5404	..	..	..	..	..	..	..	..	-5404	..
International marine bunkers	..	..	..	..	..	..	..	..	..	..	..
International aviation bunkers	..	..	..	-485	..	..	..	..	..	-485	..
Stock changes	..	..	..	..	..	..	..	..	..	..	..
Total energy supply	46982	..	..	40737	..	6389	..	4644	..	98752	6396
Statistical difference	0	..	..	-5253	..	0	..	50	..	-5202	7
Transfers	..	..	..	..	..	..	..	..	..	..	..
Transformation	-45212	..	..	-129	..	*-1901	..	10872	..	-36370	*-1901
Electricity plants	-45212	..	..	-129	..	..	..	10872	..	-34469	..
CHP plants	..	..	..	..	..	..	..	..	..	..	..
Heat plants	..	..	..	..	..	..	..	..	..	..	..
Coke ovens	..	..	..	..	..	..	..	..	..	..	..
Briquetting plants	..	..	..	..	..	..	..	..	..	..	..
Liquefaction plants	..	..	..	..	..	..	..	..	..	..	..
Gas works	..	..	..	..	..	..	..	..	..	..	..
Blast furnaces	..	..	..	..	..	..	..	..	..	..	..
NGL plants & gas blending	..	..	..	..	..	..	..	..	..	..	..
Oil refineries	..	..	..	..	..	..	..	..	..	..	..
Other transformation	..	..	..	..	..	*-1901	..	..	..	*-1901	*-1901
Energy industries own use	..	..	..	..	..	..	..	-1584	..	-1584	..
Losses	..	..	..	..	..	..	..	-2074	..	-2074	..
Final consumption	1770	..	..	45861	..	*4488	..	11808	..	63927	*4488
Final energy consumption	1770	..	..	44977	..	*4488	..	11808	..	63042	*4488
Manufacturing, const., mining	1605	..	..	7853	..	..	..	3924	..	13382	..
Iron and steel	..	..	..	..	..	..	..	58	..	58	..
Chemical and petrochemical	..	..	..	..	..	..	..	79	..	79	..
Non-ferrous metals	..	..	..	..	..	..	..	79	..	79	..
Non-metallic minerals	..	..	..	..	..	..	..	68	..	68	..
Transport equipment	..	..	..	..	..	..	..	..	..	..	..
Machinery	..	..	..	..	..	..	..	..	..	..	..
Mining and quarrying	1605	..	..	5811	..	..	..	3013	..	10429	..
Food and tobacco	..	..	..	176	..	..	..	320	..	497	..
Paper, pulp and printing	..	..	..	40	..	..	..	29	..	69	..
Wood and wood products	..	..	..	..	..	..	..	29	..	29	..
Textile and leather	..	..	..	43	..	..	..	94	..	137	..
Construction	..	..	..	946	..	..	..	22	..	968	..
Industries n.e.s	0	..	..	837	..	..	..	133	..	970	..
Transport	..	..	..	35276	..	..	..	..	..	35276	..
Road	..	..	..	34714	..	..	..	..	..	34714	..
Rail	..	..	..	473	..	..	..	..	..	473	..
Domestic aviation	..	..	..	89	..	..	..	..	..	89	..
Domestic navigation	..	..	..	..	..	..	..	..	..	..	..
Pipeline transport	..	..	..	..	..	..	..	..	..	..	..
Transport, n.e.s	..	..	..	..	..	..	..	..	..	..	..
Other	165	..	..	1848	..	*4488	..	7884	..	14385	*4488
Agriculture, forestry, fishing	118	..	..	434	..	..	..	673	..	1225	..
Commerce, public services	47	..	..	864	..	..	..	3074	..	3986	..
Households	..	..	..	506	..	*2272	..	3679	..	6457	*2272
Other consumers	..	..	..	43	..	*2216	..	457	..	*2716	*2216
Non-energy use	..	..	..	884	..	..	..	..	..	884	..

Botswana

Terajoules

2018	Primary coal and peat	Coal and peat products	Primary Oil	Oil Products	Natural Gas	Biofuels and waste	Nuclear	Electricity	Heat	Total energy	of which: renewables
Primary production	58575	..	..	..	..	6389	..	18	..	64982	6407
Imports	..	..	..	43140	..	1	..	998	..	44139	1
Exports	-7487	..	..	..	..	..	..	..	..	-7487	..
International marine bunkers	..	..	..	..	..	..	..	..	..	..	..
International aviation bunkers	..	..	..	-529	..	..	..	..	..	-529	..
Stock changes	..	..	..	..	..	..	..	..	..	..	..
Total energy supply	51088	..	..	42611	..	6390	..	1016	..	101105	6408
Statistical difference	15599	..	..	-5547	..	0	..	-2201	..	7850	18
Transfers	..	..	..	..	..	..	..	..	..	..	..
Transformation	-33673	..	..	-129	..	*-1901	..	11159	..	-24543	*-1901
Electricity plants	-33673	..	..	-129	..	..	..	11159	..	-22642	..
CHP plants	..	..	..	..	..	..	..	..	..	..	..
Heat plants	..	..	..	..	..	..	..	..	..	..	..
Coke ovens	..	..	..	..	..	..	..	..	..	..	..
Briquetting plants	..	..	..	..	..	..	..	..	..	..	..
Liquefaction plants	..	..	..	..	..	..	..	..	..	..	..
Gas works	..	..	..	..	..	..	..	..	..	..	..
Blast furnaces	..	..	..	..	..	..	..	..	..	..	..
NGL plants & gas blending	..	..	..	..	..	..	..	..	..	..	..
Oil refineries	..	..	..	..	..	..	..	..	..	..	..
Other transformation	..	..	..	..	..	*-1901	..	..	..	*-1901	*-1901
Energy industries own use	..	..	..	..	..	..	..	-1350	..	-1350	..
Losses	..	..	..	..	..	..	..	-1475	..	-1475	..
Final consumption	1817	..	..	48029	..	*4488	..	11552	..	65887	*4488
Final energy consumption	1817	..	..	47105	..	*4488	..	11552	..	64962	*4488
Manufacturing, const., mining	1652	..	..	8278	..	..	..	3359	..	13289	..
Iron and steel	..	..	..	..	..	..	..	58	..	58	..
Chemical and petrochemical	..	..	..	..	..	..	..	79	..	79	..
Non-ferrous metals	..	..	..	..	..	..	..	79	..	79	..
Non-metallic minerals	..	..	..	..	..	..	..	68	..	68	..
Transport equipment	..	..	..	..	..	..	..	..	..	..	..
Machinery	..	..	..	..	..	..	..	..	..	..	..
Mining and quarrying	1652	..	..	6112	..	..	..	2434	..	10197	..
Food and tobacco	..	..	..	176	..	..	..	324	..	500	..
Paper, pulp and printing	..	..	..	40	..	..	..	32	..	73	..
Wood and wood products	..	..	..	..	..	..	..	32	..	32	..
Textile and leather	..	..	..	43	..	..	..	97	..	140	..
Construction	..	..	..	989	..	..	..	22	..	1011	..
Industries n.e.s	0	..	..	917	..	..	..	133	..	1051	..
Transport	..	..	..	36893	..	..	..	..	..	36893	..
Road	..	..	..	36374	..	..	..	..	..	36374	..
Rail	..	..	..	430	..	..	..	..	..	430	..
Domestic aviation	..	..	..	89	..	..	..	..	..	89	..
Domestic navigation	..	..	..	..	..	..	..	..	..	..	..
Pipeline transport	..	..	..	..	..	..	..	..	..	..	..
Transport, n.e.s	..	..	..	..	..	..	..	..	..	..	..
Other	165	..	..	1934	..	*4488	..	8194	..	14781	*4488
Agriculture, forestry, fishing	118	..	..	477	..	..	..	684	..	1279	..
Commerce, public services	47	..	..	907	..	..	..	3211	..	4166	..
Households	..	..	..	506	..	*2272	..	3834	..	6613	*2272
Other consumers	..	..	..	43	..	*2216	..	464	..	*2723	*2216
Non-energy use	..	..	..	925	..	..	..	..	..	925	..

Brazil

Terajoules

2017	Primary coal and peat	Coal and peat products	Primary Oil	Oil Products	Natural Gas	Biofuels and waste	Nuclear	Electricity	Heat	Total energy	of which: renewables
Primary production	80848	..	5964200	..	896891	3763144	169981	1490800	..	12365863	5253944
Imports	587540	44431	313617	1207311	373649	38699	..	131440	..	2696688	38699
Exports	..	..	-2255888	-235444	..	-29439	..	-562	..	-2521333	-29439
International marine bunkers	..	..	..	-140518	..	..	..	..	..	-140518	..
International aviation bunkers	..	..	..	-93051	..	..	..	..	..	-93051	..
Stock changes	-2718	-3264	9432	-11647	..	-10179	..	..	..	-18376	-10179
Total energy supply	665670	41167	4031361	726651	1270540	3762226	169981	1621678	..	12289273	5253025
Statistical difference	969	-36	3637	-190562	3800	1287	0	7	..	-180898	1492087
Transfers	..	..	55258	-37108	..	-141200	..	..	..	-123051	-141200
Transformation	-493248	345644	-4082981	3941055	-519556	-667840	-169981	630774	..	-1016133	-667840
Electricity plants	-205225	-16320	..	-135218	-519556	-575969	-169981	630774	..	-991495	-575969
CHP plants	..	..	..	..	..	..	..	..	..	..	..
Heat plants	..	..	..	..	..	..	..	..	..	..	..
Coke ovens	-288024	361964	..	-37960	..	..	..	..	..	35980	..
Briquetting plants	..	..	..	..	..	..	..	..	..	..	..
Liquefaction plants	..	..	0	..	..	..	..	..	..	0	..
Gas works	..	..	..	..	..	..	..	..	..	..	..
Blast furnaces	..	..	..	..	..	..	..	..	..	..	..
NGL plants & gas blending	..	..	-133882	134437	..	..	..	..	..	556	..
Oil refineries	..	..	-4005720	3979796	..	..	..	..	..	-25924	..
Other transformation	..	..	56621	..	..	-91871	..	..	..	-35250	-91871
Energy industries own use	..	-8849	..	-232603	-259276	-432414	..	-106704	..	-1039846	-432414
Losses	-2106	-1098	..	-4063	-15269	-4812	..	-351428	..	-378776	-4812
Final consumption	169347	376900	..	4584495	472640	2514672	..	1794312	..	9912365	2514672
Final energy consumption	169347	376900	..	4010230	445336	2514672	..	1794312	..	9310797	2514672
Manufacturing, const., mining	169347	376900	..	449299	356281	1353279	..	718855	..	3423961	1353279
Iron and steel	103139	363120	..	11832	45968	145025	..	89903	..	758986	145025
Chemical and petrochemical	7833	..	..	106879	85659	5844	..	79747	..	285963	5844
Non-ferrous metals	32051	10082	..	72088	23225	37	..	98251	..	235734	37
Non-metallic minerals	2928	1936	..	137818	16495	184	..	21618	..	180978	184
Transport equipment	..	..	..	..	..	..	..	..	..	..	..
Machinery	..	..	..	..	..	..	..	..	..	..	..
Mining and quarrying	12456	1762	..	34301	52689	1141	..	44989	..	147338	1141
Food and tobacco	2902	..	..	25579	33660	623216	..	98939	..	784296	623216
Paper, pulp and printing	5034	..	..	21531	32156	1679	..	83675	..	144075	1679
Wood and wood products	..	..	..	..	..	..	..	..	..	..	..
Textile and leather	..	..	..	4700	8845	..	..	23450	..	36996	..
Construction	..	..	..	606	..	..	..	..	..	606	..
Industries n.e.s	3005	0	..	33964	57584	576153	..	178283	..	848988	576153
Transport	..	..	..	2980542	68700	681551	..	7398	..	3738190	681551
Road	..	..	..	2742164	68700	678496	..	..	..	3489360	678496
Rail	..	..	..	42440	..	3054	..	7398	..	52892	3054
Domestic aviation	..	..	..	144876	..	..	..	..	..	144876	..
Domestic navigation	..	..	..	51062	..	..	..	..	..	51062	..
Pipeline transport	..	..	..	..	..	..	..	..	..	..	..
Transport, n.e.s	..	..	..	..	..	..	..	..	..	..	..
Other	..	..	..	580389	20355	479842	..	1068059	..	2148645	479842
Agriculture, forestry, fishing	..	..	..	275430	..	138309	..	103450	..	517188	138309
Commerce, public services	..	..	..	..	..	3897	..	480625	..	484522	3897
Households	..	..	..	276036	15012	334190	..	483984	..	1109222	334190
Other consumers	..	..	..	28924	5343	3446	..	..	..	37713	3446
Non-energy use	..	..	..	574265	27303	..	..	..	..	601568	..

Brazil

Terajoules

2018	Primary coal and peat	Coal and peat products	Primary Oil	Oil Products	Natural Gas	Biofuels and waste	Nuclear	Electricity	Heat	Total energy	of which: renewables
Primary production	80814	..	5856948	..	846346	3997365	169279	1587265	..	12538017	5584631
Imports	578122	53127	403071	1082180	369324	37654	..	125928	..	2649406	37654
Exports	..	..	-2333161	-346924	..	-35978	..	-4	..	-2716067	-35978
International marine bunkers	..	..	..	-120978	..	..	..	..	..	-120978	..
International aviation bunkers	..	..	..	-105487	..	..	..	..	..	-105487	..
Stock changes	-6832	-15369	-6429	16686	..	-36463	..	..	..	-48406	-36463
Total energy supply	652104	37758	3920429	525476	1215670	3962578	169279	1713190	..	12196484	5549844
Statistical difference	9076	1467	0	-174605	-7386	-221	0	4	..	-171666	1587044
Transfers	..	..	49246	-62446	..	-175675	..	..	..	-188874	-175675
Transformation	-464519	358401	-3969675	3880377	-433481	-714314	-169279	577760	..	-934729	-714314
Electricity plants	-182108	-15411	..	-116719	-433481	-618089	-169279	577760	..	-957326	-618089
CHP plants	..	..	..	..	..	..	..	..	..	..	..
Heat plants	..	..	..	..	..	..	..	..	..	..	..
Coke ovens	-282411	373812	..	-47905	..	..	..	..	..	43496	..
Briquetting plants	..	..	..	..	..	..	..	..	..	..	..
Liquefaction plants	..	..	0	..	..	..	..	..	..	0	..
Gas works	..	..	..	..	..	..	..	..	..	..	..
Blast furnaces	..	..	..	..	..	..	..	..	..	..	..
NGL plants & gas blending	..	..	-129683	130235	..	..	..	..	..	552	..
Oil refineries	..	..	-3873941	3914766	..	..	..	..	..	40825	..
Other transformation	..	..	33949	..	..	-96225	..	..	..	-62276	-96225
Energy industries own use	..	-9139	..	-202821	-286685	-518354	..	-113263	..	-1130262	-518354
Losses	-2730	-1444	..	0	-15376	-5574	..	-352703	..	-377827	-5574
Final consumption	175780	384109	..	4315191	487515	2548883	..	1824980	..	9736458	2548883
Final energy consumption	175780	384109	..	3778062	464611	2548883	..	1824980	..	9176425	2548883
Manufacturing, const., mining	175780	384109	..	395491	365444	1236059	..	722736	..	3279619	1236059
Iron and steel	108341	369664	..	13228	46470	152399	..	91343	..	781445	152399
Chemical and petrochemical	10104	..	..	91370	95943	5765	..	81576	..	284758	5765
Non-ferrous metals	27787	10718	..	44208	16470	37	..	89550	..	188770	37
Non-metallic minerals	3011	1820	..	131087	17217	184	..	21193	..	174512	184
Transport equipment	..	..	..	..	..	..	..	..	..	..	..
Machinery	..	..	..	..	..	..	..	..	..	..	..
Mining and quarrying	14008	1907	..	34415	49361	1325	..	47574	..	148589	1325
Food and tobacco	2781	..	..	24885	34990	479431	..	93254	..	635342	479431
Paper, pulp and printing	5435	..	..	20506	38390	1985	..	86134	..	152449	1985
Wood and wood products	..	..	..	..	..	..	..	..	..	..	..
Textile and leather	..	..	..	3912	9140	..	..	23011	..	36062	..
Construction	..	..	..	485	..	..	..	..	..	485	..
Industries n.e.s	4312	0	..	31396	57465	594933	..	189101	..	877207	594933
Transport	..	..	..	2810273	77090	792909	..	7085	..	3687357	792909
Road	..	..	..	2561408	77090	789155	..	..	..	3427654	789155
Rail	..	..	..	47158	..	3754	..	7085	..	57997	3754
Domestic aviation	..	..	..	148756	..	..	..	..	..	148756	..
Domestic navigation	..	..	..	52951	..	..	..	..	..	52951	..
Pipeline transport	..	..	..	..	..	..	..	..	..	..	..
Transport, n.e.s	..	..	..	..	..	..	..	..	..	..	..
Other	..	..	..	572299	22076	519915	..	1095160	..	2209449	519915
Agriculture, forestry, fishing	..	..	..	270415	..	140401	..	109490	..	520307	140401
Commerce, public services	..	..	..	..	..	3814	..	489553	..	493367	3814
Households	..	..	..	272914	16028	372363	..	496116	..	1157421	372363
Other consumers	..	..	..	28969	6048	3337	..	..	..	38354	3337
Non-energy use	..	..	..	537129	22904	..	..	..	..	560033	..

British Virgin Islands

Terajoules

	All Coal	All Oil	Natural Gas	Primary biofuels / Waste	Charcoal	Electricity	Total energy	of which: renewables
2017								
Primary production	..	..	..	14	..	*4	18	18
Imports	..	*2387	..	..	1	..	*2388	1
Exports	..	..	..	..	..	..	..	..
International marine bunkers	..	..	..	..	..	..	..	..
International aviation bunkers	..	..	..	..	..	..	..	..
Stock changes	..	..	..	..	..	..	..	..
Total energy supply	..	*2387	..	14	1	*4	*2406	19
Statistical Difference	..	0	..	0	0	0	0	4
Transfers	..	..	..	..	..	..	..	..
Transformation	..	*-1518	..	*-4	2	*531	*-989	*-2
Electricity plants	..	*-1518	..	..	..	*531	*-987	..
Charcoal plants	..	..	..	*-4	2	..	*-2	*-2
Other transformation	..	0	..	0	..	..	0	0
Energy industries own use	..	..	..	..	..	*-19	*-19	..
Losses	..	..	..	..	..	*-68	*-68	..
Final consumption	..	*869	..	*10	*3	*447	*1330	*14
Final energy consumption	..	*869	..	*10	*3	*447	*1330	*14
Manufacturing, const., mining	..	..	..	..	..	*26	*26	..
Transport	..	*729	..	..	..	..	*729	..
Road	..	*514	..	..	..	..	*514	..
Domestic aviation	..	..	..	..	..	..	..	..
Domestic navigation	..	..	..	..	..	..	..	..
Other transport	..	*215	..	..	..	..	*215	..
Other	..	*140	..	*10	*3	*422	*575	*14
Agriculture, forestry, fishing	..	..	..	..	..	..	..	..
Commerce and public services	..	..	..	..	..	*288	*288	..
Households	..	*140	..	*10	*3	*134	*287	*14
Other consumers	..	..	..	..	..	..	..	..
Non-energy use	..	..	..	..	..	..	..	..
2018								
Primary production	..	..	..	15	..	*3	18	18
Imports	..	*2253	..	..	1	..	*2254	1
Exports	..	..	..	..	..	..	..	..
International marine bunkers	..	..	..	..	..	..	..	..
International aviation bunkers	..	..	..	..	..	..	..	..
Stock changes	..	..	..	..	..	..	..	..
Total energy supply	..	*2253	..	15	1	*3	*2272	19
Statistical Difference	..	0	..	0	0	0	0	3
Transfers	..	..	..	..	..	..	..	..
Transformation	..	*-1462	..	*-4	2	*522	*-942	*-2
Electricity plants	..	*-1462	..	..	..	*522	*-940	..
Charcoal plants	..	..	..	*-4	2	..	*-2	*-2
Other transformation	..	0	..	0	..	..	0	0
Energy industries own use	..	..	..	..	..	*-21	*-21	..
Losses	..	..	..	..	..	*-83	*-83	..
Final consumption	..	*791	..	*11	*3	*421	*1226	*14
Final energy consumption	..	*791	..	*11	*3	*421	*1226	*14
Manufacturing, const., mining	..	..	..	..	..	*25	*25	..
Transport	..	*659	..	..	..	..	*659	..
Road	..	*487	..	..	..	..	*487	..
Domestic aviation	..	..	..	..	..	..	..	..
Domestic navigation	..	..	..	..	..	..	..	..
Other transport	..	*172	..	..	..	..	*172	..
Other	..	*131	..	*11	*3	*396	*541	*14
Agriculture, forestry, fishing	..	..	..	..	..	..	..	..
Commerce and public services	..	..	..	..	..	*270	*270	..
Households	..	*131	..	*11	*3	*126	*271	*14
Other consumers	..	..	..	..	..	..	..	..
Non-energy use	..	..	..	..	..	..	..	..

Brunei Darussalam

Terajoules

2017	Primary coal and peat	Coal and peat products	Primary Oil	Oil Products	Natural Gas	Biofuels and waste	Nuclear	Electricity	Heat	Total energy	of which: renewables
Primary production	..	..	235333	..	416499	106	..	7	..	651946	114
Imports	..	..	120	19208	..	11	..	..	..	19339	11
Exports	..	..	-226552	0	-294493	-4	..	..	..	-521049	-4
International marine bunkers	..	..	..	..	..	..	..	..	..	..	..
International aviation bunkers	..	..	..	-3131	..	..	..	..	..	-3131	..
Stock changes	..	..	3174	-492	2813	..	..	..	..	5494	..
Total energy supply	..	..	12076	15584	124819	113	..	7	..	152599	121
Statistical difference	..	..	-811	-988	-4502	-1	..	7	..	-6296	6
Transfers	..	..	..	..	..	..	..	..	..	..	..
Transformation	..	..	-12887	10411	-46494	*-8	..	14958	..	-34021	*-8
Electricity plants	..	..	..	-559	-40840	..	..	13399	..	-28000	..
CHP plants	..	..	..	..	-5654	..	..	1559	..	-4095	..
Heat plants	..	..	..	..	..	..	..	..	..	..	..
Coke ovens	..	..	..	..	..	..	..	..	..	..	..
Briquetting plants	..	..	..	..	..	..	..	..	..	..	..
Liquefaction plants	..	..	..	..	..	..	..	..	..	..	..
Gas works	..	..	..	..	..	..	..	..	..	..	..
Blast furnaces	..	..	..	..	..	..	..	..	..	..	..
NGL plants & gas blending	..	..	-751	804	..	..	..	..	..	53	..
Oil refineries	..	..	-12136	10166	..	..	..	..	..	-1970	..
Other transformation	..	..	..	..	..	*-8	..	..	..	*-8	*-8
Energy industries own use	..	..	..	-168	-37994	..	..	-2023	..	-40185	..
Losses	..	..	..	..	-8021	..	..	-1732	..	-9752	..
Final consumption	..	..	..	26815	36813	*106	..	11203	..	74937	*106
Final energy consumption	..	..	..	26130	17644	*106	..	11203	..	55084	*106
Manufacturing, const., mining	..	..	..	5696	16910	..	..	482	..	23088	..
Iron and steel	..	..	..	..	..	..	..	..	..	..	..
Chemical and petrochemical	..	..	..	15	16910	..	..	..	..	16925	..
Non-ferrous metals	..	..	..	..	..	..	..	..	..	..	..
Non-metallic minerals	..	..	..	..	..	..	..	..	..	..	..
Transport equipment	..	..	..	..	..	..	..	..	..	..	..
Machinery	..	..	..	..	..	..	..	..	..	..	..
Mining and quarrying	..	..	..	..	..	..	..	..	..	..	..
Food and tobacco	..	..	..	..	..	..	..	..	..	..	..
Paper, pulp and printing	..	..	..	..	..	..	..	..	..	..	..
Wood and wood products	..	..	..	..	..	..	..	..	..	..	..
Textile and leather	..	..	..	..	..	..	..	..	..	..	..
Construction	..	..	..	..	..	..	..	..	..	..	..
Industries n.e.s	..	..	..	5681	0	..	..	482	..	6163	..
Transport	..	..	..	18599	..	..	..	..	..	18599	..
Road	..	..	..	18599	..	..	..	..	..	18599	..
Rail	..	..	..	..	..	..	..	..	..	..	..
Domestic aviation	..	..	..	..	..	..	..	..	..	..	..
Domestic navigation	..	..	..	..	..	..	..	..	..	..	..
Pipeline transport	..	..	..	..	..	..	..	..	..	..	..
Transport, n.e.s	..	..	..	..	..	..	..	..	..	..	..
Other	..	..	..	1836	734	*106	..	10721	..	13397	*106
Agriculture, forestry, fishing	..	..	..	..	..	..	..	..	..	..	..
Commerce, public services	..	..	..	..	..	..	..	6109	..	6109	..
Households	..	..	..	804	734	*106	..	4612	..	6256	*106
Other consumers	..	..	..	1032	..	..	..	..	..	1032	..
Non-energy use	..	..	..	684	19169	..	..	..	..	19854	..

Brunei Darussalam

Terajoules

2018	Primary coal and peat	Coal and peat products	Primary Oil	Oil Products	Natural Gas	Biofuels and waste	Nuclear	Electricity	Heat	Total energy	of which: renewables
Primary production	..	..	231983	..	407115	106	..	7	..	639212	114
Imports	..	..	270	15422	..	10	..	..	..	15702	10
Exports	..	..	-210660	0	-277182	-2	..	..	..	-487844	-2
International marine bunkers	..	..	..	..	..	..	..	..	..	..	..
International aviation bunkers	..	..	..	-3572	..	..	..	..	..	-3572	..
Stock changes	..	..	-6369	233	-1410	..	..	..	..	-7547	..
Total energy supply	..	..	15223	12083	128523	115	..	7	..	155950	122
Statistical difference	..	..	-766	-778	1770	0	..	0	..	226	7
Transfers	..	..	..	..	..	..	..	..	..	..	..
Transformation	..	..	-15990	14391	-49449	*-14	..	15451	..	-35610	*-14
Electricity plants	..	..	..	-559	-44378	..	..	13867	..	-31070	..
CHP plants	..	..	..	..	-5071	..	..	1584	..	-3487	..
Heat plants	..	..	..	..	..	..	..	..	..	..	..
Coke ovens	..	..	..	..	..	..	..	..	..	..	..
Briquetting plants	..	..	..	..	..	..	..	..	..	..	..
Liquefaction plants	..	..	..	..	..	..	..	..	..	..	..
Gas works	..	..	..	..	..	..	..	..	..	..	..
Blast furnaces	..	..	..	..	..	..	..	..	..	..	..
NGL plants & gas blending	..	..	-751	804	..	..	..	..	..	53	..
Oil refineries	..	..	-15238	14146	..	..	..	..	..	-1092	..
Other transformation	..	..	..	..	..	*-14	..	..	..	*-14	*-14
Energy industries own use	..	..	..	-153	-33886	..	..	-3758	..	-37798	..
Losses	..	..	..	..	-5234	..	..	..	..	-5234	..
Final consumption	..	..	..	27098	38184	*101	..	11700	..	77083	*101
Final energy consumption	..	..	..	26791	26309	*101	..	11700	..	64901	*101
Manufacturing, const., mining	..	..	..	5656	25490	..	..	562	..	31708	..
Iron and steel	..	..	..	..	..	..	..	..	..	..	..
Chemical and petrochemical	..	..	..	668	25490	..	..	..	..	26158	..
Non-ferrous metals	..	..	..	..	..	..	..	..	..	..	..
Non-metallic minerals	..	..	..	..	..	..	..	..	..	..	..
Transport equipment	..	..	..	..	..	..	..	..	..	..	..
Machinery	..	..	..	..	..	..	..	..	..	..	..
Mining and quarrying	..	..	..	..	..	..	..	..	..	..	..
Food and tobacco	..	..	..	..	..	..	..	..	..	..	..
Paper, pulp and printing	..	..	..	..	..	..	..	..	..	..	..
Wood and wood products	..	..	..	..	..	..	..	..	..	..	..
Textile and leather	..	..	..	..	..	..	..	..	..	..	..
Construction	..	..	..	..	..	..	..	..	..	..	..
Industries n.e.s	..	..	..	4988	0	..	..	562	..	5550	..
Transport	..	..	..	18901	..	..	..	..	..	18901	..
Road	..	..	..	18901	..	..	..	..	..	18901	..
Rail	..	..	..	..	..	..	..	..	..	..	..
Domestic aviation	..	..	..	..	..	..	..	..	..	..	..
Domestic navigation	..	..	..	..	..	..	..	..	..	..	..
Pipeline transport	..	..	..	..	..	..	..	..	..	..	..
Transport, n.e.s	..	..	..	..	..	..	..	..	..	..	..
Other	..	..	..	2234	819	*101	..	11138	..	14292	*101
Agriculture, forestry, fishing	..	..	..	..	..	..	..	..	..	..	..
Commerce, public services	..	..	..	..	..	..	..	6433	..	6433	..
Households	..	..	..	987	819	*101	..	4705	..	6612	*101
Other consumers	..	..	..	1247	..	..	..	..	..	1247	..
Non-energy use	..	..	..	306	11876	..	..	..	..	12182	..

Bulgaria

Terajoules

2017	Primary coal and peat	Coal and peat products	Primary Oil	Oil Products	Natural Gas	Biofuels and waste	Nuclear	Electricity	Heat	Total energy	of which: renewables
Primary production	238401	..	1015	..	2774	56931	168582	20646	4276	492625	77768
Imports	22634	1767	291126	111111	114006	4117	..	13338	..	558099	4117
Exports	-152	..	..	-206690	-1121	*-4508	..	-33070	..	-245541	*-4508
International marine bunkers	..	..	..	-3421	..	..	..	..	..	-3421	..
International aviation bunkers	..	..	..	-10231	..	..	..	..	..	-10231	..
Stock changes	-4415	-1250	-4308	-321	-8	*881	..	..	..	-9421	*881
Total energy supply	256468	517	287833	-109552	115650	57421	168582	914	4276	782110	78258
Statistical difference	156	-70	0	438	1334	-102	0	169	522	2447	20544
Transfers	..	..	25241	-24484	..	..	..	..	..	757	..
Transformation	-242361	1602	-313074	302378	-44145	*-3577	-168582	141163	41788	-284808	*-3573
Electricity plants	-210422	-3964	..	-1644	-905	-632	-167886	127667	-532	-258319	-632
CHP plants	-15296	-9292	..	-5506	-23936	*-2666	-696	13496	32559	-11336	*-2666
Heat plants	-50	-189	..	-98	-10113	*-217	..	..	9761	-907	*-213
Coke ovens	..	..	..	..	..	..	..	..	..	..	..
Briquetting plants	-16592	15048	..	..	..	..	..	..	..	-1544	..
Liquefaction plants	..	..	6768	..	..	..	..	..	..	6768	..
Gas works	..	..	..	..	..	..	..	..	..	..	..
Blast furnaces	..	..	..	..	..	..	..	..	..	..	..
NGL plants & gas blending	..	..	..	..	..	..	..	..	..	..	..
Oil refineries	..	..	-319842	309626	..	..	..	..	..	-10216	..
Other transformation	..	..	..	..	-9191	*-62	..	..	..	-9253	*-62
Energy industries own use	-7	-13	..	-17771	-1428	*-31	..	-21730	-8454	-49434	*-31
Losses	-202	..	..	-90	-468	..	..	-12514	-7082	-20355	..
Final consumption	13743	2177	..	150042	68275	*53916	..	107665	30006	425823	*54111
Final energy consumption	13440	524	..	143537	56636	*53916	..	107665	30006	405725	*54111
Manufacturing, const., mining	7725	57	..	13458	38889	*11815	..	35050	8292	115286	*9578
Iron and steel	..	..	..	..	2120	*2	..	2833	..	4955	*2
Chemical and petrochemical	5240	0	..	7328	12896	*573	..	5350	6487	37874	*573
Non-ferrous metals	..	57	..	498	1643	..	..	3776	841	6815	..
Non-metallic minerals	2325	..	..	3762	11649	2973	..	3362	2	24072	736
Transport equipment	..	..	..	..	332	*1	..	428	0	762	*1
Machinery	0	..	..	310	1751	*16	..	3726	24	5827	*16
Mining and quarrying	25	..	..	207	915	*1	..	3974	..	5123	*1
Food and tobacco	25	0	..	402	3731	*622	..	4514	429	9723	*622
Paper, pulp and printing	35	..	..	0	1751	*5789	..	1580	16	*9171	*5789
Wood and wood products	0	..	..	..	152	*1601	..	817	0	*2570	*1601
Textile and leather	76	..	..	43	822	*74	..	1318	447	2779	*74
Construction	0	..	..	862	554	*4	..	900	36	2356	*4
Industries n.e.s	0	0	..	47	573	*159	..	2470	10	3259	*159
Transport	..	..	..	122577	10299	6766	..	1357	..	140999	6766
Road	..	..	..	121136	3141	6766	..	191	..	131234	6766
Rail	..	..	..	559	..	0	..	1094	..	1653	0
Domestic aviation	..	..	..	882	..	..	..	..	..	882	..
Domestic navigation	..	..	..	..	..	..	..	..	..	..	..
Pipeline transport	..	..	..	..	7158	..	..	72	..	7230	..
Transport, n.e.s	..	..	..	..	..	..	..	..	..	..	..
Other	5715	467	..	7502	7448	*35335	..	71258	21714	149440	*37767
Agriculture, forestry, fishing	353	13	..	4954	634	*325	..	799	379	7456	*325
Commerce, public services	147	13	..	1465	3965	*2570	..	30362	6692	45214	*4585
Households	5215	442	..	1084	2849	*32440	..	40097	14643	96770	*32857
Other consumers	..	..	..	..	..	..	..	..	..	..	..
Non-energy use	302	1653	..	6505	11639	..	..	..	..	20099	..

Bulgaria

Terajoules

2018	Primary coal and peat	Coal and peat products	Primary Oil	Oil Products	Natural Gas	Biofuels and waste	Nuclear	Electricity	Heat	Total energy	of which: renewables
Primary production	220850	..	931	..	1195	75707	174868	28109	4311	505970	102558
Imports	22927	1739	248453	90517	108410	5604	..	8003	..	485652	5604
Exports	-301	..	..	-151901	-434	*-7695	..	-36108	..	-196439	*-7695
International marine bunkers	..	..	..	-3461	..	..	..	..	..	-3461	..
International aviation bunkers	..	..	..	-10981	..	..	..	..	..	-10981	..
Stock changes	-4930	-2688	104	6136	195	*312	..	..	..	-873	*312
Total energy supply	238546	-950	249488	-69690	109366	73926	174868	4	4311	779869	100778
Statistical difference	1208	0	254	575	1623	-88	0	306	432	4309	28020
Transfers	..	..	18456	-17923	..	..	..	..	..	533	..
Transformation	-223109	3131	-267690	264727	-42278	-19667	-174868	139511	35777	-284466	-18505
Electricity plants	-191356	-2510	..	-1138	-1408	*-9907	-174150	125881	-374	-254961	*-8800
CHP plants	-13102	-7025	..	-1887	-24408	*-9374	-718	13630	27151	-15734	*-9374
Heat plants	-603	-13	..	..	-9018	*-344	..	..	9000	-978	*-289
Coke ovens	..	..	..	..	..	..	..	..	..	..	..
Briquetting plants	-18047	12679	..	..	..	..	..	..	..	-5368	..
Liquefaction plants	..	..	5472	..	..	..	..	..	..	5472	..
Gas works	..	..	..	..	..	..	..	..	..	..	..
Blast furnaces	..	..	..	..	..	..	..	..	..	..	..
NGL plants & gas blending	..	..	..	..	..	..	..	..	..	..	..
Oil refineries	..	..	-273432	267751	..	..	..	..	..	-5681	..
Other transformation	..	..	270	..	-7444	*-42	..	..	..	-7216	*-42
Energy industries own use	-7	-13	..	-16062	-2007	..	..	-20419	-8000	-46508	..
Losses	-55	..	..	-43	-325	..	..	-11167	-6558	-18148	..
Final consumption	14167	2168	..	160435	63134	*54347	..	107622	25098	426971	*54253
Final energy consumption	13838	458	..	150513	54429	*54347	..	107622	25098	406306	*54253
Manufacturing, const., mining	9085	57	..	16876	37466	*12262	..	35539	3091	114376	*9675
Iron and steel	..	..	..	..	2322	*1	..	2941	..	5264	*1
Chemical and petrochemical	6719	..	..	10772	11059	*276	..	4910	879	34616	*276
Non-ferrous metals	..	57	..	709	1866	..	..	3895	934	7461	..
Non-metallic minerals	2249	..	..	3315	11438	3484	..	3402	4	23892	897
Transport equipment	..	..	..	..	288	*1	..	482	1	772	*1
Machinery	..	..	..	267	1706	*11	..	3856	32	5872	*11
Mining and quarrying	..	..	..	207	778	*1	..	4043	279	5308	*1
Food and tobacco	27	..	..	395	3783	*2217	..	4784	352	11558	*2217
Paper, pulp and printing	35	..	..	..	1810	*4273	..	1616	19	*7753	*4273
Wood and wood products	..	..	..	..	197	*1812	..	904	2	*2915	*1812
Textile and leather	55	..	..	43	731	*81	..	1307	524	2740	*81
Construction	..	..	..	1078	848	*13	..	824	52	2816	*13
Industries n.e.s	0	0	..	90	641	*92	..	2574	13	3410	*92
Transport	..	..	..	126195	9034	6699	..	1166	..	143095	6699
Road	..	..	..	124972	3283	6699	..	130	..	135084	6699
Rail	..	..	..	473	..	..	..	976	..	1449	..
Domestic aviation	..	..	..	750	..	..	..	..	..	750	..
Domestic navigation	..	..	..	..	..	..	..	..	..	..	..
Pipeline transport	..	..	..	..	5751	..	..	61	..	5812	..
Transport, n.e.s	..	..	..	..	..	..	..	..	..	..	..
Other	4753	401	..	7442	7929	*35386	..	70916	22007	148835	*37879
Agriculture, forestry, fishing	345	..	..	5388	599	*205	..	954	366	7857	*205
Commerce, public services	96	..	..	1109	4094	*4254	..	30496	7646	47694	*6309
Households	4312	401	..	946	3236	*30927	..	39467	13995	93283	*31365
Other consumers	..	..	..	..	..	..	..	..	..	..	..
Non-energy use	329	1710	..	9922	8705	..	..	..	..	20666	..

Burkina Faso

Terajoules

	All Coal	All Oil	Natural Gas	Primary biofuels / Waste	Charcoal	Electricity	Total energy	of which: renewables
2017								
Primary production	..	..	..	128833	..	494	129328	129328
Imports	..	51077	..	18	..	2323	53419	18
Exports	..	..	..	0	-354	..	-354	-354
International marine bunkers	..	..	..	..	..	..	..	..
International aviation bunkers	..	-1193	..	..	..	..	-1193	..
Stock changes	..	*3929	..	..	..	..	*3929	..
Total energy supply	..	53813	..	128852	-354	2818	185128	128992
Statistical Difference	..	*-2	..	0	0	0	*-2	494
Transfers	..	..	..	..	..	..	..	..
Transformation	..	*-8558	..	*-38778	20852	3448	*-23035	*-17925
Electricity plants	..	*-8558	..	*-36	..	3448	*-5145	*-36
Charcoal plants	..	..	..	*-38742	20852	..	*-17889	*-17889
Other transformation	..	0	..	0	..	..	0	0
Energy industries own use	..	..	..	..	..	-235	-235	..
Losses	..	..	..	..	..	*-805	*-805	..
Final consumption	..	*45257	..	*90074	*20498	*5227	*161056	*110572
Final energy consumption	..	*45226	..	*90074	*20498	*5227	*161025	*110572
Manufacturing, const., mining	..	*12924	..	*633	..	*1927	*15484	*633
Transport	..	28310	..	..	..	..	28310	..
Road	..	28310	..	..	..	..	28310	..
Domestic aviation	..	..	..	..	..	..	..	..
Domestic navigation	..	..	..	..	..	..	..	..
Other transport	..	..	..	..	..	..	..	..
Other	..	3992	..	*89441	*20498	*3299	*117230	*109939
Agriculture, forestry, fishing	..	..	..	..	..	*58	*58	..
Commerce and public services	..	..	..	..	..	*2052	*2052	..
Households	..	3992	..	*89441	*20498	*1190	*115120	*109939
Other consumers	..	..	..	..	..	..	..	..
Non-energy use	..	*31	..	..	..	..	*31	..
2018								
Primary production	..	..	..	130320	..	524	130844	130844
Imports	..	64783	..	0	..	3015	67798	0
Exports	..	..	..	0	-354	..	-354	-354
International marine bunkers	..	..	..	..	..	..	..	..
International aviation bunkers	..	-1314	..	..	..	..	-1314	..
Stock changes	..	*-4459	..	..	..	..	*-4459	..
Total energy supply	..	59010	..	130320	-354	3538	192515	130490
Statistical Difference	..	0	..	0	0	59	59	524
Transfers	..	..	..	..	..	..	..	..
Transformation	..	*-8357	..	*-39744	21372	3151	*-23579	*-18372
Electricity plants	..	*-8357	..	*-36	..	3151	*-5242	*-36
Charcoal plants	..	..	..	*-39708	21372	..	*-18336	*-18336
Other transformation	..	0	..	0	..	..	0	0
Energy industries own use	..	..	..	..	..	-197	-197	..
Losses	..	..	..	..	..	*-788	*-788	..
Final consumption	..	*50653	..	*90575	*21018	*5645	*167892	*111593
Final energy consumption	..	*50621	..	*90575	*21018	*5645	*167859	*111593
Manufacturing, const., mining	..	*14609	..	*633	..	*2082	*17324	*633
Transport	..	31520	..	..	..	..	31520	..
Road	..	31520	..	..	..	..	31520	..
Domestic aviation	..	..	..	..	..	..	..	..
Domestic navigation	..	..	..	..	..	..	..	..
Other transport	..	..	..	..	..	..	..	..
Other	..	4492	..	*89942	*21018	*3564	*119015	*110960
Agriculture, forestry, fishing	..	..	..	..	..	*62	*62	..
Commerce and public services	..	..	..	..	..	*2216	*2216	..
Households	..	4492	..	*89942	*21018	*1285	*116737	*110960
Other consumers	..	..	..	..	..	..	..	..
Non-energy use	..	*32	..	..	..	..	*32	..

Burundi

Terajoules

	All Coal	All Oil	Natural Gas	Primary biofuels / Waste	Charcoal	Electricity	Total energy	of which: renewables
2017								
Primary production	204	..	..	55353	..	389	55946	55743
Imports	38	*7362	..	..	..	*339	*7740	..
Exports	..	..	..	..	..	..	..	..
International marine bunkers	..	..	..	..	..	..	..	..
International aviation bunkers	..	-189	..	..	..	..	-189	..
Stock changes	..	0	..	..	..	..	0	..
Total energy supply	242	*7173	..	55353	..	729	63497	55743
Statistical Difference	0	0	..	0	0	*-21	*-21	389
Transfers	..	..	..	..	..	..	..	..
Transformation	..	*-921	..	*-14650	7788	302	*-7481	*-6862
Electricity plants	..	*-921	..	*-180	..	302	*-799	*-180
Charcoal plants	..	..	..	*-14470	7788	..	*-6682	*-6682
Other transformation	..	0	..	0	..	..	0	0
Energy industries own use	..	..	..	..	..	-97	-97	..
Losses	..	..	..	..	..	*-144	*-144	..
Final consumption	242	*6252	..	*40703	*7788	*810	*55796	*48491
Final energy consumption	242	*6000	..	*40703	*7788	*810	*55543	*48491
Manufacturing, const., mining	*38	*48	..	*372	..	*327	*786	*372
Transport	..	*5939	..	..	..	..	*5939	..
Road	..	*5939	..	..	..	..	*5939	..
Domestic aviation	..	..	..	..	..	..	..	..
Domestic navigation	..	..	..	..	..	..	..	..
Other transport	..	..	..	..	..	..	..	..
Other	204	*12	..	*40331	*7788	*483	*48818	*48119
Agriculture, forestry, fishing	..	..	..	..	..	..	..	..
Commerce and public services	..	..	..	..	..	..	..	..
Households	204	*12	..	*40331	*7788	*400	*48734	*48119
Other consumers	..	..	..	..	..	84	84	..
Non-energy use	..	*253	..	..	..	..	*253	..
2018								
Primary production	173	..	..	55293	..	507	55973	55800
Imports	6	*9521	..	..	..	*361	*9888	..
Exports	..	..	..	..	..	..	..	..
International marine bunkers	..	..	..	..	..	..	..	..
International aviation bunkers	..	*-243	..	..	..	..	*-243	..
Stock changes	..	..	..	..	..	..	..	..
Total energy supply	179	*9279	..	55293	..	868	65618	55800
Statistical Difference	0	0	..	0	0	*1	*1	507
Transfers	..	..	..	..	..	..	..	..
Transformation	..	*-1212	..	*-14630	7788	378	*-7676	*-6842
Electricity plants	..	*-1212	..	*-160	..	378	*-994	*-160
Charcoal plants	..	..	..	*-14470	7788	..	*-6682	*-6682
Other transformation	..	0	..	0	..	..	0	0
Energy industries own use	..	..	..	..	..	-109	-109	..
Losses	..	..	..	..	..	*-144	*-144	..
Final consumption	179	*8067	..	*40663	*7788	*993	*57689	*48451
Final energy consumption	179	*7741	..	*40663	*7788	*993	*57363	*48451
Manufacturing, const., mining	*6	*40	..	*332	..	*432	*810	*332
Transport	..	*7686	..	..	..	..	*7686	..
Road	..	*7686	..	..	..	..	*7686	..
Domestic aviation	..	..	..	..	..	..	..	..
Domestic navigation	..	..	..	..	..	..	..	..
Other transport	..	..	..	..	..	..	..	..
Other	173	*14	..	*40331	*7788	*561	*48867	*48119
Agriculture, forestry, fishing	..	..	..	..	..	..	..	..
Commerce and public services	..	..	..	..	..	..	..	..
Households	173	*14	..	*40331	*7788	*475	*48781	*48119
Other consumers	..	..	..	..	..	86	86	..
Non-energy use	..	*326	..	..	..	..	*326	..

Cabo Verde

Terajoules

	All Coal	All Oil	Natural Gas	Primary biofuels / Waste	Charcoal	Electricity	Total energy	of which: renewables
2017								
Primary production	..	..	..	*1413	..	298	*1711	*1711
Imports	..	*13540	..	..	..	..	*13540	..
Exports	..	..	..	..	..	..	..	..
International marine bunkers	..	*-3321	..	..	..	..	*-3321	..
International aviation bunkers	..	*-2134	..	..	..	..	*-2134	..
Stock changes	..	..	..	..	..	..	..	..
Total energy supply	..	*8084	..	*1413	..	298	*9796	*1711
Statistical Difference	..	0	..	*5	0	22	*27	*303
Transfers	..	..	..	..	..	..	..	..
Transformation	..	*-3633	..	*-34	*19	1472	*-2176	*-15
Electricity plants	..	*-3633	..	..	..	1472	*-2161	..
Charcoal plants	..	..	..	*-34	*19	..	*-15	*-15
Other transformation	..	0	..	0	..	..	0	0
Energy industries own use	..	..	..	..	..	-42	-42	..
Losses	..	..	..	..	..	*-470	*-470	..
Final consumption	..	*4451	..	*1374	*19	*1236	*7081	*1393
Final energy consumption	..	*4371	..	*1374	*19	*1236	*7000	*1393
Manufacturing, const., mining	..	0	..	..	..	*131	*131	..
Transport	..	*3753	..	..	..	..	*3753	..
Road	..	*2921	..	..	..	..	*2921	..
Domestic aviation	..	*595	..	..	..	..	*595	..
Domestic navigation	..	*237	..	..	..	..	*237	..
Other transport	..	..	..	..	..	..	..	..
Other	..	*618	..	*1374	*19	*1106	*3117	*1393
Agriculture, forestry, fishing	..	..	..	..	..	..	..	..
Commerce and public services	..	*257	..	..	*17	*194	*468	*17
Households	..	*361	..	*1374	*2	*396	*2133	*1377
Other consumers	..	..	..	..	..	*516	*516	..
Non-energy use	..	*80	..	..	..	..	*80	..
2018								
Primary production	..	..	..	*1399	..	*372	*1771	*1771
Imports	..	*14087	..	..	..	..	*14087	..
Exports	..	..	..	..	..	..	..	..
International marine bunkers	..	*-3441	..	..	..	..	*-3441	..
International aviation bunkers	..	*-2227	..	..	..	..	*-2227	..
Stock changes	..	..	..	..	..	..	..	..
Total energy supply	..	*8419	..	*1399	..	*372	*10190	*1771
Statistical Difference	..	0	..	0	0	0	0	*372
Transfers	..	..	..	..	..	..	..	..
Transformation	..	*-3828	..	*-35	*19	*1417	*-2427	*-16
Electricity plants	..	*-3828	..	..	..	*1417	*-2410	..
Charcoal plants	..	..	..	*-35	*19	..	*-16	*-16
Other transformation	..	0	..	0	..	..	0	0
Energy industries own use	..	..	..	..	..	*-54	*-54	..
Losses	..	..	..	..	..	*-454	*-454	..
Final consumption	..	*4591	..	*1364	*19	*1282	*7256	*1383
Final energy consumption	..	*4507	..	*1364	*19	*1282	*7171	*1383
Manufacturing, const., mining	..	0	..	..	..	*134	*135	..
Transport	..	*3864	..	..	..	..	*3864	..
Road	..	*3006	..	..	..	..	*3006	..
Domestic aviation	..	*613	..	..	..	..	*613	..
Domestic navigation	..	*245	..	..	..	..	*245	..
Other transport	..	..	..	..	..	..	..	..
Other	..	*642	..	*1364	*19	*1147	*3173	*1383
Agriculture, forestry, fishing	..	..	..	..	..	..	..	..
Commerce and public services	..	*264	..	..	*17	*199	*480	*17
Households	..	*378	..	*1364	*2	*411	*2155	*1366
Other consumers	..	..	..	..	..	*537	*537	..
Non-energy use	..	*84	..	..	..	..	*84	..

Cambodia

Terajoules

	All Coal	All Oil	Natural Gas	Primary biofuels / Waste	Charcoal	Electricity	Total energy	of which: renewables
2017								
Primary production	1114	..	..	186915	..	9857	197885	196772
Imports	38859	99589	..	..	..	5328	143776	..
Exports	..	..	..	..	..	..	..	..
International marine bunkers	..	..	..	..	..	..	..	..
International aviation bunkers	..	-4763	..	..	..	..	-4763	..
Stock changes	2267	-309	..	..	..	..	1958	..
Total energy supply	42240	94517	..	186915	..	15185	338857	196772
Statistical Difference	0	0	..	0	0	0	0	9857
Transfers	..	29	..	..	..	..	29	..
Transformation	-40112	-3644	..	-53585	27642	15336	-54363	-25944
Electricity plants	-40112	-3644	..	-1132	..	15336	-29552	-1132
Charcoal plants	..	..	..	-52453	27642	..	-24812	-24812
Other transformation	0	0	..	0	..	..	0	0
Energy industries own use	..	..	..	..	..	-1339	-1339	..
Losses	..	..	..	..	..	-4795	-4795	..
Final consumption	2128	90902	..	133330	27642	24386	278388	160972
Final energy consumption	2128	90339	..	133330	27642	24386	277825	160972
Manufacturing, const., mining	2128	6267	..	42448	..	5562	56405	42448
Transport	..	73847	..	..	..	..	73847	..
Road	..	62926	..	..	..	..	62926	..
Domestic aviation	..	1676	..	..	..	..	1676	..
Domestic navigation	..	1935	..	..	..	..	1935	..
Other transport	..	7310	..	..	..	..	7310	..
Other	..	10225	..	90882	27642	18824	147573	118524
Agriculture, forestry, fishing	..	..	..	..	..	..	..	..
Commerce and public services	..	5771	..	..	..	9122	14893	..
Households	..	2649	..	90882	27642	9702	130874	118524
Other consumers	..	1806	..	..	..	..	1806	..
Non-energy use	..	563	..	..	..	..	563	
2018								
Primary production	1193	..	..	192545	..	17111	210849	209656
Imports	23467	108988	..	..	..	5641	138096	..
Exports	..	..	..	..	..	..	..	..
International marine bunkers	..	..	..	..	..	..	..	..
International aviation bunkers	..	-5204	..	..	..	..	-5204	..
Stock changes	..	..	..	..	..	..	..	..
Total energy supply	24660	103784	..	192545	..	22752	343741	209656
Statistical Difference	-8969	727	..	-1	0	0	-8243	17110
Transfers	..	29	..	..	..	..	29	..
Transformation	-31342	-3644	..	-54628	28055	12312	-49247	-26574
Electricity plants	-31342	-3644	..	*-1385	..	12312	-24059	*-1385
Charcoal plants	..	..	..	-53243	28055	..	-25189	-25189
Other transformation	0	0	..	0	..	..	0	0
Energy industries own use	..	..	..	..	..	-1566	-1566	..
Losses	..	..	..	..	..	-3924	-3924	..
Final consumption	2287	99443	..	*137918	28055	29574	297276	*165973
Final energy consumption	2287	98840	..	*137918	28055	29574	296673	*165973
Manufacturing, const., mining	2287	6825	..	*45663	..	6746	*61522	*45663
Transport	..	80813	..	..	..	..	80813	..
Road	..	68856	..	..	..	..	68856	..
Domestic aviation	..	1852	..	..	..	..	1852	..
Domestic navigation	..	2107	..	..	..	..	2107	..
Other transport	..	7998	..	..	..	..	7998	..
Other	..	11202	..	*92255	28055	22828	*154339	*120309
Agriculture, forestry, fishing	..	..	..	..	..	..	..	..
Commerce and public services	..	6338	..	..	..	11063	17401	..
Households	..	2885	..	*92255	28055	11765	*134960	*120309
Other consumers	..	1978	..	..	..	..	1978	..
Non-energy use	..	603	..	..	..	..	603	..

Cameroon

Terajoules

2017	Primary coal and peat	Coal and peat products	Primary Oil	Oil Products	Natural Gas	Biofuels and waste	Nuclear	Electricity	Heat	Total energy	of which: renewables
Primary production	..	..	162644	..	20710	*274135	..	18382	..	*475870	*292517
Imports	..	..	47122	35994	..	..	..	65	..	83181	..
Exports	..	..	-146950	-18693	..	..	..	..	..	-165643	..
International marine bunkers	..	..	..	0	..	..	..	..	..	0	..
International aviation bunkers	..	..	..	-750	..	..	..	..	..	-750	..
Stock changes	..	..	..	..	..	..	..	..	..	..	..
Total energy supply	..	..	62816	16552	20710	*274135	..	18446	..	*392658	*292517
Statistical difference	..	..	0	2272	227	*1	..	540	..	*3040	*18383
Transfers	..	..	..	..	..	..	..	..	..	..	..
Transformation	..	..	-62815	42450	-20483	*-38963	..	10775	..	-69037	*-38963
Electricity plants	..	..	..	-13969	-20483	*-354	..	10775	..	-24031	*-354
CHP plants	..	..	..	..	..	..	..	..	..	..	..
Heat plants	..	..	..	..	..	..	..	..	..	..	..
Coke ovens	..	..	..	..	..	..	..	..	..	..	..
Briquetting plants	..	..	..	..	..	..	..	..	..	..	..
Liquefaction plants	..	..	..	..	..	..	..	..	..	..	..
Gas works	..	..	..	..	..	..	..	..	..	..	..
Blast furnaces	..	..	..	..	..	..	..	..	..	..	..
NGL plants & gas blending	..	..	..	..	..	..	..	..	..	..	..
Oil refineries	..	..	-62815	56419	..	..	..	..	..	-6397	..
Other transformation	..	..	..	..	..	*-38609	..	..	..	*-38609	*-38609
Energy industries own use	..	..	..	-990	..	..	..	-850	..	-1840	..
Losses	..	..	..	-1733	..	..	..	-5530	..	-7262	..
Final consumption	..	..	..	54006	..	*235171	..	22302	..	*311479	*235171
Final energy consumption	..	..	..	51313	..	*235171	..	22302	..	*308786	*235171
Manufacturing, const., mining	..	..	..	3035	..	..	..	12442	..	15477	..
Iron and steel	..	..	..	..	..	..	..	335	..	335	..
Chemical and petrochemical	..	..	..	..	..	..	..	..	..	..	..
Non-ferrous metals	..	..	..	..	..	..	..	5440	..	5440	..
Non-metallic minerals	..	..	..	161	..	..	..	522	..	683	..
Transport equipment	..	..	..	..	..	..	..	..	..	..	..
Machinery	..	..	..	..	..	..	..	..	..	..	..
Mining and quarrying	..	..	..	..	..	..	..	2200	..	2200	..
Food and tobacco	..	..	..	..	..	..	..	731	..	731	..
Paper, pulp and printing	..	..	..	..	..	..	..	..	..	..	..
Wood and wood products	..	..	..	..	..	..	..	..	..	..	..
Textile and leather	..	..	..	..	..	..	..	104	..	104	..
Construction	..	..	..	..	..	..	..	..	..	..	..
Industries n.e.s	..	..	..	2874	..	..	..	3110	..	5985	..
Transport	..	..	..	40529	..	..	..	..	..	40529	..
Road	..	..	..	40441	..	..	..	..	..	40441	..
Rail	..	..	..	..	..	..	..	..	..	..	..
Domestic aviation	..	..	..	88	..	..	..	..	..	88	..
Domestic navigation	..	..	..	..	..	..	..	..	..	..	..
Pipeline transport	..	..	..	..	..	..	..	..	..	..	..
Transport, n.e.s	..	..	..	..	..	..	..	..	..	..	..
Other	..	..	..	7749	..	*235171	..	9860	..	*252780	*235171
Agriculture, forestry, fishing	..	..	..	..	..	..	..	212	..	212	..
Commerce, public services	..	..	..	..	..	*41724	..	1742	..	*43466	*41724
Households	..	..	..	6496	..	*193441	..	4759	..	*204696	*193441
Other consumers	..	..	..	1253	..	6	..	3146	..	4405	6
Non-energy use	..	..	..	2693	..	..	..	..	..	2693	..

Cameroon

Terajoules

2018	Primary coal and peat	Coal and peat products	Primary Oil	Oil Products	Natural Gas	Biofuels and waste	Nuclear	Electricity	Heat	Total energy	of which: renewables
Primary production	..	..	147458	..	55227	281329	..	18151	..	502165	299480
Imports	..	..	42723	36844	..	..	..	68	..	79635	..
Exports	..	..	-133203	-15939	-28044	..	..	..	..	-177186	..
International marine bunkers	..	..	..	..	..	..	..	..	..	..	..
International aviation bunkers	..	..	..	-662	..	..	..	..	..	-662	..
Stock changes	..	..	..	..	..	..	..	..	..	..	..
Total energy supply	..	..	56978	20243	27183	281329	..	18220	..	403953	299480
Statistical difference	..	..	42	1269	298	1	..	562	..	2172	18152
Transfers	..	..	..	..	..	..	..	..	..	..	..
Transformation	..	..	-56936	36343	-26885	*-39930	..	12902	..	-74505	*-39930
Electricity plants	..	..	..	-14391	-26885	*-369	..	12902	..	-28743	*-369
CHP plants	..	..	..	..	..	..	..	..	..	..	..
Heat plants	..	..	..	..	..	..	..	..	..	..	..
Coke ovens	..	..	..	..	..	..	..	..	..	..	..
Briquetting plants	..	..	..	..	..	..	..	..	..	..	..
Liquefaction plants	..	..	..	..	..	..	..	..	..	..	..
Gas works	..	..	..	..	..	..	..	..	..	..	..
Blast furnaces	..	..	..	..	..	..	..	..	..	..	..
NGL plants & gas blending	..	..	..	..	..	..	..	..	..	..	..
Oil refineries	..	..	-56936	50734	..	..	..	..	..	-6202	..
Other transformation	..	..	..	..	..	*-39561	..	..	..	*-39561	*-39561
Energy industries own use	..	..	..	-891	..	..	..	-907	..	-1798	..
Losses	..	..	..	-1584	..	..	..	-5900	..	-7484	..
Final consumption	..	..	..	52842	..	*241399	..	23753	..	*317993	*241399
Final energy consumption	..	..	..	50028	..	*241399	..	23753	..	*315179	*241399
Manufacturing, const., mining	..	..	..	3075	..	..	..	13255	..	16331	..
Iron and steel	..	..	..	..	..	..	..	356	..	356	..
Chemical and petrochemical	..	..	..	..	..	..	..	..	..	..	..
Non-ferrous metals	..	..	..	..	..	..	..	5792	..	5792	..
Non-metallic minerals	..	..	..	161	..	..	..	554	..	715	..
Transport equipment	..	..	..	..	..	..	..	..	..	..	..
Machinery	..	..	..	..	..	..	..	..	..	..	..
Mining and quarrying	..	..	..	..	..	..	..	2344	..	2344	..
Food and tobacco	..	..	..	..	..	..	..	781	..	781	..
Paper, pulp and printing	..	..	..	..	..	..	..	..	..	..	..
Wood and wood products	..	..	..	..	..	..	..	..	..	..	..
Textile and leather	..	..	..	..	..	..	..	112	..	112	..
Construction	..	..	..	..	..	..	..	..	..	..	..
Industries n.e.s	..	..	..	2915	..	..	..	3316	..	6230	..
Transport	..	..	..	39403	..	..	..	..	..	39403	..
Road	..	..	..	39315	..	..	..	..	..	39315	..
Rail	..	..	..	..	..	..	..	..	..	..	..
Domestic aviation	..	..	..	88	..	..	..	..	..	88	..
Domestic navigation	..	..	..	..	..	..	..	..	..	..	..
Pipeline transport	..	..	..	..	..	..	..	..	..	..	..
Transport, n.e.s	..	..	..	..	..	..	..	..	..	..	..
Other	..	..	..	7549	..	*241399	..	10498	..	*259445	*241399
Agriculture, forestry, fishing	..	..	..	..	..	..	..	227	..	227	..
Commerce, public services	..	..	..	..	..	*46436	..	1854	..	*48290	*46436
Households	..	..	..	6391	..	*194957	..	5069	..	*206416	*194957
Other consumers	..	..	..	1158	..	6	..	3348	..	4512	6
Non-energy use	..	..	..	2814	..	..	..	..	..	2814	..

Canada

Terajoules

2017	Primary coal and peat	Coal and peat products	Primary Oil	Oil Products	Natural Gas	Biofuels and waste	Nuclear	Electricity	Heat	Total energy	of which: renewables
Primary production	1292204	..	10413199	..	6360025	568235	1094029	1546697	1797	21276186	2106763
Imports	194603	33250	1898386	482326	878804	62064	..	35654	..	3585088	62064
Exports	-776529	-137	-7467923	-1012104	-2955618	*-52590	..	-259344	..	-12524245	*-52590
International marine bunkers	..	..	..	-15780	..	..	..	..	..	-15780	..
International aviation bunkers	..	..	..	-26372	..	..	..	..	..	-26372	..
Stock changes	-20659	6617	-14012	-14312	65473	..	..	..	..	23108	..
Total energy supply	689618	39730	4829651	-586242	4348684	577709	1094029	1323007	1797	12317984	2116237
Statistical difference	-1948	17737	263186	-502575	330340	0	0	-19854	-9216	77669	1546697
Transfers	..	..	-527575	684017	..	..	..	..	..	156442	..
Transformation	-646877	47335	-4038891	3939807	-687175	*-120172	-1094029	839603	19294	-1741105	*-116343
Electricity plants	-573570	-2277	..	-78665	-505508	*-109372	-1094029	816833	..	-1546588	*-108353
CHP plants	..	..	..	-81	-56120	-2875	..	22770	14980	-21326	-2184
Heat plants	..	-36	..	..	..	-7925	..	..	4314	-3647	-5807
Coke ovens	-73307	82545	..	..	..	..	..	..	..	9238	..
Briquetting plants	..	..	..	..	..	..	..	..	..	..	..
Liquefaction plants	..	..	127153	..	..	..	..	..	..	127153	..
Gas works	..	..	..	..	..	..	..	..	..	..	..
Blast furnaces	..	-32897	..	..	..	..	..	..	..	-32897	..
NGL plants & gas blending	..	..	..	..	..	..	..	..	..	..	..
Oil refineries	..	..	-4166044	4018553	..	..	..	..	..	-147491	..
Other transformation	..	..	..	..	-125547	..	..	..	..	-125547	..
Energy industries own use	..	..	..	-656282	-1333854	-78	..	-205585	0	-2195799	-78
Losses	..	..	..	..	..	..	..	-127465	..	-127465	..
Final consumption	44690	69328	..	3883876	1997315	*457459	..	1849414	30307	8332388	*453119
Final energy consumption	40962	67379	..	3146539	1868638	*457459	..	1849414	30307	7460697	*453119
Manufacturing, const., mining	40578	67379	..	260350	610822	*229322	..	655722	26244	1890416	*223185
Iron and steel	7652	64386	..	..	85256	61	..	31000	57	188412	61
Chemical and petrochemical	..	..	..	..	151954	..	..	67194	12125	231273	..
Non-ferrous metals	9208	..	..	1419	32921	..	..	210676	..	254224	..
Non-metallic minerals	13215	1977	..	21623	31892	6137	..	7434	..	82277	..
Transport equipment	..	..	..	..	9926	..	..	12996	..	22922	..
Machinery	..	..	..	..	14009	..	..	24196	..	38205	..
Mining and quarrying	..	1016	..	61131	32024	..	..	64044	..	158215	..
Food and tobacco	..	..	..	..	35760	..	..	20999	94	56853	..
Paper, pulp and printing	..	..	..	7519	78870	*223124	..	149548	4239	463300	*223124
Wood and wood products	..	..	..	24663	10426	..	..	16337	..	51425	..
Textile and leather	..	..	..	..	3857	..	..	3046	..	6903	..
Construction	..	..	..	89244	16796	..	..	..	33	106073	..
Industries n.e.s	10502	0	..	54751	107132	0	..	48254	9696	230335	0
Transport	..	..	..	2535502	136020	89785	..	28314	..	2789621	89785
Road	..	..	..	2133117	1916	89785	..	4396	..	2229214	89785
Rail	..	..	..	92235	..	..	..	..	..	92235	..
Domestic aviation	..	..	..	259757	..	..	..	..	..	259757	..
Domestic navigation	..	..	..	46097	..	..	..	..	..	46097	..
Pipeline transport	..	..	..	477	131844	..	..	23918	..	156239	..
Transport, n.e.s	..	..	..	3818	2260	..	..	..	..	6078	..
Other	384	..	..	350687	1121796	*138352	..	1165378	4063	2780660	*140149
Agriculture, forestry, fishing	..	..	..	221018	35659	7	..	35226	1	291910	7
Commerce, public services	..	..	..	57989	492862	638	..	525841	1444	1078774	638
Households	384	..	..	71680	593276	*137707	..	604310	..	1407358	*137707
Other consumers	..	..	..	..	..	..	..	..	2618	2618	1797
Non-energy use	3728	1949	..	737337	128678	..	..	..	..	871692	..

Canada

Terajoules

2018	Primary coal and peat	Coal and peat products	Primary Oil	Oil Products	Natural Gas	Biofuels and waste	Nuclear	Electricity	Heat	Total energy	of which: renewables
Primary production	1299176	..	11185363	..	6477478	574865	1087895	1522220	1797	22148795	2088739
Imports	199301	30230	1826699	563781	807757	55705	..	47502	..	3530975	55705
Exports	-842278	-1071	-8212260	-928127	-2804370	*-58476	..	-221044	..	-13067627	*-58476
International marine bunkers	..	..	..	-18926	..	..	..	..	..	-18926	..
International aviation bunkers	..	..	..	-36956	..	..	..	..	..	-36956	..
Stock changes	-48477	2883	-31651	-13117	-19884	..	..	..	..	-110245	..
Total energy supply	607722	32042	4768152	-433345	4460981	572093	1087895	1348679	1797	12446016	2085968
Statistical difference	26293	18039	508433	-804221	79772	3238	0	-34099	-8091	-210636	1525459
Transfers	..	..	-314902	460033	..	..	..	..	..	145131	..
Transformation	-540504	60010	-3944816	3826273	-800795	*-112915	-1087895	833216	19892	-1747533	*-109086
Electricity plants	-449310	-1706	..	-81057	-554281	*-102115	-1087895	796324	..	-1480040	*-101096
CHP plants	..	..	..	-121	-92434	-2875	..	36893	15577	-42960	-2184
Heat plants	..	-38	..	..	..	-7925	..	..	4315	-3648	-5807
Coke ovens	-91194	94171	..	..	..	..	..	..	..	2977	..
Briquetting plants	..	..	..	..	..	..	..	..	..	..	..
Liquefaction plants	..	..	156084	..	..	..	..	..	..	156084	..
Gas works	..	..	..	..	..	..	..	..	..	..	..
Blast furnaces	..	-32416	..	..	..	..	..	..	..	-32416	..
NGL plants & gas blending	..	..	..	..	..	..	..	..	..	..	..
Oil refineries	..	..	-4100900	3907451	..	..	..	..	..	-193449	..
Other transformation	..	..	..	..	-154080	..	..	..	..	-154080	..
Energy industries own use	..	..	..	-660392	-1419602	-78	..	-205499	0	-2285570	-78
Losses	..	..	..	..	..	..	..	-122764	..	-122764	..
Final consumption	40925	74013	..	3996790	2160814	*455862	..	1887732	29780	8645916	*451345
Final energy consumption	37551	72064	..	3230799	2024501	*455862	..	1887732	29780	7738289	*451345
Manufacturing, const., mining	37185	72064	..	258326	639209	*227603	..	661889	25858	1922134	*221289
Iron and steel	7638	69675	..	..	87605	61	..	33217	57	198253	61
Chemical and petrochemical	..	..	..	..	163950	..	..	75301	11738	250990	..
Non-ferrous metals	8020	..	..	1376	36414	..	..	211104	..	256914	..
Non-metallic minerals	10465	1977	..	18383	32542	6314	..	7452	..	77133	..
Transport equipment	..	..	..	..	9848	..	..	13061	..	22909	..
Machinery	..	..	..	..	14610	..	..	24376	..	38985	..
Mining and quarrying	..	412	..	61368	35034	..	..	62064	..	158878	..
Food and tobacco	..	..	..	..	35882	..	..	21398	94	57375	..
Paper, pulp and printing	..	..	..	6130	83738	*221228	..	146693	4719	462508	*221228
Wood and wood products	..	..	..	25912	10087	..	..	16531	..	52531	..
Textile and leather	..	..	..	..	3830	..	..	3046	..	6875	..
Construction	..	..	..	90374	18330	..	..	..	33	108737	..
Industries n.e.s	11063	0	..	54784	107339	0	..	47646	9217	230048	0
Transport	..	..	..	2617865	153404	90112	..	28656	..	2890037	90112
Road	..	..	..	2192978	1957	90112	..	4403	..	2289449	90112
Rail	..	..	..	94213	..	..	..	..	..	94213	..
Domestic aviation	..	..	..	279381	..	..	..	..	..	279381	..
Domestic navigation	..	..	..	46689	..	..	..	..	..	46689	..
Pipeline transport	..	..	..	567	149349	..	..	24253	..	174169	..
Transport, n.e.s	..	..	..	4039	2099	..	..	..	..	6137	..
Other	365	..	..	354608	1231889	*138147	..	1197187	3922	2926117	*139944
Agriculture, forestry, fishing	..	..	..	228876	38755	7	..	36983	..	304621	7
Commerce, public services	..	..	..	54813	518063	638	..	538855	1304	1113674	638
Households	365	..	..	70918	675070	*137502	..	621349	..	1505204	*137502
Other consumers	..	..	..	..	..	..	..	..	2618	2618	1797
Non-energy use	3374	1949	..	765991	136312	..	..	..	..	907627	..

Cayman Islands

Terajoules

	All Coal	All Oil	Natural Gas	Primary biofuels / Waste	Charcoal	Electricity	Total energy	of which: renewables
2017								
Primary production	..	..	..	..	..	..	..	..
Imports	..	9963	..	0	0	..	9963	0
Exports	..	..	..	..	..	..	..	..
International marine bunkers	..	..	..	..	..	..	..	..
International aviation bunkers	..	-1676	..	..	..	..	-1676	..
Stock changes	..	..	..	..	..	..	..	..
Total energy supply	..	8287	..	0	0	..	8288	0
Statistical Difference	..	-43	..	0	0	-2	-45	0
Transfers	..	..	..	..	..	..	..	..
Transformation	..	-5547	..	..	..	2414	-3133	..
Electricity plants	..	-5547	..	..	..	2414	-3133	..
Charcoal plants	..	..	..	..	..	..	..	..
Other transformation	..	0	..	..	..	..	0	..
Energy industries own use	..	..	..	..	..	0	0	..
Losses	..	..	..	..	..	-104	-104	..
Final consumption	..	2783	..	0	0	2311	5095	0
Final energy consumption	..	2699	..	0	0	2311	5010	0
Manufacturing, const., mining	..	..	..	..	..	1123	1123	..
Transport	..	2462	..	..	..	..	2462	..
Road	..	2374	..	..	..	..	2374	..
Domestic aviation	..	88	..	..	..	..	88	..
Domestic navigation	..	..	..	..	..	..	..	..
Other transport	..	..	..	..	..	..	..	..
Other	..	237	..	0	0	1188	1425	0
Agriculture, forestry, fishing	..	..	..	..	..	..	..	..
Commerce and public services	..	..	..	..	..	25	25	..
Households	..	237	..	..	..	1163	1399	..
Other consumers	..	..	..	0	0	..	0	0
Non-energy use	..	84	..	..	..	..	84	..
2018								
Primary production	..	..	..	..	..	..	..	..
Imports	..	10349	..	0	0	..	10350	0
Exports	..	..	..	..	..	..	..	..
International marine bunkers	..	..	..	..	..	..	..	..
International aviation bunkers	..	-1614	..	..	..	..	-1614	..
Stock changes	..	..	..	..	..	..	..	..
Total energy supply	..	8735	..	0	0	..	8736	0
Statistical Difference	..	4	..	0	0	-1	3	0
Transfers	..	..	..	..	..	..	..	..
Transformation	..	-5586	..	..	..	2368	-3218	..
Electricity plants	..	-5586	..	..	..	2368	-3218	..
Charcoal plants	..	..	..	..	..	..	..	..
Other transformation	..	0	..	..	..	..	0	..
Energy industries own use	..	..	..	..	..	0	0	..
Losses	..	..	..	..	..	-32	-32	..
Final consumption	..	3145	..	0	0	2336	5482	0
Final energy consumption	..	2987	..	0	0	2336	5324	0
Manufacturing, const., mining	..	..	..	..	..	1145	1145	..
Transport	..	2793	..	..	..	..	2793	..
Road	..	2709	..	..	..	..	2709	..
Domestic aviation	..	84	..	..	..	..	84	..
Domestic navigation	..	..	..	..	..	..	..	..
Other transport	..	..	..	..	..	..	..	..
Other	..	194	..	0	0	1192	1386	0
Agriculture, forestry, fishing	..	..	..	..	..	..	..	..
Commerce and public services	..	..	..	..	..	25	25	..
Households	..	194	..	..	..	1166	1360	..
Other consumers	..	..	..	0	0	..	0	0
Non-energy use	..	158	..	..	..	..	158	..

Central African Rep.

Terajoules

	All Coal	All Oil	Natural Gas	Primary biofuels / Waste	Charcoal	Electricity	Total energy	of which: renewables
2017								
Primary production	..	..	..	18270	..	520	18790	18790
Imports	..	*3792	..	..	1	..	*3793	1
Exports	..	..	..	..	0	..	0	0
International marine bunkers	..	..	..	..	..	..	..	..
International aviation bunkers	..	-706	..	..	..	..	-706	..
Stock changes	..	..	..	..	..	..	..	..
Total energy supply	..	*3086	..	18270	1	520	21877	18791
Statistical Difference	..	0	..	0	0	0	0	520
Transfers	..	..	..	..	..	..	..	..
Transformation	..	*-15	..	*-11903	6408	*4	*-5506	*-5495
Electricity plants	..	*-15	..	..	..	*4	*-11	..
Charcoal plants	..	..	..	*-11903	6408	..	*-5495	*-5495
Other transformation	..	0	..	0	..	..	0	0
Energy industries own use	..	..	..	..	..	0	0	..
Losses	..	..	..	..	..	*-36	*-36	..
Final consumption	..	*3071	..	*6367	*6409	*487	*16334	*12776
Final energy consumption	..	*3031	..	*6367	*6409	*487	*16294	*12776
Manufacturing, const., mining	..	*81	..	..	..	*234	*315	..
Transport	..	*2724	..	..	..	..	*2724	..
Road	..	*2724	..	..	..	..	*2724	..
Domestic aviation	..	..	..	..	..	..	..	..
Domestic navigation	..	..	..	..	..	..	..	..
Other transport	..	..	..	..	..	..	..	..
Other	..	*226	..	*6367	*6409	*253	*13255	*12776
Agriculture, forestry, fishing	..	..	..	..	..	..	..	..
Commerce and public services	..	..	..	..	..	*36	*36	..
Households	..	*226	..	*6367	..	*94	*6687	*6367
Other consumers	..	..	..	..	*6409	*124	*6532	*6409
Non-energy use	..	*40	..	..	..	..	*40	..
2018								
Primary production	..	..	..	18270	..	527	18797	18797
Imports	..	*3924	..	..	1	..	*3925	1
Exports	..	..	..	..	0	..	0	0
International marine bunkers	..	..	..	..	..	..	..	..
International aviation bunkers	..	-750	..	..	..	..	-750	..
Stock changes	..	..	..	..	..	..	..	..
Total energy supply	..	*3174	..	18270	1	527	21972	18798
Statistical Difference	..	0	..	0	0	0	0	527
Transfers	..	..	..	..	..	..	..	..
Transformation	..	*-15	..	*-11903	6408	*4	*-5506	*-5495
Electricity plants	..	*-15	..	..	..	*4	*-11	..
Charcoal plants	..	..	..	*-11903	6408	..	*-5495	*-5495
Other transformation	..	0	..	0	..	..	0	0
Energy industries own use	..	..	..	..	..	*-2	*-2	..
Losses	..	..	..	..	..	*-36	*-36	..
Final consumption	..	*3159	..	*6367	*6409	*493	*16428	*12776
Final energy consumption	..	*3119	..	*6367	*6409	*493	*16388	*12776
Manufacturing, const., mining	..	*81	..	..	..	*234	*315	..
Transport	..	*2768	..	..	..	..	*2768	..
Road	..	*2768	..	..	..	..	*2768	..
Domestic aviation	..	..	..	..	..	..	..	..
Domestic navigation	..	..	..	..	..	..	..	..
Other transport	..	..	..	..	..	..	..	..
Other	..	*270	..	*6367	*6409	*259	*13305	*12776
Agriculture, forestry, fishing	..	..	..	..	..	..	..	..
Commerce and public services	..	..	..	..	..	*36	*36	..
Households	..	*270	..	*6367	..	*101	*6738	*6367
Other consumers	..	..	..	..	*6409	*122	*6531	*6409
Non-energy use	..	*40	..	..	..	..	*40	..

Chad

Terajoules

	All Coal	All Oil	Natural Gas	Primary biofuels / Waste	Charcoal	Electricity	Total energy	of which: renewables
2017								
Primary production	..	245340	..	72834	..	..	318174	72834
Imports	..	*120	..	..	..	..	*120	..
Exports	..	-232033	..	..	..	..	-232033	..
International marine bunkers	..	..	..	..	..	..	..	..
International aviation bunkers	..	*-781	..	..	..	..	*-781	..
Stock changes	..	*4	..	..	..	..	*4	..
Total energy supply	..	12650	..	72834	..	..	85484	72834
Statistical Difference	..	0	..	0	0	0	0	0
Transfers	..	..	..	..	..	..	..	..
Transformation	..	*-2948	..	*-26254	14131	*828	*-14244	*-12123
Electricity plants	..	*-2537	..	..	..	*828	*-1709	..
Charcoal plants	..	..	..	*-26254	14131	..	*-12123	*-12123
Other transformation	..	*-411	..	0	..	..	*-411	0
Energy industries own use	..	..	..	..	..	*-43	*-43	..
Losses	..	..	..	..	..	..	..	..
Final consumption	..	*9702	..	*46580	*14131	*785	*71197	*60711
Final energy consumption	..	*9617	..	*46580	*14131	*785	*71113	*60711
Manufacturing, const., mining	..	..	..	*914	..	*281	*1195	*914
Transport	..	*2125	..	..	..	..	*2125	..
Road	..	*1816	..	..	..	..	*1816	..
Domestic aviation	..	*309	..	..	..	..	*309	..
Domestic navigation	..	..	..	..	..	..	..	..
Other transport	..	..	..	..	..	..	..	..
Other	..	*7492	..	*45666	*14131	*504	*67793	*59796
Agriculture, forestry, fishing	..	..	..	..	..	..	..	..
Commerce and public services	..	..	..	..	..	*36	*36	..
Households	..	*1128	..	*45666	*14131	*396	*61321	*59796
Other consumers	..	*6364	..	..	..	*72	*6436	..
Non-energy use	..	*84	..	..	..	..	*84	..
2018								
Primary production	..	274950	..	73651	..	..	348601	73651
Imports	..	*120	..	..	..	..	*120	..
Exports	..	-261854	..	..	..	..	-261854	..
International marine bunkers	..	..	..	..	..	..	..	..
International aviation bunkers	..	*-794	..	..	..	..	*-794	..
Stock changes	..	..	..	..	..	..	..	..
Total energy supply	..	12421	..	73651	..	..	86072	73651
Statistical Difference	..	38	..	0	0	0	38	0
Transfers	..	..	..	..	..	..	..	..
Transformation	..	*-2509	..	*-26921	14485	*842	*-14103	*-12436
Electricity plants	..	*-2580	..	..	..	*842	*-1738	..
Charcoal plants	..	..	..	*-26921	14485	..	*-12436	*-12436
Other transformation	..	*71	..	0	..	..	*71	0
Energy industries own use	..	..	..	..	..	*-47	*-47	..
Losses	..	..	..	..	..	..	..	..
Final consumption	..	*9874	..	*46731	*14485	*796	*71885	*61215
Final energy consumption	..	*9789	..	*46731	*14485	*796	*71800	*61215
Manufacturing, const., mining	..	..	..	*736	..	*284	*1020	*736
Transport	..	*2174	..	..	..	..	*2174	..
Road	..	*1861	..	..	..	..	*1861	..
Domestic aviation	..	*313	..	..	..	..	*313	..
Domestic navigation	..	..	..	..	..	..	..	..
Other transport	..	..	..	..	..	..	..	..
Other	..	*7616	..	*45995	*14485	*511	*68606	*60479
Agriculture, forestry, fishing	..	..	..	..	..	..	..	..
Commerce and public services	..	..	..	..	..	*36	*36	..
Households	..	*1148	..	*45995	*14485	*403	*62031	*60479
Other consumers	..	*6467	..	..	..	*72	*6539	..
Non-energy use	..	*84	..	..	..	..	*84	..

Chile

Terajoules

2017	Primary coal and peat	Coal and peat products	Primary Oil	Oil Products	Natural Gas	Biofuels and waste	Nuclear	Electricity	Heat	Total energy	of which: renewables
Primary production	41109	..	12499	..	43139	338531	..	103500	4386	543163	446417
Imports	279996	0	373093	340779	146736	..	..	0	..	1140604	..
Exports	-15494	-1487	..	-21003	-7412	..	..	-140	..	-45536	..
International marine bunkers	..	..	..	-5737	..	..	..	..	..	-5737	..
International aviation bunkers	..	..	..	-25534	..	..	..	..	..	-25534	..
Stock changes	2221	86	-574	-6112	-549	*474	..	..	..	-4455	*474
Total energy supply	307831	-1401	385018	282394	181913	339005	..	103360	4386	1602506	446891
Statistical difference	8581	-381	-542	-6962	3527	*-14444	..	8878	0	-1344	89286
Transfers	..	..	36286	-35057	..	..	..	..	..	1229	..
Transformation	-291761	10340	-421845	391395	-96871	*-198901	..	182398	-2304	-427549	*-200974
Electricity plants	-280905	..	..	-21589	-95252	..	..	160574	-2304	-239475	-2074
CHP plants	..	..	..	..	..	*-193866	..	21823	..	*-172043	*-193866
Heat plants	..	..	..	..	..	..	..	..	..	..	..
Coke ovens	-10856	14483	..	..	0	..	..	..	..	3627	..
Briquetting plants	..	..	..	..	..	..	..	..	..	..	..
Liquefaction plants	..	..	1619	..	..	..	..	..	..	1619	..
Gas works	..	..	..	..	-72	..	..	..	..	-72	..
Blast furnaces	..	-4222	..	..	..	..	..	..	..	-4222	..
NGL plants & gas blending	..	79	..	0	0	0	..	..	..	79	0
Oil refineries	..	..	-423464	412984	..	..	..	..	..	-10480	..
Other transformation	..	0	..	0	-1547	*-5035	..	..	..	*-6582	*-5035
Energy industries own use	..	-5888	..	-12730	-7067	..	..	-11210	..	-36895	..
Losses	0	-459	..	..	-3548	-572	..	-15030	..	-19609	-572
Final consumption	7489	2973	..	632964	70901	*153977	..	250639	2082	1121025	*156059
Final energy consumption	7489	2973	..	618653	61961	*153977	..	250639	2082	1097775	*156059
Manufacturing, const., mining	7421	2914	..	150430	33516	*77997	..	149152	..	421429	*77997
Iron and steel	..	2514	..	348	223	..	..	2203	..	5288	..
Chemical and petrochemical	0	..	..	..	3092	..	..	112	..	3203	..
Non-ferrous metals	..	..	..	..	..	..	..	..	..	..	..
Non-metallic minerals	160	..	..	9154	417	0	..	1742	..	11474	0
Transport equipment	..	..	..	..	..	..	..	..	..	..	..
Machinery	..	..	..	..	..	..	..	..	..	..	..
Mining and quarrying	2794	200	..	90392	7364	*93	..	91876	..	192718	*93
Food and tobacco	3000	172	..	43	42	*8	..	..	..	3265	*8
Paper, pulp and printing	23	..	..	8810	6720	*60218	..	19674	..	*95445	*60218
Wood and wood products	..	..	..	..	..	..	..	..	..	..	..
Textile and leather	..	..	..	..	..	..	..	..	..	..	..
Construction	..	..	..	7695	1723	..	..	292	..	9709	..
Industries n.e.s	1443	29	..	33988	13936	*17679	..	33253	..	100327	*17679
Transport	..	..	..	375871	691	..	..	3467	..	380029	..
Road	..	..	..	336920	691	..	..	1750	..	339361	..
Rail	..	..	..	1763	..	..	..	1645	..	3408	..
Domestic aviation	..	..	..	21291	..	..	..	..	..	21291	..
Domestic navigation	..	..	..	15897	..	..	..	..	..	15897	..
Pipeline transport	..	..	..	..	..	..	..	0	..	0	..
Transport, n.e.s	..	..	..	..	0	..	..	72	..	72	..
Other	69	59	..	92352	27754	*75980	..	98021	2082	296317	*78062
Agriculture, forestry, fishing	69	..	..	18373	941	*233	..	6595	..	26212	*233
Commerce, public services	0	0	..	29577	6767	888	..	46163	..	83395	888
Households	..	59	..	44401	20046	*74651	..	45263	..	184419	*74651
Other consumers	..	..	..	..	..	209	..	..	2082	2291	2291
Non-energy use	..	..	..	14311	8940	..	..	..	..	23251	..

Chile

Terajoules

2018	Primary coal and peat	Coal and peat products	Primary Oil	Oil Products	Natural Gas	Biofuels and waste	Nuclear	Electricity	Heat	Total energy	of which: renewables
Primary production	37703	..	17434	..	43979	345468	..	115819	10169	570573	471456
Imports	274218	..	376969	353470	144631	..	..	0	..	1149287	..
Exports	-7050	-934	..	-31570	-5643	..	..	..	..	-45197	..
International marine bunkers	..	..	..	-5494	..	..	..	..	..	-5494	..
International aviation bunkers	..	..	..	-28048	..	..	..	..	..	-28048	..
Stock changes	-3675	-1477	2224	-2331	-339	*-972	..	..	..	-6570	*-972
Total energy supply	301196	-2412	396627	286027	182628	344496	..	115819	10169	1634550	470484
Statistical difference	19510	-485	-352	-15592	-3902	*-19217	..	9562	0	-10478	97373
Transfers	..	..	42933	-41613	..	..	..	..	..	1321	..
Transformation	-276230	11602	-439912	400119	-90784	*-195911	..	180508	-7704	-418313	*-202844
Electricity plants	-264613	..	..	-16759	-90732	..	..	160027	-7704	-219780	-6934
CHP plants	..	..	..	..	..	*-190105	..	20480	..	*-169625	*-190105
Heat plants	..	..	..	..	..	..	..	..	..	..	..
Coke ovens	-11618	16068	..	..	..	..	..	..	..	4450	..
Briquetting plants	..	..	..	..	..	..	..	..	..	..	..
Liquefaction plants	..	..	1656	..	..	..	..	..	..	1656	..
Gas works	..	..	..	..	-52	..	..	..	..	-52	..
Blast furnaces	..	-4539	..	-40	..	..	..	..	..	-4579	..
NGL plants & gas blending	..	73	..	..	..	..	..	..	..	73	..
Oil refineries	..	..	-441568	416919	..	..	..	..	..	-24650	..
Other transformation	..	..	..	0	..	*-5806	..	..	..	*-5806	*-5806
Energy industries own use	..	-5962	..	-13915	-8904	..	..	-11203	..	-39984	..
Losses	..	-712	..	..	-2910	..	..	-12640	..	-16261	..
Final consumption	5456	3002	..	646210	83933	*167802	..	262922	2465	1171791	*170267
Final energy consumption	5456	3002	..	634311	64469	*167802	..	262922	2465	1140428	*170267
Manufacturing, const., mining	5411	2949	..	150352	36197	*87703	..	158728	..	441339	*87703
Iron and steel	..	2373	..	350	239	..	..	2462	..	5425	..
Chemical and petrochemical	..	..	..	..	4700	..	..	112	..	4811	..
Non-ferrous metals	..	..	..	..	..	..	..	..	..	..	..
Non-metallic minerals	182	..	..	8895	392	*1	..	1904	..	11375	*1
Transport equipment	..	..	..	..	..	..	..	..	..	..	..
Machinery	..	..	..	..	..	..	..	..	..	..	..
Mining and quarrying	1819	60	..	95745	8255	*118	..	94543	..	200540	*118
Food and tobacco	1932	482	..	129	47	*9	..	..	..	2600	*9
Paper, pulp and printing	..	..	..	10222	6897	*62194	..	20434	..	*99746	*62194
Wood and wood products	..	..	..	..	..	..	..	..	..	..	..
Textile and leather	..	..	..	..	..	..	..	..	..	..	..
Construction	..	..	..	7956	1704	..	..	594	..	10254	..
Industries n.e.s	1478	33	..	27055	13964	*25381	..	38678	..	106588	*25381
Transport	..	..	..	388741	568	..	..	4144	..	393452	..
Road	..	..	..	348127	568	..	..	2390	..	351086	..
Rail	..	..	..	1806	..	..	..	1732	..	3538	..
Domestic aviation	..	..	..	23191	..	..	..	..	..	23191	..
Domestic navigation	..	..	..	15617	..	..	..	..	..	15617	..
Pipeline transport	..	..	..	..	..	..	..	..	..	..	..
Transport, n.e.s	..	..	..	..	..	..	..	22	..	22	..
Other	45	53	..	95218	27704	*80100	..	100051	2465	305636	*82565
Agriculture, forestry, fishing	45	..	..	19146	1258	918	..	9198	..	30566	918
Commerce, public services	..	21	..	30145	5951	*1092	..	42523	..	79732	*1092
Households	..	32	..	45927	20495	*78090	..	48330	..	192874	*78090
Other consumers	..	..	..	..	..	..	..	..	2465	2465	2465
Non-energy use	..	..	..	11899	19464	..	..	..	..	31364	..

China

Terajoules

2017	Primary coal and peat	Coal and peat products	Primary Oil	Oil Products	Natural Gas	Biofuels and waste	Nuclear	Electricity	Heat	Total energy	of which: renewables
Primary production	73173808	..	8018360	..	5441938	4211159	2679480	5703480	..	99228226	9662274
Imports	4958618	276	17562887	2590559	3173859	6312	..	23122	..	28315633	6312
Exports	-167963	-229995	-203518	-2413481	-118509	-1802	..	-70090	..	-3205358	-1802
International marine bunkers	..	..	..	-412044	..	..	..	..	..	-412044	..
International aviation bunkers	..	..	..	-409473	..	..	..	..	..	-409473	..
Stock changes	717107	392317	-712544	-306227	..	..	..	..	..	90654	..
Total energy supply	78681569	162598	24665186	-950665	8497288	4215669	2679480	5656512	..	123607637	9666784
Statistical difference	-742707	41771	2848	20079	-10193	-1116	0	-2	15	-689304	5702053
Transfers	..	..	3208694	0	..	..	..	..	..	3208694	..
Transformation	-57944192	6839323	-27699079	24187189	-2061660	-814652	-2679480	17688920	4587405	-37896226	-562598
Electricity plants	-39127978	-1202048	-5943	-103264	*-1601574	-624576	-2679480	17688920	-712676	-28368619	-412563
CHP plants	..	..	..	..	..	..	..	..	..	..	..
Heat plants	-5967883	-350985	0	-215819	..	-134717	..	..	5300081	-1369323	-94676
Coke ovens	-12130205	13774212	..	..	..	..	..	..	..	1644006	..
Briquetting plants	-56827	..	..	..	..	..	..	..	..	-56827	..
Liquefaction plants	-322927	..	253598	..	-402915	..	..	..	..	-472244	..
Gas works	-338372	620939	..	-2247	..	..	..	..	..	280320	..
Blast furnaces	..	-5999132	..	..	..	..	..	..	..	-5999132	..
NGL plants & gas blending	..	..	..	..	..	..	..	..	..	..	..
Oil refineries	..	..	-27946733	29037900	-57170	..	..	..	..	1033996	..
Other transformation	..	..	..	-4529381	..	*-55360	..	..	..	-4584741	*-55360
Energy industries own use	-4039882	-228855	-124823	-1913104	-842054	-6050	..	-2731873	-531102	-10417742	-6050
Losses	..	..	-19273	-473	-95719	..	..	-1150497	-48175	-1314137	..
Final consumption	17440202	6731295	27857	21302868	5508048	*3396083	..	19463065	4008113	77877530	*3396083
Final energy consumption	15461940	6260566	27857	16452503	5149614	*3396083	..	19463065	4008113	70219740	*3396083
Manufacturing, const., mining	11444602	6181249	27857	1946204	2463417	526578	..	12597179	2677710	37864796	526578
Iron and steel	2109520	5039491	4	75502	198184	30121	..	2028815	211729	9693366	30121
Chemical and petrochemical	1216582	331442	27479	470296	768601	32822	..	1844014	1194973	5886209	32822
Non-ferrous metals	..	..	0	106407	..	3606	..	..	..	110013	3606
Non-metallic minerals	..	..	176	353576	..	11075	..	..	..	364826	11075
Transport equipment	..	..	25	49383	..	1409	..	..	..	50817	1409
Machinery	..	..	59	89470	..	5222	..	..	..	94751	5222
Mining and quarrying	..	..	67	86820	..	1106	..	..	..	87993	1106
Food and tobacco	..	..	13	44410	..	*326327	..	..	..	*370749	*326327
Paper, pulp and printing	..	..	17	16809	..	26908	..	..	..	43734	26908
Wood and wood products	..	..	0	10832	..	39424	..	..	..	50257	39424
Textile and leather	..	..	8	32464	..	20828	..	..	..	53301	20828
Construction	..	..	..	528870	..	9408	..	..	..	538278	9408
Industries n.e.s	8118500	810316	8	81366	1496631	18323	..	8724351	1271009	20520504	18323
Transport	72627	1710	..	8636817	902382	375357	..	510474	30644	10530011	375357
Road	..	..	..	5703816	817488	375357	..	117014	..	7013675	375357
Rail	56316	2	..	135402	..	..	..	284100	..	475821	..
Domestic aviation	..	..	..	1067744	..	..	..	..	..	1067744	..
Domestic navigation	3111	..	..	1032689	..	..	..	..	..	1035801	..
Pipeline transport	..	..	..	4049	16238	..	..	12652	..	32938	..
Transport, n.e.s	13199	1708	..	693117	68657	..	..	96707	30644	904031	..
Other	3944711	77607	..	5869482	1783815	*2494147	..	6355412	1299758	21824933	*2494147
Agriculture, forestry, fishing	583533	10947	..	771407	3809	141394	..	423043	1333	1935466	141394
Commerce, public services	..	..	..	..	..	28960	..	..	..	28960	28960
Households	1911365	45093	..	3286207	1409426	754273	..	3265764	1063300	11735428	754273
Other consumers	1449813	21567	..	1811868	370580	*1569520	..	2666604	235126	8125079	*1569520
Non-energy use	1978262	470729	0	4850365	358434	..	..	..	..	7657790	..

China

Terajoules

2018	Primary coal and peat	Coal and peat products	Primary Oil	Oil Products	Natural Gas	Biofuels and waste	Nuclear	Electricity	Heat	Total energy	of which: renewables
Primary production	76868532	..	7927004	..	5412303	4233165	3179077	6272550	..	103892632	10275582
Imports	5030088	2582	19339146	2833826	4211899	9963	..	20477	..	31447980	9963
Exports	-102614	-277139	-109976	-2706924	-113647	-1809	..	-75262	..	-3387369	-1809
International marine bunkers	..	..	..	-439860	..	..	..	..	..	-439860	..
International aviation bunkers	..	..	..	-445269	..	..	..	..	..	-445269	..
Stock changes	-549171	-149597	-422527	-295841	..	..	..	..	..	-1417136	..
Total energy supply	81246835	-424154	26733647	-1054068	9510555	4241320	3179077	6217765	..	129650978	10283737
Statistical difference	-544854	217906	353730	238232	30992	-1164	0	342	186	295370	6271103
Transfers	..	..	*2857681	0	..	..	..	..	..	*2857681	..
Transformation	-62557337	9264548	-29079912	25484895	-1935780	-802522	-3179077	19407089	5233030	-38165066	-572672
Electricity plants	-42227542	-1467440	-6406	-112001	-1419024	-614151	-3179077	19407089	-972588	-30591139	-420814
CHP plants	..	..	..	..	..	..	..	..	..	..	..
Heat plants	-6665137	-345854	0	-244221	..	-133083	..	..	6205618	-1182677	-96570
Coke ovens	-12677323	14296027	..	..	..	..	..	..	..	1618704	..
Briquetting plants	-59710	..	..	..	..	..	..	..	..	-59710	..
Liquefaction plants	-513926	..	209344	..	-447254	..	..	..	..	-751836	..
Gas works	-413700	676119	..	-2237	..	..	..	..	..	260182	..
Blast furnaces	..	-3894304	..	..	..	..	..	..	..	-3894304	..
NGL plants & gas blending	..	..	..	..	..	..	..	..	..	..	..
Oil refineries	..	..	-29282849	30429495	-69503	..	..	..	..	1077143	..
Other transformation	..	..	..	-4586141	..	*-55288	..	..	..	-4641429	*-55288
Energy industries own use	-3756227	-311780	-116679	-2034281	-944364	-6171	..	-2814440	-689434	-10673376	-6171
Losses	..	..	-11841	-255	-82151	..	..	-1206616	-51836	-1352699	..
Final consumption	15478124	8310709	29167	22158058	6517268	*3433791	..	21603456	4491574	82022147	*3433791
Final energy consumption	13043088	7916929	29167	16728442	6179143	*3433791	..	21603456	4491574	73425590	*3433791
Manufacturing, const., mining	9728588	7843100	29167	1982840	3246183	*567306	..	13854290	2954926	40206402	*567306
Iron and steel	2083080	6298459	0	56900	372351	30723	..	2351023	186291	11378827	30723
Chemical and petrochemical	556876	*390652	28673	573676	798277	33478	..	1961701	1355218	5698551	33478
Non-ferrous metals	..	..	151	118667	..	3678	..	..	..	122496	3678
Non-metallic minerals	..	..	193	365573	..	11296	..	..	..	377061	11296
Transport equipment	..	..	13	43547	..	1437	..	..	..	44997	1437
Machinery	..	..	8	70889	..	5326	..	..	..	76223	5326
Mining and quarrying	..	..	50	97057	..	1128	..	..	..	98236	1128
Food and tobacco	..	..	25	30992	..	*363050	..	..	..	*394068	*363050
Paper, pulp and printing	..	..	13	13941	..	27446	..	..	..	41399	27446
Wood and wood products	..	..	0	7133	..	40213	..	..	..	47346	40213
Textile and leather	..	..	29	17874	..	21245	..	..	..	39148	21245
Construction	..	..	..	515630	..	9596	..	..	..	525226	9596
Industries n.e.s	7088632	1153989	13	70962	2075555	*18690	..	9541566	1413418	21362823	*18690
Transport	66159	*855	..	8886719	925624	*377440	..	579060	38190	10874047	*377440
Road	..	..	..	5874112	838543	*377440	..	132736	..	7222832	*377440
Rail	51301	*3	..	136780	..	..	..	322272	..	510356	..
Domestic aviation	..	..	..	1165649	..	..	..	..	..	1165649	..
Domestic navigation	2834	..	..	1004291	..	..	..	..	..	1007124	..
Pipeline transport	..	..	..	*4128	16656	..	..	14352	..	35136	..
Transport, n.e.s	12024	*852	..	701759	70425	..	..	109700	38190	932950	..
Other	3248340	72974	..	5858883	2007337	*2489045	..	7170106	1498458	22345141	*2489045
Agriculture, forestry, fishing	486228	10295	..	743752	4402	144222	..	447311	684	1836894	144222
Commerce, public services	..	..	..	..	..	29539	..	..	..	29539	29539
Households	1587553	39554	..	3334026	1582824	768297	..	3620718	1216843	12149815	768297
Other consumers	1174559	23125	..	1781105	*420110	*1546987	..	3102077	280931	8328893	*1546987
Non-energy use	2435037	393780	0	5429616	338125	..	..	..	..	8596557	..

China, Hong Kong SAR

Terajoules

2017	Primary coal and peat	Coal and peat products	Primary Oil	Oil Products	Natural Gas	Biofuels and waste	Nuclear	Electricity	Heat	Total energy	of which: renewables
Primary production	..	..	..	..	..	..	..	..	..	..	..
Imports	276964	..	..	907844	113748	118	..	45274	..	1343948	118
Exports	..	..	..	-12170	..	..	..	-4828	..	-16997	..
International marine bunkers	..	..	..	-450285	..	..	..	..	..	-450285	..
International aviation bunkers	..	..	..	-291951	..	..	..	..	..	-291951	..
Stock changes	-14372	..	..	16651	..	..	..	..	..	2279	..
Total energy supply	262592	..	..	170089	113748	118	..	40446	..	586994	118
Statistical difference	0	..	..	-75	0	30	..	0	..	-45	30
Transfers	..	..	..	..	..	..	..	..	..	..	..
Transformation	-262592	..	..	-16895	-87604	..	..	133092	..	-234000	..
Electricity plants	-262592	..	..	-4257	-96079	..	..	133092	..	-229836	..
CHP plants	..	..	..	..	..	..	..	..	..	..	..
Heat plants	..	..	..	..	..	..	..	..	..	..	..
Coke ovens	..	..	..	..	..	..	..	..	..	..	..
Briquetting plants	..	..	..	..	..	..	..	..	..	..	..
Liquefaction plants	..	..	..	..	..	..	..	..	..	..	..
Gas works	..	..	..	-12638	-17670	..	..	..	..	-30308	..
Blast furnaces	..	..	..	..	..	..	..	..	..	..	..
NGL plants & gas blending	..	..	..	..	26144	..	..	..	..	26144	..
Oil refineries	..	..	..	..	..	..	..	..	..	..	..
Other transformation	..	..	..	..	..	..	..	..	..	..	..
Energy industries own use	..	..	..	..	..	..	..	0	..	0	..
Losses	..	..	..	..	..	..	..	-15743	..	-15743	..
Final consumption	..	..	..	*153269	26144	89	..	157795	..	337296	89
Final energy consumption	..	..	..	*151620	26144	89	..	157795	..	335648	89
Manufacturing, const., mining	..	..	..	*19264	1412	..	..	11196	..	*31872	..
Iron and steel	..	..	..	..	..	..	..	..	..	..	..
Chemical and petrochemical	..	..	..	..	..	..	..	..	..	..	..
Non-ferrous metals	..	..	..	..	..	..	..	..	..	..	..
Non-metallic minerals	..	..	..	..	..	..	..	..	..	..	..
Transport equipment	..	..	..	..	..	..	..	..	..	..	..
Machinery	..	..	..	..	..	..	..	..	..	..	..
Mining and quarrying	..	..	..	..	..	..	..	..	..	..	..
Food and tobacco	..	..	..	..	..	..	..	..	..	..	..
Paper, pulp and printing	..	..	..	..	..	..	..	..	..	..	..
Wood and wood products	..	..	..	..	..	..	..	..	..	..	..
Textile and leather	..	..	..	..	..	..	..	..	..	..	..
Construction	..	..	..	..	..	..	..	..	..	..	..
Industries n.e.s	..	..	..	*19264	1412	..	..	11196	..	*31872	..
Transport	..	..	..	*96335	..	..	..	..	..	*96335	..
Road	..	..	..	*95872	..	..	..	..	..	*95872	..
Rail	..	..	..	..	..	..	..	..	..	..	..
Domestic aviation	..	..	..	463	..	..	..	..	..	463	..
Domestic navigation	..	..	..	..	..	..	..	..	..	..	..
Pipeline transport	..	..	..	..	..	..	..	..	..	..	..
Transport, n.e.s	..	..	..	..	..	..	..	..	..	..	..
Other	..	..	..	*36021	24732	89	..	146599	..	207441	89
Agriculture, forestry, fishing	..	..	..	..	..	..	..	..	..	..	..
Commerce, public services	..	..	..	..	10945	..	..	104472	..	115417	..
Households	..	..	..	*28595	13787	89	..	42127	..	84598	89
Other consumers	..	..	..	*7426	..	..	..	..	..	*7426	..
Non-energy use	..	..	..	1648	..	..	..	..	..	1648	..

China, Hong Kong SAR

Terajoules

	Primary coal and peat	Coal and peat products	Primary Oil	Oil Products	Natural Gas	Biofuels and waste	Nuclear	Electricity	Heat	Total energy	of which: renewables
2018											
Primary production	..	..	..	..	..	..	..	..	..	..	..
Imports	287011	..	..	919902	110877	118	..	45356	..	1363265	118
Exports	..	..	..	-9380	..	..	..	-2002	..	-11382	..
International marine bunkers	..	..	..	-454828	..	..	..	..	..	-454828	..
International aviation bunkers	..	..	..	-301569	..	..	..	..	..	-301569	..
Stock changes	-17351	..	..	11168	..	..	..	..	..	-6183	..
Total energy supply	269660	..	..	165294	110877	118	..	43355	..	589303	118
Statistical difference	-26	..	..	2388	0	0	..	0	..	2362	0
Transfers	..	..	..	..	..	..	..	..	..	..	..
Transformation	-269686	..	..	-15954	-84282	..	..	131634	..	-238288	..
Electricity plants	-269686	..	..	-3182	-92705	..	..	131634	..	-233939	..
CHP plants	..	..	..	..	..	..	..	..	..	..	..
Heat plants	..	..	..	..	..	..	..	..	..	..	..
Coke ovens	..	..	..	..	..	..	..	..	..	..	..
Briquetting plants	..	..	..	..	..	..	..	..	..	..	..
Liquefaction plants	..	..	..	..	..	..	..	..	..	..	..
Gas works	..	..	..	-12772	-18172	..	..	..	..	-30943	..
Blast furnaces	..	..	..	..	..	..	..	..	..	..	..
NGL plants & gas blending	..	..	..	..	26595	..	..	..	..	26595	..
Oil refineries	..	..	..	..	..	..	..	..	..	..	..
Other transformation	..	..	..	..	..	..	..	..	..	..	..
Energy industries own use	..	..	..	..	..	..	..	0	..	0	..
Losses	..	..	..	..	..	..	..	-15491	..	-15491	..
Final consumption	..	..	..	*146952	*26595	118	..	159498	..	333163	118
Final energy consumption	..	..	..	*145223	*26595	118	..	159498	..	331434	118
Manufacturing, const., mining	..	..	..	*18705	1545	..	..	11081	..	*31331	..
Iron and steel	..	..	..	..	..	..	..	..	..	..	..
Chemical and petrochemical	..	..	..	..	..	..	..	..	..	..	..
Non-ferrous metals	..	..	..	..	..	..	..	..	..	..	..
Non-metallic minerals	..	..	..	..	..	..	..	..	..	..	..
Transport equipment	..	..	..	..	..	..	..	..	..	..	..
Machinery	..	..	..	..	..	..	..	..	..	..	..
Mining and quarrying	..	..	..	..	..	..	..	..	..	..	..
Food and tobacco	..	..	..	..	..	..	..	..	..	..	..
Paper, pulp and printing	..	..	..	..	..	..	..	..	..	..	..
Wood and wood products	..	..	..	..	..	..	..	..	..	..	..
Textile and leather	..	..	..	..	..	..	..	..	..	..	..
Construction	..	..	..	..	..	..	..	..	..	..	..
Industries n.e.s	..	..	..	*18705	1545	..	..	11081	..	*31331	..
Transport	..	..	..	*93800	..	..	..	..	..	*93800	..
Road	..	..	..	*93438	..	..	..	..	..	*93438	..
Rail	..	..	..	..	..	..	..	..	..	..	..
Domestic aviation	..	..	..	362	..	..	..	..	..	362	..
Domestic navigation	..	..	..	..	..	..	..	..	..	..	..
Pipeline transport	..	..	..	..	..	..	..	..	..	..	..
Transport, n.e.s	..	..	..	..	..	..	..	..	..	..	..
Other	..	..	..	*32719	*25050	118	..	148417	..	206304	118
Agriculture, forestry, fishing	..	..	..	..	..	..	..	..	..	..	..
Commerce, public services	..	..	..	..	*11070	..	..	106452	..	117522	..
Households	..	..	..	*25198	*13980	118	..	41965	..	81261	118
Other consumers	..	..	..	*7521	..	..	..	..	..	*7521	..
Non-energy use	..	..	..	*1729	..	..	..	..	..	*1729	..

China, Macao SAR

Terajoules

	All Coal	All Oil	Natural Gas	Primary biofuels / Waste	Charcoal	Electricity	Total energy	of which: renewables
2017								
Primary production	..	..	..	*5616	..	..	*5616	*2808
Imports	..	25613	6162	..	30	14227	46032	30
Exports	..	..	..	..	..	..	..	..
International marine bunkers	..	-2838	..	..	..	..	-2838	..
International aviation bunkers	..	..	..	..	..	..	..	..
Stock changes	..	-540	-2	..	..	..	-541	..
Total energy supply	..	22236	6161	*5616	30	14227	48269	*2838
Statistical Difference	..	-62	-100	0	0	4	-159	0
Transfers	..	..	..	..	..	..	..	..
Transformation	..	-4770	-5710	*-5616	..	5274	-10821	*-2808
Electricity plants	..	-4770	-5710	*-5616	..	5274	-10821	*-2808
Charcoal plants	..	..	..	..	..	..	..	..
Other transformation	..	0	0	0	..	..	0	0
Energy industries own use	..	..	..	..	..	-245	-245	..
Losses	..	..	..	..	..	-500	-500	..
Final consumption	..	17529	551	..	*30	18752	36861	*30
Final energy consumption	..	15298	551	..	*30	18752	34631	*30
Manufacturing, const., mining	..	1462	61	..	..	734	2258	..
Transport	..	5690	104	..	..	..	5794	..
Road	..	5690	104	..	..	..	5794	..
Domestic aviation	..	..	..	..	..	..	..	..
Domestic navigation	..	..	..	..	..	..	..	..
Other transport	..	..	..	..	..	..	..	..
Other	..	*8146	386	..	*30	18018	26580	*30
Agriculture, forestry, fishing	..	..	..	..	..	..	..	..
Commerce and public services	..	88	353	..	..	14008	14448	..
Households	..	662	33	..	..	4010	4706	..
Other consumers	..	*7396	..	..	*30	..	*7426	*30
Non-energy use	..	2230	..	..	..	..	2230	..
2018								
Primary production	..	..	..	5897	..	..	5897	2948
Imports	..	17673	3271	..	30	17680	38652	30
Exports	..	..	..	..	..	..	..	..
International marine bunkers	..	-2752	..	..	..	..	-2752	..
International aviation bunkers	..	..	..	..	..	..	..	..
Stock changes	..	42	..	..	..	..	42	..
Total energy supply	..	14962	3271	5897	30	17680	41839	2978
Statistical Difference	..	-372	-51	0	0	-752	-1176	0
Transfers	..	..	..	..	..	..	..	..
Transformation	..	-1697	-2612	*-5897	..	2362	-7844	*-2948
Electricity plants	..	-1697	-2612	*-5897	..	2362	-7844	*-2948
Charcoal plants	..	..	..	..	..	..	..	..
Other transformation	..	0	0	0	..	..	0	0
Energy industries own use	..	..	..	..	..	-212	-212	..
Losses	..	..	..	..	..	-540	-540	..
Final consumption	..	13638	710	..	*30	20041	34419	*30
Final energy consumption	..	11535	710	..	*30	20041	32315	*30
Manufacturing, const., mining	..	1333	59	..	..	893	2285	..
Transport	..	5867	151	..	..	..	6018	..
Road	..	5867	151	..	..	..	6018	..
Domestic aviation	..	..	..	..	..	..	..	..
Domestic navigation	..	..	..	..	..	..	..	..
Other transport	..	..	..	..	..	..	..	..
Other	..	4334	500	..	*30	19148	24012	*30
Agriculture, forestry, fishing	..	..	..	..	..	..	..	..
Commerce and public services	..	88	463	..	..	15055	15605	..
Households	..	710	37	..	..	4093	4840	..
Other consumers	..	3537	..	..	*30	..	3567	*30
Non-energy use	..	2103	..	..	..	..	2103	..

Colombia

Terajoules

2017	Primary coal and peat	Coal and peat products	Primary Oil	Oil Products	Natural Gas	Biofuels and waste	Nuclear	Electricity	Heat	Total energy	of which: renewables
Primary production	2464200	..	1876659	..	410589	225025	..	221224	..	5197697	446248
Imports	..	..	..	277476	455	..	..	281	..	278212	..
Exports	-2794578	-50685	-1373312	-207452	..	-295	..	-32	..	-4426354	-295
International marine bunkers	..	..	..	-10849	..	..	..	..	..	-10849	..
International aviation bunkers	..	..	..	-56095	..	..	..	..	..	-56095	..
Stock changes	543300	..	191957	-26020	..	1509	..	..	..	710746	1509
Total energy supply	212922	-50685	695305	-22940	411044	226238	..	221472	..	1693357	447462
Statistical difference	17580	-5305	-8798	56237	73574	-440	..	15512	..	148360	220783
Transfers	..	..	105792	-111295	..	..	..	..	..	-5502	..
Transformation	-98923	51380	-800674	749255	-98546	-1240	..	64181	..	-134567	-1240
Electricity plants	-32521	-346	-11379	-14141	-98546	-99	..	64181	..	-92851	-99
CHP plants	..	..	..	..	..	..	..	..	..	..	..
Heat plants	..	..	..	..	..	..	..	..	..	..	..
Coke ovens	-66402	53259	..	..	..	..	..	..	..	-13143	..
Briquetting plants	..	..	..	..	..	..	..	..	..	..	..
Liquefaction plants	..	..	..	..	..	..	..	..	..	..	..
Gas works	..	..	..	..	..	..	..	..	..	..	..
Blast furnaces	..	-1532	..	..	..	..	..	..	..	-1532	..
NGL plants & gas blending	..	..	-14232	15231	..	..	..	..	..	998	..
Oil refineries	..	..	-775063	748165	..	..	..	..	..	-26898	..
Other transformation	..	..	..	..	..	-1141	..	..	..	-1141	-1141
Energy industries own use	..	-833	-8798	-22545	-69557	..	..	-28454	..	-130189	..
Losses	..	-131	..	..	..	..	..	-20016	..	-20147	..
Final consumption	96419	5036	423	536239	169366	225439	..	221670	..	1254592	225439
Final energy consumption	96419	5036	423	476221	169366	225439	..	221670	..	1194573	225439
Manufacturing, const., mining	93752	5036	423	25584	60548	82587	..	70679	..	338609	82587
Iron and steel	13879	4956	42	473	10869	..	..	9457	..	39677	..
Chemical and petrochemical	3184	60	..	2355	6400	911	..	11822	..	24733	911
Non-ferrous metals	..	..	..	135	657	..	..	929	..	1720	..
Non-metallic minerals	34916	..	42	1420	10841	..	..	7006	..	54224	..
Transport equipment	27	..	..	..	304	..	..	425	..	756	..
Machinery	..	20	..	43	484	..	..	968	..	1516	..
Mining and quarrying	..	..	..	16732	8593	..	..	15264	..	40589	..
Food and tobacco	16111	..	..	1493	12181	61871	..	14558	..	106213	61871
Paper, pulp and printing	10777	..	338	171	5561	6887	..	4752	..	28486	6887
Wood and wood products	..	..	..	95	108	..	..	576	..	779	..
Textile and leather	12600	..	..	88	4055	59	..	3445	..	20246	59
Construction	..	..	..	2537	91	..	..	601	..	3229	..
Industries n.e.s	2259	0	0	43	405	12859	..	875	..	16441	12859
Transport	..	..	..	390856	18766	27203	..	349	..	437174	27203
Road	..	..	..	389400	18766	27203	..	..	..	435369	27203
Rail	..	..	..	..	..	..	..	349	..	349	..
Domestic aviation	..	..	..	1019	..	..	..	..	..	1019	..
Domestic navigation	..	..	..	437	..	..	..	..	..	437	..
Pipeline transport	..	..	..	..	..	..	..	..	..	..	..
Transport, n.e.s	..	..	..	..	..	..	..	..	..	..	..
Other	2667	..	..	59781	90051	115649	..	150642	..	418790	115649
Agriculture, forestry, fishing	..	..	..	3017	..	..	..	2236	..	5252	..
Commerce, public services	..	..	..	2081	14621	..	..	57222	..	73925	..
Households	2667	..	..	15050	44155	103357	..	83448	..	248677	103357
Other consumers	..	..	..	39633	31275	*12292	..	7736	..	90937	*12292
Non-energy use	..	..	..	60019	..	..	..	..	..	60019	..

Colombia

Terajoules

2018	Primary coal and peat	Coal and peat products	Primary Oil	Oil Products	Natural Gas	Biofuels and waste	Nuclear	Electricity	Heat	Total energy	of which: renewables
Primary production	2293705	..	1900555	..	428515	207766	..	215989	..	5046530	423755
Imports	..	..	..	192320	455	..	..	439	..	193215	..
Exports	-2274900	-62281	-1302840	-229642	..	-325	..	-58	..	-3870044	-325
International marine bunkers	..	..	..	-5607	..	..	..	..	..	-5607	..
International aviation bunkers	..	..	..	-64254	..	..	..	..	..	-64254	..
Stock changes	189682	..	140521	177	..	-74	..	..	..	330306	-74
Total energy supply	208486	-62281	738236	-107005	428971	207368	..	216371	..	1630145	423357
Statistical difference	-15321	-5286	-8925	43393	78080	-430	..	6124	..	97636	215560
Transfers	..	..	105581	-111072	..	..	..	..	..	-5491	..
Transformation	-126518	62995	-843436	814284	-113412	-1326	..	71881	..	-135531	-1326
Electricity plants	-45583	-350	-11548	-15492	-113412	-69	..	71881	..	-114573	-69
CHP plants	..	..	..	..	..	..	..	..	..	..	..
Heat plants	..	..	..	..	..	..	..	..	..	..	..
Coke ovens	-80934	64888	..	..	..	..	..	..	..	-16047	..
Briquetting plants	..	..	..	..	..	..	..	..	..	..	..
Liquefaction plants	..	..	..	..	..	..	..	..	..	..	..
Gas works	..	..	..	..	..	..	..	..	..	..	..
Blast furnaces	..	-1542	..	..	..	..	..	..	..	-1542	..
NGL plants & gas blending	..	..	-13172	14095	..	..	..	..	..	924	..
Oil refineries	..	..	-818717	815680	..	..	..	..	..	-3036	..
Other transformation	..	..	..	..	..	-1257	..	..	..	-1257	-1257
Energy industries own use	..	-841	-8883	-23430	-66780	..	..	-30139	..	-130073	..
Losses	..	-132	..	..	..	..	..	-29358	..	-29490	..
Final consumption	97290	5027	423	529383	170699	206471	..	222631	..	1231924	206471
Final energy consumption	97290	5027	423	494088	170699	206471	..	222631	..	1196629	206471
Manufacturing, const., mining	94732	5027	423	30752	59691	62843	..	71849	..	325317	62843
Iron and steel	14015	4947	42	473	10100	..	..	8669	..	38246	..
Chemical and petrochemical	3320	60	..	2402	6939	932	..	10714	..	24367	932
Non-ferrous metals	..	..	..	135	691	..	..	828	..	1654	..
Non-metallic minerals	33936	..	42	1420	10707	..	..	7337	..	53442	..
Transport equipment	27	..	..	..	319	..	..	414	..	760	..
Machinery	..	20	..	43	500	..	..	925	..	1488	..
Mining and quarrying	..	..	..	21118	9083	..	..	19116	..	49317	..
Food and tobacco	16464	..	..	1540	12014	41598	..	12902	..	84519	41598
Paper, pulp and printing	11811	..	338	171	4895	7064	..	5627	..	29906	7064
Wood and wood products	..	..	..	95	148	..	..	403	..	645	..
Textile and leather	12899	..	..	88	3809	59	..	3323	..	20178	59
Construction	..	..	..	3225	57	..	..	346	..	3627	..
Industries n.e.s	2259	0	0	43	430	13190	..	1246	..	17168	13190
Transport	..	..	..	399465	17488	31988	..	374	..	449315	31988
Road	..	..	..	398098	17488	31988	..	..	..	447574	31988
Rail	..	..	..	..	..	..	..	374	..	374	..
Domestic aviation	..	..	..	886	..	..	..	..	..	886	..
Domestic navigation	..	..	..	481	..	..	..	..	..	481	..
Pipeline transport	..	..	..	..	..	..	..	..	..	..	..
Transport, n.e.s	..	..	..	..	..	..	..	..	..	..	..
Other	2558	..	..	63871	93520	111640	..	150408	..	421997	111640
Agriculture, forestry, fishing	..	..	..	3703	..	..	..	2783	..	6486	..
Commerce, public services	..	..	..	5723	15821	..	..	47862	..	69406	..
Households	2558	..	..	17487	45059	104046	..	88884	..	258035	104046
Other consumers	..	..	..	36957	32639	*7594	..	10879	..	88070	*7594
Non-energy use	..	..	..	35296	..	..	..	..	..	35296	..

Comoros

Terajoules

	All Coal	All Oil	Natural Gas	Primary biofuels / Waste	Charcoal	Electricity	Total energy	of which: renewables
2017								
Primary production	..	..	..	3732	..	..	3732	3732
Imports	..	*3866	..	..	..	..	*3866	..
Exports	..	..	..	..	..	..	..	..
International marine bunkers	..	..	..	..	..	..	..	..
International aviation bunkers	..	*-45	..	..	..	..	*-45	..
Stock changes	..	..	..	..	..	..	..	..
Total energy supply	..	*3820	..	3732	..	..	*7552	3732
Statistical Difference	..	0	..	0	0	0	0	0
Transfers	..	..	..	..	..	..	..	..
Transformation	..	*-1147	..	-20	5	*327	*-836	-16
Electricity plants	..	*-1147	..	..	..	*327	*-820	..
Charcoal plants	..	..	..	-20	5	..	-16	-16
Other transformation	..	0	..	0	..	..	0	0
Energy industries own use	..	..	..	..	..	*-39	*-39	..
Losses	..	..	..	..	..	*-91	*-91	..
Final consumption	..	*2673	..	3711	5	*197	6586	3716
Final energy consumption	..	*2673	..	3711	5	*197	6586	3716
Manufacturing, const., mining	..	*5	..	252	..	..	256	252
Transport	..	*2093	..	..	..	..	*2093	..
Road	..	*1709	..	..	..	..	*1709	..
Domestic aviation	..	*159	..	..	..	..	*159	..
Domestic navigation	..	*225	..	..	..	..	*225	..
Other transport	..	..	..	..	..	..	..	..
Other	..	*575	..	3460	5	*197	4237	3464
Agriculture, forestry, fishing	..	..	..	..	..	..	..	..
Commerce and public services	..	..	..	..	..	..	..	..
Households	..	*556	..	3460	5	*146	4166	3464
Other consumers	..	*19	..	..	..	*51	*71	..
Non-energy use	..	..	..	..	..	..	..	..
2018								
Primary production	..	..	..	3816	..	..	3816	3816
Imports	..	*4209	..	..	..	..	*4209	..
Exports	..	..	..	..	..	..	..	..
International marine bunkers	..	..	..	..	..	..	..	..
International aviation bunkers	..	*-71	..	..	..	..	*-71	..
Stock changes	..	..	..	..	..	..	..	..
Total energy supply	..	*4138	..	3816	..	..	*7954	3816
Statistical Difference	..	0	..	0	0	0	0	0
Transfers	..	..	..	..	..	..	..	..
Transformation	..	*-1243	..	*-21	*5	*354	*-905	*-16
Electricity plants	..	*-1243	..	..	..	*354	*-889	..
Charcoal plants	..	..	..	*-21	*5	..	*-16	*-16
Other transformation	..	0	..	0	..	..	0	0
Energy industries own use	..	..	..	..	..	*-42	*-42	..
Losses	..	..	..	..	..	*-99	*-99	..
Final consumption	..	*2895	..	*3795	*5	*214	*6908	*3800
Final energy consumption	..	*2895	..	*3795	*5	*214	*6908	*3800
Manufacturing, const., mining	..	*5	..	*257	..	..	*261	*257
Transport	..	*2324	..	..	..	..	*2324	..
Road	..	*1880	..	..	..	..	*1880	..
Domestic aviation	..	*227	..	..	..	..	*227	..
Domestic navigation	..	*216	..	..	..	..	*216	..
Other transport	..	..	..	..	..	..	..	..
Other	..	*566	..	*3538	*5	*214	*4323	*3543
Agriculture, forestry, fishing	..	..	..	..	..	..	..	..
Commerce and public services	..	..	..	..	..	..	..	..
Households	..	*543	..	*3538	*5	*158	*4245	*3543
Other consumers	..	*23	..	..	..	*55	*78	..
Non-energy use	..	..	..	..	..	..	..	..

Congo

Terajoules

2017	Primary coal and peat	Coal and peat products	Primary Oil	Oil Products	Natural Gas	Biofuels and waste	Nuclear	Electricity	Heat	Total energy	of which: renewables
Primary production	..	..	591503	..	21641	66809	..	4334	..	684287	71143
Imports	..	..	..	8612	..	..	..	79	..	8691	..
Exports	..	..	-556008	-13857	..	..	..	-79	..	-569944	..
International marine bunkers	..	..	..	..	..	..	..	..	..	..	..
International aviation bunkers	..	..	..	-1367	..	..	..	..	..	-1367	..
Stock changes	..	..	..	..	..	..	..	..	..	..	..
Total energy supply	..	..	35495	-6613	21641	66809	..	4334	..	121666	71143
Statistical difference	..	..	44	-484	0	59	..	742	..	361	4393
Transfers	..	..	..	..	..	..	..	..	..	..	..
Transformation	..	..	-35451	27728	-21641	-14725	..	8168	..	-35920	-14725
Electricity plants	..	..	..	-1611	-21641	..	..	8168	..	-15083	..
CHP plants	..	..	..	..	..	..	..	..	..	..	..
Heat plants	..	..	..	..	..	..	..	..	..	..	..
Coke ovens	..	..	..	..	..	..	..	..	..	..	..
Briquetting plants	..	..	..	..	..	..	..	..	..	..	..
Liquefaction plants	..	..	..	..	..	..	..	..	..	..	..
Gas works	..	..	..	..	..	..	..	..	..	..	..
Blast furnaces	..	..	..	..	..	..	..	..	..	..	..
NGL plants & gas blending	..	..	..	..	..	..	..	..	..	..	..
Oil refineries	..	..	-35451	29981	..	..	..	..	..	-5469	..
Other transformation	..	..	..	-643	..	-14725	..	..	..	-15368	-14725
Energy industries own use	..	..	..	..	..	..	..	-1397	..	-1397	..
Losses	..	..	..	..	..	..	..	-4766	..	-4766	..
Final consumption	..	..	..	21599	..	52026	..	5598	..	79222	52026
Final energy consumption	..	..	..	20796	..	52026	..	5598	..	78420	52026
Manufacturing, const., mining	..	..	..	1534	..	..	..	371	..	1905	..
Iron and steel	..	..	..	..	..	..	..	..	..	..	..
Chemical and petrochemical	..	..	..	..	..	..	..	..	..	..	..
Non-ferrous metals	..	..	..	..	..	..	..	..	..	..	..
Non-metallic minerals	..	..	..	..	..	..	..	..	..	..	..
Transport equipment	..	..	..	..	..	..	..	..	..	..	..
Machinery	..	..	..	..	..	..	..	..	..	..	..
Mining and quarrying	..	..	..	..	..	..	..	..	..	..	..
Food and tobacco	..	..	..	766	..	..	..	..	..	766	..
Paper, pulp and printing	..	..	..	..	..	..	..	..	..	..	..
Wood and wood products	..	..	..	..	..	..	..	122	..	122	..
Textile and leather	..	..	..	..	..	..	..	..	..	..	..
Construction	..	..	..	..	..	..	..	..	..	..	..
Industries n.e.s	..	..	..	768	..	..	..	248	..	1016	..
Transport	..	..	..	18103	..	..	..	..	..	18103	..
Road	..	..	..	16530	..	..	..	..	..	16530	..
Rail	..	..	..	645	..	..	..	..	..	645	..
Domestic aviation	..	..	..	573	..	..	..	..	..	573	..
Domestic navigation	..	..	..	354	..	..	..	..	..	354	..
Pipeline transport	..	..	..	..	..	..	..	..	..	..	..
Transport, n.e.s	..	..	..	..	..	..	..	..	..	..	..
Other	..	..	..	1160	..	52026	..	5227	..	58413	52026
Agriculture, forestry, fishing	..	..	..	..	..	..	..	..	..	..	..
Commerce, public services	..	..	..	306	..	590	..	2794	..	3689	590
Households	..	..	..	854	..	51436	..	2434	..	54724	51436
Other consumers	..	..	..	..	..	..	..	..	..	..	..
Non-energy use	..	..	..	803	..	..	..	..	..	803	..

Congo

Terajoules

2018	Primary coal and peat	Coal and peat products	Primary Oil	Oil Products	Natural Gas	Biofuels and waste	Nuclear	Electricity	Heat	Total energy	of which: renewables
Primary production	..	..	723394	..	21641	68566	..	4464	..	818065	73030
Imports	..	..	..	8612	..	..	..	68	..	8680	..
Exports	..	..	-651564	-14059	..	..	..	-94	..	-665716	..
International marine bunkers	..	..	..	..	..	..	..	..	..	..	..
International aviation bunkers	..	..	..	-1367	..	..	..	..	..	-1367	..
Stock changes	..	..	-35913	..	..	..	..	..	..	-35913	..
Total energy supply	..	..	35918	-6815	21641	68566	..	4439	..	123749	73030
Statistical difference	..	..	-42	-686	0	59	..	695	..	26	4523
Transfers	..	..	..	..	..	..	..	..	..	..	..
Transformation	..	..	-35960	27728	-21641	-13838	..	8168	..	-35542	-13838
Electricity plants	..	..	..	-1611	-21641	..	..	8168	..	-15083	..
CHP plants	..	..	..	..	..	..	..	..	..	..	..
Heat plants	..	..	..	..	..	..	..	..	..	..	..
Coke ovens	..	..	..	..	..	..	..	..	..	..	..
Briquetting plants	..	..	..	..	..	..	..	..	..	..	..
Liquefaction plants	..	..	..	..	..	..	..	..	..	..	..
Gas works	..	..	..	..	..	..	..	..	..	..	..
Blast furnaces	..	..	..	..	..	..	..	..	..	..	..
NGL plants & gas blending	..	..	..	..	..	..	..	..	..	..	..
Oil refineries	..	..	-35960	29981	..	..	..	..	..	-5979	..
Other transformation	..	..	..	-643	..	-13838	..	..	..	-14481	-13838
Energy industries own use	..	..	..	..	..	..	..	-1411	..	-1411	..
Losses	..	..	..	..	..	..	..	-4806	..	-4806	..
Final consumption	..	..	..	21599	..	54670	..	5695	..	81964	54670
Final energy consumption	..	..	..	20796	..	54670	..	5695	..	81161	54670
Manufacturing, const., mining	..	..	..	1534	..	..	..	378	..	1912	..
Iron and steel	..	..	..	..	..	..	..	..	..	..	..
Chemical and petrochemical	..	..	..	..	..	..	..	..	..	..	..
Non-ferrous metals	..	..	..	..	..	..	..	..	..	..	..
Non-metallic minerals	..	..	..	..	..	..	..	..	..	..	..
Transport equipment	..	..	..	..	..	..	..	..	..	..	..
Machinery	..	..	..	..	..	..	..	..	..	..	..
Mining and quarrying	..	..	..	..	..	..	..	..	..	..	..
Food and tobacco	..	..	..	766	..	..	..	..	..	766	..
Paper, pulp and printing	..	..	..	..	..	..	..	..	..	..	..
Wood and wood products	..	..	..	..	..	..	..	126	..	126	..
Textile and leather	..	..	..	..	..	..	..	..	..	..	..
Construction	..	..	..	..	..	..	..	..	..	..	..
Industries n.e.s	..	..	..	768	..	..	..	252	..	1020	..
Transport	..	..	..	18103	..	..	..	..	..	18103	..
Road	..	..	..	16530	..	..	..	..	..	16530	..
Rail	..	..	..	645	..	..	..	..	..	645	..
Domestic aviation	..	..	..	573	..	..	..	..	..	573	..
Domestic navigation	..	..	..	354	..	..	..	..	..	354	..
Pipeline transport	..	..	..	..	..	..	..	..	..	..	..
Transport, n.e.s	..	..	..	..	..	..	..	..	..	..	..
Other	..	..	..	1160	..	54670	..	5317	..	61147	54670
Agriculture, forestry, fishing	..	..	..	..	..	..	..	..	..	..	..
Commerce, public services	..	..	..	306	..	620	..	2822	..	3747	620
Households	..	..	..	854	..	54050	..	2495	..	57399	54050
Other consumers	..	..	..	..	..	..	..	..	..	..	..
Non-energy use	..	..	..	803	..	..	..	..	..	803	..

Cook Islands

Terajoules

	All Coal	All Oil	Natural Gas	Primary biofuels / Waste	Charcoal	Electricity	Total energy	of which: renewables
2017								
Primary production	..	..	..	..	..	21	21	21
Imports	..	*1528	..	..	..	..	*1528	..
Exports	..	..	..	..	..	..	..	
International marine bunkers	..	*-63	..	..	..	..	*-63	
International aviation bunkers	..	*-416	..	..	..	..	*-416	
Stock changes	..	..	..	..	..	..	..	
Total energy supply	..	*1049	..	..	..	21	*1070	21
Statistical Difference	..	0	..	..	..	0	0	21
Transfers	..	..	..	..	..	..	..	..
Transformation	..	*-344	..	..	..	111	*-233	..
Electricity plants	..	*-344	..	..	..	111	*-233	..
Charcoal plants	..	..	..	..	..	..	..	..
Other transformation	..	0	..	..	..	..	0	..
Energy industries own use	..	..	..	..	..	0	0	..
Losses	..	..	..	..	..	..	..	..
Final consumption	..	*705	..	..	..	132	*837	..
Final energy consumption	..	*705	..	..	..	132	*837	..
Manufacturing, const., mining	..	..	..	..	..	..	..	..
Transport	..	*705	..	..	..	..	*705	..
Road	..	323	..	..	..	..	323	..
Domestic aviation	..	..	..	..	..	..	..	..
Domestic navigation	..	*95	..	..	..	..	*95	..
Other transport	..	*288	..	..	..	..	*288	..
Other	..	..	..	..	..	132	132	..
Agriculture, forestry, fishing	..	..	..	..	..	..	..	..
Commerce and public services	..	..	..	..	..	..	..	..
Households	..	..	..	..	..	..	..	..
Other consumers	..	..	..	..	..	132	132	..
Non-energy use	..	..	..	..	..	..	..	..
2018								
Primary production	..	..	..	..	..	38	38	38
Imports	..	*1528	..	..	..	..	*1528	..
Exports	..	..	..	..	..	..	..	..
International marine bunkers	..	*-63	..	..	..	..	*-63	..
International aviation bunkers	..	*-416	..	..	..	..	*-416	..
Stock changes	..	..	..	..	..	..	..	..
Total energy supply	..	*1049	..	..	..	38	*1087	38
Statistical Difference	..	0	..	..	..	0	0	38
Transfers	..	..	..	..	..	..	..	..
Transformation	..	*-348	..	..	..	111	*-237	..
Electricity plants	..	*-348	..	..	..	111	*-237	..
Charcoal plants	..	..	..	..	..	..	..	..
Other transformation	..	0	..	..	..	..	0	..
Energy industries own use	..	..	..	..	..	0	0	..
Losses	..	..	..	..	..	..	..	..
Final consumption	..	*701	..	..	..	149	*850	..
Final energy consumption	..	*701	..	..	..	149	*850	..
Manufacturing, const., mining	..	..	..	..	..	..	..	..
Transport	..	*701	..	..	..	..	*701	..
Road	..	*318	..	..	..	..	*318	..
Domestic aviation	..	..	..	..	..	..	..	..
Domestic navigation	..	*95	..	..	..	..	*95	..
Other transport	..	*288	..	..	..	..	*288	..
Other	..	..	..	..	..	149	149	..
Agriculture, forestry, fishing	..	..	..	..	..	..	..	..
Commerce and public services	..	..	..	..	..	..	..	..
Households	..	..	..	..	..	..	..	..
Other consumers	..	..	..	..	..	149	149	..
Non-energy use	..	..	..	..	..	..	..	..

Costa Rica

Terajoules

2017	Primary coal and peat	Coal and peat products	Primary Oil	Oil Products	Natural Gas	Biofuels and waste	Nuclear	Electricity	Heat	Total energy	of which: renewables
Primary production	..	..	..	..	..	25526	..	35973	40242	101741	101741
Imports	181	..	..	121454	..	22	..	1982	..	123639	22
Exports	..	..	..	..	..	-558	..	-2669	..	-3227	-558
International marine bunkers	..	..	..	..	..	..	..	..	..	..	..
International aviation bunkers	..	..	..	-8260	..	..	..	..	..	-8260	..
Stock changes	..	..	..	-1852	..	..	..	..	..	-1852	..
Total energy supply	181	..	..	111341	..	24990	..	35286	40242	212040	101205
Statistical difference	0	..	..	1721	..	69	..	58	0	1849	40066
Transfers	..	..	..	-172	..	..	..	..	..	-172	..
Transformation	..	..	..	-363	..	-1372	..	4823	-40242	-37154	-37590
Electricity plants	..	..	..	-363	..	-1329	..	4159	-40242	-37775	-37547
CHP plants	..	..	..	..	..	..	..	664	..	664	..
Heat plants	..	..	..	..	..	..	..	..	..	..	..
Coke ovens	..	..	..	..	..	..	..	..	..	..	..
Briquetting plants	..	..	..	..	..	..	..	..	..	..	..
Liquefaction plants	..	..	..	..	..	..	..	..	..	..	..
Gas works	..	..	..	..	..	..	..	..	..	..	..
Blast furnaces	..	..	..	..	..	..	..	..	..	..	..
NGL plants & gas blending	..	..	..	..	..	..	..	..	..	..	..
Oil refineries	..	..	..	..	..	..	..	..	..	..	..
Other transformation	..	..	..	..	..	-43	..	..	..	-43	-43
Energy industries own use	..	..	..	-400	..	..	..	-464	..	-864	..
Losses	..	..	..	..	..	-4	..	-3945	..	-3949	-4
Final consumption	181	..	..	108685	..	23544	..	35642	..	168052	23544
Final energy consumption	181	..	..	104004	..	23544	..	35642	..	163372	23544
Manufacturing, const., mining	181	..	..	14945	..	18257	..	7293	..	40676	18257
Iron and steel	..	..	..	..	..	..	..	..	..	..	..
Chemical and petrochemical	..	..	..	593	..	..	..	1472	..	2064	..
Non-ferrous metals	..	..	..	..	..	..	..	..	..	..	..
Non-metallic minerals	181	..	..	4593	..	..	..	..	..	4774	..
Transport equipment	..	..	..	..	..	..	..	..	..	..	..
Machinery	..	..	..	..	..	..	..	..	..	..	..
Mining and quarrying	..	..	..	..	..	..	..	..	..	..	..
Food and tobacco	0	..	..	5328	..	12525	..	2423	..	20275	12525
Paper, pulp and printing	..	..	..	480	..	405	..	458	..	1343	405
Wood and wood products	..	..	..	239	..	4838	..	141	..	5217	4838
Textile and leather	..	..	..	567	..	..	..	255	..	823	..
Construction	..	..	..	..	..	..	..	..	..	..	..
Industries n.e.s	0	..	..	3145	..	490	..	2545	..	6180	490
Transport	..	..	..	80924	..	..	..	..	..	80924	..
Road	..	..	..	80567	..	..	..	..	..	80567	..
Rail	..	..	..	62	..	..	..	..	..	62	..
Domestic aviation	..	..	..	230	..	..	..	..	..	230	..
Domestic navigation	..	..	..	64	..	..	..	..	..	64	..
Pipeline transport	..	..	..	..	..	..	..	..	..	..	..
Transport, n.e.s	..	..	..	..	..	..	..	..	..	..	..
Other	..	..	..	8135	..	5287	..	28349	..	41772	5287
Agriculture, forestry, fishing	..	..	..	2513	..	..	..	1237	..	3751	..
Commerce, public services	..	..	..	1750	..	1172	..	13246	..	16168	1172
Households	..	..	..	2926	..	4115	..	13598	..	20638	4115
Other consumers	..	..	..	946	..	..	..	268	..	1215	..
Non-energy use	..	..	..	4680	..	..	..	..	..	4680	..

Costa Rica

Terajoules

2018	Primary coal and peat	Coal and peat products	Primary Oil	Oil Products	Natural Gas	Biofuels and waste	Nuclear	Electricity	Heat	Total energy	of which: renewables
Primary production	..	..	..	..	..	24426	..	36710	34869	96004	96004
Imports	12	..	..	116249	..	30	..	2060	..	118350	30
Exports	..	..	..	0	..	-531	..	-2927	..	-3458	-531
International marine bunkers	..	..	..	..	..	..	..	..	..	..	..
International aviation bunkers	..	..	..	-9068	..	..	..	..	..	-9068	..
Stock changes	..	..	..	2914	..	..	..	..	..	2914	..
Total energy supply	12	..	..	110094	..	23924	..	35843	34869	204742	95503
Statistical difference	0	..	..	-894	..	72	..	164	0	-658	40269
Transfers	..	..	..	-394	..	..	..	..	..	-394	..
Transformation	..	..	..	-1417	..	-1355	..	4683	-34869	-32957	-32737
Electricity plants	..	..	..	-1417	..	-1329	..	4058	-34869	-33557	-32711
CHP plants	..	..	..	..	..	..	..	625	..	625	..
Heat plants	..	..	..	..	..	..	..	..	..	..	..
Coke ovens	..	..	..	..	..	..	..	..	..	..	..
Briquetting plants	..	..	..	..	..	..	..	..	..	..	..
Liquefaction plants	..	..	..	..	..	..	..	..	..	..	..
Gas works	..	..	..	..	..	..	..	..	..	..	..
Blast furnaces	..	..	..	..	..	..	..	..	..	..	..
NGL plants & gas blending	..	..	..	..	..	..	..	..	..	..	..
Oil refineries	..	..	..	..	..	..	..	..	..	..	..
Other transformation	..	..	..	..	..	-26	..	..	..	-26	-26
Energy industries own use	..	..	..	-399	..	..	..	-437	..	-836	..
Losses	..	..	..	..	..	-4	..	-3966	..	-3970	-4
Final consumption	12	..	..	108779	..	22492	..	35959	..	167242	22492
Final energy consumption	12	..	..	103751	..	22492	..	35959	..	162214	22492
Manufacturing, const., mining	12	..	..	14468	..	18818	..	6959	..	40256	18818
Iron and steel	..	..	..	..	..	..	..	..	..	..	..
Chemical and petrochemical	..	..	..	586	..	..	..	1401	..	1986	..
Non-ferrous metals	..	..	..	..	..	..	..	..	..	..	..
Non-metallic minerals	10	..	..	4288	..	..	..	..	..	4298	..
Transport equipment	..	..	..	..	..	..	..	..	..	..	..
Machinery	..	..	..	..	..	..	..	..	..	..	..
Mining and quarrying	..	..	..	..	..	..	..	..	..	..	..
Food and tobacco	2	..	..	5120	..	13198	..	2323	..	20642	13198
Paper, pulp and printing	..	..	..	532	..	405	..	436	..	1373	405
Wood and wood products	..	..	..	232	..	4725	..	134	..	5091	4725
Textile and leather	..	..	..	544	..	..	..	243	..	787	..
Construction	..	..	..	..	..	..	..	..	..	..	..
Industries n.e.s	0	..	..	3166	..	490	..	2422	..	6078	490
Transport	..	..	..	81567	..	..	..	..	..	81567	..
Road	..	..	..	81079	..	..	..	..	..	81079	..
Rail	..	..	..	55	..	..	..	..	..	55	..
Domestic aviation	..	..	..	383	..	..	..	..	..	383	..
Domestic navigation	..	..	..	50	..	..	..	..	..	50	..
Pipeline transport	..	..	..	..	..	..	..	..	..	..	..
Transport, n.e.s	..	..	..	..	..	..	..	..	..	..	..
Other	..	..	..	7717	..	3675	..	29000	..	40392	3675
Agriculture, forestry, fishing	..	..	..	2128	..	..	..	1178	..	3306	..
Commerce, public services	..	..	..	1722	..	1172	..	13712	..	16607	1172
Households	..	..	..	3014	..	2503	..	13844	..	19360	2503
Other consumers	..	..	..	853	..	..	..	267	..	1120	..
Non-energy use	..	..	..	5027	..	..	..	..	..	5027	..

Côte d'Ivoire

Terajoules

	Primary coal and peat	Coal and peat products	Primary Oil	Oil Products	Natural Gas	Biofuels and waste	Nuclear	Electricity	Heat	Total energy	of which: renewables
2017											
Primary production	..	..	85161	..	78911	266401	..	7370	..	437843	273771
Imports	..	..	100928	58553	..	..	..	133	..	159614	..
Exports	..	..	-79101	*-46505	..	..	..	-4489	..	-130096	..
International marine bunkers	..	..	..	-3209	..	..	..	..	..	-3209	..
International aviation bunkers	..	..	..	*-7321	..	..	..	..	..	*-7321	..
Stock changes	..	..	..	753	..	..	..	..	..	753	..
Total energy supply	..	..	106988	2271	78911	266401	..	3014	..	457585	273771
Statistical difference	..	..	11083	*-2286	1	0	..	-86	..	8712	7370
Transfers	..	..	44505	-44421	..	..	..	..	..	84	..
Transformation	..	..	-140411	*131130	-66093	-81083	..	29066	..	-127391	-81083
Electricity plants	..	..	..	-975	-66093	-1941	..	29066	..	-39943	-1941
CHP plants	..	..	..	..	..	..	..	..	..	..	..
Heat plants	..	..	..	..	..	..	..	..	..	..	..
Coke ovens	..	..	..	..	..	..	..	..	..	..	..
Briquetting plants	..	..	..	..	..	..	..	..	..	..	..
Liquefaction plants	..	..	..	..	..	..	..	..	..	..	..
Gas works	..	..	..	..	..	..	..	..	..	..	..
Blast furnaces	..	..	..	..	..	..	..	..	..	..	..
NGL plants & gas blending	..	..	-265	284	..	..	..	..	..	19	..
Oil refineries	..	..	-140145	*131821	..	..	..	..	..	-8325	..
Other transformation	..	..	..	..	..	-79142	..	..	..	-79142	-79142
Energy industries own use	..	..	..	-1870	..	..	..	-5112	..	-6982	..
Losses	..	..	..	..	..	-1298	..	-4309	..	-5607	-1298
Final consumption	..	..	..	89395	12817	184020	..	22745	..	308977	184020
Final energy consumption	..	..	..	86179	12817	184020	..	22745	..	305761	184020
Manufacturing, const., mining	..	..	..	9596	12817	..	..	7837	..	30250	..
Iron and steel	..	..	..	..	..	..	..	374	..	374	..
Chemical and petrochemical	..	..	..	..	..	..	..	396	..	396	..
Non-ferrous metals	..	..	..	..	..	..	..	..	..	..	..
Non-metallic minerals	..	..	..	..	..	..	..	..	..	..	..
Transport equipment	..	..	..	..	..	..	..	..	..	..	..
Machinery	..	..	..	..	..	..	..	..	..	..	..
Mining and quarrying	..	..	..	..	..	..	..	..	..	..	..
Food and tobacco	..	..	..	687	12817	..	..	2862	..	16366	..
Paper, pulp and printing	..	..	..	..	..	..	..	..	..	..	..
Wood and wood products	..	..	..	..	..	..	..	1886	..	1886	..
Textile and leather	..	..	..	..	..	..	..	551	..	551	..
Construction	..	..	..	..	..	..	..	205	..	205	..
Industries n.e.s	..	..	..	8909	0	..	..	1562	..	10471	..
Transport	..	..	..	55218	..	..	..	..	..	55218	..
Road	..	..	..	*50093	..	..	..	..	..	*50093	..
Rail	..	..	..	645	..	..	..	..	..	645	..
Domestic aviation	..	..	..	309	..	..	..	..	..	309	..
Domestic navigation	..	..	..	4171	..	..	..	..	..	4171	..
Pipeline transport	..	..	..	..	..	..	..	..	..	..	..
Transport, n.e.s	..	..	..	..	..	..	..	..	..	..	..
Other	..	..	..	*21366	..	184020	..	14908	..	220293	184020
Agriculture, forestry, fishing	..	..	..	5848	..	..	..	..	..	5848	..
Commerce, public services	..	..	..	*5827	..	19984	..	8402	..	34212	19984
Households	..	..	..	*9691	..	164037	..	6444	..	180172	164037
Other consumers	..	..	..	..	..	..	..	61	..	61	..
Non-energy use	..	..	..	3216	..	..	..	..	..	3216	..

Côte d'Ivoire

Terajoules

2018	Primary coal and peat	Coal and peat products	Primary Oil	Oil Products	Natural Gas	Biofuels and waste	Nuclear	Electricity	Heat	Total energy	of which: renewables
Primary production	..	..	70947	..	71850	261984	..	10663	..	415444	272647
Imports	..	..	104439	54958	..	..	..	367	..	159764	..
Exports	..	..	-64042	-62472	..	..	..	-4162	..	-130676	..
International marine bunkers	..	..	..	-3465	..	..	..	..	..	-3465	..
International aviation bunkers	..	..	..	-6615	..	..	..	..	..	-6615	..
Stock changes	..	..	..	..	..	..	..	..	..	..	..
Total energy supply	..	..	111343	-17594	71850	261984	..	6869	..	434452	272647
Statistical difference	..	..	4103	-1897	3577	-30	..	40	..	5794	10634
Transfers	..	..	38829	-38834	..	..	..	..	..	-5	..
Transformation	..	..	-146069	143903	-58407	-80485	..	25549	..	-115508	-80485
Electricity plants	..	..	..	-126	-58407	-2087	..	25549	..	-35072	-2087
CHP plants	..	..	..	..	..	..	..	..	..	..	..
Heat plants	..	..	..	..	..	..	..	..	..	..	..
Coke ovens	..	..	..	..	..	..	..	..	..	..	..
Briquetting plants	..	..	..	..	..	..	..	..	..	..	..
Liquefaction plants	..	..	..	..	..	..	..	..	..	..	..
Gas works	..	..	..	..	..	..	..	..	..	..	..
Blast furnaces	..	..	..	..	..	..	..	..	..	..	..
NGL plants & gas blending	..	..	-221	237	..	..	..	..	..	16	..
Oil refineries	..	..	-145848	143793	..	..	..	..	..	-2055	..
Other transformation	..	..	..	..	..	-78398	..	..	..	-78398	-78398
Energy industries own use	..	..	..	-2040	-2651	..	..	-698	..	-5389	..
Losses	..	..	..	..	..	-1298	..	-6746	..	-8044	-1298
Final consumption	..	..	..	87333	7214	180231	..	24934	..	299712	180231
Final energy consumption	..	..	..	83634	7214	180231	..	24934	..	296013	180231
Manufacturing, const., mining	..	..	..	8085	7214	..	..	7160	..	22460	..
Iron and steel	..	..	..	..	..	..	..	374	..	374	..
Chemical and petrochemical	..	..	..	189	..	..	..	389	..	578	..
Non-ferrous metals	..	..	..	378	..	..	..	..	..	378	..
Non-metallic minerals	..	..	..	..	..	..	..	..	..	..	..
Transport equipment	..	..	..	568	..	..	..	..	..	568	..
Machinery	..	..	..	..	..	..	..	..	..	..	..
Mining and quarrying	..	..	..	869	..	..	..	882	..	1751	..
Food and tobacco	..	..	..	849	5772	..	..	2056	..	8677	..
Paper, pulp and printing	..	..	..	..	..	..	..	..	..	..	..
Wood and wood products	..	..	..	..	..	..	..	346	..	346	..
Textile and leather	..	..	..	378	1443	..	..	403	..	2224	..
Construction	..	..	..	..	..	..	..	648	..	648	..
Industries n.e.s	..	..	..	4854	0	..	..	2063	..	6917	..
Transport	..	..	..	54754	..	..	..	..	..	54754	..
Road	..	..	..	49241	..	..	..	..	..	49241	..
Rail	..	..	..	688	..	..	..	..	..	688	..
Domestic aviation	..	..	..	353	..	..	..	..	..	353	..
Domestic navigation	..	..	..	4472	..	..	..	..	..	4472	..
Pipeline transport	..	..	..	..	..	..	..	..	..	..	..
Transport, n.e.s	..	..	..	..	..	..	..	..	..	..	..
Other	..	..	..	20795	..	180231	..	17773	..	218799	180231
Agriculture, forestry, fishing	..	..	..	3440	..	..	..	767	..	4207	..
Commerce, public services	..	..	..	1565	..	*19681	..	8370	..	*29616	*19681
Households	..	..	..	15789	..	160551	..	8590	..	184930	160551
Other consumers	..	..	..	..	..	..	..	47	..	47	..
Non-energy use	..	..	..	3698	..	..	..	..	..	3698	..

Croatia

Terajoules

2017	Primary coal and peat	Coal and peat products	Primary Oil	Oil Products	Natural Gas	Biofuels and waste	Nuclear	Electricity	Heat	Total energy	of which: renewables
Primary production	..	..	31973	..	51477	67739	..	23728	884	175801	91867
Imports	15615	909	121061	97825	63095	1528	..	43769	..	343803	1528
Exports	..	..	..	-106771	-6930	-13967	..	-18734	..	-146403	-13967
International marine bunkers	..	..	..	-293	..	..	..	..	..	-293	..
International aviation bunkers	..	..	..	-6218	..	..	..	..	..	-6218	..
Stock changes	-125	..	-955	1931	-3255	-142	..	..	..	-2547	-142
Total energy supply	15490	909	152080	-13527	104387	55157	..	48762	884	364142	79286
Statistical difference	17	-29	30	-43	0	-33	..	-11	-1	-70	23695
Transfers	..	..	13373	-13373		..	..	..	..	0	..
Transformation	-13359	..	-165423	167817	-34013	-7291	..	18702	12431	-21135	-7291
Electricity plants	-13222	..	..	-43	-184	-309	..	5029	..	-8728	-309
CHP plants	-137	..	..	-1987	-28517	-6580	..	13673	10660	-12888	-6580
Heat plants	..	..	..	-293	-1902	-3	..	..	1771	-427	-3
Coke ovens	..	..	..	..	..	..	..	..	..	..	..
Briquetting plants	..	..	..	..	..	..	..	..	..	..	..
Liquefaction plants	..	..	2412	..	..	..	..	..	..	2412	..
Gas works	..	..	..	..	..	..	..	..	..	..	..
Blast furnaces	..	..	..	..	..	..	..	..	..	..	..
NGL plants & gas blending	..	..	-1856	1987	..	..	..	..	..	130	..
Oil refineries	..	..	-165978	168154	..	..	..	..	..	2175	..
Other transformation	..	..	..	..	-3411	-399	..	..	..	-3810	-399
Energy industries own use	..	..	..	-14427	-6854	-28	..	-3586	-1234	-26129	-28
Losses	..	..	..	..	-1117	0	..	-6354	-1534	-9005	0
Final consumption	2114	938	..	126533	62404	47871	..	57535	10548	307943	48272
Final energy consumption	2114	938	..	120302	45276	47871	..	57535	10548	284584	48272
Manufacturing, const., mining	1960	938	..	12811	16180	1824	..	12992	2995	49700	1341
Iron and steel	..	..	..	..	73	..	..	194	..	267	..
Chemical and petrochemical	..	..	..	131	5063	..	..	1109	671	6974	..
Non-ferrous metals	..	..	..	47	326	4	..	310	..	687	4
Non-metallic minerals	1464	791	..	6910	3661	571	..	2437	..	15835	88
Transport equipment	..	..	..	43	111	1	..	353	..	508	1
Machinery	..	..	..	268	892	12	..	1645	379	3196	12
Mining and quarrying	..	..	..	516	..	..	..	119	..	635	..
Food and tobacco	496	147	..	752	3765	174	..	2506	529	8368	174
Paper, pulp and printing	..	..	..	218	1451	52	..	1166	26	2914	52
Wood and wood products	..	..	..	..	59	689	..	1120	1218	3086	689
Textile and leather	..	..	..	83	423	6	..	551	35	1098	6
Construction	..	..	..	3755	..	..	..	277	..	4032	..
Industries n.e.s	0	0	..	86	357	315	..	1206	137	2101	315
Transport	..	..	..	90883	177	0	..	965	..	92025	0
Road	..	..	..	87732	177	0	..	..	..	87909	0
Rail	..	..	..	774	..	..	..	824	..	1598	..
Domestic aviation	..	..	..	485	..	..	..	..	..	485	..
Domestic navigation	..	..	..	1892	..	..	..	..	..	1892	..
Pipeline transport	..	..	..	..	..	..	..	140	..	140	..
Transport, n.e.s	..	..	..	..	..	..	..	..	..	..	..
Other	154	..	..	16608	28919	46047	..	43578	7553	142859	46931
Agriculture, forestry, fishing	..	..	..	8275	833		..	223	393	9724	158
Commerce, public services	..	..	..	2500	8026	347	..	20797	1883	33553	696
Households	154	..	..	5833	20060	45701	..	22558	5277	99582	46078
Other consumers	..	..	..	..	..	..	..	..	..	..	..
Non-energy use	..	..	..	6231	17128	..	..	..	..	23359	..

Croatia

Terajoules

	Primary coal and peat	Coal and peat products	Primary Oil	Oil Products	Natural Gas	Biofuels and waste	Nuclear	Electricity	Heat	Total energy	of which: renewables
2018											
Primary production	..	..	31666	..	42611	66552	..	32800	976	174604	99510
Imports	13148	879	127082	91990	55050	3054	..	45695	..	336898	3054
Exports	..	..	..	-103542	-3925	-11603	..	-26302	..	-145371	-11603
International marine bunkers	..	..	..	-890	..	..	..	..	..	-890	..
International aviation bunkers	..	..	..	-7762	..	..	..	..	..	-7762	..
Stock changes	1256	29	-2826	-3950	2235	-165	..	..	..	-3421	-165
Total energy supply	14404	909	155922	-24154	95971	57838	..	52193	976	354058	90796
Statistical difference	42	0	-44	73	-2	-32	..	4	0	41	32775
Transfers	..	..	10449	-10449	..	..	..	..	..	0	..
Transformation	-12459	..	-166415	170822	-27961	-10463	..	15973	12627	-17876	-10528
Electricity plants	-12357	..	..	-43	-17	-308	..	5310	-72	-7487	-373
CHP plants	-103	..	..	-571	-22388	-9758	..	10663	10968	-11188	-9758
Heat plants	..	..	..	-250	-1864	-3	..	..	1731	-386	-3
Coke ovens	..	..	..	..	..	..	..	..	..	..	..
Briquetting plants	..	..	..	..	..	..	..	..	..	..	..
Liquefaction plants	..	..	2700	..	..	..	..	..	..	2700	..
Gas works	..	..	..	..	..	..	..	..	..	..	..
Blast furnaces	..	..	..	..	..	..	..	..	..	..	..
NGL plants & gas blending	..	..	-1680	1797	..	..	..	..	..	118	..
Oil refineries	..	..	-167436	169889	..	..	..	..	..	2453	..
Other transformation	..	..	..	..	-3693	-394	..	..	..	-4087	-394
Energy industries own use	..	..	..	-13587	-7105	-19	..	-3370	-1556	-25636	-19
Losses	..	..	..	..	-1040	..	..	-6566	-1689	-9295	..
Final consumption	1902	909	..	122560	59867	47388	..	58226	10358	301210	47474
Final energy consumption	1902	909	..	116128	45051	47388	..	58226	10358	279963	47474
Manufacturing, const., mining	1800	909	..	12799	16037	2232	..	13255	3144	50176	1414
Iron and steel	75	29	..	..	264	..	..	630	..	998	..
Chemical and petrochemical	..	..	..	131	4514	..	..	1123	690	6458	..
Non-ferrous metals	..	..	..	47	416	3	..	356	..	823	3
Non-metallic minerals	1348	762	..	6682	3741	974	..	2462	..	15970	156
Transport equipment	..	..	..	43	167	1	..	335	..	545	1
Machinery	..	..	..	228	804	14	..	1490	352	2888	14
Mining and quarrying	..	..	..	559	4	..	..	104	..	667	..
Food and tobacco	376	117	..	750	3839	241	..	2444	522	8289	241
Paper, pulp and printing	..	..	..	178	1486	100	..	1141	25	2930	100
Wood and wood products	..	..	..	..	77	554	..	1138	1391	3159	554
Textile and leather	..	..	..	83	378	10	..	533	34	1038	10
Construction	..	..	..	4055	..	..	..	281	..	4335	..
Industries n.e.s	0	0	..	43	350	335	..	1217	130	2075	335
Transport	..	..	..	87636	176	1131	..	1015	..	89958	1131
Road	..	..	..	84484	176	1131	..	4	..	85795	1131
Rail	..	..	..	645	..	..	..	857	..	1502	..
Domestic aviation	..	..	..	485	..	..	..	..	..	485	..
Domestic navigation	..	..	..	2021	..	..	..	..	..	2021	..
Pipeline transport	..	..	..	..	..	..	..	155	..	155	..
Transport, n.e.s	..	..	..	..	..	..	..	..	..	..	..
Other	103	..	..	15693	28838	44025	..	43956	7214	139828	44929
Agriculture, forestry, fishing	..	..	..	8494	814	..	..	227	395	9930	148
Commerce, public services	..	..	..	2159	8463	439	..	21402	1739	34201	786
Households	103	..	..	5040	19562	43587	..	22327	5080	95697	43996
Other consumers	..	..	..	..	..	..	..	..	..	..	..
Non-energy use	..	..	..	6432	14816	..	..	..	..	21248	..

Cuba

Terajoules

2017	Primary coal and peat	Coal and peat products	Primary Oil	Oil Products	Natural Gas	Biofuels and waste	Nuclear	Electricity	Heat	Total energy	of which: renewables
Primary production	..	..	106689	..	36903	50487	..	591	..	194671	51079
Imports	93	14	120115	145447	..	..	..	..	..	265669	..
Exports	..	..	..	*-30509	..	..	..	..	..	*-30509	..
International marine bunkers	..	..	..	*-19023	..	..	..	..	..	*-19023	..
International aviation bunkers	..	..	..	-7012	..	..	..	..	..	-7012	..
Stock changes	..	..	..	..	..	..	..	..	..	..	..
Total energy supply	93	14	226804	88903	36903	50487	..	591	..	403796	51079
Statistical difference	31	2	0	-1894	3164	540	..	0	..	1843	1132
Transfers	..	..	*-109946	*105008	..	..	..	..	..	*-4938	..
Transformation	..	3459	*-116858	-66528	-14441	*-14945	..	73418	..	-135895	*-14945
Electricity plants	..	..	..	-166518	*-14441	*-12996	..	73418	..	-120538	*-12996
CHP plants	..	..	..	..	..	..	..	..	..	..	..
Heat plants	..	..	..	..	..	..	..	..	..	..	..
Coke ovens	..	..	..	..	..	..	..	..	..	..	..
Briquetting plants	..	..	..	..	..	..	..	..	..	..	..
Liquefaction plants	..	..	..	..	..	..	..	..	..	..	..
Gas works	..	3467	..	*-10511	..	..	..	..	..	*-7044	..
Blast furnaces	..	*-8	..	..	..	..	..	..	..	*-8	..
NGL plants & gas blending	..	..	..	..	..	..	..	..	..	..	..
Oil refineries	..	..	*-116858	110501	..	..	..	..	..	*-6357	..
Other transformation	..	..	..	..	..	*-1949	..	..	..	*-1949	*-1949
Energy industries own use	..	..	..	-94	..	..	..	-6807	..	-6901	..
Losses	..	..	..	..	..	..	..	-11438	..	-11438	..
Final consumption	62	3471	..	129183	*19298	*35002	..	55765	..	242781	*35002
Final energy consumption	62	3471	..	124705	*19298	*35002	..	55765	..	238302	*35002
Manufacturing, const., mining	62	*363	..	75186	*19263	*28742	..	11042	..	134657	*28742
Iron and steel	..	6	..	..	..	..	..	..	..	6	..
Chemical and petrochemical	..	..	..	..	..	..	..	..	..	..	..
Non-ferrous metals	..	..	..	..	..	..	..	..	..	..	..
Non-metallic minerals	..	..	..	..	..	..	..	..	..	..	..
Transport equipment	..	..	..	..	..	..	..	..	..	..	..
Machinery	..	..	..	..	..	..	..	..	..	..	..
Mining and quarrying	..	..	..	20527	..	..	..	..	..	20527	..
Food and tobacco	..	..	..	2586	..	*27591	..	..	..	*30177	*27591
Paper, pulp and printing	..	..	..	..	..	..	..	..	..	..	..
Wood and wood products	..	..	..	..	..	..	..	..	..	..	..
Textile and leather	..	..	..	..	..	..	..	..	..	..	..
Construction	..	..	..	634	..	..	..	373	..	1007	..
Industries n.e.s	62	*357	..	51439	*19263	*1151	..	10669	..	82940	*1151
Transport	..	..	..	18396	..	..	..	1056	..	19452	..
Road	..	..	..	11154	..	..	..	..	..	11154	..
Rail	..	..	..	..	..	..	..	1056	..	1056	..
Domestic aviation	..	..	..	5302	..	..	..	..	..	5302	..
Domestic navigation	..	..	..	..	..	..	..	..	..	..	..
Pipeline transport	..	..	..	..	..	..	..	..	..	..	..
Transport, n.e.s	..	..	..	1940	..	..	..	..	..	1940	..
Other	..	3108	..	31123	*35	*6260	..	43667	..	84193	*6260
Agriculture, forestry, fishing	..	..	..	5591	..	*872	..	1101	..	7565	*872
Commerce, public services	..	..	..	8916	..	..	..	1258	..	10174	..
Households	..	2104	..	12656	..	787	..	32024	..	47571	787
Other consumers	..	*1004	..	3960	*35	*4600	..	9284	..	18883	*4600
Non-energy use	..	..	..	4478	..	..	..	..	..	4478	..

Cuba

Terajoules

2018	Primary coal and peat	Coal and peat products	Primary Oil	Oil Products	Natural Gas	Biofuels and waste	Nuclear	Electricity	Heat	Total energy	of which: renewables
Primary production	..	..	104164	..	34069	57704	..	*1128	..	197065	58832
Imports	108	34	107882	129409	..	..	..	..	..	237433	..
Exports	..	..	..	*-39000	..	..	..	..	..	*-39000	..
International marine bunkers	..	..	..	*-17612	..	..	..	..	..	*-17612	..
International aviation bunkers	..	..	..	-3299	..	..	..	..	..	-3299	..
Stock changes	..	..	..	..	..	..	..	..	..	..	..
Total energy supply	108	34	212046	69498	34069	57704	..	*1128	..	374587	58832
Statistical difference	59	0	0	-33004	365	840	..	0	..	-31739	1968
Transfers	..	..	*-89883	*85846	..	..	..	..	..	*-4037	..
Transformation	..	3291	*-122162	-71708	*-14529	*-11923	..	73885	..	-143145	*-11923
Electricity plants	..	..	..	-175972	*-14529	*-10298	..	73885	..	-126914	*-10298
CHP plants	..	..	..	..	..	..	..	..	..	..	..
Heat plants	..	..	..	..	..	..	..	..	..	..	..
Coke ovens	..	..	..	..	..	..	..	..	..	..	..
Briquetting plants	..	..	..	..	..	..	..	..	..	..	..
Liquefaction plants	..	..	..	..	..	..	..	..	..	..	..
Gas works	..	3319	..	*-11227	..	..	..	..	..	*-7908	..
Blast furnaces	..	*-28	..	..	..	..	..	..	..	*-28	..
NGL plants & gas blending	..	..	..	..	..	..	..	..	..	..	..
Oil refineries	..	..	*-122162	115492	..	..	..	..	..	*-6671	..
Other transformation	..	..	..	..	..	*-1625	..	..	..	*-1625	*-1625
Energy industries own use	..	..	..	-208	..	..	..	-7050	..	-7257	..
Losses	..	..	..	..	..	..	..	-11843	..	-11843	..
Final consumption	49	3325	..	116432	*19175	*44941	..	56121	..	240044	*44941
Final energy consumption	49	3325	..	111632	*19175	*44941	..	56121	..	235244	*44941
Manufacturing, const., mining	49	*381	..	67840	*19140	*39053	..	11016	..	137478	*39053
Iron and steel	..	6	..	..	..	..	..	..	..	6	..
Chemical and petrochemical	..	..	..	..	..	..	..	..	..	..	..
Non-ferrous metals	..	..	..	..	..	..	..	..	..	..	..
Non-metallic minerals	..	..	..	..	..	..	..	..	..	..	..
Transport equipment	..	..	..	..	..	..	..	..	..	..	..
Machinery	..	..	..	..	..	..	..	..	..	..	..
Mining and quarrying	..	..	..	20455	..	..	..	..	..	20455	..
Food and tobacco	..	..	..	2145	..	*37949	..	..	..	*40094	*37949
Paper, pulp and printing	..	..	..	..	..	..	..	..	..	..	..
Wood and wood products	..	..	..	..	..	..	..	..	..	..	..
Textile and leather	..	..	..	..	..	..	..	..	..	..	..
Construction	..	..	..	638	..	..	..	352	..	990	..
Industries n.e.s	49	*375	..	44602	*19140	*1104	..	10664	..	75933	*1104
Transport	..	..	..	15026	..	..	..	1044	..	16070	..
Road	..	..	..	11361	..	..	..	..	..	11361	..
Rail	..	..	..	..	..	..	..	1044	..	1044	..
Domestic aviation	..	..	..	1809	..	..	..	..	..	1809	..
Domestic navigation	..	..	..	..	..	..	..	..	..	..	..
Pipeline transport	..	..	..	..	..	..	..	..	..	..	..
Transport, n.e.s	..	..	..	1856	..	..	..	..	..	1856	..
Other	..	2945	..	28767	*35	*5888	..	44061	..	81696	*5888
Agriculture, forestry, fishing	..	..	..	5389	..	*835	..	1169	..	7393	*835
Commerce, public services	..	..	..	6069	..	..	..	1471	..	7540	..
Households	..	1979	..	13899	..	724	..	32445	..	49047	724
Other consumers	..	*966	..	3410	*35	*4329	..	8975	..	17715	*4329
Non-energy use	..	..	..	4800	..	..	..	..	..	4800	..

Curaçao

Terajoules

2017	Primary coal and peat	Coal and peat products	Primary Oil	Oil Products	Natural Gas	Biofuels and waste	Nuclear	Electricity	Heat	Total energy	of which: renewables
Primary production	..	..	..	..	..	..	..	677	..	677	677
Imports	..	..	185892	109624	*2520	11	..	..	..	298047	11
Exports	..	..	..	-164824	..	..	..	..	..	-164824	..
International marine bunkers	..	..	..	-65279	..	..	..	..	..	-65279	..
International aviation bunkers	..	..	..	-2602	..	..	..	..	..	-2602	..
Stock changes	..	..	..	..	..	..	..	..	..	..	..
Total energy supply	..	..	185892	-123081	*2520	11	..	677	..	66019	688
Statistical difference	..	..	0	-615	0	0	..	-4	..	-619	677
Transfers	..	..	8772	-8660	..	..	..	..	..	112	..
Transformation	..	..	-194664	175505	..	..	..	2531	..	-16629	..
Electricity plants	..	..	..	-7394	..	..	..	2531	..	-4863	..
CHP plants	..	..	..	..	..	..	..	..	..	..	..
Heat plants	..	..	..	..	..	..	..	..	..	..	..
Coke ovens	..	..	..	..	..	..	..	..	..	..	..
Briquetting plants	..	..	..	..	..	..	..	..	..	..	..
Liquefaction plants	..	..	..	..	..	..	..	..	..	..	..
Gas works	..	..	..	..	..	..	..	..	..	..	..
Blast furnaces	..	..	..	..	..	..	..	..	..	..	..
NGL plants & gas blending	..	..	..	..	..	..	..	..	..	..	..
Oil refineries	..	..	-194664	182899	..	..	..	..	..	-11765	..
Other transformation	..	..	..	..	..	..	..	..	..	..	..
Energy industries own use	..	..	..	-18029	*-2520	..	..	-209	..	-20757	..
Losses	..	..	..	..	..	..	..	-353	..	-353	..
Final consumption	..	..	..	26350	..	*11	..	2650	..	29011	*11
Final energy consumption	..	..	..	22330	..	*11	..	2650	..	24991	*11
Manufacturing, const., mining	..	..	..	5171	..	..	..	731	..	5902	..
Iron and steel	..	..	..	..	..	..	..	..	..	..	..
Chemical and petrochemical	..	..	..	..	..	..	..	..	..	..	..
Non-ferrous metals	..	..	..	..	..	..	..	..	..	..	..
Non-metallic minerals	..	..	..	..	..	..	..	..	..	..	..
Transport equipment	..	..	..	..	..	..	..	..	..	..	..
Machinery	..	..	..	..	..	..	..	..	..	..	..
Mining and quarrying	..	..	..	..	..	..	..	..	..	..	..
Food and tobacco	..	..	..	..	..	..	..	..	..	..	..
Paper, pulp and printing	..	..	..	..	..	..	..	..	..	..	..
Wood and wood products	..	..	..	..	..	..	..	..	..	..	..
Textile and leather	..	..	..	..	..	..	..	..	..	..	..
Construction	..	..	..	..	..	..	..	..	..	..	..
Industries n.e.s	..	..	..	5171	..	..	..	731	..	5902	..
Transport	..	..	..	14841	..	..	..	..	..	14841	..
Road	..	..	..	14841	..	..	..	..	..	14841	..
Rail	..	..	..	..	..	..	..	..	..	..	..
Domestic aviation	..	..	..	..	..	..	..	..	..	..	..
Domestic navigation	..	..	..	..	..	..	..	..	..	..	..
Pipeline transport	..	..	..	..	..	..	..	..	..	..	..
Transport, n.e.s	..	..	..	..	..	..	..	..	..	..	..
Other	..	..	..	2318	..	*11	..	1919	..	4247	*11
Agriculture, forestry, fishing	..	..	..	..	..	..	..	..	..	..	..
Commerce, public services	..	..	..	..	..	..	..	846	..	846	..
Households	..	..	..	2318	..	*11	..	1073	..	3401	*11
Other consumers	..	..	..	..	..	..	..	..	..	..	..
Non-energy use	..	..	..	4020	..	..	..	..	..	4020	..

Curaçao

Terajoules

2018	Primary coal and peat	Coal and peat products	Primary Oil	Oil Products	Natural Gas	Biofuels and waste	Nuclear	Electricity	Heat	Total energy	of which: renewables
Primary production	..	..	..	..	..	..	..	911	..	911	911
Imports	..	..	138668	105747	*1890	11	..	..	..	246317	11
Exports	..	..	..	-121564	..	..	..	..	..	-121564	..
International marine bunkers	..	..	..	-65117	..	..	..	..	..	-65117	..
International aviation bunkers	..	..	..	-2558	..	..	..	..	..	-2558	..
Stock changes	..	..	..	..	..	..	..	..	..	..	..
Total energy supply	..	..	138668	-83492	*1890	11	..	911	..	57988	922
Statistical difference	..	..	0	-1041	0	0	..	4	..	-1037	911
Transfers	..	..	6547	-6463	..	..	..	..	..	84	..
Transformation	..	..	-145215	124491	..	..	..	2207	..	-18517	..
Electricity plants	..	..	..	-6431	..	..	..	2207	..	-4224	..
CHP plants	..	..	..	..	..	..	..	..	..	..	..
Heat plants	..	..	..	..	..	..	..	..	..	..	..
Coke ovens	..	..	..	..	..	..	..	..	..	..	..
Briquetting plants	..	..	..	..	..	..	..	..	..	..	..
Liquefaction plants	..	..	..	..	..	..	..	..	..	..	..
Gas works	..	..	..	..	..	..	..	..	..	..	..
Blast furnaces	..	..	..	..	..	..	..	..	..	..	..
NGL plants & gas blending	..	..	..	..	..	..	..	..	..	..	..
Oil refineries	..	..	-145215	130922	..	..	..	..	..	-14293	..
Other transformation	..	..	..	..	..	..	..	..	..	..	..
Energy industries own use	..	..	..	-9314	*-1890	..	..	-194	..	-11399	..
Losses	..	..	..	..	..	..	..	-342	..	-342	..
Final consumption	..	..	..	26263	..	*11	..	2578	..	28851	*11
Final energy consumption	..	..	..	22243	..	*11	..	2578	..	24831	*11
Manufacturing, const., mining	..	..	..	5171	..	..	..	659	..	5830	..
Iron and steel	..	..	..	..	..	..	..	..	..	..	..
Chemical and petrochemical	..	..	..	..	..	..	..	..	..	..	..
Non-ferrous metals	..	..	..	..	..	..	..	..	..	..	..
Non-metallic minerals	..	..	..	..	..	..	..	..	..	..	..
Transport equipment	..	..	..	..	..	..	..	..	..	..	..
Machinery	..	..	..	..	..	..	..	..	..	..	..
Mining and quarrying	..	..	..	..	..	..	..	..	..	..	..
Food and tobacco	..	..	..	..	..	..	..	..	..	..	..
Paper, pulp and printing	..	..	..	..	..	..	..	..	..	..	..
Wood and wood products	..	..	..	..	..	..	..	..	..	..	..
Textile and leather	..	..	..	..	..	..	..	..	..	..	..
Construction	..	..	..	..	..	..	..	..	..	..	..
Industries n.e.s	..	..	..	5171	..	..	..	659	..	5830	..
Transport	..	..	..	14754	..	..	..	..	..	14754	..
Road	..	..	..	14754	..	..	..	..	..	14754	..
Rail	..	..	..	..	..	..	..	..	..	..	..
Domestic aviation	..	..	..	..	..	..	..	..	..	..	..
Domestic navigation	..	..	..	..	..	..	..	..	..	..	..
Pipeline transport	..	..	..	..	..	..	..	..	..	..	..
Transport, n.e.s	..	..	..	..	..	..	..	..	..	..	..
Other	..	..	..	2318	..	*11	..	1919	..	4247	*11
Agriculture, forestry, fishing	..	..	..	..	..	..	..	..	..	..	..
Commerce, public services	..	..	..	..	..	..	..	860	..	860	..
Households	..	..	..	2318	..	*11	..	1058	..	3387	*11
Other consumers	..	..	..	..	..	..	..	..	..	..	..
Non-energy use	..	..	..	4020	..	..	..	..	..	4020	..

Cyprus

Terajoules

2017	Primary coal and peat	Coal and peat products	Primary Oil	Oil Products	Natural Gas	Biofuels and waste	Nuclear	Electricity	Heat	Total energy	of which: renewables
Primary production	..	..	..	..	..	1656	..	1380	3005	6041	5901
Imports	439	..	..	110745	..	2264	..	..	..	113448	1557
Exports	..	..	..	0	..	..	..	..	..	0	..
International marine bunkers	..	..	..	-10565	..	..	..	..	..	-10565	..
International aviation bunkers	..	..	..	-13186	..	..	..	..	..	-13186	..
Stock changes	-284	..	..	-1223	..	64	..	..	..	-1443	40
Total energy supply	155	..	..	85771	..	3984	..	1380	3005	94296	7498
Statistical difference	26	..	..	-117	..	-30	..	14	0	-106	1351
Transfers	..	..	..	242	..	..	..	..	..	242	..
Transformation	..	..	..	-42523	..	-436	..	16636	54	-26269	-436
Electricity plants	..	..	..	-42482	..	..	..	16434	..	-26048	..
CHP plants	..	..	..	-40	..	-323	..	202	54	-108	-323
Heat plants	..	..	..	..	..	..	..	..	..	..	..
Coke ovens	..	..	..	..	..	..	..	..	..	..	..
Briquetting plants	..	..	..	..	..	..	..	..	..	..	..
Liquefaction plants	..	..	..	..	..	..	..	..	..	..	..
Gas works	..	..	..	..	..	..	..	..	..	..	..
Blast furnaces	..	..	..	..	..	..	..	..	..	..	..
NGL plants & gas blending	..	..	..	..	..	..	..	..	..	..	..
Oil refineries	..	..	..	..	..	..	..	..	..	..	..
Other transformation	..	..	..	..	..	-113	..	..	..	-113	-113
Energy industries own use	..	..	..	0	..	..	..	-833	0	-833	..
Losses	..	..	..	..	..	..	..	-821	..	-821	..
Final consumption	129	..	..	43608	..	3578	..	16348	3059	66721	5711
Final energy consumption	129	..	..	41960	..	3578	..	16348	3059	65073	5711
Manufacturing, const., mining	129	..	..	5896	..	1880	..	1865	..	9770	1008
Iron and steel	..	..	..	..	..	..	..	7	..	7	..
Chemical and petrochemical	..	..	..	83	..	22	..	158	..	264	22
Non-ferrous metals	..	..	..	0	..	..	..	..	..	0	..
Non-metallic minerals	129	..	..	4037	..	1740	..	630	..	6536	868
Transport equipment	..	..	..	..	..	..	..	7	..	7	..
Machinery	..	..	..	..	..	..	..	76	..	76	..
Mining and quarrying	..	..	..	129	..	..	..	104	..	233	..
Food and tobacco	..	..	..	936	..	118	..	634	..	1688	118
Paper, pulp and printing	..	..	..	40	..	..	..	58	..	98	..
Wood and wood products	..	..	..	..	..	..	..	22	..	22	..
Textile and leather	..	..	..	..	..	..	..	18	..	18	..
Construction	..	..	..	629	..	..	..	18	..	647	..
Industries n.e.s	0	..	..	40	..	0	..	133	..	174	0
Transport	..	..	..	28151	..	368	..	..	..	28519	368
Road	..	..	..	28019	..	368	..	..	..	28387	368
Rail	..	..	..	..	..	..	..	..	..	..	..
Domestic aviation	..	..	..	88	..	..	..	..	..	88	..
Domestic navigation	..	..	..	43	..	..	..	..	..	43	..
Pipeline transport	..	..	..	..	..	..	..	..	..	..	..
Transport, n.e.s	..	..	..	..	..	..	..	..	..	..	..
Other	..	..	..	7913	..	1330	..	14483	3059	26785	4335
Agriculture, forestry, fishing	..	..	..	1127	..	96	..	616	54	1892	96
Commerce, public services	..	..	..	1291	..	277	..	7549	441	9558	718
Households	..	..	..	5102	..	957	..	5990	2564	14613	3521
Other consumers	..	..	..	394	..	..	..	328	..	721	..
Non-energy use	..	..	..	1648	..	..	..	..	..	1648	..

Cyprus

Terajoules

2018	Primary coal and peat	Coal and peat products	Primary Oil	Oil Products	Natural Gas	Biofuels and waste	Nuclear	Electricity	Heat	Total energy	of which: renewables
Primary production	..	..	..	..	..	1712	..	1517	3081	6310	6127
Imports	568	..	..	109347	..	2676	..	..	..	112590	1725
Exports	..	..	..	..	..	..	..	..	..	..	..
International marine bunkers	..	..	..	-11296	..	..	..	..	..	-11296	..
International aviation bunkers	..	..	..	-13583	..	..	..	..	..	-13583	..
Stock changes	26	..	..	694	..	45	..	..	..	764	42
Total energy supply	593	..	..	85162	..	4433	..	1517	3081	94786	7893
Statistical difference	0	..	..	758	..	7	..	0	0	766	1525
Transfers	..	..	..	202	..	..	..	..	..	202	..
Transformation	..	..	..	-43146	..	-400	..	16704	54	-26788	-400
Electricity plants	..	..	..	-43146	..	..	..	16495	..	-26650	..
CHP plants	..	..	..	..	..	-347	..	209	54	-84	-347
Heat plants	..	..	..	..	..	..	..	..	..	..	..
Coke ovens	..	..	..	..	..	..	..	..	..	..	..
Briquetting plants	..	..	..	..	..	..	..	..	..	..	..
Liquefaction plants	..	..	..	..	..	..	..	..	..	..	..
Gas works	..	..	..	..	..	..	..	..	..	..	..
Blast furnaces	..	..	..	..	..	..	..	..	..	..	..
NGL plants & gas blending	..	..	..	..	..	..	..	..	..	..	..
Oil refineries	..	..	..	..	..	..	..	..	..	..	..
Other transformation	..	..	..	..	..	-53	..	..	..	-53	-53
Energy industries own use	..	..	..	..	..	..	..	-862	0	-862	..
Losses	..	..	..	..	..	..	..	-569	..	-569	..
Final consumption	593	..	..	41460	..	4026	..	16790	3135	66004	5969
Final energy consumption	593	..	..	39812	..	4026	..	16790	3135	64356	5969
Manufacturing, const., mining	593	..	..	4679	..	2348	..	1904	17	9542	1227
Iron and steel	..	..	..	..	..	..	..	7	..	7	..
Chemical and petrochemical	..	..	..	83	..	18	..	162	17	280	35
Non-ferrous metals	..	..	..	47	..	..	..	..	..	47	..
Non-metallic minerals	593	..	..	3054	..	2197	..	619	..	6464	1059
Transport equipment	..	..	..	..	..	..	..	7	..	7	..
Machinery	..	..	..	..	..	..	..	86	..	86	..
Mining and quarrying	..	..	..	172	..	..	..	104	..	276	..
Food and tobacco	..	..	..	900	..	133	..	655	..	1688	133
Paper, pulp and printing	..	..	..	40	..	..	..	58	..	98	..
Wood and wood products	..	..	..	..	..	..	..	22	..	22	..
Textile and leather	..	..	..	..	..	..	..	18	..	18	..
Construction	..	..	..	382	..	..	..	25	..	407	..
Industries n.e.s	0	..	..	0	..	0	..	140	0	140	0
Transport	..	..	..	28096	..	368	..	..	..	28464	368
Road	..	..	..	27965	..	368	..	..	..	28333	368
Rail	..	..	..	..	..	..	..	..	..	..	..
Domestic aviation	..	..	..	88	..	..	..	..	..	88	..
Domestic navigation	..	..	..	43	..	..	..	..	..	43	..
Pipeline transport	..	..	..	..	..	..	..	..	..	..	..
Transport, n.e.s	..	..	..	..	..	..	..	..	..	..	..
Other	..	..	..	7037	..	1310	..	14886	3118	26350	4374
Agriculture, forestry, fishing	..	..	..	1131	..	96	..	637	54	1918	96
Commerce, public services	..	..	..	1559	..	239	..	7826	450	10074	689
Households	..	..	..	3998	..	975	..	6077	2614	13663	3589
Other consumers	..	..	..	349	..	..	..	346	..	695	..
Non-energy use	..	..	..	1648	..	..	..	..	..	1648	..

Czechia

Terajoules

2017	Primary coal and peat	Coal and peat products	Primary Oil	Oil Products	Natural Gas	Biofuels and waste	Nuclear	Electricity	Heat	Total energy	of which: renewables
Primary production	639846	..	8727	..	7891	176089	306980	16754	1149	1157437	180232
Imports	104567	19169	331827	163426	307090	*18784	..	54259	53	999174	*18784
Exports	-75854	-21101	-1018	-101079	..	*-15640	..	-101192	-84	-315969	*-15640
International marine bunkers	..	..	..	..	..	..	..	..	..	..	..
International aviation bunkers	..	..	..	-15126	..	..	..	..	..	-15126	..
Stock changes	4005	-715	-1323	3676	-13490	-110	..	..	..	-7957	-110
Total energy supply	672563	-2647	338213	50897	301491	179122	306980	-30179	1118	1817559	183265
Statistical difference	-3208	-1774	70	-3710	0	*-40	0	6566	3081	985	16716
Transfers	..	..	9447	-8561	..	..	..	..	..	886	..
Transformation	-614773	59668	-347591	349830	-58443	*-53200	-306980	292345	122459	-556685	*-50013
Electricity plants	-82132	..	..	-205	-11295	-539	-306072	134554	-171	-265860	-539
CHP plants	-416791	-29409	..	-1793	-21398	*-50600	-908	157856	95446	-267596	*-47826
Heat plants	-1848	-84	..	-346	-25751	*-2060	..	-65	27184	-2971	*-1647
Coke ovens	-87413	95672	..	..	..	..	..	..	..	8259	..
Briquetting plants	-2763	2981	..	..	..	..	..	..	..	218	..
Liquefaction plants	..	..	..	..	..	..	..	..	..	..	..
Gas works	-16454	15177	..	..	..	..	..	..	..	-1277	..
Blast furnaces	-7371	-28179	..	..	..	..	..	..	..	-35550	..
NGL plants & gas blending	..	..	..	..	..	..	..	..	..	..	..
Oil refineries	..	..	-348302	352174	..	..	..	..	..	3872	..
Other transformation	..	3510	711	0	..	..	..	..	..	4221	..
Energy industries own use	-10152	-15331	..	-9860	-3983	..	..	-33293	-23212	-95831	..
Losses	-827	-1116	..	..	-3843	..	..	-15750	-6912	-28448	..
Final consumption	50019	42348	..	386017	235221	*125962	..	206557	90372	1136496	*116536
Final energy consumption	49992	30920	..	282039	231506	*125962	..	206557	90372	1017348	*116536
Manufacturing, const., mining	20925	26180	..	5590	89631	*27707	..	85946	24223	280202	*18850
Iron and steel	1697	21618	..	..	8023	*1	..	8338	3268	42944	*1
Chemical and petrochemical	10927	1388	..	1618	9255	156	..	12182	7395	42921	*27
Non-ferrous metals	..	144	..	..	2467	*4	..	1480	51	4146	*4
Non-metallic minerals	4755	2563	..	342	22479	8783	..	8752	439	48113	*73
Transport equipment	238	..	..	90	6773	*9	..	10984	1837	19931	*9
Machinery	189	202	..	225	10718	*381	..	15635	3101	30451	*381
Mining and quarrying	27	..	..	81	2217	*11	..	1354	43	3732	*11
Food and tobacco	1653	202	..	218	13165	268	..	5944	3329	24778	268
Paper, pulp and printing	1163	..	..	81	4335	*11680	..	6498	1229	24986	*11680
Wood and wood products	38	..	..	164	516	*6057	..	1894	453	*9121	*6057
Textile and leather	88	..	..	47	2245	*3	..	2653	382	5418	*3
Construction	64	64	..	2070	3428	*122	..	1962	297	8007	*122
Industries n.e.s	88	0	..	653	4010	*232	..	8273	2399	15654	*214
Transport	39	..	..	258667	2929	13064	..	6109	..	280808	13064
Road	..	..	..	252762	2336	12806	..	241	..	268145	12806
Rail	39	..	..	3483	..	258	..	5670	..	9450	258
Domestic aviation	..	..	..	2250	..	..	..	..	..	2250	..
Domestic navigation	..	..	..	172	..	..	..	..	..	172	..
Pipeline transport	..	..	..	..	593	..	..	148	..	741	..
Transport, n.e.s	..	..	..	..	..	..	..	50	..	50	..
Other	29028	4740	..	17783	138947	*85191	..	114502	66149	456339	*84622
Agriculture, forestry, fishing	227	..	..	14156	2740	5857	..	3517	301	26798	5857
Commerce, public services	752	513	..	1120	49826	3516	..	56225	20575	132527	2301
Households	28050	4227	..	2034	83923	*75818	..	54760	45273	294085	*76464
Other consumers	..	..	..	472	2458	..	..	..	..	2930	..
Non-energy use	27	11428	..	103978	3715	..	..	..	..	119147	..

Czechia

Terajoules

2018	Primary coal and peat	Coal and peat products	Primary Oil	Oil Products	Natural Gas	Biofuels and waste	Nuclear	Electricity	Heat	Total energy	of which: renewables
Primary production	615424	..	8224	..	7520	181153	324011	16546	1576	1154452	183450
Imports	102355	19307	318863	185531	276475	17973	..	41663	52	962218	17973
Exports	-62341	-20963	-942	-94210	..	*-17910	..	-91732	-76	-288173	*-17910
International marine bunkers	..	..	..	..	..	..	..	..	..	..	..
International aviation bunkers	..	..	..	-17464	..	..	..	..	..	-17464	..
Stock changes	6775	667	-171	-6475	1508	-110	..	..	..	2194	-110
Total energy supply	662213	-989	325974	67382	285503	181106	324011	-33523	1552	1813227	183403
Statistical difference	-1739	-1987	573	-3403	0	1	0	5598	3068	2111	16547
Transfers	..	..	8723	-8160	..	..	..	..	..	563	..
Transformation	-605080	59298	-334124	336265	-58136	*-51695	-324011	296510	117172	-563801	*-48662
Electricity plants	-78502	..	..	-205	-11724	-554	-323147	140036	-354	-274450	-554
CHP plants	-410036	-28607	..	-1495	-21147	*-49070	-864	156546	90702	-263971	*-46483
Heat plants	-1738	-56	..	-306	-25264	*-2089	..	-76	26824	-2705	*-1643
Coke ovens	-86958	95799	..	..	..	..	..	..	..	8841	..
Briquetting plants	-3143	3326	..	..	..	..	..	..	..	183	..
Liquefaction plants	..	..	..	..	..	..	..	..	..	..	..
Gas works	-17193	13932	..	..	..	..	..	..	..	-3261	..
Blast furnaces	-7510	-30155	..	..	..	..	..	..	..	-37665	..
NGL plants & gas blending	..	..	..	..	..	..	..	..	..	..	..
Oil refineries	..	..	-335033	338271	..	..	..	..	..	3238	..
Other transformation	..	5058	909	0	..	..	..	..	..	5967	..
Energy industries own use	-10338	-15869	..	-9091	-3668	..	..	-33206	-22549	-94722	..
Losses	-1896	-1232	..	..	-3668	..	..	-15368	-5859	-28024	..
Final consumption	46638	43194	..	389799	220030	*129410	..	208814	87248	1125133	*118194
Final energy consumption	46612	32014	..	284843	216299	*129410	..	208814	87248	1005239	*118194
Manufacturing, const., mining	20427	27189	..	6820	84729	*28524	..	87131	23653	278471	*17887
Iron and steel	1852	22179	..	..	8373	0	..	8485	2991	43880	0
Chemical and petrochemical	10782	1503	..	1972	9086	150	..	11866	7249	42608	*21
Non-ferrous metals	13	113	..	..	2210	*6	..	1490	43	3875	*6
Non-metallic minerals	4145	2940	..	620	21128	10556	..	8906	505	48801	*66
Transport equipment	227	..	..	47	6530	*11	..	11668	1761	20245	*11
Machinery	252	142	..	273	9599	*141	..	15347	3048	28802	*141
Mining and quarrying	26	..	..	40	1909	*16	..	1339	40	3371	*16
Food and tobacco	1688	198	..	225	12232	*238	..	6005	3342	23928	*238
Paper, pulp and printing	1275	..	..	128	4228	*11190	..	6516	1172	24509	*11190
Wood and wood products	..	28	..	124	572	*5853	..	2012	523	*9112	*5853
Textile and leather	63	..	..	47	2045	*2	..	2725	361	5243	*2
Construction	52	85	..	2074	3152	*121	..	2232	336	8052	*121
Industries n.e.s	50	0	..	1268	3665	*240	..	8539	2282	16045	*222
Transport	26	..	..	260267	3130	12850	..	6311	..	282584	12850
Road	..	..	..	255205	2544	12629	..	245	..	270623	12629
Rail	26	..	..	3477	..	221	..	5857	..	9582	221
Domestic aviation	..	..	..	1456	..	..	..	..	..	1456	..
Domestic navigation	..	..	..	129	..	..	..	..	..	129	..
Pipeline transport	..	..	..	..	586	..	..	169	..	755	..
Transport, n.e.s	..	..	..	..	..	..	..	40	..	40	..
Other	26159	4825	..	17756	128440	*88036	..	115373	63595	444184	*87457
Agriculture, forestry, fishing	216	..	..	14125	2207	5618	..	3492	310	25967	5618
Commerce, public services	431	483	..	930	46314	3593	..	57701	20807	130258	2334
Households	25512	4342	..	2270	78664	*78825	..	54180	42478	286271	*79505
Other consumers	..	..	..	432	1256	..	..	..	..	1687	..
Non-energy use	26	11180	..	104956	3731	..	..	..	..	119894	..

Dem. Rep. of the Congo

Terajoules

2017	Primary coal and peat	Coal and peat products	Primary Oil	Oil Products	Natural Gas	Biofuels and waste	Nuclear	Electricity	Heat	Total energy	of which: renewables
Primary production	..	..	50675	..	11	1179530	..	34135	..	1264352	1213666
Imports	..	..	..	35413	..	..	..	2405	..	37818	..
Exports	..	..	-50675	..	..	..	..	-223	..	-50899	..
International marine bunkers	..	..	..	..	..	..	..	..	..	..	..
International aviation bunkers	..	..	..	-5160	..	..	..	..	..	-5160	..
Stock changes	..	..	..	..	..	..	..	..	..	..	..
Total energy supply	..	..	0	30253	11	1179530	..	36317	..	1246111	1213666
Statistical difference	..	..	0	-129	0	-8156	..	2686	..	-5599	25979
Transfers	..	..	..	..	..	..	..	..	..	..	..
Transformation	..	..	..	-86	-11	-190502	..	101	..	-190498	-190502
Electricity plants	..	..	..	-86	-11	*-301	..	101	..	*-297	*-301
CHP plants	..	..	..	..	..	..	..	..	..	..	..
Heat plants	..	..	..	..	..	..	..	..	..	..	..
Coke ovens	..	..	..	..	..	..	..	..	..	..	..
Briquetting plants	..	..	..	..	..	..	..	..	..	..	..
Liquefaction plants	..	..	..	..	..	..	..	..	..	..	..
Gas works	..	..	..	..	..	..	..	..	..	..	..
Blast furnaces	..	..	..	..	..	..	..	..	..	..	..
NGL plants & gas blending	..	..	..	..	..	..	..	..	..	..	..
Oil refineries	..	..	..	..	..	..	..	..	..	..	..
Other transformation	..	..	..	..	..	-190201	..	..	..	-190201	-190201
Energy industries own use	..	..	..	..	..	..	..	-2534	..	-2534	..
Losses	..	..	..	..	..	..	..	-5195	..	-5195	..
Final consumption	..	..	..	30296	..	*997184	..	26003	..	*1053483	*997184
Final energy consumption	..	..	..	30135	..	*997184	..	26003	..	*1053323	*997184
Manufacturing, const., mining	..	..	..	646	..	149982	..	16715	..	167343	149982
Iron and steel	..	..	..	..	..	..	..	58	..	58	..
Chemical and petrochemical	..	..	..	..	..	..	..	..	..	..	..
Non-ferrous metals	..	..	..	..	..	..	..	..	..	..	..
Non-metallic minerals	..	..	..	646	..	..	..	371	..	1017	..
Transport equipment	..	..	..	..	..	..	..	..	..	..	..
Machinery	..	..	..	..	..	..	..	..	..	..	..
Mining and quarrying	..	..	..	..	..	..	..	10379	..	10379	..
Food and tobacco	..	..	..	..	..	..	..	97	..	97	..
Paper, pulp and printing	..	..	..	..	..	..	..	..	..	..	..
Wood and wood products	..	..	..	..	..	..	..	..	..	..	..
Textile and leather	..	..	..	..	..	..	..	..	..	..	..
Construction	..	..	..	..	..	..	..	..	..	..	..
Industries n.e.s	..	..	..	0	..	149982	..	5810	..	155792	149982
Transport	..	..	..	29445	..	..	..	36	..	29481	..
Road	..	..	..	24930	..	..	..	..	..	24930	..
Rail	..	..	..	..	..	..	..	36	..	36	..
Domestic aviation	..	..	..	..	..	..	..	..	..	..	..
Domestic navigation	..	..	..	4515	..	..	..	..	..	4515	..
Pipeline transport	..	..	..	..	..	..	..	..	..	..	..
Transport, n.e.s	..	..	..	..	..	..	..	..	..	..	..
Other	..	..	..	44	..	*847202	..	9252	..	*856498	*847202
Agriculture, forestry, fishing	..	..	..	..	..	8157	..	..	..	8157	8157
Commerce, public services	..	..	..	..	..	..	..	3604	..	3604	..
Households	..	..	..	44	..	*839045	..	5648	..	*844738	*839045
Other consumers	..	..	..	..	..	..	..	..	..	..	..
Non-energy use	..	..	..	161	..	..	..	..	..	161	..

Dem. Rep. of the Congo

Terajoules

2018	Primary coal and peat	Coal and peat products	Primary Oil	Oil Products	Natural Gas	Biofuels and waste	Nuclear	Electricity	Heat	Total energy	of which: renewables
Primary production	..	..	56428	..	14	1076851	..	39926	..	1173219	1116778
Imports	..	..	..	35330	..	..	..	2876	..	38206	..
Exports	..	..	-56428	..	..	..	..	-252	..	-56680	..
International marine bunkers	..	..	..	..	..	..	..	..	..	..	..
International aviation bunkers	..	..	..	-5909	..	..	..	..	..	-5909	..
Stock changes	..	..	..	..	..	..	..	..	..	..	..
Total energy supply	..	..	0	29421	14	1076851	..	42551	..	1148836	1116778
Statistical difference	..	..	0	0	0	0	..	0	..	0	39926
Transfers	..	..	..	..	..	..	..	..	..	..	..
Transformation	..	..	..	-43	-14	-403265	..	3514	..	-399808	-403265
Electricity plants	..	..	..	-43	-14	-4654	..	3514	..	-1197	-4654
CHP plants	..	..	..	..	..	..	..	..	..	..	..
Heat plants	..	..	..	..	..	..	..	..	..	..	..
Coke ovens	..	..	..	..	..	..	..	..	..	..	..
Briquetting plants	..	..	..	..	..	..	..	..	..	..	..
Liquefaction plants	..	..	..	..	..	..	..	..	..	..	..
Gas works	..	..	..	..	..	..	..	..	..	..	..
Blast furnaces	..	..	..	..	..	..	..	..	..	..	..
NGL plants & gas blending	..	..	..	..	..	..	..	..	..	..	..
Oil refineries	..	..	..	..	..	..	..	..	..	..	..
Other transformation	..	..	..	..	..	-398611	..	..	..	-398611	-398611
Energy industries own use	..	..	..	..	..	..	..	-5543	..	-5543	..
Losses	..	..	..	..	..	..	..	-4648	..	-4648	..
Final consumption	..	..	..	29378	..	673586	..	35874	..	738837	673586
Final energy consumption	..	..	..	29217	..	673586	..	35874	..	738677	673586
Manufacturing, const., mining	..	..	..	566	..	104	..	26586	..	27256	104
Iron and steel	..	..	..	..	..	..	..	58	..	58	..
Chemical and petrochemical	..	..	..	..	..	..	..	4	..	4	..
Non-ferrous metals	..	..	..	..	..	..	..	..	..	..	..
Non-metallic minerals	..	..	..	566	..	..	..	464	..	1030	..
Transport equipment	..	..	..	..	..	..	..	..	..	..	..
Machinery	..	..	..	..	..	..	..	..	..	..	..
Mining and quarrying	..	..	..	..	..	..	..	21197	..	21197	..
Food and tobacco	..	..	..	..	..	..	..	259	..	259	..
Paper, pulp and printing	..	..	..	..	..	..	..	..	..	..	..
Wood and wood products	..	..	..	..	..	..	..	..	..	..	..
Textile and leather	..	..	..	..	..	4	..	4	..	8	4
Construction	..	..	..	..	..	..	..	..	..	..	..
Industries n.e.s	..	..	..	0	..	100	..	4601	..	4701	100
Transport	..	..	..	28594	..	..	..	36	..	28630	..
Road	..	..	..	24380	..	..	..	..	..	24380	..
Rail	..	..	..	..	..	..	..	36	..	36	..
Domestic aviation	..	..	..	..	..	..	..	..	..	..	..
Domestic navigation	..	..	..	4214	..	..	..	..	..	4214	..
Pipeline transport	..	..	..	..	..	..	..	..	..	..	..
Transport, n.e.s	..	..	..	..	..	..	..	..	..	..	..
Other	..	..	..	57	..	673481	..	9252	..	682790	673481
Agriculture, forestry, fishing	..	..	..	..	..	..	..	..	..	..	..
Commerce, public services	..	..	..	..	..	..	..	3604	..	3604	..
Households	..	..	..	57	..	673481	..	5648	..	679187	673481
Other consumers	..	..	..	..	..	..	..	..	..	..	..
Non-energy use	..	..	..	161	..	..	..	..	..	161	..

Denmark

Terajoules

2017	Primary coal and peat	Coal and peat products	Primary Oil	Oil Products	Natural Gas	Biofuels and waste	Nuclear	Electricity	Heat	Total energy	of which: renewables
Primary production	..	..	289691	..	182142	119160	..	55976	2515	649484	159847
Imports	74790	352	207389	239952	19445	*77401	..	54785	124	674239	*75380
Exports	..	0	-176214	-285706	-84036	-1730	..	-38358	..	-586044	-1730
International marine bunkers	..	..	..	-22466	..	..	..	..	..	-22466	..
International aviation bunkers	..	..	..	-41586	..	..	..	..	..	-41586	..
Stock changes	-10292	..	1376	41454	-2528	-512	..	..	..	29498	-512
Total energy supply	64499	352	322242	-68353	115024	194320	..	72403	2639	703125	232985
Statistical difference	-900	59	-688	2782	-1148	*-147	..	68	20	45	*57671
Transfers	..	..	54955	-54522	..	..	..	..	..	433	..
Transformation	-60679	..	-377885	374340	-28026	*-129382	..	54749	133754	-33129	*-110691
Electricity plants	..	..	..	-293	..	-15	..	86	..	-222	-15
CHP plants	-60557	..	..	-2728	-19562	*-101028	..	55688	92284	-35903	*-83667
Heat plants	-122	..	..	-592	-13595	*-23209	..	-1026	41470	2927	*-21880
Coke ovens	..	..	..	..	..	..	..	..	..	..	..
Briquetting plants	..	..	..	..	..	..	..	..	..	..	..
Liquefaction plants	..	..	..	..	..	..	..	..	..	..	..
Gas works	..	..	..	..	..	..	..	..	..	..	..
Blast furnaces	..	..	..	..	..	..	..	..	..	..	..
NGL plants & gas blending	..	..	..	..	5130	-5130	..	..	..	0	-5130
Oil refineries	..	..	-377885	377953	..	..	..	..	..	68	..
Other transformation	..	..	..	..	..	..	..	..	..	..	..
Energy industries own use	..	..	..	-14457	-22769	-115	..	-8406	-1292	-47039	-115
Losses	..	..	..	..	-138	..	..	-6041	-27019	-33198	..
Final consumption	4720	293	..	234227	65239	*64970	..	112637	108062	590148	*64508
Final energy consumption	4720	293	..	223936	65239	*64970	..	112637	108062	579857	*64508
Manufacturing, const., mining	4306	293	..	18708	28794	*8399	..	30863	3256	94619	*7653
Iron and steel	..	..	..	90	1886	0	..	1519	168	3663	0
Chemical and petrochemical	511	..	..	331	4929	*403	..	5526	612	12312	*403
Non-ferrous metals	..	..	..	..	..	..	..	..	..	..	..
Non-metallic minerals	2409	205	..	8978	4902	1543	..	2884	319	21239	815
Transport equipment	..	..	..	43	176	*9	..	317	35	579	*9
Machinery	..	..	..	571	2170	*502	..	4824	534	8601	*490
Mining and quarrying	122	..	..	687	864	*1060	..	331	37	3101	*1060
Food and tobacco	1265	88	..	2184	11530	154	..	8680	961	24861	154
Paper, pulp and printing	..	..	..	138	1029	394	..	1148	127	2836	391
Wood and wood products	..	..	..	83	92	*3489	..	763	85	*4512	*3488
Textile and leather	..	..	..	..	220	*28	..	403	44	695	*28
Construction	..	..	..	5517	343	..	..	1451	..	7311	..
Industries n.e.s	0	0	..	86	654	*817	..	3017	334	4908	*815
Transport	..	..	..	175737	267	8888	..	1465	..	186357	8888
Road	..	..	..	162039	267	8888	..	..	..	171195	8888
Rail	..	..	..	3311	..	..	..	1465	..	4776	..
Domestic aviation	..	..	..	1279	..	..	..	..	..	1279	..
Domestic navigation	..	..	..	6278	..	..	..	..	..	6278	..
Pipeline transport	..	..	..	..	..	..	..	..	..	..	..
Transport, n.e.s	..	..	..	2829	..	..	..	..	..	2829	..
Other	414	..	..	29491	36178	*47683	..	80309	104806	298881	*47968
Agriculture, forestry, fishing	414	..	..	17824	1802	*2291	..	6332	1579	30241	*2291
Commerce, public services	..	..	..	2444	8089	*2342	..	38466	32626	83967	*2120
Households	..	..	..	9224	26047	*43050	..	35510	70601	184432	*43557
Other consumers	..	..	..	..	240	..	..	..	..	240	..
Non-energy use	..	..	..	10291	..	..	..	..	..	10291	..

Denmark

Terajoules

2018	Primary coal and peat	Coal and peat products	Primary Oil	Oil Products	Natural Gas	Biofuels and waste	Nuclear	Electricity	Heat	Total energy	of which: renewables
Primary production	..	..	243638	..	155071	121409	..	53521	2875	576515	161025
Imports	73425	410	202702	257722	14522	*77690	..	56282	114	682868	*75252
Exports	-453	..	-120787	-276960	-57669	-2061	..	-37472	..	-495402	-2061
International marine bunkers	..	..	..	-24919	..	..	..	..	..	-24919	..
International aviation bunkers	..	..	..	-43527	..	..	..	..	..	-43527	..
Stock changes	-1439	-59	-1075	18763	6	64	..	..	..	16261	64
Total energy supply	71534	352	324478	-68920	111930	197102	..	72331	2989	711796	234279
Statistical difference	-2158	-29	-1204	3338	-894	*163	..	65	22	-697	*55900
Transfers	..	..	67381	-66465	..	..	..	..	..	916	..
Transformation	-68443	..	-393063	388005	-26081	*-129489	..	54778	132690	-41603	*-111421
Electricity plants	..	..	..	-169	..	-12	..	50	..	-131	-12
CHP plants	-68310	..	..	-2710	-19297	*-101598	..	55786	89367	-46762	*-84836
Heat plants	-133	..	..	-807	-13845	*-20819	..	-1058	43323	6661	*-19513
Coke ovens	..	..	..	..	..	..	..	..	..	..	..
Briquetting plants	..	..	..	..	..	..	..	..	..	..	..
Liquefaction plants	..	..	..	..	..	..	..	..	..	..	..
Gas works	..	..	..	..	..	..	..	..	..	..	..
Blast furnaces	..	..	..	..	..	..	..	..	..	..	..
NGL plants & gas blending	..	..	..	..	7061	-7060	..	..	..	1	-7060
Oil refineries	..	..	-393063	391691	..	..	..	..	..	-1371	..
Other transformation	..	..	..	..	..	..	..	..	..	..	..
Energy industries own use	..	..	..	-13778	-20987	-119	..	-7211	-1474	-43569	-119
Losses	..	..	..	..	-136	..	..	-7931	-26838	-34905	..
Final consumption	5248	381	..	235505	65620	*67330	..	111902	107345	593332	*66838
Final energy consumption	5248	381	..	225334	65620	*67330	..	111902	107345	583161	*66838
Manufacturing, const., mining	4875	381	..	17398	29965	*9539	..	30866	3256	96280	*8793
Iron and steel	..	..	..	90	1967	..	..	1519	168	3744	..
Chemical and petrochemical	586	..	..	250	5134	*543	..	5522	612	12647	*543
Non-ferrous metals	..	..	..	..	..	..	..	..	..	..	..
Non-metallic minerals	2717	264	..	7953	5113	1555	..	2884	319	20805	827
Transport equipment	..	..	..	43	183	*12	..	317	35	590	*12
Machinery	..	..	..	660	2263	*640	..	4820	534	8917	*628
Mining and quarrying	133	..	..	819	901	*1375	..	331	37	3596	*1375
Food and tobacco	1439	117	..	1543	12024	368	..	8672	961	25124	368
Paper, pulp and printing	..	..	..	138	1073	*397	..	1148	127	2883	*394
Wood and wood products	..	..	..	126	95	*3735	..	763	85	*4805	*3734
Textile and leather	..	..	..	..	230	*31	..	403	44	708	*31
Construction	..	..	..	5647	301	..	..	1472	..	7420	..
Industries n.e.s	0	0	..	129	683	*883	..	3013	334	5042	*882
Transport	..	..	..	178277	329	8824	..	1451	..	188881	8824
Road	..	..	..	165933	329	8824	..	..	..	175086	8824
Rail	..	..	..	3053	..	..	..	1451	..	4504	..
Domestic aviation	..	..	..	1235	..	..	..	..	..	1235	..
Domestic navigation	..	..	..	6450	..	..	..	..	..	6450	..
Pipeline transport	..	..	..	..	..	..	..	..	..	..	..
Transport, n.e.s	..	..	..	1606	..	..	..	..	..	1606	..
Other	373	..	..	29660	35326	*48967	..	79585	104089	298000	*49221
Agriculture, forestry, fishing	373	..	..	17731	1529	*2280	..	6264	1579	29756	*2280
Commerce, public services	..	..	..	2577	7839	*2672	..	38138	32398	83624	*2413
Households	..	..	..	9353	25752	*44015	..	35183	70112	184414	*44528
Other consumers	..	..	..	..	206	..	..	..	..	206	..
Non-energy use	..	..	..	10171	..	..	..	..	..	10171	..

Djibouti

Terajoules

	All Coal	All Oil	Natural Gas	Primary biofuels / Waste	Charcoal	Electricity	Total energy	of which: renewables
2017								
Primary production	..	..	..	3605	..	..	3605	3605
Imports	..	9582	..	1	0	1830	11413	1
Exports	..	..	..	-12	-422	..	-433	-433
International marine bunkers	..	*-794	..	..	..	..	*-794	..
International aviation bunkers	..	*-3563	..	..	..	..	*-3563	..
Stock changes	..	*-242	..	..	..	..	*-242	..
Total energy supply	..	4984	..	3594	-421	1830	9985	3172
Statistical Difference	..	*-13	..	0	0	*-27	-40	0
Transfers	..	..	..	..	..	..	..	..
Transformation	..	*-602	..	*-2923	1574	*211	*-1740	*-1349
Electricity plants	..	*-602	..	..	..	*211	*-391	..
Charcoal plants	..	..	..	*-2923	1574	..	*-1349	*-1349
Other transformation	..	0	..	0	..	..	0	0
Energy industries own use	..	..	..	..	..	0	0	..
Losses	..	..	..	..	..	*-408	*-408	..
Final consumption	..	*4394	..	*671	*1153	*1660	*7878	*1823
Final energy consumption	..	*4073	..	*671	*1153	*1660	*7556	*1823
Manufacturing, const., mining	..	*322	..	..	..	..	*322	..
Transport	..	*1906	..	..	..	..	*1906	..
Road	..	*1906	..	..	..	..	*1906	..
Domestic aviation	..	..	..	..	..	..	..	..
Domestic navigation	..	..	..	..	..	..	..	..
Other transport	..	..	..	..	..	..	..	..
Other	..	*1845	..	*671	*1153	*1660	*5329	*1823
Agriculture, forestry, fishing	..	..	..	..	..	..	..	..
Commerce and public services	..	*378	..	..	..	*664	*1042	..
Households	..	*607	..	*671	*1153	*996	*3426	*1823
Other consumers	..	*860	..	..	..	..	*860	..
Non-energy use	..	*322	..	..	..	..	*322	..
2018								
Primary production	..	..	..	3650	..	..	3650	3650
Imports	..	*9513	..	..	0	1894	*11407	0
Exports	..	..	..	..	-150	..	-150	-150
International marine bunkers	..	*-794	..	..	..	..	*-794	..
International aviation bunkers	..	*-3563	..	..	..	..	*-3563	..
Stock changes	..	*-430	..	..	..	..	*-430	..
Total energy supply	..	*4726	..	3650	-150	1894	*10120	3501
Statistical Difference	..	0	..	0	0	0	0	0
Transfers	..	..	..	..	..	..	..	..
Transformation	..	*-645	..	*-2963	1595	*209	*-1804	*-1368
Electricity plants	..	*-645	..	..	..	*209	*-436	..
Charcoal plants	..	..	..	*-2963	1595	..	*-1368	*-1368
Other transformation	..	0	..	0	..	..	0	0
Energy industries own use	..	..	..	..	..	0	0	..
Losses	..	..	..	..	..	*-414	*-414	..
Final consumption	..	*4081	..	*688	*1445	*1688	*7902	*2133
Final energy consumption	..	*3840	..	*688	*1445	*1688	*7661	*2133
Manufacturing, const., mining	..	*322	..	..	..	..	*322	..
Transport	..	*1888	..	..	..	..	*1888	..
Road	..	*1888	..	..	..	..	*1888	..
Domestic aviation	..	..	..	..	..	..	..	..
Domestic navigation	..	..	..	..	..	..	..	..
Other transport	..	..	..	..	..	..	..	..
Other	..	*1630	..	*688	*1445	*1688	*5451	*2133
Agriculture, forestry, fishing	..	..	..	..	..	..	..	..
Commerce and public services	..	*378	..	..	..	*684	*1062	..
Households	..	*607	..	*688	*1445	*1004	*3744	*2133
Other consumers	..	*645	..	..	..	..	*645	..
Non-energy use	..	*241	..	..	..	..	*241	..

Dominica

Terajoules

	All Coal	All Oil	Natural Gas	Primary biofuels / Waste	Charcoal	Electricity	Total energy	of which: renewables
2017								
Primary production	..	..	..	68	..	98	166	166
Imports	..	*2407	..	0	1	..	*2408	1
Exports	..	..	..	0	-1	..	-1	-1
International marine bunkers	..	*-40	..	..	..	..	*-40	..
International aviation bunkers	..	*-27	..	..	..	..	*-27	..
Stock changes	..	*-67	..	..	..	..	*-67	..
Total energy supply	..	*2272	..	68	-1	98	*2437	165
Statistical Difference	..	*-4	..	0	0	0	*-4	98
Transfers	..	..	..	..	..	..	..	..
Transformation	..	*-1180	..	*-13	7	369	*-817	*-6
Electricity plants	..	*-1180	..	..	..	369	*-811	..
Charcoal plants	..	..	..	*-13	7	..	*-6	*-6
Other transformation	..	0	..	0	..	..	0	0
Energy industries own use	..	..	..	..	..	-14	-14	..
Losses	..	*-13	..	..	..	-18	-31	..
Final consumption	..	*1083	..	*55	*6	*435	*1580	*62
Final energy consumption	..	*1083	..	*55	*6	*435	*1580	*62
Manufacturing, const., mining	..	*139	..	..	..	*76	*216	..
Transport	..	*746	..	..	..	..	*746	..
Road	..	*746	..	..	..	..	*746	..
Domestic aviation	..	..	..	..	..	..	..	..
Domestic navigation	..	..	..	..	..	..	..	..
Other transport	..	..	..	..	..	..	..	..
Other	..	*198	..	*55	*6	*359	*618	*62
Agriculture, forestry, fishing	..	*49	..	..	..	*13	*61	..
Commerce and public services	..	*46	..	..	..	*211	*256	..
Households	..	*102	..	*55	*6	124	*287	*62
Other consumers	..	*2	..	..	..	*11	*14	..
Non-energy use	..	..	..	..	..	..	..	..
2018								
Primary production	..	..	..	68	..	87	155	155
Imports	..	*2402	..	0	1	..	*2403	1
Exports	..	..	..	0	-1	..	-1	-1
International marine bunkers	..	*-41	..	..	..	..	*-41	..
International aviation bunkers	..	*-27	..	..	..	..	*-27	..
Stock changes	..	*-59	..	..	..	..	*-59	..
Total energy supply	..	*2275	..	68	-1	87	*2429	154
Statistical Difference	..	0	..	0	0	0	0	87
Transfers	..	..	..	..	..	..	..	..
Transformation	..	*-964	..	*-13	7	*307	*-662	*-6
Electricity plants	..	*-964	..	..	..	*307	*-656	..
Charcoal plants	..	..	..	*-13	7	..	*-6	*-6
Other transformation	..	0	..	0	..	..	0	0
Energy industries own use	..	..	..	..	..	-12	-12	..
Losses	..	*-9	..	..	..	-22	-31	..
Final consumption	..	*1303	..	*55	*6	*361	*1725	*61
Final energy consumption	..	*1303	..	*55	*6	*361	*1725	*61
Manufacturing, const., mining	..	*203	..	..	..	*77	*281	..
Transport	..	*849	..	..	..	..	*849	..
Road	..	*849	..	..	..	..	*849	..
Domestic aviation	..	..	..	..	..	..	..	..
Domestic navigation	..	..	..	..	..	..	..	..
Other transport	..	..	..	..	..	..	..	..
Other	..	*250	..	*55	*6	*283	*595	*61
Agriculture, forestry, fishing	..	*80	..	..	..	*13	*92	..
Commerce and public services	..	*65	..	..	..	*176	*242	..
Households	..	*103	..	*55	*6	84	*248	*61
Other consumers	..	*2	..	..	..	10	13	..
Non-energy use	..	..	..	..	..	..	..	..

Dominican Republic

Terajoules

2017	Primary coal and peat	Coal and peat products	Primary Oil	Oil Products	Natural Gas	Biofuels and waste	Nuclear	Electricity	Heat	Total energy	of which: renewables
Primary production	..	..	..	..	..	22503	..	9817	..	32319	32319
Imports	32379	..	41881	221215	41496	..	..	..	..	336972	..
Exports	..	..	..	..	..	-56	..	..	..	-56	-56
International marine bunkers	..	..	..	..	-1334	..	..	..	..	-1334	..
International aviation bunkers	..	..	..	-23770	..	..	..	..	..	-23770	..
Stock changes	137	..	-1840	-1290	-72	..	..	..	..	-3066	..
Total energy supply	32516	..	40041	196155	40090	22447	..	9817	..	341065	32263
Statistical difference	1903	..	-360	945	0	-56	..	42	..	2474	9761
Transfers	..	..	..	..	..	..	..	..	..	..	..
Transformation	-26458	..	-40401	-30951	-36190	-3150	..	58714	..	-78436	-3150
Electricity plants	-26458	..	..	-69480	-36190	-2256	..	58714	..	-75671	-2256
CHP plants	..	..	..	..	..	..	..	..	..	..	..
Heat plants	..	..	..	..	..	..	..	..	..	..	..
Coke ovens	..	..	..	..	..	..	..	..	..	..	..
Briquetting plants	..	..	..	..	..	..	..	..	..	..	..
Liquefaction plants	..	..	..	..	..	..	..	..	..	..	..
Gas works	..	..	..	..	..	..	..	..	..	..	..
Blast furnaces	..	..	..	..	..	..	..	..	..	..	..
NGL plants & gas blending	..	..	..	..	..	..	..	..	..	..	..
Oil refineries	..	..	-40401	38529	..	..	..	..	..	-1872	..
Other transformation	..	..	..	..	..	-894	..	..	..	-894	-894
Energy industries own use	..	..	..	-1704	..	..	..	-2395	..	-4098	..
Losses	-475	..	..	..	..	..	..	-8902	..	-9377	..
Final consumption	3681	..	..	162556	3900	19353	..	57191	..	246680	19353
Final energy consumption	3681	..	..	149357	3900	19353	..	57191	..	233481	19353
Manufacturing, const., mining	3681	..	..	28550	3301	9682	..	20202	..	65416	9682
Iron and steel	..	..	..	..	..	..	..	..	..	..	..
Chemical and petrochemical	..	..	..	1247	647	..	..	2470	..	4364	..
Non-ferrous metals	..	..	..	..	..	..	..	..	..	..	..
Non-metallic minerals	..	..	..	..	..	..	..	..	..	..	..
Transport equipment	..	..	..	..	..	..	..	..	..	..	..
Machinery	..	..	..	..	..	..	..	..	..	..	..
Mining and quarrying	2837	..	..	14208	380	..	..	5827	..	23252	..
Food and tobacco	843	..	..	6325	1166	9452	..	5843	..	23630	9452
Paper, pulp and printing	..	..	..	1392	..	..	..	839	..	2230	..
Wood and wood products	..	..	..	..	..	..	..	..	..	..	..
Textile and leather	..	..	..	3122	985	..	..	4123	..	8230	..
Construction	..	..	..	1722	..	..	..	..	..	1722	..
Industries n.e.s	0	..	..	535	123	229	..	1099	..	1987	229
Transport	..	..	..	94048	599	..	..	182	..	94829	..
Road	..	..	..	93695	599	..	..	..	..	94294	..
Rail	..	..	..	..	..	..	..	182	..	182	..
Domestic aviation	..	..	..	353	..	..	..	..	..	353	..
Domestic navigation	..	..	..	..	..	..	..	..	..	..	..
Pipeline transport	..	..	..	..	..	..	..	..	..	..	..
Transport, n.e.s	..	..	..	..	..	..	..	..	..	..	..
Other	..	..	..	26759	..	9671	..	36807	..	73237	9671
Agriculture, forestry, fishing	..	..	..	2696	..	..	..	3704	..	6401	..
Commerce, public services	..	..	..	3650	..	45	..	14854	..	18549	45
Households	..	..	..	20413	..	9626	..	18249	..	48288	9626
Other consumers	..	..	..	..	..	..	..	..	..	..	..
Non-energy use	..	..	..	13199	..	..	..	..	..	13199	..

Dominican Republic

Terajoules

2018	Primary coal and peat	Coal and peat products	Primary Oil	Oil Products	Natural Gas	Biofuels and waste	Nuclear	Electricity	Heat	Total energy	of which: renewables
Primary production	..	..	..	..	..	22853	..	9027	..	31880	31880
Imports	32578	..	52681	229444	40526	..	..	..	..	355229	..
Exports	..	..	..	..	..	-55	..	..	..	-55	-55
International marine bunkers	..	..	..	..	-1081	..	..	..	..	-1081	..
International aviation bunkers	..	..	..	-23971	..	..	..	..	..	-23971	..
Stock changes	-627	..	964	868	523	..	..	..	..	1728	..
Total energy supply	31950	..	53646	206341	39968	22798	..	9027	..	363731	31825
Statistical difference	2513	..	-463	1923	0	-53	..	0	..	3920	8974
Transfers	..	..	..	..	..	..	..	..	..	..	..
Transformation	-25143	..	-54108	-33958	-35797	-3882	..	61717	..	-91171	-3882
Electricity plants	-25143	..	..	-85642	-35797	-2950	..	61717	..	-87814	-2950
CHP plants	..	..	..	..	..	..	..	..	..	..	..
Heat plants	..	..	..	..	..	..	..	..	..	..	..
Coke ovens	..	..	..	..	..	..	..	..	..	..	..
Briquetting plants	..	..	..	..	..	..	..	..	..	..	..
Liquefaction plants	..	..	..	..	..	..	..	..	..	..	..
Gas works	..	..	..	..	..	..	..	..	..	..	..
Blast furnaces	..	..	..	..	..	..	..	..	..	..	..
NGL plants & gas blending	..	..	..	..	..	..	..	..	..	..	..
Oil refineries	..	..	-54108	51684	..	..	..	..	..	-2424	..
Other transformation	..	..	..	..	..	-934	..	..	..	-934	-934
Energy industries own use	..	..	..	-2279	..	..	..	-2494	..	-4773	..
Losses	-727	..	..	..	..	..	..	-9176	..	-9903	..
Final consumption	3568	..	..	168181	4172	18969	..	59073	..	253964	18969
Final energy consumption	3568	..	..	153706	4172	18969	..	59073	..	239488	18969
Manufacturing, const., mining	3568	..	..	23792	3520	9117	..	20842	..	60839	9117
Iron and steel	..	..	..	..	..	..	..	..	..	..	..
Chemical and petrochemical	..	..	..	1258	686	..	..	2538	..	4482	..
Non-ferrous metals	..	..	..	..	..	..	..	..	..	..	..
Non-metallic minerals	..	..	..	..	..	..	..	..	..	..	..
Transport equipment	..	..	..	..	..	..	..	..	..	..	..
Machinery	..	..	..	..	..	..	..	..	..	..	..
Mining and quarrying	2932	..	..	13634	402	..	..	5988	..	22957	..
Food and tobacco	636	..	..	3858	1235	8874	..	6005	..	20607	8874
Paper, pulp and printing	..	..	..	259	..	..	..	862	..	1120	..
Wood and wood products	..	..	..	..	..	..	..	..	..	..	..
Textile and leather	..	..	..	2466	1066	..	..	4319	..	7851	..
Construction	..	..	..	1754	..	..	..	..	..	1754	..
Industries n.e.s	0	..	..	563	130	244	..	1130	..	2067	244
Transport	..	..	..	102615	652	..	..	206	..	103472	..
Road	..	..	..	101580	652	..	..	..	..	102232	..
Rail	..	..	..	..	..	..	..	206	..	206	..
Domestic aviation	..	..	..	1035	..	..	..	..	..	1035	..
Domestic navigation	..	..	..	..	..	..	..	..	..	..	..
Pipeline transport	..	..	..	..	..	..	..	..	..	..	..
Transport, n.e.s	..	..	..	..	..	..	..	..	..	..	..
Other	..	..	..	27299	..	9852	..	38026	..	75177	9852
Agriculture, forestry, fishing	..	..	..	2937	..	..	..	3937	..	6875	..
Commerce, public services	..	..	..	3741	..	45	..	15483	..	19269	45
Households	..	..	..	20621	..	9807	..	18606	..	49034	9807
Other consumers	..	..	..	..	..	..	..	..	..	..	..
Non-energy use	..	..	..	14476	..	..	..	..	..	14476	..

Ecuador

Terajoules

2017	Primary coal and peat	Coal and peat products	Primary Oil	Oil Products	Natural Gas	Biofuels and waste	Nuclear	Electricity	Heat	Total energy	of which: renewables
Primary production	..	..	1136098	..	28136	25866	..	72720	*102	1262922	98688
Imports	..	..	126	253403	..	..	..	67	..	253595	..
Exports	..	..	-776226	-125470	..	..	..	-762	..	-902458	..
International marine bunkers	..	..	..	-15168	..	..	..	..	..	-15168	..
International aviation bunkers	..	..	..	-10922	..	..	..	..	..	-10922	..
Stock changes	..	..	23608	2447	..	..	..	..	..	26055	..
Total energy supply	..	..	383605	104290	28136	25866	..	72024	*102	614023	98688
Statistical difference	..	..	2627	3883	32	0	..	-115	0	6427	72720
Transfers	..	..	..	..	..	..	..	..	..	..	..
Transformation	..	..	-374941	296275	-26185	-5033	..	28198	..	-81687	-5033
Electricity plants	..	..	-14061	-39185	-20836	-1958	..	26547	..	-49492	-1958
CHP plants	..	..	..	..	..	-3075	..	1651	..	-1424	-3075
Heat plants	..	..	..	..	..	..	..	..	..	..	..
Coke ovens	..	..	..	..	..	..	..	..	..	..	..
Briquetting plants	..	..	..	..	..	..	..	..	..	..	..
Liquefaction plants	..	..	..	..	..	..	..	..	..	..	..
Gas works	..	..	..	..	-5349	..	..	..	..	-5349	..
Blast furnaces	..	..	..	..	..	..	..	..	..	..	..
NGL plants & gas blending	..	..	-7690	8185	..	..	..	..	..	494	..
Oil refineries	..	..	-353191	326270	..	..	..	..	..	-26921	..
Other transformation	..	..	..	1005	..	..	..	..	..	1005	..
Energy industries own use	..	..	-6037	-15917	..	..	..	-1379	..	-23333	..
Losses	..	..	..	..	..	..	..	-12658	..	-12658	..
Final consumption	..	..	..	380765	1919	20832	..	86300	*102	489919	20934
Final energy consumption	..	..	..	380765	1919	20832	..	86300	*102	489919	20934
Manufacturing, const., mining	..	..	..	24026	1901	11636	..	34088	..	71651	11636
Iron and steel	..	..	..	..	..	..	..	..	..	..	..
Chemical and petrochemical	..	..	..	..	..	..	..	..	..	..	..
Non-ferrous metals	..	..	..	..	..	..	..	..	..	..	..
Non-metallic minerals	..	..	..	..	..	..	..	..	..	..	..
Transport equipment	..	..	..	..	..	..	..	..	..	..	..
Machinery	..	..	..	..	..	..	..	..	..	..	..
Mining and quarrying	..	..	..	..	..	..	..	..	..	..	..
Food and tobacco	..	..	..	..	..	..	..	..	..	..	..
Paper, pulp and printing	..	..	..	..	..	..	..	..	..	..	..
Wood and wood products	..	..	..	..	..	..	..	..	..	..	..
Textile and leather	..	..	..	..	..	..	..	..	..	..	..
Construction	..	..	..	..	..	..	..	..	..	..	..
Industries n.e.s	..	..	..	24026	1901	11636	..	34088	..	71651	11636
Transport	..	..	..	261094	..	817	..	36	..	261947	817
Road	..	..	..	244642	..	817	..	36	..	245495	817
Rail	..	..	..	12198	..	..	..	..	..	12198	..
Domestic aviation	..	..	..	3832	..	..	..	..	..	3832	..
Domestic navigation	..	..	..	423	..	..	..	..	..	423	..
Pipeline transport	..	..	..	..	..	..	..	..	..	..	..
Transport, n.e.s	..	..	..	..	..	..	..	..	..	..	..
Other	..	..	..	95645	18	8379	..	52176	*102	156320	8481
Agriculture, forestry, fishing	..	..	..	5462	..	..	..	..	..	5462	..
Commerce, public services	..	..	..	15730	..	..	..	18203	*102	34035	*102
Households	..	..	..	36060	18	8379	..	26273	..	70730	8379
Other consumers	..	..	..	38392	..	..	..	7700	..	46093	..
Non-energy use	..	..	..	..	..	..	..	..	..	..	..

Ecuador

Terajoules

	Primary coal and peat	Coal and peat products	Primary Oil	Oil Products	Natural Gas	Biofuels and waste	Nuclear	Electricity	Heat	Total energy	of which: renewables
2018											
Primary production	..	..	1115480	..	25696	23939	..	74867	*102	1240084	98908
Imports	..	..	..	269001	..	..	..	..	..	269001	..
Exports	..	..	-762209	-126626	..	..	..	..	..	-888835	..
International marine bunkers	..	..	..	-29476	..	..	..	..	..	-29476	..
International aviation bunkers	..	..	..	-11061	..	..	..	..	..	-11061	..
Stock changes	..	..	16868	-862	..	..	..	..	..	16006	..
Total energy supply	..	..	370139	100977	25696	23939	..	74867	*102	595721	98908
Statistical difference	..	..	-19412	9514	833	0	..	470	0	-8595	74867
Transfers	..	..	..	..	..	..	..	..	..	..	..
Transformation	..	..	-383379	309405	-23076	-4876	..	30246	..	-71679	-4876
Electricity plants	..	..	-15659	-49063	-17900	-2146	..	28869	..	-55898	-2146
CHP plants	..	..	..	..	..	-2730	..	1541	..	-1189	-2730
Heat plants	..	..	..	..	..	..	..	..	..	..	..
Coke ovens	..	..	..	..	..	..	..	..	..	..	..
Briquetting plants	..	..	..	..	..	..	..	..	..	..	..
Liquefaction plants	..	..	..	..	..	..	..	..	..	..	..
Gas works	..	..	..	..	-5176	..	..	..	..	-5176	..
Blast furnaces	..	..	..	..	..	..	..	..	..	..	..
NGL plants & gas blending	..	..	-5522	9989		..	..	..	..	4468	..
Oil refineries	..	..	-362198	346760	..	..	..	..	..	-15438	..
Other transformation	..	..	..	1718	..	..	..	..	..	1718	..
Energy industries own use	..	..	-6172	-16814	..	..	..	-1328	..	-24314	..
Losses	..	..	..	..	..	..	..	-13644	..	-13644	..
Final consumption	..	..	..	384054	1788	19064	..	89670	*102	494678	19166
Final energy consumption	..	..	..	384054	1788	19064	..	89670	*102	494678	19166
Manufacturing, const., mining	..	..	..	33409	1768	10259	..	38011	..	83447	10259
Iron and steel	..	..	..	..	..	..	..	..	..	..	..
Chemical and petrochemical	..	..	..	..	..	..	..	..	..	..	..
Non-ferrous metals	..	..	..	..	..	..	..	..	..	..	..
Non-metallic minerals	..	..	..	..	..	..	..	..	..	..	..
Transport equipment	..	..	..	..	..	..	..	..	..	..	..
Machinery	..	..	..	..	..	..	..	..	..	..	..
Mining and quarrying	..	..	..	..	..	..	..	..	..	..	..
Food and tobacco	..	..	..	..	..	..	..	..	..	..	..
Paper, pulp and printing	..	..	..	..	..	..	..	..	..	..	..
Wood and wood products	..	..	..	..	..	..	..	..	..	..	..
Textile and leather	..	..	..	..	..	..	..	..	..	..	..
Construction	..	..	..	..	..	..	..	..	..	..	..
Industries n.e.s	..	..	..	33409	1768	10259	..	38011	..	83447	10259
Transport	..	..	..	250307	..	717	..	39	..	251063	717
Road	..	..	..	234467	..	717	..	39	..	235223	717
Rail	..	..	..	11331	..	..	..	..	..	11331	..
Domestic aviation	..	..	..	4094	..	..	..	..	..	4094	..
Domestic navigation	..	..	..	415	..	..	..	..	..	415	..
Pipeline transport	..	..	..	..	..	..	..	..	..	..	..
Transport, n.e.s	..	..	..	..	..	..	..	..	..	..	..
Other	..	..	..	100338	20	8088	..	51620	*102	160168	8190
Agriculture, forestry, fishing	..	..	..	5365	..	..	..	..	..	5365	..
Commerce, public services	..	..	..	17498	..	..	..	24979	*102	42579	*102
Households	..	..	..	38804	20	8088	..	26641	..	73553	8088
Other consumers	..	..	..	38670	..	..	..	..	..	38670	..
Non-energy use	..	..	..	..	..	..	..	..	..	..	..

Egypt

Terajoules

2017	Primary coal and peat	Coal and peat products	Primary Oil	Oil Products	Natural Gas	Biofuels and waste	Nuclear	Electricity	Heat	Total energy	of which: renewables
Primary production	..	..	1341005	..	1795134	225109	..	56268	..	3417516	281377
Imports	15398	*4164	265771	624732	269856	42	..	234	..	1180196	42
Exports	..	*-4191	-405826	-63080	-81636	-652	..	-1199	..	-556584	-652
International marine bunkers	..	..	..	-7673	..	..	..	..	..	-7673	..
International aviation bunkers	..	..	..	-19536	..	..	..	..	..	-19536	..
Stock changes	..	..	..	-1656	..	..	..	..	..	-1656	..
Total energy supply	15398	*-27	1200950	532787	1983353	224499	..	55303	..	4012263	280767
Statistical difference	0	0	-42	17766	-210796	0	..	0	..	-193072	56268
Transfers	..	..	..	..	..	..	..	..	..	..	..
Transformation	-15398	*8037	-1200992	804385	-1181400	*-42235	..	646272	..	-981330	*-42235
Electricity plants	..	..	..	-267232	-1181400	*-5668	..	646272	..	-808028	*-5668
CHP plants	..	..	..	..	..	..	..	..	..	..	..
Heat plants	..	..	..	..	..	..	..	..	..	..	..
Coke ovens	-14728	*13716	..	..	..	..	..	..	..	-1013	..
Briquetting plants	..	..	..	..	..	..	..	..	..	..	..
Liquefaction plants	..	..	..	..	..	..	..	..	..	..	..
Gas works	-669	526	..	..	..	..	..	..	..	-144	..
Blast furnaces	..	*-6204	..	..	..	..	..	..	..	*-6204	..
NGL plants & gas blending	..	..	-54366	58179	..	..	..	..	..	3813	..
Oil refineries	..	..	-1146626	1013438	..	..	..	..	..	-133188	..
Other transformation	..	..	..	..	..	*-36567	..	..	..	*-36567	*-36567
Energy industries own use	..	..	..	-39499	-217781	..	..	-64451	..	-321731	..
Losses	..	..	..	..	..	..	..	*-91343	..	*-91343	..
Final consumption	..	8010	..	1279908	794968	*182264	..	545782	..	2810932	*182264
Final energy consumption	..	8010	..	1212091	581097	*182264	..	545782	..	2529243	*182264
Manufacturing, const., mining	..	7879	..	215370	320384	*56842	..	149324	..	749799	*56842
Iron and steel	..	7879	..	..	65240	..	..	..	..	73119	..
Chemical and petrochemical	..	..	..	..	..	..	..	..	..	..	..
Non-ferrous metals	..	..	..	..	..	..	..	..	..	..	..
Non-metallic minerals	..	..	..	..	..	..	..	..	..	..	..
Transport equipment	..	..	..	..	..	..	..	..	..	..	..
Machinery	..	..	..	..	..	..	..	..	..	..	..
Mining and quarrying	..	..	..	..	..	..	..	..	..	..	..
Food and tobacco	..	..	..	..	..	..	..	..	..	..	..
Paper, pulp and printing	..	..	..	..	..	..	..	..	..	..	..
Wood and wood products	..	..	..	..	..	..	..	..	..	..	..
Textile and leather	..	..	..	..	..	..	..	..	..	..	..
Construction	..	..	..	..	..	..	..	..	..	..	..
Industries n.e.s	..	0	..	215370	255144	*56842	..	149324	..	676680	*56842
Transport	..	..	..	522326	13522	..	..	1922	..	537770	..
Road	..	..	..	486083	13522	..	..	..	..	499605	..
Rail	..	..	..	..	..	..	..	1922	..	1922	..
Domestic aviation	..	..	..	25093	..	..	..	..	..	25093	..
Domestic navigation	..	..	..	11150	..	..	..	..	..	11150	..
Pipeline transport	..	..	..	..	..	..	..	..	..	..	..
Transport, n.e.s	..	..	..	..	..	..	..	..	..	..	..
Other	..	131	..	474395	247191	*125422	..	394535	..	1241674	*125422
Agriculture, forestry, fishing	..	..	..	39301	..	..	..	24275	..	63576	..
Commerce, public services	..	..	..	..	..	..	..	139410	..	139410	..
Households	..	131	..	196616	81888	..	..	230850	..	509485	..
Other consumers	..	..	..	238478	165303	*125422	..	..	..	529203	*125422
Non-energy use	..	..	..	67817	213872	..	..	..	..	281688	..

Egypt

Terajoules

2018	Primary coal and peat	Coal and peat products	Primary Oil	Oil Products	Natural Gas	Biofuels and waste	Nuclear	Electricity	Heat	Total energy	of which: renewables
Primary production	..	..	1362371	..	1718235	227880	..	55789	..	3364275	283670
Imports	11066	*3157	255365	551481	196853	77	..	292	..	1018290	77
Exports	..	..	-446646	-142408	-36176	-669	..	-1530	..	-627429	-669
International marine bunkers	..	..	..	-3769	..	..	..	..	..	-3769	..
International aviation bunkers	..	..	..	-27518	..	..	..	..	..	-27518	..
Stock changes	*-3379	1143	..	0	..	..	..	..	..	*-2236	..
Total energy supply	7687	*4300	1171090	377785	1878913	227288	..	54551	..	3721613	283077
Statistical difference	0	0	0	11360	-32	0	..	9619	..	20947	55789
Transfers	..	..	..	..	..	..	..	..	..	..	..
Transformation	-7687	3903	-1171090	930311	-1173007	*-60507	..	674428	..	-803649	*-60507
Electricity plants	..	..	..	-237555	-1173007	*-5730	..	674428	..	-741864	*-5730
CHP plants	..	..	..	..	..	..	..	..	..	..	..
Heat plants	..	..	..	..	..	..	..	..	..	..	..
Coke ovens	-7377	7783	..	..	..	..	..	..	..	406	..
Briquetting plants	..	..	..	..	..	..	..	..	..	..	..
Liquefaction plants	..	..	..	..	..	..	..	..	..	..	..
Gas works	-310	370	..	..	..	..	..	..	..	60	..
Blast furnaces	..	-4250	..	..	..	..	..	..	..	-4250	..
NGL plants & gas blending	..	..	-57416	61443	..	..	..	..	..	4027	..
Oil refineries	..	..	-1113674	1106423	..	..	..	..	..	-7251	..
Other transformation	..	..	..	..	..	*-54777	..	..	..	*-54777	*-54777
Energy industries own use	..	..	..	-10879	-32945	..	..	-43762	..	-87585	..
Losses	..	..	..	..	..	..	..	-79402	..	-79402	..
Final consumption	..	8203	..	1285858	672994	*166781	..	596196	..	2730031	*166781
Final energy consumption	..	8203	..	1181077	665256	*166781	..	596196	..	2617512	*166781
Manufacturing, const., mining	..	8115	..	206042	422026	*59274	..	157043	..	852499	*59274
Iron and steel	..	8115	..	..	58990	..	..	..	..	67104	..
Chemical and petrochemical	..	..	..	..	..	..	..	..	..	..	..
Non-ferrous metals	..	..	..	..	..	..	..	..	..	..	..
Non-metallic minerals	..	..	..	..	..	..	..	..	..	..	..
Transport equipment	..	..	..	..	..	..	..	..	..	..	..
Machinery	..	..	..	..	..	..	..	..	..	..	..
Mining and quarrying	..	..	..	..	..	..	..	..	..	..	..
Food and tobacco	..	..	..	..	..	..	..	..	..	..	..
Paper, pulp and printing	..	..	..	..	..	..	..	..	..	..	..
Wood and wood products	..	..	..	..	..	..	..	..	..	..	..
Textile and leather	..	..	..	..	..	..	..	..	..	..	..
Construction	..	..	..	..	..	..	..	..	..	..	..
Industries n.e.s	..	0	..	206042	363037	*59274	..	157043	..	785395	*59274
Transport	..	..	..	513278	12278	..	..	1156	..	526711	..
Road	..	..	..	482747	12278	..	..	..	..	495025	..
Rail	..	..	..	..	..	..	..	1156	..	1156	..
Domestic aviation	..	..	..	22491	..	..	..	..	..	22491	..
Domestic navigation	..	..	..	8040	..	..	..	..	..	8040	..
Pipeline transport	..	..	..	..	..	..	..	..	..	..	..
Transport, n.e.s	..	..	..	..	..	..	..	..	..	..	..
Other	..	88	..	461757	230952	*107507	..	437998	..	1238301	*107507
Agriculture, forestry, fishing	..	..	..	37168	..	..	..	25405	..	62573	..
Commerce, public services	..	..	..	..	..	..	..	143280	..	143280	..
Households	..	88	..	193636	73620	..	..	240512	..	507856	..
Other consumers	..	..	..	230953	157332	*107507	..	*28800	..	524592	*107507
Non-energy use	..	..	..	104781	7738	..	..	..	..	112519	..

El Salvador

Terajoules

2017	Primary coal and peat	Coal and peat products	Primary Oil	Oil Products	Natural Gas	Biofuels and waste	Nuclear	Electricity	Heat	Total energy	of which: renewables
Primary production	..	..	..	..	..	25917	..	7088	56488	89493	89493
Imports	..	28	..	95378	..	..	..	6030	..	101436	..
Exports	..	..	..	-7798	..	..	..	-323	..	-8121	..
International marine bunkers	..	..	..	..	..	..	..	..	..	..	..
International aviation bunkers	..	..	..	-7277	..	..	..	..	..	-7277	..
Stock changes	..	..	..	..	..	..	..	..	..	..	..
Total energy supply	..	28	..	80303	..	25917	..	12795	56488	175532	89493
Statistical difference	..	0	..	87	..	0	..	150	0	237	12737
Transfers	..	..	..	..	..	..	..	..	..	..	..
Transformation	..	..	..	-11554	..	-15600	..	13125	-56488	-70517	-66439
Electricity plants	..	..	..	-11554	..	-14583	..	13125	-56488	-69500	-65422
CHP plants	..	..	..	..	..	..	..	..	..	..	..
Heat plants	..	..	..	..	..	..	..	..	..	..	..
Coke ovens	..	..	..	..	..	..	..	..	..	..	..
Briquetting plants	..	..	..	..	..	..	..	..	..	..	..
Liquefaction plants	..	..	..	..	..	..	..	..	..	..	..
Gas works	..	..	..	..	..	..	..	..	..	..	..
Blast furnaces	..	..	..	..	..	..	..	..	..	..	..
NGL plants & gas blending	..	..	..	..	..	..	..	..	..	..	..
Oil refineries	..	..	..	..	..	..	..	..	..	..	..
Other transformation	..	..	..	..	..	-1017	..	..	..	-1017	-1017
Energy industries own use	..	..	..	..	..	..	..	-1280	..	-1280	..
Losses	..	..	..	..	..	..	..	*-2342	..	*-2342	..
Final consumption	..	28	..	68662	..	10317	..	22149	..	101156	10317
Final energy consumption	..	28	..	67894	..	10317	..	22149	..	100388	10317
Manufacturing, const., mining	..	28	..	15293	..	655	..	7403	..	23380	655
Iron and steel	..	28	..	..	..	..	..	..	..	28	..
Chemical and petrochemical	..	..	..	..	..	..	..	..	..	..	..
Non-ferrous metals	..	..	..	..	..	..	..	..	..	..	..
Non-metallic minerals	..	..	..	..	..	..	..	..	..	..	..
Transport equipment	..	..	..	..	..	..	..	..	..	..	..
Machinery	..	..	..	..	..	..	..	..	..	..	..
Mining and quarrying	..	..	..	..	..	..	..	..	..	..	..
Food and tobacco	..	..	..	..	..	..	..	..	..	..	..
Paper, pulp and printing	..	..	..	..	..	..	..	..	..	..	..
Wood and wood products	..	..	..	..	..	..	..	..	..	..	..
Textile and leather	..	..	..	..	..	..	..	..	..	..	..
Construction	..	..	..	..	..	..	..	2	..	2	..
Industries n.e.s	..	0	..	15293	..	655	..	7402	..	23350	655
Transport	..	..	..	46805	..	..	..	..	..	46805	..
Road	..	..	..	46805	..	..	..	..	..	46805	..
Rail	..	..	..	..	..	..	..	..	..	..	..
Domestic aviation	..	..	..	..	..	..	..	..	..	..	..
Domestic navigation	..	..	..	..	..	..	..	..	..	..	..
Pipeline transport	..	..	..	..	..	..	..	..	..	..	..
Transport, n.e.s	..	..	..	..	..	..	..	..	..	..	..
Other	..	..	..	5796	..	9662	..	14746	..	30204	9662
Agriculture, forestry, fishing	..	..	..	..	..	..	..	..	..	..	..
Commerce, public services	..	..	..	215	..	841	..	6412	..	7467	841
Households	..	..	..	5581	..	8821	..	6761	..	21163	8821
Other consumers	..	..	..	..	..	..	..	1573	..	1573	..
Non-energy use	..	..	..	767	..	..	..	..	..	767	..

El Salvador

Terajoules

2018	Primary coal and peat	Coal and peat products	Primary Oil	Oil Products	Natural Gas	Biofuels and waste	Nuclear	Electricity	Heat	Total energy	of which: renewables
Primary production	..	..	..	..	..	24555	..	6912	55631	87098	87098
Imports	..	28	..	100973	..	..	..	6567	..	107568	..
Exports	..	..	..	-7382	..	..	..	-233	..	-7615	..
International marine bunkers	..	..	..	..	..	..	..	..	..	..	..
International aviation bunkers	..	..	..	-7673	..	..	..	..	..	-7673	..
Stock changes	..	..	..	..	..	..	..	..	..	..	..
Total energy supply	..	28	..	85918	..	24555	..	13245	55631	179377	87098
Statistical difference	..	0	..	4	..	0	..	207	0	212	12475
Transfers	..	..	..	..	..	..	..	..	..	..	..
Transformation	..	..	..	-10062	..	-15446	..	12536	-55631	-68604	-65514
Electricity plants	..	..	..	-10062	..	-14548	..	12536	-55631	-67705	-64616
CHP plants	..	..	..	..	..	..	..	..	..	..	..
Heat plants	..	..	..	..	..	..	..	..	..	..	..
Coke ovens	..	..	..	..	..	..	..	..	..	..	..
Briquetting plants	..	..	..	..	..	..	..	..	..	..	..
Liquefaction plants	..	..	..	..	..	..	..	..	..	..	..
Gas works	..	..	..	..	..	..	..	..	..	..	..
Blast furnaces	..	..	..	..	..	..	..	..	..	..	..
NGL plants & gas blending	..	..	..	..	..	..	..	..	..	..	..
Oil refineries	..	..	..	..	..	..	..	..	..	..	..
Other transformation	..	..	..	..	..	-898	..	..	..	-898	-898
Energy industries own use	..	..	..	..	..	..	..	-589	..	-589	..
Losses	..	..	..	..	..	..	..	*-2589	..	*-2589	..
Final consumption	..	28	..	75851	..	9109	..	22395	..	107384	9109
Final energy consumption	..	28	..	75204	..	9109	..	22395	..	106737	9109
Manufacturing, const., mining	..	28	..	16735	..	578	..	7728	..	25070	578
Iron and steel	..	28	..	..	..	..	..	..	..	28	..
Chemical and petrochemical	..	..	..	..	..	..	..	..	..	..	..
Non-ferrous metals	..	..	..	..	..	..	..	..	..	..	..
Non-metallic minerals	..	..	..	..	..	..	..	..	..	..	..
Transport equipment	..	..	..	..	..	..	..	..	..	..	..
Machinery	..	..	..	..	..	..	..	..	..	..	..
Mining and quarrying	..	..	..	..	..	..	..	..	..	..	..
Food and tobacco	..	..	..	..	..	..	..	..	..	..	..
Paper, pulp and printing	..	..	..	..	..	..	..	..	..	..	..
Wood and wood products	..	..	..	..	..	..	..	..	..	..	..
Textile and leather	..	..	..	..	..	..	..	..	..	..	..
Construction	..	..	..	..	..	..	..	2	..	2	..
Industries n.e.s	..	0	..	16735	..	578	..	7726	..	25039	578
Transport	..	..	..	48334	..	..	..	..	..	48334	..
Road	..	..	..	48334	..	..	..	..	..	48334	..
Rail	..	..	..	..	..	..	..	..	..	..	..
Domestic aviation	..	..	..	..	..	..	..	..	..	..	..
Domestic navigation	..	..	..	..	..	..	..	..	..	..	..
Pipeline transport	..	..	..	..	..	..	..	..	..	..	..
Transport, n.e.s	..	..	..	..	..	..	..	..	..	..	..
Other	..	..	..	10135	..	8531	..	14667	..	33333	8531
Agriculture, forestry, fishing	..	..	..	..	..	..	..	..	..	..	..
Commerce, public services	..	..	..	391	..	742	..	6268	..	7402	742
Households	..	..	..	9744	..	7788	..	6896	..	24428	7788
Other consumers	..	..	..	..	..	..	..	1503	..	1503	..
Non-energy use	..	..	..	647	..	..	..	..	..	647	..

Equatorial Guinea

Terajoules

	All Coal	All Oil	Natural Gas	Primary biofuels / Waste	Charcoal	Electricity	Total energy	of which: renewables
2017								
Primary production	..	421161	289287	4083	..	*720	715251	4803
Imports	..	*13871	..	..	..	..	*13871	..
Exports	..	-423330	-176789	..	..	..	-600119	..
International marine bunkers	..	..	..	..	..	..	..	..
International aviation bunkers	..	-2161	..	..	..	..	-2161	..
Stock changes	..	*7425	..	..	..	..	*7425	..
Total energy supply	..	16967	112498	4083	..	*720	134268	4803
Statistical Difference	..	7	0	0	0	0	6	720
Transfers	..	..	..	..	..	..	..	..
Transformation	..	-86	*-5400	*-576	310	*2340	*-3413	*-267
Electricity plants	..	*-86	*-5400	..	..	*2340	*-3146	..
Charcoal plants	..	..	..	*-576	310	..	*-267	*-267
Other transformation	..	0	0	0	..	..	0	0
Energy industries own use	..	*-4230	*-356	..	..	*-126	*-4712	..
Losses	..	..	..	..	..	*-346	*-346	..
Final consumption	..	12644	*106743	*3507	*310	*2588	*125792	*3817
Final energy consumption	..	12411	*106743	*3507	*310	*2588	*125559	*3817
Manufacturing, const., mining	..	*1333	*106743	..	..	*832	*108907	..
Transport	..	8659	..	..	..	..	8659	..
Road	..	8659	..	..	..	..	8659	..
Domestic aviation	..	..	..	..	..	..	..	..
Domestic navigation	..	..	..	..	..	..	..	..
Other transport	..	..	..	..	..	..	..	..
Other	..	*2419	..	*3507	*310	*1757	*7992	*3817
Agriculture, forestry, fishing	..	..	..	..	..	..	..	..
Commerce and public services	..	*710	..	..	..	*756	*1466	..
Households	..	310	..	*3507	*310	*900	*5027	*3817
Other consumers	..	1399	..	..	..	*101	1500	..
Non-energy use	..	*233	..	..	..	..	*233	..
2018								
Primary production	..	370080	272197	4083	..	*720	647080	4803
Imports	..	*12258	..	..	..	..	*12258	..
Exports	..	-342753	-193457	..	..	..	-536211	..
International marine bunkers	..	..	..	..	..	..	..	..
International aviation bunkers	..	-1940	..	..	..	..	-1940	..
Stock changes	..	*-22018	..	..	..	..	*-22018	..
Total energy supply	..	15626	78740	4083	..	*720	99169	4803
Statistical Difference	..	38	0	0	0	0	38	720
Transfers	..	..	..	..	..	..	..	..
Transformation	..	-86	*-5400	*-602	324	*1930	*-3834	*-278
Electricity plants	..	*-86	*-5400	..	..	*1930	*-3556	..
Charcoal plants	..	..	..	*-602	324	..	*-278	*-278
Other transformation	..	0	0	0	..	..	0	0
Energy industries own use	..	*-4230	*-356	..	..	*-126	*-4712	..
Losses	..	..	..	..	..	*-270	*-270	..
Final consumption	..	11272	*72985	*3482	*324	*2254	*90315	*3806
Final energy consumption	..	11031	*72985	*3482	*324	*2254	*90074	*3806
Manufacturing, const., mining	..	*1247	*72985	..	..	*724	*74955	..
Transport	..	7784	..	..	..	..	7784	..
Road	..	7784	..	..	..	..	7784	..
Domestic aviation	..	..	..	..	..	..	..	..
Domestic navigation	..	..	..	..	..	..	..	..
Other transport	..	..	..	..	..	..	..	..
Other	..	*1999	..	*3482	*324	*1530	*7335	*3806
Agriculture, forestry, fishing	..	..	..	..	..	..	..	..
Commerce and public services	..	*710	..	..	..	*691	*1401	..
Households	..	*331	..	*3482	*324	*738	*4875	*3806
Other consumers	..	959	..	..	..	*101	1060	..
Non-energy use	..	*241	..	..	..	..	*241	..

Eritrea

Terajoules

	All Coal	All Oil	Natural Gas	Primary biofuels / Waste	Charcoal	Electricity	Total energy	of which: renewables
2017								
Primary production	..	..	..	26231	..	47	26278	26278
Imports	..	9132	..	..	..	..	9132	..
Exports	..	..	..	..	..	..	..	..
International marine bunkers	..	..	..	..	..	..	..	..
International aviation bunkers	..	-353	..	..	..	..	-353	..
Stock changes	..	..	..	..	..	..	..	..
Total energy supply	..	8779	..	26231	..	47	35057	26278
Statistical Difference	..	3	..	0	0	25	29	47
Transfers	..	..	..	..	..	..	..	..
Transformation	..	-4364	..	-16081	5399	1361	-13686	-10682
Electricity plants	..	-4364	..	..	..	1361	-3003	..
Charcoal plants	..	..	..	-16081	5399	..	-10682	-10682
Other transformation	..	0	..	0	..	..	0	0
Energy industries own use	..	..	..	..	..	-65	-65	..
Losses	..	..	..	..	..	-173	-173	..
Final consumption	..	4411	..	10150	5399	1145	21105	15549
Final energy consumption	..	4251	..	10150	5399	1145	20944	15549
Manufacturing, const., mining	..	245	..	..	..	317	562	..
Transport	..	3068	..	..	..	..	3068	..
Road	..	2980	..	..	..	..	2980	..
Domestic aviation	..	88	..	..	..	..	88	..
Domestic navigation	..	..	..	..	..	..	..	..
Other transport	..	..	..	..	..	..	..	..
Other	..	937	..	10150	5399	828	17314	15549
Agriculture, forestry, fishing	..	..	..	..	..	..	..	..
Commerce and public services	..	84	..	856	89	378	1407	944
Households	..	853	..	9295	5310	450	15908	14605
Other consumers	..	..	..	..	..	..	..	..
Non-energy use	..	161	..	..	..	..	161	..
2018								
Primary production	..	..	..	26535	..	162	26697	26697
Imports	..	10162	..	..	..	..	10162	..
Exports	..	..	..	..	..	..	..	..
International marine bunkers	..	..	..	..	..	..	..	..
International aviation bunkers	..	-397	..	..	..	..	-397	..
Stock changes	..	..	..	..	..	..	..	..
Total energy supply	..	9765	..	26535	..	162	36462	26697
Statistical Difference	..	43	..	0	0	29	71	162
Transfers	..	..	..	..	..	..	..	..
Transformation	..	-5134	..	-16755	5605	1620	-14664	-11150
Electricity plants	..	-5134	..	..	..	1620	-3514	..
Charcoal plants	..	..	..	-16755	5605	..	-11150	-11150
Other transformation	..	0	..	0	..	..	0	0
Energy industries own use	..	..	..	..	..	-79	-79	..
Losses	..	..	..	..	..	-220	-220	..
Final consumption	..	4588	..	9781	5605	1454	21428	15386
Final energy consumption	..	4427	..	9781	5605	1454	21267	15386
Manufacturing, const., mining	..	245	..	..	..	403	648	..
Transport	..	3197	..	..	..	..	3197	..
Road	..	3109	..	..	..	..	3109	..
Domestic aviation	..	88	..	..	..	..	88	..
Domestic navigation	..	..	..	..	..	..	..	..
Other transport	..	..	..	..	..	..	..	..
Other	..	985	..	9781	5605	1051	17422	15386
Agriculture, forestry, fishing	..	..	..	..	..	..	..	..
Commerce and public services	..	84	..	892	89	479	1543	980
Households	..	901	..	8889	5517	572	15878	14405
Other consumers	..	..	..	..	..	..	..	..
Non-energy use	..	161	..	..	..	..	161	..

Estonia

Terajoules

2017	Primary coal and peat	Coal and peat products	Primary Oil	Oil Products	Natural Gas	Biofuels and waste	Nuclear	Electricity	Heat	Total energy	of which: renewables
Primary production	173950	..	..	..	..	65841	..	2747	..	242537	67073
Imports	990	..	..	80602	16997	*866	..	8212	..	107666	*866
Exports	-312	-542	-36283	-18228	..	*-22626	..	-18054	..	-96045	*-22626
International marine bunkers	..	..	..	-13179	..	..	..	..	..	-13179	..
International aviation bunkers	..	..	..	-2558	..	..	..	..	..	-2558	..
Stock changes	3732	..	..	-3383	..	*805	..	..	..	1154	*810
Total energy supply	178359	-542	-36283	43255	16997	44886	..	-7096	..	239576	46123
Statistical difference	8	0	0	-43	0	*1793	..	0	528	2286	4499
Transfers	..	..	-3699	3909	..	..	..	..	..	210	..
Transformation	-174418	542	39983	-1737	-6939	*-24301	..	43758	24261	-98852	*-23192
Electricity plants	-103725	-3679	..	-727	..	*-673	..	38387	..	-70417	*-673
CHP plants	-4836	-2936	..	-40	-474	*-13978	..	5371	11148	-5745	*-12869
Heat plants	-405	..	..	-970	-6465	*-9650	..	..	13113	-4376	*-9650
Coke ovens	-650	542	..	..	..	..	..	..	..	-109	..
Briquetting plants	..	..	..	..	..	..	..	..	..	..	..
Liquefaction plants	-57431	..	39983	..	..	..	..	..	..	-17449	..
Gas works	-7371	6615	..	..	..	..	..	..	..	-756	..
Blast furnaces	..	..	..	..	..	..	..	..	..	..	..
NGL plants & gas blending	..	..	..	..	..	..	..	..	..	..	..
Oil refineries	..	..	..	..	..	..	..	..	..	..	..
Other transformation	..	..	..	..	..	..	..	..	..	..	..
Energy industries own use	-146	..	..	-559	-189	*-40	..	-7823	-353	-9110	*-40
Losses	..	..	..	..	..	0	..	-2804	-3456	-6260	0
Final consumption	3786	..	..	44911	9869	*18752	..	26035	19924	123277	*18391
Final energy consumption	1659	..	..	42016	9869	*18752	..	26035	19924	118255	*18391
Manufacturing, const., mining	1527	..	..	2388	4114	*2355	..	8212	1550	20146	*1994
Iron and steel	..	..	..	..	11	0	..	7	..	18	0
Chemical and petrochemical	..	..	..	224	173	0	..	410	720	1527	0
Non-ferrous metals	..	..	..	..	44	0	..	..	..	44	0
Non-metallic minerals	1527	..	..	43	644	724	..	540	72	3549	363
Transport equipment	..	..	..	43	79	*14	..	259	63	458	*14
Machinery	..	..	..	47	166	*43	..	1087	216	1559	*43
Mining and quarrying	..	..	..	172	180	0	..	36	2	390	0
Food and tobacco	..	..	..	178	983	*16	..	1112	127	2416	*16
Paper, pulp and printing	..	..	..	..	928	*300	..	1768	35	3031	*300
Wood and wood products	..	..	..	172	396	*350	..	1796	62	2776	*350
Textile and leather	..	..	..	..	88	*6	..	209	65	368	*6
Construction	..	..	..	1419	298	*30	..	295	83	2125	*30
Industries n.e.s	0	..	..	90	125	*872	..	691	105	1884	*872
Transport	..	..	..	33734	196	127	..	166	..	34223	127
Road	..	..	..	32701	196	127	..	58	..	33082	127
Rail	..	..	..	688	..	..	..	47	..	735	..
Domestic aviation	..	..	..	44	..	..	..	..	..	44	..
Domestic navigation	..	..	..	301	..	..	..	..	..	301	..
Pipeline transport	..	..	..	..	..	..	..	..	..	..	..
Transport, n.e.s	..	..	..	..	..	..	..	61	..	61	..
Other	132	..	..	5894	5558	*16270	..	17658	18374	63887	*16270
Agriculture, forestry, fishing	44	..	..	4216	184	*222	..	900	74	5640	*222
Commerce, public services	..	..	..	1261	3056	*554	..	9774	4980	19625	*554
Households	88	..	..	417	2319	*15494	..	6984	13320	38622	*15494
Other consumers	..	..	..	..	..	..	..	..	..	..	..
Non-energy use	2128	..	..	2894	..	..	..	..	..	5022	..

Estonia

Terajoules

2018	Primary coal and peat	Coal and peat products	Primary Oil	Oil Products	Natural Gas	Biofuels and waste	Nuclear	Electricity	Heat	Total energy	of which: renewables
Primary production	201770	..	..	..	..	72298	..	2455	..	276523	73084
Imports	968	..	..	87220	17317	1978	..	10991	..	118474	1654
Exports	0	-371	-42029	-29145	..	*-25842	..	-17820	..	-115206	*-25842
International marine bunkers	..	..	..	-12407	..	..	..	..	..	-12407	..
International aviation bunkers	..	..	..	-2999	..	..	..	..	..	-2999	..
Stock changes	-4237	-29	..	2791	..	*-403	..	..	..	-1878	*-403
Total energy supply	198500	-399	-42029	45461	17317	48031	..	-4374	..	262506	48493
Statistical difference	-1670	0	0	559	1	896	..	1105	604	1495	3351
Transfers	..	..	-1692	1745	..	..	..	..	..	53	..
Transformation	-195712	8681	43721	-1333	-6113	*-27274	..	42041	24260	-111729	*-26030
Electricity plants	-109791	-7250	..	-525	..	*-1858	..	36641	..	-82783	*-1616
CHP plants	-5401	-2467	..	-40	-554	*-18191	..	5400	13131	-8122	*-17189
Heat plants	-726	-521	..	-768	-5559	*-7225	..	..	11129	-3670	*-7225
Coke ovens	-6718	11276	..	..	..	..	..	..	..	4558	..
Briquetting plants	..	..	..	..	..	..	..	..	..	..	..
Liquefaction plants	-57913	..	43721	..	..	..	..	..	..	-14192	..
Gas works	-15162	7643	..	..	..	..	..	..	..	-7519	..
Blast furnaces	..	..	..	..	..	..	..	..	..	..	..
NGL plants & gas blending	..	..	..	..	..	..	..	..	..	..	..
Oil refineries	..	..	..	..	..	..	..	..	..	..	..
Other transformation	..	..	..	..	..	..	..	..	..	..	..
Energy industries own use	..	-8282	..	-645	-668	*-30	..	-6916	-385	-16925	*-30
Losses	..	..	..	..	..	0	..	-2678	-3106	-5784	0
Final consumption	4459	..	..	44668	10535	*19831	..	26968	20165	126626	*19082
Final energy consumption	2073	..	..	42256	10535	*19831	..	26968	20165	121828	*19082
Manufacturing, const., mining	1963	..	..	2204	4565	*2822	..	8496	1497	21546	*2084
Iron and steel	..	..	..	..	14	0	..	11	..	24	0
Chemical and petrochemical	..	..	..	90	240	6	..	418	647	1401	6
Non-ferrous metals	..	..	..	..	45	0	..	11	..	56	0
Non-metallic minerals	1941	..	..	43	716	1143	..	698	95	4637	405
Transport equipment	..	..	..	43	70	*7	..	295	81	496	*7
Machinery	..	..	..	47	138	*56	..	1152	219	1612	*56
Mining and quarrying	..	..	..	129	206	0	..	72	5	412	0
Food and tobacco	..	..	..	86	1092	*20	..	1044	121	2363	*20
Paper, pulp and printing	..	..	..	..	1116	*344	..	1735	29	3224	*344
Wood and wood products	..	..	..	86	428	*265	..	1940	68	2788	*265
Textile and leather	..	..	..	..	79	*5	..	220	64	368	*5
Construction	22	..	..	1589	262	*20	..	256	77	2225	*20
Industries n.e.s	0	..	..	90	158	*956	..	644	91	1940	*956
Transport	..	..	..	34311	298	730	..	155	..	35493	730
Road	..	..	..	33364	298	730	..	61	..	34453	730
Rail	..	..	..	645	..	..	..	36	..	681	..
Domestic aviation	..	..	..	44	..	..	..	..	..	44	..
Domestic navigation	..	..	..	258	..	..	..	..	..	258	..
Pipeline transport	..	..	..	..	..	..	..	..	..	..	..
Transport, n.e.s	..	..	..	..	..	..	..	58	..	58	..
Other	110	..	..	5742	5673	*16279	..	18317	18668	64788	*16268
Agriculture, forestry, fishing	22	..	..	4214	180	*218	..	594	68	5296	*218
Commerce, public services	44	..	..	1158	3191	*500	..	10559	5100	20551	*489
Households	44	..	..	370	2302	*15561	..	6696	13500	38473	*15561
Other consumers	..	..	..	..	..	..	..	468	..	468	..
Non-energy use	2386	..	..	2412	..	..	..	..	..	4798	..

Eswatini

Terajoules

2017	Primary coal and peat	Coal and peat products	Primary Oil	Oil Products	Natural Gas	Biofuels and waste	Nuclear	Electricity	Heat	Total energy	of which: renewables
Primary production	4704	..	..	..	..	24427	..	422	..	29553	24849
Imports	1574	..	..	11880	..	..	..	3772	..	17226	..
Exports	-4704	..	..	..	..	-30	..	..	..	-4733	-30
International marine bunkers	..	..	..	..	..	..	..	..	..	..	..
International aviation bunkers	..	..	..	-72	..	..	..	..	..	-72	..
Stock changes	..	..	..	..	..	..	..	..	..	..	..
Total energy supply	1574	..	..	11808	..	24397	..	4194	..	41973	24819
Statistical difference	-17	..	..	-284	..	0	..	-339	..	-640	422
Transfers	..	..	..	..	..	..	..	..	..	..	..
Transformation	-422	..	..	..	..	-3763	..	1069	..	-3116	-3763
Electricity plants	..	..	..	..	..	..	..	47	..	47	..
CHP plants	-181	..	..	..	..	-2400	..	1022	..	-1558	-2400
Heat plants	-241	..	..	..	..	..	..	..	..	-241	..
Coke ovens	..	..	..	..	..	..	..	..	..	..	..
Briquetting plants	..	..	..	..	..	..	..	..	..	..	..
Liquefaction plants	..	..	..	..	..	..	..	..	..	..	..
Gas works	..	..	..	..	..	..	..	..	..	..	..
Blast furnaces	..	..	..	..	..	..	..	..	..	..	..
NGL plants & gas blending	..	..	..	..	..	..	..	..	..	..	..
Oil refineries	..	..	..	..	..	..	..	..	..	..	..
Other transformation	..	..	..	..	..	-1363	..	..	..	-1363	-1363
Energy industries own use	..	..	..	..	..	..	..	-1	..	-1	..
Losses	..	..	..	..	..	..	..	-608	..	-608	..
Final consumption	1169	..	..	12092	..	20634	..	4993	..	38888	20634
Final energy consumption	1169	..	..	12067	..	20634	..	4993	..	38863	20634
Manufacturing, const., mining	1169	..	..	2031	..	9965	..	1948	..	15113	9965
Iron and steel	..	..	..	..	..	..	..	..	..	..	..
Chemical and petrochemical	..	..	..	..	..	..	..	..	..	..	..
Non-ferrous metals	..	..	..	..	..	..	..	..	..	..	..
Non-metallic minerals	..	..	..	..	..	..	..	..	..	..	..
Transport equipment	..	..	..	..	..	..	..	..	..	..	..
Machinery	..	..	..	..	..	..	..	..	..	..	..
Mining and quarrying	..	..	..	22	..	..	..	..	..	22	..
Food and tobacco	1164	..	..	322	..	9965	..	738	..	12189	9965
Paper, pulp and printing	..	..	..	..	..	..	..	..	..	..	..
Wood and wood products	..	..	..	..	..	..	..	..	..	..	..
Textile and leather	..	..	..	..	..	..	..	..	..	..	..
Construction	..	..	..	..	..	..	..	..	..	..	..
Industries n.e.s	6	..	..	1687	..	0	..	1210	..	2902	0
Transport	..	..	..	9230	..	..	..	..	..	9230	..
Road	..	..	..	9230	..	..	..	..	..	9230	..
Rail	..	..	..	..	..	..	..	..	..	..	..
Domestic aviation	..	..	..	..	..	..	..	..	..	..	..
Domestic navigation	..	..	..	..	..	..	..	..	..	..	..
Pipeline transport	..	..	..	..	..	..	..	..	..	..	..
Transport, n.e.s	..	..	..	..	..	..	..	..	..	..	..
Other	..	..	..	805	..	10669	..	3046	..	14520	10669
Agriculture, forestry, fishing	..	..	..	443	..	..	..	1148	..	1591	..
Commerce, public services	..	..	..	289	..	..	..	407	..	696	..
Households	..	..	..	61	..	10669	..	1490	..	12221	10669
Other consumers	..	..	..	12	..	..	..	..	..	12	..
Non-energy use	..	..	..	*25	..	..	..	..	..	*25	..

Eswatini

Terajoules

2018	Primary coal and peat	Coal and peat products	Primary Oil	Oil Products	Natural Gas	Biofuels and waste	Nuclear	Electricity	Heat	Total energy	of which: renewables
Primary production	3328	..	..	..	..	25148	..	749	..	29226	25898
Imports	1574	..	..	12486	..	..	..	3672	..	17732	..
Exports	-3328	..	..	..	..	*-30	..	..	..	-3358	*-30
International marine bunkers	..	..	..	..	..	..	..	..	..	..	..
International aviation bunkers	..	..	..	-78	..	..	..	..	..	-78	..
Stock changes	..	..	..	..	..	..	..	..	..	..	..
Total energy supply	1574	..	..	12409	..	25119	..	4422	..	43523	25868
Statistical difference	-15	..	..	-44	..	0	..	75	..	16	750
Transfers	..	..	..	..	..	..	..	..	..	..	..
Transformation	-454	..	..	..	..	-3356	..	1120	..	-2690	-3356
Electricity plants	..	..	..	..	..	..	..	54	..	54	..
CHP plants	-108	..	..	..	..	-2439	..	1066	..	-1482	-2439
Heat plants	-346	..	..	..	..	..	..	..	..	-346	..
Coke ovens	..	..	..	..	..	..	..	..	..	..	..
Briquetting plants	..	..	..	..	..	..	..	..	..	..	..
Liquefaction plants	..	..	..	..	..	..	..	..	..	..	..
Gas works	..	..	..	..	..	..	..	..	..	..	..
Blast furnaces	..	..	..	..	..	..	..	..	..	..	..
NGL plants & gas blending	..	..	..	..	..	..	..	..	..	..	..
Oil refineries	..	..	..	..	..	..	..	..	..	..	..
Other transformation	..	..	..	..	..	*-917	..	..	..	*-917	*-917
Energy industries own use	..	..	..	..	..	..	..	0	..	0	..
Losses	..	..	..	..	..	..	..	-703	..	-703	..
Final consumption	1135	..	..	12453	..	21762	..	4763	..	40113	21762
Final energy consumption	1135	..	..	12448	..	21762	..	4763	..	40109	21762
Manufacturing, const., mining	1135	..	..	2454	..	11064	..	1559	..	16212	11064
Iron and steel	..	..	..	..	..	..	..	..	..	..	..
Chemical and petrochemical	..	..	..	..	..	..	..	..	..	..	..
Non-ferrous metals	..	..	..	..	..	..	..	..	..	..	..
Non-metallic minerals	..	..	..	..	..	..	..	..	..	..	..
Transport equipment	..	..	..	..	..	..	..	..	..	..	..
Machinery	..	..	..	..	..	..	..	..	..	..	..
Mining and quarrying	..	..	..	43	..	..	..	36	..	79	..
Food and tobacco	1135	..	..	467	..	10535	..	947	..	13084	10535
Paper, pulp and printing	..	..	..	..	..	..	..	..	..	..	..
Wood and wood products	..	..	..	..	..	529	..	18	..	547	529
Textile and leather	..	..	..	..	..	..	..	..	..	..	..
Construction	..	..	..	..	..	..	..	..	..	..	..
Industries n.e.s	0	..	..	1944	..	0	..	558	..	2502	0
Transport	..	..	..	7972	..	..	..	..	..	7972	..
Road	..	..	..	7972	..	..	..	..	..	7972	..
Rail	..	..	..	..	..	..	..	..	..	..	..
Domestic aviation	..	..	..	..	..	..	..	..	..	..	..
Domestic navigation	..	..	..	..	..	..	..	..	..	..	..
Pipeline transport	..	..	..	..	..	..	..	..	..	..	..
Transport, n.e.s	..	..	..	..	..	..	..	..	..	..	..
Other	..	..	..	2023	..	10698	..	3204	..	15925	10698
Agriculture, forestry, fishing	..	..	..	302	..	..	..	1285	..	1588	..
Commerce, public services	..	..	..	1681	..	..	..	439	..	2121	..
Households	..	..	..	39	..	10698	..	1480	..	12217	10698
Other consumers	..	..	..	..	..	..	..	..	..	..	..
Non-energy use	..	..	..	*5	..	..	..	..	..	*5	..

Ethiopia

Terajoules

2017	Primary coal and peat	Coal and peat products	Primary Oil	Oil Products	Natural Gas	Biofuels and waste	Nuclear	Electricity	Heat	Total energy	of which: renewables
Primary production	52	..	..	..	..	1331739	..	47650	..	1379440	1379388
Imports	14964	..	..	175644	..	10	..	..	..	190618	10
Exports	..	..	..	..	..	-25	..	-5155	..	-5180	-25
International marine bunkers	..	..	..	..	..	..	..	..	..	..	..
International aviation bunkers	..	..	..	-30076	..	..	..	..	..	-30076	..
Stock changes	..	..	..	..	..	..	..	..	..	..	..
Total energy supply	15016	..	..	145568	..	1331724	..	42494	..	1534802	1379373
Statistical difference	0	..	..	-3129	..	4	..	-40	..	-3164	47654
Transfers	..	..	..	..	..	..	..	..	..	..	..
Transformation	..	..	..	-43	..	*-106823	..	144	..	*-106722	*-106823
Electricity plants	..	..	..	-43	..	*-502	..	144	..	*-401	*-502
CHP plants	..	..	..	..	..	..	..	..	..	..	..
Heat plants	..	..	..	..	..	..	..	..	..	..	..
Coke ovens	..	..	..	..	..	..	..	..	..	..	..
Briquetting plants	..	..	..	..	..	..	..	..	..	..	..
Liquefaction plants	..	..	..	..	..	..	..	..	..	..	..
Gas works	..	..	..	..	..	..	..	..	..	..	..
Blast furnaces	..	..	..	..	..	..	..	..	..	..	..
NGL plants & gas blending	..	..	..	..	..	..	..	..	..	..	..
Oil refineries	..	..	..	..	..	..	..	..	..	..	..
Other transformation	..	..	..	..	..	*-106322	..	..	..	*-106322	*-106322
Energy industries own use	..	..	..	..	..	..	..	-202	..	-202	..
Losses	..	..	..	..	..	..	..	-10602	..	-10602	..
Final consumption	15016	..	..	148654	..	*1224896	..	31874	..	*1420440	*1224896
Final energy consumption	15016	..	..	144674	..	*1224896	..	31874	..	*1416460	*1224896
Manufacturing, const., mining	15016	..	..	36173	..	*8456	..	8438	..	68082	*8456
Iron and steel	..	..	..	..	..	..	..	..	..	..	..
Chemical and petrochemical	..	..	..	..	..	..	..	..	..	..	..
Non-ferrous metals	..	..	..	..	..	..	..	..	..	..	..
Non-metallic minerals	15016	..	..	6468	..	..	..	..	..	21483	..
Transport equipment	..	..	..	..	..	..	..	..	..	..	..
Machinery	..	..	..	..	..	..	..	..	..	..	..
Mining and quarrying	..	..	..	..	..	..	..	..	..	..	..
Food and tobacco	..	..	..	..	..	*8456	..	..	..	*8456	*8456
Paper, pulp and printing	..	..	..	..	..	..	..	..	..	..	..
Wood and wood products	..	..	..	..	..	..	..	..	..	..	..
Textile and leather	..	..	..	..	..	..	..	..	..	..	..
Construction	..	..	..	..	..	..	..	..	..	..	..
Industries n.e.s	0	..	..	29705	..	0	..	8438	..	38144	0
Transport	..	..	..	87393	..	134	..	..	..	87527	134
Road	..	..	..	87040	..	134	..	..	..	87174	134
Rail	..	..	..	..	..	..	..	..	..	..	..
Domestic aviation	..	..	..	353	..	..	..	..	..	353	..
Domestic navigation	..	..	..	..	..	..	..	..	..	..	..
Pipeline transport	..	..	..	..	..	..	..	..	..	..	..
Transport, n.e.s	..	..	..	..	..	..	..	..	..	..	..
Other	..	..	..	21109	..	*1216307	..	23436	..	*1260851	*1216307
Agriculture, forestry, fishing	..	..	..	7267	..	..	..	..	..	7267	..
Commerce, public services	..	..	..	3053	..	11642	..	8665	..	23360	11642
Households	..	..	..	3522	..	*1204665	..	14771	..	*1222957	*1204665
Other consumers	..	..	..	7267	..	..	..	..	..	7267	..
Non-energy use	..	..	..	3980	..	..	..	..	..	3980	..

Ethiopia

Terajoules

2018	Primary coal and peat	Coal and peat products	Primary Oil	Oil Products	Natural Gas	Biofuels and waste	Nuclear	Electricity	Heat	Total energy	of which: renewables
Primary production	52	..	..	..	..	1347979	..	48856	..	1396887	1396835
Imports	15970	..	..	187170	..	0	..	..	..	203140	0
Exports	..	..	..	..	..	0	..	-5292	..	-5292	0
International marine bunkers	..	..	..	..	..	..	..	..	..	..	..
International aviation bunkers	..	..	..	-32105	..	..	..	..	..	-32105	..
Stock changes	..	..	..	..	..	..	..	..	..	..	..
Total energy supply	16022	..	..	155065	..	1347979	..	43564	..	1562630	1396835
Statistical difference	-26	..	..	-3213	..	0	..	-94	..	-3332	48856
Transfers	..	..	..	..	..	..	..	..	..	..	..
Transformation	..	..	..	-43	..	*-114845	..	148	..	*-114740	*-114845
Electricity plants	..	..	..	-43	..	*-502	..	148	..	*-397	*-502
CHP plants	..	..	..	..	..	..	..	..	..	..	..
Heat plants	..	..	..	..	..	..	..	..	..	..	..
Coke ovens	..	..	..	..	..	..	..	..	..	..	..
Briquetting plants	..	..	..	..	..	..	..	..	..	..	..
Liquefaction plants	..	..	..	..	..	..	..	..	..	..	..
Gas works	..	..	..	..	..	..	..	..	..	..	..
Blast furnaces	..	..	..	..	..	..	..	..	..	..	..
NGL plants & gas blending	..	..	..	..	..	..	..	..	..	..	..
Oil refineries	..	..	..	..	..	..	..	..	..	..	..
Other transformation	..	..	..	..	..	*-114343	..	..	..	*-114343	*-114343
Energy industries own use	..	..	..	..	..	..	..	-212	..	-212	..
Losses	..	..	..	..	..	..	..	-10868	..	-10868	..
Final consumption	16048	..	..	158235	..	1233134	..	32724	..	1440141	1233134
Final energy consumption	16048	..	..	154336	..	1233134	..	32724	..	1436242	1233134
Manufacturing, const., mining	16048	..	..	38656	..	*8456	..	8665	..	71824	*8456
Iron and steel	..	..	..	..	..	..	..	..	..	..	..
Chemical and petrochemical	..	..	..	..	..	..	..	..	..	..	..
Non-ferrous metals	..	..	..	..	..	..	..	..	..	..	..
Non-metallic minerals	16048	..	..	6890	..	..	..	..	..	22938	..
Transport equipment	..	..	..	..	..	..	..	..	..	..	..
Machinery	..	..	..	..	..	..	..	..	..	..	..
Mining and quarrying	..	..	..	..	..	..	..	..	..	..	..
Food and tobacco	..	..	..	..	..	*8456	..	..	..	*8456	*8456
Paper, pulp and printing	..	..	..	..	..	..	..	..	..	..	..
Wood and wood products	..	..	..	..	..	..	..	..	..	..	..
Textile and leather	..	..	..	..	..	..	..	..	..	..	..
Construction	..	..	..	..	..	..	..	..	..	..	..
Industries n.e.s	0	..	..	31766	..	0	..	8665	..	40431	0
Transport	..	..	..	93322	..	161	..	..	..	93483	161
Road	..	..	..	92926	..	161	..	..	..	93086	161
Rail	..	..	..	..	..	..	..	..	..	..	..
Domestic aviation	..	..	..	397	..	..	..	..	..	397	..
Domestic navigation	..	..	..	..	..	..	..	..	..	..	..
Pipeline transport	..	..	..	..	..	..	..	..	..	..	..
Transport, n.e.s	..	..	..	..	..	..	..	..	..	..	..
Other	..	..	..	22357	..	1224518	..	24059	..	1270934	1224518
Agriculture, forestry, fishing	..	..	..	7740	..	..	..	..	..	7740	..
Commerce, public services	..	..	..	3268	..	11936	..	8896	..	24099	11936
Households	..	..	..	3609	..	1212582	..	15163	..	1231355	1212582
Other consumers	..	..	..	7740	..	..	..	..	..	7740	..
Non-energy use	..	..	..	3899	..	..	..	..	..	3899	..

Faeroe Islands

Terajoules

	All Coal	All Oil	Natural Gas	Primary biofuels / Waste	Charcoal	Electricity	Total energy	of which: renewables
2017								
Primary production	..	..	..	..	..	615	615	615
Imports	..	*11265	..	..	0	..	*11265	0
Exports	..	..	..	..	..	..	..	..
International marine bunkers	..	-1543	..	..	..	..	-1543	..
International aviation bunkers	..	-5	..	..	..	..	-5	..
Stock changes	..	..	..	..	..	..	..	..
Total energy supply	..	*9716	..	..	0	615	*10332	616
Statistical Difference	..	0	..	..	0	0	0	615
Transfers	..	..	..	..	..	..	..	..
Transformation	..	-1364	..	..	..	588	-776	..
Electricity plants	..	-1364	..	..	..	588	-776	..
Charcoal plants	..	..	..	..	..	..	..	..
Other transformation	..	0	..	..	..	..	0	..
Energy industries own use	..	..	..	..	..	-35	-35	..
Losses	..	..	..	..	..	*-65	*-65	..
Final consumption	..	8352	..	..	0	1103	9456	0
Final energy consumption	..	8351	..	..	0	1103	9454	0
Manufacturing, const., mining	..	1114	..	..	..	308	1422	..
Transport	..	1433	..	..	..	..	1433	..
Road	..	1433	..	..	..	..	1433	..
Domestic aviation	..	..	..	..	..	..	..	..
Domestic navigation	..	..	..	..	..	..	..	..
Other transport	..	..	..	..	..	..	..	..
Other	..	5804	..	..	0	795	6600	0
Agriculture, forestry, fishing	..	3768	..	..	..	151	3919	..
Commerce and public services	..	492	..	..	..	362	854	..
Households	..	1544	..	..	0	282	1826	0
Other consumers	..	0	..	..	..	..	0	..
Non-energy use	..	*2	..	..	..	..	*2	..
2018								
Primary production	..	..	..	..	..	619	619	619
Imports	..	*11626	..	..	0	..	*11626	0
Exports	..	..	..	..	..	..	..	..
International marine bunkers	..	-1638	..	..	..	..	-1638	..
International aviation bunkers	..	0	..	..	..	..	0	..
Stock changes	..	..	..	..	..	..	..	..
Total energy supply	..	*9988	..	..	0	619	*10607	619
Statistical Difference	..	0	..	..	0	0	0	619
Transfers	..	..	..	..	..	..	..	..
Transformation	..	-1517	..	..	..	648	-869	..
Electricity plants	..	-1517	..	..	..	648	-869	..
Charcoal plants	..	..	..	..	..	..	..	..
Other transformation	..	0	..	..	..	..	0	..
Energy industries own use	..	..	..	..	..	-40	-40	..
Losses	..	..	..	..	..	*-74	*-74	..
Final consumption	..	8471	..	..	0	1154	9625	0
Final energy consumption	..	8469	..	..	0	1154	9623	0
Manufacturing, const., mining	..	1067	..	..	..	296	1363	..
Transport	..	1467	..	..	..	..	1467	..
Road	..	1467	..	..	..	..	1467	..
Domestic aviation	..	..	..	..	..	..	..	..
Domestic navigation	..	..	..	..	..	..	..	..
Other transport	..	..	..	..	..	..	..	..
Other	..	5936	..	..	0	858	6794	0
Agriculture, forestry, fishing	..	3812	..	..	..	205	4016	..
Commerce and public services	..	526	..	..	..	366	892	..
Households	..	1597	..	..	0	288	1885	0
Other consumers	..	1	..	..	..	..	1	..
Non-energy use	..	*2	..	..	..	..	*2	..

Falkland Is. (Malvinas)

Terajoules

	All Coal	All Oil	Natural Gas	Primary biofuels / Waste	Charcoal	Electricity	Total energy	of which: renewables
2017								
Primary production	48	..	..	8	..	19	74	26
Imports	..	453	4	..	1	..	458	1
Exports	..	..	..	..	..	..	..	..
International marine bunkers	..	..	..	..	..	..	..	..
International aviation bunkers	..	..	..	..	..	..	..	..
Stock changes	..	..	..	..	..	..	..	..
Total energy supply	48	453	4	8	1	19	532	27
Statistical Difference	0	0	0	0	0	1	1	19
Transfers	..	..	..	..	..	..	..	..
Transformation	..	-114	..	*-6	3	52	-65	*-3
Electricity plants	..	-114	..	..	..	52	-62	..
Charcoal plants	..	..	..	*-6	3	..	*-3	*-3
Other transformation	..	0	..	0	..	..	0	0
Energy industries own use	..	..	..	..	..	*-7	*-7	..
Losses	..	..	..	..	..	..	..	..
Final consumption	*48	340	4	*2	*4	*63	460	*6
Final energy consumption	*48	340	4	*2	*4	*63	460	*6
Manufacturing, const., mining	..	203	..	..	..	*26	229	..
Transport	..	17	..	..	..	..	17	..
Road	..	9	..	..	..	..	9	..
Domestic aviation	..	8	..	..	..	..	8	..
Domestic navigation	..	..	..	..	..	..	..	..
Other transport	..	..	..	..	..	..	..	..
Other	*48	120	4	*2	*4	*37	214	*6
Agriculture, forestry, fishing	..	..	..	..	..	*5	*5	..
Commerce and public services	..	..	..	..	..	..	..	..
Households	*48	120	4	*2	*4	*10	187	*6
Other consumers	..	..	..	..	..	*21	*21	..
Non-energy use	..	..	..	..	..	..	..	..
2018								
Primary production	48	..	..	8	..	19	75	28
Imports	..	481	4	..	1	..	486	1
Exports	..	..	..	..	..	..	..	..
International marine bunkers	..	..	..	..	..	..	..	..
International aviation bunkers	..	..	..	..	..	..	..	..
Stock changes	..	..	..	..	..	..	..	..
Total energy supply	48	481	4	8	1	19	561	29
Statistical Difference	0	0	0	0	0	0	0	19
Transfers	..	..	..	..	..	..	..	..
Transformation	..	-122	..	*-7	4	50	-75	*-3
Electricity plants	..	-122	..	..	..	50	-72	..
Charcoal plants	..	..	..	*-7	4	..	*-3	*-3
Other transformation	..	0	..	0	..	..	0	0
Energy industries own use	..	..	..	..	..	*-5	*-5	..
Losses	..	..	..	..	..	..	..	..
Final consumption	*48	360	4	*1	*4	*64	480	*6
Final energy consumption	*48	360	4	*1	*4	*64	480	*6
Manufacturing, const., mining	..	213	..	..	..	*26	240	..
Transport	..	17	..	..	..	..	17	..
Road	..	9	..	..	..	..	9	..
Domestic aviation	..	9	..	..	..	..	9	..
Domestic navigation	..	..	..	..	..	..	..	..
Other transport	..	..	..	..	..	..	..	..
Other	*48	129	4	*1	*4	*37	223	*6
Agriculture, forestry, fishing	..	..	..	..	..	*5	*5	..
Commerce and public services	..	..	..	..	..	..	..	..
Households	*48	129	4	*1	*4	*10	197	*6
Other consumers	..	..	..	..	..	*21	*21	..
Non-energy use	..	..	..	..	..	..	..	..

Fiji

Terajoules

	All Coal	All Oil	Natural Gas	Primary biofuels / Waste	Charcoal	Electricity	Total energy	of which: renewables
2017								
Primary production	..	..	..	4871	..	1810	6681	6681
Imports	*4	34639	..	..	0	..	34644	0
Exports	..	-12843	..	-1	0	..	-12844	-1
International marine bunkers	..	*-2470	..	..	..	..	*-2470	..
International aviation bunkers	..	*-1341	..	..	..	..	*-1341	..
Stock changes	..	*617	..	..	..	..	*617	..
Total energy supply	*4	18604	..	4870	0	1810	25287	6679
Statistical Difference	0	-17	..	0	0	0	-18	1810
Transfers	..	..	..	..	..	..	..	..
Transformation	0	*-4250	..	*-136	73	1852	*-2461	*-63
Electricity plants	0	*-4250	..	..	..	1852	*-2399	..
Charcoal plants	..	..	..	*-136	73	..	*-63	*-63
Other transformation	0	0	..	0	..	..	0	0
Energy industries own use	..	..	..	..	..	-118	-118	..
Losses	..	..	..	..	..	*-295	*-295	..
Final consumption	*4	*14371	..	*4734	*73	3248	*22430	*4807
Final energy consumption	*4	*14138	..	*4734	*73	3248	*22197	*4807
Manufacturing, const., mining	..	*3462	..	*4533	..	798	*8793	*4533
Transport	..	*9303	..	..	..	..	*9303	..
Road	..	*7463	..	..	..	..	*7463	..
Domestic aviation	..	*550	..	..	..	..	*550	..
Domestic navigation	..	*1290	..	..	..	..	*1290	..
Other transport	..	..	..	..	..	..	..	..
Other	*4	*1372	..	*201	*73	2450	4101	*274
Agriculture, forestry, fishing	..	..	..	..	..	..	..	..
Commerce and public services	..	..	..	..	..	1498	1498	..
Households	..	*1290	..	*201	*73	902	*2466	*274
Other consumers	*4	*82	..	..	..	*50	*136	..
Non-energy use	..	*233	..	..	..	..	*233	..
2018								
Primary production	..	..	..	*4369	..	2084	*6452	*6452
Imports	*4	*36270	..	..	0	..	*36275	0
Exports	..	*-13016	..	-1	0	..	*-13017	-1
International marine bunkers	..	*-2782	..	..	..	..	*-2782	..
International aviation bunkers	..	*-1345	..	..	..	..	*-1345	..
Stock changes	..	*-573	..	..	..	..	*-573	..
Total energy supply	*4	*18554	..	*4368	0	2084	*25009	*6451
Statistical Difference	0	*26	..	0	0	0	*26	*2084
Transfers	..	..	..	..	..	..	..	..
Transformation	0	*-3942	..	*-136	73	1669	*-2336	*-63
Electricity plants	0	*-3942	..	..	..	1669	*-2273	..
Charcoal plants	..	..	..	*-136	73	..	*-63	*-63
Other transformation	0	0	..	0	..	..	0	0
Energy industries own use	..	..	..	..	..	-178	-178	..
Losses	..	..	..	..	..	*-310	*-310	..
Final consumption	*4	*14586	..	*4232	*73	*3265	*22160	*4305
Final energy consumption	*4	*14377	..	*4232	*73	*3265	*21951	*4305
Manufacturing, const., mining	..	*3459	..	*4031	..	*799	*8289	*4031
Transport	..	*9361	..	..	..	..	*9361	..
Road	..	*7949	..	..	..	..	*7949	..
Domestic aviation	..	*551	..	..	..	..	*551	..
Domestic navigation	..	*860	..	..	..	..	*860	..
Other transport	..	..	..	..	..	..	..	..
Other	*4	*1557	..	*201	*73	*2466	*4302	*274
Agriculture, forestry, fishing	..	..	..	..	..	..	..	..
Commerce and public services	..	..	..	..	..	*1501	*1501	..
Households	..	*1415	..	*201	*73	*914	*2604	*274
Other consumers	*4	*142	..	..	..	*50	*196	..
Non-energy use	..	*209	..	..	..	..	*209	..

Finland

Terajoules

2017	Primary coal and peat	Coal and peat products	Primary Oil	Oil Products	Natural Gas	Biofuels and waste	Nuclear	Electricity	Heat	Total energy	of which: renewables
Primary production	30603	..	..	..	..	404291	242752	70614	4806	753066	461075
Imports	106007	7472	532130	221809	80189	5937	..	79934	..	1033478	5937
Exports	..	-3965	..	-386102	..	*-1168	..	-6404	..	-397639	*-1168
International marine bunkers	..	..	..	-14645	-194	..	..	..	..	-14839	..
International aviation bunkers	..	..	..	-29018	..	..	..	..	..	-29018	..
Stock changes	34709	-1223	5802	7115	900	..	..	..	..	47302	..
Total energy supply	171319	2283	537932	-200842	80896	409060	242752	144144	4806	1392350	465844
Statistical difference	373	0	42	-6631	-840	-35	0	4	0	-7087	70579
Transfers	..	..	86233	-86190	..	..	..	..	..	43	..
Transformation	-156695	17859	-624123	626506	-47538	*-164082	-242752	170942	186307	-233574	*-152799
Electricity plants	-16567	-5466	..	-700	-148	*-12041	-242752	94424	-1887	-185135	*-11548
CHP plants	-88945	-946	..	-4731	-28077	*-113973	..	78044	119935	-38693	*-104404
Heat plants	-11920	-382	..	-5243	-8299	*-37708	..	-1526	68259	3181	*-36487
Coke ovens	-31618	34520	..	..	..	..	..	..	..	2902	..
Briquetting plants	..	..	..	..	..	..	..	..	..	..	..
Liquefaction plants	..	..	10216	..	..	..	..	..	..	10216	..
Gas works	..	..	..	..	..	..	..	..	..	..	..
Blast furnaces	-7618	-7622	..	..	..	..	..	..	..	-15241	..
NGL plants & gas blending	..	..	..	..	360	-360	..	..	..	0	-360
Oil refineries	..	..	-634339	637856	..	..	..	..	..	3517	..
Other transformation	-27	-2245	..	-677	-11374	..	..	..	..	-14322	..
Energy industries own use	..	-8285	..	-27315	-3115	-932	..	-13378	-5477	-58501	-932
Losses	..	-2183	..	-891	-296	..	..	-9965	-16756	-30091	..
Final consumption	14251	9675	..	317898	30786	*244082	..	291740	168880	1077313	*241535
Final energy consumption	14251	9675	..	260869	26523	*244082	..	291740	168880	1016020	*241535
Manufacturing, const., mining	11850	9675	..	50327	23796	*165255	..	139352	52806	453061	*162632
Iron and steel	1145	7824	..	4906	2320	*2	..	15199	3673	35070	*2
Chemical and petrochemical	..	..	..	9639	1428	804	..	16610	11110	39592	*305
Non-ferrous metals	37	234	..	1378	47	..	..	6822	1984	10502	..
Non-metallic minerals	1928	1587	..	3780	1062	1928	..	2952	540	13777	1082
Transport equipment	..	..	..	436	24	..	..	1174	961	2595	..
Machinery	..	..	..	1244	187	*48	..	7769	3597	12845	*48
Mining and quarrying	..	..	..	1735	4	7	..	5245	224	7214	7
Food and tobacco	453	29	..	1987	697	*342	..	6955	6934	17397	*342
Paper, pulp and printing	8228	..	..	6253	17577	*151955	..	65185	13516	*262714	*150738
Wood and wood products	50	..	..	431	1	9936	..	5825	8164	24406	9936
Textile and leather	..	..	..	81	152	*1	..	392	298	924	*1
Construction	..	..	..	14537	..	..	..	1620	..	16157	..
Industries n.e.s	10	0	..	3920	297	*232	..	3604	1805	9867	*171
Transport	..	..	..	161310	366	14297	..	2790	..	178763	14297
Road	..	..	..	152320	190	14216	..	79	..	166805	14216
Rail	..	..	..	903	..	..	..	2711	..	3614	..
Domestic aviation	..	..	..	2734	..	..	..	..	..	2734	..
Domestic navigation	..	..	..	5353	..	80	..	..	..	5434	80
Pipeline transport	..	..	..	..	50	..	..	..	..	50	..
Transport, n.e.s	..	..	..	..	126	..	..	..	..	126	..
Other	2401	..	..	49232	2361	*64531	..	149598	116074	384196	*64606
Agriculture, forestry, fishing	2153	..	..	15712	43	*7097	..	5483	561	31049	*7097
Commerce, public services	99	..	..	11184	1220	*4007	..	63072	42847	122428	*4007
Households	149	..	..	15101	1098	*53427	..	81043	69591	220409	*53502
Other consumers	..	..	..	7235	..	..	..	..	3075	10310	..
Non-energy use	..	..	..	57029	4263	..	..	..	..	61292	..

Finland

Terajoules

2018	Primary coal and peat	Coal and peat products	Primary Oil	Oil Products	Natural Gas	Biofuels and waste	Nuclear	Electricity	Heat	Total energy	of which: renewables
Primary production	75848	..	..	..	..	416710	246164	69228	4529	812480	471540
Imports	110385	9112	544820	209446	91225	6396	..	81173	..	1052557	6396
Exports	..	-3088	..	-377216	..	*-1560	..	-9403	..	-391268	*-1560
International marine bunkers	..	..	..	-13601	-44	..	..	..	..	-13646	..
International aviation bunkers	..	..	..	-33207	..	..	..	..	..	-33207	..
Stock changes	-15075	-1082	-512	5436	-231	..	..	..	..	-11464	..
Total energy supply	171158	4943	544308	-209143	90950	421546	246164	140998	4529	1415453	476376
Statistical difference	-4442	0	-6751	-15546	406	27	0	7	-8	-26306	69255
Transfers	..	..	73823	-75071	..	..	..	..	..	-1249	..
Transformation	-161357	15598	-624882	616226	-55912	*-167757	-246164	182200	183286	-258763	*-155879
Electricity plants	-24250	-5944	..	-1048	-1036	*-18457	-246164	101563	-1831	-197167	*-17610
CHP plants	-85311	-1393	..	-1657	-33647	*-112761	..	82156	113585	-39029	*-102735
Heat plants	-11526	-401	..	-7019	-11556	*-36172	..	-1519	71532	3340	*-35168
Coke ovens	-32136	34568	..	..	..	..	..	..	..	2432	..
Briquetting plants	..	..	..	..	..	..	..	..	..	..	..
Liquefaction plants	..	..	9064	..	..	..	..	..	..	9064	..
Gas works	..	..	..	..	..	..	..	..	..	..	..
Blast furnaces	-8134	-8545	..	..	..	..	..	..	..	-16679	..
NGL plants & gas blending	..	..	..	..	366	-367	..	..	..	-1	-367
Oil refineries	..	..	-633946	626725	..	..	..	..	..	-7221	..
Other transformation	..	-2688	..	-775	-10040	..	..	..	..	-13502	..
Energy industries own use	..	-8371	..	-25327	-4338	-986	..	-14335	-5603	-58961	-986
Losses	..	-1293	..	-396	-548	..	..	-10886	-14122	-27246	..
Final consumption	14243	10876	..	321834	29746	*252775	..	297968	168098	1095541	*250256
Final energy consumption	14243	10876	..	265635	25093	*252775	..	297968	168098	1034688	*250256
Manufacturing, const., mining	11884	10876	..	55154	22447	*175535	..	142153	53268	471318	*172933
Iron and steel	1231	9302	..	4248	2784	*1	..	15509	3648	36723	*1
Chemical and petrochemical	..	..	..	14694	1736	774	..	17593	11490	46288	*238
Non-ferrous metals	..	322	..	1603	50	69	..	6959	1971	10975	*26
Non-metallic minerals	1749	1252	..	3844	1178	1794	..	2902	563	13281	1050
Transport equipment	..	..	..	496	31	..	..	1062	925	2514	..
Machinery	..	..	..	1302	226	*47	..	8417	3510	13502	*47
Mining and quarrying	..	..	..	1390	4	*68	..	5206	200	6867	*68
Food and tobacco	562	..	..	1452	680	*394	..	7373	7414	17874	*394
Paper, pulp and printing	8114	..	..	6324	15514	*163224	..	65826	13102	*272104	*162022
Wood and wood products	228	..	..	510	..	*8948	..	5980	8334	24000	*8945
Textile and leather	..	..	..	43	111	97	..	410	318	979	49
Construction	..	..	..	15655	..	..	..	1494	..	17149	..
Industries n.e.s	0	0	..	3594	134	*119	..	3424	1793	9063	*93
Transport	..	..	..	163890	501	13628	..	3035	..	181054	13628
Road	..	..	..	154549	288	13548	..	166	..	168550	13548
Rail	..	..	..	989	..	..	..	2869	..	3858	..
Domestic aviation	..	..	..	2999	..	..	..	..	..	2999	..
Domestic navigation	..	..	..	5353	..	80	..	..	..	5434	80
Pipeline transport	..	..	..	..	140	..	..	..	..	140	..
Transport, n.e.s	..	..	..	..	74	..	..	..	..	74	..
Other	2359	..	..	46591	2145	*63612	..	152780	114830	382316	*63695
Agriculture, forestry, fishing	2111	..	..	14848	40	*7091	..	5429	545	30063	*7091
Commerce, public services	99	..	..	11097	1079	*4021	..	65520	45302	127118	*4021
Households	149	..	..	13894	1026	*52500	..	81832	67497	216898	*52583
Other consumers	..	..	..	6752	..	..	..	..	1486	8238	..
Non-energy use	..	..	..	56200	4653	..	..	..	..	60853	..

France

Terajoules

2017	Primary coal and peat	Coal and peat products	Primary Oil	Oil Products	Natural Gas	Biofuels and waste	Nuclear	Electricity	Heat	Total energy	of which: renewables
Primary production	..	..	37603	..	592	704154	4302277	304981	24594	5374201	964242
Imports	406735	15628	2469992	1771218	1806840	56039	..	76028	..	6602482	56039
Exports	..	-168	-4147	-866660	-227027	-32165	..	-220493	..	-1350660	-32165
International marine bunkers	..	..	..	-69811	..	..	..	..	..	-69811	..
International aviation bunkers	..	..	..	-241448	..	..	..	..	..	-241448	..
Stock changes	-2799	-6132	-15550	1441	31160	-274	..	..	..	7846	-274
Total energy supply	403937	9328	2487897	594741	1611565	727754	4302277	160517	24594	10322610	987842
Statistical difference	12597	-1307	4707	13998	0	-332	0	8654	1	38318	310574
Transfers	..	..	73928	-64623	..	..	..	..	..	9305	..
Transformation	-316130	74609	-2557119	2486741	-303810	-220288	-4302277	1699333	158976	-3279966	-175890
Electricity plants	-122626	-25795	..	-58843	-180645	-47013	-4302277	1622858	-4824	-3119166	-30731
CHP plants	-11101	-212	..	-12587	-97040	-130309	..	76644	100459	-74146	-103642
Heat plants	-8326	..	..	-1129	-27441	*-41651	..	-169	63341	-15375	*-40202
Coke ovens	-122899	118797	..	..	..	..	..	..	..	-4102	..
Briquetting plants	..	..	..	..	..	..	..	..	..	..	..
Liquefaction plants	..	..	..	..	..	..	..	..	..	..	..
Gas works	..	..	..	..	..	..	..	..	..	..	..
Blast furnaces	-51178	-25239	..	..	..	..	..	..	..	-76417	..
NGL plants & gas blending	..	..	0	0	1316	-1315	..	..	..	1	-1315
Oil refineries	..	..	-2557119	2562036	..	..	..	..	..	4918	..
Other transformation	..	7058	..	-2737	..	..	..	..	..	4321	..
Energy industries own use	..	-40453	..	-71006	-51422	..	..	-118512	1	-281391	..
Losses	..	..	..	..	-18214	..	..	-138956	-24144	-181315	..
Final consumption	75209	44792	..	2931854	1238119	*507797	..	1593727	159426	6550925	*501377
Final energy consumption	67809	40648	..	2396012	1183743	*507797	..	1593727	159426	5949162	*501377
Manufacturing, const., mining	65360	39784	..	111248	391199	*66364	..	445745	62170	1181869	*54756
Iron and steel	30082	35857	..	2039	32363	*15	..	42739	..	143095	*15
Chemical and petrochemical	15498	421	..	5042	62174	*4192	..	73357	..	160685	*3657
Non-ferrous metals	..	..	..	6044	14079	..	..	32159	..	52281	..
Non-metallic minerals	7853	1401	..	26331	70697	14928	..	29624	..	150834	*5187
Transport equipment	..	196	..	1094	17951	*278	..	25970	..	45489	*278
Machinery	54	784	..	4902	25999	*150	..	46804	..	78693	*147
Mining and quarrying	..	..	..	8278	1539	438	..	5868	..	16123	438
Food and tobacco	11301	1124	..	9445	98032	*12770	..	77936	..	210609	*12768
Paper, pulp and printing	571	..	..	1645	35480	*24002	..	28768	..	90465	*22680
Wood and wood products	..	..	..	1398	2321	*12712	..	7952	..	*24384	*12712
Textile and leather	..	..	..	713	6989	*6	..	5861	..	13568	*6
Construction	..	..	..	39904	12650	99	..	24512	..	77165	75
Industries n.e.s	0	0	..	4413	10928	*-3227	..	44194	62170	118478	*-3208
Transport	..	..	..	1798104	4986	135416	..	39107	..	1977613	135416
Road	..	..	..	1702112	3578	135416	..	752	..	1841857	135416
Rail	..	..	..	5977	..	..	..	34844	..	40821	..
Domestic aviation	..	..	..	68976	..	..	..	..	..	68976	..
Domestic navigation	..	..	..	21039	..	..	..	..	..	21039	..
Pipeline transport	..	..	..	..	1409	..	..	2830	..	4238	..
Transport, n.e.s	..	..	..	..	..	..	..	680	..	680	..
Other	2449	864	..	486660	787558	*306018	..	1108876	97256	2789680	*311206
Agriculture, forestry, fishing	54	32	..	136780	8732	*6835	..	31806	1381	185620	*7886
Commerce, public services	1496	224	..	112458	304092	23194	..	501775	35803	979043	20744
Households	898	608	..	219088	474733	*275989	..	573145	60072	1604533	*282576
Other consumers	..	..	..	18334	1	..	..	2149	..	20484	..
Non-energy use	7401	4144	..	535842	54376	..	..	..	..	601763	..

France

Terajoules

2018	Primary coal and peat	Coal and peat products	Primary Oil	Oil Products	Natural Gas	Biofuels and waste	Nuclear	Electricity	Heat	Total energy	of which: renewables
Primary production	..	..	36604	..	324	721635	4459774	377759	26232	5622328	1050249
Imports	365362	18169	2273226	1818141	1833072	60355	..	48823	..	6417148	60355
Exports	..	-1400	-955	-855621	-222716	-44210	..	-275522	..	-1400423	-44210
International marine bunkers	..	..	..	-77651	..	..	..	..	..	-77651	..
International aviation bunkers	..	..	..	-249165	..	..	..	..	..	-249165	..
Stock changes	-4839	1092	19116	16345	-73045	572	..	..	..	-40759	572
Total energy supply	360523	17861	2327991	652050	1537636	738352	4459774	151060	26232	10271478	1066965
Statistical difference	17705	3032	-3422	33327	-1	732	0	4684	0	56056	385116
Transfers	..	..	67310	-58140	..	..	..	..	..	9170	..
Transformation	-282675	70509	-2398724	2337167	-242267	-227842	-4459774	1697890	157964	-3347752	-182519
Electricity plants	-82210	-25654	..	-50606	-121562	-50783	-4459774	1622480	-4644	-3172753	-34540
CHP plants	-6591	-79	..	-11465	-94426	-131768	..	75654	97885	-70790	-103842
Heat plants	-6067	..	..	-799	-28591	*-42978	..	-245	64723	-13957	*-41824
Coke ovens	-122943	92512	..	..	..	..	..	..	..	-30431	..
Briquetting plants	..	..	..	..	..	..	..	..	..	..	..
Liquefaction plants	..	..	..	..	..	..	..	..	..	..	..
Gas works	..	..	..	..	..	..	..	..	..	..	..
Blast furnaces	-64863	3730	..	..	..	..	..	..	..	-61133	..
NGL plants & gas blending	..	..	0	0	2313	-2313	..	..	..	0	-2313
Oil refineries	..	..	-2398724	2401946	..	..	..	..	..	3222	..
Other transformation	..	0	..	-1910	..	..	..	..	..	-1910	..
Energy industries own use	..	-60225	..	-65020	-54682	..	..	-120262	0	-300189	..
Losses	..	..	..	..	-17850	..	..	-138974	-21776	-178600	..
Final consumption	60143	25113	..	2832729	1222838	*509778	..	1585030	162420	6398051	*499331
Final energy consumption	53001	20829	..	2332963	1167357	*509778	..	1585030	162420	5831377	*499331
Manufacturing, const., mining	50684	20445	..	106043	405213	*74865	..	445813	64241	1167304	*58608
Iron and steel	10921	16100	..	1266	33598	*14	..	43445	..	105344	*14
Chemical and petrochemical	15007	354	..	4432	69802	*3558	..	72252	..	165405	*2982
Non-ferrous metals	..	..	..	3491	13673	..	..	29650	..	46814	..
Non-metallic minerals	9774	1518	..	24698	75948	20262	..	29700	..	161900	*5829
Transport equipment	..	280	..	1094	18056	*237	..	26467	..	46134	*234
Machinery	55	952	..	4521	25392	*152	..	46483	..	77555	*146
Mining and quarrying	..	..	..	8411	1343	428	..	5796	..	15978	427
Food and tobacco	14459	1241	..	9075	97710	*7420	..	82012	..	211916	*6557
Paper, pulp and printing	469	..	..	1806	35211	*28632	..	28573	..	94691	*28391
Wood and wood products	..	..	..	1397	2888	*10998	..	8082	..	23365	*10978
Textile and leather	..	..	..	948	6416	2	..	5854	..	13220	..
Construction	..	..	..	40592	13864	361	..	25164	..	79981	209
Industries n.e.s	0	0	..	4312	11313	*2801	..	42336	64241	125003	*2841
Transport	..	..	..	1762578	5821	137462	..	37296	..	1943158	137462
Road	..	..	..	1661469	4210	137462	..	943	..	1804085	137462
Rail	..	..	..	5332	..	..	..	33210	..	38542	..
Domestic aviation	..	..	..	72901	..	..	..	..	..	72901	..
Domestic navigation	..	..	..	22877	..	..	..	..	..	22877	..
Pipeline transport	..	..	..	..	1611	..	..	2736	..	4347	..
Transport, n.e.s	..	..	..	..	..	..	..	407	..	407	..
Other	2317	384	..	464342	756322	*297451	..	1101920	98179	2720915	*303261
Agriculture, forestry, fishing	28	32	..	136178	9912	*7177	..	30784	1579	185689	*8229
Commerce, public services	1434	96	..	108490	299629	22925	..	498557	35576	966707	20763
Households	855	256	..	200070	446781	*267349	..	569988	61024	1546323	*274269
Other consumers	..	..	..	19603	1	..	..	2592	..	22196	..
Non-energy use	7143	4284	..	499766	55481	..	..	..	..	566674	..

French Polynesia

Terajoules

	All Coal	All Oil	Natural Gas	Primary biofuels / Waste	Charcoal	Electricity	Total energy	of which: renewables
2017								
Primary production	..	..	..	42	..	760	802	802
Imports	..	12305	..	0	4	..	12309	4
Exports	..	..	..	..	..	..	..	..
International marine bunkers	..	-707	..	..	..	..	-707	..
International aviation bunkers	..	*-425	..	..	..	..	*-425	..
Stock changes	..	*-386	..	..	..	..	*-386	..
Total energy supply	..	10786	..	42	4	760	11592	806
Statistical Difference	..	0	..	0	0	2	2	760
Transfers	..	..	..	..	..	..	..	..
Transformation	..	-4388	..	*-29	16	1754	-2647	*-14
Electricity plants	..	-4388	..	..	..	1754	-2634	..
Charcoal plants	..	..	..	*-29	16	..	*-14	*-14
Other transformation	..	0	..	0	..	..	0	0
Energy industries own use	..	..	..	..	..	-47	-47	..
Losses	..	..	..	..	..	-230	-230	..
Final consumption	..	6398	..	*13	*20	*2234	8665	*33
Final energy consumption	..	6282	..	*13	*20	*2234	8548	*33
Manufacturing, const., mining	..	..	..	..	..	..	..	..
Transport	..	5366	..	..	..	..	5366	..
Road	..	2014	..	..	..	..	2014	..
Domestic aviation	..	*186	..	..	..	..	*186	..
Domestic navigation	..	..	..	..	..	..	..	..
Other transport	..	3166	..	..	..	..	3166	..
Other	..	915	..	*13	*20	*2234	*3182	*33
Agriculture, forestry, fishing	..	412	..	..	..	..	412	..
Commerce and public services	..	..	..	..	..	*1007	*1007	..
Households	..	503	..	*13	*20	*1227	*1763	*33
Other consumers	..	..	..	..	..	..	..	..
Non-energy use	..	*117	..	..	..	..	*117	..
2018								
Primary production	..	..	..	42	..	724	766	766
Imports	..	12373	..	..	7	..	12380	7
Exports	..	..	..	..	..	..	..	..
International marine bunkers	..	-680	..	..	..	..	-680	..
International aviation bunkers	..	*-405	..	..	..	..	*-405	..
Stock changes	..	0	..	..	..	..	0	..
Total energy supply	..	11288	..	42	7	724	12062	774
Statistical Difference	..	0	..	0	0	40	40	724
Transfers	..	..	..	..	..	..	..	..
Transformation	..	-4544	..	*-29	16	1780	-2777	*-14
Electricity plants	..	-4544	..	..	..	1780	-2764	..
Charcoal plants	..	..	..	*-29	16	..	*-14	*-14
Other transformation	..	0	..	0	..	..	0	0
Energy industries own use	..	..	..	..	..	-34	-34	..
Losses	..	..	..	..	..	-239	-239	..
Final consumption	..	6745	..	*13	*23	*2190	8971	*36
Final energy consumption	..	6633	..	*13	*23	*2190	8859	*36
Manufacturing, const., mining	..	..	..	..	..	..	..	..
Transport	..	5647	..	..	..	..	5647	..
Road	..	2325	..	..	..	..	2325	..
Domestic aviation	..	*179	..	..	..	..	*179	..
Domestic navigation	..	..	..	..	..	..	..	..
Other transport	..	3143	..	..	..	..	3143	..
Other	..	986	..	*13	*23	*2190	*3212	*36
Agriculture, forestry, fishing	..	435	..	..	..	..	435	..
Commerce and public services	..	..	..	..	..	*986	*986	..
Households	..	551	..	*13	*23	*1205	*1791	*36
Other consumers	..	..	..	..	..	..	..	..
Non-energy use	..	*112	..	..	..	..	*112	..

Gabon

Terajoules

2017	Primary coal and peat	Coal and peat products	Primary Oil	Oil Products	Natural Gas	Biofuels and waste	Nuclear	Electricity	Heat	Total energy	of which: renewables
Primary production	..	..	444108	..	16524	*53590	..	3352	..	517573	*56942
Imports	..	..	..	12406	..	..	..	1246	..	13652	..
Exports	..	..	-396563	-9997	..	..	..	..	..	-406560	..
International marine bunkers	..	..	..	-4770	..	..	..	..	..	-4770	..
International aviation bunkers	..	..	..	-2077	..	..	..	..	..	-2077	..
Stock changes	..	..	-12690	-426	..	..	..	..	..	-13116	..
Total energy supply	..	..	34855	-4863	16524	*53590	..	4597	..	104704	*56942
Statistical difference	..	..	550	2199	-1288	0	..	4	..	1465	*3352
Transfers	..	..	..	..	..	..	..	..	..	..	..
Transformation	..	..	-34305	30430	-13728	*-914	..	4846	..	-13672	*-914
Electricity plants	..	..	..	-2881	-13728	-334	..	4846	..	-12097	-334
CHP plants	..	..	..	..	..	..	..	..	..	..	..
Heat plants	..	..	..	..	..	..	..	..	..	..	..
Coke ovens	..	..	..	..	..	..	..	..	..	..	..
Briquetting plants	..	..	..	..	..	..	..	..	..	..	..
Liquefaction plants	..	..	..	..	..	..	..	..	..	..	..
Gas works	..	..	..	..	..	..	..	..	..	..	..
Blast furnaces	..	..	..	..	..	..	..	..	..	..	..
NGL plants & gas blending	..	..	..	..	..	..	..	..	..	..	..
Oil refineries	..	..	-34305	33311	..	..	..	..	..	-994	..
Other transformation	..	..	..	..	..	*-580	..	..	..	*-580	*-580
Energy industries own use	..	..	..	-5272	-3980	..	..	-526	..	-9777	..
Losses	..	..	..	..	..	..	..	-1156	..	-1156	..
Final consumption	..	..	..	18097	104	*52676	..	7758	..	*78635	*52676
Final energy consumption	..	..	..	17570	104	*52676	..	7758	..	*78108	*52676
Manufacturing, const., mining	..	..	..	6714	104	*11535	..	2333	..	*20686	*11535
Iron and steel	..	..	..	..	..	..	..	..	..	..	..
Chemical and petrochemical	..	..	..	..	..	..	..	7	..	7	..
Non-ferrous metals	..	..	..	..	..	..	..	..	..	..	..
Non-metallic minerals	..	..	..	..	..	..	..	..	..	..	..
Transport equipment	..	..	..	..	..	..	..	..	..	..	..
Machinery	..	..	..	..	..	..	..	..	..	..	..
Mining and quarrying	..	..	..	..	..	..	..	342	..	342	..
Food and tobacco	..	..	..	..	50	*618	..	662	..	1331	*618
Paper, pulp and printing	..	..	..	..	..	..	..	..	..	..	..
Wood and wood products	..	..	..	..	54	..	..	842	..	896	..
Textile and leather	..	..	..	..	..	..	..	7	..	7	..
Construction	..	..	..	..	..	..	..	385	..	385	..
Industries n.e.s	..	..	..	6714	0	*10917	..	86	..	*17717	*10917
Transport	..	..	..	*7506	..	..	..	29	..	*7535	..
Road	..	..	..	*7418	..	..	..	..	..	*7418	..
Rail	..	..	..	..	..	..	..	29	..	29	..
Domestic aviation	..	..	..	88	..	..	..	..	..	88	..
Domestic navigation	..	..	..	..	..	..	..	..	..	..	..
Pipeline transport	..	..	..	..	..	..	..	..	..	..	..
Transport, n.e.s	..	..	..	..	..	..	..	..	..	..	..
Other	..	..	..	3350	..	*41141	..	5396	..	*49887	*41141
Agriculture, forestry, fishing	..	..	..	44	..	..	..	115	..	160	..
Commerce, public services	..	..	..	747	..	..	..	1087	..	1834	..
Households	..	..	..	2417	..	*41141	..	4136	..	*47694	*41141
Other consumers	..	..	..	142	..	..	..	58	..	199	..
Non-energy use	..	..	..	527	..	..	..	..	..	527	..

Gabon

Terajoules

2018	Primary coal and peat	Coal and peat products	Primary Oil	Oil Products	Natural Gas	Biofuels and waste	Nuclear	Electricity	Heat	Total energy	of which: renewables
Primary production	..	..	401300	..	16085	*54751	..	3811	..	475946	*58561
Imports	..	..	..	12024	..	..	..	1256	..	13280	..
Exports	..	..	-366487	-10038	..	..	..	..	..	-376525	..
International marine bunkers	..	..	..	-4684	..	..	..	..	..	-4684	..
International aviation bunkers	..	..	..	-2385	..	..	..	..	..	-2385	..
Stock changes	..	..	..	..	..	..	..	..	..	..	..
Total energy supply	..	..	34813	-5083	16085	*54751	..	5067	..	105633	*58561
Statistical difference	..	..	296	-375	-1869	0	..	467	..	-1482	*3811
Transfers	..	..	..	..	..	..	..	..	..	..	..
Transformation	..	..	-34517	30684	-13843	*-964	..	5599	..	-13042	*-964
Electricity plants	..	..	..	-2881	-13843	*-336	..	5599	..	-11461	*-336
CHP plants	..	..	..	..	..	..	..	..	..	..	..
Heat plants	..	..	..	..	..	..	..	..	..	..	..
Coke ovens	..	..	..	..	..	..	..	..	..	..	..
Briquetting plants	..	..	..	..	..	..	..	..	..	..	..
Liquefaction plants	..	..	..	..	..	..	..	..	..	..	..
Gas works	..	..	..	..	..	..	..	..	..	..	..
Blast furnaces	..	..	..	..	..	..	..	..	..	..	..
NGL plants & gas blending	..	..	..	..	..	..	..	..	..	..	..
Oil refineries	..	..	-34517	33565	..	..	..	..	..	-952	..
Other transformation	..	..	..	..	..	*-628	..	..	..	*-628	*-628
Energy industries own use	..	..	..	-5315	-4005	..	..	-256	..	-9575	..
Losses	..	..	..	..	..	..	..	-1037	..	-1037	..
Final consumption	..	..	..	*20661	106	*53786	..	8906	..	*83460	*53786
Final energy consumption	..	..	..	*20095	106	*53786	..	8906	..	*82893	*53786
Manufacturing, const., mining	..	..	..	*9024	106	*12374	..	2347	..	*23852	*12374
Iron and steel	..	..	..	..	..	..	..	..	..	..	..
Chemical and petrochemical	..	..	..	..	..	..	..	7	..	7	..
Non-ferrous metals	..	..	..	..	..	..	..	..	..	..	..
Non-metallic minerals	..	..	..	..	..	..	..	..	..	..	..
Transport equipment	..	..	..	..	..	..	..	..	..	..	..
Machinery	..	..	..	..	..	..	..	..	..	..	..
Mining and quarrying	..	..	..	..	..	..	..	346	..	346	..
Food and tobacco	..	..	..	..	51	*633	..	666	..	1351	*633
Paper, pulp and printing	..	..	..	..	..	..	..	..	..	..	..
Wood and wood products	..	..	..	..	55	..	..	850	..	905	..
Textile and leather	..	..	..	..	..	..	..	7	..	7	..
Construction	..	..	..	..	..	..	..	385	..	385	..
Industries n.e.s	..	..	..	*9024	0	*11741	..	86	..	*20851	*11741
Transport	..	..	..	*7721	..	..	..	29	..	*7750	..
Road	..	..	..	*7633	..	..	..	..	..	*7633	..
Rail	..	..	..	..	..	..	..	29	..	29	..
Domestic aviation	..	..	..	88	..	..	..	..	..	88	..
Domestic navigation	..	..	..	..	..	..	..	..	..	..	..
Pipeline transport	..	..	..	..	..	..	..	..	..	..	..
Transport, n.e.s	..	..	..	..	..	..	..	..	..	..	..
Other	..	..	..	3350	..	*41412	..	6530	..	*51292	*41412
Agriculture, forestry, fishing	..	..	..	44	..	..	..	115	..	160	..
Commerce, public services	..	..	..	747	..	..	..	1098	..	1845	..
Households	..	..	..	2417	..	*41412	..	4172	..	*48001	*41412
Other consumers	..	..	..	142	..	..	..	*1145	..	*1287	..
Non-energy use	..	..	..	567	..	..	..	..	..	567	..

Gambia

Terajoules

	All Coal	All Oil	Natural Gas	Primary biofuels / Waste	Charcoal	Electricity	Total energy	of which: renewables
2017								
Primary production	..	..	..	6921	..	*13	6934	6934
Imports	..	*8006	*96	0	22	..	*8124	22
Exports	..	*-87	..	0	-83	..	*-170	-83
International marine bunkers	..	..	..	..	..	..	..	..
International aviation bunkers	..	*-626	..	..	..	..	*-626	..
Stock changes	..	..	..	..	..	..	..	..
Total energy supply	..	*7293	*96	6921	-61	*13	*14261	6873
Statistical Difference	..	0	0	0	0	0	0	13
Transfers	..	..	..	..	..	..	..	..
Transformation	..	*-3522	..	*-3731	2008	1129	*-4116	*-1723
Electricity plants	..	*-3522	..	..	..	1129	*-2393	..
Charcoal plants	..	..	..	*-3731	2008	..	*-1723	*-1723
Other transformation	..	0	..	0	..	..	0	0
Energy industries own use	..	..	..	..	..	*-43	*-43	..
Losses	..	..	..	..	..	*-245	*-245	..
Final consumption	..	*3771	*96	*3190	*1947	*854	*9858	*5137
Final energy consumption	..	*3771	*96	*3190	*1947	*854	*9858	*5137
Manufacturing, const., mining	..	*1879	..	..	..	*144	*2023	..
Transport	..	*1125	..	..	..	..	*1125	..
Road	..	*1125	..	..	..	..	*1125	..
Domestic aviation	..	..	..	..	..	..	..	..
Domestic navigation	..	..	..	..	..	..	..	..
Other transport	..	..	..	..	..	..	..	..
Other	..	*767	*96	*3190	*1947	*710	*6710	*5137
Agriculture, forestry, fishing	..	..	..	..	..	..	..	..
Commerce and public services	..	..	..	..	..	..	..	..
Households	..	..	..	*3190	*1947	..	*5137	*5137
Other consumers	..	*767	*96	..	..	*710	*1573	..
Non-energy use	..	..	..	..	..	..	..	..
2018								
Primary production	..	..	..	6997	..	*13	7010	7010
Imports	..	*8129	*98	0	21	..	*8248	21
Exports	..	*-87	..	0	-29	..	*-116	-29
International marine bunkers	..	..	..	..	..	..	..	..
International aviation bunkers	..	*-657	..	..	..	..	*-657	..
Stock changes	..	..	..	..	..	..	..	..
Total energy supply	..	*7385	*98	6997	-8	*13	*14484	7002
Statistical Difference	..	0	0	0	0	0	0	13
Transfers	..	..	..	..	..	..	..	..
Transformation	..	*-3569	..	*-3800	2045	*1144	*-4179	*-1755
Electricity plants	..	*-3569	..	..	..	*1144	*-2424	..
Charcoal plants	..	..	..	*-3800	2045	..	*-1755	*-1755
Other transformation	..	0	..	0	..	..	0	0
Energy industries own use	..	..	..	..	..	*-46	*-46	..
Losses	..	..	..	..	..	*-249	*-249	..
Final consumption	..	*3817	*98	*3197	*2037	*862	*10010	*5234
Final energy consumption	..	*3817	*98	*3197	*2037	*862	*10010	*5234
Manufacturing, const., mining	..	*1903	..	..	..	*146	*2049	..
Transport	..	*1139	..	..	..	..	*1139	..
Road	..	*1139	..	..	..	..	*1139	..
Domestic aviation	..	..	..	..	..	..	..	..
Domestic navigation	..	..	..	..	..	..	..	..
Other transport	..	..	..	..	..	..	..	..
Other	..	*775	*98	*3197	*2037	*716	*6823	*5234
Agriculture, forestry, fishing	..	..	..	..	..	..	..	..
Commerce and public services	..	..	..	..	..	..	..	..
Households	..	..	..	*3197	*2037	..	*5234	*5234
Other consumers	..	*775	*98	..	..	*716	*1589	..
Non-energy use	..	..	..	..	..	..	..	..

Georgia

Terajoules

2017	Primary coal and peat	Coal and peat products	Primary Oil	Oil Products	Natural Gas	Biofuels and waste	Nuclear	Electricity	Heat	Total energy	of which: renewables
Primary production	4558	..	1360	..	300	15277	..	33474	786	55754	49537
Imports	4489	3974	2533	62207	85737	..	..	6304	..	165244	..
Exports	-38	-376	-315	*-7235	..	-66	..	-3383	..	*-11413	-66
International marine bunkers	..	..	..	..	..	..	..	..	..	..	..
International aviation bunkers	..	..	..	-4194	..	..	..	..	..	-4194	..
Stock changes	-486	519	200	487	..	..	..	..	..	720	..
Total energy supply	8522	4117	3778	51265	86036	15211	..	36395	786	206111	49470
Statistical difference	376	20	183	-8	0	0	..	0	0	570	33474
Transfers	..	..	-2533	*2722	..	..	..	..	..	*189	..
Transformation	-634	..	-1063	1008	-18367	..	..	8039	..	-11017	..
Electricity plants	-634	..	..	..	-18367	..	..	8039	..	-10963	..
CHP plants	..	..	..	..	..	..	..	..	..	..	..
Heat plants	..	..	..	..	..	..	..	..	..	..	..
Coke ovens	..	..	..	..	..	..	..	..	..	..	..
Briquetting plants	..	..	..	..	..	..	..	..	..	..	..
Liquefaction plants	..	..	..	..	..	..	..	..	..	..	..
Gas works	..	..	..	..	..	..	..	..	..	..	..
Blast furnaces	..	..	..	..	..	..	..	..	..	..	..
NGL plants & gas blending	..	..	..	..	..	..	..	..	..	..	..
Oil refineries	..	..	-1063	1008	..	..	..	..	..	-55	..
Other transformation	..	..	..	..	..	..	..	..	..	..	..
Energy industries own use	-15	..	..	..	..	..	..	-830	..	-845	..
Losses	..	..	..	..	-3367	..	..	-3253	..	-6620	..
Final consumption	7497	4098	..	55003	64302	15211	..	40351	786	187247	15997
Final energy consumption	7497	4098	..	49930	55648	15211	..	40351	786	173519	15997
Manufacturing, const., mining	7443	4098	..	3479	4886	46	..	11860	..	31812	46
Iron and steel	38	4098	..	4	575	..	..	6625	..	11340	..
Chemical and petrochemical	..	..	..	..	201	..	..	1021	..	1222	..
Non-ferrous metals	..	..	..	..	..	..	..	0	..	0	..
Non-metallic minerals	7242	..	..	23	1371	1	..	1060	..	9698	1
Transport equipment	..	..	..	..	4	..	..	8	..	11	..
Machinery	..	..	..	..	4	..	..	21	..	24	..
Mining and quarrying	..	..	..	774	32	..	..	453	..	1259	..
Food and tobacco	144	..	..	20	1738	44	..	893	..	2839	44
Paper, pulp and printing	..	..	..	..	63	..	..	61	..	124	..
Wood and wood products	..	..	..	..	25	1	..	28	..	54	1
Textile and leather	..	..	..	..	49	..	..	63	..	112	..
Construction	..	..	..	2657	747	1	..	524	..	3929	1
Industries n.e.s	20	0	..	0	78	0	..	1103	..	1200	0
Transport	..	..	..	44839	12254	..	..	1211	..	58305	..
Road	..	..	..	44276	8849	..	..	..	..	53125	..
Rail	..	..	..	455	..	..	..	1211	..	1666	..
Domestic aviation	..	..	..	26	..	..	..	..	..	26	..
Domestic navigation	..	..	..	82	..	..	..	..	..	82	..
Pipeline transport	..	..	..	..	3406	..	..	..	..	3406	..
Transport, n.e.s	..	..	..	..	..	..	..	..	..	..	..
Other	53	..	..	1612	38507	15165	..	27279	786	83402	15951
Agriculture, forestry, fishing	10	..	..	551	441	1	..	226	38	1267	39
Commerce, public services	21	..	..	413	6903	156	..	10987	483	18963	640
Households	22	..	..	648	31164	15008	..	8859	265	55966	15273
Other consumers	..	..	..	..	..	..	..	7206	..	7206	..
Non-energy use	..	..	..	5073	8655	..	..	..	..	13728	..

Georgia

Terajoules

2018	Primary coal and peat	Coal and peat products	Primary Oil	Oil Products	Natural Gas	Biofuels and waste	Nuclear	Electricity	Heat	Total energy	of which: renewables
Primary production	2344	..	1284	..	363	11399	..	36121	799	52310	48319
Imports	7134	4775	84	62730	85270	0	..	5480	..	165473	0
Exports	-63	-30	-395	-4244	..	-69	..	-2167	..	-6968	-69
International marine bunkers	..	..	..	-69	..	..	..	..	..	-69	..
International aviation bunkers	..	..	..	-4520	..	..	..	..	..	-4520	..
Stock changes	-862	-79	-55	-1079	..	..	..	..	..	-2075	..
Total energy supply	8554	4665	917	52818	85633	11331	..	39434	799	204150	48251
Statistical difference	-4	-4	-82	109	0	2	..	65	0	86	36123
Transfers	..	..	..	..	..	..	..	..	..	..	..
Transformation	-359	..	-999	937	-17373	..	..	7614	..	-10180	..
Electricity plants	-359	..	..	..	-17373	..	..	7614	..	-10118	..
CHP plants	..	..	..	..	..	..	..	..	..	..	..
Heat plants	..	..	..	..	..	..	..	..	..	..	..
Coke ovens	..	..	..	..	..	..	..	..	..	..	..
Briquetting plants	..	..	..	..	..	..	..	..	..	..	..
Liquefaction plants	..	..	..	..	..	..	..	..	..	..	..
Gas works	..	..	..	..	..	..	..	..	..	..	..
Blast furnaces	..	..	..	..	..	..	..	..	..	..	..
NGL plants & gas blending	..	..	..	..	..	..	..	..	..	..	..
Oil refineries	..	..	-999	937	..	..	..	..	..	-62	..
Other transformation	..	..	..	..	..	..	..	..	..	..	..
Energy industries own use	-12	..	..	..	..	..	..	-819	..	-831	..
Losses	..	..	..	..	-3929	..	..	-3190	..	-7119	..
Final consumption	8187	4669	..	53646	64330	11329	..	42974	799	185934	12127
Final energy consumption	8187	4669	..	48558	54769	11329	..	42974	799	171284	12127
Manufacturing, const., mining	8163	4669	..	3959	4537	70	..	11901	..	33299	70
Iron and steel	726	4669	..	9	668	..	..	6881	..	12953	..
Chemical and petrochemical	..	..	..	..	110	..	..	1160	..	1271	..
Non-ferrous metals	..	..	..	..	..	..	..	..	..	..	..
Non-metallic minerals	7237	..	..	12	1237	0	..	922	..	9409	0
Transport equipment	..	..	..	..	7	..	..	6	..	13	..
Machinery	..	..	..	..	21	..	..	33	..	55	..
Mining and quarrying	..	..	..	899	50	..	..	444	..	1392	..
Food and tobacco	200	..	..	3	1511	69	..	885	..	2667	69
Paper, pulp and printing	..	..	..	..	149	..	..	56	..	205	..
Wood and wood products	..	..	..	..	11	2	..	26	..	39	2
Textile and leather	..	..	..	0	39	..	..	56	..	95	..
Construction	..	..	..	3141	544	0	..	419	..	4104	0
Industries n.e.s	0	0	..	-104	188	-1	..	1013	..	1097	-1
Transport	..	..	..	43217	12449	..	..	1316	..	56981	..
Road	..	..	..	42429	8143	..	..	..	..	50572	..
Rail	..	..	..	462	..	..	..	1282	..	1744	..
Domestic aviation	..	..	..	13	..	..	..	..	..	13	..
Domestic navigation	..	..	..	24	..	..	..	..	..	24	..
Pipeline transport	..	..	..	288	4306	..	..	..	..	4594	..
Transport, n.e.s	..	..	..	..	..	..	..	34	..	34	..
Other	24	..	..	1382	37783	11259	..	29758	799	81004	12057
Agriculture, forestry, fishing	8	..	..	506	288	0	..	286	39	1127	39
Commerce, public services	8	..	..	63	7236	140	..	13612	492	21550	632
Households	8	..	..	813	30259	11119	..	8942	268	51409	11386
Other consumers	..	..	..	..	..	..	..	6918	..	6918	..
Non-energy use	..	..	..	5088	9561	..	..	..	..	14650	..

Germany

Terajoules

2017	Primary coal and peat	Coal and peat products	Primary Oil	Oil Products	Natural Gas	Biofuels and waste	Nuclear	Electricity	Heat	Total energy	of which: renewables
Primary production	1651374	..	147776	..	252419	1284461	824299	594878	38985	4794192	1729332
Imports	1345650	69594	3856819	1768937	4008494	86837	..	100231	..	11236562	86837
Exports	-6454	-55444	..	-989092	-1126265	-81249	..	-289084	-124	-2547711	-81249
International marine bunkers	..	..	..	-95969	..	..	..	..	..	-95969	..
International aviation bunkers	..	..	..	-410968	..	..	..	..	..	-410968	..
Stock changes	-16964	-860	10584	23291	19715	..	..	..	..	35767	..
Total energy supply	2973607	13290	4015178	296200	3154363	1290049	824299	406026	38861	13011873	1734919
Statistical difference	14094	23935	340	-8032	12620	-564	0	0	0	42393	595549
Transfers	..	..	394995	-362346	..	..	..	..	..	32649	..
Transformation	-2862223	262439	-4409833	4300244	-766636	-633931	-824299	1736906	462645	-2734689	-498032
Electricity plants	-2010580	-85731	..	-34876	-144441	-209850	-824299	1257350	-5868	-2058295	-167860
CHP plants	-259332	-36853	..	-17537	-530301	-368745	..	479556	340265	-392947	-296756
Heat plants	-12587	-2316	..	-4958	-91895	-54923	..	..	128248	-38430	-33003
Coke ovens	-334656	337125	..	-16965	..	..	..	..	..	-14496	..
Briquetting plants	-112796	141180	..	..	..	..	..	..	..	28385	..
Liquefaction plants	..	..	..	..	..	..	..	..	..	..	..
Gas works	..	..	..	..	..	..	..	..	..	..	..
Blast furnaces	-132273	-114256	..	-1131	..	..	..	..	..	-247661	..
NGL plants & gas blending	..	..	..	..	..	..	..	..	..	..	..
Oil refineries	..	..	-4409833	4386706	..	..	..	..	..	-23127	..
Other transformation	..	23289	..	-10995	..	*-413	..	..	..	11881	*-413
Energy industries own use	-6339	-28283	..	-230139	-57558	-22382	..	-177415	-14168	-536284	-22382
Losses	..	-23600	..	..	..	-3495	..	-97286	-44912	-169293	-3495
Final consumption	90950	199911	..	4011990	2317550	*630804	..	1868231	442426	9561862	*615460
Final energy consumption	90019	183719	..	3166501	2209442	*630804	..	1868231	442426	8591142	*615460
Manufacturing, const., mining	86641	164739	..	91257	874346	*162816	..	836017	172093	2387910	*115644
Iron and steel	28289	98162	..	1277	93811	1	..	96102	1283	318924	1
Chemical and petrochemical	28437	5165	..	46364	245610	11629	..	195188	99041	631433	1697
Non-ferrous metals	644	487	..	2575	34952	279	..	58594	925	98454	11
Non-metallic minerals	10752	46232	..	14122	106295	47448	..	45904	732	271485	13853
Transport equipment	6623	1734	..	1690	39127	33	..	64012	12591	125810	31
Machinery	1260	745	..	9788	75497	359	..	122069	10825	220541	285
Mining and quarrying	27	2422	..	1350	4273	63	..	6365	129	14629	63
Food and tobacco	4094	3939	..	6459	118075	774	..	67100	10912	211352	774
Paper, pulp and printing	6355	5834	..	1575	87099	7262	..	77062	25839	211026	3978
Wood and wood products	..	..	..	647	5749	64	..	17341	2675	26477	50
Textile and leather	161	..	..	821	10170	..	..	7841	653	19646	..
Construction	..	..	..	..	21886	..	..	14890	..	36776	..
Industries n.e.s	0	20	..	4592	31803	*94903	..	63551	6488	201357	*94900
Transport	..	..	..	2297738	19133	108758	..	43045	..	2468675	108758
Road	..	..	..	2240943	5989	108170	..	565	..	2355667	108170
Rail	..	..	..	11537	..	589	..	42480	..	54606	589
Domestic aviation	..	..	..	29064	..	..	..	..	..	29064	..
Domestic navigation	..	..	..	10234	..	..	..	..	..	10234	..
Pipeline transport	..	..	..	..	13145	..	..	..	..	13145	..
Transport, n.e.s	..	..	..	5960	..	..	..	..	..	5960	..
Other	3379	18980	..	777506	1315962	*359230	..	989168	270333	3734557	*391058
Agriculture, forestry, fishing	..	..	..	..	10618	30442	..	18324	..	59385	30442
Commerce, public services	697	..	..	295609	401070	*79001	..	509324	56629	1342330	*82648
Households	2681	18980	..	478204	904274	*249786	..	461520	213704	2329150	*277967
Other consumers	..	..	..	3693	..	..	..	..	..	3693	..
Non-energy use	931	16191	..	845489	108108	..	..	..	..	970720	..

Germany

Terajoules

2018	Primary coal and peat	Coal and peat products	Primary Oil	Oil Products	Natural Gas	Biofuels and waste	Nuclear	Electricity	Heat	Total energy	of which: renewables
Primary production	1574911	..	146171	..	197396	1257902	820854	625352	43732	4666318	1750403
Imports	1198094	69674	3621894	1738732	2953008	107987	..	114217	..	9803605	107987
Exports	-5871	-55140	..	-948897	..	-106327	..	-289667	..	-1405902	-106327
International marine bunkers	..	..	..	-71235	..	..	..	..	..	-71235	..
International aviation bunkers	..	..	..	-423845	..	..	..	..	..	-423845	..
Stock changes	104828	-890	21380	21310	-70929	..	..	..	..	75700	..
Total energy supply	2871961	13644	3789445	316066	3079475	1259561	820854	449903	43732	12644642	1752062
Statistical difference	41128	18034	43	4338	-97222	-509	0	0	0	-34187	626397
Transfers	..	..	429250	-403593	..	..	..	..	..	25657	..
Transformation	-2760720	252457	-4218652	4124474	-724268	-607022	-820854	1667812	459049	-2627725	-489966
Electricity plants	-1925857	-103488	..	-26535	-155009	-214293	-820854	1226671	-6408	-2025773	-174863
CHP plants	-229909	-17358	..	-17115	-493761	-351526	..	441140	354630	-313898	-290249
Heat plants	-8086	-4072	..	-4604	-75498	-40791	..	..	110827	-22225	-24441
Coke ovens	-334850	332839	..	-12513	..	..	..	..	..	-14524	..
Briquetting plants	-126935	139222	..	..	..	..	..	..	..	12287	..
Liquefaction plants	..	..	..	..	..	..	..	..	..	..	..
Gas works	..	..	..	..	..	..	..	..	..	..	..
Blast furnaces	-135084	-119684	..	-1818	..	..	..	..	..	-256586	..
NGL plants & gas blending	..	..	..	..	..	..	..	..	..	..	..
Oil refineries	..	..	-4218652	4195212	..	..	..	..	..	-23441	..
Other transformation	..	24999	..	-8152	..	*-413	..	..	..	16435	*-413
Energy industries own use	-6132	-27462	..	-215866	-65204	-21780	..	-175172	-15265	-526881	-21037
Losses	..	-11504	..	..	..	-3448	..	-95980	-52222	-163154	-3448
Final consumption	63981	209101	..	3816743	2387225	*627820	..	1846562	435294	9386726	*611214
Final energy consumption	63031	193260	..	3041909	2261309	*627820	..	1846562	435294	8469185	*611214
Manufacturing, const., mining	59404	174648	..	155526	844452	*166748	..	829897	191473	2422149	*114645
Iron and steel	20092	111227	..	640	92985	..	..	94828	1377	321149	..
Chemical and petrochemical	10931	5872	..	56271	225758	9380	..	192838	111912	612962	1418
Non-ferrous metals	672	458	..	1744	36128	279	..	56826	1046	97152	17
Non-metallic minerals	10288	42759	..	17401	107050	52856	..	45724	4267	280343	15001
Transport equipment	4674	1509	..	1730	38050	3	..	63889	12933	122788	4
Machinery	295	532	..	9354	74118	702	..	122472	10603	218076	419
Mining and quarrying	27	2700	..	1189	4131	102	..	6386	180	14715	102
Food and tobacco	4637	3989	..	6519	118279	871	..	68263	12042	214599	871
Paper, pulp and printing	6339	5582	..	1913	78737	11940	..	75082	27799	207393	6394
Wood and wood products	..	..	..	733	5230	218	..	16805	2636	25621	77
Textile and leather	188	..	..	692	9841	1	..	7675	644	19041	1
Construction	..	..	..	51599	23599	1937	..	16056	..	93191	1937
Industries n.e.s	1262	19	..	5743	30547	*88458	..	63054	6034	195118	*88403
Transport	..	..	..	2221700	25670	112833	..	43513	..	2403716	112833
Road	..	..	..	2165695	5252	112318	..	817	..	2284082	112318
Rail	..	..	..	9590	..	515	..	42696	..	52801	515
Domestic aviation	..	..	..	28094	..	..	..	..	..	28094	..
Domestic navigation	..	..	..	10707	..	..	..	..	..	10707	..
Pipeline transport	..	..	..	..	20417	..	..	..	..	20417	..
Transport, n.e.s	..	..	..	7615	..	..	..	..	..	7615	..
Other	3626	18612	..	664683	1391188	*348239	..	973152	243821	3643320	*383736
Agriculture, forestry, fishing	..	..	..	91246	10478	32227	..	18083	44	152078	32271
Commerce, public services	806	..	..	138104	448520	*74540	..	493549	59172	1214692	*78477
Households	2820	18612	..	432075	932189	*241472	..	461520	184605	2273293	*272988
Other consumers	..	..	..	3257	..	..	..	..	..	3257	..
Non-energy use	950	15841	..	774834	125915	..	..	..	..	917540	..

Ghana

Terajoules

2017	Primary coal and peat	Coal and peat products	Primary Oil	Oil Products	Natural Gas	Biofuels and waste	Nuclear	Electricity	Heat	Total energy	of which: renewables
Primary production	..	..	359424	..	32046	107237	..	20318	..	519026	127555
Imports	..	..	9856	165672	11122	..	..	1152	..	187802	..
Exports	..	..	-344364	-20395	..	-12	..	-965	..	-365736	-12
International marine bunkers	..	..	..	-3823	..	..	..	..	..	-3823	..
International aviation bunkers	..	..	..	-7058	..	..	..	..	..	-7058	..
Stock changes	..	..	-12944	-2608	..	..	..	..	..	-15552	..
Total energy supply	..	..	11972	131789	43168	107225	..	20506	..	314660	127543
Statistical difference	..	..	-6260	-11787	-5556	32	..	32	..	-23538	20351
Transfers	..	..	..	..	..	..	..	..	..	..	..
Transformation	..	..	-16414	-4060	-39165	-18133	..	30974	..	-46797	-18133
Electricity plants	..	..	-10448	-10147	-39165	..	..	30974	..	-28786	..
CHP plants	..	..	..	..	..	..	..	..	..	..	..
Heat plants	..	..	..	..	..	..	..	..	..	..	..
Coke ovens	..	..	..	..	..	..	..	..	..	..	..
Briquetting plants	..	..	..	..	..	..	..	..	..	..	..
Liquefaction plants	..	..	..	..	..	..	..	..	..	..	..
Gas works	..	..	..	..	..	..	..	..	..	..	..
Blast furnaces	..	..	..	..	..	..	..	..	..	..	..
NGL plants & gas blending	..	..	-4950	5392	..	..	..	..	..	442	..
Oil refineries	..	..	-1015	695	..	..	..	..	..	-320	..
Other transformation	..	..	..	..	..	-18133	..	..	..	-18133	-18133
Energy industries own use	..	..	-169	-3259	-8473	..	..	-904	..	-12805	..
Losses	..	..	-1650	..	..	..	..	-6912	..	-8562	..
Final consumption	..	..	..	136256	1086	89060	..	43632	..	270034	89060
Final energy consumption	..	..	..	133002	1086	89060	..	43632	..	266780	89060
Manufacturing, const., mining	..	..	..	12316	1086	5479	..	11081	..	29961	5479
Iron and steel	..	..	..	..	..	..	..	..	..	..	..
Chemical and petrochemical	..	..	..	..	..	..	..	..	..	..	..
Non-ferrous metals	..	..	..	..	..	..	..	..	..	..	..
Non-metallic minerals	..	..	..	..	..	..	..	..	..	..	..
Transport equipment	..	..	..	..	..	..	..	..	..	..	..
Machinery	..	..	..	..	..	..	..	..	..	..	..
Mining and quarrying	..	..	..	..	..	..	..	..	..	..	..
Food and tobacco	..	..	..	..	..	..	..	..	..	..	..
Paper, pulp and printing	..	..	..	..	..	..	..	..	..	..	..
Wood and wood products	..	..	..	..	..	..	..	..	..	..	..
Textile and leather	..	..	..	..	..	..	..	..	..	..	..
Construction	..	..	..	..	..	..	..	..	..	..	..
Industries n.e.s	..	..	..	12316	1086	5479	..	11081	..	29961	5479
Transport	..	..	..	106073	..	..	..	22	..	106095	..
Road	..	..	..	101067	..	..	..	..	..	101067	..
Rail	..	..	..	*1557	..	..	..	..	..	*1557	..
Domestic aviation	..	..	..	736	..	..	..	..	..	736	..
Domestic navigation	..	..	..	*2713	..	..	..	..	..	*2713	..
Pipeline transport	..	..	..	..	..	..	..	22	..	22	..
Transport, n.e.s	..	..	..	..	..	..	..	..	..	..	..
Other	..	..	..	14613	..	83581	..	32530	..	130723	83581
Agriculture, forestry, fishing	..	..	..	6198	..	..	..	14	..	6212	..
Commerce, public services	..	..	..	700	..	4680	..	10174	..	15554	4680
Households	..	..	..	7714	..	78901	..	22342	..	108957	78901
Other consumers	..	..	..	..	..	..	..	..	..	..	..
Non-energy use	..	..	..	*3254	..	..	..	..	..	*3254	..

Ghana

Terajoules

2018	Primary coal and peat	Coal and peat products	Primary Oil	Oil Products	Natural Gas	Biofuels and waste	Nuclear	Electricity	Heat	Total energy	of which: renewables
Primary production	..	..	378973	..	30929	107702	..	21779	..	539383	129481
Imports	..	..	8333	165726	24041	..	..	504	..	198604	..
Exports	..	..	-374778	-6844	..	-12	..	-2664	..	-384298	-12
International marine bunkers	..	..	..	-443	..	..	..	..	..	-443	..
International aviation bunkers	..	..	..	-8152	..	..	..	..	..	-8152	..
Stock changes	..	..	8206	0	..	..	..	..	..	8206	..
Total energy supply	..	..	20734	150287	54970	107690	..	19619	..	353301	129469
Statistical difference	..	..	-2073	9957	-8722	-9	..	29	..	-818	21770
Transfers	..	..	..	..	..	..	..	..	..	..	..
Transformation	..	..	-20692	7410	-50267	-19535	..	37350	..	-45734	-19535
Electricity plants	..	..	-42	-9778	-50267	..	..	37350	..	-22737	..
CHP plants	..	..	..	..	..	..	..	..	..	..	..
Heat plants	..	..	..	..	..	..	..	..	..	..	..
Coke ovens	..	..	..	..	..	..	..	..	..	..	..
Briquetting plants	..	..	..	..	..	..	..	..	..	..	..
Liquefaction plants	..	..	..	..	..	..	..	..	..	..	..
Gas works	..	..	..	..	..	..	..	..	..	..	..
Blast furnaces	..	..	..	..	..	..	..	..	..	..	..
NGL plants & gas blending	..	..	-3518	3765	..	..	..	..	..	247	..
Oil refineries	..	..	-17132	13423	..	..	..	..	..	-3709	..
Other transformation	..	..	..	..	..	-19535	..	..	..	-19535	-19535
Energy industries own use	..	..	-973	-3793	-10984	..	..	-824	..	-16574	..
Losses	..	..	-1142	..	..	..	..	-8651	..	-9793	..
Final consumption	..	..	..	*143948	2441	88164	..	47466	..	282019	88164
Final energy consumption	..	..	..	*139857	2441	88164	..	47466	..	277928	88164
Manufacturing, const., mining	..	..	..	14570	2441	6216	..	14623	..	37850	6216
Iron and steel	..	..	..	..	..	..	..	..	..	..	..
Chemical and petrochemical	..	..	..	..	..	..	..	..	..	..	..
Non-ferrous metals	..	..	..	..	..	..	..	..	..	..	..
Non-metallic minerals	..	..	..	..	..	..	..	..	..	..	..
Transport equipment	..	..	..	..	..	..	..	..	..	..	..
Machinery	..	..	..	..	..	..	..	..	..	..	..
Mining and quarrying	..	..	..	..	..	..	..	..	..	..	..
Food and tobacco	..	..	..	..	..	..	..	..	..	..	..
Paper, pulp and printing	..	..	..	..	..	..	..	..	..	..	..
Wood and wood products	..	..	..	..	..	..	..	..	..	..	..
Textile and leather	..	..	..	..	..	..	..	..	..	..	..
Construction	..	..	..	..	..	..	..	..	..	..	..
Industries n.e.s	..	..	..	14570	2441	6216	..	14623	..	37850	6216
Transport	..	..	..	*110569	..	..	..	29	..	*110598	..
Road	..	..	..	*104736	..	..	..	..	..	*104736	..
Rail	..	..	..	*1763	..	..	..	..	..	*1763	..
Domestic aviation	..	..	..	1129	..	..	..	..	..	1129	..
Domestic navigation	..	..	..	*2941	..	..	..	..	..	*2941	..
Pipeline transport	..	..	..	..	..	..	..	29	..	29	..
Transport, n.e.s	..	..	..	..	..	..	..	..	..	..	..
Other	..	..	..	14718	..	81948	..	32814	..	129480	81948
Agriculture, forestry, fishing	..	..	..	6040	..	..	..	14	..	6054	..
Commerce, public services	..	..	..	727	..	4083	..	9569	..	14380	4083
Households	..	..	..	7951	..	77864	..	23231	..	109046	77864
Other consumers	..	..	..	..	..	..	..	..	..	..	..
Non-energy use	..	..	..	*4091	..	..	..	..	..	*4091	..

Gibraltar

Terajoules

	All Coal	All Oil	Natural Gas	Primary biofuels / Waste	Charcoal	Electricity	Total energy	of which: renewables
2017								
Primary production	..	..	..	..	..	0	0	0
Imports	..	183729	..	1	0	..	183729	1
Exports	..	..	..	..	..	..	..	..
International marine bunkers	..	-173733	..	..	..	..	-173733	..
International aviation bunkers	..	-353	..	..	..	..	-353	..
Stock changes	..	..	..	..	..	..	..	..
Total energy supply	..	9643	..	1	0	0	9644	1
Statistical Difference	..	0	..	0	0	-1	-1	0
Transfers	..	..	..	..	..	..	..	..
Transformation	..	-1737	..	..	..	648	-1089	..
Electricity plants	..	-1737	..	..	..	648	-1089	..
Charcoal plants	..	..	..	..	..	..	..	..
Other transformation	..	0	..	..	..	..	0	..
Energy industries own use	..	..	..	..	..	-14	-14	..
Losses	..	..	..	..	..	-20	-20	..
Final consumption	..	7906	..	*1	0	616	8522	*1
Final energy consumption	..	6821	..	*1	0	616	7437	*1
Manufacturing, const., mining	..	..	..	..	..	..	..	..
Transport	..	6821	..	..	..	..	6821	..
Road	..	6821	..	..	..	..	6821	..
Domestic aviation	..	..	..	..	..	..	..	..
Domestic navigation	..	..	..	..	..	..	..	..
Other transport	..	..	..	..	..	..	..	..
Other	..	..	..	*1	0	616	616	*1
Agriculture, forestry, fishing	..	..	..	..	..	..	..	..
Commerce and public services	..	..	..	..	0	97	97	0
Households	..	..	..	*1	..	..	*1	*1
Other consumers	..	..	..	..	..	518	518	..
Non-energy use	..	1085	..	..	..	..	1085	..
2018								
Primary production	..	..	..	..	..	0	0	0
Imports	..	180556	..	1	0	..	180557	1
Exports	..	..	..	..	..	..	..	..
International marine bunkers	..	-169704	..	..	..	..	-169704	..
International aviation bunkers	..	-265	..	..	..	..	-265	..
Stock changes	..	..	..	..	..	..	..	..
Total energy supply	..	10587	..	1	0	0	10588	1
Statistical Difference	..	-40	..	0	0	2	-38	0
Transfers	..	..	..	..	..	..	..	..
Transformation	..	-2101	..	..	..	774	-1327	..
Electricity plants	..	-2101	..	..	..	774	-1327	..
Charcoal plants	..	..	..	..	..	..	..	..
Other transformation	..	0	..	..	..	..	0	..
Energy industries own use	..	..	..	..	..	-14	-14	..
Losses	..	..	..	..	..	-23	-23	..
Final consumption	..	8527	..	*1	0	734	9262	*1
Final energy consumption	..	7401	..	*1	0	734	8136	*1
Manufacturing, const., mining	..	..	..	..	..	..	..	..
Transport	..	7401	..	..	..	..	7401	..
Road	..	7401	..	..	..	..	7401	..
Domestic aviation	..	..	..	..	..	..	..	..
Domestic navigation	..	..	..	..	..	..	..	..
Other transport	..	..	..	..	..	..	..	..
Other	..	..	..	*1	0	734	735	*1
Agriculture, forestry, fishing	..	..	..	..	..	..	..	..
Commerce and public services	..	..	..	..	0	115	115	0
Households	..	..	..	*1	..	..	*1	*1
Other consumers	..	..	..	..	..	619	619	..
Non-energy use	..	1126	..	..	..	..	1126	..

Greece

Terajoules

2017	Primary coal and peat	Coal and peat products	Primary Oil	Oil Products	Natural Gas	Biofuels and waste	Nuclear	Electricity	Heat	Total energy	of which: renewables
Primary production	191221	..	5418	..	380	44005	..	48568	11735	301327	104308
Imports	9573	..	991845	392634	176895	5909	..	31306	..	1608162	5909
Exports	..	..	-6716	-806418	..	*-546	..	-8852	..	-822531	*-546
International marine bunkers	..	..	..	-90207	..	..	..	..	..	-90207	..
International aviation bunkers	..	..	..	-42336	..	..	..	..	..	-42336	..
Stock changes	857	..	14897	-10783	-1275	-37	..	..	..	3660	-37
Total energy supply	201651	..	1005446	-557109	176000	49331	..	71021	11735	958074	109634
Statistical difference	890	..	5977	-5210	1010	-51	..	-7	0	2610	48517
Transfers	..	..	311331	-311082	..	..	..	..	..	250	..
Transformation	-192614	..	-1310799	1297674	-119410	-3892	..	150113	2137	-176791	-3892
Electricity plants	-114243	..	..	-49730	-110837	-687	..	115744	..	-159753	-687
CHP plants	-78372	..	..	-7707	-8573	-3169	..	34369	2137	-61315	-3169
Heat plants	..	..	..	..	..	..	..	..	..	..	..
Coke ovens	..	..	..	..	..	..	..	..	..	..	..
Briquetting plants	..	..	..	..	..	..	..	..	..	..	..
Liquefaction plants	..	..	..	..	..	..	..	..	..	..	..
Gas works	..	..	..	..	..	..	..	..	..	..	..
Blast furnaces	..	..	..	..	..	..	..	..	..	..	..
NGL plants & gas blending	..	..	..	..	..	..	..	..	..	..	..
Oil refineries	..	..	-1310799	1355112	..	..	..	..	..	44313	..
Other transformation	..	..	..	0	..	*-36	..	..	..	*-36	*-36
Energy industries own use	..	..	..	-61493	-2712	-43	..	-22878	0	-87126	-43
Losses	..	..	..	..	-394	..	..	-3967	..	-4361	..
Final consumption	8146	..	..	373201	52474	*45448	..	194296	13872	687436	*57183
Final energy consumption	8146	..	..	353674	35447	*45448	..	194296	13872	650882	*57183
Manufacturing, const., mining	7923	..	..	44961	13485	*5601	..	44230	67	116267	*5668
Iron and steel	..	..	..	703	1170	..	..	3604	..	5477	..
Chemical and petrochemical	..	..	..	881	1775	0	..	2408	..	5064	..
Non-ferrous metals	6386	..	..	310	5359	..	..	16456	..	28510	..
Non-metallic minerals	1537	..	..	22811	689	*137	..	3643	..	28816	*137
Transport equipment	..	..	..	606	..	0	..	191	..	797	0
Machinery	..	..	..	439	118	0	..	1530	..	2087	0
Mining and quarrying	..	..	..	3658	..	0	..	227	..	3884	0
Food and tobacco	..	..	..	6871	2523	*4721	..	3737	..	17851	*4721
Paper, pulp and printing	..	..	..	677	481	*124	..	763	..	2044	*124
Wood and wood products	..	..	..	90	180	*619	..	238	..	*1127	*619
Textile and leather	..	..	..	263	464	..	..	828	..	1556	..
Construction	..	..	..	4662	507	0	..	1789	..	6957	0
Industries n.e.s	0	..	..	2992	221	0	..	8816	67	12095	*67
Transport	..	..	..	238787	536	6955	..	677	..	246955	6955
Road	..	..	..	204539	536	6845	..	86	..	212006	6845
Rail	..	..	..	1689	..	74	..	590	..	2353	74
Domestic aviation	..	..	..	8379	..	..	..	..	..	8379	..
Domestic navigation	..	..	..	24093	..	37	..	..	..	24130	37
Pipeline transport	..	..	..	..	..	..	..	..	..	..	..
Transport, n.e.s	..	..	..	86	..	..	..	0	..	86	..
Other	223	..	..	69925	21426	*32892	..	149389	13805	287660	*44560
Agriculture, forestry, fishing	20	..	..	1998	16	*1141	..	9454	120	12749	*1261
Commerce, public services	..	..	..	5228	6310	784	..	69275	665	82262	1449
Households	188	..	..	52738	15100	*30967	..	70661	13020	182673	*41850
Other consumers	15	..	..	9961	0	0	..	0	..	9976	0
Non-energy use	..	..	..	19527	17027	..	..	..	..	36554	..

Greece

Terajoules

2018	Primary coal and peat	Coal and peat products	Primary Oil	Oil Products	Natural Gas	Biofuels and waste	Nuclear	Electricity	Heat	Total energy	of which: renewables
Primary production	178979	..	7861	..	530	45013	..	57006	11978	301366	112784
Imports	9808	..	1019056	393248	173526	5862	..	30780	..	1632280	5862
Exports	..	..	-8245	-852101	..	*-772	..	-8179	..	-869297	*-772
International marine bunkers	..	..	..	-92385	..	..	..	..	..	-92385	..
International aviation bunkers	..	..	..	-46746	..	..	..	..	..	-46746	..
Stock changes	8222	..	-226	3671	-1677	..	..	..	..	9990	..
Total energy supply	197008	..	1018445	-594313	172380	50103	..	79607	11978	935208	117874
Statistical difference	-175	..	7641	-14068	1331	-5	..	0	0	-5275	57001
Transfers	..	..	341659	-341795	..	..	..	..	..	-136	..
Transformation	-185399	..	-1352463	1345380	-112748	-5261	..	134683	2167	-173641	-4048
Electricity plants	-111540	..	..	-46048	-104357	-900	..	102002	..	-160842	-900
CHP plants	-73859	..	..	-9222	-8392	-4309	..	32681	2167	-60934	-3096
Heat plants	..	..	..	..	..	..	..	..	..	..	..
Coke ovens	..	..	..	..	..	..	..	..	..	..	..
Briquetting plants	..	..	..	..	..	..	..	..	..	..	..
Liquefaction plants	..	..	..	..	..	..	..	..	..	..	..
Gas works	..	..	..	..	..	..	..	..	..	..	..
Blast furnaces	..	..	..	..	..	..	..	..	..	..	..
NGL plants & gas blending	..	..	..	..	..	..	..	..	..	..	..
Oil refineries	..	..	-1352463	1400650	..	..	..	..	..	48187	..
Other transformation	..	..	..	..	..	*-52	..	..	..	*-52	*-52
Energy industries own use	..	..	..	-62877	-3581	-115	..	-17327	0	-83900	-115
Losses	..	..	..	..	-429	..	..	-18871	..	-19301	..
Final consumption	11784	..	..	360463	54290	*44732	..	178092	14145	663506	*56710
Final energy consumption	11784	..	..	342757	33979	*44732	..	178092	14145	625488	*56710
Manufacturing, const., mining	11607	..	..	39551	13421	*5896	..	44687	69	115230	*5965
Iron and steel	..	..	..	529	1094	..	..	3827	..	5451	..
Chemical and petrochemical	..	..	..	888	1150	..	..	3370	..	5408	..
Non-ferrous metals	6380	..	..	284	5458	..	..	17521	..	29642	..
Non-metallic minerals	4813	..	..	17590	743	*156	..	4187	..	27490	*156
Transport equipment	..	..	..	692	8	..	..	270	..	970	..
Machinery	..	..	..	571	91	37	..	1994	..	2693	37
Mining and quarrying	..	..	..	4091	..	37	..	738	..	4866	37
Food and tobacco	..	..	..	6916	2099	*4799	..	5483	..	19296	*4799
Paper, pulp and printing	..	..	..	677	768	*121	..	734	..	2300	*121
Wood and wood products	..	..	..	90	16	*636	..	958	..	1700	*636
Textile and leather	..	..	..	270	673	..	..	3132	..	4075	..
Construction	..	..	..	4016	657	110	..	1685	..	6468	110
Industries n.e.s	414	..	..	2937	663	0	..	788	69	4872	*69
Transport	..	..	..	242320	636	6624	..	727	..	250308	6624
Road	..	..	..	205032	636	6550	..	83	..	212301	6550
Rail	..	..	..	1603	..	74	..	644	..	2321	74
Domestic aviation	..	..	..	9526	..	..	..	..	..	9526	..
Domestic navigation	..	..	..	26033	..	..	..	..	..	26033	..
Pipeline transport	..	..	..	..	..	..	..	..	..	..	..
Transport, n.e.s	..	..	..	126	..	..	..	..	..	126	..
Other	177	..	..	60886	19922	*32212	..	132678	14076	259950	*44121
Agriculture, forestry, fishing	25	..	..	2095	23	*1203	..	8222	121	11688	*1324
Commerce, public services	..	..	..	5131	6027	1151	..	64109	674	77092	1825
Households	152	..	..	43880	13872	*29822	..	60347	13281	161353	*40936
Other consumers	..	..	..	9780	..	37	..	..	..	9817	37
Non-energy use	..	..	..	17707	20311	..	..	..	..	38018	..

Greenland

Terajoules

2017	Primary coal and peat	Coal and peat products	Primary Oil	Oil Products	Natural Gas	Biofuels and waste	Nuclear	Electricity	Heat	Total energy	of which: renewables
Primary production	..	..	..	..	..	94	..	1398	..	1492	1445
Imports	..	..	..	8426	..	..	..	..	..	8426	..
Exports	..	..	..	..	..	..	..	..	..	..	..
International marine bunkers	..	..	..	-824	..	..	..	..	..	-824	..
International aviation bunkers	..	..	..	..	..	..	..	..	..	..	..
Stock changes	..	..	..	-290	..	..	..	..	..	-290	..
Total energy supply	..	..	..	7311	..	94	..	1398	..	8803	1445
Statistical difference	..	..	..	-76	..	0	..	-57	-91	-224	1398
Transfers	..	..	..	..	..	..	..	..	..	..	..
Transformation	..	..	..	-1107	..	-94	..	*-173	*1201	*-172	-47
Electricity plants	..	..	..	..	..	..	..	..	..	..	..
CHP plants	..	..	..	-1107	..	-94	..	467	*625	-108	-47
Heat plants	..	..	..	..	..	..	..	*-640	*576	*-64	..
Coke ovens	..	..	..	..	..	..	..	..	..	..	..
Briquetting plants	..	..	..	..	..	..	..	..	..	..	..
Liquefaction plants	..	..	..	..	..	..	..	..	..	..	..
Gas works	..	..	..	..	..	..	..	..	..	..	..
Blast furnaces	..	..	..	..	..	..	..	..	..	..	..
NGL plants & gas blending	..	..	..	..	..	..	..	..	..	..	..
Oil refineries	..	..	..	..	..	..	..	..	..	..	..
Other transformation	..	..	..	..	..	..	..	..	..	..	..
Energy industries own use	..	..	..	-1	..	..	..	-57	*-7	-65	..
Losses	..	..	..	-73	..	..	..	-46	-532	-651	..
Final consumption	..	..	..	6206	..	..	..	1180	754	8139	..
Final energy consumption	..	..	..	6093	..	..	..	1180	754	8027	..
Manufacturing, const., mining	..	..	..	349	..	..	..	188	4	541	..
Iron and steel	..	..	..	9	..	..	..	7	..	16	..
Chemical and petrochemical	..	..	..	..	..	..	..	..	..	..	..
Non-ferrous metals	..	..	..	..	..	..	..	..	..	..	..
Non-metallic minerals	..	..	..	..	..	..	..	..	..	..	..
Transport equipment	..	..	..	..	..	..	..	..	..	..	..
Machinery	..	..	..	..	..	..	..	..	..	..	..
Mining and quarrying	..	..	..	11	..	..	..	0	..	11	..
Food and tobacco	..	..	..	175	..	..	..	144	2	321	..
Paper, pulp and printing	..	..	..	1	..	..	..	..	..	1	..
Wood and wood products	..	..	..	..	..	..	..	2	..	2	..
Textile and leather	..	..	..	5	..	..	..	3	..	9	..
Construction	..	..	..	142	..	..	..	31	2	175	..
Industries n.e.s	..	..	..	6	..	..	..	1	0	7	..
Transport	..	..	..	1736	..	..	..	..	..	1736	..
Road	..	..	..	564	..	..	..	..	..	564	..
Rail	..	..	..	..	..	..	..	..	..	..	..
Domestic aviation	..	..	..	667	..	..	..	..	..	667	..
Domestic navigation	..	..	..	501	..	..	..	..	..	501	..
Pipeline transport	..	..	..	..	..	..	..	..	..	..	..
Transport, n.e.s	..	..	..	4	..	..	..	..	..	4	..
Other	..	..	..	4008	..	..	..	992	750	5750	..
Agriculture, forestry, fishing	..	..	..	1980	..	..	..	2	..	1982	..
Commerce, public services	..	..	..	619	..	..	..	565	299	1482	..
Households	..	..	..	1273	..	..	..	368	445	2086	..
Other consumers	..	..	..	137	..	..	..	57	6	200	..
Non-energy use	..	..	..	113	..	..	..	..	..	113	..

Greenland

Terajoules

2018	Primary coal and peat	Coal and peat products	Primary Oil	Oil Products	Natural Gas	Biofuels and waste	Nuclear	Electricity	Heat	Total energy	of which: renewables
Primary production	..	..	..	..	..	*94	..	*1440	..	*1534	*1487
Imports	..	..	..	*8252	..	..	..	..	..	*8252	..
Exports	..	..	..	..	..	..	..	..	..	..	..
International marine bunkers	..	..	..	*-835	..	..	..	..	..	*-835	..
International aviation bunkers	..	..	..	..	..	..	..	..	..	..	..
Stock changes	..	..	..	*27	..	..	..	..	..	*27	..
Total energy supply	..	..	..	*7444	..	*94	..	*1440	..	*8978	*1487
Statistical difference	..	..	..	*-14	..	0	..	*-31	*-94	*-139	*1440
Transfers	..	..	..	..	..	..	..	..	..	..	..
Transformation	..	..	..	*-1118	..	*-94	..	*-180	*1201	*-191	*-47
Electricity plants	..	..	..	..	..	..	..	..	..	..	..
CHP plants	..	..	..	*-1118	..	*-94	..	*468	*615	*-129	*-47
Heat plants	..	..	..	..	..	..	..	*-648	*576	*-72	..
Coke ovens	..	..	..	..	..	..	..	..	..	..	..
Briquetting plants	..	..	..	..	..	..	..	..	..	..	..
Liquefaction plants	..	..	..	..	..	..	..	..	..	..	..
Gas works	..	..	..	..	..	..	..	..	..	..	..
Blast furnaces	..	..	..	..	..	..	..	..	..	..	..
NGL plants & gas blending	..	..	..	..	..	..	..	..	..	..	..
Oil refineries	..	..	..	..	..	..	..	..	..	..	..
Other transformation	..	..	..	..	..	..	..	..	..	..	..
Energy industries own use	..	..	..	*-2	..	..	..	*-54	*-6	*-62	..
Losses	..	..	..	-71	..	..	..	*-36	*-532	*-639	..
Final consumption	..	..	..	*6267	..	..	..	*1201	*757	*8225	..
Final energy consumption	..	..	..	*6151	..	..	..	*1201	*757	*8108	..
Manufacturing, const., mining	..	..	..	*343	..	..	..	*191	*4	*538	..
Iron and steel	..	..	..	*9	..	..	..	*7	..	*16	..
Chemical and petrochemical	..	..	..	..	..	..	..	..	..	..	..
Non-ferrous metals	..	..	..	..	..	..	..	..	..	..	..
Non-metallic minerals	..	..	..	..	..	..	..	..	..	..	..
Transport equipment	..	..	..	..	..	..	..	..	..	..	..
Machinery	..	..	..	..	..	..	..	..	..	..	..
Mining and quarrying	..	..	..	*12	..	..	..	..	..	*12	..
Food and tobacco	..	..	..	*172	..	..	..	*144	*2	*318	..
Paper, pulp and printing	..	..	..	..	..	..	..	..	..	..	..
Wood and wood products	..	..	..	..	..	..	..	*2	..	*2	..
Textile and leather	..	..	..	*4	..	..	..	*4	..	*8	..
Construction	..	..	..	*145	..	..	..	*32	*2	*179	..
Industries n.e.s	..	..	..	*1	..	..	..	*2	0	*3	..
Transport	..	..	..	*1743	..	..	..	..	..	*1743	..
Road	..	..	..	*566	..	..	..	..	..	*566	..
Rail	..	..	..	..	..	..	..	..	..	..	..
Domestic aviation	..	..	..	*668	..	..	..	..	..	*668	..
Domestic navigation	..	..	..	*505	..	..	..	..	..	*505	..
Pipeline transport	..	..	..	..	..	..	..	..	..	..	..
Transport, n.e.s	..	..	..	*4	..	..	..	..	..	*4	..
Other	..	..	..	*4064	..	..	..	*1010	*753	*5827	..
Agriculture, forestry, fishing	..	..	..	*1989	..	..	..	*2	..	*1991	..
Commerce, public services	..	..	..	*645	..	..	..	*576	*300	*1521	..
Households	..	..	..	*1291	..	..	..	*374	*446	*2112	..
Other consumers	..	..	..	*139	..	..	..	*58	*7	*203	..
Non-energy use	..	..	..	*117	..	..	..	..	..	*117	..

Grenada

Terajoules

	All Coal	All Oil	Natural Gas	Primary biofuels / Waste	Charcoal	Electricity	Total energy	of which: renewables
2017								
Primary production	..	..	..	397	..	0	398	398
Imports	..	4464	..	..	..	..	4464	..
Exports	..	..	..	..	..	..	..	..
International marine bunkers	..	..	..	..	..	..	..	..
International aviation bunkers	..	-330	..	..	..	..	-330	..
Stock changes	..	-198	..	..	..	..	-198	..
Total energy supply	..	3936	..	397	..	0	4334	398
Statistical Difference	..	6	..	0	0	0	6	0
Transfers	..	..	..	..	..	..	..	..
Transformation	..	-2016	..	-86	65	815	-1221	-20
Electricity plants	..	-2016	..	..	..	815	-1201	..
Charcoal plants	..	..	..	-86	65	..	-20	-20
Other transformation	..	0	..	0	..	..	0	0
Energy industries own use	..	..	..	..	..	-43	-43	..
Losses	..	..	..	..	..	-67	-67	..
Final consumption	..	1915	..	312	65	706	2997	377
Final energy consumption	..	1915	..	312	65	706	2997	377
Manufacturing, const., mining	..	9	..	21	..	20	50	21
Transport	..	1391	..	..	..	..	1391	..
Road	..	1391	..	..	..	..	1391	..
Domestic aviation	..	..	..	..	..	..	..	..
Domestic navigation	..	..	..	..	..	..	..	..
Other transport	..	..	..	..	..	..	..	..
Other	..	514	..	291	65	686	1556	356
Agriculture, forestry, fishing	..	1	..	..	..	..	1	..
Commerce and public services	..	237	..	..	..	417	654	..
Households	..	276	..	291	65	*269	901	356
Other consumers	..	..	..	..	..	..	..	..
Non-energy use	..	..	..	..	..	..	..	..
2018								
Primary production	..	..	..	412	..	0	413	413
Imports	..	4647	..	..	..	..	4647	..
Exports	..	..	..	..	..	..	..	..
International marine bunkers	..	..	..	..	..	..	..	..
International aviation bunkers	..	-342	..	..	..	..	-342	..
Stock changes	..	86	..	..	..	..	86	..
Total energy supply	..	4391	..	412	..	0	4804	413
Statistical Difference	..	0	..	0	0	0	0	0
Transfers	..	..	..	..	..	..	..	..
Transformation	..	-2173	..	-89	69	*831	-1362	-20
Electricity plants	..	-2173	..	..	..	*831	-1342	..
Charcoal plants	..	..	..	-89	69	..	-20	-20
Other transformation	..	0	..	0	..	..	0	0
Energy industries own use	..	..	..	..	..	-23	-23	..
Losses	..	..	..	..	..	-59	-59	..
Final consumption	..	2218	..	323	69	749	3359	392
Final energy consumption	..	2218	..	323	69	749	3359	392
Manufacturing, const., mining	..	155	..	22	..	21	198	22
Transport	..	1477	..	..	..	..	1477	..
Road	..	1477	..	..	..	..	1477	..
Domestic aviation	..	..	..	..	..	..	..	..
Domestic navigation	..	..	..	..	..	..	..	..
Other transport	..	..	..	..	..	..	..	..
Other	..	585	..	302	69	728	1684	371
Agriculture, forestry, fishing	..	218	..	..	..	..	218	..
Commerce and public services	..	116	..	..	..	438	554	..
Households	..	251	..	302	69	290	912	371
Other consumers	..	..	..	..	..	..	..	..
Non-energy use	..	..	..	..	..	..	..	..

Guatemala

Terajoules

	Primary coal and peat	Coal and peat products	Primary Oil	Oil Products	Natural Gas	Biofuels and waste	Nuclear	Electricity	Heat	Total energy	of which: renewables
2017											
Primary production	..	..	20335	..	..	291653	..	22331	9110	343429	323094
Imports	47161	..	..	200090	..	..	..	3209	..	250460	..
Exports	..	..	-16608	-13732	..	..	..	-6688	..	-37028	..
International marine bunkers	..	..	..	-17718	..	..	..	..	..	-17718	..
International aviation bunkers	..	..	..	-4295	..	..	..	..	..	-4295	..
Stock changes	-3943	..	-19	-332	..	5	..	..	..	-4289	5
Total energy supply	43218	..	3708	164013	..	291658	..	18852	9110	530559	323099
Statistical difference	0	..	0	44	..	0	..	-245	0	-201	23242
Transfers	..	..	..	..	..	..	..	..	..	..	..
Transformation	-43218	..	-3708	-632	..	-56425	..	21850	-9110	-91243	-64624
Electricity plants	-43218	..	..	-4187	..	-54113	..	21850	-9110	-88779	-62312
CHP plants	..	..	..	..	..	..	..	..	..	..	..
Heat plants	..	..	..	..	..	..	..	..	..	..	..
Coke ovens	..	..	..	..	..	..	..	..	..	..	..
Briquetting plants	..	..	..	..	..	..	..	..	..	..	..
Liquefaction plants	..	..	..	..	..	..	..	..	..	..	..
Gas works	..	..	..	..	..	..	..	..	..	..	..
Blast furnaces	..	..	..	..	..	..	..	..	..	..	..
NGL plants & gas blending	..	..	..	..	..	..	..	..	..	..	..
Oil refineries	..	..	-3708	3555	..	..	..	..	..	-153	..
Other transformation	..	..	..	..	..	*-2311	..	..	..	*-2311	*-2311
Energy industries own use	..	..	..	-2029	..	..	..	-3190	..	-5218	..
Losses	..	..	..	..	..	..	..	-1344	..	-1344	..
Final consumption	..	..	..	161308	..	*235233	..	36413	..	*432954	*235233
Final energy consumption	..	..	..	160206	..	*235233	..	36413	..	*431853	*235233
Manufacturing, const., mining	..	..	..	30085	..	..	..	13345	..	43430	..
Iron and steel	..	..	..	..	..	..	..	..	..	..	..
Chemical and petrochemical	..	..	..	..	..	..	..	..	..	..	..
Non-ferrous metals	..	..	..	..	..	..	..	..	..	..	..
Non-metallic minerals	..	..	..	..	..	..	..	..	..	..	..
Transport equipment	..	..	..	..	..	..	..	..	..	..	..
Machinery	..	..	..	..	..	..	..	..	..	..	..
Mining and quarrying	..	..	..	..	..	..	..	..	..	..	..
Food and tobacco	..	..	..	..	..	..	..	..	..	..	..
Paper, pulp and printing	..	..	..	..	..	..	..	..	..	..	..
Wood and wood products	..	..	..	..	..	..	..	..	..	..	..
Textile and leather	..	..	..	..	..	..	..	..	..	..	..
Construction	..	..	..	..	..	..	..	..	..	..	..
Industries n.e.s	..	..	..	30085	..	..	..	13345	..	43430	..
Transport	..	..	..	115006	..	..	..	..	..	115006	..
Road	..	..	..	114819	..	..	..	..	..	114819	..
Rail	..	..	..	..	..	..	..	..	..	..	..
Domestic aviation	..	..	..	..	..	..	..	..	..	..	..
Domestic navigation	..	..	..	..	..	..	..	..	..	..	..
Pipeline transport	..	..	..	..	..	..	..	..	..	..	..
Transport, n.e.s	..	..	..	187	..	..	..	..	..	187	..
Other	..	..	..	15115	..	*235233	..	23068	..	*273417	*235233
Agriculture, forestry, fishing	..	..	..	..	..	..	..	..	..	..	..
Commerce, public services	..	..	..	713	..	7628	..	8899	..	17240	7628
Households	..	..	..	14402	..	*227606	..	12550	..	*254557	*227606
Other consumers	..	..	..	..	..	..	..	*1620	..	*1620	..
Non-energy use	..	..	..	1101	..	..	..	..	..	1101	..

Guatemala

Terajoules

2018	Primary coal and peat	Coal and peat products	Primary Oil	Oil Products	Natural Gas	Biofuels and waste	Nuclear	Electricity	Heat	Total energy	of which: renewables
Primary production	..	..	19436	..	..	294044	..	20687	8991	343158	323722
Imports	52182	..	..	201368	..	..	..	2970	..	256520	..
Exports	..	..	-13058	-11574	..	..	..	-9001	..	-33633	..
International marine bunkers	..	..	..	-18194	..	..	..	..	..	-18194	..
International aviation bunkers	..	..	..	-4613	..	..	..	..	..	-4613	..
Stock changes	-1152	..	-601	4526	..	2	..	..	..	2775	2
Total energy supply	51029	..	5777	171513	..	294047	..	14655	8991	546013	323724
Statistical difference	0	..	0	88	..	0	..	-21	0	68	21586
Transfers	..	..	..	..	..	..	..	..	..	..	..
Transformation	-51029	..	-5777	796	..	-53428	..	28158	-8991	-90272	-61520
Electricity plants	-51029	..	..	-5235	..	-51801	..	28158	-8991	-88899	-59893
CHP plants	..	..	..	..	..	..	..	..	..	..	..
Heat plants	..	..	..	..	..	..	..	..	..	..	..
Coke ovens	..	..	..	..	..	..	..	..	..	..	..
Briquetting plants	..	..	..	..	..	..	..	..	..	..	..
Liquefaction plants	..	..	..	..	..	..	..	..	..	..	..
Gas works	..	..	..	..	..	..	..	..	..	..	..
Blast furnaces	..	..	..	..	..	..	..	..	..	..	..
NGL plants & gas blending	..	..	..	..	..	..	..	..	..	..	..
Oil refineries	..	..	-5777	6032	..	..	..	..	..	255	..
Other transformation	..	..	..	..	..	*-1627	..	..	..	*-1627	*-1627
Energy industries own use	..	..	..	-8424	..	..	..	-2789	..	-11213	..
Losses	..	..	..	..	..	..	..	-3252	..	-3252	..
Final consumption	..	..	..	163797	..	*240618	..	36793	..	*441208	*240618
Final energy consumption	..	..	..	160853	..	*240618	..	36793	..	*438265	*240618
Manufacturing, const., mining	..	..	..	25643	..	..	..	13304	..	38946	..
Iron and steel	..	..	..	..	..	..	..	..	..	..	..
Chemical and petrochemical	..	..	..	..	..	..	..	..	..	..	..
Non-ferrous metals	..	..	..	..	..	..	..	..	..	..	..
Non-metallic minerals	..	..	..	..	..	..	..	..	..	..	..
Transport equipment	..	..	..	..	..	..	..	..	..	..	..
Machinery	..	..	..	..	..	..	..	..	..	..	..
Mining and quarrying	..	..	..	..	..	..	..	..	..	..	..
Food and tobacco	..	..	..	..	..	..	..	..	..	..	..
Paper, pulp and printing	..	..	..	..	..	..	..	..	..	..	..
Wood and wood products	..	..	..	..	..	..	..	..	..	..	..
Textile and leather	..	..	..	..	..	..	..	..	..	..	..
Construction	..	..	..	..	..	..	..	..	..	..	..
Industries n.e.s	..	..	..	25643	..	..	..	13304	..	38946	..
Transport	..	..	..	119461	..	..	..	..	..	119461	..
Road	..	..	..	119266	..	..	..	..	..	119266	..
Rail	..	..	..	..	..	..	..	..	..	..	..
Domestic aviation	..	..	..	..	..	..	..	..	..	..	..
Domestic navigation	..	..	..	..	..	..	..	..	..	..	..
Pipeline transport	..	..	..	..	..	..	..	..	..	..	..
Transport, n.e.s	..	..	..	195	..	..	..	..	..	195	..
Other	..	..	..	15750	..	*240618	..	23489	..	*279858	*240618
Agriculture, forestry, fishing	..	..	..	..	..	..	..	..	..	..	..
Commerce, public services	..	..	..	744	..	7835	..	10273	..	18853	7835
Households	..	..	..	15006	..	*232783	..	13216	..	*261005	*232783
Other consumers	..	..	..	..	..	..	..	..	..	..	..
Non-energy use	..	..	..	2943	..	..	..	..	..	2943	..

Guinea

Terajoules

	All Coal	All Oil	Natural Gas	Primary biofuels / Waste	Charcoal	Electricity	Total energy	of which: renewables
2017								
Primary production	..	..	3	113017	..	4364	117384	117381
Imports	..	48940	..	..	1	..	48941	1
Exports	..	..	..	..	-24	..	-24	-24
International marine bunkers	..	..	..	..	..	..	..	..
International aviation bunkers	..	*-1127	..	..	..	..	*-1127	..
Stock changes	..	..	..	..	..	..	..	..
Total energy supply	..	47813	3	113017	-23	4364	165174	117358
Statistical Difference	..	0	0	0	0	0	0	4364
Transfers	..	..	..	..	..	..	..	..
Transformation	..	*-5647	..	*-22125	11907	1947	*-13917	*-10218
Electricity plants	..	*-5647	..	..	..	1947	*-3700	..
Charcoal plants	..	..	..	*-22125	11907	..	*-10218	*-10218
Other transformation	..	0	..	0	..	..	0	0
Energy industries own use	..	..	..	..	..	-126	-126	..
Losses	..	..	..	..	..	*-947	*-947	..
Final consumption	..	*42166	*3	*90892	*11884	*5238	*150184	*102777
Final energy consumption	..	*39835	*3	*90892	*11884	*5238	*147852	*102777
Manufacturing, const., mining	..	*15430	..	*629	..	*2230	*18290	*629
Transport	..	*23367	..	..	..	..	*23367	..
Road	..	*23145	..	..	..	..	*23145	..
Domestic aviation	..	*222	..	..	..	..	*222	..
Domestic navigation	..	..	..	..	..	..	..	..
Other transport	..	..	..	..	..	..	..	..
Other	..	*1038	*3	*90263	*11884	*3007	*106196	*102147
Agriculture, forestry, fishing	..	..	..	..	..	..	..	..
Commerce and public services	..	..	..	..	..	*1233	*1233	..
Households	..	*1038	..	*90263	*11884	*1774	*104959	*102147
Other consumers	..	..	*3	..	..	..	*3	..
Non-energy use	..	*2332	..	..	..	..	*2332	..
2018								
Primary production	..	..	3	113367	..	4253	117624	117621
Imports	..	54617	..	..	1	..	54619	1
Exports	..	..	..	..	-1	..	-1	-1
International marine bunkers	..	..	..	..	..	..	..	..
International aviation bunkers	..	*-1140	..	..	..	..	*-1140	..
Stock changes	..	..	..	..	..	..	..	..
Total energy supply	..	53477	3	113367	0	4253	171102	117621
Statistical Difference	..	0	0	0	0	0	0	4253
Transfers	..	..	..	..	..	..	..	..
Transformation	..	*-7357	..	*-22556	12140	2636	*-15136	*-10416
Electricity plants	..	*-7357	..	..	..	2636	*-4720	..
Charcoal plants	..	..	..	*-22556	12140	..	*-10416	*-10416
Other transformation	..	0	..	0	..	..	0	0
Energy industries own use	..	..	..	..	..	-138	-138	..
Losses	..	..	..	..	..	*-1034	*-1034	..
Final consumption	..	*46121	*3	*90811	*12140	*5718	*154794	*102952
Final energy consumption	..	*43696	*3	*90811	*12140	*5718	*152370	*102952
Manufacturing, const., mining	..	*22959	..	*638	..	*2435	*26031	*638
Transport	..	*19805	..	..	..	..	*19805	..
Road	..	*19588	..	..	..	..	*19588	..
Domestic aviation	..	*217	..	..	..	..	*217	..
Domestic navigation	..	..	..	..	..	..	..	..
Other transport	..	..	..	..	..	..	..	..
Other	..	*933	*3	*90173	*12140	3284	*106534	*102314
Agriculture, forestry, fishing	..	..	..	..	..	..	..	..
Commerce and public services	..	..	..	..	..	*1347	*1347	..
Households	..	*933	..	*90173	*12140	1937	*105184	*102314
Other consumers	..	..	*3	..	..	..	*3	..
Non-energy use	..	*2424	..	..	..	..	*2424	..

Guinea-Bissau

Terajoules

	All Coal	All Oil	Natural Gas	Primary biofuels / Waste	Charcoal	Electricity	Total energy	of which: renewables
2017								
Primary production	..	..	..	26119	..	*24	26144	26144
Imports	..	*5778	..	..	..	..	*5778	..
Exports	..	..	..	..	-3	..	-3	-3
International marine bunkers	..	..	..	..	..	..	..	..
International aviation bunkers	..	*-556	..	..	..	..	*-556	..
Stock changes	..	..	..	..	..	..	..	..
Total energy supply	..	*5223	..	26119	-3	*24	31363	26141
Statistical Difference	..	*4	..	0	0	0	*4	24
Transfers	..	..	..	..	..	..	..	..
Transformation	..	*-796	..	*-4127	2221	*284	*-2417	*-1906
Electricity plants	..	*-796	..	..	..	*284	*-511	..
Charcoal plants	..	..	..	*-4127	2221	..	*-1906	*-1906
Other transformation	..	0	..	0	..	..	0	0
Energy industries own use	..	..	..	..	..	0	0	..
Losses	..	..	..	..	..	..	..	..
Final consumption	..	*4423	..	*21993	*2218	*308	*28942	*24211
Final energy consumption	..	*3402	..	*21993	*2218	*308	*27921	*24211
Manufacturing, const., mining	..	..	..	..	..	*82	*82	..
Transport	..	*1495	..	..	..	..	*1495	..
Road	..	*1185	..	..	..	..	*1185	..
Domestic aviation	..	..	..	..	..	..	..	..
Domestic navigation	..	*310	..	..	..	..	*310	..
Other transport	..	..	..	..	..	..	..	..
Other	..	*1907	..	*21993	*2218	*227	*26345	*24211
Agriculture, forestry, fishing	..	..	..	..	..	..	..	..
Commerce and public services	..	..	..	..	..	*37	*37	..
Households	..	*405	..	*21993	..	*178	*22577	*21993
Other consumers	..	*1502	..	..	*2218	*11	*3731	*2218
Non-energy use	..	*1021	..	..	..	..	*1021	..
2018								
Primary production	..	..	..	26434	..	*25	26459	26459
Imports	..	*5888	..	..	..	..	*5888	..
Exports	..	..	..	..	-3	..	-3	-3
International marine bunkers	..	..	..	..	..	..	..	..
International aviation bunkers	..	*-564	..	..	..	..	*-564	..
Stock changes	..	..	..	..	..	..	..	..
Total energy supply	..	*5324	..	26434	-3	*25	31780	26456
Statistical Difference	..	0	..	0	0	0	0	25
Transfers	..	..	..	..	..	..	..	..
Transformation	..	*-843	..	*-4219	2271	*287	*-2504	*-1948
Electricity plants	..	*-843	..	..	..	*287	*-556	..
Charcoal plants	..	..	..	*-4219	2271	..	*-1948	*-1948
Other transformation	..	0	..	0	..	..	0	0
Energy industries own use	..	..	..	..	..	0	0	..
Losses	..	..	..	..	..	..	..	..
Final consumption	..	*4481	..	*22215	*2268	*312	*29275	*24483
Final energy consumption	..	*3444	..	*22215	*2268	*312	*28238	*24483
Manufacturing, const., mining	..	..	..	..	..	*83	*83	..
Transport	..	*1508	..	..	..	..	*1508	..
Road	..	*1194	..	..	..	..	*1194	..
Domestic aviation	..	..	..	..	..	..	..	..
Domestic navigation	..	*314	..	..	..	..	*314	..
Other transport	..	..	..	..	..	..	..	..
Other	..	*1936	..	*22215	*2268	*229	*26648	*24483
Agriculture, forestry, fishing	..	..	..	..	..	..	..	..
Commerce and public services	..	..	..	..	..	*38	*38	..
Households	..	*410	..	*22215	..	*180	*22805	*22215
Other consumers	..	*1526	..	..	*2268	*11	*3806	*2268
Non-energy use	..	*1037	..	..	..	..	*1037	..

Guyana

Terajoules

	All Coal	All Oil	Natural Gas	Primary biofuels / Waste	Charcoal	Electricity	Total energy	of which: renewables
2017								
Primary production	..	..	..	6609	..	26	6635	6635
Imports	..	30748	..	..	..	..	30748	..
Exports	..	..	..	..	..	..	..	..
International marine bunkers	..	..	..	..	..	..	..	..
International aviation bunkers	..	-774	..	..	..	..	-774	..
Stock changes	..	251	..	..	..	..	251	..
Total energy supply	..	30225	..	6609	..	26	36860	6635
Statistical Difference	..	-69	..	0	0	0	-69	26
Transfers	..	..	..	..	..	..	..	..
Transformation	..	-11004	..	-409	43	3951	-7418	-366
Electricity plants	..	-11004	..	-327	..	3951	-7380	-327
Charcoal plants	..	..	..	-81	43	..	-38	-38
Other transformation	..	0	..	0	..	..	0	0
Energy industries own use	..	..	..	..	..	-45	-45	..
Losses	..	..	..	..	..	-838	-838	..
Final consumption	..	19290	..	6200	43	3094	28627	6244
Final energy consumption	..	19073	..	6200	43	3094	28411	6244
Manufacturing, const., mining	..	987	..	5226	2	1202	7417	5228
Transport	..	9813	..	..	..	..	9813	..
Road	..	9774	..	..	..	..	9774	..
Domestic aviation	..	*40	..	..	..	..	*40	..
Domestic navigation	..	..	..	..	..	..	..	..
Other transport	..	..	..	..	..	..	..	..
Other	..	8273	..	974	41	1892	11181	1015
Agriculture, forestry, fishing	..	6741	..	..	..	197	6938	..
Commerce and public services	..	323	..	..	..	596	919	..
Households	..	1210	..	974	41	1099	3324	1015
Other consumers	..	..	..	..	..	..	..	..
Non-energy use	..	216	..	..	..	..	216	..
2018								
Primary production	..	..	..	4987	..	41	5028	5028
Imports	..	33162	..	..	..	..	33162	..
Exports	..	..	..	..	..	..	..	..
International marine bunkers	..	..	..	..	..	..	..	..
International aviation bunkers	..	-754	..	..	..	..	-754	..
Stock changes	..	186	..	..	..	..	186	..
Total energy supply	..	32594	..	4987	..	41	37622	5028
Statistical Difference	..	0	..	0	0	0	0	41
Transfers	..	..	..	..	..	..	..	..
Transformation	..	-11691	..	-312	40	4049	-7914	-272
Electricity plants	..	-11691	..	-231	..	4049	-7872	-231
Charcoal plants	..	..	..	*-81	40	..	*-41	*-41
Other transformation	..	0	..	0	..	..	0	0
Energy industries own use	..	..	..	..	..	-119	-119	..
Losses	..	..	..	..	..	-847	-847	..
Final consumption	..	20903	..	4674	40	3125	28742	4714
Final energy consumption	..	20557	..	4674	40	3125	28396	4714
Manufacturing, const., mining	..	1060	..	3684	2	1214	5960	3686
Transport	..	10793	..	..	..	..	10793	..
Road	..	10753	..	..	..	..	10753	..
Domestic aviation	..	*40	..	..	..	..	*40	..
Domestic navigation	..	..	..	..	..	..	..	..
Other transport	..	..	..	..	..	..	..	..
Other	..	8703	..	990	38	1911	11643	1028
Agriculture, forestry, fishing	..	7136	..	..	..	199	7334	..
Commerce and public services	..	340	..	..	..	602	942	..
Households	..	1228	..	990	38	1110	3367	1028
Other consumers	..	..	..	..	..	..	..	..
Non-energy use	..	346	..	..	..	..	346	..

Haiti

Terajoules

	All Coal	All Oil	Natural Gas	Primary biofuels / Waste	Charcoal	Electricity	Total energy	of which: renewables
2017								
Primary production	..	..	..	142274	..	461	142735	142735
Imports	..	43843	..	..	..	..	43843	..
Exports	..	..	..	..	..	..	..	..
International marine bunkers	..	..	..	..	..	..	..	..
International aviation bunkers	..	-970	..	..	..	..	-970	..
Stock changes	..	..	..	..	..	..	..	..
Total energy supply	..	42873	..	142274	..	461	185608	142735
Statistical Difference	..	-2170	..	0	0	-25	-2195	461
Transfers	..	..	..	..	..	..	..	..
Transformation	..	-12152	..	-75126	38026	3341	-45912	-37101
Electricity plants	..	-12152	..	..	..	3341	-8811	..
Charcoal plants	..	..	..	-75126	38026	..	-37101	-37101
Other transformation	..	0	..	0	..	..	0	0
Energy industries own use	..	..	..	..	..	-61	-61	..
Losses	..	-667	..	..	..	-2246	-2913	..
Final consumption	..	32224	..	67148	38026	1519	138917	105174
Final energy consumption	..	31903	..	67148	38026	1519	138596	105174
Manufacturing, const., mining	..	8148	..	3457	..	680	12286	3457
Transport	..	19891	..	..	..	..	19891	..
Road	..	19891	..	..	..	..	19891	..
Domestic aviation	..	..	..	..	..	..	..	..
Domestic navigation	..	..	..	..	..	..	..	..
Other transport	..	..	..	..	..	..	..	..
Other	..	3863	..	63691	38026	839	106419	101717
Agriculture, forestry, fishing	..	..	..	..	..	..	..	..
Commerce and public services	..	47	..	..	1977	137	2161	1977
Households	..	3816	..	63691	36049	702	104258	99740
Other consumers	..	..	..	..	..	..	..	..
Non-energy use	..	322	..	..	..	..	322	..
2018								
Primary production	..	..	..	144382	..	713	145095	145095
Imports	..	48091	..	..	..	..	48091	..
Exports	..	..	..	..	..	..	..	..
International marine bunkers	..	..	..	..	..	..	..	..
International aviation bunkers	..	-970	..	..	..	..	-970	..
Stock changes	..	..	..	..	..	..	..	..
Total energy supply	..	47121	..	144382	..	713	192216	145095
Statistical Difference	..	2194	..	0	0	-126	2068	713
Transfers	..	..	..	..	..	..	..	..
Transformation	..	-11199	..	-76241	38586	3053	-45802	-37655
Electricity plants	..	-11199	..	..	..	3053	-8147	..
Charcoal plants	..	..	..	-76241	38586	..	-37655	-37655
Other transformation	..	0	..	0	..	..	0	0
Energy industries own use	..	..	..	..	..	-65	-65	..
Losses	..	-667	..	..	..	-2282	-2949	..
Final consumption	..	33061	..	68141	38586	1544	141333	106727
Final energy consumption	..	32338	..	68141	38586	1544	140609	106727
Manufacturing, const., mining	..	8277	..	3509	..	691	12478	3509
Transport	..	20153	..	..	..	..	20153	..
Road	..	20153	..	..	..	..	20153	..
Domestic aviation	..	..	..	..	..	..	..	..
Domestic navigation	..	..	..	..	..	..	..	..
Other transport	..	..	..	..	..	..	..	..
Other	..	3907	..	64632	38586	853	107978	103218
Agriculture, forestry, fishing	..	..	..	..	..	..	..	..
Commerce and public services	..	47	..	..	2006	140	2194	2006
Households	..	3860	..	64632	36580	713	105785	101212
Other consumers	..	..	..	..	..	..	..	..
Non-energy use	..	724	..	..	..	..	724	..

Honduras

Terajoules

	All Coal	All Oil	Natural Gas	Primary biofuels / Waste	Charcoal	Electricity	Total energy	of which: renewables
2017								
Primary production	..	..	..	85751	..	19872	105623	100844
Imports	26	130651	..	..	..	1184	131862	..
Exports	..	-11429	..	..	..	-90	-11519	..
International marine bunkers	..	-2868	..	..	..	..	-2868	..
International aviation bunkers	..	-2602	..	..	..	..	-2602	..
Stock changes	..	-2902	..	0	..	..	-2902	0
Total energy supply	26	110850	..	85751	..	20966	217594	100844
Statistical Difference	0	-496	..	0	0	-335	-831	16859
Transfers	..	..	..	..	..	..	..	..
Transformation	-26	-31786	..	*-18095	3	13432	-36472	*-21105
Electricity plants	-26	-31786	..	*-18075	..	13432	-36455	*-21088
Charcoal plants	..	..	..	*-20	3	..	*-17	*-17
Other transformation	0	0	..	0	..	..	0	0
Energy industries own use	..	..	..	..	..	-43	-43	..
Losses	..	..	..	..	..	-10782	-10782	..
Final consumption	..	79561	..	*67656	3	23908	171127	*62879
Final energy consumption	..	79400	..	*67656	3	23908	170966	*62879
Manufacturing, const., mining	..	16254	..	*17116	..	6656	40026	*17116
Transport	..	54180	..	..	..	..	54180	..
Road	..	53648	..	..	..	..	53648	..
Domestic aviation	..	485	..	..	..	..	485	..
Domestic navigation	..	..	..	..	..	..	..	..
Other transport	..	47	..	..	..	..	47	..
Other	..	8966	..	*50540	3	17251	*76760	*45763
Agriculture, forestry, fishing	..	603	..	..	..	..	603	..
Commerce and public services	..	5752	..	..	..	8352	14104	..
Households	..	2167	..	*40981	3	8899	*52050	*40984
Other consumers	..	443	..	*9559	..	..	*10002	*4780
Non-energy use	..	161	..	..	..	..	161	..
2018								
Primary production	..	..	..	100279	..	29354	129633	125910
Imports	..	148812	..	..	..	1325	150137	..
Exports	..	-12834	..	..	..	-29	-12863	..
International marine bunkers	..	-2949	..	..	..	..	-2949	..
International aviation bunkers	..	-2249	..	..	..	..	-2249	..
Stock changes	..	-4731	..	..	..	..	-4731	..
Total energy supply	..	126049	..	100279	..	30650	256978	125910
Statistical Difference	..	4774	..	0	0	36	4810	19732
Transfers	..	..	..	..	..	..	..	..
Transformation	..	-36880	..	*-16974	*6	4939	-48908	*-26591
Electricity plants	..	-36880	..	*-16959	..	4939	-48899	*-26582
Charcoal plants	..	..	..	*-15	*6	..	*-9	*-9
Other transformation	..	0	..	0	..	..	0	0
Energy industries own use	..	..	..	..	..	-72	-72	..
Losses	..	..	..	..	..	-10692	-10692	..
Final consumption	..	84395	..	*83305	*6	24790	192496	*79588
Final energy consumption	..	83591	..	*83305	*6	24790	191692	*79588
Manufacturing, const., mining	..	13933	..	*11860	..	7654	33447	*11860
Transport	..	56751	..	..	..	..	56751	..
Road	..	56307	..	..	..	..	56307	..
Domestic aviation	..	397	..	..	..	..	397	..
Domestic navigation	..	..	..	..	..	..	..	..
Other transport	..	47	..	..	..	..	47	..
Other	..	12907	..	*71445	*6	17136	*101493	*67728
Agriculture, forestry, fishing	..	3271	..	..	..	..	3271	..
Commerce and public services	..	5782	..	..	..	8244	14026	..
Households	..	3677	..	*63999	*6	8892	*76574	*64005
Other consumers	..	177	..	*7446	..	..	*7623	*3723
Non-energy use	..	804	..	..	..	..	804	..

Hungary

Terajoules

2017	Primary coal and peat	Coal and peat products	Primary Oil	Oil Products	Natural Gas	Biofuels and waste	Nuclear	Electricity	Heat	Total energy	of which: renewables
Primary production	53723	..	44061	..	59064	128082	174495	4777	8615	472819	135895
Imports	49205	3481	250131	160985	467390	11283	..	71291	..	1013766	9736
Exports	-13	-11000	-7547	-127176	-123173	-19030	..	-24930	..	-312870	-19030
International marine bunkers	..	..	..	..	..	..	..	..	..	..	..
International aviation bunkers	..	..	..	-9526	..	..	..	..	..	-9526	..
Stock changes	-1024	-265	-2394	762	-45652	-167	..	..	..	-48739	-167
Total energy supply	101891	-7784	284252	25045	357629	120168	174495	51138	8615	1115449	126433
Statistical difference	8	-57	0	-1538	-10599	38	0	1706	-112	-10554	7567
Transfers	..	..	20440	-20440	..	..	..	..	..	0	..
Transformation	-93971	20579	-304692	307266	-92111	*-32000	-174495	113609	46954	-208862	*-30952
Electricity plants	-53445	-2560	..	-824	-25213	*-14524	-173102	93870	-36	-175834	*-13184
CHP plants	-1394	-2057	..	-166	-37383	*-14213	-1393	19739	20422	-16446	*-12491
Heat plants	-267	-2712	..	-162	-23001	*-3077	..	..	26568	-2651	-5092
Coke ovens	-38865	38419	..	..	..	..	..	..	..	-446	..
Briquetting plants	..	..	..	..	..	..	..	..	..	..	..
Liquefaction plants	..	..	1320	..	..	..	..	..	..	1320	..
Gas works	..	..	..	..	..	..	..	..	..	..	..
Blast furnaces	..	-11059	..	..	-1301	..	..	..	..	-12361	..
NGL plants & gas blending	..	..	-3827	4210	186	-186	..	..	..	383	-186
Oil refineries	..	..	-302185	304990	..	..	..	..	..	2805	..
Other transformation	..	549	..	-782	-5399	..	..	..	..	-5632	..
Energy industries own use	..	-7088	..	-14923	-9115	-583	..	-12024	-4787	-48520	-583
Losses	..	-641	..	..	-4501	..	..	-12442	-4297	-21881	..
Final consumption	7912	5124	..	298485	262501	*87547	..	138575	46597	846741	*87331
Final energy consumption	7912	4984	..	226979	239175	*87547	..	138575	46597	751769	*87331
Manufacturing, const., mining	4046	4749	..	28354	57160	*10698	..	60246	15109	180362	*7624
Iron and steel	88	4453	..	86	2426	*5	..	2477	807	10342	*5
Chemical and petrochemical	..	..	..	15678	10878	*58	..	12139	10311	49064	*44
Non-ferrous metals	..	..	..	90	3419	..	..	1544	369	5423	..
Non-metallic minerals	912	207	..	3755	8130	3819	..	5062	162	22046	*1086
Transport equipment	..	..	..	138	3074	*6	..	6174	510	9901	12
Machinery	..	30	..	409	7586	*139	..	9904	261	18328	*149
Mining and quarrying	..	..	..	688	145	*1	..	360	..	1194	*1
Food and tobacco	..	59	..	550	12338	*2782	..	8831	1343	25903	*2830
Paper, pulp and printing	2974	..	..	131	1904	*1275	..	3190	836	10309	*861
Wood and wood products	..	..	..	262	437	*2096	..	1213	34	*4042	*2096
Textile and leather	..	..	..	..	873	*21	..	814	23	1731	*21
Construction	65	..	..	6430	2027	*150	..	1210	127	10008	*160
Industries n.e.s	7	0	..	138	3923	*346	..	7330	326	12069	*359
Transport	..	..	..	178601	2765	6814	..	4349	..	192528	6814
Road	..	..	..	176580	366	6814	..	86	..	183846	6814
Rail	..	..	..	1806	..	..	..	4223	..	6029	..
Domestic aviation	..	..	..	..	..	..	..	..	..	..	..
Domestic navigation	..	..	..	215	..	..	..	..	..	215	..
Pipeline transport	..	..	..	..	2399	..	..	40	..	2438	..
Transport, n.e.s	..	..	..	..	..	..	..	..	..	..	..
Other	3866	235	..	20024	179250	*70035	..	73980	31488	378879	*72893
Agriculture, forestry, fishing	7	..	..	15142	5129	*614	..	3254	1563	25709	2160
Commerce, public services	51	..	..	1273	49000	*1443	..	29963	8459	90188	*2272
Households	3809	235	..	3216	124420	*67978	..	40496	21361	261515	*68461
Other consumers	..	..	..	393	702	..	..	266	105	1467	..
Non-energy use	..	140	..	71506	23326	..	..	..	..	94972	..

Hungary

Terajoules

2018	Primary coal and peat	Coal and peat products	Primary Oil	Oil Products	Natural Gas	Biofuels and waste	Nuclear	Electricity	Heat	Total energy	of which: renewables
Primary production	53225	..	46396	..	61427	119533	170536	5216	8697	465030	127416
Imports	49575	3029	279099	176170	444714	12381	..	67007	..	1031975	9902
Exports	-20	-8854	-16469	-146991	-174713	-18533	..	-15354	..	-380935	-18533
International marine bunkers	..	..	..	..	..	..	..	..	..	..	..
International aviation bunkers	..	..	..	-11775	..	..	..	..	..	-11775	..
Stock changes	-615	-1647	-2519	3774	14979	-378	..	..	..	13593	-378
Total energy supply	102165	-7473	306506	21177	346407	113002	170536	56869	8697	1117888	118405
Statistical difference	67	-61	-1	-2909	-8172	45	0	821	250	-9962	7844
Transfers	..	..	18643	-18643	..	..	..	..	..	0	..
Transformation	-96277	19475	-325150	328773	-87705	*-33034	-170536	109998	44433	-210024	*-31722
Electricity plants	-54475	-2154	..	-735	-21849	*-16096	-169214	90853	-432	-174102	*-14910
CHP plants	-1268	-2957	..	-222	-36094	*-13997	-1322	19145	20154	-16561	*-12151
Heat plants	-252	-2590	..	-40	-21713	*-2757	..	..	24711	-2642	-4477
Coke ovens	-40283	38100	..	..	..	..	..	..	..	-2183	..
Briquetting plants	..	..	..	..	..	..	..	..	..	..	..
Liquefaction plants	..	..	1600	..	..	..	..	..	..	1600	..
Gas works	..	..	..	..	..	..	..	..	..	..	..
Blast furnaces	..	-11625	..	..	-1752	..	..	..	..	-13377	..
NGL plants & gas blending	..	..	-3225	3548	185	-184	..	..	..	323	-184
Oil refineries	..	..	-323525	327105	..	..	..	..	..	3580	..
Other transformation	..	701	..	-882	-6481	..	..	..	..	-6662	..
Energy industries own use	-7	-7132	..	-16305	-8709	-557	..	-12028	-4931	-49669	-557
Losses	..	-1355	..	..	-4351	..	..	-12085	-3949	-21740	..
Final consumption	5814	3577	..	317913	253814	*79366	..	141934	44000	846418	*78282
Final energy consumption	5814	3549	..	241839	233420	*79366	..	141934	44000	749921	*78282
Manufacturing, const., mining	3276	3336	..	31160	60177	*12754	..	62125	14135	186963	*8744
Iron and steel	90	3012	..	86	2818	*4	..	2635	736	9381	*4
Chemical and petrochemical	..	..	..	15814	10789	*76	..	11999	9972	48650	*61
Non-ferrous metals	..	..	..	43	3370	..	..	1577	333	5322	..
Non-metallic minerals	599	206	..	4138	8447	4733	..	5134	122	23378	*1162
Transport equipment	..	..	..	90	3160	*20	..	6336	484	10090	*27
Machinery	7	29	..	452	7572	*136	..	10177	289	18662	*144
Mining and quarrying	..	..	..	907	142	*1	..	421	..	1472	*1
Food and tobacco	..	88	..	550	14135	*2909	..	9094	944	27720	*2954
Paper, pulp and printing	2396	..	..	90	2010	*1506	..	3197	732	9931	*999
Wood and wood products	..	..	..	305	560	*2859	..	1361	29	*5114	*2859
Textile and leather	..	..	..	..	887	*9	..	878	20	1794	*9
Construction	178	..	..	8503	2279	*173	..	1678	149	12959	*180
Industries n.e.s	7	0	..	181	4010	*328	..	7639	325	12489	*344
Transport	..	..	..	188774	3279	8005	..	4334	..	204393	8005
Road	..	..	..	186753	405	8005	..	94	..	195257	8005
Rail	..	..	..	1806	..	..	..	4198	..	6004	..
Domestic aviation	..	..	..	..	..	..	..	..	..	..	..
Domestic navigation	..	..	..	215	..	..	..	..	..	215	..
Pipeline transport	..	..	..	..	2874	..	..	43	..	2917	..
Transport, n.e.s	..	..	..	..	..	..	..	..	..	..	..
Other	2538	213	..	21905	169964	*58607	..	75474	29865	358565	*61533
Agriculture, forestry, fishing	37	..	..	16625	4496	*653	..	3535	1676	27023	2314
Commerce, public services	51	..	..	1579	46156	*1338	..	30744	8004	87871	*2086
Households	2450	213	..	3264	118510	*56616	..	40932	20084	242068	*57133
Other consumers	..	..	..	437	802	..	..	263	101	1603	..
Non-energy use	..	28	..	76074	20395	..	..	..	..	96496	..

Iceland

Terajoules

2017	Primary coal and peat	Coal and peat products	Primary Oil	Oil Products	Natural Gas	Biofuels and waste	Nuclear	Electricity	Heat	Total energy	of which: renewables
Primary production	..	..	..	..	..	756	..	50641	247735	299132	299132
Imports	3562	587	..	42190	..	671	..	..	..	47010	671
Exports	..	..	..	..	..	..	..	..	..	..	..
International marine bunkers	..	..	..	-2542	..	..	..	..	..	-2542	..
International aviation bunkers	..	..	..	-16052	..	..	..	..	..	-16052	..
Stock changes	..	..	..	186	..	0	..	..	..	186	0
Total energy supply	3562	587	..	23781	..	1427	..	50641	247735	327734	299804
Statistical difference	-84	-80	..	-1088	..	0	..	0	63	-1189	98366
Transfers	..	..	..	0	..	..	..	..	..	0	..
Transformation	..	..	..	-129	..	..	..	17921	-214350	-196558	-196621
Electricity plants	..	..	..	-43	..	..	..	2020	-20124	-18147	-18112
CHP plants	..	..	..	..	..	..	..	16600	-175893	-159293	-159293
Heat plants	..	..	..	-86	..	..	..	-698	-18333	-19117	-19216
Coke ovens	..	..	..	..	..	..	..	..	..	..	..
Briquetting plants	..	..	..	..	..	..	..	..	..	..	..
Liquefaction plants	..	..	..	..	..	..	..	..	..	..	..
Gas works	..	..	..	..	..	..	..	..	..	..	..
Blast furnaces	..	..	..	..	..	..	..	..	..	..	..
NGL plants & gas blending	..	..	..	..	..	..	..	..	..	..	..
Oil refineries	..	..	..	..	..	..	..	..	..	..	..
Other transformation	..	..	..	..	..	..	..	..	..	..	..
Energy industries own use	..	..	..	..	..	..	..	-2020	0	-2020	..
Losses	..	..	..	..	..	..	..	-2128	-2987	-5115	..
Final consumption	3647	667	..	24740	..	1427	..	64415	30335	125231	4816
Final energy consumption	3647	667	..	23936	..	1427	..	64415	30335	124427	4816
Manufacturing, const., mining	3647	667	..	1757	..	739	..	55400	507	62717	1246
Iron and steel	3647	667	..	260	..	739	..	3647	..	8959	739
Chemical and petrochemical	..	..	..	..	..	..	..	302	..	302	..
Non-ferrous metals	..	..	..	0	..	..	..	48568	..	48568	..
Non-metallic minerals	..	..	..	..	..	..	..	446	..	446	..
Transport equipment	..	..	..	..	..	..	..	18	..	18	..
Machinery	..	..	..	..	..	..	..	40	..	40	..
Mining and quarrying	..	..	..	..	..	..	..	7	..	7	..
Food and tobacco	..	..	..	129	..	..	..	2070	..	2199	..
Paper, pulp and printing	..	..	..	..	..	..	..	54	..	54	..
Wood and wood products	..	..	..	..	..	..	..	14	..	14	..
Textile and leather	..	..	..	..	..	..	..	11	..	11	..
Construction	..	..	..	1247	..	..	..	137	..	1384	..
Industries n.e.s	0	0	..	121	..	0	..	86	507	715	507
Transport	..	..	..	14195	..	688	..	274	..	15157	688
Road	..	..	..	13456	..	688	..	43	..	14188	688
Rail	..	..	..	..	..	..	..	..	..	..	..
Domestic aviation	..	..	..	309	..	..	..	..	..	309	..
Domestic navigation	..	..	..	430	..	..	..	..	..	430	..
Pipeline transport	..	..	..	..	..	..	..	..	..	..	..
Transport, n.e.s	..	..	..	..	..	..	..	230	..	230	..
Other	..	..	..	7984	..	..	..	8741	29828	46553	2882
Agriculture, forestry, fishing	..	..	..	7386	..	..	..	1026	2916	11328	790
Commerce, public services	..	..	..	0	..	..	..	4795	11914	16709	1587
Households	..	..	..	133	..	..	..	2920	14615	17668	505
Other consumers	..	..	..	465	..	..	..	..	383	848	..
Non-energy use	..	..	..	804	..	..	..	..	..	804	..

Iceland

Terajoules

2018	Primary coal and peat	Coal and peat products	Primary Oil	Oil Products	Natural Gas	Biofuels and waste	Nuclear	Electricity	Heat	Total energy	of which: renewables
Primary production	..	..	..	..	..	980	..	49745	285403	336128	336128
Imports	3635	583	..	48637	..	659	..	..	..	53514	659
Exports	..	..	..	..	..	..	..	..	..	..	..
International marine bunkers	..	..	..	-3180	..	..	..	..	..	-3180	
International aviation bunkers	..	..	..	-17993	..	..	..	..	..	-17993	
Stock changes	361	..	..	-2736	..	..	..	..	..	-2376	
Total energy supply	3996	583	..	24729	..	1639	..	49745	285403	366094	336787
Statistical difference	0	0	..	-1243	..	-84	..	4	-3395	-4718	104118
Transfers	..	..	..	-9	..	..	..	..	..	-9	..
Transformation	..	..	..	-43	..	..	..	20873	-248275	-227445	-227545
Electricity plants	..	..	..	-43	..	..	..	4111	-41040	-36972	-36936
CHP plants	..	..	..	..	..	..	..	17532	-185480	-167948	-167948
Heat plants	..	..	..	..	..	..	..	-770	-21755	-22525	-22661
Coke ovens	..	..	..	..	..	..	..	..	..	..	..
Briquetting plants	..	..	..	..	..	..	..	..	..	..	..
Liquefaction plants	..	..	..	..	..	..	..	..	..	..	..
Gas works	..	..	..	..	..	..	..	..	..	..	..
Blast furnaces	..	..	..	..	..	..	..	..	..	..	..
NGL plants & gas blending	..	..	..	..	..	..	..	..	..	..	..
Oil refineries	..	..	..	..	..	..	..	..	..	..	..
Other transformation	..	..	..	..	..	..	..	..	..	..	..
Energy industries own use	..	..	..	..	..	..	..	-2066	0	-2066	..
Losses	..	..	..	..	..	..	..	-1994	-3394	-5388	..
Final consumption	3996	583	..	25919	..	1722	..	66553	37129	135903	5123
Final energy consumption	3996	583	..	23950	..	1722	..	66553	37129	133933	5123
Manufacturing, const., mining	3996	583	..	1755	..	934	..	55886	519	63672	1453
Iron and steel	3996	583	..	423	..	932	..	3650	..	9583	932
Chemical and petrochemical	..	..	..	..	..	..	..	346	..	346	..
Non-ferrous metals	..	..	..	47	..	..	..	48690	..	48737	..
Non-metallic minerals	..	..	..	..	..	..	..	637	..	637	..
Transport equipment	..	..	..	..	..	..	..	18	..	18	..
Machinery	..	..	..	..	..	..	..	40	..	40	..
Mining and quarrying	..	..	..	..	..	..	..	14	..	14	..
Food and tobacco	..	..	..	129	..	..	..	2250	..	2379	..
Paper, pulp and printing	..	..	..	..	..	..	..	40	..	40	..
Wood and wood products	..	..	..	..	..	..	..	11	..	11	..
Textile and leather	..	..	..	..	..	..	..	11	..	11	..
Construction	..	..	..	1075	..	..	..	137	..	1212	..
Industries n.e.s	0	0	..	81	..	2	..	43	519	645	521
Transport	..	..	..	14376	..	789	..	320	..	15485	789
Road	..	..	..	13521	..	789	..	65	..	14375	789
Rail	..	..	..	..	..	..	..	..	..	..	..
Domestic aviation	..	..	..	309	..	..	..	..	..	309	..
Domestic navigation	..	..	..	546	..	..	..	..	..	546	..
Pipeline transport	..	..	..	..	..	..	..	..	..	..	..
Transport, n.e.s	..	..	..	..	..	..	..	256	..	256	..
Other	..	..	..	7819	..	..	..	10346	36610	54776	2882
Agriculture, forestry, fishing	..	..	..	7682	..	..	..	1123	2927	11732	790
Commerce, public services	..	..	..	..	..	..	..	6170	15251	21421	1587
Households	..	..	..	138	..	..	..	3053	18001	21191	505
Other consumers	..	..	..	0	..	..	..	..	431	431	..
Non-energy use	..	..	..	1970	..	..	..	..	..	1970	..

India

Terajoules

	Primary coal and peat	Coal and peat products	Primary Oil	Oil Products	Natural Gas	Biofuels and waste	Nuclear	Electricity	Heat	Total energy	of which: renewables
2017											
Primary production	11297930	..	1746314	..	1131875	8138102	414137	681732	..	23410090	8819834
Imports	5546490	129297	9529429	1991808	688853	..	..	20200	..	17906076	..
Exports	-24197	-3046	..	-3200868	..	..	..	-25931	..	-3254042	..
International marine bunkers	..	..	..	-63751	..	..	..	..	..	-63751	..
International aviation bunkers	..	..	..	*-167227	..	..	..	..	..	*-167227	..
Stock changes	252535	..	..	*-441	..	..	..	..	..	252094	..
Total energy supply	17072758	126251	11275743	-1440480	1820728	8138102	414137	676001	..	38083240	8819834
Statistical difference	-467249	9	415174	-115251	63165	29500	0	-26181	..	-100833	711232
Transfers	..	..	*387000	*-24179	..	..	..	..	..	*362821	..
Transformation	-11231378	765942	-11247568	11280492	-569318	*-1162999	-414137	4683323	..	-7895642	*-1162999
Electricity plants	-10586237	*-36321	..	-30566	-569318	*-1025626	-414137	4683323	..	-7978881	*-1025626
CHP plants	..	..	..	..	..	..	..	..	..	..	..
Heat plants	..	..	..	..	..	..	..	..	..	..	..
Coke ovens	-562061	501113	..	..	..	..	..	..	..	-60948	..
Briquetting plants	*-15514	*9280	..	..	..	..	..	..	..	*-6234	..
Liquefaction plants	..	..	..	..	..	..	..	..	..	..	..
Gas works	-2022	*1060	..	..	..	..	..	..	..	-962	..
Blast furnaces	-65545	290810	..	..	..	..	..	..	..	225266	..
NGL plants & gas blending	..	..	*-203718	158823	..	..	..	..	..	*-44895	..
Oil refineries	..	..	-11043851	11152235	..	..	..	..	..	108385	..
Other transformation	..	..	..	..	..	-137373	..	..	..	-137373	-137373
Energy industries own use	-4256	*-72643	..	*-486338	-116346	..	..	-380945	..	*-1060527	..
Losses	..	..	..	..	..	..	..	-935377	..	-935377	..
Final consumption	6304372	*819542	..	9444747	1071900	*6945604	..	4069182	..	28655347	*6945604
Final energy consumption	6304372	*819542	..	9037963	351637	*6945604	..	4069182	..	27528300	*6945604
Manufacturing, const., mining	5757403	*810262	..	2689975	30265	*1968809	..	*1688074	..	12944788	*1968809
Iron and steel	1190311	*810262	..	46493	..	..	..	..	..	2047066	..
Chemical and petrochemical	43557	..	..	513834	..	..	..	..	..	557391	..
Non-ferrous metals	..	..	..	11073	..	..	..	..	..	11073	..
Non-metallic minerals	..	..	..	..	..	..	..	..	..	..	..
Transport equipment	..	..	..	..	..	..	..	..	..	..	..
Machinery	..	..	..	6806	..	..	..	..	..	6806	..
Mining and quarrying	..	..	..	56212	..	..	..	..	..	56212	..
Food and tobacco	..	..	..	..	..	..	..	..	..	..	..
Paper, pulp and printing	34756	..	..	..	..	..	..	..	..	34756	..
Wood and wood products	..	..	..	..	..	..	..	..	..	..	..
Textile and leather	27772	..	..	3277	..	..	..	..	..	31050	..
Construction	155060	..	..	35453	..	..	..	..	..	190512	..
Industries n.e.s	4305946	0	..	2016827	30265	*1968809	..	*1688074	..	10009922	*1968809
Transport	..	..	..	1927851	17195	..	..	51682	..	1996728	..
Road	..	..	..	1286584	..	..	..	..	..	1286584	..
Rail	..	..	..	129	..	..	..	51682	..	51811	..
Domestic aviation	..	..	..	*282381	..	..	..	..	..	*282381	..
Domestic navigation	..	..	..	358756	..	..	..	..	..	358756	..
Pipeline transport	..	..	..	..	17195	..	..	..	..	17195	..
Transport, n.e.s	..	..	..	..	..	..	..	..	..	..	..
Other	*546970	*9280	..	4420137	304177	*4976795	..	2329427	..	12586785	*4976795
Agriculture, forestry, fishing	..	..	..	28844	6552	..	..	735455	..	770851	..
Commerce, public services	*207949	..	..	3767	..	294066	..	346108	..	851889	294066
Households	*115856	*9280	..	1122257	297625	*4682729	..	984780	..	*7212526	*4682729
Other consumers	*223165	..	..	3265269	..	..	..	263084	..	3751518	..
Non-energy use	..	..	..	406784	720263	..	..	..	..	1127047	..

India

Terajoules

2018	Primary coal and peat	Coal and peat products	Primary Oil	Oil Products	Natural Gas	Biofuels and waste	Nuclear	Electricity	Heat	Total energy	of which: renewables
Primary production	12096820	..	1664654	..	1154464	*7662018	408380	860447	..	23846783	*8522465
Imports	6312772	*139054	9580950	1723906	1009317	..	..	16765	..	18782765	..
Exports	-21416	*-705	..	-3052894	..	..	..	-30578	..	-3105593	..
International marine bunkers	..	..	..	*-68074	..	..	..	..	..	*-68074	..
International aviation bunkers	..	..	..	*-182089	..	..	..	..	..	*-182089	..
Stock changes	-85186	..	..	*-4322	..	..	..	..	..	-89508	..
Total energy supply	18302990	*138349	11245604	-1583472	2163781	*7662018	408380	846634	..	39184284	*8522465
Statistical difference	883383	0	147839	-67180	33539	0	0	-83992	..	913589	*860447
Transfers	..	..	*355180	*794	..	..	..	..	..	*355974	..
Transformation	*-11551355	*663989	-11452946	11839984	-421602	*-1189475	-408380	4617979	..	-7901807	*-1189475
Electricity plants	*-10519834	*-38643	..	-35833	*-421602	*-1026504	-408380	4617979	..	*-7832818	*-1026504
CHP plants	..	..	..	..	..	..	..	..	..	..	..
Heat plants	..	..	..	..	..	..	..	..	..	..	..
Coke ovens	*-942483	*1255370	..	..	..	..	..	..	..	*312887	..
Briquetting plants	*-15418	*9220	..	..	..	..	..	..	..	*-6198	..
Liquefaction plants	..	..	..	..	..	..	..	..	..	..	..
Gas works	*-2207	*1167	..	..	..	..	..	..	..	*-1040	..
Blast furnaces	*-71413	*-563125	..	..	..	..	..	..	..	*-634538	..
NGL plants & gas blending	..	..	*-217994	*154293	..	..	..	..	..	*-63702	..
Oil refineries	..	..	-11234952	11721524	..	..	..	..	..	486573	..
Other transformation	..	..	..	..	..	*-162971	..	..	..	*-162971	*-162971
Energy industries own use	*-4484	*-77287	..	*-698792	-578724	..	..	-409691	..	-1768978	..
Losses	..	..	..	..	-2880	..	..	-968994	..	-971874	..
Final consumption	5863768	*725051	..	9625693	1127036	*6472543	..	4169920	..	27984011	*6472543
Final energy consumption	5863768	*725051	..	9197081	416580	*6472543	..	4169920	..	26844943	*6472543
Manufacturing, const., mining	5863768	*715831	..	*2610675	38139	*1878607	..	1745435	..	12852455	*1878607
Iron and steel	1432963	*715831	..	50375	..	..	..	..	..	2199169	..
Chemical and petrochemical	35742	..	..	524408	..	..	..	..	..	560150	..
Non-ferrous metals	..	..	..	17486	..	..	..	..	..	17486	..
Non-metallic minerals	..	..	..	..	..	..	..	..	..	..	..
Transport equipment	..	..	..	..	..	..	..	..	..	..	..
Machinery	..	..	..	8003	..	..	..	..	..	8003	..
Mining and quarrying	..	..	..	66123	..	..	..	..	..	66123	..
Food and tobacco	..	..	..	..	..	..	..	..	..	..	..
Paper, pulp and printing	34462	..	..	..	..	..	..	..	..	34462	..
Wood and wood products	..	..	..	..	..	..	..	..	..	..	..
Textile and leather	28130	..	..	3305	..	..	..	..	..	31435	..
Construction	176535	..	..	45123	..	..	..	..	..	221658	..
Industries n.e.s	4155935	0	..	*1895853	38139	*1878607	..	1745435	..	9713969	*1878607
Transport	..	..	..	2078358	342304	..	..	60563	..	2481225	..
Road	..	..	..	1383506	323305	..	..	..	..	1706810	..
Rail	..	..	..	116788	..	..	..	60563	..	177351	..
Domestic aviation	..	..	..	*184070	..	..	..	..	..	*184070	..
Domestic navigation	..	..	..	393994	..	..	..	..	..	393994	..
Pipeline transport	..	..	..	..	18999	..	..	..	..	18999	..
Transport, n.e.s	..	..	..	..	..	..	..	..	..	..	..
Other	..	*9220	..	4508048	36137	*4593936	..	2363922	..	11511263	*4593936
Agriculture, forestry, fishing	..	..	..	32637	6743	..	..	748048	..	787427	..
Commerce, public services	..	..	..	4249	..	*296110	..	350104	..	650462	*296110
Households	..	*9220	..	1169252	..	*4297826	..	1009634	..	*6485933	*4297826
Other consumers	..	..	..	3301910	29395	..	..	256136	..	3587441	..
Non-energy use	..	..	..	428612	710455	..	..	..	..	1139068	..

Indonesia

Terajoules

2017	Primary coal and peat	Coal and peat products	Primary Oil	Oil Products	Natural Gas	Biofuels and waste	Nuclear	Electricity	Heat	Total energy	of which: renewables
Primary production	11935751	..	1961809	..	2246745	1606025	..	67203	459500	18277033	2132728
Imports	122726	14831	763113	1398092	..	..	..	4030	..	2302792	..
Exports	-10085528	0	-581392	-45673	-703724	-23260	..	..	..	-11439578	-23260
International marine bunkers	..	..	..	-13816	..	..	..	..	..	-13816	..
International aviation bunkers	..	..	..	-42504	..	..	..	..	..	-42504	..
Stock changes	-9191	*-952	-1438	1939	..	*-25834	..	..	..	*-35476	*-25834
Total energy supply	1963758	13879	2142092	1298039	1543020	1556931	..	71233	459500	9048452	2083634
Statistical difference	-438633	*21	115165	111237	179428	0	..	4228	0	-28554	113153
Transfers	..	..	..	-2348	..	..	..	..	..	-2348	..
Transformation	-2100939	*83816	-2025742	1708949	-503557	-49807	..	*953927	-459500	-2392853	-463357
Electricity plants	-2013593	..	..	-121003	-503557	*-7000	..	*953927	-459500	-2150726	-420550
CHP plants	..	..	..	..	..	..	..	..	..	..	..
Heat plants	..	..	..	..	..	..	..	..	..	..	..
Coke ovens	-84437	*78819	..	..	..	..	..	..	..	-5618	..
Briquetting plants	-2910	*1697	..	..	..	..	..	..	..	-1212	..
Liquefaction plants	..	..	..	..	..	..	..	..	..	..	..
Gas works	..	*3300	..	..	..	..	..	..	..	*3300	..
Blast furnaces	..	..	..	..	..	..	..	..	..	..	..
NGL plants & gas blending	..	..	*-147186	*151005	..	..	..	..	..	*3819	..
Oil refineries	..	..	-1878556	1678947	..	..	..	..	..	-199609	..
Other transformation	..	..	..	..	..	-42807	..	..	..	-42807	-42807
Energy industries own use	-44349	*-254	..	-93303	*-165205	..	..	*-50645	..	*-353756	..
Losses	-104	*-550	-1184	0	-207307	..	..	-89593	..	-298738	..
Final consumption	256999	*96871	..	2800100	487524	1507124	..	880693	..	6029311	1507124
Final energy consumption	256999	*96617	..	2568361	318106	1507124	..	880693	..	5627901	1507124
Manufacturing, const., mining	256999	*96067	..	285263	304862	331324	..	336474	..	1610990	331324
Iron and steel	1949	*78819	..	8882	58455	..	..	9731	..	157835	..
Chemical and petrochemical	17173	0	..	20185	61212	..	..	36569	..	135139	..
Non-ferrous metals	..	..	..	..	..	..	..	..	..	..	..
Non-metallic minerals	..	..	..	..	..	..	..	..	..	..	..
Transport equipment	..	..	..	..	..	..	..	..	..	..	..
Machinery	..	..	..	..	..	..	..	..	..	..	..
Mining and quarrying	..	..	..	..	..	..	..	..	..	..	..
Food and tobacco	..	..	..	..	..	..	..	..	..	..	..
Paper, pulp and printing	..	..	..	..	..	..	..	..	..	..	..
Wood and wood products	..	..	..	..	..	..	..	..	..	..	..
Textile and leather	..	..	..	..	..	..	..	..	..	..	..
Construction	..	..	..	..	..	..	..	..	..	..	..
Industries n.e.s	237877	*17248	..	256196	185196	331324	..	290174	..	1318016	331324
Transport	..	..	..	1293098	964	*95581	..	864	..	1390506	*95581
Road	..	..	..	1098043	964	*95581	..	..	..	1194587	*95581
Rail	..	..	..	9457	..	..	..	864	..	10321	..
Domestic aviation	..	..	..	149402	..	..	..	..	..	149402	..
Domestic navigation	..	..	..	35874	..	..	..	..	..	35874	..
Pipeline transport	..	..	..	..	..	..	..	..	..	..	..
Transport, n.e.s	..	..	..	322	..	..	..	..	..	322	..
Other	..	*550	..	990000	12280	1080219	..	543355	..	2626404	1080219
Agriculture, forestry, fishing	..	..	..	14436	..	..	..	1987	..	16424	..
Commerce, public services	..	..	..	29807	11270	..	..	198317	..	239394	..
Households	..	*200	..	929859	1010	1072064	..	343051	..	2346184	1072064
Other consumers	..	*350	..	15898	..	8155	..	..	..	24403	8155
Non-energy use	0	*254	..	*231739	169418	..	..	..	..	*401411	..

Indonesia

Terajoules

2018	Primary coal and peat	Coal and peat products	Primary Oil	Oil Products	Natural Gas	Biofuels and waste	Nuclear	Electricity	Heat	Total energy	of which: renewables
Primary production	14216216	..	1901742	..	2287177	1634161	..	71210	460944	20571451	2166316
Imports	151096	*4898	719038	1373024	..	195921	..	..	..	2443977	195921
Exports	-11130700	0	-434494	-45335	-747640	-133928	..	..	..	-12492097	-133928
International marine bunkers	..	..	..	-8557	..	..	..	..	..	-8557	..
International aviation bunkers	..	..	..	-45569	..	..	..	..	..	-45569	..
Stock changes	26720	*-1076	-74829	-5499	..	..	..	..	..	-54684	..
Total energy supply	3263331	*3821	2111458	1268065	1539537	1696155	..	71210	460944	10414522	2228309
Statistical difference	-4821	0	117280	141875	96000	-93114	..	-11146	0	246075	24191
Transfers	..	..	..	-5442	..	..	..	..	..	-5442	..
Transformation	-2497081	*95943	-1994009	1726436	-418583	*-40369	..	984320	-460944	-2604287	-455219
Electricity plants	-2393869	..	..	-153573	-418583	..	..	984320	-460944	-2442648	-414850
CHP plants	..	..	..	..	..	..	..	..	..	..	..
Heat plants	..	..	..	..	..	..	..	..	..	..	..
Coke ovens	-98336	*90635	..	..	..	..	..	..	..	-7702	..
Briquetting plants	-4876	*2008	..	..	..	..	..	..	..	-2868	..
Liquefaction plants	..	..	..	..	..	..	..	..	..	..	..
Gas works	..	*3300	..	..	..	..	..	..	..	*3300	..
Blast furnaces	..	..	..	..	..	..	..	..	..	..	..
NGL plants & gas blending	..	..	-201419	205304	..	..	..	..	..	3885	..
Oil refineries	..	..	-1792590	1674705	..	..	..	..	..	-117885	..
Other transformation	..	..	..	..	..	*-40369	..	..	..	*-40369	*-40369
Energy industries own use	-55727	..	..	-111475	-273666	..	..	-69876	..	-510743	..
Losses	-104	*-550	-169	0	-187709	..	..	-90335	..	-278868	..
Final consumption	*715240	*99214	..	2735710	563579	1748899	..	906466	..	6769107	1748899
Final energy consumption	*715240	*99214	..	2507684	375870	1748899	..	906466	..	6353372	1748899
Manufacturing, const., mining	*715240	*98664	..	383283	363186	743349	..	334685	..	2638407	743349
Iron and steel	85924	*79101	..	10438	45502	..	..	9594	..	230559	..
Chemical and petrochemical	*44644	0	..	21358	74234	1175	..	36792	..	178203	1175
Non-ferrous metals	..	..	..	..	..	..	..	..	..	..	..
Non-metallic minerals	..	..	..	..	..	..	..	..	..	..	..
Transport equipment	..	..	..	..	..	..	..	..	..	..	..
Machinery	..	..	..	..	..	..	..	..	..	..	..
Mining and quarrying	..	..	..	..	..	..	..	..	..	..	..
Food and tobacco	..	..	..	..	..	..	..	..	..	..	..
Paper, pulp and printing	..	..	..	..	..	..	..	..	..	..	..
Wood and wood products	..	..	..	..	..	..	..	..	..	..	..
Textile and leather	..	..	..	..	..	..	..	..	..	..	..
Construction	..	..	..	..	..	..	..	..	..	..	..
Industries n.e.s	*584672	*19563	..	351487	243450	742174	..	288299	..	2229645	742174
Transport	..	..	..	1079928	2939	212594	..	958	..	1296419	212594
Road	..	..	..	892420	2939	212594	..	..	..	1107953	212594
Rail	..	..	..	8377	..	..	..	958	..	9334	..
Domestic aviation	..	..	..	140274	..	..	..	..	..	140274	..
Domestic navigation	..	..	..	38496	..	..	..	..	..	38496	..
Pipeline transport	..	..	..	..	..	..	..	..	..	..	..
Transport, n.e.s	..	..	..	362	..	..	..	..	..	362	..
Other	..	*550	..	1044473	9744	792957	..	570823	..	2418547	792957
Agriculture, forestry, fishing	..	..	..	14984	..	..	..	2063	..	17046	..
Commerce, public services	..	..	..	26055	9103	40976	..	213376	..	289509	40976
Households	..	*200	..	989764	642	734862	..	355385	..	2080853	734862
Other consumers	..	*350	..	13670	..	17119	..	..	..	31138	17119
Non-energy use	0	..	..	*228025	187709	..	..	..	..	*415735	..

Iran (Islamic Rep. of)

Terajoules

2017	Primary coal and peat	Coal and peat products	Primary Oil	Oil Products	Natural Gas	Biofuels and waste	Nuclear	Electricity	Heat	Total energy	of which: renewables
Primary production	42562	..	9432932	..	7640818	*84172	81151	55591	..	17337226	*139763
Imports	9456	3440	47430	155541	136759	0	..	13867	..	366493	0
Exports	-1903	-1438	-5327442	-1130024	-468502	..	..	-29419	..	-6958728	..
International marine bunkers	..	..	..	-58425	..	..	..	..	..	-58425	..
International aviation bunkers	..	..	..	*-70172	..	..	..	..	..	*-70172	..
Stock changes	..	-28	185735	0	..	..	..	..	..	185707	..
Total energy supply	50115	1974	4338654	-1103080	7309075	*84172	81151	40039	..	10802101	*139763
Statistical difference	-7343	-10035	-19287	-65981	-6956	0	0	22230	..	-87371	*55591
Transfers	..	..	8987	-8402	..	..	..	..	..	585	..
Transformation	-48176	16629	-4358485	4470983	-2463971	-288	-81151	1053180	..	-1411280	-288
Electricity plants	..	-9920	..	-322808	-2457527	-288	-81151	1053180	..	-1818515	-288
CHP plants	..	..	..	..	..	..	..	..	..	..	..
Heat plants	..	..	..	..	..	..	..	..	..	..	..
Coke ovens	-48176	46913	..	..	..	..	..	..	..	-1263	..
Briquetting plants	..	..	..	..	..	..	..	..	..	..	..
Liquefaction plants	..	..	..	..	..	..	..	..	..	..	..
Gas works	..	..	..	..	..	..	..	..	..	..	..
Blast furnaces	..	-20364	..	..	-6444	..	..	..	..	-26808	..
NGL plants & gas blending	..	..	-577075	608246	..	..	..	..	..	31171	..
Oil refineries	..	..	-3781410	3757975	..	..	..	..	..	-23435	..
Other transformation	..	..	..	*427569	..	0	..	..	..	*427569	0
Energy industries own use	..	*-6933	-8442	-98006	-534668	..	..	-43409	..	-691458	..
Losses	..	-1467	0	..	-6955	..	..	-121399	..	-129821	..
Final consumption	*9282	20238	..	3327477	4310437	*83884	..	906181	..	8657498	*83884
Final energy consumption	387	7612	..	2290838	3780968	*83884	..	906181	..	7069869	*83884
Manufacturing, const., mining	..	7612	..	156396	1475230	..	..	290696	..	1929934	..
Iron and steel	..	7612	..	..	1	..	..	..	..	7613	..
Chemical and petrochemical	..	..	..	..	405341	..	..	..	..	405341	..
Non-ferrous metals	..	..	..	..	..	..	..	..	..	..	..
Non-metallic minerals	..	..	..	..	..	..	..	..	..	..	..
Transport equipment	..	..	..	..	..	..	..	..	..	..	..
Machinery	..	..	..	..	..	..	..	..	..	..	..
Mining and quarrying	..	..	..	..	..	..	..	..	..	..	..
Food and tobacco	..	..	..	..	..	..	..	..	..	..	..
Paper, pulp and printing	..	..	..	..	..	..	..	..	..	..	..
Wood and wood products	..	..	..	..	..	..	..	..	..	..	..
Textile and leather	..	..	..	..	..	..	..	..	..	..	..
Construction	..	..	..	..	..	..	..	..	..	..	..
Industries n.e.s	..	0	..	156396	1069888	..	..	290696	..	1516980	..
Transport	..	..	..	1800018	*287775	..	..	1717	..	2089511	..
Road	..	..	..	1799749	..	..	..	..	..	1799749	..
Rail	..	..	..	..	..	..	..	1717	..	1717	..
Domestic aviation	..	..	..	*27	..	..	..	..	..	*27	..
Domestic navigation	..	..	..	242	..	..	..	..	..	242	..
Pipeline transport	..	..	..	..	..	..	..	..	..	..	..
Transport, n.e.s	..	..	..	..	*287775	..	..	..	..	*287775	..
Other	387	..	..	334424	2017963	*83884	..	613768	..	3050425	*83884
Agriculture, forestry, fishing	..	..	..	105613	78265	..	..	141764	..	325643	..
Commerce, public services	..	..	..	31084	259405	..	..	154832	..	445321	..
Households	387	..	..	195911	1680293	*83884	..	300251	..	2260725	*83884
Other consumers	..	..	..	1816	..	..	..	16920	..	18736	..
Non-energy use	*8895	12626	..	*1036639	529469	..	..	..	..	*1587628	..

Iran (Islamic Rep. of)

Terajoules

2018	Primary coal and peat	Coal and peat products	Primary Oil	Oil Products	Natural Gas	Biofuels and waste	Nuclear	Electricity	Heat	Total energy	of which: renewables
Primary production	46024	..	8809126	..	7978593	*83830	81151	57319	..	17056042	*141149
Imports	7794	9983	47700	210699	56378	..	..	9313	..	341866	..
Exports	-6375	-2566	-4567454	-1126283	-550430	..	..	-22662	..	-6275770	..
International marine bunkers	..	..	..	-58425	..	..	..	..	..	-58425	..
International aviation bunkers	..	..	..	*-72024	..	..	..	..	..	*-72024	..
Stock changes	..	..	..	..	..	..	..	..	..	..	..
Total energy supply	47443	7417	4289372	-1046033	7484540	*83830	81151	43970	..	10991689	*141149
Statistical difference	-12812	-4967	-43625	42118	112556	0	0	-11380	..	81890	*57319
Transfers	..	..	9073	-8482	..	..	..	..	..	591	..
Transformation	-51303	17632	-4334689	4432285	-2392506	-288	-81151	1051366	..	-1358654	-288
Electricity plants	..	-10709	..	-348258	-2385777	-288	-81151	1051366	..	-1774817	-288
CHP plants	..	..	..	..	..	..	..	..	..	..	..
Heat plants	..	..	..	..	..	..	..	..	..	..	..
Coke ovens	-51303	49886	..	..	..	..	..	..	..	-1417	..
Briquetting plants	..	..	..	..	..	..	..	..	..	..	..
Liquefaction plants	..	..	..	..	..	..	..	..	..	..	..
Gas works	..	..	..	..	..	..	..	..	..	..	..
Blast furnaces	..	-21545	..	..	-6729	..	..	..	..	-28274	..
NGL plants & gas blending	..	..	-591882	623733	..	..	..	..	..	31851	..
Oil refineries	..	..	-3742806	3729241	..	..	..	..	..	-13565	..
Other transformation	..	..	..	*427569	..	..	..	..	..	*427569	..
Energy industries own use	..	*-7343	-7381	-95773	-558302	..	..	-53334	..	-722134	..
Losses	..	-1562	..	..	-7262	..	..	-118271	..	-127095	..
Final consumption	*8951	21111	..	3239879	4413914	*83542	..	935111	..	8702508	*83542
Final energy consumption	387	8457	..	2193844	3871734	*83542	..	935111	..	7093075	*83542
Manufacturing, const., mining	..	8457	..	158545	1510644	..	..	318748	..	1996393	..
Iron and steel	..	8457	..	..	..	..	..	..	..	8457	..
Chemical and petrochemical	..	..	..	..	415072	..	..	..	..	415072	..
Non-ferrous metals	..	..	..	..	..	..	..	..	..	..	..
Non-metallic minerals	..	..	..	..	..	..	..	..	..	..	..
Transport equipment	..	..	..	..	..	..	..	..	..	..	..
Machinery	..	..	..	..	..	..	..	..	..	..	..
Mining and quarrying	..	..	..	..	..	..	..	..	..	..	..
Food and tobacco	..	..	..	..	..	..	..	..	..	..	..
Paper, pulp and printing	..	..	..	..	..	..	..	..	..	..	..
Wood and wood products	..	..	..	..	..	..	..	..	..	..	..
Textile and leather	..	..	..	..	..	..	..	..	..	..	..
Construction	..	..	..	..	..	..	..	..	..	..	..
Industries n.e.s	..	0	..	158545	1095572	..	..	318748	..	1572864	..
Transport	..	..	..	1692297	*294683	..	..	1717	..	1988698	..
Road	..	..	..	1690757	..	..	..	..	..	1690757	..
Rail	..	..	..	..	..	..	..	1717	..	1717	..
Domestic aviation	..	..	..	*27	..	..	..	..	..	*27	..
Domestic navigation	..	..	..	242	..	..	..	..	..	242	..
Pipeline transport	..	..	..	1270	..	..	..	..	..	1270	..
Transport, n.e.s	..	..	..	..	*294683	..	..	..	..	*294683	..
Other	387	..	..	343003	2066407	*83542	..	614646	..	3107984	*83542
Agriculture, forestry, fishing	..	..	..	110867	80143	..	..	136919	..	327929	..
Commerce, public services	..	..	..	31994	265633	..	..	153310	..	450937	..
Households	387	..	..	198281	1720631	*83542	..	306356	..	2309197	*83542
Other consumers	..	..	..	1861	..	..	..	18061	..	19922	..
Non-energy use	*8564	12654	..	*1046035	542180	..	..	..	..	*1609433	..

Iraq

Terajoules

2017	Primary coal and peat	Coal and peat products	Primary Oil	Oil Products	Natural Gas	Biofuels and waste	Nuclear	Electricity	Heat	Total energy	of which: renewables
Primary production	..	..	9574545	..	296997	1982	..	8039	..	9881563	10021
Imports	..	..	..	700062	54720	..	..	42433	..	797215	..
Exports	..	..	-7900540	-147783	..	..	..	..	..	-8048323	..
International marine bunkers	..	..	..	-11554	..	..	..	..	..	-11554	..
International aviation bunkers	..	..	..	-28180	..	..	..	..	..	-28180	..
Stock changes	..	..	-16285	1372	..	..	..	..	..	-14914	..
Total energy supply	..	..	1657720	513916	351717	1982	..	50472	..	2575807	10021
Statistical difference	..	..	262471	146686	-23385	0	..	2315	..	388087	8039
Transfers	..	..	265433	-253776	..	..	..	..	..	11656	..
Transformation	..	..	-1530481	583481	-318483	-894	..	294170	..	-972206	-894
Electricity plants	..	..	-338781	-482207	-318483	..	..	294170	..	-845300	..
CHP plants	..	..	..	..	..	..	..	..	..	..	..
Heat plants	..	..	..	..	..	..	..	..	..	..	..
Coke ovens	..	..	..	..	..	..	..	..	..	..	..
Briquetting plants	..	..	..	..	..	..	..	..	..	..	..
Liquefaction plants	..	..	..	..	..	..	..	..	..	..	..
Gas works	..	..	..	..	..	..	..	..	..	..	..
Blast furnaces	..	..	..	..	..	..	..	..	..	..	..
NGL plants & gas blending	..	..	-64046	68538	..	..	..	..	..	4492	..
Oil refineries	..	..	-1127655	997150	..	..	..	..	..	-130504	..
Other transformation	..	..	..	..	..	-894	..	..	..	-894	-894
Energy industries own use	..	..	-120978	-54457	..	..	..	-14209	..	-189644	..
Losses	..	..	-9221	..	..	..	..	-189961	..	-199183	..
Final consumption	..	..	..	642478	56619	1089	..	138157	..	838343	1089
Final energy consumption	..	..	..	630338	47218	1089	..	138157	..	816801	1089
Manufacturing, const., mining	..	..	..	90301	47218	..	..	18576	..	156095	..
Iron and steel	..	..	..	..	..	..	..	..	..	..	..
Chemical and petrochemical	..	..	..	..	..	..	..	..	..	..	..
Non-ferrous metals	..	..	..	..	..	..	..	..	..	..	..
Non-metallic minerals	..	..	..	..	..	..	..	..	..	..	..
Transport equipment	..	..	..	..	..	..	..	..	..	..	..
Machinery	..	..	..	..	..	..	..	..	..	..	..
Mining and quarrying	..	..	..	..	..	..	..	..	..	..	..
Food and tobacco	..	..	..	..	..	..	..	..	..	..	..
Paper, pulp and printing	..	..	..	..	..	..	..	..	..	..	..
Wood and wood products	..	..	..	..	..	..	..	..	..	..	..
Textile and leather	..	..	..	..	..	..	..	..	..	..	..
Construction	..	..	..	..	..	..	..	..	..	..	..
Industries n.e.s	..	..	..	90301	47218	..	..	18576	..	156095	..
Transport	..	..	..	399617	..	..	..	..	..	399617	..
Road	..	..	..	399617	..	..	..	..	..	399617	..
Rail	..	..	..	..	..	..	..	..	..	..	..
Domestic aviation	..	..	..	..	..	..	..	..	..	..	..
Domestic navigation	..	..	..	..	..	..	..	..	..	..	..
Pipeline transport	..	..	..	..	..	..	..	..	..	..	..
Transport, n.e.s	..	..	..	..	..	..	..	..	..	..	..
Other	..	..	..	140420	..	1089	..	119581	..	261089	1089
Agriculture, forestry, fishing	..	..	..	..	..	..	..	2556	..	2556	..
Commerce, public services	..	..	..	..	..	..	..	8942	..	8942	..
Households	..	..	..	140420	..	..	..	89975	..	230395	..
Other consumers	..	..	..	..	..	1089	..	18108	..	19197	1089
Non-energy use	..	..	..	12140	9401	..	..	..	..	21542	..

Iraq

Terajoules

2018	Primary coal and peat	Coal and peat products	Primary Oil	Oil Products	Natural Gas	Biofuels and waste	Nuclear	Electricity	Heat	Total energy	of which: renewables
Primary production	..	..	9579717	..	403916	1977	..	7902	..	9993511	9879
Imports	..	..	..	596055	153900	..	..	78455	..	828410	..
Exports	..	..	-8025198	-54103	..	..	..	..	..	-8079301	..
International marine bunkers	..	..	..	-11756	..	..	..	..	..	-11756	..
International aviation bunkers	..	..	..	-27298	..	..	..	..	..	-27298	..
Stock changes	..	..	-26818	..	..	..	..	..	..	-26818	..
Total energy supply	..	..	1527700	502898	557816	1977	..	86357	..	2676747	9879
Statistical difference	..	..	38070	114040	87286	-1	..	25769	..	265164	7901
Transfers	..	..	331209	-316632	..	..	..	..	..	14577	..
Transformation	..	..	-1689329	716522	-414230	-1126	..	289123	..	-1099038	-1126
Electricity plants	..	..	-345929	-488772	-414230	..	..	289123	..	-959808	..
CHP plants	..	..	..	..	..	..	..	..	..	..	..
Heat plants	..	..	..	..	..	..	..	..	..	..	..
Coke ovens	..	..	..	..	..	..	..	..	..	..	..
Briquetting plants	..	..	..	..	..	..	..	..	..	..	..
Liquefaction plants	..	..	..	..	..	..	..	..	..	..	..
Gas works	..	..	..	..	..	..	..	..	..	..	..
Blast furnaces	..	..	..	..	..	..	..	..	..	..	..
NGL plants & gas blending	..	..	-68068	72842	..	..	..	..	..	4774	..
Oil refineries	..	..	-1275331	1132452	..	..	..	..	..	-142879	..
Other transformation	..	..	..	..	..	-1126	..	..	..	-1126	-1126
Energy industries own use	..	..	-122458	-61701	..	..	..	-7474	..	-191633	..
Losses	..	..	-9052	..	..	..	..	-199699	..	-208751	..
Final consumption	..	..	..	727047	56300	852	..	142538	..	926738	852
Final energy consumption	..	..	..	714666	46952	852	..	142538	..	905008	852
Manufacturing, const., mining	..	..	..	111899	46952	..	..	17222	..	176074	..
Iron and steel	..	..	..	..	..	..	..	..	..	..	..
Chemical and petrochemical	..	..	..	..	..	..	..	..	..	..	..
Non-ferrous metals	..	..	..	..	..	..	..	..	..	..	..
Non-metallic minerals	..	..	..	..	..	..	..	..	..	..	..
Transport equipment	..	..	..	..	..	..	..	..	..	..	..
Machinery	..	..	..	..	..	..	..	..	..	..	..
Mining and quarrying	..	..	..	..	..	..	..	..	..	..	..
Food and tobacco	..	..	..	..	..	..	..	..	..	..	..
Paper, pulp and printing	..	..	..	..	..	..	..	..	..	..	..
Wood and wood products	..	..	..	..	..	..	..	..	..	..	..
Textile and leather	..	..	..	..	..	..	..	..	..	..	..
Construction	..	..	..	..	..	..	..	..	..	..	..
Industries n.e.s	..	..	..	111899	46952	..	..	17222	..	176074	..
Transport	..	..	..	467077	..	..	..	..	..	467077	..
Road	..	..	..	467077	..	..	..	..	..	467077	..
Rail	..	..	..	..	..	..	..	..	..	..	..
Domestic aviation	..	..	..	..	..	..	..	..	..	..	..
Domestic navigation	..	..	..	..	..	..	..	..	..	..	..
Pipeline transport	..	..	..	..	..	..	..	..	..	..	..
Transport, n.e.s	..	..	..	..	..	..	..	..	..	..	..
Other	..	..	..	135690	..	852	..	125316	..	261858	852
Agriculture, forestry, fishing	..	..	..	..	..	..	..	1814	..	1814	..
Commerce, public services	..	..	..	..	..	..	..	8320	..	8320	..
Households	..	..	..	135690	..	..	..	84042	..	219732	..
Other consumers	..	..	..	..	..	852	..	31140	..	31992	852
Non-energy use	..	..	..	12382	9348	..	..	..	..	21730	..

Ireland

Terajoules

2017	Primary coal and peat	Coal and peat products	Primary Oil	Oil Products	Natural Gas	Biofuels and waste	Nuclear	Electricity	Heat	Total energy	of which: renewables
Primary production	31144	..	..	..	119248	23253	..	29383	648	203677	48481
Imports	51199	277	124931	256297	59009	7010	..	4018	..	502740	7010
Exports	-309	-137	..	-78204	..	*-9	..	-6462	..	-85121	*-9
International marine bunkers	..	..	..	-6500	..	..	..	..	..	-6500	..
International aviation bunkers	..	..	..	-42601	..	..	..	..	..	-42601	..
Stock changes	-6364	-86	11346	-5667	2301	331	..	..	..	1861	331
Total energy supply	75670	54	136277	123326	180558	30585	..	26939	648	574056	55813
Statistical difference	-26	0	0	1205	-853	637	..	3110	0	4074	30060
Transfers	..	..	-1487	1125	..	..	..	..	..	-362	..
Transformation	-62976	1659	-134790	134641	-103144	-10035	..	81119	-119	-93645	-7816
Electricity plants	-59700	..	..	-1392	-89504	-9633	..	73238	-119	-87109	-7414
CHP plants	-286	..	..	-47	-11756	-402	..	7880	..	-4611	-402
Heat plants	..	..	..	..	..	..	..	..	..	..	..
Coke ovens	..	..	..	..	..	..	..	..	..	..	..
Briquetting plants	-2990	1659	..	..	..	..	..	..	..	-1331	..
Liquefaction plants	..	..	1889	..	..	..	..	..	..	1889	..
Gas works	..	..	..	..	..	..	..	..	..	..	..
Blast furnaces	..	..	..	..	..	..	..	..	..	..	..
NGL plants & gas blending	..	..	..	..	..	..	..	..	..	..	..
Oil refineries	..	..	-136678	136080	..	..	..	..	..	-599	..
Other transformation	..	..	..	..	-1884	..	..	..	..	-1884	..
Energy industries own use	-555	..	..	-5407	..	..	..	-4050	..	-10011	..
Losses	..	..	..	..	-2075	..	..	-7834	..	-9909	..
Final consumption	12164	1714	..	252480	76192	*19913	..	93064	529	456055	*17937
Final energy consumption	12164	1714	..	241786	76192	*19913	..	93064	529	445362	*17937
Manufacturing, const., mining	3962	..	..	20320	31903	*11336	..	36918	..	104439	*8831
Iron and steel	..	..	..	0	..	..	..	..	..	0	..
Chemical and petrochemical	..	..	..	1046	2689	..	..	6721	..	10456	..
Non-ferrous metals	..	..	..	323	17516	..	..	2866	..	20704	..
Non-metallic minerals	3119	..	..	7601	701	5087	..	2354	..	18863	2582
Transport equipment	..	..	..	185	77	..	..	781	..	1044	..
Machinery	..	..	..	2013	5342	..	..	5512	..	12867	..
Mining and quarrying	..	..	..	1292	495	..	..	2653	..	4441	..
Food and tobacco	842	..	..	5609	4356	*968	..	7888	..	19663	*968
Paper, pulp and printing	..	..	..	87	140	..	..	868	..	1095	..
Wood and wood products	..	..	..	86	85	*5281	..	1588	..	*7039	*5281
Textile and leather	..	..	..	127	48	..	..	472	..	647	..
Construction	..	..	..	..	..	..	..	263	..	263	..
Industries n.e.s	0	..	..	1952	454	0	..	4954	..	7359	0
Transport	..	..	..	162132	845	6254	..	187	..	169419	6254
Road	..	..	..	157313	1	6254	..	25	..	163593	6254
Rail	..	..	..	1548	..	..	..	162	..	1710	..
Domestic aviation	..	..	..	132	..	..	..	..	..	132	..
Domestic navigation	..	..	..	3139	..	..	..	..	..	3139	..
Pipeline transport	..	..	..	..	844	..	..	..	..	844	..
Transport, n.e.s	..	..	..	..	..	..	..	..	..	..	..
Other	8203	1714	..	59334	43444	*2323	..	55958	529	171504	*2852
Agriculture, forestry, fishing	..	..	..	7826	..	..	..	2009	..	9835	..
Commerce, public services	..	..	..	10696	20234	*1199	..	25297	7	57433	*1206
Households	8203	1714	..	40812	23210	*1124	..	28652	522	104237	*1646
Other consumers	..	..	..	..	..	..	..	..	..	..	..
Non-energy use	..	..	..	10693	..	..	..	..	..	10693	..

Ireland

Terajoules

2018	Primary coal and peat	Coal and peat products	Primary Oil	Oil Products	Natural Gas	Biofuels and waste	Nuclear	Electricity	Heat	Total energy	of which: renewables
Primary production	33554	..	..	..	115022	25505	..	33541	751	208372	53820
Imports	34225	297	127843	254341	72865	6240	..	5839	..	501650	6240
Exports	..	-176	..	-70962	..	-385	..	-5936	..	-77459	-385
International marine bunkers	..	..	..	-6752	..	..	..	..	..	-6752	..
International aviation bunkers	..	..	..	-45908	..	..	..	..	..	-45908	..
Stock changes	-10104	362	1627	4689	..	48	..	..	..	-3379	48
Total energy supply	57675	483	129470	135407	187887	31408	..	33444	751	576524	59723
Statistical difference	-34	78	0	-2328	-442	-577	..	1138	0	-2165	33026
Transfers	..	..	-62	-301	..	..	..	..	..	-362	..
Transformation	-44891	1425	-129408	129223	-104512	-12731	..	77627	-184	-83450	-8874
Electricity plants	-42004	..	..	-1435	-91405	-12350	..	69876	-184	-77502	-8493
CHP plants	-243	..	..	-47	-11405	-381	..	7751	..	-4325	-381
Heat plants	..	..	..	..	..	..	..	..	..	..	..
Coke ovens	..	..	..	..	..	..	..	..	..	..	..
Briquetting plants	-2644	1425	..	..	..	..	..	..	..	-1219	..
Liquefaction plants	..	..	1711	..	..	..	..	..	..	1711	..
Gas works	..	..	..	..	..	..	..	..	..	..	..
Blast furnaces	..	..	..	..	..	..	..	..	..	..	..
NGL plants & gas blending	..	..	..	..	..	..	..	..	..	..	..
Oil refineries	..	..	-131119	130706	..	..	..	..	..	-414	..
Other transformation	..	..	..	..	-1702	..	..	..	..	-1702	..
Energy industries own use	-425	..	..	-5338	..	..	..	-4162	..	-9925	..
Losses	..	..	..	..	-2404	..	..	-8050	..	-10454	..
Final consumption	12394	1830	..	261320	81413	*19254	..	97722	567	474500	*17823
Final energy consumption	12394	1830	..	250989	81413	*19254	..	97722	567	464168	*17823
Manufacturing, const., mining	4115	..	..	21790	32996	*10599	..	39204	..	108704	*8601
Iron and steel	..	..	..	..	..	..	..	..	..	..	..
Chemical and petrochemical	..	..	..	1177	2870	..	..	7153	..	11200	..
Non-ferrous metals	..	..	..	363	17645	..	..	2966	..	20974	..
Non-metallic minerals	3376	..	..	8174	748	4089	..	2506	..	18893	2091
Transport equipment	..	..	..	185	83	..	..	832	..	1099	..
Machinery	..	..	..	2155	5701	..	..	5864	..	13720	..
Mining and quarrying	..	..	..	1378	528	..	..	2822	..	4729	..
Food and tobacco	739	..	..	5925	4648	*1092	..	8395	..	20799	*1092
Paper, pulp and printing	..	..	..	87	149	..	..	922	..	1158	..
Wood and wood products	..	..	..	86	90	*5418	..	1688	..	*7282	*5418
Textile and leather	..	..	..	87	50	..	..	504	..	641	..
Construction	..	..	..	..	..	..	..	263	..	263	..
Industries n.e.s	0	..	..	2173	484	0	..	5288	..	7946	0
Transport	..	..	..	164767	942	6415	..	220	..	172344	6415
Road	..	..	..	159428	1	6415	..	43	..	165887	6415
Rail	..	..	..	1591	..	..	..	176	..	1767	..
Domestic aviation	..	..	..	265	..	..	..	..	..	265	..
Domestic navigation	..	..	..	3483	..	..	..	..	..	3483	..
Pipeline transport	..	..	..	..	941	..	..	..	..	941	..
Transport, n.e.s	..	..	..	..	..	..	..	..	..	..	..
Other	8279	1830	..	64432	47475	*2240	..	58298	567	183121	*2807
Agriculture, forestry, fishing	..	..	..	8428	..	..	..	2009	..	10437	..
Commerce, public services	..	..	..	11042	22234	*1073	..	26863	7	61219	*1080
Households	8279	1830	..	44961	25241	*1167	..	29426	560	111465	*1727
Other consumers	..	..	..	..	..	..	..	..	..	..	..
Non-energy use	..	..	..	10331	..	..	..	..	..	10331	..

Israel

Terajoules

2017	Primary coal and peat	Coal and peat products	Primary Oil	Oil Products	Natural Gas	Biofuels and waste	Nuclear	Electricity	Heat	Total energy	of which: renewables
Primary production	1783	..	3233	..	292070	1143	..	6088	16135	320451	23366
Imports	212185	..	499567	210592	15450	649	..	..	..	938443	649
Exports	..	..	..	-242788	-2169	..	..	-20336	..	-265293	..
International marine bunkers	..	..	..	-9886	..	..	..	..	..	-9886	..
International aviation bunkers	..	..	..	-45026	..	..	..	..	..	-45026	..
Stock changes	-5905	..	-27607	405	..	..	..	..	..	-33108	..
Total energy supply	208062	..	475193	-86703	305351	1792	..	-14249	16135	905581	24015
Statistical difference	-1470	..	1873	-24815	-54725	0	..	1048	0	-78090	6088
Transfers	..	..	127543	-127543	..	..	..	..	..	0	..
Transformation	-208735	..	-600863	600720	-312750	-960	..	237542	..	-285046	-960
Electricity plants	-208735	..	..	-7872	-308213	-960	..	237542	..	-288237	-960
CHP plants	..	..	..	..	..	..	..	..	..	..	..
Heat plants	..	..	..	..	..	..	..	..	..	..	..
Coke ovens	..	..	..	..	..	..	..	..	..	..	..
Briquetting plants	..	..	..	..	..	..	..	..	..	..	..
Liquefaction plants	..	..	4773	..	..	..	..	..	..	4773	..
Gas works	..	..	..	..	..	..	..	..	..	..	..
Blast furnaces	..	..	..	..	..	..	..	..	..	..	..
NGL plants & gas blending	..	..	..	..	..	..	..	..	..	..	..
Oil refineries	..	..	-605636	608592	..	..	..	..	..	2955	..
Other transformation	..	..	..	..	-4537	..	..	..	..	-4537	..
Energy industries own use	-772	..	..	-28166	..	..	..	-10998	..	-39936	..
Losses	..	..	..	..	..	..	..	-8593	..	-8593	..
Final consumption	25	..	..	383123	47327	832	..	202655	16135	650096	16967
Final energy consumption	..	..	..	303779	47327	832	..	202655	16135	570727	16967
Manufacturing, const., mining	..	..	..	32194	43965	..	..	46591	..	122751	..
Iron and steel	..	..	..	..	..	..	..	1667	..	1667	..
Chemical and petrochemical	..	..	..	..	..	..	..	..	..	..	..
Non-ferrous metals	..	..	..	..	..	..	..	..	..	..	..
Non-metallic minerals	..	..	..	12904	..	..	..	..	..	12904	..
Transport equipment	..	..	..	..	..	..	..	1674	..	1674	..
Machinery	..	..	..	..	..	..	..	9248	..	9248	..
Mining and quarrying	..	..	..	..	..	..	..	8129	..	8129	..
Food and tobacco	..	..	..	..	..	..	..	5969	..	5969	..
Paper, pulp and printing	..	..	..	..	..	..	..	277	..	277	..
Wood and wood products	..	..	..	..	..	..	..	2149	..	2149	..
Textile and leather	..	..	..	..	..	..	..	752	..	752	..
Construction	..	..	..	..	..	..	..	..	..	..	..
Industries n.e.s	..	..	..	19290	43965	..	..	16726	..	79981	..
Transport	..	..	..	247933	..	..	..	..	..	247933	..
Road	..	..	..	246787	..	..	..	..	..	246787	..
Rail	..	..	..	..	..	..	..	..	..	..	..
Domestic aviation	..	..	..	1147	..	..	..	..	..	1147	..
Domestic navigation	..	..	..	..	..	..	..	..	..	..	..
Pipeline transport	..	..	..	..	..	..	..	..	..	..	..
Transport, n.e.s	..	..	..	..	..	..	..	..	..	..	..
Other	..	..	..	23651	3362	832	..	156064	16135	200043	16967
Agriculture, forestry, fishing	..	..	..	..	..	..	..	10530	..	10530	..
Commerce, public services	..	..	..	5487	..	..	..	64368	..	69855	..
Households	..	..	..	5624	..	183	..	66856	16135	88798	16318
Other consumers	..	..	..	12540	3362	649	..	14310	..	30860	649
Non-energy use	25	..	..	79345	..	..	..	..	..	79370	..

Israel

Terajoules

2018	Primary coal and peat	Coal and peat products	Primary Oil	Oil Products	Natural Gas	Biofuels and waste	Nuclear	Electricity	Heat	Total energy	of which: renewables
Primary production	1648	..	3743	..	310789	1061	..	6325	15100	338666	22486
Imports	192176	..	492521	199312	19907	649	..	..	..	904564	649
Exports	..	..	..	-253214	..	..	..	-21107	..	-274321	..
International marine bunkers	..	..	..	-11949	..	..	..	..	..	-11949	..
International aviation bunkers	..	..	..	-47937	..	..	..	..	..	-47937	..
Stock changes	6447	..	19057	297	..	..	..	..	..	25800	..
Total energy supply	200270	..	515321	-113491	330696	1710	..	-14782	15100	934825	23135
Statistical difference	3016	..	11799	-3215	0	0	..	-338	0	11261	6325
Transfers	..	..	127543	-127543	..	..	..	..	..	0	..
Transformation	-196108	..	-631065	635529	-274448	-878	..	241690	..	-225281	-878
Electricity plants	-195461	..	..	-3552	-251457	-878	..	228125	..	-223224	-878
CHP plants	-647	..	..	-40	-19093	..	..	13565	..	-6215	..
Heat plants	..	..	..	..	..	..	..	..	..	..	..
Coke ovens	..	..	..	..	..	..	..	..	..	..	..
Briquetting plants	..	..	..	..	..	..	..	..	..	..	..
Liquefaction plants	..	..	4103	..	..	..	..	..	..	4103	..
Gas works	..	..	..	..	..	..	..	..	..	..	..
Blast furnaces	..	..	..	..	..	..	..	..	..	..	..
NGL plants & gas blending	..	..	..	..	..	..	..	..	..	..	..
Oil refineries	..	..	-635168	639121	..	..	..	..	..	3953	..
Other transformation	..	..	..	..	-3898	..	..	..	..	-3898	..
Energy industries own use	-1146	..	..	-28067	..	..	..	-11264	..	-40477	..
Losses	..	..	..	..	..	..	..	-9050	..	-9050	..
Final consumption	..	..	..	369643	56248	832	..	206932	15100	648755	15932
Final energy consumption	..	..	..	290251	56248	832	..	206932	15100	569362	15932
Manufacturing, const., mining	..	..	..	17939	52255	..	..	50386	..	120579	..
Iron and steel	..	..	..	..	..	..	..	1804	..	1804	..
Chemical and petrochemical	..	..	..	..	..	..	..	..	..	..	..
Non-ferrous metals	..	..	..	..	..	..	..	..	..	..	..
Non-metallic minerals	..	..	..	..	..	..	..	..	..	..	..
Transport equipment	..	..	..	..	..	..	..	1807	..	1807	..
Machinery	..	..	..	..	..	..	..	10001	..	10001	..
Mining and quarrying	..	..	..	..	..	..	..	8791	..	8791	..
Food and tobacco	..	..	..	..	..	..	..	6455	..	6455	..
Paper, pulp and printing	..	..	..	..	..	..	..	302	..	302	..
Wood and wood products	..	..	..	..	..	..	..	2326	..	2326	..
Textile and leather	..	..	..	..	..	..	..	814	..	814	..
Construction	..	..	..	..	..	..	..	..	..	..	..
Industries n.e.s	..	..	..	17939	52255	..	..	18086	..	88280	..
Transport	..	..	..	250135	..	..	..	..	..	250135	..
Road	..	..	..	248900	..	..	..	..	..	248900	..
Rail	..	..	..	..	..	..	..	..	..	..	..
Domestic aviation	..	..	..	1235	..	..	..	..	..	1235	..
Domestic navigation	..	..	..	..	..	..	..	..	..	..	..
Pipeline transport	..	..	..	..	..	..	..	..	..	..	..
Transport, n.e.s	..	..	..	..	..	..	..	..	..	..	..
Other	..	..	..	22177	3993	832	..	156546	15100	198648	15932
Agriculture, forestry, fishing	..	..	..	..	..	..	..	10721	..	10721	..
Commerce, public services	..	..	..	5250	..	..	..	64566	..	69816	..
Households	..	..	..	5388	..	183	..	66690	15100	87361	15283
Other consumers	..	..	..	11539	3993	649	..	14569	..	30750	649
Non-energy use	..	..	..	79393	..	..	..	..	..	79393	..

Italy

Terajoules

2017	Primary coal and peat	Coal and peat products	Primary Oil	Oil Products	Natural Gas	Biofuels and waste	Nuclear	Electricity	Heat	Total energy	of which: renewables
Primary production	0	..	186570	..	189910	523857	..	281948	239044	1421329	997362
Imports	382267	19405	2783408	782978	2388299	103732	..	154422	..	6614512	103732
Exports	0	-9903	-29367	-1326337	-9347	-13779	..	-18482	..	-1407215	-13779
International marine bunkers	..	..	..	-97283	..	..	..	..	..	-97283	..
International aviation bunkers	..	..	..	-146809	..	..	..	..	..	-146809	..
Stock changes	-1004	-58	13208	5041	8071	-1325	..	..	..	23934	-1325
Total energy supply	381263	9444	2953819	-782409	2576934	612485	..	417888	239044	6408468	1085991
Statistical difference	-25	-34	18924	-29613	-1	-7	..	0	0	-10755	305061
Transfers	..	..	233283	-233283	..	..	..	..	..	0	..
Transformation	-372446	16085	-3168177	3047094	-1056159	-254456	..	776477	8593	-1002989	-418939
Electricity plants	-301929	0	..	-21163	-360914	-108434	..	380009	-223236	-635667	-292096
CHP plants	-2259	-28414	..	-154021	-685207	-141272	..	396468	219888	-394816	-121300
Heat plants	..	..	..	-86	-10339	*-4127	..	..	11941	-2612	*-4920
Coke ovens	-56690	64855	..	..	..	..	..	..	..	8165	..
Briquetting plants	..	..	..	..	..	..	..	..	..	..	..
Liquefaction plants	..	..	..	..	..	..	..	..	..	..	..
Gas works	..	..	..	..	..	..	..	..	..	..	..
Blast furnaces	-11569	-24215	..	..	..	..	..	..	..	-35784	..
NGL plants & gas blending	..	..	..	..	302	-302	..	..	..	-1	-302
Oil refineries	..	..	-3168177	3226173	..	..	..	..	..	57996	..
Other transformation	..	3859	..	-3808	..	*-321	..	..	..	-270	*-321
Energy industries own use	0	-1942		-128755	-59320	..	..	-76082	-58757	-324857	..
Losses	..	..	..	..	-13788	..	..	-67205	-2423	-83416	..
Final consumption	8842	23620	..	1932260	1447668	*358037	..	1051078	186457	5007962	*361991
Final energy consumption	6759	23620	..	1627911	1420223	*358037	..	1051078	186457	4674084	*361991
Manufacturing, const., mining	6759	23620	..	82937	371392	*26162	..	416196	120858	1047925	*16429
Iron and steel	552	23620	..	2909	52580	..	..	67410	6795	153866	..
Chemical and petrochemical	..	0	..	12821	42211	3396	..	51422	43264	153114	309
Non-ferrous metals	..	0	..	1976	17898	..	..	9202	10	29086	..
Non-metallic minerals	6207	0	..	37514	83905	*11175	..	32058	5294	176154	*5599
Transport equipment	..	..	..	..	..	..	..	12924	4656	17580	..
Machinery	..	..	..	10668	59433	219	..	75197	1221	146738	*95
Mining and quarrying	..	..	..	1232	1302	..	..	2182	33	4749	..
Food and tobacco	..	..	..	7975	49154	*1862	..	44687	15855	119533	*1862
Paper, pulp and printing	..	..	..	2345	27528	18	..	30974	34889	95754	18
Wood and wood products	..	..	..	..	1378	*6696	..	10724	1507	20305	*6459
Textile and leather	..	..	..	2950	25511	4	..	18590	1678	48733	4
Construction	..	..	..	1333	9581	*32	..	4990	7	15943	*32
Industries n.e.s	0	0	..	1216	910	*2760	..	55836	5649	66371	*2051
Transport	..	..	..	1336985	44553	43855	..	40979	..	1466371	43855
Road	..	..	..	1265311	35465	43855	..	299	..	1344930	43855
Rail	..	..	..	1419	..	..	..	19854	..	21273	..
Domestic aviation	..	..	..	33516	..	..	..	..	..	33516	..
Domestic navigation	..	..	..	36739	..	..	..	..	..	36739	..
Pipeline transport	..	..	..	..	9087	..	..	1368	..	10455	..
Transport, n.e.s	..	..	..	..	..	..	..	19458	..	19458	..
Other	..	..	..	207989	1004278	*288020	..	593903	65599	2159788	*301707
Agriculture, forestry, fishing	..	..	..	91762	5693	*1477	..	21564	2528	123023	3566
Commerce, public services	..	..	..	23407	275918	*3697	..	336571	17993	657586	8790
Households	..	..	..	89160	722668	*282846	..	235768	44393	1374834	*289351
Other consumers	..	..	..	3660	..	..	..	..	685	4345	..
Non-energy use	2083	..	..	304349	27446	..	..	..	..	333878	..

Italy

Terajoules

2018	Primary coal and peat	Coal and peat products	Primary Oil	Oil Products	Natural Gas	Biofuels and waste	Nuclear	Electricity	Heat	Total energy	of which: renewables
Primary production	..	..	213130	..	186811	494615	..	320965	236050	1451571	1004194
Imports	352869	18863	2601550	820740	2327346	*115579	..	169812	..	6406759	*115579
Exports	-75	-10369	-22646	-1237759	-13390	-12115	..	-11776	..	-1308129	-12115
International marine bunkers	..	..	..	-114973	..	..	..	..	..	-114973	..
International aviation bunkers	..	..	..	-164669	..	..	..	..	..	-164669	..
Stock changes	-4239	405	31879	-822	-9060	147	..	..	..	18309	147
Total energy supply	348554	8898	2823913	-697483	2491707	598226	..	479002	236050	6288868	1107806
Statistical difference	25	27	-2052	-63366	3	-20	..	4	-2	-65381	343807
Transfers	..	..	205828	-205828	..	..	..	..	..	0	..
Transformation	-337286	20241	-3031792	2917553	-978124	-252726	..	715813	8014	-938308	-414530
Electricity plants	-264667	..	..	-13783	-320309	-105290	..	338087	-219780	-585742	-286352
CHP plants	-2244	-28333	..	-158785	-647314	-141857	..	377726	214636	-386172	-121721
Heat plants	..	..	..	-169	-11469	*-4289	..	..	13158	-2770	*-5167
Coke ovens	-60425	68718	..	..	..	..	..	..	..	8293	..
Briquetting plants	..	..	..	..	..	..	..	..	..	..	..
Liquefaction plants	..	..	..	..	..	..	..	..	..	..	..
Gas works	..	..	..	..	..	..	..	..	..	..	..
Blast furnaces	-9950	-21795	..	..	..	..	..	..	..	-31745	..
NGL plants & gas blending	..	..	..	..	968	-969	..	..	..	-1	-969
Oil refineries	..	..	-3031792	3094738	..	..	..	..	..	62946	..
Other transformation	..	1651	..	-4448	..	*-321	..	..	..	-3118	*-321
Energy industries own use	..	-2599	..	-126279	-66283	..	..	-74966	-50384	-320511	..
Losses	..	..	..	..	-13544	..	..	-64757	-2446	-80747	..
Final consumption	11243	26513	..	1951330	1433753	*345520	..	1055088	191236	5014683	*349468
Final energy consumption	9373	26513	..	1676972	1407959	*345520	..	1055088	191236	4712661	*349468
Manufacturing, const., mining	9373	26513	..	85644	362120	*27050	..	417852	94023	1022575	*16993
Iron and steel	723	26283	..	3306	53757	..	..	68069	3763	155900	..
Chemical and petrochemical	..	58	..	15763	39430	3556	..	52070	26513	137390	313
Non-ferrous metals	1197	115	..	2641	16855	..	..	9101	10	29919	..
Non-metallic minerals	6979	58	..	38193	85124	11869	..	32134	6154	180510	*5550
Transport equipment	..	..	..	..	..	..	..	12838	4308	17146	..
Machinery	..	..	..	11030	57160	246	..	76097	1185	145718	*112
Mining and quarrying	..	..	..	1518	1265	..	..	2214	33	5030	..
Food and tobacco	..	..	..	6865	47321	*2007	..	45119	16008	117320	*2007
Paper, pulp and printing	..	..	..	2012	25871	19	..	30532	27876	86310	19
Wood and wood products	..	..	..	..	1327	*7223	..	10760	1381	20691	*6977
Textile and leather	474	..	..	2538	24121	4	..	18432	1631	47200	4
Construction	..	..	..	817	9014	*60	..	5108	8	15008	*60
Industries n.e.s	0	0	..	961	875	*2066	..	55379	5153	64434	*1951
Transport	..	..	..	1373048	45766	51693	..	41540	..	1512048	51693
Road	..	..	..	1306779	35920	51693	..	356	..	1394748	51693
Rail	..	..	..	1892	..	..	..	20524	..	22416	..
Domestic aviation	..	..	..	37751	..	..	..	..	..	37751	..
Domestic navigation	..	..	..	26627	..	..	..	..	..	26627	..
Pipeline transport	..	..	..	..	9846	..	..	1310	..	11156	..
Transport, n.e.s	..	..	..	..	..	..	..	19350	..	19350	..
Other	..	..	..	218281	1000073	*266777	..	595696	97213	2178039	*280782
Agriculture, forestry, fishing	..	..	..	97184	5727	*1433	..	21035	2513	127891	3497
Commerce, public services	..	..	..	23274	303549	*3658	..	340164	35027	705673	8791
Households	..	..	..	93853	690797	*261686	..	234497	58805	1339638	*268494
Other consumers	..	..	..	3969	..	..	..	..	868	4837	..
Non-energy use	1870	..	..	274357	25794	..	..	..	..	302022	..

Jamaica

Terajoules

2017	Primary coal and peat	Coal and peat products	Primary Oil	Oil Products	Natural Gas	Biofuels and waste	Nuclear	Electricity	Heat	Total energy	of which: renewables
Primary production	..	..	..	..	..	6971	..	1753	..	8724	8724
Imports	2482	..	49288	74255	3680	1404	..	..	..	131110	1404
Exports	..	..	..	-12281	..	..	..	..	..	-12281	..
International marine bunkers	..	..	..	-2189	..	..	..	..	..	-2189	..
International aviation bunkers	..	..	..	-7598	..	..	..	..	..	-7598	..
Stock changes	-359	..	..	-2055	..	..	..	..	..	-2414	..
Total energy supply	2123	..	49288	50132	3680	8376	..	1753	..	115352	10129
Statistical difference	21	..	-317	5568	0	0	..	-4	..	5268	1753
Transfers	..	..	..	..	..	..	..	..	..	..	..
Transformation	..	..	-47156	13032	*-3680	*-2456	..	13943	..	-26318	*-2456
Electricity plants	..	..	..	*-30594	*-3680	..	..	13943	..	*-20331	..
CHP plants	..	..	..	..	..	*-1853	..	..	..	*-1853	*-1853
Heat plants	..	..	..	..	..	..	..	..	..	..	..
Coke ovens	..	..	..	..	..	..	..	..	..	..	..
Briquetting plants	..	..	..	..	..	..	..	..	..	..	..
Liquefaction plants	..	..	..	..	..	..	..	..	..	..	..
Gas works	..	..	..	..	..	..	..	..	..	..	..
Blast furnaces	..	..	..	..	..	..	..	..	..	..	..
NGL plants & gas blending	..	..	..	..	..	..	..	..	..	..	..
Oil refineries	..	..	-47156	43626	..	..	..	..	..	-3530	..
Other transformation	..	..	..	..	..	*-603	..	..	..	*-603	*-603
Energy industries own use	..	..	-2449	..	..	..	..	-65	..	-2514	..
Losses	..	..	0	..	..	..	..	-4147	..	-4147	..
Final consumption	2103	..	..	57596	..	5919	..	11488	..	77106	5919
Final energy consumption	2103	..	..	55119	..	5919	..	11488	..	74628	5919
Manufacturing, const., mining	2103	..	..	20527	..	*171	..	4889	..	27690	*171
Iron and steel	..	..	..	..	..	..	..	..	..	..	..
Chemical and petrochemical	..	..	..	..	..	..	..	..	..	..	..
Non-ferrous metals	..	..	..	..	..	..	..	..	..	..	..
Non-metallic minerals	..	..	..	..	..	..	..	*180	..	*180	..
Transport equipment	..	..	..	..	..	..	..	..	..	..	..
Machinery	..	..	..	..	..	..	..	..	..	..	..
Mining and quarrying	..	..	..	19398	..	..	..	*3053	..	22451	..
Food and tobacco	..	..	..	..	..	*112	..	*180	..	*292	*112
Paper, pulp and printing	..	..	..	..	..	..	..	..	..	..	..
Wood and wood products	..	..	..	..	..	..	..	..	..	..	..
Textile and leather	..	..	..	..	..	..	..	..	..	..	..
Construction	2103	..	..	516	..	..	..	*144	..	2763	..
Industries n.e.s	0	..	..	614	..	*59	..	1332	..	2005	*59
Transport	..	..	..	27869	..	1404	..	..	..	29273	1404
Road	..	..	..	26549	..	1404	..	..	..	27954	1404
Rail	..	..	..	..	..	..	..	..	..	..	..
Domestic aviation	..	..	..	273	..	..	..	..	..	273	..
Domestic navigation	..	..	..	1046	..	..	..	..	..	1046	..
Pipeline transport	..	..	..	..	..	..	..	..	..	..	..
Transport, n.e.s	..	..	..	..	..	..	..	..	..	..	..
Other	..	..	..	6722	..	4344	..	6599	..	17665	4344
Agriculture, forestry, fishing	..	..	..	1347	..	..	..	151	..	1498	..
Commerce, public services	..	..	..	3933	..	*738	..	2394	..	7064	*738
Households	..	..	..	1443	..	3607	..	3848	..	8898	3607
Other consumers	..	..	..	..	..	..	..	205	..	205	..
Non-energy use	..	..	..	2477	..	..	..	..	..	2477	..

Jamaica

Terajoules

2018	Primary coal and peat	Coal and peat products	Primary Oil	Oil Products	Natural Gas	Biofuels and waste	Nuclear	Electricity	Heat	Total energy	of which: renewables
Primary production	..	..	..	..	..	*6550	..	1897	..	*8448	*8448
Imports	2735	..	43781	79907	3410	1501	..	..	..	131333	1501
Exports	..	..	..	-11777	..	..	..	..	..	-11777	..
International marine bunkers	..	..	..	-1892	..	..	..	..	..	-1892	..
International aviation bunkers	..	..	..	-9261	..	..	..	..	..	-9261	..
Stock changes	-490	..	..	864	..	..	..	..	..	374	..
Total energy supply	2245	..	43781	57841	3410	*8051	..	1897	..	117225	*9948
Statistical difference	0	..	0	-4838	0	*-30	..	-216	..	-5084	*1868
Transfers	..	..	..	..	..	..	..	..	..	..	..
Transformation	..	..	-43781	12737	-3410	*-924	..	13950	..	-21427	*-924
Electricity plants	..	..	..	-30588	-3410	..	..	13882	..	-20116	..
CHP plants	..	..	..	..	..	*-309	..	68	..	*-240	*-309
Heat plants	..	..	..	..	..	..	..	..	..	..	..
Coke ovens	..	..	..	..	..	..	..	..	..	..	..
Briquetting plants	..	..	..	..	..	..	..	..	..	..	..
Liquefaction plants	..	..	..	..	..	..	..	..	..	..	..
Gas works	..	..	..	..	..	..	..	..	..	..	..
Blast furnaces	..	..	..	..	..	..	..	..	..	..	..
NGL plants & gas blending	..	..	..	..	..	..	..	..	..	..	..
Oil refineries	..	..	-43781	43325	..	..	..	..	..	-456	..
Other transformation	..	..	..	..	..	*-615	..	..	..	*-615	*-615
Energy industries own use	..	..	..	..	..	..	..	-68	..	-68	..
Losses	..	..	..	..	..	..	..	-4118	..	-4118	..
Final consumption	2245	..	..	75417	..	*7157	..	11876	..	96695	*7157
Final energy consumption	2245	..	..	74412	..	*7157	..	11876	..	95690	*7157
Manufacturing, const., mining	2245	..	..	35284	..	*1295	..	6480	..	45303	*1295
Iron and steel	..	..	..	..	..	..	..	..	..	..	..
Chemical and petrochemical	..	..	..	..	..	..	..	..	..	..	..
Non-ferrous metals	..	..	..	..	..	..	..	..	..	..	..
Non-metallic minerals	2245	..	..	366	..	..	..	2099	..	4710	..
Transport equipment	..	..	..	..	..	..	..	..	..	..	..
Machinery	..	..	..	..	..	..	..	..	..	..	..
Mining and quarrying	..	..	..	32612	..	..	..	1750	..	34361	..
Food and tobacco	..	..	..	288	..	*1236	..	1400	..	2924	*1236
Paper, pulp and printing	..	..	..	..	..	..	..	..	..	..	..
Wood and wood products	..	..	..	..	..	..	..	..	..	..	..
Textile and leather	..	..	..	..	..	..	..	..	..	..	..
Construction	..	..	..	473	..	..	..	*108	..	581	..
Industries n.e.s	0	..	..	1545	..	*59	..	1123	..	2727	*59
Transport	..	..	..	33225	..	1501	..	..	..	34726	1501
Road	..	..	..	31597	..	1501	..	..	..	33098	1501
Rail	..	..	..	..	..	..	..	..	..	..	..
Domestic aviation	..	..	..	*132	..	..	..	..	..	*132	..
Domestic navigation	..	..	..	*1496	..	..	..	..	..	*1496	..
Pipeline transport	..	..	..	..	..	..	..	..	..	..	..
Transport, n.e.s	..	..	..	..	..	..	..	..	..	..	..
Other	..	..	..	5902	..	*4362	..	5396	..	15661	*4362
Agriculture, forestry, fishing	..	..	..	567	..	..	..	*108	..	675	..
Commerce, public services	..	..	..	4595	..	738	..	1418	..	6751	738
Households	..	..	..	741	..	*3624	..	3870	..	8235	*3624
Other consumers	..	..	..	..	..	..	..	..	..	..	..
Non-energy use	..	..	..	1005	..	..	..	..	..	1005	..

Japan

Terajoules

	Primary coal and peat	Coal and peat products	Primary Oil	Oil Products	Natural Gas	Biofuels and waste	Nuclear	Electricity	Heat	Total energy	of which: renewables
2017											
Primary production	32402	..	18438	..	107250	580400	355450	523116	103495	1720550	957460
Imports	4838251	37077	6641313	1889700	4112001	*49555	..	..	..	17567898	*49555
Exports	-73	-35940	..	-734271	..	..	..	..	..	-770285	..
International marine bunkers	..	..	..	-169024	..	..	..	..	..	-169024	..
International aviation bunkers	..	..	..	-293353	..	..	..	..	..	-293353	..
Stock changes	..	2334	37675	6646	5131	..	..	..	..	51786	..
Total energy supply	4870580	3471	6697426	699697	4224382	629955	355450	523116	103495	18107572	1007015
Statistical difference	-162873	32313	19339	149246	23872	13260	0	31957	1	107115	544524
Transfers	..	..	175015	-177352	..	..	..	..	..	-2337	..
Transformation	-4584409	651584	-6838804	6259849	-2907205	-353741	-355450	3303299	-65387	-4890264	*-264545
Electricity plants	-2973094	-270466	-57104	-522432	-2962993	-348368	-355450	3306895	-88452	-4271463	*-263919
CHP plants	..	..	..	..	..	..	..	..	..	..	..
Heat plants	..	..	..	-162	-13552	..	..	-3596	23065	5755	..
Coke ovens	-1239264	1256225	..	-18409	..	-4747	..	..	..	-6194	..
Briquetting plants	..	..	..	..	..	..	..	..	..	..	..
Liquefaction plants	..	..	..	..	..	..	..	..	..	..	..
Gas works	..	..	..	..	..	..	..	..	..	..	..
Blast furnaces	-372051	-409374	..	..	..	..	..	..	..	-781425	..
NGL plants & gas blending	..	..	..	-57503	69340	-129	..	..	..	11708	-129
Oil refineries	..	..	-6781700	6869835	..	..	..	..	..	88136	..
Other transformation	..	75198	..	-11482	..	*-497	..	..	..	63220	*-497
Energy industries own use	-16693	-121041	-2817	-264925	-58432	-3108	..	-175111	-660	-642787	-3108
Losses	..	..	..	..	..	..	..	-146311	..	-146311	..
Final consumption	432351	501700	11481	6368023	1234874	*259846	..	3473035	37447	12318757	*194838
Final energy consumption	432351	472202	974	4873534	1225500	*259846	..	3473035	37447	10774889	*194838
Manufacturing, const., mining	429220	467883	974	766011	474386	*158240	..	1247868	27	3544609	*115368
Iron and steel	100803	414343	..	56320	102930	1444	..	255028	..	930867	..
Chemical and petrochemical	112578	32471	974	388793	87165	5980	..	200160	..	828121	..
Non-ferrous metals	1863	6955	..	15719	18770	1334	..	46670	..	91311	..
Non-metallic minerals	136646	11633	..	83376	32007	27733	..	63954	..	355349	*5559
Transport equipment	181	2422	..	13361	30259	..	..	100876	..	147099	..
Machinery	..	29	..	29975	60269	*4	..	182156	..	272433	*4
Mining and quarrying	0	0	..	8043	..	..	..	3913	..	11957	..
Food and tobacco	26	29	..	48856	80636	*252	..	89420	4	219223	*256
Paper, pulp and printing	76553	0	..	30673	30160	*120003	..	129899	..	387288	*108036
Wood and wood products	..	..	..	5127	629	*1490	..	13158	..	20404	*1490
Textile and leather	0	..	..	8457	9239	..	..	14386	..	32081	..
Construction	..	..	..	63599	2630	..	..	22723	..	88952	..
Industries n.e.s	569	0	0	13712	19695	0	..	125525	23	159524	*23
Transport	52	..	..	2910601	2153	17577	..	62856	..	2993238	17577
Road	..	..	..	2632100	2153	17577	..	..	..	2651830	17577
Rail	52	..	..	6837	..	..	..	62856	..	69745	..
Domestic aviation	..	..	..	144869	..	..	..	..	..	144869	..
Domestic navigation	..	..	..	126795	..	..	..	..	..	126795	..
Pipeline transport	..	..	..	..	..	..	..	..	..	..	..
Transport, n.e.s	..	..	..	..	..	..	..	..	..	..	..
Other	3080	4319	..	1196922	748961	*84029	..	2162311	37420	4237041	*61893
Agriculture, forestry, fishing	..	..	..	185751	79	..	..	11563	470	197863	470
Commerce, public services	3080	4319	..	464292	363349	*59820	..	1166929	24190	2085978	*48466
Households	..	..	..	546879	385533	354	..	983819	12459	1929044	11675
Other consumers	..	..	..	..	..	23855	..	..	301	24156	*1282
Non-energy use	0	29498	10507	1494489	9374	..	..	..	..	1543869	..

Japan

Terajoules

2018	Primary coal and peat	Coal and peat products	Primary Oil	Oil Products	Natural Gas	Biofuels and waste	Nuclear	Electricity	Heat	Total energy	of which: renewables
Primary production	30848	..	16704	..	93099	607486	701233	544025	106617	2100011	991279
Imports	4757717	46449	6347185	1851420	3950033	*57935	..	..	..	17010738	*57935
Exports	-743	-41928	..	-735031	..	..	..	..	..	-777703	..
International marine bunkers	..	..	..	-178131	..	..	..	..	..	-178131	..
International aviation bunkers	..	..	..	-301644	..	..	..	..	..	-301644	..
Stock changes	..	-1809	-18571	9342	17021	..	..	..	..	5983	..
Total energy supply	4787821	2712	6345318	645956	4060152	665421	701233	544025	106617	17859255	1049215
Statistical difference	-116077	44629	-11726	217904	49338	11744	0	36943	1	232757	566399
Transfers	..	..	158270	-161190	..	..	..	..	..	-2920	..
Transformation	-4460470	652695	-6509583	6086992	-2742233	-386191	-701233	3233732	-67799	-4894090	*-280177
Electricity plants	-2868155	-262242	-21137	-421034	-2798211	-381076	-701233	3237329	-90864	-4306624	*-279574
CHP plants	..	..	..	..	..	..	..	..	..	..	..
Heat plants	..	..	..	-162	-13498	..	..	-3596	23065	5809	..
Coke ovens	-1240647	1258153	..	-18438	..	-4512	..	..	..	-5444	..
Briquetting plants	..	..	..	..	..	..	..	..	..	..	..
Liquefaction plants	..	..	..	..	..	..	..	..	..	..	..
Gas works	..	..	..	..	..	..	..	..	..	..	..
Blast furnaces	-351668	-417574	..	..	..	..	..	..	..	-769242	..
NGL plants & gas blending	..	..	..	-58741	69476	-106	..	..	..	10629	-106
Oil refineries	..	..	-6488445	6597338	..	..	..	..	..	108892	..
Other transformation	..	74358	..	-11971	..	*-497	..	..	..	61890	*-497
Energy industries own use	-18968	-121317	-1723	-273630	-51921	-6110	..	-174895	-660	-649223	-6110
Losses	..	..	..	..	..	..	..	-161996	..	-161996	..
Final consumption	424460	489460	4008	6080224	1216661	*261376	..	3403922	38157	11918268	*196529
Final energy consumption	424435	459832	931	4674664	1207320	*261376	..	3403922	38157	10470638	*196529
Manufacturing, const., mining	421303	455514	931	721303	479071	*160779	..	1239552	27	3478480	*115820
Iron and steel	98747	400633	..	50746	108847	1495	..	252626	..	913094	..
Chemical and petrochemical	111996	33726	931	360385	87449	6140	..	197939	..	798564	..
Non-ferrous metals	1708	6471	..	14919	18711	1358	..	46357	..	89524	..
Non-metallic minerals	132102	12611	..	81845	31808	29533	..	63216	..	351115	*5561
Transport equipment	181	2013	..	12257	30240	..	..	100325	..	145016	..
Machinery	..	29	..	27972	59270	*4	..	183388	..	270663	*4
Mining and quarrying	..	..	..	8000	..	..	..	3866	..	11867	..
Food and tobacco	26	29	..	46154	80629	*252	..	88326	4	215420	*256
Paper, pulp and printing	75975	..	..	29520	29930	*120507	..	129895	..	385827	*108486
Wood and wood products	..	..	..	5036	628	*1490	..	13000	..	20154	*1490
Textile and leather	..	..	..	7921	9239	..	..	14206	..	31365	..
Construction	..	..	..	63419	2630	..	..	22450	..	88498	..
Industries n.e.s	569	0	0	13130	19691	0	..	123959	23	157372	*23
Transport	52	..	..	2874395	1782	17979	..	62856	..	2957064	17979
Road	..	..	..	2593673	1782	17979	..	..	..	2613434	17979
Rail	52	..	..	6837	..	..	..	62856	..	69745	..
Domestic aviation	..	..	..	146677	..	..	..	..	..	146677	..
Domestic navigation	..	..	..	127208	..	..	..	..	..	127208	..
Pipeline transport	..	..	..	..	..	..	..	..	..	..	..
Transport, n.e.s	..	..	..	..	..	..	..	..	..	..	..
Other	3079	4319	..	1078966	726467	*82618	..	2101514	38130	4035094	*62730
Agriculture, forestry, fishing	..	..	..	184073	79	..	..	11534	470	196157	470
Commerce, public services	3079	4319	..	429188	365701	*59855	..	1151366	24214	2037722	*48525
Households	..	..	..	465705	360688	354	..	938614	13145	1778505	12361
Other consumers	..	..	..	..	..	22409	..	..	301	22710	*1374
Non-energy use	26	29628	3077	1405559	9340	..	..	..	..	1447630	..

Jordan

Terajoules

2017	Primary coal and peat	Coal and peat products	Primary Oil	Oil Products	Natural Gas	Biofuels and waste	Nuclear	Electricity	Heat	Total energy	of which: renewables
Primary production	..	..	12	..	3462	3361	..	3882	..	10718	7243
Imports	5222	1253	125008	116744	181812	587	..	184	..	430809	587
Exports	..	..	..	..	-38326	-9	..	-205	..	-38541	-9
International marine bunkers	..	..	..	-3108	..	..	..	..	..	-3108	..
International aviation bunkers	..	..	..	-2799	..	..	..	..	..	-2799	..
Stock changes	..	..	-685	-5585	..	..	..	..	..	-6270	..
Total energy supply	5222	1253	124336	105251	146948	3939	..	3861	..	390809	7821
Statistical difference	0	0	0	-6275	0	0	..	-2908	..	-9183	3882
Transfers	..	..	..	..	..	..	..	..	..	..	..
Transformation	..	..	-124336	101027	-146948	*-1310	..	66073	..	-105494	*-1310
Electricity plants	..	..	..	*-13272	-146948	-100	..	66073	..	-94248	-100
CHP plants	..	..	..	..	..	..	..	..	..	..	..
Heat plants	..	..	..	..	..	..	..	..	..	..	..
Coke ovens	..	..	..	..	..	..	..	..	..	..	..
Briquetting plants	..	..	..	..	..	..	..	..	..	..	..
Liquefaction plants	..	..	..	..	..	..	..	..	..	..	..
Gas works	..	..	..	..	..	..	..	..	..	..	..
Blast furnaces	..	..	..	..	..	..	..	..	..	..	..
NGL plants & gas blending	..	..	..	..	..	..	..	..	..	..	..
Oil refineries	..	..	-124336	114299	..	..	..	..	..	-10036	..
Other transformation	..	..	..	..	..	*-1210	..	..	..	*-1210	*-1210
Energy industries own use	..	..	..	*-1781	..	..	..	-2524	..	-4305	..
Losses	..	..	..	..	..	..	..	-7304	..	-7304	..
Final consumption	5222	1253	..	210772	..	*2629	..	63014	..	282889	*2629
Final energy consumption	5222	1253	..	200762	..	*2629	..	63014	..	272879	*2629
Manufacturing, const., mining	5222	1253	..	20181	..	..	..	14075	..	40731	..
Iron and steel	..	..	..	..	..	..	..	..	..	..	..
Chemical and petrochemical	..	..	..	..	..	..	..	421	..	421	..
Non-ferrous metals	..	..	..	..	..	..	..	..	..	..	..
Non-metallic minerals	..	..	..	..	..	..	..	1757	..	1757	..
Transport equipment	..	..	..	..	..	..	..	..	..	..	..
Machinery	..	..	..	..	..	..	..	..	..	..	..
Mining and quarrying	..	..	..	..	..	..	..	1584	..	1584	..
Food and tobacco	..	..	..	..	..	..	..	..	..	..	..
Paper, pulp and printing	..	..	..	..	..	..	..	..	..	..	..
Wood and wood products	..	..	..	..	..	..	..	..	..	..	..
Textile and leather	..	..	..	..	..	..	..	..	..	..	..
Construction	..	..	..	..	..	..	..	..	..	..	..
Industries n.e.s	5222	1253	..	20181	..	..	..	10313	..	36969	..
Transport	..	..	..	136967	..	..	..	..	..	136967	..
Road	..	..	..	122365	..	..	..	..	..	122365	..
Rail	..	..	..	..	..	..	..	..	..	..	..
Domestic aviation	..	..	..	*14509	..	..	..	..	..	*14509	..
Domestic navigation	..	..	..	..	..	..	..	..	..	..	..
Pipeline transport	..	..	..	..	..	..	..	..	..	..	..
Transport, n.e.s	..	..	..	94	..	..	..	..	..	94	..
Other	..	..	..	43613	..	*2629	..	48939	..	95181	*2629
Agriculture, forestry, fishing	..	..	..	..	..	..	..	9660	..	9660	..
Commerce, public services	..	..	..	7246	..	..	..	10484	..	17730	..
Households	..	..	..	26706	..	*644	..	28796	..	56145	*644
Other consumers	..	..	..	9662	..	*1985	..	..	..	11647	*1985
Non-energy use	..	..	..	10010	..	..	..	..	..	10010	..

Jordan

Terajoules

2018	Primary coal and peat	Coal and peat products	Primary Oil	Oil Products	Natural Gas	Biofuels and waste	Nuclear	Electricity	Heat	Total energy	of which: renewables
Primary production	..	..	42	..	3262	3425	..	5637	..	12366	9062
Imports	7036	1792	105032	116516	151093	627	..	677	..	382773	627
Exports	..	..	..	..	-10429	-14	..	-338	..	-10782	-14
International marine bunkers	..	..	..	-181	..	..	..	..	..	-181	..
International aviation bunkers	..	..	..	-2528	..	..	..	..	..	-2528	..
Stock changes	..	..	-470	619	..	..	..	..	..	150	..
Total energy supply	7036	1792	104605	114426	143926	4038	..	5976	..	381798	9675
Statistical difference	0	0	0	-5595	0	0	..	-4518	..	-10113	5637
Transfers	..	..	..	..	..	..	..	..	..	..	..
Transformation	..	..	-104605	92586	-143925	*-1337	..	62254	..	-95027	*-1337
Electricity plants	..	..	..	*-5433	-143925	*-100	..	62254	..	-87204	*-100
CHP plants	..	..	..	..	..	..	..	..	..	..	..
Heat plants	..	..	..	..	..	..	..	..	..	..	..
Coke ovens	..	..	..	..	..	..	..	..	..	..	..
Briquetting plants	..	..	..	..	..	..	..	..	..	..	..
Liquefaction plants	..	..	..	..	..	..	..	..	..	..	..
Gas works	..	..	..	..	..	..	..	..	..	..	..
Blast furnaces	..	..	..	..	..	..	..	..	..	..	..
NGL plants & gas blending	..	..	..	..	..	..	..	..	..	..	..
Oil refineries	..	..	-104605	98019	..	..	..	..	..	-6586	..
Other transformation	..	..	..	..	..	*-1237	..	..	..	*-1237	*-1237
Energy industries own use	..	..	..	-8449	..	..	..	-2232	..	-10681	..
Losses	..	..	..	..	..	..	..	-7538	..	-7538	..
Final consumption	7036	1792	..	204158	..	*2701	..	62977	..	278665	*2701
Final energy consumption	7036	1792	..	198309	..	*2701	..	62977	..	272816	*2701
Manufacturing, const., mining	7036	1792	..	16724	..	..	..	13901	..	39453	..
Iron and steel	..	..	..	..	..	..	..	..	..	..	..
Chemical and petrochemical	..	..	..	..	..	..	..	522	..	522	..
Non-ferrous metals	..	..	..	..	..	..	..	..	..	..	..
Non-metallic minerals	..	..	..	..	..	..	..	1393	..	1393	..
Transport equipment	..	..	..	..	..	..	..	..	..	..	..
Machinery	..	..	..	..	..	..	..	..	..	..	..
Mining and quarrying	..	..	..	..	..	..	..	1523	..	1523	..
Food and tobacco	..	..	..	..	..	..	..	..	..	..	..
Paper, pulp and printing	..	..	..	..	..	..	..	..	..	..	..
Wood and wood products	..	..	..	..	..	..	..	..	..	..	..
Textile and leather	..	..	..	..	..	..	..	..	..	..	..
Construction	..	..	..	..	..	..	..	..	..	..	..
Industries n.e.s	7036	1792	..	16724	..	..	..	10463	..	36015	..
Transport	..	..	..	138115	..	..	..	..	..	138115	..
Road	..	..	..	121889	..	..	..	..	..	121889	..
Rail	..	..	..	..	..	..	..	..	..	..	..
Domestic aviation	..	..	..	15982	..	..	..	..	..	15982	..
Domestic navigation	..	..	..	..	..	..	..	..	..	..	..
Pipeline transport	..	..	..	..	..	..	..	..	..	..	..
Transport, n.e.s	..	..	..	244	..	..	..	..	..	244	..
Other	..	..	..	43469	..	*2701	..	49076	..	95247	*2701
Agriculture, forestry, fishing	..	..	..	..	..	..	..	9701	..	9701	..
Commerce, public services	..	..	..	7239	..	..	..	10961	..	18201	..
Households	..	..	..	24782	..	*651	..	28414	..	53847	*651
Other consumers	..	..	..	11448	..	*2051	..	..	..	13499	*2051
Non-energy use	..	..	..	5849	..	..	..	..	..	5849	..

Kazakhstan

Terajoules

2017	Primary coal and peat	Coal and peat products	Primary Oil	Oil Products	Natural Gas	Biofuels and waste	Nuclear	Electricity	Heat	Total energy	of which: renewables
Primary production	2010051	..	3671262	..	1663122	2202	..	41915	..	7388551	44116
Imports	74	25587	1777	83278	220390	112	..	4777	..	335995	112
Exports	-544829	-1309	-2929548	-185370	-624407	-3	..	-20491	..	-4305956	-3
International marine bunkers	..	..	..	0	..	..	..	..	..	0	..
International aviation bunkers	..	..	..	*-21036	..	..	..	..	..	*-21036	..
Stock changes	-48924	..	*-2411	16630	-10204	..	..	..	..	-44910	..
Total energy supply	1416372	24278	741079	-106498	1248901	2310	..	26201	..	3352644	44225
Statistical difference	-196595	0	-4568	-70513	36900	8	..	-28897	39401	-224264	41923
Transfers	..	..	..	..	..	..	..	..	..	..	..
Transformation	-994820	47565	*-669042	628245	-235655	*-13	..	329346	371187	-523188	*-13
Electricity plants	-317957	..	..	..	-235655	..	..	..	..	-553612	..
CHP plants	..	..	..	-8888	..	..	..	329346	371187	691645	..
Heat plants	-592785	..	..	..	..	..	..	..	..	-592785	..
Coke ovens	-84098	97867	..	..	..	..	..	..	..	13770	..
Briquetting plants	..	..	..	..	..	..	..	..	..	..	..
Liquefaction plants	..	..	..	..	..	..	..	..	..	..	..
Gas works	..	..	..	..	..	..	..	..	..	..	..
Blast furnaces	..	-50303	..	..	..	..	..	..	..	-50303	..
NGL plants & gas blending	..	..	-54720	58557	..	..	..	..	..	3838	..
Oil refineries	..	..	*-614323	578576	..	..	..	..	..	*-35747	..
Other transformation	..	..	..	..	..	*-13	..	..	..	*-13	*-13
Energy industries own use	-8391	-17517	-36928	-26600	-811725	..	..	-110891	-88883	-1100935	..
Losses	-234	-81	-16835	-464	-20174	..	..	-23080	-34561	-95430	..
Final consumption	609522	54245	*22842	565195	*144446	*2289	..	250474	208342	1857356	*2289
Final energy consumption	609522	54245	*22842	536613	*127957	*2289	..	250474	208342	1812284	*2289
Manufacturing, const., mining	401675	54245	*22842	150674	*63812	..	..	170662	79179	943089	..
Iron and steel	97344	54061	..	22020	*11854	..	..	47282	29034	261595	..
Chemical and petrochemical	847	..	..	1556	*16488	..	..	14562	4897	38349	..
Non-ferrous metals	30521	..	..	18905	*7110	..	..	21769	648	78953	..
Non-metallic minerals	78	..	..	18774	..	..	..	5688	..	24540	..
Transport equipment	58	..	..	86	*257	..	..	166	644	1211	..
Machinery	853	..	..	343	*573	..	..	1415	1256	4440	..
Mining and quarrying	39157	..	..	47597	*16950	..	..	13910	11015	128629	..
Food and tobacco	1586	..	..	4360	*8282	..	..	4460	6366	25054	..
Paper, pulp and printing	26	..	..	288	*683	..	..	288	666	1951	..
Wood and wood products	19	..	..	86	*36	..	..	112	135	387	..
Textile and leather	63	..	..	86	*285	..	..	457	218	1110	..
Construction	989	..	..	15995	*1293	..	..	1588	5674	25538	..
Industries n.e.s	230135	185	*22842	20579	0	..	..	58964	18626	351332	..
Transport	0	..	..	227135	..	..	..	14468	..	241603	..
Road	..	..	..	201370	..	..	..	407	..	201777	..
Rail	0	..	..	11223	..	..	..	4838	..	16061	..
Domestic aviation	..	..	..	3275	..	..	..	..	..	3275	..
Domestic navigation	..	..	..	258	..	..	..	..	..	258	..
Pipeline transport	..	..	..	..	..	..	..	1674	..	1674	..
Transport, n.e.s	0	..	..	11008	..	..	..	7549	..	18557	..
Other	207848	..	..	158804	*64145	*2289	..	65344	129163	627592	*2289
Agriculture, forestry, fishing	4638	..	..	23508	*964	..	..	2585	3762	35457	..
Commerce, public services	36329	..	..	21400	*35738	..	..	19516	88089	201071	..
Households	166648	..	..	91817	*10955	*1476	..	43243	32935	347074	*1476
Other consumers	*233	..	..	22080	*16488	*813	..	..	4377	43991	*813
Non-energy use	..	..	..	28582	16490	..	..	..	..	45072	..

Kazakhstan

Terajoules

2018	Primary coal and peat	Coal and peat products	Primary Oil	Oil Products	Natural Gas	Biofuels and waste	Nuclear	Electricity	Heat	Total energy	of which: renewables
Primary production	2037951	..	3888210	..	1410422	2189	..	39143	..	7377915	41332
Imports	9756	25076	1058	65186	349055	230	..	5620	..	455981	230
Exports	-504866	-1801	-2952752	-233489	-964566	-108	..	-18151	..	-4675732	-108
International marine bunkers	..	..	..	-655	..	..	..	..	..	-655	..
International aviation bunkers	..	..	..	-26513	..	..	..	..	..	-26513	..
Stock changes	8371	..	-18697	-1860	-15375	4	..	..	..	-27556	4
Total energy supply	1551213	23275	917819	-197331	779536	2315	..	26611	..	3103439	41458
Statistical difference	112676	1132	79735	-57261	192836	0	..	-788	46963	375292	39143
Transfers	..	..	..	33	..	..	..	..	..	33	..
Transformation	-1065401	62080	-753653	684390	-281795	-101	..	346273	383651	-624555	-101
Electricity plants	-349529	..	..	..	-281795	-19	..	..	..	-631342	-19
CHP plants	..	..	..	-8601	..	..	..	346273	383651	721323	..
Heat plants	-652097	..	..	..	..	..	..	..	..	-652097	..
Coke ovens	-63775	92972	..	..	..	..	..	..	..	29197	..
Briquetting plants	..	..	..	..	..	..	..	..	..	..	..
Liquefaction plants	..	..	..	..	..	..	..	..	..	..	..
Gas works	..	..	..	..	..	..	..	..	..	..	..
Blast furnaces	..	-30892	..	..	..	..	..	..	..	-30892	..
NGL plants & gas blending	..	..	-65982	70609	..	..	..	..	..	4628	..
Oil refineries	..	..	-687671	622382	..	..	..	..	..	-65289	..
Other transformation	..	..	..	..	..	-82	..	..	..	-82	-82
Energy industries own use	-8355	-16668	-76986	-15018	-67151	..	..	-76399	-102484	-363061	..
Losses	-135	..	-7360	-4872	-16250	..	..	-8093	-36400	-73110	..
Final consumption	364646	67556	85	524463	221504	2215	..	289181	197804	1667454	2215
Final energy consumption	364646	67556	85	490655	221504	2215	..	289181	197804	1633646	2215
Manufacturing, const., mining	153357	67556	85	98791	59664	..	..	181429	77440	638321	..
Iron and steel	29441	57910	..	28281	6225	..	..	81684	28300	231840	..
Chemical and petrochemical	600	..	..	909	20137	..	..	12121	4500	38267	..
Non-ferrous metals	69178	8297	..	1508	5211	..	..	47516	570	132281	..
Non-metallic minerals	33681	258	..	14182	..	..	..	5926	..	54047	..
Transport equipment	87	13	..	100	984	..	..	191	600	1976	..
Machinery	993	..	..	855	257	..	..	2315	1300	5719	..
Mining and quarrying	16693	1040	..	27114	14844	..	..	22939	11000	93630	..
Food and tobacco	1582	..	..	3609	8204	..	..	5767	6300	25461	..
Paper, pulp and printing	34	..	..	211	715	..	..	407	700	2067	..
Wood and wood products	25	38	..	56	8	..	..	47	150	323	..
Textile and leather	91	..	..	75	342	..	..	515	220	1243	..
Construction	951	..	..	12259	2739	..	..	2002	5600	23551	..
Industries n.e.s	0	0	85	9632	0	..	..	0	18200	27917	..
Transport	..	..	..	240652	11786	..	..	11642	..	264080	..
Road	..	..	..	232757	11786	..	..	..	..	244543	..
Rail	..	..	..	..	..	..	..	11642	..	11642	..
Domestic aviation	..	..	..	6418	..	..	..	..	..	6418	..
Domestic navigation	..	..	..	829	..	..	..	..	..	829	..
Pipeline transport	..	..	..	..	..	..	..	..	..	..	..
Transport, n.e.s	..	..	..	648	..	..	..	..	..	648	..
Other	211290	..	..	151213	150054	2215	..	96109	120364	731244	2215
Agriculture, forestry, fishing	4628	..	..	27082	1925	..	..	2866	..	36500	..
Commerce, public services	37910	..	..	23122	32295	..	..	29452	89864	212642	..
Households	168600	..	..	101009	115835	1697	..	63756	30500	481396	1697
Other consumers	152	..	..	..	..	518	..	36	..	706	518
Non-energy use	..	..	..	*33808	..	..	..	..	..	*33808	..

Kenya

Terajoules

2017	Primary coal and peat	Coal and peat products	Primary Oil	Oil Products	Natural Gas	Biofuels and waste	Nuclear	Electricity	Heat	Total energy	of which: renewables
Primary production	..	..	..	..	..	556330	..	10217	171227	737774	737774
Imports	11945	..	0	287882	..	..	..	827	..	300654	..
Exports	..	..	0	-72626	..	..	..	-44	..	-72670	..
International marine bunkers	..	..	..	-320	..	..	..	..	..	-320	..
International aviation bunkers	..	..	..	-33592	..	..	..	..	..	-33592	..
Stock changes	..	..	0	0	..	..	..	..	..	0	..
Total energy supply	11945	..	0	181345	..	556330	..	11000	171227	931847	737774
Statistical difference	0	..	0	-14913	..	0	..	-1478	0	-16390	27340
Transfers	..	..	..	..	..	..	..	..	..	..	..
Transformation	..	..	0	-12205	..	-197059	..	26245	-171227	-354246	-351163
Electricity plants	..	..	..	-12205	..	-16800	..	26065	-171227	-174167	-170904
CHP plants	..	..	..	..	..	..	..	180	..	180	..
Heat plants	..	..	..	..	..	..	..	..	..	..	..
Coke ovens	..	..	..	..	..	..	..	..	..	..	..
Briquetting plants	..	..	..	..	..	..	..	..	..	..	..
Liquefaction plants	..	..	..	..	..	..	..	..	..	..	..
Gas works	..	..	..	..	..	..	..	..	..	..	..
Blast furnaces	..	..	..	..	..	..	..	..	..	..	..
NGL plants & gas blending	..	..	..	..	..	..	..	..	..	..	..
Oil refineries	..	..	0	0	..	..	..	..	..	0	..
Other transformation	..	..	..	..	..	-180259	..	..	..	-180259	-180259
Energy industries own use	..	..	..	0	..	..	..	-180	..	-180	..
Losses	..	..	..	..	..	..	..	-7075	..	-7075	..
Final consumption	11945	..	..	184052	..	*359271	..	31467	..	*586736	*359271
Final energy consumption	11945	..	..	181716	..	*359271	..	31467	..	*584400	*359271
Manufacturing, const., mining	11945	..	..	16085	..	14367	..	19433	..	61830	14367
Iron and steel	..	..	..	..	..	..	..	..	..	..	..
Chemical and petrochemical	..	..	..	..	..	..	..	..	..	..	..
Non-ferrous metals	..	..	..	..	..	..	..	..	..	..	..
Non-metallic minerals	11945	..	..	..	..	..	..	..	..	11945	..
Transport equipment	..	..	..	..	..	..	..	..	..	..	..
Machinery	..	..	..	..	..	..	..	..	..	..	..
Mining and quarrying	..	..	..	..	..	..	..	..	..	..	..
Food and tobacco	..	..	..	..	..	..	..	1292	..	1292	..
Paper, pulp and printing	..	..	..	..	..	..	..	..	..	..	..
Wood and wood products	..	..	..	..	..	..	..	..	..	..	..
Textile and leather	..	..	..	..	..	..	..	..	..	..	..
Construction	..	..	..	..	..	..	..	..	..	..	..
Industries n.e.s	0	..	..	16085	..	14367	..	18140	..	48592	14367
Transport	..	..	..	138054	..	..	..	..	..	138054	..
Road	..	..	..	137482	..	..	..	..	..	137482	..
Rail	..	..	..	508	..	..	..	..	..	508	..
Domestic aviation	..	..	..	64	..	..	..	..	..	64	..
Domestic navigation	..	..	..	..	..	..	..	..	..	..	..
Pipeline transport	..	..	..	..	..	..	..	..	..	..	..
Transport, n.e.s	..	..	..	..	..	..	..	..	..	..	..
Other	..	..	..	27577	..	*344904	..	12035	..	*384516	*344904
Agriculture, forestry, fishing	..	..	..	2243	..	..	..	..	..	2243	..
Commerce, public services	..	..	..	..	..	..	..	3020	..	3020	..
Households	..	..	..	25121	..	227921	..	9014	..	262056	227921
Other consumers	..	..	..	213	..	*116983	..	0	..	*117196	*116983
Non-energy use	..	..	..	2336	..	..	..	..	..	2336	..

Kenya

Terajoules

2018	Primary coal and peat	Coal and peat products	Primary Oil	Oil Products	Natural Gas	Biofuels and waste	Nuclear	Electricity	Heat	Total energy	of which: renewables
Primary production	..	..	..	..	..	*553469	..	15703	184608	*753780	*753780
Imports	17879	..	0	233335	..	..	..	468	..	251682	..
Exports	..	..	..	-1045	..	..	..	-248	..	-1294	..
International marine bunkers	..	..	..	-1987	..	..	..	..	..	-1987	..
International aviation bunkers	..	..	..	-29723	..	..	..	..	..	-29723	..
Stock changes	..	..	..	..	..	..	..	..	..	..	..
Total energy supply	17879	..	0	200579	..	*553469	..	15923	184608	*972458	*753780
Statistical difference	0	..	0	-7054	..	0	..	603	0	*-6450	*34164
Transfers	..	..	..	..	..	..	..	..	..	..	..
Transformation	..	..	..	-25075	..	*-232047	..	24484	-184608	-417246	*-398194
Electricity plants	..	..	..	-25075	..	*-16506	..	24304	-184608	-201885	-182653
CHP plants	..	..	..	..	..	..	..	*180	..	*180	..
Heat plants	..	..	..	..	..	..	..	..	..	..	..
Coke ovens	..	..	..	..	..	..	..	..	..	..	..
Briquetting plants	..	..	..	..	..	..	..	..	..	..	..
Liquefaction plants	..	..	..	..	..	..	..	..	..	..	..
Gas works	..	..	..	..	..	..	..	..	..	..	..
Blast furnaces	..	..	..	..	..	..	..	..	..	..	..
NGL plants & gas blending	..	..	..	..	..	..	..	..	..	..	..
Oil refineries	..	..	..	..	..	..	..	..	..	..	..
Other transformation	..	..	..	..	..	*-215541	..	..	..	*-215541	*-215541
Energy industries own use	..	..	..	..	..	..	..	-396	..	-396	..
Losses	..	..	..	..	..	..	..	-8078	..	-8078	..
Final consumption	*17879	..	..	182558	..	*321422	..	31329	..	*553188	*321422
Final energy consumption	*17879	..	..	179864	..	*321422	..	31329	..	*550494	*321422
Manufacturing, const., mining	*17879	..	..	29381	..	11676	..	15611	..	74547	11676
Iron and steel	..	..	..	..	..	..	..	..	..	..	..
Chemical and petrochemical	..	..	..	..	..	..	..	..	..	..	..
Non-ferrous metals	..	..	..	..	..	..	..	..	..	..	..
Non-metallic minerals	*17879	..	..	..	..	..	..	..	..	*17879	..
Transport equipment	..	..	..	..	..	..	..	..	..	..	..
Machinery	..	..	..	..	..	..	..	..	..	..	..
Mining and quarrying	..	..	..	..	..	..	..	..	..	..	..
Food and tobacco	..	..	..	..	..	..	..	439	..	439	..
Paper, pulp and printing	..	..	..	..	..	..	..	..	..	..	..
Wood and wood products	..	..	..	..	..	..	..	..	..	..	..
Textile and leather	..	..	..	..	..	..	..	..	..	..	..
Construction	..	..	..	..	..	..	..	..	..	..	..
Industries n.e.s	0	..	..	29381	..	11676	..	15172	..	56229	11676
Transport	..	..	..	128106	..	..	..	..	..	128106	..
Road	..	..	..	126712	..	..	..	..	..	126712	..
Rail	..	..	..	516	..	..	..	..	..	516	..
Domestic aviation	..	..	..	797	..	..	..	..	..	797	..
Domestic navigation	..	..	..	81	..	..	..	..	..	81	..
Pipeline transport	..	..	..	..	..	..	..	..	..	..	..
Transport, n.e.s	..	..	..	..	..	..	..	..	..	..	..
Other	..	..	..	22377	..	*309746	..	15717	..	*347841	*309746
Agriculture, forestry, fishing	..	..	..	2127	..	..	..	..	..	2127	..
Commerce, public services	..	..	..	..	..	..	..	4963	..	4963	..
Households	..	..	..	17576	..	192764	..	10645	..	220985	192764
Other consumers	..	..	..	2675	..	*116983	..	109	..	*119767	*116983
Non-energy use	..	..	..	2693	..	..	..	..	..	2693	..

Kiribati

Terajoules

	All Coal	All Oil	Natural Gas	Primary biofuels / Waste	Charcoal	Electricity	Total energy	of which: renewables
2017								
Primary production	..	..	..	*540	..	17	*557	*557
Imports	..	1034	..	1	..	..	1035	1
Exports	..	..	..	..	..	..	..	..
International marine bunkers	..	..	..	..	..	..	..	..
International aviation bunkers	..	*-28	..	..	..	..	*-28	..
Stock changes	..	..	..	..	..	..	..	..
Total energy supply	..	1006	..	*541	..	17	1564	*558
Statistical Difference	..	0	..	0	0	0	0	*17
Transfers	..	..	..	..	..	..	..	..
Transformation	..	*-301	..	*-22	12	*94	*-217	*-10
Electricity plants	..	*-301	..	..	..	*94	*-207	..
Charcoal plants	..	..	..	*-22	12	..	*-10	*-10
Other transformation	..	0	..	0	..	..	0	0
Energy industries own use	..	..	..	..	..	-5	-5	..
Losses	..	..	..	..	..	*-16	*-16	..
Final consumption	..	*705	..	*519	*12	*90	*1326	*531
Final energy consumption	..	*701	..	*519	*12	*90	*1322	*531
Manufacturing, const., mining	..	*9	..	..	..	*8	*17	..
Transport	..	*435	..	..	..	..	*435	..
Road	..	*341	..	..	..	..	*341	..
Domestic aviation	..	*34	..	..	..	..	*34	..
Domestic navigation	..	*60	..	..	..	..	*60	..
Other transport	..	..	..	..	..	..	..	..
Other	..	*257	..	*519	*12	*82	*870	*531
Agriculture, forestry, fishing	..	*116	..	..	..	..	*116	..
Commerce and public services	..	*35	..	..	..	*44	*79	..
Households	..	*106	..	*519	*12	*35	*671	*531
Other consumers	..	..	..	..	..	*4	*4	..
Non-energy use	..	*4	..	..	..	..	*4	..
2018								
Primary production	..	..	..	*542	..	*18	*560	*560
Imports	..	*1041	..	0	..	..	*1041	0
Exports	..	..	..	..	..	..	..	..
International marine bunkers	..	..	..	..	..	..	..	..
International aviation bunkers	..	*-28	..	..	..	..	*-28	..
Stock changes	..	..	..	..	..	..	..	..
Total energy supply	..	*1013	..	*542	..	*18	*1573	*560
Statistical Difference	..	0	..	0	0	*4	*4	*18
Transfers	..	..	..	..	..	..	..	..
Transformation	..	*-301	..	*-22	12	*95	*-216	*-10
Electricity plants	..	*-301	..	..	..	*95	*-206	..
Charcoal plants	..	..	..	*-22	12	..	*-10	*-10
Other transformation	..	0	..	0	..	..	0	0
Energy industries own use	..	..	..	..	..	*-5	*-5	..
Losses	..	..	..	..	..	*-17	*-17	..
Final consumption	..	*712	..	*520	*12	*87	*1331	*532
Final energy consumption	..	*708	..	*520	*12	*87	*1327	*532
Manufacturing, const., mining	..	*9	..	..	..	*8	*17	..
Transport	..	*444	..	..	..	..	*444	..
Road	..	*347	..	..	..	..	*347	..
Domestic aviation	..	*35	..	..	..	..	*35	..
Domestic navigation	..	*62	..	..	..	..	*62	..
Other transport	..	..	..	..	..	..	..	..
Other	..	*255	..	*520	*12	*79	*867	*532
Agriculture, forestry, fishing	..	*117	..	..	..	..	*117	..
Commerce and public services	..	*34	..	..	..	*44	*78	..
Households	..	*104	..	*520	*12	*35	*671	*532
Other consumers	..	..	..	..	..	..	..	..
Non-energy use	..	*4	..	..	..	..	*4	..

Korea, Dem.Ppl's.Rep.

Terajoules

	Primary coal and peat	Coal and peat products	Primary Oil	Oil Products	Natural Gas	Biofuels and waste	Nuclear	Electricity	Heat	Total energy	of which: renewables
2017											
Primary production	556687	..	..	..	..	46604	..	42890	..	646181	89494
Imports	18222	5048	22504	17341	..	..	..	..	..	63114	..
Exports	*-129965	..	..	..	..	..	..	..	..	*-129965	..
International marine bunkers	..	..	..	..	..	..	..	..	..	..	..
International aviation bunkers	..	..	..	..	..	..	..	..	..	..	..
Stock changes	*-271851	..	..	..	..	..	..	..	..	*-271851	..
Total energy supply	173093	5048	22504	17341	..	46604	..	42890	..	307480	89494
Statistical difference	-333	56	0	0	..	0	..	-4	..	-280	42890
Transfers	..	..	..	..	..	..	..	..	..	..	..
Transformation	-23360	-2585	-22504	7983	..	-9692	..	10804	..	-39355	-9692
Electricity plants	-23360	..	..	-14140	..	..	..	10804	..	-26697	..
CHP plants	..	..	..	..	..	..	..	..	..	..	..
Heat plants	..	..	..	..	..	..	..	..	..	..	..
Coke ovens	..	..	..	..	..	..	..	..	..	..	..
Briquetting plants	..	..	..	..	..	..	..	..	..	..	..
Liquefaction plants	..	..	..	..	..	..	..	..	..	..	..
Gas works	..	..	..	..	..	..	..	..	..	..	..
Blast furnaces	..	-2585	..	..	..	..	..	..	..	-2585	..
NGL plants & gas blending	..	..	..	..	..	..	..	..	..	..	..
Oil refineries	..	..	-22504	22123	..	..	..	..	..	-381	..
Other transformation	..	..	..	..	..	-9692	..	..	..	-9692	-9692
Energy industries own use	..	..	..	-646	..	..	..	-5087	..	-5733	..
Losses	..	..	..	..	..	..	..	-8485	..	-8485	..
Final consumption	150066	2406	..	24677	..	36912	..	40126	..	254187	36912
Final energy consumption	150066	2406	..	24677	..	36912	..	40126	..	254187	36912
Manufacturing, const., mining	114170	2406	..	3757	..	..	..	20063	..	140396	..
Iron and steel	..	2406	..	..	..	..	..	..	..	2406	..
Chemical and petrochemical	..	..	..	..	..	..	..	..	..	..	..
Non-ferrous metals	..	..	..	..	..	..	..	..	..	..	..
Non-metallic minerals	..	..	..	..	..	..	..	..	..	..	..
Transport equipment	..	..	..	..	..	..	..	..	..	..	..
Machinery	..	..	..	..	..	..	..	..	..	..	..
Mining and quarrying	..	..	..	..	..	..	..	..	..	..	..
Food and tobacco	..	..	..	..	..	..	..	..	..	..	..
Paper, pulp and printing	..	..	..	..	..	..	..	..	..	..	..
Wood and wood products	..	..	..	..	..	..	..	..	..	..	..
Textile and leather	..	..	..	..	..	..	..	..	..	..	..
Construction	..	..	..	..	..	..	..	..	..	..	..
Industries n.e.s	114170	0	..	3757	..	..	..	20063	..	137990	..
Transport	..	..	..	19256	..	..	..	..	..	19256	..
Road	..	..	..	19256	..	..	..	..	..	19256	..
Rail	..	..	..	..	..	..	..	..	..	..	..
Domestic aviation	..	..	..	..	..	..	..	..	..	..	..
Domestic navigation	..	..	..	..	..	..	..	..	..	..	..
Pipeline transport	..	..	..	..	..	..	..	..	..	..	..
Transport, n.e.s	..	..	..	..	..	..	..	..	..	..	..
Other	35896	..	..	1664	..	36912	..	20063	..	94535	36912
Agriculture, forestry, fishing	..	..	..	..	..	..	..	..	..	..	..
Commerce, public services	..	..	..	..	..	..	..	..	..	..	..
Households	..	..	..	1664	..	4897	..	..	..	6561	4897
Other consumers	35896	..	..	..	..	32015	..	20063	..	87974	32015
Non-energy use	..	..	..	..	..	..	..	..	..	..	..

Korea, Dem.Ppl's.Rep.

Terajoules

2018	Primary coal and peat	Coal and peat products	Primary Oil	Oil Products	Natural Gas	Biofuels and waste	Nuclear	Electricity	Heat	Total energy	of which: renewables
Primary production	464706	..	..	..	..	46740	..	46134	..	557580	92874
Imports	..	3751	22504	17015	..	..	..	..	..	43269	..
Exports	..	..	..	..	..	..	..	..	..	..	..
International marine bunkers	..	..	..	..	..	..	..	..	..	..	..
International aviation bunkers	..	..	..	..	..	..	..	..	..	..	..
Stock changes	*-335389	..	..	..	..	..	..	..	..	*-335389	..
Total energy supply	129318	3751	22504	17015	..	46740	..	46134	..	265461	92874
Statistical difference	26	28	0	0	..	1	..	4	..	59	46135
Transfers	..	..	..	..	..	..	..	..	..	..	..
Transformation	-19487	-1936	-22504	8265	..	-9781	..	9418	..	-36024	-9781
Electricity plants	-19487	..	..	-13857	..	..	..	9418	..	-23926	..
CHP plants	..	..	..	..	..	..	..	..	..	..	..
Heat plants	..	..	..	..	..	..	..	..	..	..	..
Coke ovens	..	..	..	..	..	..	..	..	..	..	..
Briquetting plants	..	..	..	..	..	..	..	..	..	..	..
Liquefaction plants	..	..	..	..	..	..	..	..	..	..	..
Gas works	..	..	..	..	..	..	..	..	..	..	..
Blast furnaces	..	-1936	..	..	..	..	..	..	..	-1936	..
NGL plants & gas blending	..	..	..	..	..	..	..	..	..	..	..
Oil refineries	..	..	-22504	22123	..	..	..	..	..	-381	..
Other transformation	..	..	..	..	..	-9781	..	..	..	-9781	-9781
Energy industries own use	..	..	..	-646	..	..	..	-5260	..	-5906	..
Losses	..	..	..	..	..	..	..	-8780	..	-8780	..
Final consumption	109804	1786	..	24634	..	36959	..	41508	..	214691	36959
Final energy consumption	109804	1786	..	24634	..	36959	..	41508	..	214691	36959
Manufacturing, const., mining	83512	1786	..	3757	..	..	..	20754	..	109810	..
Iron and steel	..	1786	..	..	..	..	..	..	..	1786	..
Chemical and petrochemical	..	..	..	..	..	..	..	..	..	..	..
Non-ferrous metals	..	..	..	..	..	..	..	..	..	..	..
Non-metallic minerals	..	..	..	..	..	..	..	..	..	..	..
Transport equipment	..	..	..	..	..	..	..	..	..	..	..
Machinery	..	..	..	..	..	..	..	..	..	..	..
Mining and quarrying	..	..	..	..	..	..	..	..	..	..	..
Food and tobacco	..	..	..	..	..	..	..	..	..	..	..
Paper, pulp and printing	..	..	..	..	..	..	..	..	..	..	..
Wood and wood products	..	..	..	..	..	..	..	..	..	..	..
Textile and leather	..	..	..	..	..	..	..	..	..	..	..
Construction	..	..	..	..	..	..	..	..	..	..	..
Industries n.e.s	83512	0	..	3757	..	..	..	20754	..	108024	..
Transport	..	..	..	19213	..	..	..	..	..	19213	..
Road	..	..	..	19213	..	..	..	..	..	19213	..
Rail	..	..	..	..	..	..	..	..	..	..	..
Domestic aviation	..	..	..	..	..	..	..	..	..	..	..
Domestic navigation	..	..	..	..	..	..	..	..	..	..	..
Pipeline transport	..	..	..	..	..	..	..	..	..	..	..
Transport, n.e.s	..	..	..	..	..	..	..	..	..	..	..
Other	26292	..	..	1664	..	36959	..	20754	..	85669	36959
Agriculture, forestry, fishing	..	..	..	..	..	..	..	..	..	..	..
Commerce, public services	..	..	..	..	..	..	..	..	..	..	..
Households	..	..	..	1664	..	4927	..	..	..	6591	4927
Other consumers	26292	..	..	..	..	32032	..	20754	..	79078	32032
Non-energy use	..	..	..	..	..	..	..	..	..	..	..

Korea, Republic of

Terajoules

2017	Primary coal and peat	Coal and peat products	Primary Oil	Oil Products	Natural Gas	Biofuels and waste	Nuclear	Electricity	Heat	Total energy	of which: renewables
Primary production	28806	..	31592	..	12783	295074	1603012	45126	11557	2027949	195585
Imports	3409567	9678	6359891	1646672	1826517	..	..	..	..	13252324	..
Exports	..	..	-132	-2799244	..	..	..	..	..	-2799376	..
International marine bunkers	..	..	..	-408601	..	..	..	..	..	-408601	..
International aviation bunkers	..	..	..	-209122	..	..	..	..	..	-209122	..
Stock changes	5816	..	1356	-19549	-30017	37	..	..	..	-42357	37
Total energy supply	3444189	9678	6392707	-1789844	1809283	295110	1603012	45126	11557	11820817	195621
Statistical difference	58226	3323	-38086	-87906	-21090	-38	0	-60682	18698	-127553	45088
Transfers	..	..	454614	-448618	..	..	..	..	..	5996	..
Transformation	-3208146	317221	-6885407	6558182	-896287	-99235	-1603012	1980576	236465	-3599642	*-65628
Electricity plants	-2165537	-90007	..	-53053	-551732	*-53032	-1603012	1748344	-1250	-2769278	*-50195
CHP plants	-160949	-94473	..	-68639	-342437	-23254	..	232232	213238	-244283	*-9379
Heat plants	..	..	..	-8854	-2117	-22948	..	..	24477	-9442	-6054
Coke ovens	-663063	633011	..	..	..	..	..	..	..	-30052	..
Briquetting plants	-26660	20897	..	..	..	..	..	..	..	-5763	..
Liquefaction plants	..	..	..	..	..	..	..	..	..	..	..
Gas works	..	..	..	..	..	..	..	..	..	..	..
Blast furnaces	-191937	-181019	..	..	..	..	..	..	..	-372956	..
NGL plants & gas blending	..	..	..	-4541	..	..	..	..	..	-4541	..
Oil refineries	..	..	-6885407	6663543	..	..	..	..	..	-221864	..
Other transformation	..	28812	..	29726	..	..	..	..	..	58538	..
Energy industries own use	..	-127920	..	-270315	-5949	..	..	-135083	-4217	-543484	..
Losses	..	..	..	..	..	..	..	-67644	-2849	-70493	..
Final consumption	177816	195655	..	4137310	928137	195914	..	1883657	222258	7740746	84905
Final energy consumption	177816	179415	..	1903305	928137	195914	..	1883657	222258	5490501	84905
Manufacturing, const., mining	177816	158518	..	147769	313251	134992	..	987944	121656	2041947	*29857
Iron and steel	61184	148840	..	3562	64759	355	..	196250	212	475163	..
Chemical and petrochemical	594	..	..	25957	45348	16647	..	186869	79033	354447	482
Non-ferrous metals	..	..	..	1313	10849	..	..	32407	2	44571	..
Non-metallic minerals	103277	..	..	19849	22784	29386	..	46382	108	221786	*112
Transport equipment	..	..	..	9383	22226	*121	..	91397	245	123373	*121
Machinery	..	..	..	3094	40707	*4	..	287950	149	331903	*4
Mining and quarrying	..	..	..	1746	..	*3	..	6286	..	8035	*3
Food and tobacco	965	..	..	3334	28257	5295	..	41065	4910	83826	*1808
Paper, pulp and printing	..	..	..	1454	9952	30006	..	36230	10093	87735	*11743
Wood and wood products	..	..	..	167	1127	*4932	..	6970	394	13589	*4631
Textile and leather	2201	..	..	3650	11936	5497	..	41328	16658	81270	*2656
Construction	..	..	..	30580	143	1286	..	..	..	32009	369
Industries n.e.s	9596	9678	..	43680	55163	41460	..	14810	9852	184239	*7928
Transport	..	..	..	1415249	49645	19394	..	10314	..	1494601	19394
Road	..	..	..	1338916	49645	19394	..	162	..	1408116	19394
Rail	..	..	..	4042	..	..	..	10152	..	14194	..
Domestic aviation	..	..	..	54636	..	..	..	..	..	54636	..
Domestic navigation	..	..	..	17612	..	..	..	..	..	17612	..
Pipeline transport	..	..	..	43	..	..	..	..	..	43	..
Transport, n.e.s	..	..	..	..	..	..	..	..	..	..	..
Other	..	20897	..	340287	565241	41528	..	885398	100602	1953953	35655
Agriculture, forestry, fishing	..	..	..	47762	128	*2927	..	57528	1164	109509	*4079
Commerce, public services	..	..	..	80365	171619	32089	..	588323	18653	891049	23069
Households	..	20897	..	154727	393494	*6512	..	239548	80785	895963	*8507
Other consumers	..	..	..	57432	..	..	..	..	..	57432	..
Non-energy use	..	16240	..	2234005	..	..	..	..	..	2250245	..

Korea, Republic of

Terajoules

2018	Primary coal and peat	Coal and peat products	Primary Oil	Oil Products	Natural Gas	Biofuels and waste	Nuclear	Electricity	Heat	Total energy	of which: renewables
Primary production	22099	..	34068	..	10932	287913	1441854	55861	12782	1865510	226164
Imports	3332079	9360	6345924	1792574	2078478	..	..	..	..	13558414	..
Exports	..	..	-1895	-2964842	..	..	..	..	..	-2966738	..
International marine bunkers	..	..	..	-381782	..	..	..	..	..	-381782	..
International aviation bunkers	..	..	..	-220324	..	..	..	..	..	-220324	..
Stock changes	6513	..	90087	-34080	-91350	74	..	..	..	-28757	74
Total energy supply	3360691	9360	6468183	-1808455	1998060	287987	1441854	55861	12782	11826324	226238
Statistical difference	-45538	3844	99096	27565	-33440	35	0	-6937	12292	56917	55897
Transfers	..	..	671840	-653681	..	..	..	..	..	18159	..
Transformation	-3213466	336554	-7040926	6763021	-1087108	-113116	-1441854	2054448	249191	-3493256	*-79642
Electricity plants	-2174564	-88995	..	-61597	-685818	*-67004	-1441854	1789960	-1304	-2731177	*-64088
CHP plants	-149176	-96692	..	-67942	-398218	-22822	..	264488	225023	-245338	*-9320
Heat plants	..	..	..	-8854	-3073	-23289	..	..	25472	-9744	-6234
Coke ovens	-682441	661226	..	..	..	..	..	..	..	-21215	..
Briquetting plants	-22550	19230	..	..	..	..	..	..	..	-3320	..
Liquefaction plants	..	..	..	..	..	..	..	..	..	..	..
Gas works	..	..	..	..	..	..	..	..	..	..	..
Blast furnaces	-184735	-187046	..	..	..	..	..	..	..	-371781	..
NGL plants & gas blending	..	..	..	-8493	..	..	..	..	..	-8493	..
Oil refineries	..	..	-7040926	6884375	..	..	..	..	..	-156551	..
Other transformation	..	28831	..	25533	..	..	..	..	..	54364	..
Energy industries own use	..	-126765	..	-250997	-6377	..	..	-138845	-4299	-527283	..
Losses	..	..	..	..	..	..	..	-65459	-2524	-67983	..
Final consumption	192764	215305	..	4022324	938015	174836	..	1912943	242858	7699044	90699
Final energy consumption	192764	199233	..	1862413	938015	174836	..	1912943	242858	5523062	90699
Manufacturing, const., mining	192764	180003	..	150964	315145	109352	..	1003727	132669	2084624	30085
Iron and steel	70078	170672	..	2670	65462	362	..	199922	231	509397	..
Chemical and petrochemical	570	..	..	31863	45010	17631	..	190501	86565	372140	484
Non-ferrous metals	..	..	..	1498	10801	..	..	32548	2	44848	..
Non-metallic minerals	100309	..	..	20604	23647	30786	..	46444	116	221905	*112
Transport equipment	..	..	..	7483	21036	*121	..	94428	263	123331	*121
Machinery	..	..	..	3058	41693	*5	..	290603	161	335520	*5
Mining and quarrying	..	..	..	1679	..	*4	..	6365	..	8047	*4
Food and tobacco	942	..	..	3757	28107	5398	..	41296	5369	84869	*1961
Paper, pulp and printing	..	..	..	1497	9826	30724	..	37836	10847	90730	*11548
Wood and wood products	..	..	..	124	1136	*4938	..	7135	431	13764	*4635
Textile and leather	2181	..	..	2440	11812	5768	..	41807	17966	81973	2785
Construction	..	..	..	30138	153	1327	..	..	..	31618	360
Industries n.e.s	18684	9331	..	44154	56462	12288	..	14843	10718	166481	8071
Transport	..	..	..	1389566	50881	23552	..	10681	..	1474680	23552
Road	..	..	..	1316333	50881	23552	..	162	..	1390927	23552
Rail	..	..	..	4042	..	..	..	10519	..	14561	..
Domestic aviation	..	..	..	55831	..	..	..	..	..	55831	..
Domestic navigation	..	..	..	13277	..	..	..	..	..	13277	..
Pipeline transport	..	..	..	83	..	..	..	..	..	83	..
Transport, n.e.s	..	..	..	..	..	..	..	..	..	..	..
Other	..	19230	..	321883	571990	41932	..	898535	110189	1963758	37062
Agriculture, forestry, fishing	..	..	..	45067	137	*2949	..	60484	1219	109855	*4157
Commerce, public services	..	..	..	78036	172040	32362	..	594547	21015	898001	24087
Households	..	19230	..	142967	399812	*6621	..	243504	87955	900090	*8818
Other consumers	..	..	..	55812	..	..	..	..	..	55812	..
Non-energy use	..	16072	..	2159910	..	..	..	..	..	2175982	..

Kosovo

Terajoules

2017	Primary coal and peat	Coal and peat products	Primary Oil	Oil Products	Natural Gas	Biofuels and waste	Nuclear	Electricity	Heat	Total energy	of which: renewables
Primary production	59100	..	..	..	..	15305	..	649	14	75068	15968
Imports	115	..	..	31364	..	237	..	4471	..	36188	237
Exports	-109	..	..	-98	..	-5	..	-3168	..	-3380	-5
International marine bunkers	..	..	..	..	..	..	..	..	..	..	..
International aviation bunkers	..	..	..	-265	..	..	..	..	..	-265	..
Stock changes	257	..	..	..	..	..	..	..	..	257	..
Total energy supply	59364	..	..	31002	..	15537	..	1952	14	107868	16200
Statistical difference	-62	..	..	680	..	-2	..	32	9	657	647
Transfers	..	..	..	..	..	..	..	..	..	..	..
Transformation	-55792	..	..	-207	..	..	..	20660	817	-34522	..
Electricity plants	-55792	..	..	-167	..	..	..	20660	..	-35299	..
CHP plants	..	..	..	..	..	..	..	..	..	..	..
Heat plants	..	..	..	-40	..	..	..	..	817	777	..
Coke ovens	..	..	..	..	..	..	..	..	..	..	..
Briquetting plants	..	..	..	..	..	..	..	..	..	..	..
Liquefaction plants	..	..	..	..	..	..	..	..	..	..	..
Gas works	..	..	..	..	..	..	..	..	..	..	..
Blast furnaces	..	..	..	..	..	..	..	..	..	..	..
NGL plants & gas blending	..	..	..	..	..	..	..	..	..	..	..
Oil refineries	..	..	..	..	..	..	..	..	..	..	..
Other transformation	..	..	..	..	..	..	..	..	..	..	..
Energy industries own use	..	..	..	..	..	..	..	-2225	-98	-2323	..
Losses	..	..	..	..	..	..	..	-4741	-99	-4840	..
Final consumption	3634	..	..	30115	..	15539	..	15613	625	65526	15553
Final energy consumption	3634	..	..	28346	..	15539	..	15613	625	63757	15553
Manufacturing, const., mining	966	..	..	7847	..	559	..	3823	..	13195	559
Iron and steel	778	..	..	648	..	2	..	1710	..	3138	2
Chemical and petrochemical	..	..	..	47	..	2	..	7	..	57	2
Non-ferrous metals	..	..	..	920	..	..	..	58	..	978	..
Non-metallic minerals	..	..	..	4469	..	14	..	223	..	4706	14
Transport equipment	..	..	..	..	..	..	..	..	..	..	..
Machinery	..	..	..	..	..	3	..	47	..	50	3
Mining and quarrying	..	..	..	172	..	..	..	..	..	172	..
Food and tobacco	179	..	..	482	..	236	..	1325	..	2222	236
Paper, pulp and printing	..	..	..	..	..	..	..	4	..	4	..
Wood and wood products	..	..	..	..	..	..	..	..	..	..	..
Textile and leather	..	..	..	..	..	..	..	..	..	..	..
Construction	8	..	..	..	..	..	..	..	..	8	..
Industries n.e.s	0	..	..	1109	..	302	..	450	..	1861	302
Transport	..	..	..	17401	..	..	..	..	..	17401	..
Road	..	..	..	17272	..	..	..	..	..	17272	..
Rail	..	..	..	129	..	..	..	..	..	129	..
Domestic aviation	..	..	..	..	..	..	..	..	..	..	..
Domestic navigation	..	..	..	..	..	..	..	..	..	..	..
Pipeline transport	..	..	..	..	..	..	..	..	..	..	..
Transport, n.e.s	..	..	..	..	..	..	..	..	..	..	..
Other	2668	..	..	3098	..	14980	..	11790	625	33161	14994
Agriculture, forestry, fishing	..	..	..	688	..	136	..	403	..	1227	136
Commerce, public services	2247	..	..	1957	..	453	..	3139	226	8022	463
Households	421	..	..	453	..	14391	..	8248	399	23912	14395
Other consumers	..	..	..	..	..	..	..	..	..	..	..
Non-energy use	..	..	..	1769	..	..	..	..	..	1769	..

Kosovo

Terajoules

2018	Primary coal and peat	Coal and peat products	Primary Oil	Oil Products	Natural Gas	Biofuels and waste	Nuclear	Electricity	Heat	Total energy	of which: renewables
Primary production	59771	..	..	..	..	15415	..	1098	15	76299	16528
Imports	97	..	..	31773	..	383	..	2970	..	35223	383
Exports	-70	..	..	-421	..	0	..	-2437	..	-2928	0
International marine bunkers	..	..	..	..	..	..	..	..	..	..	..
International aviation bunkers	..	..	..	-132	..	..	..	..	..	-132	..
Stock changes	250	..	..	..	..	..	..	..	..	250	..
Total energy supply	60048	..	..	31220	..	15798	..	1631	15	108712	16911
Statistical difference	-203	..	..	133	..	7	..	18	14	-31	1105
Transfers	..	..	..	..	..	..	..	..	..	..	..
Transformation	-59498	..	..	-164	..	..	..	20203	832	-38627	..
Electricity plants	-59498	..	..	-124	..	..	..	20203	..	-39419	..
CHP plants	..	..	..	..	..	..	..	..	..	..	..
Heat plants	..	..	..	-40	..	..	..	..	832	792	..
Coke ovens	..	..	..	..	..	..	..	..	..	..	..
Briquetting plants	..	..	..	..	..	..	..	..	..	..	..
Liquefaction plants	..	..	..	..	..	..	..	..	..	..	..
Gas works	..	..	..	..	..	..	..	..	..	..	..
Blast furnaces	..	..	..	..	..	..	..	..	..	..	..
NGL plants & gas blending	..	..	..	..	..	..	..	..	..	..	..
Oil refineries	..	..	..	..	..	..	..	..	..	..	..
Other transformation	..	..	..	..	..	..	..	..	..	..	..
Energy industries own use	..	..	..	..	..	..	..	-1933	-100	-2033	..
Losses	..	..	..	..	..	..	..	-4050	-99	-4149	..
Final consumption	753	..	..	30923	..	15791	..	15833	634	63933	15806
Final energy consumption	753	..	..	28993	..	15791	..	15833	634	62003	15806
Manufacturing, const., mining	300	..	..	7514	..	616	..	3524	..	11955	616
Iron and steel	206	..	..	659	..	2	..	1548	..	2415	2
Chemical and petrochemical	..	..	..	47	..	2	..	7	..	56	2
Non-ferrous metals	..	..	..	923	..	..	..	54	..	977	..
Non-metallic minerals	..	..	..	4175	..	15	..	202	..	4392	15
Transport equipment	..	..	..	..	..	..	..	..	..	..	..
Machinery	..	..	..	..	..	4	..	43	..	47	4
Mining and quarrying	..	..	..	172	..	..	..	..	..	172	..
Food and tobacco	86	..	..	525	..	270	..	1260	..	2141	270
Paper, pulp and printing	..	..	..	..	..	..	..	4	..	4	..
Wood and wood products	..	..	..	..	..	..	..	..	..	..	..
Textile and leather	..	..	..	..	..	..	..	..	..	..	..
Construction	8	..	..	..	..	..	..	..	..	8	..
Industries n.e.s	0	..	..	1014	..	323	..	407	..	1744	323
Transport	..	..	..	18209	..	..	..	..	..	18209	..
Road	..	..	..	18080	..	..	..	..	..	18080	..
Rail	..	..	..	129	..	..	..	..	..	129	..
Domestic aviation	..	..	..	..	..	..	..	..	..	..	..
Domestic navigation	..	..	..	..	..	..	..	..	..	..	..
Pipeline transport	..	..	..	..	..	..	..	..	..	..	..
Transport, n.e.s	..	..	..	..	..	..	..	..	..	..	..
Other	453	..	..	3270	..	15175	..	12308	634	31840	15190
Agriculture, forestry, fishing	..	..	..	731	..	138	..	425	..	1294	138
Commerce, public services	351	..	..	2043	..	482	..	3402	230	6509	493
Households	101	..	..	496	..	14555	..	8482	404	24038	14559
Other consumers	..	..	..	..	..	..	..	..	..	..	..
Non-energy use	..	..	..	1930	..	..	..	..	..	1930	..

Kuwait

Terajoules

2017	Primary coal and peat	Coal and peat products	Primary Oil	Oil Products	Natural Gas	Biofuels and waste	Nuclear	Electricity	Heat	Total energy	of which: renewables
Primary production	..	..	6187027	..	584879	185	..	7	..	6772099	192
Imports	..	..	..	..	189126	1274	..	1991	..	192391	1274
Exports	..	..	-4347679	-1208045	..	-28	..	-1404	..	-5557156	-28
International marine bunkers	..	..	..	-39485	..	..	..	..	..	-39485	..
International aviation bunkers	..	..	..	-40087	..	..	..	..	..	-40087	..
Stock changes	..	..	..	127164	..	..	..	..	..	127164	..
Total energy supply	..	..	1839349	-1160453	774005	1430	..	594	..	1454925	1437
Statistical difference	..	..	-33079	-41136	0	0	..	0	..	-74215	7
Transfers	..	..	..	..	..	..	..	..	..	..	..
Transformation	..	..	-1872427	1508881	-363129	*-78	..	262037	..	-464716	*-78
Electricity plants	..	..	-54017	-282269	-363129	..	..	241672	..	-457744	..
CHP plants	..	..	..	..	..	..	..	20365	..	20365	..
Heat plants	..	..	..	..	..	..	..	..	..	..	..
Coke ovens	..	..	..	..	..	..	..	..	..	..	..
Briquetting plants	..	..	..	..	..	..	..	..	..	..	..
Liquefaction plants	..	..	..	..	..	..	..	..	..	..	..
Gas works	..	..	..	..	..	..	..	..	..	..	..
Blast furnaces	..	..	..	..	..	..	..	..	..	..	..
NGL plants & gas blending	..	..	-388120	413458	..	..	..	..	..	25337	..
Oil refineries	..	..	-1430290	1377692	..	..	..	..	..	-52598	..
Other transformation	..	..	..	..	..	*-78	..	..	..	*-78	*-78
Energy industries own use	..	..	..	-15345	-227527	..	..	-86280	..	-329152	..
Losses	..	..	..	..	..	..	..	-23412	..	-23412	..
Final consumption	..	..	..	374220	183349	*1352	..	152939	..	711860	*1352
Final energy consumption	..	..	..	252904	183349	*1352	..	152939	..	590544	*1352
Manufacturing, const., mining	..	..	..	29627	183349	..	..	..	..	212976	..
Iron and steel	..	..	..	..	..	..	..	..	..	..	..
Chemical and petrochemical	..	..	..	7353	111119	..	..	..	..	118472	..
Non-ferrous metals	..	..	..	..	..	..	..	..	..	..	..
Non-metallic minerals	..	..	..	..	..	..	..	..	..	..	..
Transport equipment	..	..	..	3655	..	..	..	..	..	3655	..
Machinery	..	..	..	..	..	..	..	..	..	..	..
Mining and quarrying	..	..	..	4859	..	..	..	..	..	4859	..
Food and tobacco	..	..	..	430	..	..	..	..	..	430	..
Paper, pulp and printing	..	..	..	..	..	..	..	..	..	..	..
Wood and wood products	..	..	..	..	..	..	..	..	..	..	..
Textile and leather	..	..	..	..	..	..	..	..	..	..	..
Construction	..	..	..	13330	..	..	..	..	..	13330	..
Industries n.e.s	..	..	..	0	72230	..	..	..	..	72230	..
Transport	..	..	..	209782	..	..	..	..	..	209782	..
Road	..	..	..	209782	..	..	..	..	..	209782	..
Rail	..	..	..	..	..	..	..	..	..	..	..
Domestic aviation	..	..	..	..	..	..	..	..	..	..	..
Domestic navigation	..	..	..	..	..	..	..	..	..	..	..
Pipeline transport	..	..	..	..	..	..	..	..	..	..	..
Transport, n.e.s	..	..	..	..	..	..	..	..	..	..	..
Other	..	..	..	13495	..	*1352	..	152939	..	167786	*1352
Agriculture, forestry, fishing	..	..	..	..	..	..	..	4720	..	4720	..
Commerce, public services	..	..	..	..	..	..	..	51454	..	51454	..
Households	..	..	..	13495	..	*1352	..	94374	..	109221	*1352
Other consumers	..	..	..	..	..	..	..	2391	..	2391	..
Non-energy use	..	..	..	121316	..	..	..	..	..	121316	..

Kuwait

Terajoules

2018	Primary coal and peat	Coal and peat products	Primary Oil	Oil Products	Natural Gas	Biofuels and waste	Nuclear	Electricity	Heat	Total energy	of which: renewables
Primary production	..	..	6263558	..	606632	187	..	14	..	6870391	201
Imports	..	..	..	..	170316	1548	..	727	..	172591	1548
Exports	..	..	-4406489	-1226025	..	-20	..	-1926	..	-5634460	-20
International marine bunkers	..	..	..	-39078	..	..	..	..	..	-39078	..
International aviation bunkers	..	..	..	-40307	..	..	..	..	..	-40307	..
Stock changes	..	..	..	130440	..	..	..	..	..	130440	..
Total energy supply	..	..	1857069	-1174971	776948	1715	..	-1184	..	1459577	1729
Statistical difference	..	..	-59572	-50620	0	0	..	0	..	-110192	14
Transfers	..	..	..	..	..	..	..	..	..	..	..
Transformation	..	..	-1916641	1530451	-390704	*-79	..	266771	..	-510201	*-79
Electricity plants	..	..	-36632	-281478	-390704	..	..	244256	..	-464558	..
CHP plants	..	..	..	..	..	..	..	22514	..	22514	..
Heat plants	..	..	..	..	..	..	..	..	..	..	..
Coke ovens	..	..	..	..	..	..	..	..	..	..	..
Briquetting plants	..	..	..	..	..	..	..	..	..	..	..
Liquefaction plants	..	..	..	..	..	..	..	..	..	..	..
Gas works	..	..	..	..	..	..	..	..	..	..	..
Blast furnaces	..	..	..	..	..	..	..	..	..	..	..
NGL plants & gas blending	..	..	-395236	421073	..	..	..	..	..	25836	..
Oil refineries	..	..	-1484772	1390856	..	..	..	..	..	-93916	..
Other transformation	..	..	..	..	..	*-79	..	..	..	*-79	*-79
Energy industries own use	..	..	..	-15939	-235990	..	..	-88080	..	-340009	..
Losses	..	..	..	..	..	..	..	-23565	..	-23565	..
Final consumption	..	..	..	390162	150254	*1636	..	153941	..	695993	*1636
Final energy consumption	..	..	..	264866	150254	*1636	..	153941	..	570698	*1636
Manufacturing, const., mining	..	..	..	29326	150254	..	..	..	..	179580	..
Iron and steel	..	..	..	..	..	..	..	..	..	..	..
Chemical and petrochemical	..	..	..	7267	111541	..	..	..	..	118808	..
Non-ferrous metals	..	..	..	..	..	..	..	..	..	..	..
Non-metallic minerals	..	..	..	..	..	..	..	..	..	..	..
Transport equipment	..	..	..	3655	..	..	..	..	..	3655	..
Machinery	..	..	..	..	..	..	..	..	..	..	..
Mining and quarrying	..	..	..	4816	..	..	..	..	..	4816	..
Food and tobacco	..	..	..	387	..	..	..	..	..	387	..
Paper, pulp and printing	..	..	..	..	..	..	..	..	..	..	..
Wood and wood products	..	..	..	..	..	..	..	..	..	..	..
Textile and leather	..	..	..	..	..	..	..	..	..	..	..
Construction	..	..	..	13201	..	..	..	..	..	13201	..
Industries n.e.s	..	..	..	0	38714	..	..	..	..	38714	..
Transport	..	..	..	221549	..	..	..	..	..	221549	..
Road	..	..	..	221549	..	..	..	..	..	221549	..
Rail	..	..	..	..	..	..	..	..	..	..	..
Domestic aviation	..	..	..	..	..	..	..	..	..	..	..
Domestic navigation	..	..	..	..	..	..	..	..	..	..	..
Pipeline transport	..	..	..	..	..	..	..	..	..	..	..
Transport, n.e.s	..	..	..	..	..	..	..	..	..	..	..
Other	..	..	..	13991	..	*1636	..	153941	..	169568	*1636
Agriculture, forestry, fishing	..	..	..	..	..	..	..	4751	..	4751	..
Commerce, public services	..	..	..	..	..	..	..	51791	..	51791	..
Households	..	..	..	13991	..	*1636	..	94992	..	110619	*1636
Other consumers	..	..	..	..	..	..	..	2407	..	2407	..
Non-energy use	..	..	..	125295	..	..	..	..	..	125295	..

Kyrgyzstan

Terajoules

2017	Primary coal and peat	Coal and peat products	Primary Oil	Oil Products	Natural Gas	Biofuels and waste	Nuclear	Electricity	Heat	Total energy	of which: renewables
Primary production	28388	..	7318	..	845	60	..	51131	..	87741	51191
Imports	18993	..	12563	54323	9779	..	..	..	..	95658	..
Exports	-7851	..	-846	-3273	..	..	..	-4374	..	-16344	..
International marine bunkers	..	..	..	..	..	..	..	..	..	..	..
International aviation bunkers	..	..	..	-838	..	..	..	..	..	-838	..
Stock changes	-2854	..	-212	-1580	..	..	..	..	..	-4646	..
Total energy supply	36675	..	18824	48631	10625	60	..	46757	..	161571	51191
Statistical difference	228	..	0	138	1	0	..	464	-6527	-5696	51131
Transfers	..	..	..	..	..	..	..	..	..	..	..
Transformation	-12726	..	-18824	17774	-3244	..	..	4720	7966	-4333	..
Electricity plants	-181	..	..	..	..	..	..	54	..	-127	..
CHP plants	-12402	..	..	-566	-1527	..	..	4666	6207	-3623	..
Heat plants	-143	..	..	-404	-1716	..	..	..	1759	-504	..
Coke ovens	..	..	..	..	..	..	..	..	..	..	..
Briquetting plants	..	..	..	..	..	..	..	..	..	..	..
Liquefaction plants	..	..	..	..	..	..	..	..	..	..	..
Gas works	..	..	..	..	..	..	..	..	..	..	..
Blast furnaces	..	..	..	..	..	..	..	..	..	..	..
NGL plants & gas blending	..	..	..	..	..	..	..	..	..	..	..
Oil refineries	..	..	-18824	18864	..	..	..	..	..	40	..
Other transformation	..	..	..	-121	..	..	..	..	..	-121	..
Energy industries own use	..	..	..	-283	-288	..	..	-1145	-674	-2389	..
Losses	..	..	..	-44	-557	..	..	-10238	-857	-11697	..
Final consumption	23721	..	..	65941	6535	60	..	39629	12962	148847	60
Final energy consumption	23721	..	..	65908	6535	60	..	39629	12962	148815	60
Manufacturing, const., mining	5327	..	..	3588	1651	..	..	6347	1265	18177	..
Iron and steel	..	..	..	..	..	..	..	..	..	..	..
Chemical and petrochemical	20	..	..	202	..	..	..	61	..	283	..
Non-ferrous metals	..	..	..	..	..	..	..	425	..	425	..
Non-metallic minerals	1706	..	..	124	558	..	..	1192	135	3714	..
Transport equipment	..	..	..	..	..	..	..	7	..	7	..
Machinery	..	..	..	..	295	..	..	137	37	469	..
Mining and quarrying	..	..	..	854	..	..	..	356	..	1210	..
Food and tobacco	330	..	..	43	626	..	..	659	977	2636	..
Paper, pulp and printing	20	..	..	..	92	..	..	..	..	112	..
Wood and wood products	..	..	..	..	..	..	..	97	2	99	..
Textile and leather	20	..	..	..	14	..	..	130	..	164	..
Construction	..	..	..	1586	..	..	..	378	25	1989	..
Industries n.e.s	3231	..	..	779	65	..	..	2905	89	7069	..
Transport	20	..	..	25804	..	..	..	166	..	25989	..
Road	..	..	..	25415	..	..	..	72	..	25487	..
Rail	20	..	..	301	..	..	..	61	..	382	..
Domestic aviation	..	..	..	88	..	..	..	..	..	88	..
Domestic navigation	..	..	..	..	..	..	..	..	..	..	..
Pipeline transport	..	..	..	..	..	..	..	..	..	..	..
Transport, n.e.s	..	..	..	..	..	..	..	32	..	32	..
Other	18374	..	..	36517	4884	60	..	33116	11697	104649	60
Agriculture, forestry, fishing	15	..	..	83	..	1	..	788	..	887	1
Commerce, public services	2849	..	..	332	1418	21	..	3496	3985	12101	21
Households	15470	..	..	35662	3465	38	..	28476	7711	90822	38
Other consumers	40	..	..	439	2	..	..	356	1	838	..
Non-energy use	..	..	..	33	..	..	..	..	..	33	..

Kyrgyzstan

Terajoules

2018	Primary coal and peat	Coal and peat products	Primary Oil	Oil Products	Natural Gas	Biofuels and waste	Nuclear	Electricity	Heat	Total energy	of which: renewables
Primary production	36369	..	8460	..	887	96	..	51545	..	97356	51641
Imports	17145	..	*17343	71570	10814	..	..	..	..	116871	..
Exports	-12699	..	-2961	-5780	..	..	..	-2718	..	-24158	..
International marine bunkers	..	..	..	..	..	..	..	..	..	..	..
International aviation bunkers	..	..	..	-176	..	..	..	..	..	-176	..
Stock changes	2674	..	381	-1160	..	-6	..	..	..	1888	-6
Total energy supply	43488	..	*23223	64453	11701	90	..	48827	..	191782	51635
Statistical difference	661	..	0	40	-1	-12	..	0	0	689	51533
Transfers	..	..	..	..	..	..	..	..	..	..	..
Transformation	-12671	..	*-23223	19244	-3253	..	..	5076	13798	-1028	..
Electricity plants	-182	..	..	..	..	..	..	140	..	-42	..
CHP plants	-12229	..	..	-1010	-1028	..	..	4936	9488	157	..
Heat plants	-260	..	..	0	-2225	..	..	..	4310	1825	..
Coke ovens	..	..	..	..	..	..	..	..	..	..	..
Briquetting plants	..	..	..	..	..	..	..	..	..	..	..
Liquefaction plants	..	..	..	..	..	..	..	..	..	..	..
Gas works	..	..	..	..	..	..	..	..	..	..	..
Blast furnaces	..	..	..	..	..	..	..	..	..	..	..
NGL plants & gas blending	..	..	..	..	..	..	..	..	..	..	..
Oil refineries	..	..	*-23223	23410	..	..	..	..	..	187	..
Other transformation	..	..	..	-3156	..	..	..	..	..	-3156	..
Energy industries own use	..	..	..	-358	-397	..	..	-1062	0	-1816	..
Losses	0	..	..	..	-995	..	..	-10130	-1060	-12185	..
Final consumption	30156	..	..	83299	7058	102	..	42710	12738	176063	102
Final energy consumption	30156	..	..	83299	7058	102	..	42710	12738	176063	102
Manufacturing, const., mining	7151	..	..	2719	1278	..	..	9036	1053	21236	..
Iron and steel	..	..	..	..	..	..	..	..	..	..	..
Chemical and petrochemical	20	..	..	242	..	..	..	40	..	302	..
Non-ferrous metals	..	..	..	..	..	..	..	277	..	277	..
Non-metallic minerals	2113	..	..	83	62	..	..	3971	129	6359	..
Transport equipment	..	..	..	..	..	..	..	14	..	14	..
Machinery	..	..	..	..	313	..	..	137	44	494	..
Mining and quarrying	20	..	..	129	..	..	..	371	..	520	..
Food and tobacco	327	..	..	288	668	..	..	796	765	2843	..
Paper, pulp and printing	20	..	..	..	104	..	..	..	..	125	..
Wood and wood products	..	..	..	..	..	..	..	97	..	97	..
Textile and leather	20	..	..	43	19	..	..	108	..	190	..
Construction	20	..	..	1803	..	..	..	662	11	2496	..
Industries n.e.s	4609	..	..	130	112	..	..	2563	104	7518	..
Transport	20	..	..	16481	..	..	..	158	..	16659	..
Road	..	..	..	16173	..	..	..	90	..	16263	..
Rail	20	..	..	43	..	..	..	36	..	99	..
Domestic aviation	..	..	..	265	..	..	..	..	..	265	..
Domestic navigation	..	..	..	..	..	..	..	..	..	..	..
Pipeline transport	..	..	..	..	..	..	..	..	..	..	..
Transport, n.e.s	..	..	..	..	..	..	..	32	..	32	..
Other	22985	..	..	64100	5780	102	..	33516	11685	138168	102
Agriculture, forestry, fishing	61	..	..	218	..	2	..	803	3	1086	2
Commerce, public services	3667	..	..	3193	1315	36	..	3424	3753	15388	36
Households	19075	..	..	59317	4460	64	..	28685	7899	119500	64
Other consumers	182	..	..	1373	5	0	..	605	30	2195	0
Non-energy use	..	..	..	0	..	..	..	..	..	0	..

Lao People's Dem. Rep.

Terajoules

	All Coal	All Oil	Natural Gas	Primary biofuels / Waste	Charcoal	Electricity	Total energy	of which: renewables
2017								
Primary production	148586	..	..	56349	..	71522	276456	127871
Imports	..	*43811	..	..	..	1800	*45611	..
Exports	0	..	..	..	..	-89644	-89644	..
International marine bunkers	..	..	..	..	..	..	..	..
International aviation bunkers	..	*-1513	..	..	..	..	*-1513	..
Stock changes	*1231	..	..	..	..	..	*1231	..
Total energy supply	149817	*42298	..	56349	..	-16322	232142	127871
Statistical Difference	*-3	0	..	0	0	0	-4	71522
Transfers	..	..	..	..	..	..	..	..
Transformation	*-124378	..	..	*-10851	*6048	*42060	*-87122	*-4804
Electricity plants	*-124378	..	..	*-425	..	*42060	*-82743	*-425
Charcoal plants	..	..	..	*-10427	*6048	..	*-4379	*-4379
Other transformation	0	..	..	0	..	..	0	0
Energy industries own use	..	..	..	..	..	*-1152	*-1152	..
Losses	..	..	..	..	..	-6477	-6477	..
Final consumption	*25442	*42298	..	*45498	*6048	*18109	*137395	*51545
Final energy consumption	*25442	*42190	..	*45498	*6048	*18109	*137286	*51545
Manufacturing, const., mining	*16536	*440	..	*4871	..	*7447	*29294	*4871
Transport	..	*39078	..	..	..	..	*39078	..
Road	..	*38419	..	..	..	..	*38419	..
Domestic aviation	..	*526	..	..	..	..	*526	..
Domestic navigation	..	..	..	..	..	..	..	..
Other transport	..	*133	..	..	..	..	*133	..
Other	*8907	*2671	..	*40627	*6048	*10662	*68915	*46674
Agriculture, forestry, fishing	..	*2227	..	..	..	*133	*2361	..
Commerce and public services	..	*92	..	*6927	*3334	*2655	*13008	*10261
Households	..	*336	..	*33700	*2714	*6743	*43493	*36414
Other consumers	*8907	*16	..	..	..	*1131	*10053	..
Non-energy use	..	*109	..	..	..	..	*109	..
2018								
Primary production	156838	..	..	55930	..	*78679	291447	*134609
Imports	..	*44690	..	..	..	1087	*45777	..
Exports	0	..	..	..	..	-97978	-97978	..
International marine bunkers	..	..	..	..	..	..	..	..
International aviation bunkers	..	*-1574	..	..	..	..	*-1574	..
Stock changes	*1303	..	..	..	..	..	*1303	..
Total energy supply	158141	*43115	..	55930	..	-18212	238975	*134609
Statistical Difference	0	0	..	0	0	0	0	*78679
Transfers	..	..	..	..	..	..	..	..
Transformation	*-131235	..	..	*-11000	*6136	*45197	*-90902	*-4864
Electricity plants	*-131235	..	..	*-421	..	*45197	*-86458	*-421
Charcoal plants	..	..	..	*-10579	*6136	..	*-4443	*-4443
Other transformation	0	..	..	0	..	..	0	0
Energy industries own use	..	..	..	..	..	*-1296	*-1296	..
Losses	..	..	..	..	..	-7177	-7177	..
Final consumption	*26906	*43115	..	*44930	*6136	*18512	*139600	*51066
Final energy consumption	*26906	*43007	..	*44930	*6136	*18512	*139491	*51066
Manufacturing, const., mining	*17494	*444	..	*4785	..	*7613	*30337	*4785
Transport	..	*39856	..	..	..	..	*39856	..
Road	..	*39277	..	..	..	..	*39277	..
Domestic aviation	..	*535	..	..	..	..	*535	..
Domestic navigation	..	..	..	..	..	..	..	..
Other transport	..	*44	..	..	..	..	*44	..
Other	*9412	*2706	..	*40145	*6136	*10899	*69298	*46281
Agriculture, forestry, fishing	..	*2262	..	..	..	*136	*2398	..
Commerce and public services	..	*92	..	*6845	*3393	*2714	*13044	*10237
Households	..	*339	..	*33300	*2744	*6893	*43275	*36043
Other consumers	*9412	*14	..	..	..	*1156	*10582	..
Non-energy use	..	*109	..	..	..	..	*109	..

Latvia

Terajoules

2017	Primary coal and peat	Coal and peat products	Primary Oil	Oil Products	Natural Gas	Biofuels and waste	Nuclear	Electricity	Heat	Total energy	of which: renewables
Primary production	20	..	..	..	..	91887	..	16312	..	108218	107944
Imports	1641	3	39	110072	42400	7458	..	14663	..	176274	6663
Exports	-155	..	-39	-32810	..	-38717	..	-14893	..	-86614	-38717
International marine bunkers	..	..	..	-10938	..	..	..	..	..	-10938	..
International aviation bunkers	..	..	..	-5998	..	..	..	..	..	-5998	..
Stock changes	213	..	..	-707	-827	5066	..	..	..	3744	5075
Total energy supply	1719	3	0	59619	41573	65693	..	16081	..	184687	80965
Statistical difference	48	0	0	-588	-2	-35	..	0	1	-575	16276
Transfers	..	..	..	563	..	..	..	..	..	563	..
Transformation	-175	10	..	-40	-26925	-23462	..	10793	29990	-9811	-23462
Electricity plants	..	..	..	..	..	..	..	..	..	..	..
CHP plants	-48	..	..	..	-16727	-14663	..	10800	13865	-6774	-14663
Heat plants	-97	..	..	-40	-10198	-8250	..	-7	16125	-2467	-8250
Coke ovens	..	..	..	..	..	..	..	..	..	..	..
Briquetting plants	-30	10	..	..	..	..	..	..	..	-20	..
Liquefaction plants	..	..	..	..	..	..	..	..	..	..	..
Gas works	..	..	..	..	..	..	..	..	..	..	..
Blast furnaces	..	..	..	..	..	..	..	..	..	..	..
NGL plants & gas blending	..	..	..	..	..	..	..	..	..	..	..
Oil refineries	..	..	..	..	..	..	..	..	..	..	..
Other transformation	..	..	..	..	..	-550	..	..	..	-550	-550
Energy industries own use	..	..	..	-258	-439	..	..	-1822	-1093	-3612	..
Losses	..	..	..	..	-476	..	..	-1706	-3576	-5759	..
Final consumption	1496	12	..	60471	13734	42265	..	23346	25320	166644	41226
Final energy consumption	1496	12	..	56893	13734	42265	..	23346	25320	163066	41226
Manufacturing, const., mining	941	3	..	2270	4505	15778	..	6347	3290	33133	14740
Iron and steel	..	..	..	..	6	..	..	54	4	64	..
Chemical and petrochemical	..	..	..	142	446	209	..	230	41	1069	209
Non-ferrous metals	..	..	..	..	26	..	..	18	..	44	..
Non-metallic minerals	893	..	..	334	1282	2004	..	940	11	5462	966
Transport equipment	..	3	..	43	42	4	..	169	71	332	4
Machinery	..	..	..	..	212	134	..	320	18	684	134
Mining and quarrying	..	..	..	172	32	4	..	101	..	308	4
Food and tobacco	48	..	..	358	1238	373	..	1037	219	3273	373
Paper, pulp and printing	..	..	..	..	105	9	..	101	10	225	9
Wood and wood products	..	..	..	477	628	12825	..	2743	2812	19486	12825
Textile and leather	..	..	..	..	183	13	..	108	27	331	13
Construction	..	..	..	744	253	56	..	245	40	1338	56
Industries n.e.s	0	0	..	0	52	147	..	281	37	517	147
Transport	..	..	..	45285	..	395	..	374	..	46054	395
Road	..	..	..	42826	..	358	..	194	..	43379	358
Rail	..	..	..	2242	..	37	..	140	..	2419	37
Domestic aviation	..	..	..	44	..	..	..	..	..	44	..
Domestic navigation	..	..	..	172	..	..	..	..	..	172	..
Pipeline transport	..	..	..	..	..	..	..	40	..	40	..
Transport, n.e.s	..	..	..	..	..	..	..	..	..	..	..
Other	555	10	..	9338	9230	26092	..	16625	22030	83879	26092
Agriculture, forestry, fishing	..	..	..	5314	337	1337	..	702	475	8165	1337
Commerce, public services	145	10	..	1536	4231	3603	..	9954	5956	25435	3603
Households	410	..	..	2316	4662	21152	..	5962	15593	50094	21152
Other consumers	..	..	..	172	..	..	..	7	6	185	..
Non-energy use	..	..	..	3578	..	..	..	..	..	3578	..

Latvia

Terajoules

2018	Primary coal and peat	Coal and peat products	Primary Oil	Oil Products	Natural Gas	Biofuels and waste	Nuclear	Electricity	Heat	Total energy	of which: renewables
Primary production	70	..	..	..	..	110222	..	9198	..	119490	119022
Imports	1977	..	..	105682	48375	11552	..	18626	..	186213	10232
Exports	-251	-10	..	-37910	..	-41968	..	-15354	..	-95492	-41968
International marine bunkers	..	..	..	-1629	..	..	..	..	..	-1629	..
International aviation bunkers	..	..	..	-6571	..	..	..	..	..	-6571	..
Stock changes	229	10	..	938	571	-9236	..	..	..	-7489	-9173
Total energy supply	2025	0	..	60511	48946	70570	..	12470	..	194522	78113
Statistical difference	24	0	..	-1187	-1	57	..	4	-1	-1104	9254
Transfers	..	..	..	442	..	..	..	..	..	442	..
Transformation	-269	10	..	-83	-33475	-23881	..	15005	29686	-13008	-23881
Electricity plants	..	..	..	..	..	..	..	..	..	..	..
CHP plants	-177	..	..	..	-24352	-14984	..	15012	14735	-9766	-14984
Heat plants	-72	..	..	-83	-9122	-8542	..	-7	14951	-2876	-8542
Coke ovens	..	..	..	..	..	..	..	..	..	..	..
Briquetting plants	-20	10	..	..	..	..	..	..	..	-10	..
Liquefaction plants	..	..	..	..	..	..	..	..	..	..	..
Gas works	..	..	..	..	..	..	..	..	..	..	..
Blast furnaces	..	..	..	..	..	..	..	..	..	..	..
NGL plants & gas blending	..	..	..	..	..	..	..	..	..	..	..
Oil refineries	..	..	..	..	..	..	..	..	..	..	..
Other transformation	..	..	..	..	..	-356	..	..	..	-356	-356
Energy industries own use	..	..	..	-301	-519	..	..	-1879	-1001	-3701	..
Losses	..	..	..	..	-529	..	..	-1613	-3491	-5633	..
Final consumption	1732	10	..	61756	14423	46631	..	23980	25195	173726	44977
Final energy consumption	1732	10	..	57535	14423	46631	..	23980	25195	169505	44977
Manufacturing, const., mining	1326	..	..	2415	4764	18711	..	6631	3782	37629	17058
Iron and steel	..	..	..	..	4	1	..	50	3	58	1
Chemical and petrochemical	..	..	..	232	474	150	..	234	44	1135	150
Non-ferrous metals	..	..	..	..	25	..	..	18	..	43	..
Non-metallic minerals	1278	..	..	387	1236	3164	..	1012	12	7088	1511
Transport equipment	..	..	..	90	47	1	..	169	72	379	1
Machinery	..	..	..	47	214	137	..	331	23	753	137
Mining and quarrying	..	..	..	172	32	22	..	108	..	334	22
Food and tobacco	24	..	..	354	1314	447	..	1022	322	3484	447
Paper, pulp and printing	..	..	..	..	106	8	..	101	2	217	8
Wood and wood products	..	..	..	477	779	13016	..	2905	3199	20377	13016
Textile and leather	..	..	..	..	175	7	..	104	32	318	7
Construction	24	..	..	655	296	81	..	252	44	1352	81
Industries n.e.s	0	..	..	0	61	1677	..	324	29	2091	1677
Transport	..	..	..	45458	3	1489	..	371	..	47320	1489
Road	..	..	..	42951	3	1416	..	101	..	44470	1416
Rail	..	..	..	2291	..	74	..	245	..	2610	74
Domestic aviation	..	..	..	..	..	..	..	..	..	..	..
Domestic navigation	..	..	..	215	..	..	..	..	..	215	..
Pipeline transport	..	..	..	..	..	..	..	25	..	25	..
Transport, n.e.s	..	..	..	..	..	..	..	..	..	..	..
Other	406	10	..	9662	9657	26431	..	16978	21413	84556	26431
Agriculture, forestry, fishing	..	..	..	5521	270	1044	..	684	475	7994	1044
Commerce, public services	141	10	..	1575	4397	2944	..	10282	5399	24748	2944
Households	265	..	..	2307	4990	22443	..	6012	15533	51550	22443
Other consumers	..	..	..	259	..	..	..	..	6	265	..
Non-energy use	..	..	..	4221	..	..	..	..	..	4221	..

Lebanon

Terajoules

2017	Primary coal and peat	Coal and peat products	Primary Oil	Oil Products	Natural Gas	Biofuels and waste	Nuclear	Electricity	Heat	Total energy	of which: renewables
Primary production	..	..	..	..	..	*4971	..	1642	*1060	*7673	*7673
Imports	*6919	..	..	365014	..	587	..	1922	..	374442	587
Exports	..	..	..	..	..	..	..	..	..	..	..
International marine bunkers	..	..	..	*-1212	..	..	..	..	..	*-1212	..
International aviation bunkers	..	..	..	*-11891	..	..	..	..	..	*-11891	..
Stock changes	..	..	..	..	..	..	..	..	..	..	..
Total energy supply	*6919	..	..	351911	..	*5558	..	3564	*1060	369012	*8260
Statistical difference	0	..	..	-168	..	0	..	0	0	-168	*1642
Transfers	..	..	..	..	..	..	..	..	..	..	..
Transformation	..	..	..	-202007	..	*-186	..	82638	..	-119555	*-186
Electricity plants	..	..	..	-202007	..	..	..	82638	..	-119369	..
CHP plants	..	..	..	..	..	..	..	..	..	..	..
Heat plants	..	..	..	..	..	..	..	..	..	..	..
Coke ovens	..	..	..	..	..	..	..	..	..	..	..
Briquetting plants	..	..	..	..	..	..	..	..	..	..	..
Liquefaction plants	..	..	..	..	..	..	..	..	..	..	..
Gas works	..	..	..	..	..	..	..	..	..	..	..
Blast furnaces	..	..	..	..	..	..	..	..	..	..	..
NGL plants & gas blending	..	..	..	..	..	..	..	..	..	..	..
Oil refineries	..	..	..	..	..	..	..	..	..	..	..
Other transformation	..	..	..	..	..	*-186	..	..	..	*-186	*-186
Energy industries own use	..	..	..	..	..	..	..	-148	..	-148	..
Losses	..	..	..	..	..	..	..	*-7744	..	*-7744	..
Final consumption	*6919	..	..	*150072	..	5373	..	*78311	*1060	*241734	6433
Final energy consumption	*6919	..	..	*146314	..	5373	..	*78311	*1060	*237976	6433
Manufacturing, const., mining	*6919	..	..	6182	..	..	..	*20520	*50	*33671	*50
Iron and steel	..	..	..	..	..	..	..	..	..	..	..
Chemical and petrochemical	..	..	..	..	..	..	..	..	..	..	..
Non-ferrous metals	..	..	..	..	..	..	..	..	..	..	..
Non-metallic minerals	*6919	..	..	..	..	..	..	..	..	*6919	..
Transport equipment	..	..	..	..	..	..	..	..	..	..	..
Machinery	..	..	..	..	..	..	..	..	..	..	..
Mining and quarrying	..	..	..	..	..	..	..	..	..	..	..
Food and tobacco	..	..	..	..	..	..	..	..	..	..	..
Paper, pulp and printing	..	..	..	..	..	..	..	..	..	..	..
Wood and wood products	..	..	..	..	..	..	..	..	..	..	..
Textile and leather	..	..	..	..	..	..	..	..	..	..	..
Construction	..	..	..	..	..	..	..	..	..	..	..
Industries n.e.s	0	..	..	6182	..	..	..	*20520	*50	*26752	*50
Transport	..	..	..	*96500	..	..	..	..	..	*96500	..
Road	..	..	..	*96500	..	..	..	..	..	*96500	..
Rail	..	..	..	..	..	..	..	..	..	..	..
Domestic aviation	..	..	..	..	..	..	..	..	..	..	..
Domestic navigation	..	..	..	..	..	..	..	..	..	..	..
Pipeline transport	..	..	..	..	..	..	..	..	..	..	..
Transport, n.e.s	..	..	..	..	..	..	..	..	..	..	..
Other	..	..	..	*43631	..	5373	..	*57791	*1010	*107805	6383
Agriculture, forestry, fishing	..	..	..	..	..	..	..	..	..	..	..
Commerce, public services	..	..	..	..	..	..	..	*13093	*310	*13403	*310
Households	..	..	..	*43631	..	4697	..	*29797	*700	*78825	5397
Other consumers	..	..	..	..	..	676	..	*14900	..	*15576	676
Non-energy use	..	..	..	3759	..	..	..	..	..	3759	..

Lebanon

Terajoules

2018	Primary coal and peat	Coal and peat products	Primary Oil	Oil Products	Natural Gas	Biofuels and waste	Nuclear	Electricity	Heat	Total energy	of which: renewables
Primary production	..	..	..	..	..	*4971	..	1426	*1060	*7457	*7457
Imports	*6919	..	..	344588	..	1481	..	40	..	353027	1481
Exports	..	..	..	..	..	..	..	..	..	..	..
International marine bunkers	..	..	..	-1212	..	..	..	..	..	-1212	..
International aviation bunkers	..	..	..	*-11632	..	..	..	..	..	*-11632	..
Stock changes	..	..	..	..	..	..	..	..	..	..	..
Total energy supply	*6919	..	..	331744	..	*6452	..	1465	*1060	347639	*8938
Statistical difference	0	..	..	-329	..	0	..	0	0	-329	1426
Transfers	..	..	..	..	..	..	..	..	..	..	..
Transformation	..	..	..	-197791	..	*-186	..	81914	..	-116062	*-186
Electricity plants	..	..	..	-197791	..	..	..	81914	..	-115877	..
CHP plants	..	..	..	..	..	..	..	..	..	..	..
Heat plants	..	..	..	..	..	..	..	..	..	..	..
Coke ovens	..	..	..	..	..	..	..	..	..	..	..
Briquetting plants	..	..	..	..	..	..	..	..	..	..	..
Liquefaction plants	..	..	..	..	..	..	..	..	..	..	..
Gas works	..	..	..	..	..	..	..	..	..	..	..
Blast furnaces	..	..	..	..	..	..	..	..	..	..	..
NGL plants & gas blending	..	..	..	..	..	..	..	..	..	..	..
Oil refineries	..	..	..	..	..	..	..	..	..	..	..
Other transformation	..	..	..	..	..	*-186	..	..	..	*-186	*-186
Energy industries own use	..	..	..	..	..	..	..	-173	..	-173	..
Losses	..	..	..	..	..	..	..	*-7488	..	*-7488	..
Final consumption	*6919	..	..	*134282	..	6266	..	*75719	*1060	*224246	7326
Final energy consumption	*6919	..	..	*130038	..	6266	..	*75719	*1060	*220002	7326
Manufacturing, const., mining	*6919	..	..	6277	..	..	..	*19840	*50	*33085	*50
Iron and steel	..	..	..	..	..	..	..	..	..	..	..
Chemical and petrochemical	..	..	..	..	..	..	..	..	..	..	..
Non-ferrous metals	..	..	..	..	..	..	..	..	..	..	..
Non-metallic minerals	*6919	..	..	..	..	..	..	..	..	*6919	..
Transport equipment	..	..	..	..	..	..	..	..	..	..	..
Machinery	..	..	..	..	..	..	..	..	..	..	..
Mining and quarrying	..	..	..	..	..	..	..	..	..	..	..
Food and tobacco	..	..	..	..	..	..	..	..	..	..	..
Paper, pulp and printing	..	..	..	..	..	..	..	..	..	..	..
Wood and wood products	..	..	..	..	..	..	..	..	..	..	..
Textile and leather	..	..	..	..	..	..	..	..	..	..	..
Construction	..	..	..	..	..	..	..	..	..	..	..
Industries n.e.s	0	..	..	6277	..	..	..	*19840	*50	*26166	*50
Transport	..	..	..	*90325	..	..	..	..	..	*90325	..
Road	..	..	..	*90325	..	..	..	..	..	*90325	..
Rail	..	..	..	..	..	..	..	..	..	..	..
Domestic aviation	..	..	..	..	..	..	..	..	..	..	..
Domestic navigation	..	..	..	..	..	..	..	..	..	..	..
Pipeline transport	..	..	..	..	..	..	..	..	..	..	..
Transport, n.e.s	..	..	..	..	..	..	..	..	..	..	..
Other	..	..	..	*33437	..	6266	..	*55879	*1010	*96592	7276
Agriculture, forestry, fishing	..	..	..	..	..	..	..	..	..	..	..
Commerce, public services	..	..	..	..	..	..	..	*12661	*310	*12971	*310
Households	..	..	..	*33437	..	4697	..	*28811	*700	*67645	5397
Other consumers	..	..	..	..	..	1569	..	*14407	..	*15977	1569
Non-energy use	..	..	..	4244	..	..	..	..	..	4244	..

Lesotho

Terajoules

	All Coal	All Oil	Natural Gas	Primary biofuels / Waste	Charcoal	Electricity	Total energy	of which: renewables
2017								
Primary production	..	..	..	16012	..	1804	17815	17815
Imports	*17492	9499	..	..	..	1393	*28384	..
Exports	..	..	..	..	..	-3	-3	..
International marine bunkers	..	..	..	..	..	..	..	..
International aviation bunkers	..	*-18	..	..	..	..	*-18	..
Stock changes	..	..	..	..	..	..	..	..
Total energy supply	*17492	9481	..	16012	..	3194	*46179	17815
Statistical Difference	0	-137	..	0	0	258	*121	1804
Transfers	..	..	..	..	..	..	..	..
Transformation	..	*-4	..	*-968	510	*2	*-460	*-458
Electricity plants	..	*-4	..	..	..	*2	*-2	..
Charcoal plants	..	..	..	*-968	510	..	*-458	*-458
Other transformation	..	0	..	0	..	..	0	0
Energy industries own use	..	..	..	..	..	-2	-2	..
Losses	..	..	..	..	..	-418	-418	..
Final consumption	*17492	9614	..	*15043	*510	2518	*45179	*15554
Final energy consumption	*17492	9477	..	*15043	*510	2518	*45042	*15554
Manufacturing, const., mining	*17492	*1017	..	..	..	1111	*19621	..
Transport	..	6861	..	..	..	..	6861	..
Road	..	6860	..	..	..	..	6860	..
Domestic aviation	..	1	..	..	..	..	1	..
Domestic navigation	..	..	..	..	..	..	..	..
Other transport	..	..	..	..	..	..	..	..
Other	..	*1599	..	*15043	*510	1407	*18560	*15554
Agriculture, forestry, fishing	..	..	..	..	..	5	5	..
Commerce and public services	..	*429	..	..	..	509	938	..
Households	..	*1170	..	*15043	*510	894	*17617	*15554
Other consumers	..	..	..	..	..	..	..	..
Non-energy use	..	137	..	..	..	..	137	..
2018								
Primary production	..	..	..	*14934	..	1860	*16794	*16794
Imports	*18421	9969	..	..	..	1428	*29819	..
Exports	..	..	..	..	..	-10	-10	..
International marine bunkers	..	..	..	..	..	..	..	..
International aviation bunkers	..	*-18	..	..	..	..	*-18	..
Stock changes	..	..	..	..	..	..	..	..
Total energy supply	*18421	9952	..	*14934	..	3278	*46584	*16794
Statistical Difference	0	*-137	..	0	0	-42	*-178	*1860
Transfers	..	..	..	..	..	..	..	..
Transformation	..	*-4	..	*-290	153	2	*-139	*-137
Electricity plants	..	*-4	..	..	..	2	*-2	..
Charcoal plants	..	..	..	*-290	153	..	*-137	*-137
Other transformation	..	0	..	0	..	..	0	0
Energy industries own use	..	..	..	..	..	-2	-2	..
Losses	..	..	..	..	..	-414	-414	..
Final consumption	*18421	*10084	..	*14644	*153	2905	*46207	*14796
Final energy consumption	*18421	9948	..	*14644	*153	2905	*46070	*14796
Manufacturing, const., mining	*18421	1078	..	..	..	1151	*20651	..
Transport	..	7182	..	..	..	..	7182	..
Road	..	7180	..	..	..	..	7180	..
Domestic aviation	..	2	..	..	..	..	2	..
Domestic navigation	..	..	..	..	..	..	..	..
Other transport	..	..	..	..	..	..	..	..
Other	..	*1687	..	*14644	*153	1754	*18238	*14796
Agriculture, forestry, fishing	..	..	..	..	..	5	5	..
Commerce and public services	..	*434	..	..	..	797	1231	..
Households	..	*1253	..	*14644	*153	951	*17001	*14796
Other consumers	..	..	..	..	..	..	..	..
Non-energy use	..	*137	..	..	..	..	*137	..

Liberia

Terajoules

	All Coal	All Oil	Natural Gas	Primary biofuels / Waste	Charcoal	Electricity	Total energy	of which: renewables
2017								
Primary production	..	..	..	81091	..	*155	81246	81246
Imports	..	*16670	..	..	1	..	*16671	1
Exports	..	..	..	..	-12	..	-12	-12
International marine bunkers	..	*-215	..	..	..	..	*-215	..
International aviation bunkers	..	*-287	..	..	..	..	*-287	..
Stock changes	..	..	..	..	..	..	..	..
Total energy supply	..	*16168	..	81091	-11	*155	97403	81235
Statistical Difference	..	0	..	0	0	*2	*2	155
Transfers	..	..	..	..	..	..	..	..
Transformation	..	*-3870	..	*-16519	8891	*1429	*-10068	*-7628
Electricity plants	..	*-3870	..	..	..	*1429	*-2441	..
Charcoal plants	..	..	..	*-16519	8891	..	*-7628	*-7628
Other transformation	..	0	..	0	..	..	0	0
Energy industries own use	..	..	..	..	..	*-448	*-448	..
Losses	..	..	..	..	..	*-108	*-108	..
Final consumption	..	*12298	..	*64573	*8880	*1026	*86777	*73453
Final energy consumption	..	*12037	..	*64573	*8880	*1026	*86516	*73453
Manufacturing, const., mining	..	*1290	..	..	..	..	*1290	..
Transport	..	*10390	..	..	..	..	*10390	..
Road	..	*10059	..	..	..	..	*10059	..
Domestic aviation	..	*331	..	..	..	..	*331	..
Domestic navigation	..	..	..	..	..	..	..	..
Other transport	..	..	..	..	..	..	..	..
Other	..	*357	..	*64573	*8880	*1026	*74836	*73453
Agriculture, forestry, fishing	..	..	..	*64573	..	..	*64573	*64573
Commerce and public services	..	..	..	..	..	..	..	..
Households	..	..	..	..	*8880	..	*8880	*8880
Other consumers	..	*357	..	..	..	*1026	*1383	..
Non-energy use	..	*261	..	..	..	..	*261	..
2018								
Primary production	..	..	..	83734	..	*454	84188	84188
Imports	..	*14389	..	..	0	..	*14389	0
Exports	..	..	..	..	-12	..	-12	-12
International marine bunkers	..	*-172	..	..	..	..	*-172	..
International aviation bunkers	..	*-287	..	..	..	..	*-287	..
Stock changes	..	..	..	..	..	..	..	..
Total energy supply	..	*13931	..	83734	-11	*454	98107	84176
Statistical Difference	..	0	..	0	0	0	0	454
Transfers	..	..	..	..	..	..	..	..
Transformation	..	*-3311	..	*-17087	9197	*1145	*-10057	*-7890
Electricity plants	..	*-3311	..	..	..	*1145	*-2166	..
Charcoal plants	..	..	..	*-17087	9197	..	*-7890	*-7890
Other transformation	..	0	..	0	..	..	0	0
Energy industries own use	..	..	..	..	..	*-421	*-421	..
Losses	..	..	..	..	..	*-97	*-97	..
Final consumption	..	*10620	..	*66647	*9185	*1080	*87532	*75832
Final energy consumption	..	*10378	..	*66647	*9185	*1080	*87291	*75832
Manufacturing, const., mining	..	*1118	..	..	..	..	*1118	..
Transport	..	*8946	..	..	..	..	*8946	..
Road	..	*8615	..	..	..	..	*8615	..
Domestic aviation	..	*331	..	..	..	..	*331	..
Domestic navigation	..	..	..	..	..	..	..	..
Other transport	..	..	..	..	..	..	..	..
Other	..	*314	..	*66647	*9185	*1080	*77226	*75832
Agriculture, forestry, fishing	..	..	..	*66647	..	..	*66647	*66647
Commerce and public services	..	..	..	..	..	..	..	..
Households	..	..	..	..	*9185	..	*9185	*9185
Other consumers	..	*314	..	..	..	*1080	*1394	..
Non-energy use	..	*241	..	..	..	..	*241	..

Libya

Terajoules

2017	Primary coal and peat	Coal and peat products	Primary Oil	Oil Products	Natural Gas	Biofuels and waste	Nuclear	Electricity	Heat	Total energy	of which: renewables
Primary production	..	..	1915351	..	489377	24602	..	29	..	2429358	24631
Imports	..	..	..	248320	..	..	..	1087	..	249407	..
Exports	..	..	-1698007	-59780	-157320	..	..	..	..	-1915107	..
International marine bunkers	..	..	..	-8888	..	..	..	..	..	-8888	..
International aviation bunkers	..	..	..	-2470	..	..	..	..	..	-2470	..
Stock changes	..	..	..	..	..	..	..	..	..	..	..
Total energy supply	..	..	217344	177182	332057	24602	..	1116	..	752301	24631
Statistical difference	..	..	-19796	86	-72796	0	..	42372	..	-50135	29
Transfers	..	..	..	..	..	..	..	..	..	..	..
Transformation	..	..	-237140	133819	-239803	-14090	..	119786	..	-237428	-14090
Electricity plants	..	..	..	-103486	-239803	..	..	119786	..	-223503	..
CHP plants	..	..	..	..	..	..	..	..	..	..	..
Heat plants	..	..	..	..	..	..	..	..	..	..	..
Coke ovens	..	..	..	..	..	..	..	..	..	..	..
Briquetting plants	..	..	..	..	..	..	..	..	..	..	..
Liquefaction plants	..	..	..	..	..	..	..	..	..	..	..
Gas works	..	..	..	..	..	..	..	..	..	..	..
Blast furnaces	..	..	..	..	..	..	..	..	..	..	..
NGL plants & gas blending	..	..	-32620	33617	..	..	..	..	..	997	..
Oil refineries	..	..	-204521	203688	..	..	..	..	..	-832	..
Other transformation	..	..	..	..	..	-14090	..	..	..	-14090	-14090
Energy industries own use	..	..	..	-7306	-2748	..	..	-3596	..	-13650	..
Losses	..	..	..	..	..	..	..	-24059	..	-24059	..
Final consumption	..	..	..	303609	162302	10512	..	50875	..	527299	10512
Final energy consumption	..	..	..	278310	57341	10512	..	50875	..	397038	10512
Manufacturing, const., mining	..	..	..	18342	57341	..	..	4410	..	80092	..
Iron and steel	..	..	..	..	..	..	..	..	..	..	..
Chemical and petrochemical	..	..	..	..	..	..	..	..	..	..	..
Non-ferrous metals	..	..	..	..	..	..	..	..	..	..	..
Non-metallic minerals	..	..	..	..	..	..	..	..	..	..	..
Transport equipment	..	..	..	..	..	..	..	..	..	..	..
Machinery	..	..	..	..	..	..	..	..	..	..	..
Mining and quarrying	..	..	..	..	..	..	..	..	..	..	..
Food and tobacco	..	..	..	..	..	..	..	..	..	..	..
Paper, pulp and printing	..	..	..	..	..	..	..	..	..	..	..
Wood and wood products	..	..	..	..	..	..	..	..	..	..	..
Textile and leather	..	..	..	..	..	..	..	..	..	..	..
Construction	..	..	..	..	..	..	..	..	..	..	..
Industries n.e.s	..	..	..	18342	57341	..	..	4410	..	80092	..
Transport	..	..	..	241169	..	..	..	..	..	241169	..
Road	..	..	..	241080	..	..	..	..	..	241080	..
Rail	..	..	..	..	..	..	..	..	..	..	..
Domestic aviation	..	..	..	89	..	..	..	..	..	89	..
Domestic navigation	..	..	..	..	..	..	..	..	..	..	..
Pipeline transport	..	..	..	..	..	..	..	..	..	..	..
Transport, n.e.s	..	..	..	..	..	..	..	..	..	..	..
Other	..	..	..	18800	..	10512	..	46465	..	75777	10512
Agriculture, forestry, fishing	..	..	..	..	..	..	..	4486	..	4486	..
Commerce, public services	..	..	..	..	..	..	..	5476	..	5476	..
Households	..	..	..	18800	..	10512	..	21431	..	50743	10512
Other consumers	..	..	..	..	..	..	..	15073	..	15073	..
Non-energy use	..	..	..	25299	104962	..	..	..	..	130261	..

Libya

Terajoules

2018	Primary coal and peat	Coal and peat products	Primary Oil	Oil Products	Natural Gas	Biofuels and waste	Nuclear	Electricity	Heat	Total energy	of which: renewables
Primary production	..	..	2405372	..	474695	24884	..	29	..	2904980	24913
Imports	..	..	..	239796	..	..	..	1674	..	241470	..
Exports	..	..	-2158149	-75688	-153900	..	..	..	..	-2387737	..
International marine bunkers	..	..	..	-11352	..	..	..	..	..	-11352	..
International aviation bunkers	..	..	..	-2470	..	..	..	..	..	-2470	..
Stock changes	..	..	..	..	..	..	..	..	..	..	..
Total energy supply	..	..	247224	150286	320795	24884	..	1703	..	744892	24913
Statistical difference	..	..	-33502	-222	-92274	0	..	33466	..	-92532	29
Transfers	..	..	..	..	..	..	..	..	..	..	..
Transformation	..	..	-280726	165611	-235319	-14235	..	122987	..	-241682	-14235
Electricity plants	..	..	..	-116571	-235319	..	..	122987	..	-228904	..
CHP plants	..	..	..	..	..	..	..	..	..	..	..
Heat plants	..	..	..	..	..	..	..	..	..	..	..
Coke ovens	..	..	..	..	..	..	..	..	..	..	..
Briquetting plants	..	..	..	..	..	..	..	..	..	..	..
Liquefaction plants	..	..	..	..	..	..	..	..	..	..	..
Gas works	..	..	..	..	..	..	..	..	..	..	..
Blast furnaces	..	..	..	..	..	..	..	..	..	..	..
NGL plants & gas blending	..	..	-41857	42959	..	..	..	..	..	1102	..
Oil refineries	..	..	-238868	239223	..	..	..	..	..	355	..
Other transformation	..	..	..	..	..	-14235	..	..	..	-14235	-14235
Energy industries own use	..	..	..	-8462	-2723	..	..	-3031	..	-14216	..
Losses	..	..	..	..	..	..	..	-24815	..	-24815	..
Final consumption	..	..	..	307656	175028	10649	..	63378	..	556711	10649
Final energy consumption	..	..	..	273754	61836	10649	..	63378	..	409618	10649
Manufacturing, const., mining	..	..	..	20281	61836	..	..	4208	..	86326	..
Iron and steel	..	..	..	..	..	..	..	..	..	..	..
Chemical and petrochemical	..	..	..	..	..	..	..	..	..	..	..
Non-ferrous metals	..	..	..	..	..	..	..	..	..	..	..
Non-metallic minerals	..	..	..	..	..	..	..	..	..	..	..
Transport equipment	..	..	..	..	..	..	..	..	..	..	..
Machinery	..	..	..	..	..	..	..	..	..	..	..
Mining and quarrying	..	..	..	..	..	..	..	..	..	..	..
Food and tobacco	..	..	..	..	..	..	..	..	..	..	..
Paper, pulp and printing	..	..	..	..	..	..	..	..	..	..	..
Wood and wood products	..	..	..	..	..	..	..	..	..	..	..
Textile and leather	..	..	..	..	..	..	..	..	..	..	..
Construction	..	..	..	..	..	..	..	..	..	..	..
Industries n.e.s	..	..	..	20281	61836	..	..	4208	..	86326	..
Transport	..	..	..	235364	..	..	..	..	..	235364	..
Road	..	..	..	235099	..	..	..	..	..	235099	..
Rail	..	..	..	..	..	..	..	..	..	..	..
Domestic aviation	..	..	..	265	..	..	..	..	..	265	..
Domestic navigation	..	..	..	..	..	..	..	..	..	..	..
Pipeline transport	..	..	..	..	..	..	..	..	..	..	..
Transport, n.e.s	..	..	..	..	..	..	..	..	..	..	..
Other	..	..	..	18109	..	10649	..	59170	..	87928	10649
Agriculture, forestry, fishing	..	..	..	..	..	..	..	4554	..	4554	..
Commerce, public services	..	..	..	..	..	..	..	6988	..	6988	..
Households	..	..	..	18109	..	10649	..	31939	..	60698	10649
Other consumers	..	..	..	..	..	..	..	15689	..	15689	..
Non-energy use	..	..	..	33902	113191	..	..	..	..	147093	..

Lithuania

Terajoules

2017	Primary coal and peat	Coal and peat products	Primary Oil	Oil Products	Natural Gas	Biofuels and waste	Nuclear	Electricity	Heat	Total energy	of which: renewables
Primary production	281	..	2370	..	..	64102	..	7322	11795	85870	70033
Imports	6901	1045	417883	56375	87081	6662	..	42934	..	618881	6662
Exports	-12	-39	-1777	-352868	-7182	-11449	..	-11696	..	-385024	-11449
International marine bunkers	..	..	..	-7421	..	..	..	..	..	-7421	..
International aviation bunkers	..	..	..	-4542	..	..	..	..	..	-4542	..
Stock changes	-238	78	-549	4368	547	900	..	..	..	5107	912
Total energy supply	6932	1084	417927	-304088	80447	60215	..	38560	11795	312871	66158
Statistical difference	12	0	0	-616	0	50	..	4	0	-550	7388
Transfers	..	..	10499	-11217	..	..	..	..	..	-717	..
Transformation	-486	49	-428426	431479	-14138	-31478	..	5656	32163	-5182	-30090
Electricity plants	..	..	..	..	..	..	..	..	-2788	-2788	..
CHP plants	..	..	..	-943	-10062	-10821	..	5666	13105	-3055	-9418
Heat plants	-415	..	..	-340	-4076	-20636	..	-11	21846	-3632	-20651
Coke ovens	..	..	..	..	..	..	..	..	..	..	..
Briquetting plants	-70	49	..	..	..	..	..	..	..	-22	..
Liquefaction plants	..	..	..	..	..	..	..	..	..	..	..
Gas works	..	..	..	..	..	..	..	..	..	..	..
Blast furnaces	..	..	..	..	..	..	..	..	..	..	..
NGL plants & gas blending	..	..	..	..	..	..	..	..	..	..	..
Oil refineries	..	..	-428426	432762	..	..	..	..	..	4335	..
Other transformation	..	..	..	..	..	-21	..	..	..	-21	-21
Energy industries own use	..	..	..	-22915	-773	..	..	-4712	-396	-28797	..
Losses	-35	..	..	..	..	-12	..	-3290	-5017	-8355	-6
Final consumption	6400	1133	..	93875	65535	28675	..	36209	38545	270371	28675
Final energy consumption	6400	1133	..	84990	23857	28675	..	36209	38545	219808	28675
Manufacturing, const., mining	3067	518	..	1640	12213	*3635	..	13082	10011	44166	*3635
Iron and steel	..	29	..	..	1	..	..	68	..	99	..
Chemical and petrochemical	..	..	..	47	4876	*704	..	2992	8894	17513	*704
Non-ferrous metals	..	..	..	..	..	..	..	..	..	..	..
Non-metallic minerals	2992	440	..	167	986	..	..	878	1	5464	..
Transport equipment	..	..	..	..	60	..	..	83	10	153	..
Machinery	..	..	..	..	362	..	..	878	94	1334	..
Mining and quarrying	..	..	..	86	9	..	..	112	1	208	..
Food and tobacco	50	39	..	646	3477	49	..	2830	415	7505	49
Paper, pulp and printing	..	..	..	..	587	..	..	688	23	1297	..
Wood and wood products	..	..	..	86	473	..	..	1314	313	2186	..
Textile and leather	..	..	..	43	554	..	..	587	102	1286	..
Construction	25	..	..	475	612	..	..	500	89	1701	..
Industries n.e.s	0	10	..	90	216	*2882	..	2153	69	5420	*2882
Transport	..	..	..	78453	1412	2540	..	266	..	82671	2540
Road	..	..	..	75688	328	2466	..	130	..	78611	2466
Rail	..	..	..	2291	..	74	..	43	..	2408	74
Domestic aviation	..	..	..	..	..	..	..	..	..	..	..
Domestic navigation	..	..	..	215	..	..	..	..	..	215	..
Pipeline transport	..	..	..	..	1085	..	..	94	..	1178	..
Transport, n.e.s	..	..	..	258	..	..	..	..	..	258	..
Other	3333	615	..	4898	10232	22500	..	22860	28534	92971	22500
Agriculture, forestry, fishing	100	20	..	2034	911	617	..	738	191	4611	617
Commerce, public services	1452	156	..	133	2883	1476	..	11905	8464	26469	1476
Households	1780	439	..	2378	6439	20407	..	10217	19879	61539	20407
Other consumers	..	..	..	353	..	..	..	..	..	353	..
Non-energy use	..	..	..	8884	41678	..	..	..	..	50562	..

Lithuania

Terajoules

2018	Primary coal and peat	Coal and peat products	Primary Oil	Oil Products	Natural Gas	Biofuels and waste	Nuclear	Electricity	Heat	Total energy	of which: renewables
Primary production	328	..	1947	..	..	62250	..	5983	11272	81780	66792
Imports	6627	1269	410817	46146	79844	8240	..	46253	..	599196	8240
Exports	-35	-10	-1904	-322307	-6301	-11446	..	-11574	..	-353577	-11446
International marine bunkers	..	..	..	-8498	..	..	..	..	..	-8498	..
International aviation bunkers	..	..	..	-5380	..	..	..	..	..	-5380	..
Stock changes	380	-10	1439	-1499	803	325	..	..	..	1439	335
Total energy supply	7300	1250	412299	-291538	74345	59370	..	40662	11272	314960	63922
Statistical difference	-2	0	-42	-993	0	-733	..	-14	0	-1785	5250
Transfers	..	..	6212	-6852	..	..	..	..	..	-640	..
Transformation	-497	39	-418553	420554	-12663	-30798	..	4752	32100	-5066	-29375
Electricity plants	..	..	..	..	..	..	..	..	-2532	-2532	..
CHP plants	..	..	..	-953	-8141	-11358	..	4763	13417	-2271	-9935
Heat plants	-439	..	..	-380	-4523	-19443	..	-11	21215	-3580	-19443
Coke ovens	..	..	..	..	..	..	..	..	..	..	..
Briquetting plants	-59	39	..	..	..	..	..	..	..	-20	..
Liquefaction plants	..	..	..	..	..	..	..	..	..	..	..
Gas works	..	..	..	..	..	..	..	..	..	..	..
Blast furnaces	..	..	..	..	..	..	..	..	..	..	..
NGL plants & gas blending	..	..	..	..	..	..	..	..	..	..	..
Oil refineries	..	..	-418553	421886	..	..	..	..	..	3333	..
Other transformation	..	..	..	..	..	4	..	..	..	4	4
Energy industries own use	..	..	..	-21687	-779	..	..	-4612	-421	-27498	..
Losses	..	..	..	..	..	-13	..	-3366	-4850	-8229	-5
Final consumption	6805	1289	..	101470	60904	29292	..	37451	38101	275312	29292
Final energy consumption	6805	1289	..	90093	24993	29292	..	37451	38101	228024	29292
Manufacturing, const., mining	3449	576	..	1526	13028	*4615	..	13277	9718	46189	*4615
Iron and steel	..	29	..	..	2	1	..	61	..	93	1
Chemical and petrochemical	..	..	..	47	5135	*558	..	2898	8592	17231	*558
Non-ferrous metals	..	..	..	..	2	..	..	..	..	2	..
Non-metallic minerals	3399	469	..	129	1002	..	..	1022	9	6030	..
Transport equipment	..	..	..	..	74	..	..	115	12	201	..
Machinery	..	..	..	..	417	..	..	788	94	1299	..
Mining and quarrying	..	..	..	86	11	..	..	112	1	209	..
Food and tobacco	25	68	..	520	3816	42	..	2750	409	7631	42
Paper, pulp and printing	..	..	..	47	707	..	..	637	18	1409	..
Wood and wood products	..	..	..	86	394	..	..	1282	308	2070	..
Textile and leather	..	..	..	43	638	..	..	572	115	1369	..
Construction	25	..	..	477	616	..	..	565	75	1758	..
Industries n.e.s	0	10	..	90	215	*4014	..	2473	85	6887	*4014
Transport	..	..	..	83722	1132	3229	..	292	..	88374	3229
Road	..	..	..	80569	323	3155	..	133	..	84180	3155
Rail	..	..	..	2592	..	74	..	61	..	2727	74
Domestic aviation	..	..	..	44	..	..	..	..	..	44	..
Domestic navigation	..	..	..	215	..	..	..	..	..	215	..
Pipeline transport	..	..	..	..	809	..	..	97	..	906	..
Transport, n.e.s	..	..	..	301	..	..	..	..	..	301	..
Other	3356	712	..	4845	10833	21449	..	23882	28383	93461	21449
Agriculture, forestry, fishing	100	20	..	1987	876	633	..	763	179	4558	633
Commerce, public services	1464	195	..	90	3061	1543	..	12373	8441	27167	1543
Households	1792	498	..	2460	6897	19273	..	10746	19763	61428	19273
Other consumers	..	..	..	309	..	..	..	..	..	309	..
Non-energy use	..	..	..	11377	35911	..	..	..	..	47288	..

Luxembourg

Terajoules

2017	Primary coal and peat	Coal and peat products	Primary Oil	Oil Products	Natural Gas	Biofuels and waste	Nuclear	Electricity	Heat	Total energy	of which: renewables
Primary production	..	..	..	..	..	5930	..	1544	91	7565	6209
Imports	1670	240	..	118911	29021	5799	..	27241	..	182883	5799
Exports	..	..	..	-1101	..	*-920	..	-5000	..	-7021	*-920
International marine bunkers	..	..	..	..	..	..	..	..	..	..	..
International aviation bunkers	..	..	..	-24608	..	..	..	..	..	-24608	..
Stock changes	..	..	..	359	..	-37	..	..	..	322	-37
Total energy supply	1670	240	..	93562	29021	10773	..	23785	91	159141	11051
Statistical difference	0	-2	..	-114	-1	-10	..	-4	0	-131	1534
Transfers	..	..	..	..	..	..	..	..	..	..	..
Transformation	..	..	..	0	-2913	-3554	..	1692	2760	-2015	-2776
Electricity plants	..	..	..	..	0	-1557	..	446	..	-1111	-779
CHP plants	..	..	..	0	-2894	*-1569	..	1246	2396	-821	*-1569
Heat plants	..	..	..	..	-242	*-206	..	..	364	-84	*-206
Coke ovens	..	..	..	..	..	..	..	..	..	..	..
Briquetting plants	..	..	..	..	..	..	..	..	..	..	..
Liquefaction plants	..	..	..	..	..	..	..	..	..	..	..
Gas works	..	..	..	..	..	..	..	..	..	..	..
Blast furnaces	..	..	..	..	..	..	..	..	..	..	..
NGL plants & gas blending	..	..	..	..	223	-223	..	..	..	0	-223
Oil refineries	..	..	..	..	..	..	..	..	..	..	..
Other transformation	..	..	..	..	..	..	..	..	..	..	..
Energy industries own use	..	..	..	..	..	..	..	-1901	-1	-1902	..
Losses	..	..	..	..	..	..	..	-562	-288	-850	..
Final consumption	1670	242	..	93676	26108	7229	..	23018	2562	154506	6742
Final energy consumption	1670	242	..	92225	26108	7229	..	23018	2562	153055	6742
Manufacturing, const., mining	1670	226	..	769	11136	*1507	..	10814	22	26144	*929
Iron and steel	123	29	..	43	5646	..	..	5803	3	11646	..
Chemical and petrochemical	..	..	..	43	536	..	..	1210	1	1790	..
Non-ferrous metals	..	..	..	..	..	..	..	..	..	..	..
Non-metallic minerals	1547	..	..	129	2771	779	..	760	..	5986	*201
Transport equipment	..	..	..	..	13	..	..	43	..	56	..
Machinery	..	..	..	86	97	..	..	266	..	450	..
Mining and quarrying	..	..	..	43	4	..	..	29	..	75	..
Food and tobacco	..	..	..	129	242	..	..	500	..	872	..
Paper, pulp and printing	..	..	..	..	83	..	..	126	..	209	..
Wood and wood products	..	..	..	..	62	*728	..	54	..	*844	*728
Textile and leather	..	..	..	..	1150	..	..	320	12	1483	..
Construction	..	198	..	172	212	..	..	652	..	1234	..
Industries n.e.s	0	0	..	124	319	0	..	1051	6	1501	0
Transport	..	..	..	79231	..	4574	..	486	..	84291	4574
Road	..	..	..	78629	..	4574	..	4	..	83206	4574
Rail	..	..	..	602	..	..	..	482	..	1084	..
Domestic aviation	..	..	..	..	..	..	..	..	..	..	..
Domestic navigation	..	..	..	..	..	..	..	..	..	..	..
Pipeline transport	..	..	..	..	..	..	..	..	..	..	..
Transport, n.e.s	..	..	..	..	..	..	..	..	..	..	..
Other	..	16	..	12225	14972	*1148	..	11718	2540	42620	*1239
Agriculture, forestry, fishing	..	..	..	774	7	153	..	119	..	1053	153
Commerce, public services	..	..	..	4807	3767	45	..	8107	2449	19175	45
Households	..	16	..	6644	11199	*950	..	3492	91	22392	*1041
Other consumers	..	..	..	..	..	..	..	..	..	..	..
Non-energy use	..	..	..	1451	..	..	..	..	..	1451	..

Luxembourg

Terajoules

2018	Primary coal and peat	Coal and peat products	Primary Oil	Oil Products	Natural Gas	Biofuels and waste	Nuclear	Electricity	Heat	Total energy	of which: renewables
Primary production	..	..	..	..	..	6929	..	1681	99	8709	7309
Imports	1573	205	..	124912	28623	5845	..	27191	..	188348	5845
Exports	..	..	..	-174	..	-864	..	-5011	..	-6049	-864
International marine bunkers	..	..	..	..	..	..	..	..	..	..	..
International aviation bunkers	..	..	..	-26328	..	..	..	..	..	-26328	..
Stock changes	..	..	..	365	..	..	..	..	..	365	..
Total energy supply	1573	205	..	98775	28623	11910	..	23861	99	165045	12290
Statistical difference	0	0	..	45	-1	-28	..	130	0	145	1653
Transfers	..	..	..	..	..	..	..	..	..	..	..
Transformation	..	..	..	..	-2529	-4430	..	1764	3127	-2068	-3654
Electricity plants	..	..	..	..	..	-1552	..	446	..	-1106	-776
CHP plants	..	..	..	..	-2492	-2461	..	1318	2749	-886	-2461
Heat plants	..	..	..	..	-245	-209	..	..	378	-76	-209
Coke ovens	..	..	..	..	..	..	..	..	..	..	..
Briquetting plants	..	..	..	..	..	..	..	..	..	..	..
Liquefaction plants	..	..	..	..	..	..	..	..	..	..	..
Gas works	..	..	..	..	..	..	..	..	..	..	..
Blast furnaces	..	..	..	..	..	..	..	..	..	..	..
NGL plants & gas blending	..	..	..	..	208	-208	..	..	..	0	-208
Oil refineries	..	..	..	..	..	..	..	..	..	..	..
Other transformation	..	..	..	..	..	..	..	..	..	..	..
Energy industries own use	..	..	..	..	..	..	..	-1811	-2	-1813	..
Losses	..	..	..	..	..	..	..	-558	-320	-878	..
Final consumption	1573	205	..	98730	26095	7508	..	23126	2904	160142	6983
Final energy consumption	1573	205	..	97060	26095	7508	..	23126	2904	158472	6983
Manufacturing, const., mining	1573	196	..	766	11589	1274	..	11020	22	26440	650
Iron and steel	123	11	..	43	5892	..	..	5810	3	11883	..
Chemical and petrochemical	..	..	..	43	590	..	..	1285	1	1919	..
Non-ferrous metals	..	..	..	..	..	..	..	..	..	..	..
Non-metallic minerals	1450	..	..	129	2829	832	..	806	..	6046	*208
Transport equipment	..	..	..	..	14	..	..	47	..	61	..
Machinery	..	..	..	86	112	..	..	284	..	482	..
Mining and quarrying	..	..	..	..	5	..	..	32	..	37	..
Food and tobacco	..	..	..	129	257	..	..	533	..	919	..
Paper, pulp and printing	..	..	..	..	95	..	..	137	..	231	..
Wood and wood products	..	..	..	..	53	442	..	58	..	553	442
Textile and leather	..	..	..	..	1125	..	..	338	12	1475	..
Construction	..	184	..	172	233	..	..	691	..	1281	..
Industries n.e.s	0	0	..	164	385	0	..	997	6	1553	0
Transport	..	..	..	84593	..	4992	..	493	..	90078	4992
Road	..	..	..	83905	..	4992	..	4	..	88901	4992
Rail	..	..	..	688	..	..	..	490	..	1178	..
Domestic aviation	..	..	..	..	..	..	..	..	..	..	..
Domestic navigation	..	..	..	..	..	..	..	..	..	..	..
Pipeline transport	..	..	..	..	..	..	..	..	..	..	..
Transport, n.e.s	..	..	..	..	..	..	..	..	..	..	..
Other	..	9	..	11701	14505	1242	..	11614	2882	41953	1341
Agriculture, forestry, fishing	..	..	..	688	8	184	..	119	..	999	184
Commerce, public services	..	..	..	4846	4262	40	..	8143	2783	20075	40
Households	..	9	..	6167	10235	1018	..	3352	99	20879	1117
Other consumers	..	..	..	..	..	..	..	..	..	..	..
Non-energy use	..	..	..	1670	..	..	..	..	..	1670	..

Madagascar

Terajoules

	All Coal	All Oil	Natural Gas	Primary biofuels / Waste	Charcoal	Electricity	Total energy	of which: renewables
2017								
Primary production	..	..	..	269345	..	2839	272184	272184
Imports	14151	39342	..	..	..	..	53493	..
Exports	..	..	..	..	..	..	..	..
International marine bunkers	..	-186	..	..	..	..	-186	..
International aviation bunkers	..	-1741	..	..	..	..	-1741	..
Stock changes	..	1487	..	..	..	..	1487	..
Total energy supply	14151	38902	..	269345	..	2839	325238	272184
Statistical Difference	5	-50	..	-41	0	54	-33	2798
Transfers	..	..	..	..	..	..	..	..
Transformation	-963	-9777	..	-107343	24702	4255	-89126	-82641
Electricity plants	-963	-9777	..	-368	..	4255	-6853	-368
Charcoal plants	..	..	..	-106975	24702	..	-82273	-82273
Other transformation	0	0	..	0	..	..	0	0
Energy industries own use	..	..	..	..	..	-92	-92	..
Losses	..	..	..	..	..	-460	-460	..
Final consumption	*13184	29175	..	162043	24702	6488	235592	186745
Final energy consumption	*13184	26522	..	162043	24702	6488	232939	186745
Manufacturing, const., mining	*13184	..	..	9140	1214	1590	*25128	10354
Transport	..	17764	..	..	..	..	17764	..
Road	..	17368	..	..	..	..	17368	..
Domestic aviation	..	396	..	..	..	..	396	..
Domestic navigation	..	..	..	..	..	..	..	..
Other transport	..	..	..	..	..	..	..	..
Other	..	*8758	..	152903	23488	4898	190047	176391
Agriculture, forestry, fishing	..	..	..	..	..	84	84	..
Commerce and public services	..	..	..	37597	..	712	38309	37597
Households	..	1645	..	115306	23488	2260	142699	138794
Other consumers	..	*7113	..	..	..	1842	*8955	..
Non-energy use	..	*2653	..	..	..	..	*2653	..
2018								
Primary production	..	..	..	*274278	..	3486	*277764	*277764
Imports	*14448	36336	..	..	..	..	50784	..
Exports	..	..	..	..	..	..	..	..
International marine bunkers	..	*-192	..	..	..	..	*-192	..
International aviation bunkers	..	*-1797	..	..	..	..	*-1797	..
Stock changes	..	4595	..	..	..	..	4595	..
Total energy supply	*14448	38942	..	*274278	..	3486	*331154	*277764
Statistical Difference	0	13	..	0	0	0	*13	*3486
Transfers	..	..	..	..	..	..	..	..
Transformation	*-1032	*-8861	..	*-106101	*25075	3973	*-86946	*-81026
Electricity plants	*-1032	*-8861	..	*-324	..	3973	*-6245	*-324
Charcoal plants	..	..	..	*-105777	*25075	..	*-80702	*-80702
Other transformation	0	0	..	0	..	..	0	0
Energy industries own use	..	..	..	..	..	*-90	*-90	..
Losses	..	..	..	..	..	*-468	*-468	..
Final consumption	*13416	*30068	..	*168177	*25075	6901	*243637	*193252
Final energy consumption	*13416	*27390	..	*168177	*25075	6901	*240959	*193252
Manufacturing, const., mining	*13416	..	..	*9234	*1475	2190	*26315	*10709
Transport	..	*18856	..	..	..	..	*18856	..
Road	..	*18142	..	..	..	..	*18142	..
Domestic aviation	..	*714	..	..	..	..	*714	..
Domestic navigation	..	..	..	..	..	..	..	..
Other transport	..	..	..	..	..	..	..	..
Other	..	*8534	..	*158943	*23600	4711	*195788	*182543
Agriculture, forestry, fishing	..	..	..	..	..	*90	*90	..
Commerce and public services	..	..	..	*43461	..	*720	*44181	*43461
Households	..	1667	..	*115482	*23600	2379	*143127	*139082
Other consumers	..	*6868	..	..	..	*1523	*8390	..
Non-energy use	..	*2677	..	..	..	..	*2677	..

Malawi

Terajoules

	All Coal	All Oil	Natural Gas	Primary biofuels / Waste	Charcoal	Electricity	Total energy	of which: renewables
2017								
Primary production	*1237	..	..	60305	..	*6511	68054	66718
Imports	*1061	15732	..	0	0	..	16793	1
Exports	*-206	..	..	-2	0	-74	*-282	-2
International marine bunkers	..	..	..	..	..	..	..	..
International aviation bunkers	..	*-296	..	..	..	..	*-296	..
Stock changes	..	..	..	..	..	..	..	..
Total energy supply	*2092	15435	..	60304	0	*6438	84269	66717
Statistical Difference	0	0	..	-3	0	0	*-3	6508
Transfers	..	..	..	..	..	..	..	..
Transformation	..	*-1905	..	*-32625	17047	*658	*-16824	*-15529
Electricity plants	..	*-1905	..	*-903	..	*658	*-2150	*-903
Charcoal plants	..	..	..	*-31673	17047	..	*-14626	*-14626
Other transformation	..	0	..	*-48	..	..	*-48	0
Energy industries own use	..	..	..	..	..	*-692	*-692	..
Losses	..	..	..	..	..	*-1620	*-1620	..
Final consumption	*2092	*13531	..	*27683	*17048	4784	*65136	*44680
Final energy consumption	*2092	*13145	..	*27683	*17048	4784	*64750	*44680
Manufacturing, const., mining	*1413	*226	..	*5922	..	2064	*9625	*5872
Transport	..	*12689	..	..	..	..	*12689	..
Road	..	*12635	..	..	..	..	*12635	..
Domestic aviation	..	*54	..	..	..	..	*54	..
Domestic navigation	..	..	..	..	..	..	..	..
Other transport	..	..	..	..	..	..	..	..
Other	*678	*229	..	*21761	*17048	2720	*42436	*38808
Agriculture, forestry, fishing	..	..	..	..	..	..	..	..
Commerce and public services	..	..	..	..	..	224	224	..
Households	..	*141	..	*21761	..	2496	*24398	*21761
Other consumers	*678	*89	..	..	*17048	..	*17815	*17048
Non-energy use	..	*386	..	..	..	..	*386	..
2018								
Primary production	*1284	..	..	60880	..	*7490	69654	68272
Imports	*1228	18344	..	0	0	..	19572	0
Exports	*-249	..	..	0	0	-296	-545	0
International marine bunkers	..	..	..	..	..	..	..	..
International aviation bunkers	..	*-339	..	..	..	..	*-339	..
Stock changes	..	..	..	..	..	..	..	..
Total energy supply	*2263	18005	..	60880	0	*7194	88341	68272
Statistical Difference	0	0	..	0	0	0	0	7490
Transfers	..	..	..	..	..	..	..	..
Transformation	..	*-1943	..	*-33333	17429	*666	*-17182	*-15857
Electricity plants	..	*-1943	..	*-903	..	*666	*-2181	*-903
Charcoal plants	..	..	..	*-32382	17429	..	*-14953	*-14953
Other transformation	..	0	..	*-48	..	..	*-48	0
Energy industries own use	..	..	..	..	..	*-756	*-756	..
Losses	..	..	..	..	..	*-1656	*-1656	..
Final consumption	*2263	*16061	..	*27546	*17429	*5448	*68748	*44925
Final energy consumption	*2263	*15663	..	*27546	*17429	*5448	*68350	*44925
Manufacturing, const., mining	*1529	*233	..	*5918	..	*2674	*10354	*5868
Transport	..	*15197	..	..	..	..	*15197	..
Road	..	*15139	..	..	..	..	*15139	..
Domestic aviation	..	*58	..	..	..	..	*58	..
Domestic navigation	..	..	..	..	..	..	..	..
Other transport	..	..	..	..	..	..	..	..
Other	*734	*233	..	*21628	*17429	*2775	*42798	*39057
Agriculture, forestry, fishing	..	..	..	..	..	..	..	..
Commerce and public services	..	..	..	..	..	*559	*559	..
Households	..	*140	..	*21628	..	*2216	*23983	*21628
Other consumers	*734	*93	..	..	*17429	..	*18256	*17429
Non-energy use	..	*398	..	..	..	..	*398	..

Malaysia

Terajoules

2017	Primary coal and peat	Coal and peat products	Primary Oil	Oil Products	Natural Gas	Biofuels and waste	Nuclear	Electricity	Heat	Total energy	of which: renewables
Primary production	78892	..	1417643	..	2187786	50298	..	96876	..	3831494	147174
Imports	803064	..	414244	560851	263506	354	..	25	..	2042044	354
Exports	-16021	..	-611362	-459860	-1162814	-10278	..	-4046	..	-2264380	-10278
International marine bunkers	..	..	..	-16033	..	..	..	..	..	-16033	..
International aviation bunkers	..	..	..	-110003	..	..	..	..	..	-110003	..
Stock changes	2402	..	-12140	4662	..	1709	..	..	..	-3368	1709
Total energy supply	868336	..	1208385	-20382	1288478	42083	..	92855	..	3479754	138959
Statistical difference	-1267	..	-17808	3589	-208290	-4315	..	-14	..	-228105	92562
Transfers	..	..	-18324	20858	..	..	..	..	..	2534	..
Transformation	-794090	..	-1198902	1232791	-604663	*-8940	..	495356	..	-878448	*-8940
Electricity plants	-794090	..	..	-19778	-486145	*-8196	..	494175	..	-814034	*-8196
CHP plants	..	..	..	..	..	..	..	1181	..	1181	..
Heat plants	..	..	..	..	..	..	..	..	..	..	..
Coke ovens	..	..	..	..	..	..	..	..	..	..	..
Briquetting plants	..	..	..	..	..	..	..	..	..	..	..
Liquefaction plants	..	..	18324	..	-42924	..	..	..	..	-24600	..
Gas works	..	..	..	..	..	..	..	..	..	..	..
Blast furnaces	..	..	..	..	..	..	..	..	..	..	..
NGL plants & gas blending	..	..	-103340	99283	..	..	..	..	..	-4057	..
Oil refineries	..	..	-1113886	1153329	..	..	..	..	..	39443	..
Other transformation	..	..	..	..	-75595	*-744	..	..	..	-76338	*-744
Energy industries own use	..	..	-8968	-9686	-229088	..	..	-16517	..	-264258	..
Losses	..	..	..	..	-28982	..	..	-44237	..	-73219	..
Final consumption	75513	..	..	1219992	634035	*37458	..	527472	..	2494469	*37458
Final energy consumption	75513	..	..	1084184	263597	*37458	..	527472	..	1988225	*37458
Manufacturing, const., mining	75513	..	..	113027	257090	*2394	..	257101	..	705125	*2394
Iron and steel	..	..	..	..	..	..	..	..	..	..	..
Chemical and petrochemical	..	..	..	..	..	..	..	..	..	..	..
Non-ferrous metals	..	..	..	..	..	..	..	..	..	..	..
Non-metallic minerals	75513	..	..	..	..	..	..	..	..	75513	..
Transport equipment	..	..	..	..	..	..	..	..	..	..	..
Machinery	..	..	..	..	..	..	..	..	..	..	..
Mining and quarrying	..	..	..	..	..	..	..	..	..	..	..
Food and tobacco	..	..	..	..	..	..	..	..	..	..	..
Paper, pulp and printing	..	..	..	..	..	..	..	..	..	..	..
Wood and wood products	..	..	..	..	..	..	..	..	..	..	..
Textile and leather	..	..	..	..	..	..	..	..	..	..	..
Construction	..	..	..	..	..	..	..	..	..	..	..
Industries n.e.s	0	..	..	113027	257090	*2394	..	257101	..	629612	*2394
Transport	..	..	..	846968	5557	13763	..	1652	..	867940	13763
Road	..	..	..	819427	5557	13763	..	..	..	838747	13763
Rail	..	..	..	40	..	..	..	1652	..	1693	..
Domestic aviation	..	..	..	27501	..	..	..	..	..	27501	..
Domestic navigation	..	..	..	..	..	..	..	..	..	..	..
Pipeline transport	..	..	..	..	..	..	..	..	..	..	..
Transport, n.e.s	..	..	..	..	..	..	..	..	..	..	..
Other	..	..	..	124189	951	*21301	..	268718	..	415160	*21301
Agriculture, forestry, fishing	..	..	..	41563	..	0	..	2102	..	43665	0
Commerce, public services	..	..	..	33587	929	..	..	157406	..	191922	..
Households	..	..	..	49040	23	*21153	..	109210	..	179425	*21153
Other consumers	..	..	..	..	..	*148	..	..	..	*148	*148
Non-energy use	..	..	..	135807	370437	..	..	..	..	506245	..

Malaysia

Terajoules

2018	Primary coal and peat	Coal and peat products	Primary Oil	Oil Products	Natural Gas	Biofuels and waste	Nuclear	Electricity	Heat	Total energy	of which: renewables
Primary production	70023	..	1413781	..	2308652	62903	..	97045	..	3952404	159948
Imports	868468	..	377612	836424	261932	1490	..	72	..	2345998	1490
Exports	0	..	-613604	-664496	-1029002	-16294	..	-5432	..	-2328827	-16294
International marine bunkers	..	..	..	-17225	..	..	..	..	..	-17225	..
International aviation bunkers	..	..	..	-106634	..	..	..	..	..	-106634	..
Stock changes	-8948	..	-18401	9495	..	4370	..	..	..	-13483	4370
Total energy supply	929544	..	1159389	57564	1541582	52469	..	91685	..	3832232	149515
Statistical difference	-3273	..	1523	24147	52955	5	..	5105	..	80462	97051
Transfers	..	..	*-17568	20427	..	..	..	..	..	2859	..
Transformation	-857092	..	-1132853	1133757	-605236	-13325	..	517036	..	-957713	-13325
Electricity plants	-857092	..	..	-15135	-482587	*-12581	..	515513	..	-851883	*-12581
CHP plants	..	..	..	..	..	..	..	1523	..	1523	..
Heat plants	..	..	..	..	..	..	..	..	..	..	..
Coke ovens	..	..	..	..	..	..	..	..	..	..	..
Briquetting plants	..	..	..	..	..	..	..	..	..	..	..
Liquefaction plants	..	..	*19116	..	-41530	..	..	..	..	-22414	..
Gas works	..	..	..	..	..	..	..	..	..	..	..
Blast furnaces	..	..	..	..	..	..	..	..	..	..	..
NGL plants & gas blending	..	..	-105992	103846	..	..	..	..	..	-2146	..
Oil refineries	..	..	-1045977	1045046	..	..	..	..	..	-931	..
Other transformation	..	..	..	..	-81119	*-744	..	..	..	-81862	*-744
Energy industries own use	..	..	-7445	-6982	-142293	..	..	-2506	..	-159226	..
Losses	..	..	..	..	-31236	..	..	-50792	..	-82029	..
Final consumption	75724	..	..	1180618	709862	*39139	..	550318	..	2555662	*39139
Final energy consumption	75724	..	..	1045730	316308	*39139	..	550318	..	2027219	*39139
Manufacturing, const., mining	75724	..	..	102735	310837	*2394	..	273917	..	765607	*2394
Iron and steel	..	..	..	..	..	..	..	..	..	..	..
Chemical and petrochemical	..	..	..	..	..	..	..	..	..	..	..
Non-ferrous metals	..	..	..	..	..	..	..	..	..	..	..
Non-metallic minerals	75724	..	..	..	..	..	..	..	..	75724	..
Transport equipment	..	..	..	..	..	..	..	..	..	..	..
Machinery	..	..	..	..	..	..	..	..	..	..	..
Mining and quarrying	..	..	..	..	..	..	..	..	..	..	..
Food and tobacco	..	..	..	..	..	..	..	..	..	..	..
Paper, pulp and printing	..	..	..	..	..	..	..	..	..	..	..
Wood and wood products	..	..	..	..	..	..	..	..	..	..	..
Textile and leather	..	..	..	..	..	..	..	..	..	..	..
Construction	..	..	..	..	..	..	..	..	..	..	..
Industries n.e.s	0	..	..	102735	310837	*2394	..	273917	..	689883	*2394
Transport	..	..	..	848472	4552	15787	..	1735	..	870546	15787
Road	..	..	..	821791	4552	15787	..	..	..	842130	15787
Rail	..	..	..	0	..	..	..	1735	..	1735	..
Domestic aviation	..	..	..	26681	..	..	..	..	..	26681	..
Domestic navigation	..	..	..	..	..	..	..	..	..	..	..
Pipeline transport	..	..	..	..	..	..	..	..	..	..	..
Transport, n.e.s	..	..	..	..	..	..	..	..	..	..	..
Other	..	..	..	94524	919	*20958	..	274666	..	391066	*20958
Agriculture, forestry, fishing	..	..	..	40965	..	0	..	2221	..	43186	0
Commerce, public services	..	..	..	19281	896	..	..	159642	..	179819	..
Households	..	..	..	34278	23	*20811	..	112802	..	167914	*20811
Other consumers	..	..	..	..	..	*148	..	..	..	*148	*148
Non-energy use	..	..	..	134888	393555	..	..	..	..	528443	..

Maldives

Terajoules

	All Coal	All Oil	Natural Gas	Primary biofuels / Waste	Charcoal	Electricity	Total energy	of which: renewables
2017								
Primary production	..	..	..	149	..	58	207	207
Imports	..	24453	..	4	13	..	24470	17
Exports	..	..	..	..	..	..	..	..
International marine bunkers	..	*-2117	..	..	..	..	*-2117	..
International aviation bunkers	..	*-882	..	..	..	..	*-882	..
Stock changes	..	..	..	..	..	..	..	..
Total energy supply	..	21453	..	153	13	58	21677	224
Statistical Difference	..	0	..	0	0	0	0	58
Transfers	..	..	..	..	..	..	..	..
Transformation	..	*-8109	..	*-48	26	2552	*-5579	*-22
Electricity plants	..	*-8109	..	..	..	2552	*-5557	..
Charcoal plants	..	..	..	*-48	26	..	*-22	*-22
Other transformation	..	0	..	0	..	..	0	0
Energy industries own use	..	..	..	..	..	*-76	*-76	..
Losses	..	..	..	..	..	*-72	*-72	..
Final consumption	..	*13343	..	*106	*39	*2462	*15950	*145
Final energy consumption	..	*13245	..	*106	*39	*2462	*15852	*145
Manufacturing, const., mining	..	*516	..	..	..	*133	*649	..
Transport	..	*12024	..	..	..	..	*12024	..
Road	..	*5621	..	..	..	..	*5621	..
Domestic aviation	..	*963	..	..	..	..	*963	..
Domestic navigation	..	*5440	..	..	..	..	*5440	..
Other transport	..	..	..	..	..	..	..	..
Other	..	*705	..	*106	*39	*2329	*3178	*145
Agriculture, forestry, fishing	..	..	..	..	..	..	..	..
Commerce and public services	..	..	..	..	..	*1026	*1026	..
Households	..	*705	..	*106	*39	*839	*1688	*145
Other consumers	..	..	..	..	..	*464	*464	..
Non-energy use	..	*98	..	..	..	..	*98	..
2018								
Primary production	..	..	..	150	..	58	208	208
Imports	..	27918	..	11	13	..	27943	25
Exports	..	..	..	..	..	..	..	..
International marine bunkers	..	*-2504	..	..	..	..	*-2504	..
International aviation bunkers	..	*-882	..	..	..	..	*-882	..
Stock changes	..	..	..	..	..	..	..	..
Total energy supply	..	24532	..	162	13	58	24764	232
Statistical Difference	..	7	..	0	0	0	7	58
Transfers	..	..	..	..	..	..	..	..
Transformation	..	*-8790	..	*-49	26	2722	*-6091	*-22
Electricity plants	..	*-8790	..	..	..	2722	*-6069	..
Charcoal plants	..	..	..	*-49	26	..	*-22	*-22
Other transformation	..	0	..	0	..	..	0	0
Energy industries own use	..	..	..	..	..	*-76	*-76	..
Losses	..	..	..	..	..	*-76	*-76	..
Final consumption	..	*15734	..	*113	*39	*2628	*18514	*152
Final energy consumption	..	*15712	..	*113	*39	*2628	*18492	*152
Manufacturing, const., mining	..	*860	..	..	..	*140	*1000	..
Transport	..	*14140	..	..	..	..	*14140	..
Road	..	*7190	..	..	..	..	*7190	..
Domestic aviation	..	*832	..	..	..	..	*832	..
Domestic navigation	..	*6118	..	..	..	..	*6118	..
Other transport	..	..	..	..	..	..	..	..
Other	..	*712	..	*113	*39	*2488	*3352	*152
Agriculture, forestry, fishing	..	..	..	..	..	..	..	..
Commerce and public services	..	..	..	..	..	*1087	*1087	..
Households	..	*712	..	*113	*39	*922	*1786	*152
Other consumers	..	..	..	..	..	*479	*479	..
Non-energy use	..	*22	..	..	..	..	*22	..

Mali

Terajoules

	All Coal	All Oil	Natural Gas	Primary biofuels / Waste	Charcoal	Electricity	Total energy	of which: renewables
2017								
Primary production	..	..	..	*155044	..	4078	*159122	*159122
Imports	..	*49832	..	..	..	*421	*50253	..
Exports	..	*-443	..	-25	..	*-1926	*-2394	-25
International marine bunkers	..	..	..	..	..	..	..	..
International aviation bunkers	..	*-2647	..	..	..	..	*-2647	..
Stock changes	..	*-610	..	..	..	..	*-610	..
Total energy supply	..	*46132	..	*155019	..	2573	*203725	*159097
Statistical Difference	..	*-17	..	*3	0	0	*-15	*4081
Transfers	..	..	..	..	..	..	..	..
Transformation	..	*-17200	..	*-63575	15340	*6965	*-58470	*-48235
Electricity plants	..	*-17200	..	*-1457	..	*6965	*-11692	*-1457
Charcoal plants	..	..	..	*-62118	15340	..	*-46778	*-46778
Other transformation	..	0	..	0	..	..	0	0
Energy industries own use	..	..	..	..	..	*-42	*-42	..
Losses	..	..	..	..	..	*-1145	*-1145	..
Final consumption	..	*28950	..	*91441	15340	*8352	*144083	*106781
Final energy consumption	..	*28950	..	*91441	15340	*8352	*144083	*106781
Manufacturing, const., mining	..	*4319	..	..	..	*3312	*7631	..
Transport	..	*18665	..	..	..	..	*18665	..
Road	..	*14998	..	..	..	..	*14998	..
Domestic aviation	..	..	..	..	..	..	..	..
Domestic navigation	..	*13	..	..	..	..	*13	..
Other transport	..	*3655	..	..	..	..	*3655	..
Other	..	*5965	..	*91441	15340	*5040	*117786	*106781
Agriculture, forestry, fishing	..	*989	..	..	..	..	*989	..
Commerce and public services	..	*14	..	*8313	..	*2016	*10343	*8313
Households	..	*1436	..	*83129	15340	*3024	*102928	*98469
Other consumers	..	*3526	..	..	..	..	*3526	..
Non-energy use	..	..	..	..	..	..	..	..
2018								
Primary production	..	..	..	*156706	..	*4078	*160785	*160785
Imports	..	*51369	..	..	..	*713	*52082	..
Exports	..	*-443	..	..	..	*-1980	*-2423	..
International marine bunkers	..	..	..	..	..	..	..	..
International aviation bunkers	..	*-2736	..	..	..	..	*-2736	..
Stock changes	..	*-416	..	..	..	..	*-416	..
Total energy supply	..	*47774	..	*156706	..	*2811	*207292	*160785
Statistical Difference	..	*-13	..	0	0	0	*-13	*4078
Transfers	..	..	..	..	..	..	..	..
Transformation	..	*-19608	..	*-64260	15488	*7661	*-60720	*-48773
Electricity plants	..	*-19608	..	*-1457	..	*7661	*-13404	*-1457
Charcoal plants	..	..	..	*-62803	15488	..	*-47316	*-47316
Other transformation	..	0	..	0	..	..	0	0
Energy industries own use	..	..	..	..	..	*-46	*-46	..
Losses	..	..	..	..	..	*-1282	*-1282	..
Final consumption	..	*28179	..	*92446	15488	*9144	*145257	*107934
Final energy consumption	..	*28179	..	*92446	15488	*9144	*145257	*107934
Manufacturing, const., mining	..	*4418	..	..	..	*3636	*8054	..
Transport	..	*20088	..	..	..	..	*20088	..
Road	..	*16205	..	..	..	..	*16205	..
Domestic aviation	..	..	..	..	..	..	..	..
Domestic navigation	..	*13	..	..	..	..	*13	..
Other transport	..	*3870	..	..	..	..	*3870	..
Other	..	*3673	..	*92446	15488	*5508	*117115	*107934
Agriculture, forestry, fishing	..	*1075	..	..	..	..	*1075	..
Commerce and public services	..	*14	..	*8404	..	*2196	*10614	*8404
Households	..	*1552	..	*84042	15488	*3312	*104394	*99530
Other consumers	..	*1032	..	..	..	..	*1032	..
Non-energy use	..	..	..	..	..	..	..	..

Malta

Terajoules

2017	Primary coal and peat	Coal and peat products	Primary Oil	Oil Products	Natural Gas	Biofuels and waste	Nuclear	Electricity	Heat	Total energy	of which: renewables
Primary production	..	..	..	..	..	77	..	583	209	869	869
Imports	..	..	..	119246	10646	289	..	3229	..	133409	289
Exports	..	..	..	-6320	..	..	..	-130	..	-6450	..
International marine bunkers	..	..	..	-88323	..	..	..	..	..	-88323	..
International aviation bunkers	..	..	..	-5998	..	..	..	..	..	-5998	..
Stock changes	..	..	..	-4452	-526	110	..	..	..	-4867	110
Total energy supply	..	..	..	14153	10121	476	..	3683	209	28641	1268
Statistical difference	..	..	..	174	0	0	..	4	0	177	583
Transfers	..	..	..	..	..	..	..	..	..	..	..
Transformation	..	..	..	-2157	-9698	-46	..	5364	3	-6534	-46
Electricity plants	..	..	..	-2157	-9698	..	..	5328	..	-6527	..
CHP plants	..	..	..	..	..	-46	..	36	3	-7	-46
Heat plants	..	..	..	..	..	..	..	..	..	..	..
Coke ovens	..	..	..	..	..	..	..	..	..	..	..
Briquetting plants	..	..	..	..	..	..	..	..	..	..	..
Liquefaction plants	..	..	..	..	..	..	..	..	..	..	..
Gas works	..	..	..	..	..	..	..	..	..	..	..
Blast furnaces	..	..	..	..	..	..	..	..	..	..	..
NGL plants & gas blending	..	..	..	..	..	..	..	..	..	..	..
Oil refineries	..	..	..	..	..	..	..	..	..	..	..
Other transformation	..	..	..	..	..	..	..	..	..	..	..
Energy industries own use	..	..	..	..	..	..	..	-177	0	-177	..
Losses	..	..	..	..	-422	..	..	-518	..	-941	..
Final consumption	..	..	..	11822	..	430	..	8348	212	20813	639
Final energy consumption	..	..	..	11420	..	430	..	8348	212	20411	639
Manufacturing, const., mining	..	..	..	739	..	..	..	1652	..	2391	..
Iron and steel	..	..	..	..	..	..	..	..	..	..	..
Chemical and petrochemical	..	..	..	..	..	..	..	180	..	180	..
Non-ferrous metals	..	..	..	..	..	..	..	..	..	..	..
Non-metallic minerals	..	..	..	..	..	..	..	32	..	32	..
Transport equipment	..	..	..	..	..	..	..	76	..	76	..
Machinery	..	..	..	..	..	..	..	414	..	414	..
Mining and quarrying	..	..	..	43	..	..	..	4	..	47	..
Food and tobacco	..	..	..	..	..	..	..	245	..	245	..
Paper, pulp and printing	..	..	..	..	..	..	..	90	..	90	..
Wood and wood products	..	..	..	..	..	..	..	7	..	7	..
Textile and leather	..	..	..	..	..	..	..	108	..	108	..
Construction	..	..	..	43	..	..	..	101	..	144	..
Industries n.e.s	..	..	..	653	..	..	..	396	..	1049	..
Transport	..	..	..	8534	..	331	..	..	..	8865	331
Road	..	..	..	7930	..	331	..	..	..	8262	331
Rail	..	..	..	..	..	..	..	..	..	..	..
Domestic aviation	..	..	..	44	..	..	..	..	..	44	..
Domestic navigation	..	..	..	559	..	..	..	..	..	559	..
Pipeline transport	..	..	..	..	..	..	..	..	..	..	..
Transport, n.e.s	..	..	..	..	..	..	..	..	..	..	..
Other	..	..	..	2148	..	99	..	6696	212	9155	308
Agriculture, forestry, fishing	..	..	..	215	..	..	..	47	..	262	..
Commerce, public services	..	..	..	1224	..	31	..	3935	3	5193	31
Households	..	..	..	710	..	68	..	2617	209	3603	277
Other consumers	..	..	..	..	..	..	..	97	..	97	..
Non-energy use	..	..	..	402	..	..	..	..	..	402	..

Malta

Terajoules

2018	Primary coal and peat	Coal and peat products	Primary Oil	Oil Products	Natural Gas	Biofuels and waste	Nuclear	Electricity	Heat	Total energy	of which: renewables
Primary production	..	..	..	..	..	69	..	684	211	964	964
Imports	..	..	..	124418	13427	799	..	2272	..	140916	799
Exports	..	..	..	-14846	..	..	..	-40	..	-14886	..
International marine bunkers	..	..	..	-93169	..	..	..	..	..	-93169	..
International aviation bunkers	..	..	..	-6747	..	..	..	..	..	-6747	..
Stock changes	..	..	..	2805	-1163	-294	..	..	..	1348	-294
Total energy supply	..	..	..	12460	12264	574	..	2916	211	28426	1469
Statistical difference	..	..	..	-131	11	74	..	-7	0	-53	758
Transfers	..	..	..	..	..	..	..	..	..	..	..
Transformation	..	..	..	-215	-12242	-42	..	6379	0	-6120	-42
Electricity plants	..	..	..	-215	-12242	..	..	6347	..	-6110	..
CHP plants	..	..	..	..	..	-42	..	32	0	-10	-42
Heat plants	..	..	..	..	..	..	..	..	..	..	..
Coke ovens	..	..	..	..	..	..	..	..	..	..	..
Briquetting plants	..	..	..	..	..	..	..	..	..	..	..
Liquefaction plants	..	..	..	..	..	..	..	..	..	..	..
Gas works	..	..	..	..	..	..	..	..	..	..	..
Blast furnaces	..	..	..	..	..	..	..	..	..	..	..
NGL plants & gas blending	..	..	..	..	..	..	..	..	..	..	..
Oil refineries	..	..	..	..	..	..	..	..	..	..	..
Other transformation	..	..	..	..	..	..	..	..	..	..	..
Energy industries own use	..	..	..	..	..	..	..	-180	0	-180	..
Losses	..	..	..	..	-12	..	..	-515	..	-527	..
Final consumption	..	..	..	12376	..	458	..	8608	211	21653	669
Final energy consumption	..	..	..	11893	..	458	..	8608	211	21170	669
Manufacturing, const., mining	..	..	..	657	..	..	..	1728	..	2385	..
Iron and steel	..	..	..	..	..	..	..	..	..	..	..
Chemical and petrochemical	..	..	..	..	..	..	..	169	..	169	..
Non-ferrous metals	..	..	..	..	..	..	..	..	..	..	..
Non-metallic minerals	..	..	..	..	..	..	..	22	..	22	..
Transport equipment	..	..	..	..	..	..	..	76	..	76	..
Machinery	..	..	..	..	..	..	..	432	..	432	..
Mining and quarrying	..	..	..	43	..	..	..	7	..	50	..
Food and tobacco	..	..	..	..	..	..	..	263	..	263	..
Paper, pulp and printing	..	..	..	..	..	..	..	97	..	97	..
Wood and wood products	..	..	..	..	..	..	..	7	..	7	..
Textile and leather	..	..	..	..	..	..	..	115	..	115	..
Construction	..	..	..	43	..	..	..	97	..	140	..
Industries n.e.s	..	..	..	571	..	..	..	443	..	1014	..
Transport	..	..	..	9303	..	368	..	..	..	9671	368
Road	..	..	..	8743	..	368	..	..	..	9111	368
Rail	..	..	..	..	..	..	..	..	..	..	..
Domestic aviation	..	..	..	44	..	..	..	..	..	44	..
Domestic navigation	..	..	..	516	..	..	..	..	..	516	..
Pipeline transport	..	..	..	..	..	..	..	..	..	..	..
Transport, n.e.s	..	..	..	..	..	..	..	..	..	..	..
Other	..	..	..	1933	..	90	..	6880	211	9114	301
Agriculture, forestry, fishing	..	..	..	215	..	..	..	43	..	258	..
Commerce, public services	..	..	..	1056	..	27	..	4025	0	5108	27
Households	..	..	..	662	..	63	..	2722	211	3658	274
Other consumers	..	..	..	..	..	..	..	90	..	90	..
Non-energy use	..	..	..	482	..	..	..	..	..	482	..

Mauritania

Terajoules

	All Coal	All Oil	Natural Gas	Primary biofuels / Waste	Charcoal	Electricity	Total energy	of which: renewables
2017								
Primary production	..	3689	..	19448	..	580	23717	20028
Imports	..	53143	..	..	..	*666	53809	..
Exports	..	*-3689	..	..	..	..	*-3689	..
International marine bunkers	..	..	..	..	..	..	..	..
International aviation bunkers	..	-900	..	..	..	..	-900	..
Stock changes	..	*-2062	..	..	..	..	*-2062	..
Total energy supply	..	50182	..	19448	..	*1246	70876	20028
Statistical Difference	..	-17	..	0	0	0	-17	580
Transfers	..	..	..	..	..	..	..	..
Transformation	..	*-10081	..	*-12140	6534	3678	*-12009	*-5606
Electricity plants	..	*-10081	..	..	..	3678	*-6403	..
Charcoal plants	..	..	..	*-12140	6534	..	*-5606	*-5606
Other transformation	..	0	..	0	..	..	0	0
Energy industries own use	..	..	..	..	..	-341	-341	..
Losses	..	..	..	..	..	*-756	*-756	..
Final consumption	..	*40117	..	*7308	*6534	3826	*57786	*13842
Final energy consumption	..	*39362	..	*7308	*6534	3826	*57030	*13842
Manufacturing, const., mining	..	13992	..	..	..	1231	15224	..
Transport	..	*19050	..	..	..	..	*19050	..
Road	..	*19006	..	..	..	..	*19006	..
Domestic aviation	..	*44	..	..	..	..	*44	..
Domestic navigation	..	..	..	..	..	..	..	..
Other transport	..	..	..	..	..	..	..	..
Other	..	*6319	..	*7308	*6534	2595	*22757	*13842
Agriculture, forestry, fishing	..	*3311	..	..	..	..	*3311	..
Commerce and public services	..	..	..	..	..	930	930	..
Households	..	3008	..	*7308	*6534	1370	*18221	*13842
Other consumers	..	..	..	..	..	*295	*295	..
Non-energy use	..	*756	..	..	..	..	*756	..
2018								
Primary production	..	0	..	19805	..	893	20697	20697
Imports	..	70229	..	..	..	711	70940	..
Exports	..	0	..	..	..	..	0	..
International marine bunkers	..	..	..	..	..	..	..	..
International aviation bunkers	..	-988	..	..	..	..	-988	..
Stock changes	..	*-16334	..	..	..	..	*-16334	..
Total energy supply	..	52908	..	19805	..	1604	74316	20697
Statistical Difference	..	2	..	0	0	0	2	893
Transfers	..	..	..	..	..	..	..	..
Transformation	..	*-9760	..	*-12387	6667	3683	*-11797	*-5720
Electricity plants	..	*-9760	..	..	..	3683	*-6077	..
Charcoal plants	..	..	..	*-12387	6667	..	*-5720	*-5720
Other transformation	..	0	..	0	..	..	0	0
Energy industries own use	..	..	..	..	..	-343	-343	..
Losses	..	..	..	..	..	*-810	*-810	..
Final consumption	..	*43146	..	*7418	*6667	4133	*61363	*14085
Final energy consumption	..	*41037	..	*7418	*6667	4133	*59255	*14085
Manufacturing, const., mining	..	14081	..	..	..	*1246	15327	..
Transport	..	*21700	..	..	..	..	*21700	..
Road	..	*21656	..	..	..	..	*21656	..
Domestic aviation	..	*44	..	..	..	..	*44	..
Domestic navigation	..	..	..	..	..	..	..	..
Other transport	..	..	..	..	..	..	..	..
Other	..	5255	..	*7418	*6667	2888	*22227	*14085
Agriculture, forestry, fishing	..	*2365	..	..	..	..	*2365	..
Commerce and public services	..	..	..	..	..	1066	1066	..
Households	..	2890	..	*7418	*6667	1386	*18360	*14085
Other consumers	..	..	..	..	..	*436	*436	..
Non-energy use	..	*2109	..	..	..	..	*2109	..

Mauritius

Terajoules

	All Coal	All Oil	Natural Gas	Primary biofuels / Waste	Charcoal	Electricity	Total energy	of which: renewables
2017								
Primary production	..	..	..	9596	..	517	10113	10113
Imports	37146	70362	..	..	..	..	107508	..
Exports	..	..	..	..	..	..	..	..
International marine bunkers	..	-19302	..	..	..	..	-19302	..
International aviation bunkers	..	-6791	..	..	..	..	-6791	..
Stock changes	-17413	-4906	..	..	..	..	-22319	..
Total energy supply	19733	39362	..	9596	..	517	69208	10113
Statistical Difference	-21	0	..	11	0	33	23	528
Transfers	..	..	..	..	..	..	..	..
Transformation	-18871	-9768	..	-8404	15	10714	-26314	-8389
Electricity plants	-18871	-9768	..	-8385	..	10714	-26311	-8385
Charcoal plants	..	..	..	*-18	15	..	*-4	*-4
Other transformation	0	0	..	0	..	..	0	0
Energy industries own use	..	..	..	..	..	-1116	-1116	..
Losses	..	..	..	..	..	-673	-673	..
Final consumption	883	29594	..	1181	15	9409	41081	1196
Final energy consumption	883	28794	..	1181	15	9409	40281	1196
Manufacturing, const., mining	883	3287	..	1059	..	2618	7846	1059
Transport	..	22268	..	..	..	..	22268	..
Road	..	15084	..	..	..	..	15084	..
Domestic aviation	..	6791	..	..	..	..	6791	..
Domestic navigation	..	393	..	..	..	..	393	..
Other transport	..	..	..	..	..	..	..	..
Other	..	3239	..	122	15	6791	10168	137
Agriculture, forestry, fishing	..	94	..	..	..	84	178	..
Commerce and public services	..	780	..	..	12	3427	4220	12
Households	..	2365	..	122	3	3142	5632	125
Other consumers	..	..	..	..	..	138	138	..
Non-energy use	..	800	..	..	..	..	800	..
2018								
Primary production	..	..	..	8919	..	680	9599	9599
Imports	33304	71023	..	..	..	..	104327	..
Exports	..	..	..	..	..	..	..	..
International marine bunkers	..	-23897	..	..	..	..	-23897	..
International aviation bunkers	..	-6880	..	..	..	..	-6880	..
Stock changes	-14570	80	..	..	..	..	-14490	..
Total energy supply	18734	40326	..	8919	..	680	68659	9599
Statistical Difference	-13	-219	..	-1	1	-45	-277	680
Transfers	..	..	..	..	..	..	..	..
Transformation	-17916	-10053	..	-7889	15	10593	-25250	-7874
Electricity plants	-17916	-10053	..	-7872	..	10593	-25248	-7872
Charcoal plants	..	..	..	-17	15	..	-2	-2
Other transformation	0	0	..	0	..	..	0	0
Energy industries own use	..	..	..	..	..	-1121	-1121	..
Losses	..	..	..	..	..	-657	-657	..
Final consumption	831	30491	..	1031	14	9540	41907	1045
Final energy consumption	831	29611	..	1031	14	9540	41027	1045
Manufacturing, const., mining	831	3332	..	911	..	2643	7718	911
Transport	..	22905	..	..	..	..	22905	..
Road	..	15608	..	..	..	..	15608	..
Domestic aviation	..	6880	..	..	..	..	6880	..
Domestic navigation	..	417	..	..	..	..	417	..
Other transport	..	..	..	..	..	..	..	..
Other	..	3374	..	120	14	6897	10404	134
Agriculture, forestry, fishing	..	91	..	..	..	67	158	..
Commerce and public services	..	814	..	..	11	3452	4277	11
Households	..	2454	..	120	3	3243	5820	122
Other consumers	..	15	..	..	..	135	150	..
Non-energy use	..	880	..	..	..	..	880	..

Mexico

Terajoules

2017	Primary coal and peat	Coal and peat products	Primary Oil	Oil Products	Natural Gas	Biofuels and waste	Nuclear	Electricity	Heat	Total energy	of which: renewables
Primary production	275508	..	4721455	..	1112254	380323	117536	156632	224908	6988617	760966
Imports	253696	34087	26086	2118068	1494916	..	..	7744	..	3934598	..
Exports	-88	-2810	-2723968	-331940	-596	..	..	-6494	..	-3065896	..
International marine bunkers	..	..	..	-33565	..	..	..	..	..	-33565	..
International aviation bunkers	..	..	..	-164627	..	..	..	..	..	-164627	..
Stock changes	-29597	..	-24409	2884	14289	..	..	..	..	-36832	..
Total energy supply	499520	31278	1999165	1590819	2620864	380323	117536	157882	224908	7622295	760966
Statistical difference	-2460	-42	-209514	114508	-69963	*-118	0	-37778	0	-205367	177916
Transfers	..	..	6995	-7099	..	..	..	..	..	-104	..
Transformation	-389651	17418	-2215673	1758170	-1602740	*-80237	-117536	1002794	-214020	-1841475	*-271958
Electricity plants	-339425	-3654	..	-361570	-1379389	*-52850	-117536	934528	-214020	-1533917	*-244571
CHP plants	..	..	..	-17708	-224787	*-27387	..	68267	..	-201615	*-27387
Heat plants	..	..	..	..	..	..	..	..	..	..	..
Coke ovens	-50226	49901	..	..	..	..	..	..	..	-325	..
Briquetting plants	..	..	..	..	..	..	..	..	..	..	..
Liquefaction plants	..	..	1382	..	..	..	..	..	..	1382	..
Gas works	..	..	..	..	..	..	..	..	..	..	..
Blast furnaces	..	-28829	..	..	..	..	..	..	..	-28829	..
NGL plants & gas blending	..	..	-244780	245342	1436	..	..	..	..	1997	..
Oil refineries	..	..	-1972275	1892219	..	..	..	..	..	-80056	..
Other transformation	..	..	..	-112	..	..	..	..	..	-112	..
Energy industries own use	..	-16045	..	-185641	-454487	..	..	-61445	..	-717617	..
Losses	..	..	..	..	..	..	..	-158094	..	-158094	..
Final consumption	112330	32692	..	3041742	633601	*300204	..	978916	10888	5110372	*311092
Final energy consumption	112330	30200	..	2849489	617008	*300204	..	978916	10888	4899033	*311092
Manufacturing, const., mining	112330	30200	..	271218	574484	*49896	..	530874	598	1569599	*50494
Iron and steel	..	30164	..	5677	133081	..	..	19350	..	188272	..
Chemical and petrochemical	..	..	..	16108	118109	..	..	22061	..	156278	..
Non-ferrous metals	..	..	..	..	..	..	..	2988	..	2988	..
Non-metallic minerals	7073	..	..	122019	46554	..	..	41296	..	216941	..
Transport equipment	..	..	..	946	4953	..	..	9587	..	15486	..
Machinery	..	..	..	2417	..	..	..	..	..	2417	..
Mining and quarrying	..	..	..	15941	9905	..	..	43150	..	68996	..
Food and tobacco	..	..	..	8520	16839	*43800	..	8334	..	*77493	*43800
Paper, pulp and printing	..	..	..	10490	28406	..	..	11578	..	50474	..
Wood and wood products	..	..	..	..	..	..	..	..	..	..	..
Textile and leather	..	..	..	..	..	..	..	281	..	281	..
Construction	..	..	..	10879	..	..	..	1998	..	12877	..
Industries n.e.s	105257	36	..	78221	216636	*6096	..	370253	598	777097	*6694
Transport	..	..	..	2135929	1979	..	..	3877	..	2141786	..
Road	..	..	..	2078613	1979	..	..	..	..	2080592	..
Rail	..	..	..	28380	..	..	..	3877	..	32257	..
Domestic aviation	..	..	..	576	..	..	..	..	..	576	..
Domestic navigation	..	..	..	28361	..	..	..	..	..	28361	..
Pipeline transport	..	..	..	..	..	..	..	..	..	..	..
Transport, n.e.s	..	..	..	..	..	..	..	..	..	..	..
Other	..	..	..	442341	40545	*250308	..	444164	10290	1187648	*260598
Agriculture, forestry, fishing	..	..	..	136452	..	..	..	41656	..	178108	..
Commerce, public services	..	..	..	64896	10861	..	..	85208	3870	164835	3870
Households	..	..	..	240994	29684	*250308	..	212951	6420	740356	*256728
Other consumers	..	..	..	..	..	..	..	104350	..	104350	..
Non-energy use	..	2492	..	192253	16593	..	..	..	..	211338	..

Mexico

Terajoules

2018	Primary coal and peat	Coal and peat products	Primary Oil	Oil Products	Natural Gas	Biofuels and waste	Nuclear	Electricity	Heat	Total energy	of which: renewables
Primary production	286281	..	4424714	..	1078887	387086	147690	170521	202165	6697343	756079
Imports	226928	34615	31409	2379486	1615705	..	..	13532	..	4301676	..
Exports	-146	-1249	-2765258	-301926	-468	..	..	-8194	..	-3077240	..
International marine bunkers	..	..	..	-34983	..	..	..	..	..	-34983	..
International aviation bunkers	..	..	..	-181032	..	..	..	..	..	-181032	..
Stock changes	-44478	..	-43204	-19598	35181	..	..	..	..	-72100	..
Total energy supply	468584	33366	1647660	1841948	2729305	387086	147690	175860	202165	7633664	756079
Statistical difference	-1647	6	-128309	-18784	-64494	1	0	-38218	0	-251445	189541
Transfers	..	..	5380	-5494	..	..	..	..	..	-113	..
Transformation	-363360	14483	-1781350	1376599	-1664364	*-82281	-147690	1037570	-190188	-1800581	*-249757
Electricity plants	-317383	-2578	..	-330869	-1431806	*-55083	-147690	967154	-190188	-1508442	*-222559
CHP plants	..	..	..	-15438	-233329	*-27198	..	70416	..	-205549	*-27198
Heat plants	..	..	..	..	..	..	..	..	..	..	..
Coke ovens	-45977	45469	..	..	..	..	..	..	..	-508	..
Briquetting plants	..	..	..	..	..	..	..	..	..	..	..
Liquefaction plants	..	..	1507	..	..	..	..	..	..	1507	..
Gas works	..	..	..	..	..	..	..	..	..	..	..
Blast furnaces	..	-28408	..	..	..	..	..	..	..	-28408	..
NGL plants & gas blending	..	..	-212118	208138	770	..	..	..	..	-3210	..
Oil refineries	..	..	-1570739	1514837	..	..	..	..	..	-55902	..
Other transformation	..	..	..	-69	..	..	..	..	..	-69	..
Energy industries own use	..	-15191	..	-160080	-471757	..	..	-62395	..	-709423	..
Losses	..	..	..	..	..	..	..	-168984	..	-168984	..
Final consumption	106871	32651	..	3071757	657679	*304804	..	1020269	11977	5206008	*316781
Final energy consumption	106871	30383	..	2899348	640454	*304804	..	1020269	11977	5014107	*316781
Manufacturing, const., mining	106871	30383	..	241010	596314	*55726	..	539060	658	1570023	*56384
Iron and steel	..	30365	..	5505	138138	..	..	18904	..	192912	..
Chemical and petrochemical	..	..	..	14014	122597	..	..	21254	..	157866	..
Non-ferrous metals	..	..	..	..	..	..	..	3056	..	3056	..
Non-metallic minerals	7136	..	..	107103	48324	..	..	41663	..	204225	..
Transport equipment	..	..	..	946	5141	..	..	9896	..	15983	..
Machinery	..	..	..	1750	..	..	..	..	..	1750	..
Mining and quarrying	..	..	..	12855	10282	..	..	46206	..	69343	..
Food and tobacco	..	..	..	7581	17479	*48918	..	8474	..	*82453	*48918
Paper, pulp and printing	..	..	..	4473	29485	..	..	11851	..	45809	..
Wood and wood products	..	..	..	..	..	..	..	..	..	..	..
Textile and leather	..	..	..	..	..	..	..	292	..	292	..
Construction	..	..	..	10879	..	..	..	2027	..	12906	..
Industries n.e.s	99736	18	..	75903	224869	*6808	..	375437	658	783428	*7466
Transport	..	..	..	2211349	2055	..	..	3859	..	2217263	..
Road	..	..	..	2157167	2055	..	..	..	..	2159222	..
Rail	..	..	..	26832	..	..	..	3859	..	30691	..
Domestic aviation	..	..	..	576	..	..	..	..	..	576	..
Domestic navigation	..	..	..	26774	..	..	..	..	..	26774	..
Pipeline transport	..	..	..	..	..	..	..	..	..	..	..
Transport, n.e.s	..	..	..	..	..	..	..	..	..	..	..
Other	..	..	..	446989	42086	*249078	..	477349	11319	1226821	*260397
Agriculture, forestry, fishing	..	..	..	142235	..	..	..	44561	..	186796	..
Commerce, public services	..	..	..	63760	11274	..	..	91152	4257	170444	4257
Households	..	..	..	240994	30812	*249078	..	227801	7062	755746	*256140
Other consumers	..	..	..	..	..	..	..	113836	..	113836	..
Non-energy use	..	2268	..	172409	17224	..	..	..	..	191901	..

Micronesia (Fed. States of)

Terajoules

	All Coal	All Oil	Natural Gas	Primary biofuels / Waste	Charcoal	Electricity	Total energy	of which: renewables
2017								
Primary production	..	..	..	24	..	7	31	31
Imports	..	*2534	..	0	..	..	*2534	0
Exports	..	..	..	..	..	..	..	..
International marine bunkers	..	*-138	..	..	..	..	*-138	..
International aviation bunkers	..	*-278	..	..	..	..	*-278	..
Stock changes	..	..	..	..	..	..	..	..
Total energy supply	..	*2119	..	24	..	7	*2150	31
Statistical Difference	..	*10	..	0	0	0	*10	7
Transfers	..	..	..	..	..	..	..	..
Transformation	..	*-830	..	*-21	11	*235	*-604	*-10
Electricity plants	..	*-830	..	..	..	*235	*-595	..
Charcoal plants	..	..	..	*-21	11	..	*-10	*-10
Other transformation	..	0	..	0	..	..	0	0
Energy industries own use	..	..	..	..	..	*-8	*-8	..
Losses	..	..	..	..	..	*-70	*-70	..
Final consumption	..	*1278	..	*4	*11	*164	*1457	*15
Final energy consumption	..	*1186	..	*4	*11	*164	*1365	*15
Manufacturing, const., mining	..	..	..	..	..	*53	*53	..
Transport	..	*1142	..	..	..	..	*1142	..
Road	..	226	..	..	..	..	226	..
Domestic aviation	..	*35	..	..	..	..	*35	..
Domestic navigation	..	*571	..	..	..	..	*571	..
Other transport	..	*310	..	..	..	..	*310	..
Other	..	*44	..	*4	*11	*111	*169	*15
Agriculture, forestry, fishing	..	..	..	..	..	..	..	..
Commerce and public services	..	..	..	..	..	*52	*52	..
Households	..	..	..	*4	..	*59	*63	*4
Other consumers	..	*44	..	..	*11	..	*55	*11
Non-energy use	..	*92	..	..	..	..	*92	..
2018								
Primary production	..	..	..	24	..	*14	39	39
Imports	..	*2555	..	0	..	..	*2555	0
Exports	..	..	..	..	..	..	..	..
International marine bunkers	..	*-142	..	..	..	..	*-142	..
International aviation bunkers	..	*-281	..	..	..	..	*-281	..
Stock changes	..	..	..	..	..	..	..	..
Total energy supply	..	*2132	..	24	..	*14	*2171	39
Statistical Difference	..	*5	..	0	0	0	*5	14
Transfers	..	..	..	..	..	..	..	..
Transformation	..	*-830	..	*-21	11	*233	*-607	*-10
Electricity plants	..	*-830	..	..	..	*233	*-597	..
Charcoal plants	..	..	..	*-21	11	..	*-10	*-10
Other transformation	..	0	..	0	..	..	0	0
Energy industries own use	..	..	..	..	..	*-8	*-8	..
Losses	..	..	..	..	..	*-74	*-74	..
Final consumption	..	*1297	..	*4	*11	*165	*1477	*15
Final energy consumption	..	*1205	..	*4	*11	*165	*1385	*15
Manufacturing, const., mining	..	..	..	..	..	*53	*53	..
Transport	..	*1161	..	..	..	..	*1161	..
Road	..	*230	..	..	..	..	*230	..
Domestic aviation	..	*41	..	..	..	..	*41	..
Domestic navigation	..	*576	..	..	..	..	*576	..
Other transport	..	*314	..	..	..	..	*314	..
Other	..	*44	..	*4	*11	*112	*171	*15
Agriculture, forestry, fishing	..	..	..	..	..	..	..	..
Commerce and public services	..	..	..	..	..	*52	*52	..
Households	..	..	..	*4	..	*60	*64	*4
Other consumers	..	*44	..	..	*11	..	*55	*11
Non-energy use	..	*92	..	..	..	..	*92	..

Mongolia

Terajoules

	Primary coal and peat	Coal and peat products	Primary Oil	Oil Products	Natural Gas	Biofuels and waste	Nuclear	Electricity	Heat	Total energy	of which: renewables
2017											
Primary production	1267330	..	38167	..	..	5481	..	..	..	1310979	5481
Imports	51	..	..	55097	..	..	..	5667	..	60815	..
Exports	-813257	..	-37617	..	..	..	..	-93	..	-850967	..
International marine bunkers	..	..	..	..	..	..	..	..	..	..	..
International aviation bunkers	..	..	..	..	..	..	..	..	..	..	..
Stock changes	-125704	..	-550	..	..	..	..	..	..	-126254	..
Total energy supply	328421	..	0	55097	..	5481	..	5575	..	394574	5481
Statistical difference	-66483	..	0	-4	..	0	..	0	0	-66488	0
Transfers	..	..	..	..	..	..	..	..	..	..	..
Transformation	-130299	..	..	-4002	..	..	..	21698	47296	-65307	..
Electricity plants	..	..	..	-3913	..	..	..	868	..	-3045	..
CHP plants	-130299	..	..	-89	..	..	..	20830	47296	-62262	..
Heat plants	..	..	..	..	..	..	..	..	..	..	..
Coke ovens	..	..	..	..	..	..	..	..	..	..	..
Briquetting plants	..	..	..	..	..	..	..	..	..	..	..
Liquefaction plants	..	..	..	..	..	..	..	..	..	..	..
Gas works	..	..	..	..	..	..	..	..	..	..	..
Blast furnaces	..	..	..	..	..	..	..	..	..	..	..
NGL plants & gas blending	..	..	..	..	..	..	..	..	..	..	..
Oil refineries	..	..	..	..	..	..	..	..	..	..	..
Other transformation	..	..	..	..	..	..	..	..	..	..	..
Energy industries own use	..	..	..	..	..	..	..	-2939	-2311	-5250	..
Losses	-10863	..	..	..	..	..	..	-2919	-2053	-15836	..
Final consumption	253742	..	..	51099	..	*5481	..	21415	42932	374669	*5481
Final energy consumption	253742	..	..	51099	..	*5481	..	21415	42932	374669	*5481
Manufacturing, const., mining	1776	..	..	..	..	..	..	13291	10461	25528	..
Iron and steel	..	..	..	..	..	..	..	..	..	..	..
Chemical and petrochemical	..	..	..	..	..	..	..	..	..	..	..
Non-ferrous metals	..	..	..	..	..	..	..	..	..	..	..
Non-metallic minerals	..	..	..	..	..	..	..	..	..	..	..
Transport equipment	..	..	..	..	..	..	..	..	..	..	..
Machinery	..	..	..	..	..	..	..	..	..	..	..
Mining and quarrying	..	..	..	..	..	..	..	..	..	..	..
Food and tobacco	..	..	..	..	..	..	..	..	..	..	..
Paper, pulp and printing	..	..	..	..	..	..	..	..	..	..	..
Wood and wood products	..	..	..	..	..	..	..	..	..	..	..
Textile and leather	..	..	..	..	..	..	..	..	..	..	..
Construction	837	..	..	..	..	..	..	..	..	837	..
Industries n.e.s	939	..	..	..	..	..	..	13291	10461	24691	..
Transport	1109	..	..	18203	..	..	..	891	..	20203	..
Road	..	..	..	18203	..	..	..	..	..	18203	..
Rail	..	..	..	..	..	..	..	..	..	..	..
Domestic aviation	..	..	..	..	..	..	..	..	..	..	..
Domestic navigation	..	..	..	..	..	..	..	..	..	..	..
Pipeline transport	..	..	..	..	..	..	..	..	..	..	..
Transport, n.e.s	1109	..	..	..	..	..	..	891	..	2000	..
Other	250857	..	..	32896	..	*5481	..	7233	32472	328938	*5481
Agriculture, forestry, fishing	136	..	..	..	..	..	..	226	214	576	..
Commerce, public services	9539	..	..	..	..	..	..	..	14605	24144	..
Households	13835	..	..	..	..	*5481	..	5136	16195	40647	*5481
Other consumers	227347	..	..	32896	..	..	..	1871	1458	263571	..
Non-energy use	..	..	..	..	..	..	..	..	..	..	..

Mongolia

Terajoules

2018	Primary coal and peat	Coal and peat products	Primary Oil	Oil Products	Natural Gas	Biofuels and waste	Nuclear	Electricity	Heat	Total energy	of which: renewables
Primary production	1356322	..	31983	..	..	5481	..	..	..	1393786	5481
Imports	60	..	..	60677	..	..	..	5997	..	66734	..
Exports	-898291	..	-30985	..	..	..	..	-96	..	-929372	..
International marine bunkers	..	..	..	..	..	..	..	..	..	..	..
International aviation bunkers	..	..	..	..	..	..	..	..	..	..	..
Stock changes	11260	..	-994	..	..	..	..	..	..	10266	..
Total energy supply	469351	..	4	60677	..	5481	..	5900	..	541414	5481
Statistical difference	22445	..	4	0	..	0	..	0	0	22450	0
Transfers		..	..	..	..	..	..	..	..	..	..
Transformation	-142533	..	..	-4245	..	..	..	23527	52355	-70895	..
Electricity plants	..	..	..	-4124	..	..	..	1472	..	-2651	..
CHP plants	-142533	..	..	-121	..	..	..	22055	52355	-68244	..
Heat plants	..	..	..	..	..	..	..	..	..	..	..
Coke ovens	..	..	..	..	..	..	..	..	..	..	..
Briquetting plants	..	..	..	..	..	..	..	..	..	..	..
Liquefaction plants	..	..	..	..	..	..	..	..	..	..	..
Gas works	..	..	..	..	..	..	..	..	..	..	..
Blast furnaces	..	..	..	..	..	..	..	..	..	..	..
NGL plants & gas blending	..	..	..	..	..	..	..	..	..	..	..
Oil refineries	..	..	..	..	..	..	..	..	..	..	..
Other transformation	..	..	..	..	..	..	..	..	..	..	..
Energy industries own use	..	..	..	..	..	..	..	-3057	-5756	-8814	..
Losses	-10453	..	..	..	..	..	..	-3151	-2052	-15656	..
Final consumption	293920	..	..	56433	..	*5481	..	23219	44547	423599	*5481
Final energy consumption	293920	..	..	56433	..	*5481	..	23219	44547	423599	*5481
Manufacturing, const., mining	2837	..	..	..	..	..	..	14411	12193	29441	..
Iron and steel	..	..	..	..	..	..	..	..	..	..	..
Chemical and petrochemical	..	..	..	..	..	..	..	..	..	..	..
Non-ferrous metals	..	..	..	..	..	..	..	..	..	..	..
Non-metallic minerals	..	..	..	..	..	..	..	..	..	..	..
Transport equipment	..	..	..	..	..	..	..	..	..	..	..
Machinery	..	..	..	..	..	..	..	..	..	..	..
Mining and quarrying	..	..	..	..	..	..	..	..	..	..	..
Food and tobacco	..	..	..	..	..	..	..	..	..	..	..
Paper, pulp and printing	..	..	..	..	..	..	..	..	..	..	..
Wood and wood products	..	..	..	..	..	..	..	..	..	..	..
Textile and leather	..	..	..	..	..	..	..	..	..	..	..
Construction	2257	..	..	..	..	..	..	..	..	2257	..
Industries n.e.s	580	..	..	..	..	..	..	14411	12193	27184	..
Transport	631	..	..	19271	..	..	..	966	..	20867	..
Road	..	..	..	19271	..	..	..	..	..	19271	..
Rail	..	..	..	..	..	..	..	..	..	..	..
Domestic aviation	..	..	..	..	..	..	..	..	..	..	..
Domestic navigation	..	..	..	..	..	..	..	..	..	..	..
Pipeline transport	..	..	..	..	..	..	..	..	..	..	..
Transport, n.e.s	631	..	..	..	..	..	..	966	..	1597	..
Other	290452	..	..	37162	..	*5481	..	7842	32353	373291	*5481
Agriculture, forestry, fishing	62	..	..	..	..	..	..	245	229	536	..
Commerce, public services	17598	..	..	..	..	..	..	..	13479	31076	..
Households	16383	..	..	..	..	*5481	..	5568	17181	44613	*5481
Other consumers	256410	..	..	37162	..	..	..	2029	1465	297065	..
Non-energy use	..	..	..	..	..	..	..	..	..	..	..

Montenegro

Terajoules

2017	Primary coal and peat	Coal and peat products	Primary Oil	Oil Products	Natural Gas	Biofuels and waste	Nuclear	Electricity	Heat	Total energy	of which: renewables
Primary production	13585	..	..	..	..	9235	..	4086	..	26906	13321
Imports	46	..	..	17161	..	36	..	5533	..	22777	36
Exports	-893	..	..	-1457	..	-1574	..	-1501	..	-5425	-1574
International marine bunkers	..	..	..	..	..	..	..	..	..	..	..
International aviation bunkers	..	..	..	-882	..	..	..	..	..	-882	..
Stock changes	..	..	..	-434	..	..	..	..	..	-434	..
Total energy supply	12737	..	..	14388	..	7698	..	8118	..	42941	11784
Statistical difference	0	..	..	-43	..	0	..	421	..	378	4086
Transfers	..	..	..	..	..	..	..	..	..	..	..
Transformation	-12341	..	..	..	..	-683	..	4853	..	-8171	-683
Electricity plants	-12341	..	..	..	..	..	..	4853	..	-7489	..
CHP plants	..	..	..	..	..	..	..	..	..	..	..
Heat plants	..	..	..	..	..	..	..	..	..	..	..
Coke ovens	..	..	..	..	..	..	..	..	..	..	..
Briquetting plants	..	..	..	..	..	..	..	..	..	..	..
Liquefaction plants	..	..	..	..	..	..	..	..	..	..	..
Gas works	..	..	..	..	..	..	..	..	..	..	..
Blast furnaces	..	..	..	..	..	..	..	..	..	..	..
NGL plants & gas blending	..	..	..	..	..	..	..	..	..	..	..
Oil refineries	..	..	..	..	..	..	..	..	..	..	..
Other transformation	..	..	..	..	..	-683	..	..	..	-683	-683
Energy industries own use	..	..	..	..	..	..	..	-428	..	-428	..
Losses	..	..	..	..	..	..	..	-1843	..	-1843	..
Final consumption	396	..	..	14431	..	7015	..	10278	..	32120	7015
Final energy consumption	396	..	..	12801	..	7015	..	10278	..	30490	7015
Manufacturing, const., mining	230	..	..	2344	..	347	..	2635	..	5556	347
Iron and steel	175	..	..	..	..	..	..	144	..	319	..
Chemical and petrochemical	..	..	..	83	..	64	..	18	..	165	64
Non-ferrous metals	..	..	..	..	..	..	..	2124	..	2124	..
Non-metallic minerals	..	..	..	86	..	0	..	22	..	108	0
Transport equipment	..	..	..	..	..	..	..	..	..	..	..
Machinery	9	..	..	90	..	18	..	22	..	139	18
Mining and quarrying	..	..	..	559	..	..	..	32	..	591	..
Food and tobacco	28	..	..	393	..	238	..	108	..	766	238
Paper, pulp and printing	..	..	..	..	..	..	..	22	..	22	..
Wood and wood products	9	..	..	473	..	9	..	47	..	538	9
Textile and leather	..	..	..	..	..	9	..	4	..	13	9
Construction	..	..	..	..	..	..	..	..	..	..	..
Industries n.e.s	9	..	..	659	..	9	..	94	..	771	9
Transport	..	..	..	9798	..	..	..	72	..	9870	..
Road	..	..	..	9798	..	..	..	..	..	9798	..
Rail	..	..	..	..	..	..	..	72	..	72	..
Domestic aviation	..	..	..	..	..	..	..	..	..	..	..
Domestic navigation	..	..	..	..	..	..	..	..	..	..	..
Pipeline transport	..	..	..	..	..	..	..	..	..	..	..
Transport, n.e.s	..	..	..	..	..	..	..	..	..	..	..
Other	166	..	..	659	..	6668	..	7571	..	15063	6668
Agriculture, forestry, fishing	..	..	..	173	..	..	..	65	..	238	..
Commerce, public services	74	..	..	439	..	301	..	2876	..	3690	301
Households	92	..	..	47	..	6367	..	4630	..	11136	6367
Other consumers	..	..	..	..	..	..	..	..	..	..	..
Non-energy use	..	..	..	1630	..	..	..	..	..	1630	..

Montenegro

Terajoules

2018	Primary coal and peat	Coal and peat products	Primary Oil	Oil Products	Natural Gas	Biofuels and waste	Nuclear	Electricity	Heat	Total energy	of which: renewables
Primary production	15317	..	..	..	..	7964	..	8047	..	31329	16011
Imports	49	..	177	17752	..	33	..	2808	..	20818	33
Exports	-897	..	..	-1281	..	-958	..	-3514	..	-6650	-958
International marine bunkers	..	..	..	..	..	..	..	..	..	..	..
International aviation bunkers	..	..	..	-1160	..	..	..	..	..	-1160	..
Stock changes	626	..	..	115	..	..	..	..	..	741	..
Total energy supply	15095	..	177	15426	..	7039	..	7341	..	45078	15086
Statistical difference	0	..	0	0	..	-1	..	0	..	-1	8046
Transfers	..	..	..	..	..	..	..	..	..	..	..
Transformation	-14816	..	..	..	..	-740	..	5198	..	-10358	-740
Electricity plants	-14816	..	..	..	..	..	..	5198	..	-9618	..
CHP plants	..	..	..	..	..	..	..	..	..	..	..
Heat plants	..	..	..	..	..	..	..	..	..	..	..
Coke ovens	..	..	..	..	..	..	..	..	..	..	..
Briquetting plants	..	..	..	..	..	..	..	..	..	..	..
Liquefaction plants	..	..	..	..	..	..	..	..	..	..	..
Gas works	..	..	..	..	..	..	..	..	..	..	..
Blast furnaces	..	..	..	..	..	..	..	..	..	..	..
NGL plants & gas blending	..	..	..	..	..	..	..	..	..	..	..
Oil refineries	..	..	..	..	..	..	..	..	..	..	..
Other transformation	..	..	..	..	..	-740	..	..	..	-740	-740
Energy industries own use	..	..	..	..	..	..	..	-481	..	-481	..
Losses	..	..	..	..	..	..	..	-1811	..	-1811	..
Final consumption	278	..	177	15426	..	6300	..	10248	..	32429	6300
Final energy consumption	278	..	177	13676	..	6300	..	10248	..	30678	6300
Manufacturing, const., mining	114	..	177	2390	..	348	..	2655	..	5684	348
Iron and steel	54	..	141	14	..	..	..	139	..	348	..
Chemical and petrochemical	..	..	..	42	..	66	..	17	..	125	66
Non-ferrous metals	..	..	35	73	..	..	..	2145	..	2253	..
Non-metallic minerals	..	..	..	138	..	..	..	35	..	172	..
Transport equipment	..	..	..	..	..	..	..	..	..	..	..
Machinery	9	..	..	103	..	19	..	22	..	152	19
Mining and quarrying	..	..	..	443	..	..	..	26	..	469	..
Food and tobacco	33	..	..	412	..	247	..	112	..	804	247
Paper, pulp and printing	..	..	..	13	..	..	..	14	..	27	..
Wood and wood products	10	..	..	482	..	8	..	*47	..	546	8
Textile and leather	..	..	..	9	..	..	..	3	..	11	..
Construction	..	..	..	..	..	..	..	..	..	..	..
Industries n.e.s	10	..	0	663	..	8	..	96	..	776	8
Transport	..	..	..	10635	..	..	..	69	..	10704	..
Road	..	..	..	10635	..	..	..	..	..	10635	..
Rail	..	..	..	..	..	..	..	69	..	69	..
Domestic aviation	..	..	..	..	..	..	..	..	..	..	..
Domestic navigation	..	..	..	..	..	..	..	..	..	..	..
Pipeline transport	..	..	..	..	..	..	..	..	..	..	..
Transport, n.e.s	..	..	..	..	..	..	..	..	..	..	..
Other	164	..	..	651	..	5952	..	7524	..	14291	5952
Agriculture, forestry, fishing	..	..	..	151	..	20	..	63	..	234	20
Commerce, public services	76	..	..	429	..	298	..	2882	..	3684	298
Households	88	..	..	71	..	5634	..	4580	..	10373	5634
Other consumers	..	..	..	..	..	..	..	..	..	..	..
Non-energy use	..	..	..	1751	..	..	..	..	..	1751	..

Montserrat

Terajoules

	All Coal	All Oil	Natural Gas	Primary biofuels / Waste	Charcoal	Electricity	Total energy	of which: renewables
2017								
Primary production	..	..	..	..	..	..	..	..
Imports	..	419	..	..	..	..	419	..
Exports	..	..	..	..	..	..	..	..
International marine bunkers	..	*-43	..	..	..	..	*-43	..
International aviation bunkers	..	*-4	..	..	..	..	*-4	..
Stock changes	..	0	..	..	..	..	0	..
Total energy supply	..	372	..	..	..	..	372	..
Statistical Difference	..	0	..	..	..	0	0	..
Transfers	..	..	..	..	..	..	..	..
Transformation	..	*-172	..	..	..	*68	*-104	..
Electricity plants	..	*-172	..	..	..	*68	*-104	..
Charcoal plants	..	..	..	..	..	..	..	..
Other transformation	..	0	..	..	..	..	0	..
Energy industries own use	..	..	..	..	..	0	0	..
Losses	..	..	..	..	..	*-4	*-4	..
Final consumption	..	*200	..	..	..	*65	*265	..
Final energy consumption	..	*196	..	..	..	*65	*261	..
Manufacturing, const., mining	..	..	..	..	..	*28	*28	..
Transport	..	*150	..	..	..	..	*150	..
Road	..	*128	..	..	..	..	*128	..
Domestic aviation	..	..	..	..	..	..	..	..
Domestic navigation	..	..	..	..	..	..	..	..
Other transport	..	*22	..	..	..	..	*22	..
Other	..	*46	..	..	..	36	*82	..
Agriculture, forestry, fishing	..	..	..	..	..	..	..	..
Commerce and public services	..	..	..	..	..	*18	*18	..
Households	..	*46	..	..	..	18	*64	..
Other consumers	..	..	..	..	..	..	..	..
Non-energy use	..	4	..	..	..	..	4	..
2018								
Primary production	..	..	..	..	..	..	..	..
Imports	..	*434	..	..	..	..	*434	..
Exports	..	..	..	..	..	..	..	..
International marine bunkers	..	*-43	..	..	..	..	*-43	..
International aviation bunkers	..	*-4	..	..	..	..	*-4	..
Stock changes	..	..	..	..	..	..	..	..
Total energy supply	..	*386	..	..	..	..	*386	..
Statistical Difference	..	0	..	..	..	0	0	..
Transfers	..	..	..	..	..	..	..	..
Transformation	..	*-177	..	..	..	*70	*-107	..
Electricity plants	..	*-177	..	..	..	*70	*-107	..
Charcoal plants	..	..	..	..	..	..	..	..
Other transformation	..	0	..	..	..	..	0	..
Energy industries own use	..	..	..	..	..	0	0	..
Losses	..	..	..	..	..	*-4	*-4	..
Final consumption	..	*209	..	..	..	*67	*276	..
Final energy consumption	..	*205	..	..	..	*67	*272	..
Manufacturing, const., mining	..	..	..	..	..	*29	*29	..
Transport	..	*158	..	..	..	..	*158	..
Road	..	*133	..	..	..	..	*133	..
Domestic aviation	..	..	..	..	..	..	..	..
Domestic navigation	..	..	..	..	..	..	..	..
Other transport	..	*25	..	..	..	..	*25	..
Other	..	*47	..	..	..	*38	*85	..
Agriculture, forestry, fishing	..	..	..	..	..	..	..	..
Commerce and public services	..	..	..	..	..	*19	*19	..
Households	..	*47	..	..	..	*19	*66	..
Other consumers	..	..	..	..	..	..	..	..
Non-energy use	..	*4	..	..	..	..	*4	..

Morocco

Terajoules

2017	Primary coal and peat	Coal and peat products	Primary Oil	Oil Products	Natural Gas	Biofuels and waste	Nuclear	Electricity	Heat	Total energy	of which: renewables
Primary production	..	..	212	..	2583	66748	..	15196	4471	89210	83407
Imports	188153	..	..	566850	40337	..	..	21809	..	817149	..
Exports	..	..	..	..	..	..	..	-580	..	-580	..
International marine bunkers	..	..	..	-5595	..	..	..	..	..	-5595	..
International aviation bunkers	..	..	..	-29900	..	..	..	..	..	-29900	..
Stock changes	-1741	..	..	241	..	..	..	..	..	-1500	..
Total energy supply	186412	..	212	531596	42920	66748	..	36425	4471	868785	83407
Statistical difference	0	..	212	-1250	150	0	..	0	0	-888	16687
Transfers	..	..	..	..	..	..	..	..	..	..	..
Transformation	-185666	..	..	-35134	-40186	-1740	..	102928	-4471	-164269	-4721
Electricity plants	-185666	..	..	-35134	-40186	..	..	102928	-4471	-162529	-2981
CHP plants	..	..	..	..	..	..	..	..	..	..	..
Heat plants	..	..	..	..	..	..	..	..	..	..	..
Coke ovens	..	..	..	..	..	..	..	..	..	..	..
Briquetting plants	..	..	..	..	..	..	..	..	..	..	..
Liquefaction plants	..	..	..	..	..	..	..	..	..	..	..
Gas works	..	..	..	..	..	..	..	..	..	..	..
Blast furnaces	..	..	..	..	..	..	..	..	..	..	..
NGL plants & gas blending	..	..	..	..	..	..	..	..	..	..	..
Oil refineries	..	..	..	..	..	..	..	..	..	..	..
Other transformation	..	..	..	..	..	-1740	..	..	..	-1740	-1740
Energy industries own use	..	..	..	..	..	..	..	-684	..	-684	..
Losses	..	..	..	..	..	..	..	-21838	..	-21838	..
Final consumption	746	..	..	497713	2584	65009	..	116831	..	682882	62000
Final energy consumption	746	..	..	477211	2584	65009	..	116831	..	662380	62000
Manufacturing, const., mining	746	..	..	89088	2584	5303	..	42574	..	140295	2294
Iron and steel	..	..	..	..	..	..	..	..	..	..	..
Chemical and petrochemical	..	..	..	2898	..	445	..	3902	..	7246	*85
Non-ferrous metals	83	..	..	3117	..	..	..	5036	..	8236	..
Non-metallic minerals	..	..	..	48811	1063	4556	..	8258	..	62688	1907
Transport equipment	..	..	..	176	..	..	..	709	..	886	..
Machinery	..	..	..	47	..	..	..	2261	..	2308	..
Mining and quarrying	..	..	..	17410	789	..	..	10145	..	28344	..
Food and tobacco	663	..	..	9648	..	210	..	6271	..	16792	210
Paper, pulp and printing	..	..	..	1172	732	..	..	1105	..	3009	..
Wood and wood products	..	..	..	..	..	11	..	119	..	130	11
Textile and leather	..	..	..	2518	..	50	..	2869	..	5437	50
Construction	..	..	..	2383	..	31	..	1073	..	3486	31
Industries n.e.s	0	..	..	907	0	1	..	824	..	1733	1
Transport	..	..	..	238690	..	..	..	1325	..	240015	..
Road	..	..	..	237200	..	..	..	..	..	237200	..
Rail	..	..	..	387	..	..	..	1325	..	1712	..
Domestic aviation	..	..	..	1103	..	..	..	..	..	1103	..
Domestic navigation	..	..	..	..	..	..	..	..	..	..	..
Pipeline transport	..	..	..	..	..	..	..	..	..	..	..
Transport, n.e.s	..	..	..	..	..	..	..	..	..	..	..
Other	..	..	..	149434	..	59705	..	72932	..	282071	59705
Agriculture, forestry, fishing	..	..	..	37567	..	..	..	13388	..	50956	..
Commerce, public services	..	..	..	6219	..	32779	..	20088	..	59087	32779
Households	..	..	..	105526	..	26926	..	39456	..	171909	26926
Other consumers	..	..	..	121	..	..	..	..	..	121	..
Non-energy use	..	..	..	20502	..	..	..	..	..	20502	..

Morocco

Terajoules

2018	Primary coal and peat	Coal and peat products	Primary Oil	Oil Products	Natural Gas	Biofuels and waste	Nuclear	Electricity	Heat	Total energy	of which: renewables
Primary production	..	..	212	..	2762	65471	..	19930	10249	98623	92641
Imports	233775	..	..	553010	35934	..	..	13410	..	836130	..
Exports	..	..	..	..	..	..	..	-1260	..	-1260	..
International marine bunkers	..	..	..	-5595	..	..	..	..	..	-5595	..
International aviation bunkers	..	..	..	-32325	..	..	..	..	..	-32325	..
Stock changes	-26970	..	..	2678	..	..	..	..	..	-24291	..
Total energy supply	206805	..	212	517769	38696	65471	..	32080	10249	871282	92641
Statistical difference	0	..	212	-1333	122	-1	..	0	0	-1000	23346
Transfers	..	..	..	..	..	..	..	..	..	..	..
Transformation	-205976	..	..	-12661	-35813	-1785	..	107996	-10249	-158488	-8618
Electricity plants	-205976	..	..	-12661	-35813	..	..	107996	-10249	-156703	-6833
CHP plants	..	..	..	..	..	..	..	..	..	..	..
Heat plants	..	..	..	..	..	..	..	..	..	..	..
Coke ovens	..	..	..	..	..	..	..	..	..	..	..
Briquetting plants	..	..	..	..	..	..	..	..	..	..	..
Liquefaction plants	..	..	..	..	..	..	..	..	..	..	..
Gas works	..	..	..	..	..	..	..	..	..	..	..
Blast furnaces	..	..	..	..	..	..	..	..	..	..	..
NGL plants & gas blending	..	..	..	..	..	..	..	..	..	..	..
Oil refineries	..	..	..	..	..	..	..	..	..	..	..
Other transformation	..	..	..	..	..	-1785	..	..	..	-1785	-1785
Energy industries own use	..	..	..	..	..	..	..	-590	..	-590	..
Losses	..	..	..	..	..	..	..	-22172	..	-22172	..
Final consumption	829	..	..	506441	2761	63686	..	117313	..	691031	60677
Final energy consumption	829	..	..	487748	2761	63686	..	117313	..	672338	60677
Manufacturing, const., mining	829	..	..	87867	2761	5359	..	43510	..	140326	2350
Iron and steel	..	..	..	..	..	..	..	..	..	..	..
Chemical and petrochemical	..	..	..	2737	..	445	..	3989	..	7170	*85
Non-ferrous metals	83	..	..	2955	..	..	..	5148	..	8186	..
Non-metallic minerals	..	..	..	49988	1136	4600	..	8438	..	64162	1951
Transport equipment	..	..	..	176	..	..	..	724	..	900	..
Machinery	..	..	..	47	..	..	..	2311	..	2359	..
Mining and quarrying	..	..	..	16416	843	..	..	10368	..	27627	..
Food and tobacco	746	..	..	8802	..	217	..	6412	..	16177	217
Paper, pulp and printing	..	..	..	1050	782	..	..	1130	..	2963	..
Wood and wood products	..	..	..	..	..	12	..	122	..	134	12
Textile and leather	..	..	..	2276	..	52	..	2930	..	5258	52
Construction	..	..	..	2469	..	33	..	1094	..	3596	33
Industries n.e.s	0	..	..	950	0	0	..	842	..	1793	0
Transport	..	..	..	246648	..	..	..	1350	..	247998	..
Road	..	..	..	245071	..	..	..	..	..	245071	..
Rail	..	..	..	387	..	..	..	1350	..	1737	..
Domestic aviation	..	..	..	1191	..	..	..	..	..	1191	..
Domestic navigation	..	..	..	..	..	..	..	..	..	..	..
Pipeline transport	..	..	..	..	..	..	..	..	..	..	..
Transport, n.e.s	..	..	..	..	..	..	..	..	..	..	..
Other	..	..	..	153233	..	58327	..	72454	..	284014	58327
Agriculture, forestry, fishing	..	..	..	38861	..	..	..	12118	..	50979	..
Commerce, public services	..	..	..	6400	..	32789	..	20304	..	59493	32789
Households	..	..	..	107891	..	25538	..	40032	..	173461	25538
Other consumers	..	..	..	80	..	..	..	..	..	80	..
Non-energy use	..	..	..	18693	..	..	..	..	..	18693	..

Mozambique

Terajoules

2017	Primary coal and peat	Coal and peat products	Primary Oil	Oil Products	Natural Gas	Biofuels and waste	Nuclear	Electricity	Heat	Total energy	of which: renewables
Primary production	316530	..	2030	..	173163	291136	..	50623	..	833482	341759
Imports	..	..	..	99391	..	..	..	35766	..	135157	..
Exports	-316530	..	-2030	..	-147607	..	..	-35802	..	-501970	..
International marine bunkers	..	..	..	..	..	..	..	..	..	..	..
International aviation bunkers	..	..	..	-1676	..	..	..	..	..	-1676	..
Stock changes	994	..	..	-7900	..	..	..	..	..	-6905	..
Total energy supply	994	..	0	89816	25556	291136	..	50587	..	458088	341759
Statistical difference	0	..	0	470	4	-59	..	4	..	418	50565
Transfers	..	..	..	-8	..	..	..	..	..	-8	..
Transformation	..	..	..	..	-21187	-197533	..	10548	..	-208172	-197533
Electricity plants	..	..	..	..	-21187	..	..	10548	..	-10639	..
CHP plants	..	..	..	..	..	..	..	..	..	..	..
Heat plants	..	..	..	..	..	..	..	..	..	..	..
Coke ovens	..	..	..	..	..	..	..	..	..	..	..
Briquetting plants	..	..	..	..	..	..	..	..	..	..	..
Liquefaction plants	..	..	..	..	..	..	..	..	..	..	..
Gas works	..	..	..	..	..	..	..	..	..	..	..
Blast furnaces	..	..	..	..	..	..	..	..	..	..	..
NGL plants & gas blending	..	..	..	..	..	..	..	..	..	..	..
Oil refineries	..	..	..	..	..	..	..	..	..	..	..
Other transformation	..	..	..	..	..	-197533	..	..	..	-197533	-197533
Energy industries own use	-994	..	..	..	..	..	..	-209	..	-1203	..
Losses	..	..	..	..	..	..	..	-8928	..	-8928	..
Final consumption	..	..	..	89338	4365	93661	..	51995	..	239359	93661
Final energy consumption	..	..	..	83260	4365	93661	..	51995	..	233281	93661
Manufacturing, const., mining	..	..	..	6934	4230	*8046	..	44957	..	64167	*8046
Iron and steel	..	..	..	..	25	..	..	..	..	25	..
Chemical and petrochemical	..	..	..	..	15	..	..	..	..	15	..
Non-ferrous metals	..	..	..	..	1548	..	..	38934	..	40482	..
Non-metallic minerals	..	..	..	..	2254	..	..	..	..	2254	..
Transport equipment	..	..	..	..	..	..	..	..	..	..	..
Machinery	..	..	..	..	..	..	..	..	..	..	..
Mining and quarrying	..	..	..	..	..	..	..	..	..	..	..
Food and tobacco	..	..	..	..	253	..	..	..	..	253	..
Paper, pulp and printing	..	..	..	..	27	..	..	..	..	27	..
Wood and wood products	..	..	..	..	..	..	..	..	..	..	..
Textile and leather	..	..	..	..	..	..	..	..	..	..	..
Construction	..	..	..	6934	..	..	..	..	..	6934	..
Industries n.e.s	..	..	..	0	108	*8046	..	6023	..	14177	*8046
Transport	..	..	..	56712	103	..	..	..	..	56814	..
Road	..	..	..	53874	103	..	..	..	..	53976	..
Rail	..	..	..	..	..	..	..	..	..	..	..
Domestic aviation	..	..	..	..	..	..	..	..	..	..	..
Domestic navigation	..	..	..	2838	..	..	..	..	..	2838	..
Pipeline transport	..	..	..	..	..	..	..	..	..	..	..
Transport, n.e.s	..	..	..	..	..	..	..	..	..	..	..
Other	..	..	..	19614	32	85615	..	7038	..	112300	85615
Agriculture, forestry, fishing	..	..	..	16426	..	..	..	68	..	16494	..
Commerce, public services	..	..	..	1618	10	15517	..	1393	..	18539	15517
Households	..	..	..	1570	23	*70098	..	5501	..	*77191	*70098
Other consumers	..	..	..	..	..	..	..	76	..	76	..
Non-energy use	..	..	..	6078	..	..	..	..	..	6078	..

Mozambique

Terajoules

2018	Primary coal and peat	Coal and peat products	Primary Oil	Oil Products	Natural Gas	Biofuels and waste	Nuclear	Electricity	Heat	Total energy	of which: renewables
Primary production	330656	..	1903	..	173221	298524	..	50123	..	854428	348647
Imports	..	..	..	67429	..	..	..	35636	..	103065	..
Exports	-355555	..	-1903	-1539	-143106	..	..	-37606	..	-539709	..
International marine bunkers	..	..	..	-344	..	..	..	..	..	-344	..
International aviation bunkers	..	..	..	-132	..	..	..	..	..	-132	..
Stock changes	26186	..	..	47	..	..	..	..	..	26233	..
Total energy supply	1286	..	0	65461	30115	298524	..	48154	..	443541	348647
Statistical difference	214	..	0	-308	4576	-88	..	2884	..	7278	50035
Transfers	..	..	..	-8	..	..	..	..	..	-8	..
Transformation	..	..	..	..	-20714	-203377	..	9850	..	-214241	-203377
Electricity plants	..	..	..	..	-20714	..	..	9850	..	-10865	..
CHP plants	..	..	..	..	..	..	..	..	..	..	..
Heat plants	..	..	..	..	..	..	..	..	..	..	..
Coke ovens	..	..	..	..	..	..	..	..	..	..	..
Briquetting plants	..	..	..	..	..	..	..	..	..	..	..
Liquefaction plants	..	..	..	..	..	..	..	..	..	..	..
Gas works	..	..	..	..	..	..	..	..	..	..	..
Blast furnaces	..	..	..	..	..	..	..	..	..	..	..
NGL plants & gas blending	..	..	..	..	..	..	..	..	..	..	..
Oil refineries	..	..	..	..	..	..	..	..	..	..	..
Other transformation	..	..	..	..	..	-203377	..	..	..	-203377	-203377
Energy industries own use	-1072	..	..	..	..	..	..	-392	..	-1464	..
Losses	..	..	..	..	..	..	..	-8928	..	-8928	..
Final consumption	..	..	..	65761	4824	95236	..	45799	..	211620	95236
Final energy consumption	..	..	..	59748	4824	95236	..	45799	..	205608	95236
Manufacturing, const., mining	..	..	..	8998	3058	*7344	..	37195	..	56595	*7344
Iron and steel	..	..	..	..	23	..	..	..	..	23	..
Chemical and petrochemical	..	..	..	..	14	..	..	..	..	14	..
Non-ferrous metals	..	..	..	..	893	..	..	29664	..	30557	..
Non-metallic minerals	..	..	..	..	1689	..	..	..	..	1689	..
Transport equipment	..	..	..	..	..	..	..	..	..	..	..
Machinery	..	..	..	..	..	..	..	..	..	..	..
Mining and quarrying	..	..	..	7138	..	..	..	..	..	7138	..
Food and tobacco	..	..	..	..	272	..	..	..	..	272	..
Paper, pulp and printing	..	..	..	..	24	..	..	..	..	24	..
Wood and wood products	..	..	..	..	..	..	..	..	..	..	..
Textile and leather	..	..	..	..	..	..	..	..	..	..	..
Construction	..	..	..	613	..	..	..	..	..	613	..
Industries n.e.s	..	..	..	1247	144	*7344	..	7531	..	16266	*7344
Transport	..	..	..	48443	74	..	..	..	..	48517	..
Road	..	..	..	42815	74	..	..	..	..	42889	..
Rail	..	..	..	817	..	..	..	..	..	817	..
Domestic aviation	..	..	..	1499	..	..	..	..	..	1499	..
Domestic navigation	..	..	..	3182	..	..	..	..	..	3182	..
Pipeline transport	..	..	..	..	..	..	..	..	..	..	..
Transport, n.e.s	..	..	..	129	..	..	..	..	..	129	..
Other	..	..	..	2307	1692	87892	..	8604	..	100496	87892
Agriculture, forestry, fishing	..	..	..	86	..	..	..	68	..	154	..
Commerce, public services	..	..	..	415	119	15989	..	1465	..	17988	15989
Households	..	..	..	1806	1573	*71903	..	5400	..	*80683	*71903
Other consumers	..	..	..	..	..	..	..	1670	..	1670	..
Non-energy use	..	..	..	6013	..	..	..	..	..	6013	..

Myanmar

Terajoules

2017	Primary coal and peat	Coal and peat products	Primary Oil	Oil Products	Natural Gas	Biofuels and waste	Nuclear	Electricity	Heat	Total energy	of which: renewables
Primary production	21601	..	25437	..	639292	460092	..	40289	..	1186710	500381
Imports	0	..	..	166441	..	..	..	..	..	166441	..
Exports	0	..	-10177	..	*-484435	..	..	..	..	*-494612	..
International marine bunkers	..	..	..	..	..	..	..	..	..	..	..
International aviation bunkers	..	..	..	..	..	..	..	..	..	..	..
Stock changes	..	..	58	1518	..	..	..	..	..	1576	..
Total energy supply	21601	..	15317	167959	154857	460092	..	40289	..	860115	500381
Statistical difference	0	..	-4326	5580	0	0	..	493	..	1747	40289
Transfers	..	..	..	-168	..	..	..	..	..	-168	..
Transformation	-6070	..	*-17892	13292	-113500	*-1839	..	31912	..	-94098	*-1839
Electricity plants	-6070	..	..	-4597	*-113500	..	..	31912	..	*-92255	..
CHP plants	..	..	..	..	..	..	..	..	..	..	..
Heat plants	..	..	..	..	..	..	..	..	..	..	..
Coke ovens	..	..	..	..	..	..	..	..	..	..	..
Briquetting plants	0	..	..	..	..	..	..	..	..	0	..
Liquefaction plants	..	..	..	..	..	..	..	..	..	..	..
Gas works	..	..	..	..	..	..	..	..	..	..	..
Blast furnaces	..	..	..	..	..	..	..	..	..	..	..
NGL plants & gas blending	..	..	-535	558	..	..	..	..	..	23	..
Oil refineries	..	..	*-17357	17330	..	..	..	..	..	*-27	..
Other transformation	..	..	..	..	..	*-1839	..	..	..	*-1839	*-1839
Energy industries own use	..	..	..	-193	-18677	..	..	-2	..	-18871	..
Losses	..	..	-1752	..	..	..	..	-10091	..	-11842	..
Final consumption	*15531	..	..	175309	22680	*458253	..	61615	..	*733388	*458253
Final energy consumption	*15531	..	..	164978	16972	*458253	..	61615	..	*717349	*458253
Manufacturing, const., mining	*15531	..	..	28242	10304	*16791	..	9982	..	80851	*16791
Iron and steel	*2859	..	..	..	386	..	..	..	..	*3245	..
Chemical and petrochemical	..	..	..	..	5328	..	..	..	..	5328	..
Non-ferrous metals	..	..	..	..	71	..	..	..	..	71	..
Non-metallic minerals	*9444	..	..	..	3497	..	..	..	..	*12941	..
Transport equipment	..	..	..	..	125	..	..	..	..	125	..
Machinery	..	..	..	..	198	..	..	..	..	198	..
Mining and quarrying	..	..	..	..	..	..	..	..	..	..	..
Food and tobacco	..	..	..	..	359	..	..	..	..	359	..
Paper, pulp and printing	..	..	..	..	9	..	..	..	..	9	..
Wood and wood products	..	..	..	..	..	..	..	..	..	..	..
Textile and leather	..	..	..	..	330	..	..	..	..	330	..
Construction	..	..	..	..	0	..	..	..	..	0	..
Industries n.e.s	*3228	..	..	28242	0	*16791	..	9982	..	58244	*16791
Transport	..	..	..	68137	6654	..	..	..	..	74790	..
Road	..	..	..	58833	6654	..	..	..	..	65486	..
Rail	..	..	..	36	..	..	..	..	..	36	..
Domestic aviation	..	..	..	9268	..	..	..	..	..	9268	..
Domestic navigation	..	..	..	..	..	..	..	..	..	..	..
Pipeline transport	..	..	..	..	..	..	..	..	..	..	..
Transport, n.e.s	..	..	..	..	..	..	..	..	..	..	..
Other	0	..	..	68599	14	*441462	..	51633	..	*561708	*441462
Agriculture, forestry, fishing	..	..	..	14651	..	..	..	..	..	14651	..
Commerce, public services	..	..	..	..	14	..	..	6131	..	6145	..
Households	..	..	..	14152	..	*441462	..	16235	..	*471848	*441462
Other consumers	0	..	..	39797	0	..	..	29267	..	69063	..
Non-energy use	..	..	..	10331	5708	..	..	..	..	16039	..

Myanmar

Terajoules

2018	Primary coal and peat	Coal and peat products	Primary Oil	Oil Products	Natural Gas	Biofuels and waste	Nuclear	Electricity	Heat	Total energy	of which: renewables
Primary production	26993	..	21175	..	651889	461288	..	53410	..	1214754	514698
Imports	..	..	..	277630	..	..	..	..	..	277630	..
Exports	..	..	-10237	..	-479378	..	..	-8482	..	-498096	..
International marine bunkers	..	..	..	-43	..	..	..	..	..	-43	..
International aviation bunkers	..	..	..	-3087	..	..	..	..	..	-3087	..
Stock changes	..	..	..	..	..	..	..	..	..	..	..
Total energy supply	26993	..	10938	274500	172511	461288	..	44928	..	991158	514698
Statistical difference	16	..	42	-127	10711	0	..	0	..	10642	53410
Transfers	..	..	..	*-134	..	..	..	..	..	*-134	..
Transformation	*-13242	..	-10008	9113	-119662	*-1847	..	42760	..	-92884	*-1847
Electricity plants	*-13242	..	..	-860	*-119662	..	..	42760	..	*-91003	..
CHP plants	..	..	..	..	..	..	..	..	..	..	..
Heat plants	..	..	..	..	..	..	..	..	..	..	..
Coke ovens	..	..	..	..	..	..	..	..	..	..	..
Briquetting plants	..	..	..	..	..	..	..	..	..	..	..
Liquefaction plants	..	..	..	..	..	..	..	..	..	..	..
Gas works	..	..	..	..	..	..	..	..	..	..	..
Blast furnaces	..	..	..	..	..	..	..	..	..	..	..
NGL plants & gas blending	..	..	-575	606	..	..	..	..	..	32	..
Oil refineries	..	..	-9433	9367	..	..	..	..	..	-66	..
Other transformation	..	..	..	..	..	*-1847	..	..	..	*-1847	*-1847
Energy industries own use	..	..	..	-502	-18101	..	..	-8575	..	-27178	..
Losses	..	..	-888	..	..	..	..	-12355	..	-13244	..
Final consumption	*13735	..	..	283105	24037	*459442	..	66758	..	*847077	*459442
Final energy consumption	*13735	..	..	269035	18026	*459442	..	66758	..	*826996	*459442
Manufacturing, const., mining	*13735	..	..	91870	10945	*16825	..	25621	..	158996	*16825
Iron and steel	*2721	..	..	..	410	..	..	..	..	*3132	..
Chemical and petrochemical	..	..	..	..	5658	..	..	..	..	5658	..
Non-ferrous metals	..	..	..	..	76	..	..	..	..	76	..
Non-metallic minerals	*8699	..	..	..	3714	..	..	..	..	*12414	..
Transport equipment	..	..	..	..	133	..	..	..	..	133	..
Machinery	..	..	..	..	211	..	..	..	..	211	..
Mining and quarrying	..	..	..	18576	..	..	..	..	..	18576	..
Food and tobacco	..	..	..	3655	382	..	..	..	..	4037	..
Paper, pulp and printing	..	..	..	..	10	..	..	..	..	10	..
Wood and wood products	..	..	..	6364	..	..	..	..	..	6364	..
Textile and leather	..	..	..	..	351	..	..	..	..	351	..
Construction	..	..	..	54954	..	..	..	..	..	54954	..
Industries n.e.s	*2314	..	..	8321	0	*16825	..	25621	..	53081	*16825
Transport	..	..	..	80189	7066	..	..	..	..	87254	..
Road	..	..	..	57276	7066	..	..	..	..	64342	..
Rail	..	..	..	14488	..	..	..	..	..	14488	..
Domestic aviation	..	..	..	4984	..	..	..	..	..	4984	..
Domestic navigation	..	..	..	3440	..	..	..	..	..	3440	..
Pipeline transport	..	..	..	..	..	..	..	..	..	..	..
Transport, n.e.s	..	..	..	..	..	..	..	..	..	..	..
Other	..	..	..	96977	15	*442617	..	41137	..	*580746	*442617
Agriculture, forestry, fishing	..	..	..	55521	..	..	..	..	..	55521	..
Commerce, public services	..	..	..	17802	15	..	..	12622	..	30439	..
Households	..	..	..	576	..	*442617	..	28062	..	*471255	*442617
Other consumers	..	..	..	23078	..	..	..	454	..	23531	..
Non-energy use	..	..	..	14070	6011	..	..	..	..	20081	..

Namibia

Terajoules

	Primary coal and peat	Coal and peat products	Primary Oil	Oil Products	Natural Gas	Biofuels and waste	Nuclear	Electricity	Heat	Total energy	of which: renewables
2017											
Primary production	..	..	..	..	..	15192	..	6142	126	21459	21459
Imports	953	..	..	55655	..	..	..	10580	..	67189	..
Exports	..	..	..	-161	..	-2950	..	-360	..	-3471	-2950
International marine bunkers	..	..	..	..	..	..	..	..	..	..	..
International aviation bunkers	..	..	..	-1632	..	..	..	..	..	-1632	..
Stock changes	..	..	..	..	..	..	..	..	..	..	..
Total energy supply	953	..	..	53862	..	12242	..	16362	126	83545	18509
Statistical difference	0	..	..	469	..	29	..	97	0	595	6171
Transfers	..	..	..	..	..	..	..	..	..	..	..
Transformation	-953	..	..	0	..	*-5008	..	238	..	*-5723	*-5008
Electricity plants	-953	..	..	0	..	..	..	238	..	-715	..
CHP plants	..	..	..	..	..	..	..	..	..	..	..
Heat plants	..	..	..	..	..	..	..	..	..	..	..
Coke ovens	..	..	..	..	..	..	..	..	..	..	..
Briquetting plants	..	..	..	..	..	..	..	..	..	..	..
Liquefaction plants	..	..	..	..	..	..	..	..	..	..	..
Gas works	..	..	..	..	..	..	..	..	..	..	..
Blast furnaces	..	..	..	..	..	..	..	..	..	..	..
NGL plants & gas blending	..	..	..	..	..	..	..	..	..	..	..
Oil refineries	..	..	..	..	..	..	..	..	..	..	..
Other transformation	..	..	..	..	..	*-5008	..	..	..	*-5008	*-5008
Energy industries own use	..	..	..	..	..	..	..	-295	..	-295	..
Losses	..	..	..	..	..	..	..	-1602	..	-1602	..
Final consumption	..	..	..	53394	..	*7205	..	14605	126	75330	*7331
Final energy consumption	..	..	..	52228	..	*7205	..	14605	126	74164	*7331
Manufacturing, const., mining	..	..	..	3915	..	*1199	..	2171	..	7285	*1199
Iron and steel	..	..	..	..	..	..	..	..	..	..	..
Chemical and petrochemical	..	..	..	..	..	..	..	..	..	..	..
Non-ferrous metals	..	..	..	..	..	..	..	..	..	..	..
Non-metallic minerals	..	..	..	..	..	*1199	..	..	..	*1199	*1199
Transport equipment	..	..	..	..	..	..	..	..	..	..	..
Machinery	..	..	..	..	..	..	..	..	..	..	..
Mining and quarrying	..	..	..	2928	..	..	..	1696	..	4624	..
Food and tobacco	..	..	..	..	..	..	..	..	..	..	..
Paper, pulp and printing	..	..	..	..	..	..	..	..	..	..	..
Wood and wood products	..	..	..	..	..	..	..	..	..	..	..
Textile and leather	..	..	..	..	..	..	..	..	..	..	..
Construction	..	..	..	986	..	..	..	..	..	986	..
Industries n.e.s	..	..	..	0	..	0	..	475	..	475	0
Transport	..	..	..	27746	..	..	..	..	..	27746	..
Road	..	..	..	26168	..	..	..	..	..	26168	..
Rail	..	..	..	..	..	..	..	..	..	..	..
Domestic aviation	..	..	..	265	..	..	..	..	..	265	..
Domestic navigation	..	..	..	1029	..	..	..	..	..	1029	..
Pipeline transport	..	..	..	..	..	..	..	..	..	..	..
Transport, n.e.s	..	..	..	284	..	..	..	..	..	284	..
Other	..	..	..	20568	..	*6006	..	12434	126	39134	*6132
Agriculture, forestry, fishing	..	..	..	15850	..	..	..	..	..	15850	..
Commerce, public services	..	..	..	81	..	..	..	..	..	81	..
Households	..	..	..	88	..	*6006	..	..	..	*6093	*6006
Other consumers	..	..	..	4549	..	..	..	12434	126	17109	126
Non-energy use	..	..	..	1166	..	..	..	..	..	1166	..

Namibia

Terajoules

2018	Primary coal and peat	Coal and peat products	Primary Oil	Oil Products	Natural Gas	Biofuels and waste	Nuclear	Electricity	Heat	Total energy	of which: renewables
Primary production	..	..	..	..	..	17340	..	4832	151	22323	22323
Imports	499	..	..	54573	..	..	..	12416	..	67489	..
Exports	..	..	..	-161	..	-3481	..	-410	..	-4052	-3481
International marine bunkers	..	..	..	..	..	..	..	..	..	..	..
International aviation bunkers	..	..	..	-1632	..	..	..	..	..	-1632	..
Stock changes	-204	..	..	..	..	..	..	..	..	-204	..
Total energy supply	295	..	..	52781	..	13859	..	16838	151	83923	18842
Statistical difference	0	..	..	1190	..	0	..	94	0	1284	4832
Transfers	..	..	..	..	..	..	..	..	..	..	..
Transformation	-295	..	..	..	..	*-5599	..	76	..	*-5818	*-5599
Electricity plants	-295	..	..	..	..	..	..	76	..	-219	..
CHP plants	..	..	..	..	..	..	..	..	..	..	..
Heat plants	..	..	..	..	..	..	..	..	..	..	..
Coke ovens	..	..	..	..	..	..	..	..	..	..	..
Briquetting plants	..	..	..	..	..	..	..	..	..	..	..
Liquefaction plants	..	..	..	..	..	..	..	..	..	..	..
Gas works	..	..	..	..	..	..	..	..	..	..	..
Blast furnaces	..	..	..	..	..	..	..	..	..	..	..
NGL plants & gas blending	..	..	..	..	..	..	..	..	..	..	..
Oil refineries	..	..	..	..	..	..	..	..	..	..	..
Other transformation	..	..	..	..	..	*-5599	..	..	..	*-5599	*-5599
Energy industries own use	..	..	..	..	..	..	..	-242	..	-242	..
Losses	..	..	..	..	..	..	..	-1562	..	-1562	..
Final consumption	..	..	..	51591	..	*8261	..	15016	151	75018	*8412
Final energy consumption	..	..	..	50465	..	*8261	..	15016	151	73892	*8412
Manufacturing, const., mining	..	..	..	3958	..	*1622	..	2110	..	7689	*1622
Iron and steel	..	..	..	..	..	..	..	..	..	..	..
Chemical and petrochemical	..	..	..	..	..	..	..	..	..	..	..
Non-ferrous metals	..	..	..	..	..	..	..	..	..	..	..
Non-metallic minerals	..	..	..	..	..	*1622	..	..	..	*1622	*1622
Transport equipment	..	..	..	..	..	..	..	..	..	..	..
Machinery	..	..	..	..	..	..	..	..	..	..	..
Mining and quarrying	..	..	..	2971	..	..	..	1598	..	4570	..
Food and tobacco	..	..	..	..	..	..	..	..	..	..	..
Paper, pulp and printing	..	..	..	..	..	..	..	..	..	..	..
Wood and wood products	..	..	..	..	..	..	..	..	..	..	..
Textile and leather	..	..	..	..	..	..	..	..	..	..	..
Construction	..	..	..	986	..	..	..	..	..	986	..
Industries n.e.s	..	..	..	0	..	0	..	511	..	511	0
Transport	..	..	..	27746	..	..	..	..	..	27746	..
Road	..	..	..	26168	..	..	..	..	..	26168	..
Rail	..	..	..	..	..	..	..	..	..	..	..
Domestic aviation	..	..	..	265	..	..	..	..	..	265	..
Domestic navigation	..	..	..	1029	..	..	..	..	..	1029	..
Pipeline transport	..	..	..	..	..	..	..	..	..	..	..
Transport, n.e.s	..	..	..	284	..	..	..	..	..	284	..
Other	..	..	..	18762	..	*6639	..	12906	151	38457	*6790
Agriculture, forestry, fishing	..	..	..	14001	..	..	..	..	..	14001	..
Commerce, public services	..	..	..	81	..	..	..	..	..	81	..
Households	..	..	..	88	..	*6639	..	..	..	*6726	*6639
Other consumers	..	..	..	4592	..	..	..	12906	151	17649	151
Non-energy use	..	..	..	1126	..	..	..	..	..	1126	..

Nauru

Terajoules

	All Coal	All Oil	Natural Gas	Primary biofuels / Waste	Charcoal	Electricity	Total energy	of which: renewables
2017								
Primary production	..	..	..	..	..	4	4	4
Imports	..	*1107	..	..	..	..	*1107	..
Exports	..	..	..	..	..	..	..	..
International marine bunkers	..	*-162	..	..	..	..	*-162	..
International aviation bunkers	..	*-172	..	..	..	..	*-172	..
Stock changes	..	..	..	..	..	..	..	..
Total energy supply	..	*773	..	..	..	4	*777	4
Statistical Difference	..	0	..	..	..	0	0	4
Transfers	..	..	..	..	..	..	..	..
Transformation	..	-360	..	..	..	121	-239	..
Electricity plants	..	-360	..	..	..	121	-239	..
Charcoal plants	..	..	..	..	..	..	..	..
Other transformation	..	0	..	..	..	..	0	..
Energy industries own use	..	..	..	..	..	-1	-1	..
Losses	..	..	..	..	..	-32	-32	..
Final consumption	..	*413	..	..	..	93	*506	..
Final energy consumption	..	*413	..	..	..	93	*506	..
Manufacturing, const., mining	..	..	..	..	..	2	2	..
Transport	..	*210	..	..	..	..	*210	..
Road	..	..	..	..	..	..	..	..
Domestic aviation	..	..	..	..	..	..	..	..
Domestic navigation	..	..	..	..	..	..	..	..
Other transport	..	*210	..	..	..	..	*210	..
Other	..	*203	..	..	..	90	*293	..
Agriculture, forestry, fishing	..	..	..	..	..	..	..	..
Commerce and public services	..	..	..	..	..	41	41	..
Households	..	*1	..	..	..	46	47	..
Other consumers	..	*202	..	..	..	3	*205	..
Non-energy use	..	..	..	..	..	..	..	..
2018								
Primary production	..	..	..	..	..	4	4	4
Imports	..	*1074	..	..	..	..	*1074	..
Exports	..	..	..	..	..	..	..	..
International marine bunkers	..	*-162	..	..	..	..	*-162	..
International aviation bunkers	..	*-167	..	..	..	..	*-167	..
Stock changes	..	..	..	..	..	..	..	..
Total energy supply	..	*746	..	..	..	4	*750	4
Statistical Difference	..	0	..	..	..	0	0	4
Transfers	..	..	..	..	..	..	..	..
Transformation	..	-344	..	..	..	126	-218	..
Electricity plants	..	-344	..	..	..	126	-218	..
Charcoal plants	..	..	..	..	..	..	..	..
Other transformation	..	0	..	..	..	..	0	..
Energy industries own use	..	..	..	..	..	-1	-1	..
Losses	..	..	..	..	..	-28	-28	..
Final consumption	..	*401	..	..	..	101	*502	..
Final energy consumption	..	*401	..	..	..	101	*502	..
Manufacturing, const., mining	..	..	..	..	..	3	3	..
Transport	..	*211	..	..	..	..	*211	..
Road	..	..	..	..	..	..	..	..
Domestic aviation	..	..	..	..	..	..	..	..
Domestic navigation	..	..	..	..	..	..	..	..
Other transport	..	*211	..	..	..	..	*211	..
Other	..	*191	..	..	..	98	*288	..
Agriculture, forestry, fishing	..	..	..	..	..	..	..	..
Commerce and public services	..	..	..	..	..	46	46	..
Households	..	*1	..	..	..	49	50	..
Other consumers	..	*190	..	..	..	3	*193	..
Non-energy use	..	..	..	..	..	..	..	..

Nepal

Terajoules

	All Coal	All Oil	Natural Gas	Primary biofuels / Waste	Charcoal	Electricity	Total energy	of which: renewables
2017								
Primary production	603	..	..	421143	..	16700	438446	437843
Imports	32507	97269	..	..	..	9295	139071	..
Exports	..	..	..	..	..	-11	-11	..
International marine bunkers	..	..	..	..	..	..	..	..
International aviation bunkers	..	-5601	..	..	..	..	-5601	..
Stock changes	..	..	..	..	..	..	..	..
Total energy supply	33109	91669	..	421143	..	25985	571905	437843
Statistical Difference	0	-2422	..	-3	0	36	-2389	16697
Transfers	..	..	..	..	..	..	..	..
Transformation	..	-1	..	-899	325	0	-575	-574
Electricity plants	..	-1	..	..	..	0	-1	..
Charcoal plants	..	..	..	-899	325	..	-574	-574
Other transformation	..	0	..	0	..	..	0	0
Energy industries own use	..	..	..	..	..	-198	-198	..
Losses	..	..	..	..	..	-5195	-5195	..
Final consumption	33109	94089	..	*420247	325	20556	*568326	*420572
Final energy consumption	33109	93647	..	*420247	325	20556	*567884	*420572
Manufacturing, const., mining	33009	862	..	14334	89	7236	55529	14423
Transport	..	62553	..	..	..	18	62571	..
Road	..	61494	..	..	..	..	61494	..
Domestic aviation	..	1058	..	..	..	..	1058	..
Domestic navigation	..	..	..	..	..	..	..	..
Other transport	..	..	..	..	..	18	18	..
Other	100	30233	..	*405913	236	13302	*449784	*406149
Agriculture, forestry, fishing	..	10535	..	..	..	454	10989	..
Commerce and public services	..	8409	..	*2295	236	2416	13356	*2531
Households	100	11289	..	*403618	..	9594	*424602	*403618
Other consumers	..	..	..	..	..	839	839	..
Non-energy use	..	442	..	..	..	..	442	..
2018								
Primary production	628	..	..	427985	..	17687	446300	445672
Imports	34667	107353	..	..	..	10127	152147	..
Exports	..	..	..	..	..	-126	-126	..
International marine bunkers	..	..	..	..	..	..	..	..
International aviation bunkers	..	-5468	..	..	..	..	-5468	..
Stock changes	..	..	..	..	..	..	..	..
Total energy supply	35295	101885	..	427985	..	27688	592853	445672
Statistical Difference	0	-2932	..	-4	0	-101	-3037	17682
Transfers	..	..	..	..	..	..	..	..
Transformation	..	-1	..	-914	325	0	-590	-590
Electricity plants	..	-1	..	..	..	0	-1	..
Charcoal plants	..	..	..	-914	325	..	-590	-590
Other transformation	..	0	..	0	..	..	0	0
Energy industries own use	..	..	..	..	..	-213	-213	..
Losses	..	..	..	..	..	-4165	-4165	..
Final consumption	35295	104816	..	*427076	325	23411	*590922	*427400
Final energy consumption	35295	104333	..	*427076	325	23411	*590440	*427400
Manufacturing, const., mining	35195	991	..	*14388	89	8777	59439	*14476
Transport	..	69138	..	..	..	18	69156	..
Road	..	67771	..	..	..	..	67771	..
Domestic aviation	..	1367	..	..	..	..	1367	..
Domestic navigation	..	..	..	..	..	..	..	..
Other transport	..	..	..	..	..	18	18	..
Other	100	34204	..	*412688	236	14616	*461845	*412924
Agriculture, forestry, fishing	..	11395	..	..	..	637	12032	..
Commerce and public services	..	9777	..	*2334	236	2696	15044	*2570
Households	100	13032	..	*410354	..	10238	*433725	*410354
Other consumers	..	..	..	..	..	1044	1044	..
Non-energy use	..	482	..	..	..	..	482	..

Netherlands

Terajoules

2017	Primary coal and peat	Coal and peat products	Primary Oil	Oil Products	Natural Gas	Biofuels and waste	Nuclear	Electricity	Heat	Total energy	of which: renewables
Primary production	..	..	61604	..	1387107	201848	36742	46213	9970	1743484	222060
Imports	390108	3975	2581451	3839983	1627155	28590	..	80849	..	8552111	19039
Exports	..	-6976	-36747	-4743562	-1683891	-72812	..	-68227	..	-6612215	-71202
International marine bunkers	..	..	..	-481386	-153	..	..	..	..	-481539	..
International aviation bunkers	..	..	..	-170358	..	..	..	..	..	-170358	..
Stock changes	-4946	2281	13768	79682	-31376	-3908	..	..	..	55500	-3908
Total energy supply	385162	-720	2620075	-1475641	1298842	153718	36742	58835	9970	3086983	165990
Statistical difference	-46	29	299	-15158	-3305	56	0	-2556	-1	-20682	46269
Transfers	..	..	82967	-35024	..	..	..	..	..	47943	..
Transformation	-378915	38473	-2612631	2579805	-405120	-105134	-36742	375937	97748	-446579	-68413
Electricity plants	-228778	-17941	..	..	-170025	*-11789	-36742	216490	-14988	-263773	*-11789
CHP plants	-39203	-7474	..	-12192	-233608	-89049	..	159448	99074	-123003	-52327
Heat plants	..	..	..	-10494	-5942	*-1196	..	..	13662	-3970	*-1196
Coke ovens	-72020	76829	..	..	..	..	..	..	..	4809	..
Briquetting plants	..	..	..	..	..	..	..	..	..	..	..
Liquefaction plants	..	..	..	..	..	..	..	..	..	..	..
Gas works	..	..	..	..	..	..	..	..	..	..	..
Blast furnaces	-38915	-12942	..	..	..	..	..	..	..	-51856	..
NGL plants & gas blending	..	..	-4884	-1023	4455	-3100	..	..	..	-4552	-3100
Oil refineries	..	..	-2564671	2572737	..	..	..	..	..	8066	..
Other transformation	..	..	-43272	30776	..	..	..	..	..	-12495	..
Energy industries own use	..	-8928	..	-96426	-57482	..	..	-34369	-10919	-208124	..
Losses	..	..	..	..	..	..	..	-19490	-4030	-23520	..
Final consumption	6293	28796	90112	987872	839545	*48528	..	383468	92770	2477385	*51308
Final energy consumption	6162	28711	..	614081	732405	*48528	..	383468	92770	1906124	*51308
Manufacturing, const., mining	6162	28591	..	145907	221286	*5572	..	128732	64651	600900	*5572
Iron and steel	4030	26788	..	219	11128	..	..	9306	6	51477	..
Chemical and petrochemical	..	..	..	126714	89797	..	..	46235	54801	317546	..
Non-ferrous metals	..	..	..	..	3089	..	..	7182	1065	11336	..
Non-metallic minerals	800	1026	..	550	17678	..	..	4550	4	24609	..
Transport equipment	..	..	..	172	2096	..	..	2120	3	4392	..
Machinery	..	..	..	133	11079	..	..	11704	39	22955	..
Mining and quarrying	180	..	..	129	2006	..	..	893	1709	4917	..
Food and tobacco	1151	..	..	47	57298	429	..	25243	4966	89135	429
Paper, pulp and printing	..	..	..	0	13698	216	..	8975	1795	24684	216
Wood and wood products	..	..	..	0	459	*968	..	562	0	1989	*968
Textile and leather	..	..	..	..	2580	..	..	1332	169	4081	..
Construction	..	57	..	17895	4801	713	..	3506	..	26972	713
Industries n.e.s	0	720	..	47	5578	*3246	..	7124	94	16810	*3246
Transport	..	..	..	434204	2437	12794	..	7189	..	456624	12794
Road	..	..	..	419953	2437	12757	..	1555	..	436702	12757
Rail	..	..	..	1124	..	37	..	5634	..	6795	37
Domestic aviation	..	..	..	441	..	..	..	..	..	441	..
Domestic navigation	..	..	..	12685	..	..	..	..	..	12685	..
Pipeline transport	..	..	..	..	..	..	..	..	..	..	..
Transport, n.e.s	..	..	..	..	..	..	..	..	..	..	..
Other	..	120	..	33970	508682	*30163	..	247547	28119	848600	*32943
Agriculture, forestry, fishing	..	..	..	22421	89609	*6412	..	34384	6747	159574	9459
Commerce, public services	..	80	..	7254	130632	7356	..	131814	8520	285656	6178
Households	..	40	..	1604	288294	*16395	..	81349	12852	400534	*17306
Other consumers	..	..	..	2690	146	..	..	..	..	2836	..
Non-energy use	131	86	90112	373792	107141	..	..	..	..	571261	..

Netherlands

Terajoules

2018	Primary coal and peat	Coal and peat products	Primary Oil	Oil Products	Natural Gas	Biofuels and waste	Nuclear	Electricity	Heat	Total energy	of which: renewables
Primary production	..	..	61985	..	1162782	199140	37962	51581	10465	1523914	225552
Imports	344672	3895	2630592	3721878	1827315	29480	..	96318	..	8654150	20755
Exports	..	-4410	-36210	-4664829	-1634850	-58721	..	-67626	..	-6466645	-57111
International marine bunkers	..	..	..	-462051	-486	-699	..	..	..	-463237	-699
International aviation bunkers	..	..	..	-172387	..	..	..	..	..	-172387	..
Stock changes	1611	-1140	-10976	41870	-68194	-6382	..	..	..	-43210	-6382
Total energy supply	346283	-1654	2645391	-1535518	1286567	162818	37962	80273	10465	3032585	182115
Statistical difference	26	1	122	-18889	13319	-318	0	-1274	-2	-7016	51263
Transfers	..	..	90118	-45461	..	..	..	..	..	44657	..
Transformation	-340306	39621	-2662744	2642362	-392883	-102311	-37962	360497	93755	-399971	-66855
Electricity plants	-205647	-15239	..	..	-170213	*-4456	-37962	206899	-6762	-233379	*-4456
CHP plants	-25802	-8815	..	-15558	-223989	-93014	..	153598	91077	-122503	-57558
Heat plants	..	..	..	-6435	-3335	*-1466	..	..	9440	-1796	*-1466
Coke ovens	-71938	76834	..	..	..	..	..	..	..	4896	..
Briquetting plants	..	..	..	..	..	..	..	..	..	..	..
Liquefaction plants	..	..	..	..	..	..	..	..	..	..	..
Gas works	..	..	..	..	..	..	..	..	..	..	..
Blast furnaces	-36920	-13159	..	..	..	..	..	..	..	-50079	..
NGL plants & gas blending	..	..	-13288	7785	4652	-3375	..	..	..	-4226	-3375
Oil refineries	..	..	-2608932	2629767	..	..	..	..	..	20835	..
Other transformation	..	..	-40708	26803	..	..	..	..	..	-13905	..
Energy industries own use	..	-8716	..	-93609	-62886	..	..	-34160	-11442	-210813	..
Losses	..	..	..	..	..	..	..	-19202	-3964	-23166	..
Final consumption	5950	29250	72644	986664	817479	*60824	..	388681	88816	2450308	*63998
Final energy consumption	5791	29079	..	619832	716144	*60824	..	388681	88816	1909168	*63998
Manufacturing, const., mining	5791	28959	..	149826	214102	*7706	..	129805	59022	595211	*7706
Iron and steel	3829	27179	..	219	10894	..	..	8993	6	51120	..
Chemical and petrochemical	..	..	..	129486	84716	192	..	46530	47228	308151	192
Non-ferrous metals	..	..	..	43	2977	..	..	8057	1173	12250	..
Non-metallic minerals	800	1083	..	348	19038	..	..	4802	..	26071	..
Transport equipment	..	..	..	262	2291	..	..	2581	3	5137	..
Machinery	..	..	..	138	8388	..	..	11326	44	19895	..
Mining and quarrying	..	..	..	129	2240	..	..	983	1936	5288	..
Food and tobacco	1162	..	..	133	57844	2079	..	24689	3182	89089	2079
Paper, pulp and printing	..	..	..	..	12038	377	..	8089	4444	24948	377
Wood and wood products	..	..	..	..	577	*1311	..	522	..	*2410	*1311
Textile and leather	..	..	..	..	2424	..	..	1451	807	4682	..
Construction	..	57	..	19020	5060	1279	..	3733	..	29149	1279
Industries n.e.s	0	640	..	47	5617	*2469	..	8050	199	17022	*2469
Transport	..	..	..	437020	2644	20976	..	7639	..	468279	20976
Road	..	..	..	422965	2644	20828	..	1818	..	448255	20828
Rail	..	..	..	958	..	74	..	5821	..	6853	74
Domestic aviation	..	..	..	485	..	..	..	..	..	485	..
Domestic navigation	..	..	..	12611	..	74	..	..	..	12685	74
Pipeline transport	..	..	..	..	..	..	..	..	..	..	..
Transport, n.e.s	..	..	..	..	..	..	..	..	..	..	..
Other	..	120	..	32986	499398	*32142	..	251237	29794	845678	*35316
Agriculture, forestry, fishing	..	..	..	21841	86481	*7658	..	35676	7430	159086	11389
Commerce, public services	..	80	..	6936	126386	8033	..	132865	8937	283238	6551
Households	..	40	..	1604	286385	*16451	..	82696	13427	400603	*17376
Other consumers	..	..	..	2605	146	..	..	..	..	2751	..
Non-energy use	158	171	72644	366832	101335	..	..	..	..	541140	..

New Caledonia

Terajoules

2017	Primary coal and peat	Coal and peat products	Primary Oil	Oil Products	Natural Gas	Biofuels and waste	Nuclear	Electricity	Heat	Total energy	of which: renewables
Primary production	..	..	..	..	..	120	..	1562	141	1823	1823
Imports	27180	..	..	38914	..	2	..	..	..	66096	2
Exports	..	..	..	..	..	..	..	..	..	..	..
International marine bunkers	..	..	..	-297	..	..	..	..	..	-297	..
International aviation bunkers	..	..	..	-1151	..	..	..	..	..	-1151	..
Stock changes	3081	..	..	-1666	..	..	..	..	..	1415	..
Total energy supply	30261	..	..	35801	..	122	..	1562	141	67887	1825
Statistical difference	-159	..	..	-307	..	0	..	-2	0	-467	1562
Transfers	..	..	..	..	..	..	..	..	..	..	..
Transformation	-19141	..	..	-17058	..	*-20	..	10059	..	-26160	*-20
Electricity plants	-19141	..	..	-17058	..	*-5	..	10059	..	-26144	*-5
CHP plants	..	..	..	..	..	..	..	..	..	..	..
Heat plants	..	..	..	..	..	..	..	..	..	..	..
Coke ovens	..	..	..	..	..	..	..	..	..	..	..
Briquetting plants	..	..	..	..	..	..	..	..	..	..	..
Liquefaction plants	..	..	..	..	..	..	..	..	..	..	..
Gas works	..	..	..	..	..	..	..	..	..	..	..
Blast furnaces	..	..	..	..	..	..	..	..	..	..	..
NGL plants & gas blending	..	..	..	..	..	..	..	..	..	..	..
Oil refineries	..	..	..	..	..	..	..	..	..	..	..
Other transformation	..	..	..	..	..	*-15	..	..	..	*-15	*-15
Energy industries own use	..	..	..	..	..	..	..	-2	..	-2	..
Losses	..	..	..	..	..	..	..	-244	..	-244	..
Final consumption	11279	..	..	19050	..	*101	..	11378	141	41949	242
Final energy consumption	4865	..	..	18399	..	*101	..	11378	141	34883	242
Manufacturing, const., mining	4865	..	..	8327	..	..	..	8957	..	22148	..
Iron and steel	..	..	..	..	..	..	..	..	..	..	..
Chemical and petrochemical	..	..	..	..	..	..	..	..	..	..	..
Non-ferrous metals	..	..	..	*2222	..	..	..	8505	..	10727	..
Non-metallic minerals	4865	..	..	2759	..	..	..	..	..	7624	..
Transport equipment	..	..	..	..	..	..	..	..	..	..	..
Machinery	..	..	..	..	..	..	..	..	..	..	..
Mining and quarrying	..	..	..	2804	..	..	..	112	..	2916	..
Food and tobacco	..	..	..	..	..	..	..	..	..	..	..
Paper, pulp and printing	..	..	..	..	..	..	..	..	..	..	..
Wood and wood products	..	..	..	..	..	..	..	..	..	..	..
Textile and leather	..	..	..	..	..	..	..	..	..	..	..
Construction	..	..	..	..	..	..	..	..	..	..	..
Industries n.e.s	0	..	..	542	..	..	..	339	..	882	..
Transport	..	..	..	9319	..	..	..	..	..	9319	..
Road	..	..	..	8371	..	..	..	..	..	8371	..
Rail	..	..	..	..	..	..	..	..	..	..	..
Domestic aviation	..	..	..	265	..	..	..	..	..	265	..
Domestic navigation	..	..	..	683	..	..	..	..	..	683	..
Pipeline transport	..	..	..	..	..	..	..	..	..	..	..
Transport, n.e.s	..	..	..	..	..	..	..	..	..	..	..
Other	..	..	..	753	..	*101	..	2421	141	3416	242
Agriculture, forestry, fishing	..	..	..	211	..	..	..	..	..	211	..
Commerce, public services	..	..	..	164	..	..	..	1360	141	1665	141
Households	..	..	..	378	..	*101	..	1061	..	1541	*101
Other consumers	..	..	..	..	..	..	..	..	..	..	..
Non-energy use	6414	..	..	*651	..	..	..	..	..	7065	..

New Caledonia

Terajoules

2018	Primary coal and peat	Coal and peat products	Primary Oil	Oil Products	Natural Gas	Biofuels and waste	Nuclear	Electricity	Heat	Total energy	of which: renewables
Primary production	..	..	..	..	..	123	..	1472	141	1736	1736
Imports	33415	..	..	41701	..	1	..	..	..	75117	1
Exports	..	..	..	..	..	..	..	..	..	..	..
International marine bunkers	..	..	..	*-374	..	..	..	..	..	*-374	..
International aviation bunkers	..	..	..	-1574	..	..	..	..	..	-1574	..
Stock changes	*-746	..	..	*-814	..	..	..	..	..	*-1561	..
Total energy supply	32669	..	..	38938	..	124	..	1472	141	73344	1737
Statistical difference	0	..	..	0	..	0	..	0	0	0	1472
Transfers	..	..	..	..	..	..	..	..	..	..	..
Transformation	*-21078	..	..	*-17707	..	*-22	..	11077	..	*-27730	*-22
Electricity plants	*-21078	..	..	*-17707	..	*-5	..	11077	..	*-27714	*-5
CHP plants	..	..	..	..	..	..	..	..	..	..	..
Heat plants	..	..	..	..	..	..	..	..	..	..	..
Coke ovens	..	..	..	..	..	..	..	..	..	..	..
Briquetting plants	..	..	..	..	..	..	..	..	..	..	..
Liquefaction plants	..	..	..	..	..	..	..	..	..	..	..
Gas works	..	..	..	..	..	..	..	..	..	..	..
Blast furnaces	..	..	..	..	..	..	..	..	..	..	..
NGL plants & gas blending	..	..	..	..	..	..	..	..	..	..	..
Oil refineries	..	..	..	..	..	..	..	..	..	..	..
Other transformation	..	..	..	..	..	*-16	..	..	..	*-16	*-16
Energy industries own use	..	..	..	..	..	..	..	-3	..	-3	..
Losses	..	..	..	..	..	..	..	*-231	..	*-231	..
Final consumption	11591	..	..	*21231	..	*102	..	12315	141	*45380	243
Final energy consumption	*5000	..	..	*20564	..	*102	..	12315	141	*38121	243
Manufacturing, const., mining	*5000	..	..	*9199	..	..	..	9860	..	*24059	..
Iron and steel	..	..	..	..	..	..	..	..	..	..	..
Chemical and petrochemical	..	..	..	..	..	..	..	..	..	..	..
Non-ferrous metals	..	..	..	*2238	..	..	..	9422	..	11660	..
Non-metallic minerals	*5000	..	..	*2917	..	..	..	..	..	*7917	..
Transport equipment	..	..	..	..	..	..	..	..	..	..	..
Machinery	..	..	..	..	..	..	..	..	..	..	..
Mining and quarrying	..	..	..	*3380	..	..	..	94	..	*3474	..
Food and tobacco	..	..	..	..	..	..	..	..	..	..	..
Paper, pulp and printing	..	..	..	..	..	..	..	..	..	..	..
Wood and wood products	..	..	..	..	..	..	..	..	..	..	..
Textile and leather	..	..	..	..	..	..	..	..	..	..	..
Construction	..	..	..	..	..	..	..	..	..	..	..
Industries n.e.s	0	..	..	*664	..	..	..	344	..	*1008	..
Transport	..	..	..	*10558	..	..	..	..	..	*10558	..
Road	..	..	..	*9429	..	..	..	..	..	*9429	..
Rail	..	..	..	..	..	..	..	..	..	..	..
Domestic aviation	..	..	..	357	..	..	..	..	..	357	..
Domestic navigation	..	..	..	*772	..	..	..	..	..	*772	..
Pipeline transport	..	..	..	..	..	..	..	..	..	..	..
Transport, n.e.s	..	..	..	..	..	..	..	..	..	..	..
Other	..	..	..	*807	..	*102	..	*2454	141	*3504	243
Agriculture, forestry, fishing	..	..	..	*254	..	..	..	..	..	*254	..
Commerce, public services	..	..	..	*194	..	..	..	*1379	141	*1713	141
Households	..	..	..	*359	..	*102	..	*1076	..	*1537	*102
Other consumers	..	..	..	..	..	..	..	..	..	..	..
Non-energy use	6591	..	..	*667	..	..	..	..	..	7258	..

New Zealand

Terajoules

2017	Primary coal and peat	Coal and peat products	Primary Oil	Oil Products	Natural Gas	Biofuels and waste	Nuclear	Electricity	Heat	Total energy	of which: renewables
Primary production	69181	..	69521	..	174972	52711	..	98420	293164	757969	444296
Imports	9891	..	222952	114495	..	59	..	..	..	347396	59
Exports	-34718	..	-58477	-9862	..	..	..	..	..	-103057	..
International marine bunkers	..	..	..	-11532	..	..	..	..	..	-11532	..
International aviation bunkers	..	..	..	-51200	..	..	..	..	..	-51200	..
Stock changes	4327	..	1171	7427	2810	..	..	..	..	15734	..
Total energy supply	48680	..	235166	49328	177782	52770	..	98420	293164	955310	444355
Statistical difference	-832	1	-4331	-9440	-3466	0	..	997	0	-17072	126882
Transfers	..	..	7021	-7044	..	..	..	..	..	-23	..
Transformation	-23586	4135	-246518	241493	-53798	-7149	..	60671	-284616	-309368	-263303
Electricity plants	-5278	..	..	-43	-41605	-2198	..	52535	-283253	-279843	-256052
CHP plants	-314	-7631	..	..	-12179	-4951	..	8136	-1363	-18302	-7251
Heat plants	..	..	..	..	..	..	..	..	..	..	..
Coke ovens	-17993	19385	..	..	-14	..	..	..	..	1377	..
Briquetting plants	..	..	..	..	..	..	..	..	..	..	..
Liquefaction plants	..	..	..	..	..	..	..	..	..	..	..
Gas works	..	..	..	..	..	..	..	..	..	..	..
Blast furnaces	..	-7934	..	..	..	..	..	..	..	-7934	..
NGL plants & gas blending	..	..	-8287	8561	..	..	..	..	..	275	..
Oil refineries	..	..	-238232	232975	..	..	..	..	..	-5257	..
Other transformation	..	315	..	..	..	..	..	..	..	315	..
Energy industries own use	-2906	-2118	..	-15158	-9519	..	..	-7416	0	-37117	..
Losses	..	-299	..	..	-619	..	..	-10609	..	-11527	..
Final consumption	23021	1717	..	278059	117311	45621	..	140069	8548	614345	54169
Final energy consumption	23021	1717	..	264461	69326	45621	..	140069	8548	552763	54169
Manufacturing, const., mining	19185	1717	..	18448	54808	38395	..	49874	4732	187160	43127
Iron and steel	..	1717	..	..	2222	..	..	4860	..	8799	..
Chemical and petrochemical	..	..	..	..	28694	..	..	1462	..	30155	..
Non-ferrous metals	216	..	..	..	..	..	..	18022	..	18237	..
Non-metallic minerals	2181	..	..	..	1949	..	..	990	..	5120	..
Transport equipment	..	..	..	..	..	..	..	112	..	112	..
Machinery	20	..	..	..	234	..	..	425	..	678	..
Mining and quarrying	..	..	..	2580	127	..	..	1246	..	3953	..
Food and tobacco	14834	..	..	..	15474	45	..	9554	..	39907	45
Paper, pulp and printing	..	..	..	..	3613	..	..	4475	..	8087	..
Wood and wood products	530	..	..	..	1499	38350	..	5234	..	45614	38350
Textile and leather	20	..	..	..	430	..	..	335	..	785	..
Construction	..	..	..	5375	456	..	..	1343	..	7174	..
Industries n.e.s	1385	0	..	10493	110	0	..	1818	4732	18538	4732
Transport	..	..	..	218845	8	107	..	223	..	219184	107
Road	..	..	..	199542	8	107	..	..	..	199657	107
Rail	..	..	..	1505	..	..	..	..	..	1505	..
Domestic aviation	..	..	..	13805	..	..	..	..	..	13805	..
Domestic navigation	..	..	..	3994	..	..	..	..	..	3994	..
Pipeline transport	..	..	..	..	..	..	..	..	..	..	..
Transport, n.e.s	..	..	..	..	..	..	..	223	..	223	..
Other	3836	..	..	27168	14510	7119	..	89971	3816	146420	10935
Agriculture, forestry, fishing	2502	..	..	16296	1305	..	..	9086	681	29871	681
Commerce, public services	1060	..	..	7340	7127	253	..	34294	2496	52569	2749
Households	275	..	..	3532	6078	6866	..	44899	639	62288	7505
Other consumers	..	..	..	..	..	..	..	1692	..	1692	..
Non-energy use	..	..	..	13598	47984	..	..	..	..	61582	..

New Zealand

Terajoules

2018	Primary coal and peat	Coal and peat products	Primary Oil	Oil Products	Natural Gas	Biofuels and waste	Nuclear	Electricity	Heat	Total energy	of which: renewables
Primary production	75972	..	55301	..	155026	51003	..	102434	294991	734727	448428
Imports	12645	..	211537	134652	..	59	..	..	..	358893	59
Exports	-36451	..	-46748	-8423	..	..	..	..	..	-91622	..
International marine bunkers	..	..	..	-12410	..	..	..	..	..	-12410	..
International aviation bunkers	..	..	..	-53934	..	..	..	..	..	-53934	..
Stock changes	-2470	..	1919	3784	6147	..	..	..	..	9379	..
Total energy supply	49695	..	222009	63668	161173	51062	..	102434	294991	945032	448487
Statistical difference	331	0	-9004	-6623	0	1	..	2236	0	-13059	131095
Transfers	..	..	15930	-15953	..	..	..	..	..	-23	..
Transformation	-25555	4012	-246943	241055	-47839	-6270	..	57334	-286596	-310802	-264206
Electricity plants	-9244	..	..	-129	-32740	-2256	..	49766	-285307	-279910	-257892
CHP plants	-337	-7255	..	..	-11511	-4014	..	7567	-1289	-16838	-6314
Heat plants	..	..	..	..	..	..	..	..	..	..	..
Coke ovens	-15975	18650	..	..	-14	..	..	..	..	2661	..
Briquetting plants	..	..	..	..	..	..	..	..	..	..	..
Liquefaction plants	..	..	..	..	..	..	..	..	..	..	..
Gas works	..	..	..	..	..	..	..	..	..	..	..
Blast furnaces	..	-7695	..	..	..	..	..	..	..	-7695	..
NGL plants & gas blending	..	..	-8332	8703	..	..	..	..	..	371	..
Oil refineries	..	..	-238610	232481	..	..	..	..	..	-6130	..
Other transformation	..	312	..	..	-3573	..	..	..	..	-3261	..
Energy industries own use	-733	-2073	..	-14465	-8465	..	..	-7024	0	-32760	..
Losses	..	-296	..	..	-551	..	..	-10660	..	-11506	..
Final consumption	23076	1643	..	280927	104318	44791	..	139849	8395	603000	53186
Final energy consumption	23076	1643	..	268650	61648	44791	..	139849	8395	548053	53186
Manufacturing, const., mining	20173	1643	..	19016	48739	37490	..	50116	4579	181755	42069
Iron and steel	..	1643	..	..	1976	..	..	4748	..	8367	..
Chemical and petrochemical	20	..	..	..	25516	..	..	1436	..	26972	..
Non-ferrous metals	..	..	..	..	..	..	..	18248	..	18248	..
Non-metallic minerals	2147	..	..	..	1734	..	..	950	..	4832	..
Transport equipment	..	..	..	..	..	..	..	112	..	112	..
Machinery	..	..	..	..	208	..	..	392	..	600	..
Mining and quarrying	..	..	..	2623	113	..	..	1289	..	4024	..
Food and tobacco	16923	..	..	..	13760	45	..	9950	..	40678	45
Paper, pulp and printing	..	..	..	..	3213	..	..	4464	..	7677	..
Wood and wood products	385	..	..	..	1334	37445	..	5126	..	44290	37445
Textile and leather	154	..	..	..	383	..	..	335	..	871	..
Construction	..	..	..	5633	406	..	..	1321	..	7360	..
Industries n.e.s	544	0	..	10760	97	0	..	1742	4579	17722	4579
Transport	..	..	..	223620	7	107	..	223	..	223957	107
Road	..	..	..	203080	7	107	..	..	..	203194	107
Rail	..	..	..	1591	..	..	..	..	..	1591	..
Domestic aviation	..	..	..	14995	..	..	..	..	..	14995	..
Domestic navigation	..	..	..	3954	..	..	..	..	..	3954	..
Pipeline transport	..	..	..	..	..	..	..	..	..	..	..
Transport, n.e.s	..	..	..	..	..	..	..	223	..	223	..
Other	2903	..	..	26015	12902	7194	..	89510	3816	142341	11010
Agriculture, forestry, fishing	1859	..	..	15864	1160	..	..	8550	681	28114	681
Commerce, public services	739	..	..	6569	6338	253	..	33952	2496	50346	2749
Households	306	..	..	3582	5405	6941	..	45220	639	62092	7580
Other consumers	..	..	..	..	..	..	..	1789	..	1789	..
Non-energy use	..	..	..	12277	42670	..	..	..	..	54947	..

Nicaragua

Terajoules

2017	Primary coal and peat	Coal and peat products	Primary Oil	Oil Products	Natural Gas	Biofuels and waste	Nuclear	Electricity	Heat	Total energy	of which: renewables
Primary production	..	..	..	..	..	60343	..	4021	27036	91401	91401
Imports	..	..	29991	44676	..	..	..	1177	..	75844	..
Exports	..	..	..	-846	..	..	..	-4	..	-850	..
International marine bunkers	..	..	..	..	..	..	..	..	..	..	..
International aviation bunkers	..	..	..	-1103	..	..	..	..	..	-1103	..
Stock changes	..	..	*-338	692	..	..	..	..	..	354	..
Total energy supply	..	..	29652	43419	..	60343	..	5195	27036	165646	91401
Statistical difference	..	..	0	925	..	*-1	..	-11	0	913	6724
Transfers	..	..	..	..	..	..	..	..	..	..	..
Transformation	..	..	-29652	10570	..	*-17097	..	12269	-27036	-50947	*-41430
Electricity plants	..	..	..	-17812	..	*-16153	..	12269	-27036	-48733	*-40485
CHP plants	..	..	..	..	..	..	..	..	..	..	..
Heat plants	..	..	..	..	..	..	..	..	..	..	..
Coke ovens	..	..	..	..	..	..	..	..	..	..	..
Briquetting plants	..	..	..	..	..	..	..	..	..	..	..
Liquefaction plants	..	..	..	..	..	..	..	..	..	..	..
Gas works	..	..	..	..	..	..	..	..	..	..	..
Blast furnaces	..	..	..	..	..	..	..	..	..	..	..
NGL plants & gas blending	..	..	..	..	..	..	..	..	..	..	..
Oil refineries	..	..	-29652	28382	..	..	..	..	..	-1270	..
Other transformation	..	..	..	..	..	-944	..	..	..	-944	-944
Energy industries own use	..	..	..	-446	..	..	..	-1465	..	-1911	..
Losses	..	..	..	..	..	..	..	-3586	..	-3586	..
Final consumption	..	..	..	52619	..	*43247	..	12424	..	*108289	*43247
Final energy consumption	..	..	..	51091	..	*43247	..	12424	..	*106761	*43247
Manufacturing, const., mining	..	..	..	8282	..	*2720	..	4129	..	15131	*2720
Iron and steel	..	..	..	..	..	..	..	..	..	..	..
Chemical and petrochemical	..	..	..	..	..	..	..	..	..	..	..
Non-ferrous metals	..	..	..	..	..	..	..	..	..	..	..
Non-metallic minerals	..	..	..	..	..	..	..	..	..	..	..
Transport equipment	..	..	..	..	..	..	..	..	..	..	..
Machinery	..	..	..	..	..	..	..	..	..	..	..
Mining and quarrying	..	..	..	215	..	..	..	..	..	215	..
Food and tobacco	..	..	..	..	..	..	..	..	..	..	..
Paper, pulp and printing	..	..	..	..	..	..	..	..	..	..	..
Wood and wood products	..	..	..	..	..	..	..	..	..	..	..
Textile and leather	..	..	..	..	..	..	..	..	..	..	..
Construction	..	..	..	431	..	..	..	328	..	759	..
Industries n.e.s	..	..	..	7635	..	*2720	..	3802	..	14157	*2720
Transport	..	..	..	32712	..	..	..	..	..	32712	..
Road	..	..	..	29139	..	..	..	..	..	29139	..
Rail	..	..	..	..	..	..	..	..	..	..	..
Domestic aviation	..	..	..	176	..	..	..	..	..	176	..
Domestic navigation	..	..	..	3397	..	..	..	..	..	3397	..
Pipeline transport	..	..	..	..	..	..	..	..	..	..	..
Transport, n.e.s	..	..	..	..	..	..	..	..	..	..	..
Other	..	..	..	10097	..	*40527	..	8294	..	*58918	*40527
Agriculture, forestry, fishing	..	..	..	655	..	*1242	..	414	..	*2311	*1242
Commerce, public services	..	..	..	6895	..	*1584	..	3884	..	12364	*1584
Households	..	..	..	2547	..	*37701	..	3996	..	*44244	*37701
Other consumers	..	..	..	..	..	..	..	..	..	..	..
Non-energy use	..	..	..	1528	..	..	..	..	..	1528	..

Nicaragua

Terajoules

2018	Primary coal and peat	Coal and peat products	Primary Oil	Oil Products	Natural Gas	Biofuels and waste	Nuclear	Electricity	Heat	Total energy	of which: renewables
Primary production	..	..	..	..	..	63457	..	4450	28836	96743	96743
Imports	..	..	27410	43628	..	..	..	724	..	71762	..
Exports	..	..	..	-1128	..	..	..	0	..	-1128	..
International marine bunkers	..	..	..	..	..	..	..	..	..	..	..
International aviation bunkers	..	..	..	-617	..	..	..	..	..	-617	..
Stock changes	..	..	*1269	-868	..	..	..	..	..	*401	..
Total energy supply	..	..	28679	41016	..	63457	..	5173	28836	167161	96743
Statistical difference	..	..	*-42	386	..	0	..	-497	0	-153	7333
Transfers	..	..	..	..	..	..	..	..	..	..	..
Transformation	..	..	*-28679	10720	..	*-17062	..	12240	-28836	-51617	*-43014
Electricity plants	..	..	..	-16999	..	*-16211	..	12240	-28836	-49806	*-42163
CHP plants	..	..	..	..	..	..	..	..	..	..	..
Heat plants	..	..	..	..	..	..	..	..	..	..	..
Coke ovens	..	..	..	..	..	..	..	..	..	..	..
Briquetting plants	..	..	..	..	..	..	..	..	..	..	..
Liquefaction plants	..	..	..	..	..	..	..	..	..	..	..
Gas works	..	..	..	..	..	..	..	..	..	..	..
Blast furnaces	..	..	..	..	..	..	..	..	..	..	..
NGL plants & gas blending	..	..	..	..	..	..	..	..	..	..	..
Oil refineries	..	..	*-28679	27720	..	..	..	..	..	*-960	..
Other transformation	..	..	..	..	..	-851	..	..	..	-851	-851
Energy industries own use	..	..	..	-1433	..	..	..	-1451	..	-2883	..
Losses	..	..	-42	..	..	..	..	-3521	..	-3563	..
Final consumption	..	..	..	49917	..	*46395	..	12938	..	*109251	*46395
Final energy consumption	..	..	..	48591	..	*46395	..	12938	..	*107924	*46395
Manufacturing, const., mining	..	..	..	7790	..	*2992	..	3848	..	14631	*2992
Iron and steel	..	..	..	..	..	..	..	..	..	..	..
Chemical and petrochemical	..	..	..	..	..	..	..	..	..	..	..
Non-ferrous metals	..	..	..	..	..	..	..	..	..	..	..
Non-metallic minerals	..	..	..	..	..	..	..	..	..	..	..
Transport equipment	..	..	..	..	..	..	..	..	..	..	..
Machinery	..	..	..	..	..	..	..	..	..	..	..
Mining and quarrying	..	..	..	0	..	..	..	..	..	0	..
Food and tobacco	..	..	..	..	..	..	..	..	..	..	..
Paper, pulp and printing	..	..	..	..	..	..	..	..	..	..	..
Wood and wood products	..	..	..	..	..	..	..	..	..	..	..
Textile and leather	..	..	..	..	..	..	..	..	..	..	..
Construction	..	..	..	431	..	..	..	..	..	431	..
Industries n.e.s	..	..	..	7359	..	*2992	..	3848	..	14199	*2992
Transport	..	..	..	30920	..	..	..	..	..	30920	..
Road	..	..	..	27563	..	..	..	..	..	27563	..
Rail	..	..	..	..	..	..	..	..	..	..	..
Domestic aviation	..	..	..	88	..	..	..	..	..	88	..
Domestic navigation	..	..	..	3268	..	..	..	..	..	3268	..
Pipeline transport	..	..	..	..	..	..	..	..	..	..	..
Transport, n.e.s	..	..	..	..	..	..	..	..	..	..	..
Other	..	..	..	9881	..	*43403	..	9090	..	*62374	*43403
Agriculture, forestry, fishing	..	..	..	612	..	*1210	..	457	..	*2279	*1210
Commerce, public services	..	..	..	6722	..	*1612	..	4140	..	12474	*1612
Households	..	..	..	2547	..	*40582	..	4493	..	*47622	*40582
Other consumers	..	..	..	..	..	..	..	..	..	..	..
Non-energy use	..	..	..	1327	..	..	..	..	..	1327	..

Niger

Terajoules

2017	Primary coal and peat	Coal and peat products	Primary Oil	Oil Products	Natural Gas	Biofuels and waste	Nuclear	Electricity	Heat	Total energy	of which: renewables
Primary production	3581	..	38517	..	..	*55550	..	53	..	*97701	*55603
Imports	..	..	..	4535	..	..	..	3043	..	7578	..
Exports	..	..	..	*-15772	..	..	..	0	..	*-15772	..
International marine bunkers	..	..	..	..	..	..	..	..	..	..	..
International aviation bunkers	..	..	..	*-2523	..	..	..	..	..	*-2523	..
Stock changes	0	..	*-1354	*-912	..	..	..	..	..	*-2265	..
Total energy supply	3581	..	37164	*-14671	..	*55550	..	3096	..	*84719	*55603
Statistical difference	11	0	*-95	*1077	..	0	..	388	..	*1381	*53
Transfers	..	..	..	..	..	..	..	..	..	..	..
Transformation	-3570	*104	*-37259	*31779	..	*-3161	..	1986	..	*-10121	*-3161
Electricity plants	-3495	..	..	*-2885	..	..	..	1986	..	-4393	..
CHP plants	..	..	..	..	..	..	..	..	..	..	..
Heat plants	..	..	..	..	..	..	..	..	..	..	..
Coke ovens	..	..	..	..	..	..	..	..	..	..	..
Briquetting plants	-75	*104	..	..	..	..	..	..	..	*28	..
Liquefaction plants	..	..	..	..	..	..	..	..	..	..	..
Gas works	..	..	..	..	..	..	..	..	..	..	..
Blast furnaces	..	..	..	..	..	..	..	..	..	..	..
NGL plants & gas blending	..	..	..	..	..	..	..	..	..	..	..
Oil refineries	..	..	*-37259	*34664	..	..	..	..	..	*-2595	..
Other transformation	..	..	..	..	..	*-3161	..	..	..	*-3161	*-3161
Energy industries own use	..	..	..	..	..	..	..	-259	..	-259	..
Losses	0	..	..	0	..	..	..	*-785	..	*-785	..
Final consumption	..	*104	..	16031	..	*52389	..	*3650	..	*72174	*52389
Final energy consumption	..	*104	..	15870	..	*52389	..	*3650	..	*72013	*52389
Manufacturing, const., mining	..	..	..	*3936	..	..	..	*1026	..	*4962	..
Iron and steel	..	..	..	..	..	..	..	..	..	..	..
Chemical and petrochemical	..	..	..	..	..	..	..	..	..	..	..
Non-ferrous metals	..	..	..	..	..	..	..	..	..	..	..
Non-metallic minerals	..	..	..	..	..	..	..	..	..	..	..
Transport equipment	..	..	..	..	..	..	..	..	..	..	..
Machinery	..	..	..	..	..	..	..	..	..	..	..
Mining and quarrying	..	..	..	..	..	..	..	..	..	..	..
Food and tobacco	..	..	..	..	..	..	..	..	..	..	..
Paper, pulp and printing	..	..	..	..	..	..	..	..	..	..	..
Wood and wood products	..	..	..	..	..	..	..	..	..	..	..
Textile and leather	..	..	..	..	..	..	..	..	..	..	..
Construction	..	..	..	..	..	..	..	..	..	..	..
Industries n.e.s	..	..	..	*3936	..	..	..	*1026	..	*4962	..
Transport	..	..	..	11034	..	..	..	..	..	11034	..
Road	..	..	..	11034	..	..	..	..	..	11034	..
Rail	..	..	..	..	..	..	..	..	..	..	..
Domestic aviation	..	..	..	..	..	..	..	..	..	..	..
Domestic navigation	..	..	..	..	..	..	..	..	..	..	..
Pipeline transport	..	..	..	..	..	..	..	..	..	..	..
Transport, n.e.s	..	..	..	..	..	..	..	..	..	..	..
Other	..	*104	..	*900	..	*52389	..	*2624	..	*56017	*52389
Agriculture, forestry, fishing	..	..	..	..	..	..	..	*22	..	*22	..
Commerce, public services	..	..	..	..	..	..	..	*414	..	*414	..
Households	..	..	..	*900	..	*52389	..	*2189	..	*55478	*52389
Other consumers	..	*104	..	..	..	..	..	..	..	*104	..
Non-energy use	..	..	..	*161	..	..	..	..	..	*161	..

Niger

Terajoules

2018	Primary coal and peat	Coal and peat products	Primary Oil	Oil Products	Natural Gas	Biofuels and waste	Nuclear	Electricity	Heat	Total energy	of which: renewables
Primary production	4414	..	35047	..	..	*67027	..	118	..	*106606	*67145
Imports	..	..	..	2789	..	..	..	4511	..	7300	..
Exports	..	..	..	*-14695	..	..	..	0	..	*-14695	..
International marine bunkers	..	..	..	..	..	..	..	..	..	..	..
International aviation bunkers	..	..	..	*-1967	..	..	..	..	..	*-1967	..
Stock changes	..	..	..	*-1548	..	..	..	..	..	*-1548	..
Total energy supply	4414	..	35047	*-15421	..	*67027	..	4629	..	*95696	*67145
Statistical difference	179	0	0	1314	..	0	..	281	..	*1774	*118
Transfers	..	..	..	..	..	..	..	..	..	..	..
Transformation	-4236	*104	*-35047	29747	..	-3288	..	1610	..	-11110	-3288
Electricity plants	-4164	..	..	*-2636	..	..	..	1610	..	-5190	..
CHP plants	..	..	..	..	..	..	..	..	..	..	..
Heat plants	..	..	..	..	..	..	..	..	..	..	..
Coke ovens	..	..	..	..	..	..	..	..	..	..	..
Briquetting plants	-71	*104	..	..	..	..	..	..	..	*32	..
Liquefaction plants	..	..	..	..	..	..	..	..	..	..	..
Gas works	..	..	..	..	..	..	..	..	..	..	..
Blast furnaces	..	..	..	..	..	..	..	..	..	..	..
NGL plants & gas blending	..	..	..	..	..	..	..	..	..	..	..
Oil refineries	..	..	*-35047	32383	..	..	..	..	..	*-2664	..
Other transformation	..	..	..	..	..	-3288	..	..	..	-3288	-3288
Energy industries own use	..	..	..	..	..	..	..	-137	..	-137	..
Losses	..	..	..	0	..	..	..	*-857	..	*-857	..
Final consumption	..	*104	..	*13012	..	*63739	..	*4964	..	*81819	*63739
Final energy consumption	..	*104	..	*12832	..	*63739	..	*4964	..	*81639	*63739
Manufacturing, const., mining	..	..	..	*1973	..	..	..	*1393	..	*3366	..
Iron and steel	..	..	..	..	..	..	..	..	..	..	..
Chemical and petrochemical	..	..	..	..	..	..	..	..	..	..	..
Non-ferrous metals	..	..	..	..	..	..	..	..	..	..	..
Non-metallic minerals	..	..	..	..	..	..	..	..	..	..	..
Transport equipment	..	..	..	..	..	..	..	..	..	..	..
Machinery	..	..	..	..	..	..	..	..	..	..	..
Mining and quarrying	..	..	..	..	..	..	..	..	..	..	..
Food and tobacco	..	..	..	..	..	..	..	..	..	..	..
Paper, pulp and printing	..	..	..	..	..	..	..	..	..	..	..
Wood and wood products	..	..	..	..	..	..	..	..	..	..	..
Textile and leather	..	..	..	..	..	..	..	..	..	..	..
Construction	..	..	..	..	..	..	..	..	..	..	..
Industries n.e.s	..	..	..	*1973	..	..	..	*1393	..	*3366	..
Transport	..	..	..	*9596	..	..	..	..	..	*9596	..
Road	..	..	..	*9596	..	..	..	..	..	*9596	..
Rail	..	..	..	..	..	..	..	..	..	..	..
Domestic aviation	..	..	..	..	..	..	..	..	..	..	..
Domestic navigation	..	..	..	..	..	..	..	..	..	..	..
Pipeline transport	..	..	..	..	..	..	..	..	..	..	..
Transport, n.e.s	..	..	..	..	..	..	..	..	..	..	..
Other	..	*104	..	1264	..	*63739	..	*3571	..	*68678	*63739
Agriculture, forestry, fishing	..	..	..	..	..	..	..	*32	..	*32	..
Commerce, public services	..	..	..	476	..	..	..	*565	..	*1041	..
Households	..	..	..	789	..	*63739	..	*2974	..	*67501	*63739
Other consumers	..	*104	..	..	..	..	..	..	..	*104	..
Non-energy use	..	..	..	180	..	..	..	..	..	180	..

Nigeria

Terajoules

2017	Primary coal and peat	Coal and peat products	Primary Oil	Oil Products	Natural Gas	Biofuels and waste	Nuclear	Electricity	Heat	Total energy	of which: renewables
Primary production	1187	..	3942396	..	1542420	4895957	..	27990	..	10409950	4923947
Imports	..	..	..	766337	..	..	..	..	..	766337	..
Exports	..	..	-3771370	-35863	-949392	..	..	..	..	-4756625	..
International marine bunkers	..	..	..	-13021	..	..	..	..	..	-13021	..
International aviation bunkers	..	..	..	-22271	..	..	..	..	..	-22271	..
Stock changes	..	..	-30283	4442	..	..	..	..	..	-25841	..
Total energy supply	1187	..	140744	699624	593028	4895957	..	27990	..	6358529	4923947
Statistical difference	0	..	-31714	62071	2879	*-1	..	8564	..	41800	27989
Transfers	..	..	23158	-19781	..	..	..	..	..	3377	..
Transformation	..	..	-193035	186468	-258443	*-387891	..	96012	..	-556889	*-387891
Electricity plants	..	..	..	..	-240023	..	..	96012	..	-144011	..
CHP plants	..	..	..	..	..	..	..	..	..	..	..
Heat plants	..	..	..	..	..	..	..	..	..	..	..
Coke ovens	..	..	..	..	..	..	..	..	..	..	..
Briquetting plants	..	..	..	..	..	..	..	..	..	..	..
Liquefaction plants	..	..	7200	..	-18420	..	..	..	..	-11220	..
Gas works	..	..	..	..	..	..	..	..	..	..	..
Blast furnaces	..	..	..	..	..	..	..	..	..	..	..
NGL plants & gas blending	..	..	..	..	..	..	..	..	..	..	..
Oil refineries	..	..	-200235	186468	..	..	..	..	..	-13767	..
Other transformation	..	..	..	..	..	*-387891	..	..	..	*-387891	*-387891
Energy industries own use	..	..	..	-17621	-186529	..	..	-4403	..	-208552	..
Losses	..	..	-2580	-2673	..	..	..	-18601	..	-23855	..
Final consumption	1187	..	..	783946	145177	*4508067	..	92434	..	*5530810	*4508067
Final energy consumption	1187	..	..	777715	94257	*4508067	..	92434	..	*5473659	*4508067
Manufacturing, const., mining	1187	..	..	18396	94257	*172950	..	13039	..	*299829	*172950
Iron and steel	..	..	..	..	9844	..	..	..	..	9844	..
Chemical and petrochemical	..	..	..	..	16252	..	..	..	..	16252	..
Non-ferrous metals	..	..	..	..	..	..	..	..	..	..	..
Non-metallic minerals	1187	..	..	..	..	..	..	..	..	1187	..
Transport equipment	..	..	..	..	..	..	..	..	..	..	..
Machinery	..	..	..	..	..	..	..	..	..	..	..
Mining and quarrying	..	..	..	..	..	..	..	..	..	..	..
Food and tobacco	..	..	..	..	..	..	..	..	..	..	..
Paper, pulp and printing	..	..	..	..	..	..	..	..	..	..	..
Wood and wood products	..	..	..	..	..	..	..	..	..	..	..
Textile and leather	..	..	..	..	..	..	..	..	..	..	..
Construction	..	..	..	..	..	..	..	..	..	..	..
Industries n.e.s	0	..	..	18396	68161	*172950	..	13039	..	*272545	*172950
Transport	..	..	..	722246	..	..	..	..	..	722246	..
Road	..	..	..	709400	..	..	..	..	..	709400	..
Rail	..	..	..	2322	..	..	..	..	..	2322	..
Domestic aviation	..	..	..	8203	..	..	..	..	..	8203	..
Domestic navigation	..	..	..	2322	..	..	..	..	..	2322	..
Pipeline transport	..	..	..	..	..	..	..	..	..	..	..
Transport, n.e.s	..	..	..	..	..	..	..	..	..	..	..
Other	..	..	..	37072	..	*4335117	..	79394	..	*4451584	*4335117
Agriculture, forestry, fishing	..	..	..	172	..	..	..	..	..	172	..
Commerce, public services	..	..	..	44	..	*114186	..	24847	..	*139077	*114186
Households	..	..	..	25381	..	*4220931	..	54547	..	*4300859	*4220931
Other consumers	..	..	..	11476	..	..	..	..	..	11476	..
Non-energy use	..	..	..	6231	50920	..	..	..	..	57151	..

Nigeria

Terajoules

	Primary coal and peat	Coal and peat products	Primary Oil	Oil Products	Natural Gas	Biofuels and waste	Nuclear	Electricity	Heat	Total energy	of which: renewables
2018											
Primary production	1213	..	4045990	..	1597140	4923946	..	23350	..	10591638	4947295
Imports	..	..	..	854081	..	..	..	..	..	854081	..
Exports	..	..	-3948764	-10586	-934686	..	..	..	..	-4894036	..
International marine bunkers	..	..	..	-13640	..	..	..	..	..	-13640	..
International aviation bunkers	..	..	..	-28665	..	..	..	..	..	-28665	..
Stock changes	..	..	-32200	108103	..	..	..	..	..	75903	..
Total energy supply	1213	..	65027	909292	662454	4923946	..	23350	..	6585280	4947295
Statistical difference	0	..	-31248	-14737	32738	30	..	11707	..	-1511	23379
Transfers	..	..	13354	-10616	..	..	..	..	..	2738	..
Transformation	..	..	-109206	114021	-286542	*-397779	..	107251	..	-572254	*-397779
Electricity plants	..	..	..	..	-268122	..	..	107251	..	-160871	..
CHP plants	..	..	..	..	..	..	..	..	..	..	..
Heat plants	..	..	..	..	..	..	..	..	..	..	..
Coke ovens	..	..	..	..	..	..	..	..	..	..	..
Briquetting plants	..	..	..	..	..	..	..	..	..	..	..
Liquefaction plants	..	..	7200	..	-18420	..	..	..	..	-11220	..
Gas works	..	..	..	..	..	..	..	..	..	..	..
Blast furnaces	..	..	..	..	..	..	..	..	..	..	..
NGL plants & gas blending	..	..	..	..	..	..	..	..	..	..	..
Oil refineries	..	..	-116406	114021	..	..	..	..	..	-2385	..
Other transformation	..	..	..	..	..	*-397779	..	..	..	*-397779	*-397779
Energy industries own use	..	..	..	-23270	-181001	..	..	-4565	..	-208836	..
Losses	..	..	-423	-3515	..	..	..	-19591	..	-23529	..
Final consumption	1213	..	..	1000650	162174	*4526138	..	94738	..	*5784911	*4526138
Final energy consumption	1213	..	..	993856	105293	*4526138	..	94738	..	*5721237	*4526138
Manufacturing, const., mining	1213	..	..	18672	105293	*176283	..	13262	..	*314723	*176283
Iron and steel	..	..	..	..	10997	..	..	..	..	10997	..
Chemical and petrochemical	..	..	..	..	18155	..	..	..	..	18155	..
Non-ferrous metals	..	..	..	..	..	..	..	..	..	..	..
Non-metallic minerals	1213	..	..	..	..	..	..	..	..	1213	..
Transport equipment	..	..	..	..	..	..	..	..	..	..	..
Machinery	..	..	..	..	..	..	..	..	..	..	..
Mining and quarrying	..	..	..	..	..	..	..	..	..	..	..
Food and tobacco	..	..	..	..	..	..	..	..	..	..	..
Paper, pulp and printing	..	..	..	..	..	..	..	..	..	..	..
Wood and wood products	..	..	..	..	..	..	..	..	..	..	..
Textile and leather	..	..	..	..	..	..	..	..	..	..	..
Construction	..	..	..	..	..	..	..	..	..	..	..
Industries n.e.s	0	..	..	18672	76141	*176283	..	13262	..	*284358	*176283
Transport	..	..	..	940805	..	..	..	..	..	940805	..
Road	..	..	..	921367	..	..	..	..	..	921367	..
Rail	..	..	..	5375	..	..	..	..	..	5375	..
Domestic aviation	..	..	..	8688	..	..	..	..	..	8688	..
Domestic navigation	..	..	..	5375	..	..	..	..	..	5375	..
Pipeline transport	..	..	..	..	..	..	..	..	..	..	..
Transport, n.e.s	..	..	..	..	..	..	..	..	..	..	..
Other	..	..	..	34380	..	*4349855	..	81475	..	*4465709	*4349855
Agriculture, forestry, fishing	..	..	..	172	..	..	..	..	..	172	..
Commerce, public services	..	..	..	44	..	*116397	..	25499	..	*141939	*116397
Households	..	..	..	26893	..	*4233458	..	55976	..	*4316327	*4233458
Other consumers	..	..	..	7271	..	..	..	..	..	7271	..
Non-energy use	..	..	..	6794	56881	..	..	..	..	63675	..

Niue

Terajoules

	All Coal	All Oil	Natural Gas	Primary biofuels / Waste	Charcoal	Electricity	Total energy	of which: renewables
2017								
Primary production	..	..	..	1	..	*16	*17	1
Imports	..	*101	..	..	..	..	*101	..
Exports	..	..	..	..	..	..	..	..
International marine bunkers	..	..	..	..	..	..	..	..
International aviation bunkers	..	*-21	..	..	..	..	*-21	..
Stock changes	..	..	..	..	..	..	..	..
Total energy supply	..	*80	..	1	..	*16	*97	1
Statistical Difference	..	0	..	0	0	0	0	*-16
Transfers	..	..	..	..	..	..	..	..
Transformation	..	*-33	..	0	0	*12	*-21	0
Electricity plants	..	*-33	..	..	..	*12	*-21	..
Charcoal plants	..	..	..	0	0	..	0	0
Other transformation	..	0	..	0	..	..	0	0
Energy industries own use	..	..	..	..	..	0	0	..
Losses	..	..	..	..	..	*-1	*-1	..
Final consumption	..	*47	..	0	0	*27	*74	*16
Final energy consumption	..	*47	..	0	0	*27	*74	*16
Manufacturing, const., mining	..	*2	..	..	..	*2	*4	..
Transport	..	*41	..	..	..	..	*41	..
Road	..	*40	..	..	..	..	*40	..
Domestic aviation	..	1	..	..	..	..	1	..
Domestic navigation	..	0	..	..	..	..	0	..
Other transport	..	..	..	..	..	..	..	..
Other	..	*4	..	0	0	*25	*29	*16
Agriculture, forestry, fishing	..	*1	..	..	..	..	*1	..
Commerce and public services	..	*1	..	..	..	*5	*6	..
Households	..	*2	..	0	0	*20	*22	*16
Other consumers	..	..	..	..	..	..	..	..
Non-energy use	..	..	..	..	..	..	..	..
2018								
Primary production	..	..	..	1	..	*18	*18	2
Imports	..	*107	..	..	..	..	*107	..
Exports	..	..	..	..	..	..	..	..
International marine bunkers	..	..	..	..	..	..	..	..
International aviation bunkers	..	-21	..	..	..	..	-21	..
Stock changes	..	..	..	..	..	..	..	..
Total energy supply	..	*85	..	1	..	*18	*104	2
Statistical Difference	..	*3	..	0	0	0	*3	*-14
Transfers	..	..	..	..	..	..	..	..
Transformation	..	-34	..	0	0	*12	-22	0
Electricity plants	..	-34	..	..	..	*12	-22	..
Charcoal plants	..	..	..	0	0	..	0	0
Other transformation	..	0	..	0	..	..	0	0
Energy industries own use	..	..	..	..	..	*-1	*-1	..
Losses	..	..	..	..	..	*-1	*-1	..
Final consumption	..	*48	..	0	0	*28	*76	*16
Final energy consumption	..	*48	..	0	0	*28	*76	*16
Manufacturing, const., mining	..	*2	..	..	..	*3	*5	..
Transport	..	*42	..	..	..	..	*42	..
Road	..	*41	..	..	..	..	*41	..
Domestic aviation	..	*1	..	..	..	..	*1	..
Domestic navigation	..	0	..	..	..	..	0	..
Other transport	..	..	..	..	..	..	..	..
Other	..	*4	..	0	0	*25	*29	*16
Agriculture, forestry, fishing	..	*1	..	..	..	..	*1	..
Commerce and public services	..	*1	..	..	..	*5	*6	..
Households	..	*2	..	0	0	*20	*23	*16
Other consumers	..	..	..	..	..	..	..	..
Non-energy use	..	..	..	..	..	..	..	..

North Macedonia

Terajoules

2017	Primary coal and peat	Coal and peat products	Primary Oil	Oil Products	Natural Gas	Biofuels and waste	Nuclear	Electricity	Heat	Total energy	of which: renewables
Primary production	35692	..	..	..	..	12295	..	4480	198	52665	16973
Imports	3682	134	0	47361	8539	1720	..	8257	..	69692	1720
Exports	-13	-1	0	-3862	..	-9	..	-1120	..	-5004	-9
International marine bunkers	0	..	..	..	..	..	..	..	..	0	..
International aviation bunkers	..	..	..	..	..	..	..	..	..	..	..
Stock changes	1073	-103	0	142	-7	433	..	..	..	1538	433
Total energy supply	40434	29	0	43641	8532	14438	..	11617	198	118890	19116
Statistical difference	-55	0	0	0	-9	0	..	0	0	-64	4480
Transfers	..	..	0	6	..	..	..	..	..	6	..
Transformation	-38362	..	0	-986	-6858	-191	..	15680	2419	-28297	-191
Electricity plants	-38362	..	..	-986	..	..	..	12697	..	-26651	..
CHP plants	0	..	..	..	-5852	-191	..	2984	1303	-1756	-191
Heat plants	..	..	..	..	-1005	..	..	..	1116	110	..
Coke ovens	..	..	..	..	..	..	..	..	..	..	..
Briquetting plants	..	..	..	..	..	..	..	..	..	..	..
Liquefaction plants	..	..	..	..	..	..	..	..	..	..	..
Gas works	..	..	..	..	..	..	..	..	..	..	..
Blast furnaces	..	..	..	..	..	..	..	..	..	..	..
NGL plants & gas blending	..	..	..	..	..	..	..	..	..	..	..
Oil refineries	..	..	0	0	..	..	..	..	..	0	..
Other transformation	..	..	..	..	..	..	..	..	..	..	..
Energy industries own use	0	..	..	-69	..	-1	..	-1716	-15	-1801	-1
Losses	..	..	..	..	-22	..	..	-3615	-314	-3950	..
Final consumption	2128	29	..	42593	1661	14245	..	21967	2289	84912	14443
Final energy consumption	2128	29	..	39165	1661	14245	..	21967	2289	81484	14443
Manufacturing, const., mining	2037	29	..	5130	1408	302	..	5299	91	14297	302
Iron and steel	690	29	..	1841	944	2	..	2344	91	5941	2
Chemical and petrochemical	..	..	..	85	38	0	..	270	..	393	0
Non-ferrous metals	0	..	..	56	0	0	..	50	..	106	0
Non-metallic minerals	1319	..	..	901	55	1	..	490	..	2766	1
Transport equipment	..	..	..	32	119	2	..	316	..	469	2
Machinery	0	0	..	109	7	11	..	194	..	320	11
Mining and quarrying	..	..	..	569	..	1	..	555	..	1124	1
Food and tobacco	0	..	..	683	218	216	..	532	..	1649	216
Paper, pulp and printing	0	..	..	24	15	3	..	40	..	82	3
Wood and wood products	..	..	..	3	..	12	..	20	..	34	12
Textile and leather	28	..	..	211	3	27	..	225	..	494	27
Construction	0	..	..	596	..	9	..	68	..	673	9
Industries n.e.s	0	0	..	21	10	18	..	195	0	244	18
Transport	..	..	..	30434	8	5	..	49	..	30497	5
Road	..	..	..	29456	8	5	..	..	..	29469	5
Rail	..	..	..	85	..	..	..	49	..	135	..
Domestic aviation	..	..	..	893	..	..	..	..	..	893	..
Domestic navigation	..	..	..	..	..	..	..	..	..	..	..
Pipeline transport	..	..	..	..	..	..	..	..	..	..	..
Transport, n.e.s	..	..	..	..	0	..	..	..	..	0	..
Other	91	..	..	3600	246	13938	..	16619	2198	36691	14136
Agriculture, forestry, fishing	23	..	..	508	..	89	..	141	154	915	243
Commerce, public services	..	..	..	..	..	28	..	..	..	28	28
Households	31	..	..	499	6	13564	..	11148	1469	26716	13564
Other consumers	37	..	..	2593	240	257	..	5330	575	9032	301
Non-energy use	0	..	..	3429	..	..	..	..	..	3429	..

North Macedonia

Terajoules

	Primary coal and peat	Coal and peat products	Primary Oil	Oil Products	Natural Gas	Biofuels and waste	Nuclear	Electricity	Heat	Total energy	of which: renewables
2018											
Primary production	33500	..	..	..	..	10379	..	6881	190	50951	17450
Imports	4908	10	..	46406	7874	1709	..	8270	..	69176	1709
Exports	-23	0	..	-4956	..	-17	..	-1359	..	-6355	-17
International marine bunkers	0	..	..	..	..	..	..	..	..	0	..
International aviation bunkers	..	..	..	..	..	..	..	..	..	..	..
Stock changes	-2186	-3	..	343	-5	49	..	..	..	-1802	49
Total energy supply	36199	7	..	41793	7869	12120	..	13792	190	111970	19191
Statistical difference	67	0	..	-12	0	0	..	0	0	55	6881
Transfers	..	..	..	4	..	..	..	..	..	4	..
Transformation	-32774	..	..	-548	-6214	-200	..	13304	2245	-24188	-200
Electricity plants	-32774	..	..	-548	..	..	..	10619	..	-22703	..
CHP plants	..	..	..	..	-5312	-200	..	2685	1262	-1565	-200
Heat plants	..	..	..	..	-903	..	..	..	983	81	..
Coke ovens	..	..	..	..	..	..	..	..	..	..	..
Briquetting plants	..	..	..	..	..	..	..	..	..	..	..
Liquefaction plants	..	..	..	..	..	..	..	..	..	..	..
Gas works	..	..	..	..	..	..	..	..	..	..	..
Blast furnaces	..	..	..	..	..	..	..	..	..	..	..
NGL plants & gas blending	..	..	..	..	..	..	..	..	..	..	..
Oil refineries	..	..	..	..	..	..	..	..	..	..	..
Other transformation	..	..	..	..	..	..	..	..	..	..	..
Energy industries own use	..	..	..	-83	..	-1	..	-1536	-19	-1639	-1
Losses	..	..	..	..	-22	..	..	-3581	-277	-3880	..
Final consumption	3359	7	..	41178	1633	11919	..	21980	2138	82212	12109
Final energy consumption	3359	7	..	39038	1633	11919	..	21980	2138	80073	12109
Manufacturing, const., mining	3295	7	..	5240	1375	312	..	5565	21	15815	312
Iron and steel	870	7	..	1922	896	0	..	2554	21	6269	0
Chemical and petrochemical	..	..	..	84	36	0	..	271	..	391	0
Non-ferrous metals	..	..	..	60	0	0	..	48	..	108	0
Non-metallic minerals	2401	..	..	1048	60	1	..	496	..	4006	1
Transport equipment	..	..	..	31	135	2	..	346	..	515	2
Machinery	0	0	..	109	6	11	..	203	..	329	11
Mining and quarrying	..	..	..	578	..	0	..	557	..	1136	0
Food and tobacco	..	..	..	620	217	229	..	540	..	1605	229
Paper, pulp and printing	0	..	..	19	15	3	..	41	..	78	3
Wood and wood products	..	..	..	3	..	12	..	20	..	35	12
Textile and leather	23	..	..	196	3	26	..	225	..	474	26
Construction	0	..	..	550	..	9	..	67	..	626	9
Industries n.e.s	0	0	..	21	7	18	..	196	0	242	18
Transport	..	..	..	30458	27	4	..	42	..	30531	4
Road	..	..	..	29361	27	4	..	..	..	29391	4
Rail	..	..	..	92	..	..	..	42	..	134	..
Domestic aviation	..	..	..	1005	..	..	..	..	..	1005	..
Domestic navigation	..	..	..	..	..	..	..	..	..	..	..
Pipeline transport	..	..	..	..	..	..	..	..	..	..	..
Transport, n.e.s	..	..	..	..	..	..	..	..	..	..	..
Other	64	..	..	3340	231	11603	..	16373	2117	33728	11793
Agriculture, forestry, fishing	18	..	..	450	..	91	..	140	148	848	240
Commerce, public services	..	..	..	..	..	32	..	..	..	32	32
Households	23	..	..	465	7	11238	..	10796	1418	23946	11238
Other consumers	23	..	..	2425	224	242	..	5437	551	8902	283
Non-energy use	..	..	..	2139	..	..	..	..	..	2139	..

Norway

Terajoules

2017	Primary coal and peat	Coal and peat products	Primary Oil	Oil Products	Natural Gas	Biofuels and waste	Nuclear	Electricity	Heat	Total energy	of which: renewables
Primary production	3681	..	3891839	..	4551886	61525	..	522792	3535	9035259	573346
Imports	21946	11714	78590	252401	0	21974	..	22000	..	408625	21974
Exports	-2108	..	-2933502	-854964	-4353988	-3364	..	-76594	..	-8224519	-3364
International marine bunkers	..	..	..	-6296	-1580	..	..	..	..	-7877	..
International aviation bunkers	..	..	..	-23108	..	..	..	..	..	-23108	..
Stock changes	-141	399	39623	8098	-3851	..	..	..	..	44128	..
Total energy supply	23379	12113	1076550	-623870	192467	80136	..	468198	3535	1232508	591957
Statistical difference	731	513	32932	104799	-54715	217	..	1411	29	85917	523011
Transfers	..	..	70838	-69127	..	..	..	..	..	1712	..
Transformation	-3653	-4453	-1114457	1146236	-13916	-22261	..	8942	19509	15948	-15158
Electricity plants	..	-1255	..	-129	0	-169	..	1879	-3535	-3209	-169
CHP plants	-815	..	..	-43	-13386	-10309	..	10771	7126	-6656	-5931
Heat plants	..	-28	..	-546	-530	-11782	..	-3708	15918	-676	-9058
Coke ovens	..	..	..	..	..	..	..	..	..	..	..
Briquetting plants	..	..	..	..	..	..	..	..	..	..	..
Liquefaction plants	..	..	..	..	..	..	..	..	..	..	..
Gas works	..	..	..	..	..	..	..	..	..	..	..
Blast furnaces	-2838	-3170	..	..	..	..	..	..	..	-6008	..
NGL plants & gas blending	..	..	-415001	443825	..	..	..	..	..	28824	..
Oil refineries	..	..	-699456	703302	..	..	..	..	..	3846	..
Other transformation	..	..	..	-172	..	..	..	..	..	-172	..
Energy industries own use	..	..	..	-34920	-194145	..	..	-33473	0	-262538	..
Losses	..	-157	..	..	..	..	..	-32951	-2496	-35604	..
Final consumption	18996	6990	..	313521	39121	57658	..	409306	20519	866110	53787
Final energy consumption	16495	6990	..	233590	17956	57658	..	409306	20519	762512	53787
Manufacturing, const., mining	16495	6990	..	35977	12170	13892	..	165636	1974	253133	10195
Iron and steel	5732	4570	..	400	37	191	..	19951	7	30888	177
Chemical and petrochemical	7728	1864	..	13118	4525	2792	..	26834	425	57285	2014
Non-ferrous metals	..	..	..	923	1642	..	..	74981	39	77585	..
Non-metallic minerals	3035	557	..	2302	2165	3242	..	3377	25	14701	871
Transport equipment	..	..	..	176	46	1	..	1429	86	1738	0
Machinery	..	..	..	353	128	7	..	3816	156	4459	2
Mining and quarrying	..	..	..	2159	103	0	..	1480	0	3741	0
Food and tobacco	..	..	..	3342	2718	66	..	10674	712	17512	66
Paper, pulp and printing	..	..	..	378	452	4273	..	14069	125	19297	3808
Wood and wood products	..	..	..	258	164	3219	..	2214	317	6172	3157
Textile and leather	..	..	..	47	24	0	..	248	3	323	0
Construction	..	..	..	12010	20	..	..	5008	64	17101	..
Industries n.e.s	0	0	..	512	148	101	..	1555	15	2330	101
Transport	..	..	..	169975	4094	21149	..	3287	..	198505	21149
Road	..	..	..	123197	956	20961	..	1210	..	146323	20961
Rail	..	..	..	602	..	..	..	2077	..	2679	..
Domestic aviation	..	..	..	15436	..	..	..	..	..	15436	..
Domestic navigation	..	..	..	30741	3138	188	..	..	..	34067	188
Pipeline transport	..	..	..	..	..	..	..	..	..	..	..
Transport, n.e.s	..	..	..	..	..	..	..	..	..	..	..
Other	..	..	..	27637	1692	22617	..	240383	18545	310874	22444
Agriculture, forestry, fishing	..	..	..	10380	561	..	..	7420	20	18381	..
Commerce, public services	..	..	..	11116	996	1627	..	90043	13949	117732	1454
Households	..	..	..	2739	135	20990	..	142920	4576	171360	20990
Other consumers	..	..	..	3402	..	..	..	..	..	3402	..
Non-energy use	2501	..	..	79932	21165	..	..	..	..	103598	..

Norway

Terajoules

2018	Primary coal and peat	Coal and peat products	Primary Oil	Oil Products	Natural Gas	Biofuels and waste	Nuclear	Electricity	Heat	Total energy	of which: renewables
Primary production	4215	..	3624135	..	4455448	62687	..	513626	3648	8663760	564549
Imports	20963	11856	141763	242104	..	17490	..	30024	..	464199	17490
Exports	-3175	..	-2657143	-917543	-4239613	-2575	..	-66560	..	-7886609	-2575
International marine bunkers	..	..	..	-6931	-1974	..	..	..	..	-8905	..
International aviation bunkers	..	..	..	-24123	..	..	..	..	..	-24123	..
Stock changes	281	314	-29277	-8110	1805	58	..	..	..	-34930	58
Total energy supply	22283	12170	1079479	-714604	215666	77660	..	477090	3648	1173393	579522
Statistical difference	-365	1398	16193	20763	-27285	538	..	-277	1	10965	514024
Transfers	..	..	59413	-58340	..	..	..	..	..	1073	..
Transformation	-4075	-4334	-1122699	1152646	-14338	-23272	..	8939	19915	12783	-16120
Electricity plants	..	-1247	..	-129	-2	-129	..	1847	-3648	-3308	-129
CHP plants	-871	..	..	-43	-13675	-10413	..	10760	7303	-6938	-5982
Heat plants	..	-16	..	-641	-662	-12731	..	-3668	16260	-1458	-10010
Coke ovens	..	..	..	..	..	..	..	..	..	..	..
Briquetting plants	..	..	..	..	..	..	..	..	..	..	..
Liquefaction plants	..	..	..	..	..	..	..	..	..	..	..
Gas works	..	..	..	..	..	..	..	..	..	..	..
Blast furnaces	-3203	-3071	..	..	..	..	..	..	..	-6274	..
NGL plants & gas blending	..	..	-389338	416538	..	..	..	..	..	27201	..
Oil refineries	..	..	-733361	737102	..	..	..	..	..	3740	..
Other transformation	..	..	..	-182	..	..	..	..	..	-182	..
Energy industries own use	..	..	..	-36799	-191561	-4	..	-36626	-1	-264990	-4
Losses	..	-148	..	..	..	-610	..	-32418	-2655	-35831	-610
Final consumption	18574	6291	..	322141	37053	53236	..	417262	20906	875462	48764
Final energy consumption	15848	6291	..	238847	18110	53236	..	417262	20906	770499	48764
Manufacturing, const., mining	15848	6291	..	35383	11555	15295	..	169214	1981	255568	11124
Iron and steel	5704	3511	..	357	39	396	..	19609	8	29624	354
Chemical and petrochemical	7503	2181	..	14220	4289	3021	..	27500	404	59118	2013
Non-ferrous metals	..	..	..	880	1781	..	..	77944	56	80661	..
Non-metallic minerals	2641	599	..	2579	1939	3484	..	3532	34	14808	878
Transport equipment	..	..	..	176	33	..	..	1555	55	1820	..
Machinery	..	..	..	348	156	3	..	3640	175	4322	3
Mining and quarrying	..	..	..	2679	113	..	..	1436	..	4228	..
Food and tobacco	..	..	..	3222	2100	187	..	10746	670	16925	187
Paper, pulp and printing	..	..	..	331	689	4486	..	13921	13	19440	4041
Wood and wood products	..	..	..	301	211	3662	..	2207	267	6647	3593
Textile and leather	..	..	..	..	25	..	..	263	1	289	..
Construction	..	..	..	9727	14	..	..	5090	282	15113	..
Industries n.e.s	0	0	..	563	167	56	..	1771	16	2574	56
Transport	..	..	..	173071	5067	16089	..	3823	..	198050	16089
Road	..	..	..	125537	1271	15901	..	1710	..	144419	15901
Rail	..	..	..	602	..	..	..	2113	..	2715	..
Domestic aviation	..	..	..	16538	..	..	..	..	..	16538	..
Domestic navigation	..	..	..	30394	3796	188	..	..	..	34378	188
Pipeline transport	..	..	..	..	..	..	..	..	..	..	..
Transport, n.e.s	..	..	..	..	..	..	..	..	..	..	..
Other	..	..	..	30393	1488	21852	..	244224	18925	316881	21551
Agriculture, forestry, fishing	..	..	..	10544	561	..	..	7542	29	18675	..
Commerce, public services	..	..	..	15352	793	1558	..	91606	14274	123582	1257
Households	..	..	..	2269	134	20294	..	145076	4622	172396	20294
Other consumers	..	..	..	2228	..	..	..	..	..	2228	..
Non-energy use	2726	..	..	83294	18943	..	..	..	..	104963	..

Oman

Terajoules

2017	Primary coal and peat	Coal and peat products	Primary Oil	Oil Products	Natural Gas	Biofuels and waste	Nuclear	Electricity	Heat	Total energy	of which: renewables
Primary production	..	..	2027595	..	1214034	436	..	13	..	3242078	449
Imports	..	..	6720	14339	73402	652	..	..	..	95113	652
Exports	..	..	-1674911	-86639	-418460	-279	..	..	..	-2180288	-279
International marine bunkers	..	..	..	-41329	..	..	..	..	..	-41329	..
International aviation bunkers	..	..	..	-10937	..	..	..	..	..	-10937	..
Stock changes	..	..	..	-177	..	..	..	..	..	-177	..
Total energy supply	..	..	359404	-124743	868977	809	..	13	..	1104460	822
Statistical difference	..	..	-98559	26613	-27007	-4	..	0	..	-98957	9
Transfers	..	..	50353	-47308		..	..	..	..	3045	..
Transformation	..	..	*-508316	507702	-282853	*-171	..	130054	..	-153584	*-171
Electricity plants	..	..	..	-8256	-282853	..	..	130054	..	-161055	..
CHP plants	..	..	..	..	..	..	..	..	..	..	..
Heat plants	..	..	..	..	..	..	..	..	..	..	..
Coke ovens	..	..	..	..	..	..	..	..	..	..	..
Briquetting plants	..	..	..	..	..	..	..	..	..	..	..
Liquefaction plants	..	..	..	..	..	..	..	..	..	..	..
Gas works	..	..	..	..	..	..	..	..	..	..	..
Blast furnaces	..	..	..	..	..	..	..	..	..	..	..
NGL plants & gas blending	..	..	-10520	11257	..	..	..	..	..	738	..
Oil refineries	..	..	*-497797	504701	..	..	..	..	..	6904	..
Other transformation	..	..	..	..	..	*-171	..	..	..	*-171	*-171
Energy industries own use	..	..	..	-6138	-144848	..	..	-1644	..	-152630	..
Losses	..	..	..	..	..	..	..	-11963	..	-11963	..
Final consumption	..	..	..	302900	468284	*642	..	116460	..	888285	*642
Final energy consumption	..	..	..	253822	400206	*642	..	116460	..	771130	*642
Manufacturing, const., mining	..	..	..	39778	241347	..	..	18076	..	299201	..
Iron and steel	..	..	..	..	26374	..	..	..	..	26374	..
Chemical and petrochemical	..	..	..	..	..	..	..	..	..	..	..
Non-ferrous metals	..	..	..	..	..	..	..	..	..	..	..
Non-metallic minerals	..	..	..	..	11687	..	..	..	..	11687	..
Transport equipment	..	..	..	..	..	..	..	..	..	..	..
Machinery	..	..	..	..	..	..	..	..	..	..	..
Mining and quarrying	..	..	..	..	2606	..	..	..	..	2606	..
Food and tobacco	..	..	..	..	..	..	..	..	..	..	..
Paper, pulp and printing	..	..	..	..	..	..	..	..	..	..	..
Wood and wood products	..	..	..	..	..	..	..	..	..	..	..
Textile and leather	..	..	..	..	..	..	..	..	..	..	..
Construction	..	..	..	..	..	..	..	..	..	..	..
Industries n.e.s	..	..	..	39778	200679	..	..	18076	..	258533	..
Transport	..	..	..	173469	..	..	..	..	..	173469	..
Road	..	..	..	171309	..	..	..	..	..	171309	..
Rail	..	..	..	..	..	..	..	..	..	..	..
Domestic aviation	..	..	..	2161	..	..	..	..	..	2161	..
Domestic navigation	..	..	..	..	..	..	..	..	..	..	..
Pipeline transport	..	..	..	..	..	..	..	..	..	..	..
Transport, n.e.s	..	..	..	..	..	..	..	..	..	..	..
Other	..	..	..	40575	158859	*642	..	98384	..	298460	*642
Agriculture, forestry, fishing	..	..	..	..	..	..	..	1530	..	1530	..
Commerce, public services	..	..	..	..	152299	..	..	43243	..	195542	..
Households	..	..	..	9271	..	*642	..	53611	..	63524	*642
Other consumers	..	..	..	31304	6560	..	..	..	..	37864	..
Non-energy use	..	..	..	49077	68078	..	..	..	..	117155	..

Oman

Terajoules

2018	Primary coal and peat	Coal and peat products	Primary Oil	Oil Products	Natural Gas	Biofuels and waste	Nuclear	Electricity	Heat	Total energy	of which: renewables
Primary production	..	..	2074135	..	1371245	436	..	14	..	3445830	450
Imports	..	..	6360	23938	59616	658	..	..	..	90571	658
Exports	..	..	-1671776	-175549	-492394	-284	..	..	..	-2340003	-284
International marine bunkers	..	..	..	-100394	..	..	..	..	..	-100394	..
International aviation bunkers	..	..	..	-12524	..	..	..	..	..	-12524	..
Stock changes	..	..	..	*7044	..	..	..	..	..	*7044	..
Total energy supply	..	..	408719	-257486	938467	809	..	14	..	1090523	823
Statistical difference	..	..	-134755	-63313	-22570	-1	..	-4	..	-220642	14
Transfers	..	..	45537	-42784			..	..	..	2753	..
Transformation	..	..	*-589011	575737	-284897	*-173	..	135601	..	-162743	*-173
Electricity plants	..	..	..	-11524	-284897	..	..	135601	..	-160820	..
CHP plants	..	..	..	..	..	..	..	..	..	..	..
Heat plants	..	..	..	..	..	..	..	..	..	..	..
Coke ovens	..	..	..	..	..	..	..	..	..	..	..
Briquetting plants	..	..	..	..	..	..	..	..	..	..	..
Liquefaction plants	..	..	..	..	..	..	..	..	..	..	..
Gas works	..	..	..	..	..	..	..	..	..	..	..
Blast furnaces	..	..	..	..	..	..	..	..	..	..	..
NGL plants & gas blending	..	..	-10564	11305	..	..	..	..	..	741	..
Oil refineries	..	..	*-578447	575957	..	..	..	..	..	*-2491	..
Other transformation	..	..	..	..	..	*-173	..	..	..	*-173	*-173
Energy industries own use	..	..	..	-7376	-143278	..	..	-1724	..	-152378	..
Losses	..	..	..	..	..	..	..	-13122	..	-13122	..
Final consumption	..	..	..	331405	532862	*636	..	120773	..	985676	*636
Final energy consumption	..	..	..	243476	463474	*636	..	120773	..	828359	*636
Manufacturing, const., mining	..	..	..	29457	205476	..	..	18608	..	253542	..
Iron and steel	..	..	..	..	26323	..	..	..	..	26323	..
Chemical and petrochemical	..	..	..	..	..	..	..	..	..	..	..
Non-ferrous metals	..	..	..	..	..	..	..	..	..	..	..
Non-metallic minerals	..	..	..	..	2802	..	..	..	..	2802	..
Transport equipment	..	..	..	..	..	..	..	..	..	..	..
Machinery	..	..	..	..	..	..	..	..	..	..	..
Mining and quarrying	..	..	..	..	625	..	..	..	..	625	..
Food and tobacco	..	..	..	..	..	..	..	..	..	..	..
Paper, pulp and printing	..	..	..	..	..	..	..	..	..	..	..
Wood and wood products	..	..	..	..	..	..	..	..	..	..	..
Textile and leather	..	..	..	..	..	..	..	..	..	..	..
Construction	..	..	..	..	..	..	..	..	..	..	..
Industries n.e.s	..	..	..	29457	175727	..	..	18608	..	223793	..
Transport	..	..	..	171620	..	..	..	..	..	171620	..
Road	..	..	..	169238	..	..	..	..	..	169238	..
Rail	..	..	..	..	..	..	..	..	..	..	..
Domestic aviation	..	..	..	2381	..	..	..	..	..	2381	..
Domestic navigation	..	..	..	..	..	..	..	..	..	..	..
Pipeline transport	..	..	..	..	..	..	..	..	..	..	..
Transport, n.e.s	..	..	..	..	..	..	..	..	..	..	..
Other	..	..	..	42399	257998	*636	..	102164	..	403197	*636
Agriculture, forestry, fishing	..	..	..	..	..	..	..	1872	..	1872	..
Commerce, public services	..	..	..	..	256424	..	..	45119	..	301543	..
Households	..	..	..	10450	..	*636	..	55174	..	66260	*636
Other consumers	..	..	..	31949	1573	..	..	..	..	33522	..
Non-energy use	..	..	..	87929	69388	..	..	..	..	157317	..

Pakistan

Terajoules

2017	Primary coal and peat	Coal and peat products	Primary Oil	Oil Products	Natural Gas	Biofuels and waste	Nuclear	Electricity	Heat	Total energy	of which: renewables
Primary production	74375	..	213380	..	1137548	*590022	74164	123149	..	2212637	713171
Imports	378294	..	700074	661934	221655	184405	..	1559	..	2147920	184405
Exports	..	..	-17428	-15267	..	-197	..	..	..	-32892	-197
International marine bunkers	..	..	..	-1834	..	..	..	..	..	-1834	..
International aviation bunkers	..	..	..	*-11025	..	..	..	..	..	*-11025	..
Stock changes	..	..	..	*3085	..	..	..	..	..	*3085	..
Total energy supply	452669	..	896026	636894	1359203	*774229	74164	124708	..	4317892	897378
Statistical difference	-15952	..	259984	46410	39650	0	0	-13374	..	316719	123149
Transfers	..	..	..	..	..	..	..	..	..	..	..
Transformation	-115611	..	*-636042	357482	-430916	*-25721	-74164	321570	..	-603402	*-25721
Electricity plants	-115611	..	..	*-257546	-430916	*-23560	-74164	321570	..	-580227	*-23560
CHP plants	..	..	..	..	..	..	..	..	..	..	..
Heat plants	..	..	..	..	..	..	..	..	..	..	..
Coke ovens	..	..	..	..	..	..	..	..	..	..	..
Briquetting plants	..	..	..	..	..	..	..	..	..	..	..
Liquefaction plants	..	..	..	..	..	..	..	..	..	..	..
Gas works	..	..	..	..	..	..	..	..	..	..	..
Blast furnaces	..	..	..	..	..	..	..	..	..	..	..
NGL plants & gas blending	..	..	-25238	*27008	..	..	..	..	..	*1770	..
Oil refineries	..	..	*-610804	588020	..	..	..	..	..	*-22784	..
Other transformation	..	..	..	..	..	*-2161	..	..	..	*-2161	*-2161
Energy industries own use	..	..	..	..	-8726	..	..	-13655	..	-22380	..
Losses	..	..	..	..	*-76500	..	..	-74214	..	*-150714	..
Final consumption	353010	..	..	947966	803410	*748509	..	371783	..	3224678	*748509
Final energy consumption	353010	..	..	866198	664134	*748509	..	371783	..	3003634	*748509
Manufacturing, const., mining	353010	..	..	72741	303886	*117708	..	98633	..	945978	*117708
Iron and steel	..	..	..	..	684	..	..	..	..	684	..
Chemical and petrochemical	..	..	..	..	..	..	..	..	..	..	..
Non-ferrous metals	..	..	..	..	..	..	..	..	..	..	..
Non-metallic minerals	..	..	..	33047	..	..	..	..	..	33047	..
Transport equipment	..	..	..	..	..	..	..	..	..	..	..
Machinery	..	..	..	..	..	..	..	..	..	..	..
Mining and quarrying	..	..	..	..	..	..	..	..	..	..	..
Food and tobacco	..	..	..	..	..	..	..	..	..	..	..
Paper, pulp and printing	..	..	..	..	..	..	..	..	..	..	..
Wood and wood products	..	..	..	..	..	..	..	..	..	..	..
Textile and leather	..	..	..	..	..	..	..	..	..	..	..
Construction	..	..	..	..	..	..	..	..	..	..	..
Industries n.e.s	353010	..	..	39694	303202	*117708	..	98633	..	912247	*117708
Transport	..	..	..	712471	65588	..	..	..	..	778059	..
Road	..	..	..	669169	65588	..	..	..	..	734758	..
Rail	..	..	..	12771	..	..	..	..	..	12771	..
Domestic aviation	..	..	..	*30531	..	..	..	..	..	*30531	..
Domestic navigation	..	..	..	..	..	..	..	..	..	..	..
Pipeline transport	..	..	..	..	..	..	..	..	..	..	..
Transport, n.e.s	..	..	..	..	..	..	..	..	..	..	..
Other	..	..	..	80986	294660	*630801	..	273150	..	1279597	*630801
Agriculture, forestry, fishing	..	..	..	645	..	..	..	34078	..	34723	..
Commerce, public services	..	..	..	..	..	..	..	47250	..	47250	..
Households	..	..	..	27298	264781	*630801	..	191822	..	*1114701	*630801
Other consumers	..	..	..	53043	29879	..	..	..	..	82923	..
Non-energy use	..	..	..	*81768	139276	..	..	..	..	221044	..

Pakistan

Terajoules

2018	Primary coal and peat	Coal and peat products	Primary Oil	Oil Products	Natural Gas	Biofuels and waste	Nuclear	Electricity	Heat	Total energy	of which: renewables
Primary production	84231	..	209695	..	1125635	*598263	106369	110041	..	2234234	708304
Imports	433639	..	687879	619148	260845	*356616	..	1070	..	2359198	*356616
Exports	..	..	-24196	-12872	..	*-713	..	..	..	-37780	*-713
International marine bunkers	..	..	..	-1672	..	..	..	..	..	-1672	..
International aviation bunkers	..	..	..	*-9217	..	..	..	..	..	*-9217	..
Stock changes	..	..	..	219	..	..	..	..	..	219	..
Total energy supply	517871	..	873379	595607	1386480	*954166	106369	111111	..	4544982	1064208
Statistical difference	21911	..	262341	10696	31715	0	0	-996	..	325667	*110041
Transfers	..	..	..	..	..	..	..	..	..	..	..
Transformation	-122361	..	-611038	327870	-468518	-25824	-106369	375890	..	-630350	-25824
Electricity plants	-122361	..	..	*-272520	-468518	*-23622	-106369	375890	..	-617500	*-23622
CHP plants	..	..	..	..	..	..	..	..	..	..	..
Heat plants	..	..	..	..	..	..	..	..	..	..	..
Coke ovens	..	..	..	..	..	..	..	..	..	..	..
Briquetting plants	..	..	..	..	..	..	..	..	..	..	..
Liquefaction plants	..	..	..	..	..	..	..	..	..	..	..
Gas works	..	..	..	..	..	..	..	..	..	..	..
Blast furnaces	..	..	..	..	..	..	..	..	..	..	..
NGL plants & gas blending	..	..	-24929	*26677	..	..	..	..	..	*1748	..
Oil refineries	..	..	-586109	573713	..	..	..	..	..	-12396	..
Other transformation	..	..	..	..	..	*-2202	..	..	..	*-2202	*-2202
Energy industries own use	..	..	..	..	-8564	..	..	-15516	..	-24080	..
Losses	..	..	..	..	-37370	..	..	-86321	..	-123691	..
Final consumption	373599	..	..	912780	840313	*928342	..	*386161	..	3441196	*928342
Final energy consumption	373599	..	..	843446	692916	*928342	..	*386161	..	3224465	*928342
Manufacturing, const., mining	373599	..	..	76994	321602	*125886	..	*102085	..	1000166	*125886
Iron and steel	..	..	..	..	725	..	..	..	..	725	..
Chemical and petrochemical	..	..	..	..	..	..	..	..	..	..	..
Non-ferrous metals	..	..	..	..	..	..	..	..	..	..	..
Non-metallic minerals	..	..	..	34946	..	..	..	..	..	34946	..
Transport equipment	..	..	..	..	..	..	..	..	..	..	..
Machinery	..	..	..	..	..	..	..	..	..	..	..
Mining and quarrying	..	..	..	..	..	..	..	..	..	..	..
Food and tobacco	..	..	..	..	..	..	..	..	..	..	..
Paper, pulp and printing	..	..	..	..	..	..	..	..	..	..	..
Wood and wood products	..	..	..	..	..	..	..	..	..	..	..
Textile and leather	..	..	..	..	..	..	..	..	..	..	..
Construction	..	..	..	..	..	..	..	..	..	..	..
Industries n.e.s	373599	..	..	42048	320878	*125886	..	*102085	..	964496	*125886
Transport	..	..	..	701988	69413	..	..	..	..	771401	..
Road	..	..	..	660193	69413	..	..	..	..	729605	..
Rail	..	..	..	14233	..	..	..	..	..	14233	..
Domestic aviation	..	..	..	*27563	..	..	..	..	..	*27563	..
Domestic navigation	..	..	..	..	..	..	..	..	..	..	..
Pipeline transport	..	..	..	..	..	..	..	..	..	..	..
Transport, n.e.s	..	..	..	..	..	..	..	..	..	..	..
Other	..	..	..	*64464	301901	*802457	..	*284076	..	*1452898	*802457
Agriculture, forestry, fishing	..	..	..	645	..	..	..	*35441	..	*36086	..
Commerce, public services	..	..	..	..	..	..	..	*49140	..	*49140	..
Households	..	..	..	26868	270280	*802457	..	*199495	..	*1299100	*802457
Other consumers	..	..	..	*36950	31622	..	..	..	..	*68572	..
Non-energy use	..	..	..	*69334	147397	..	..	..	..	216731	..

Palau

Terajoules

	All Coal	All Oil	Natural Gas	Primary biofuels / Waste	Charcoal	Electricity	Total energy	of which: renewables
2017								
Primary production	..	..	..	..	..	1	1	1
Imports	..	*3511	..	..	0	..	*3512	0
Exports	..	..	..	..	..	..	..	..
International marine bunkers	..	..	..	..	..	..	..	..
International aviation bunkers	..	*-529	..	..	..	..	*-529	..
Stock changes	..	..	..	..	..	..	..	..
Total energy supply	..	*2982	..	..	0	1	*2983	1
Statistical Difference	..	0	..	..	0	0	0	1
Transfers	..	..	..	..	..	..	..	..
Transformation	..	*-1062	..	..	..	*342	*-720	..
Electricity plants	..	*-1062	..	..	..	*342	*-720	..
Charcoal plants	..	..	..	..	..	..	..	..
Other transformation	..	0	..	..	..	..	0	..
Energy industries own use	..	..	..	..	..	*-19	*-19	..
Losses	..	..	..	..	..	*-58	*-58	..
Final consumption	..	*1920	..	..	0	*267	*2187	0
Final energy consumption	..	*1880	..	..	0	*267	*2147	0
Manufacturing, const., mining	..	..	..	..	..	*22	*22	..
Transport	..	*1788	..	..	..	..	*1788	..
Road	..	*491	..	..	..	..	*491	..
Domestic aviation	..	..	..	..	..	..	..	..
Domestic navigation	..	*1297	..	..	..	..	*1297	..
Other transport	..	..	..	..	..	..	..	..
Other	..	*92	..	..	0	*245	*338	0
Agriculture, forestry, fishing	..	..	..	..	..	..	..	..
Commerce and public services	..	..	..	..	..	*159	*159	..
Households	..	*92	..	..	0	*86	*178	0
Other consumers	..	..	..	..	..	..	..	..
Non-energy use	..	*40	..	..	..	..	*40	..
2018								
Primary production	..	..	..	..	..	*1	*1	*1
Imports	..	*3537	..	..	0	..	*3537	0
Exports	..	..	..	..	..	..	..	..
International marine bunkers	..	..	..	..	..	..	..	..
International aviation bunkers	..	*-574	..	..	..	..	*-574	..
Stock changes	..	..	..	..	..	..	..	..
Total energy supply	..	*2963	..	..	0	*1	*2965	*1
Statistical Difference	..	0	..	..	0	0	0	*1
Transfers	..	..	..	..	..	..	..	..
Transformation	..	*-1054	..	..	..	*340	*-713	..
Electricity plants	..	*-1054	..	..	..	*340	*-713	..
Charcoal plants	..	..	..	..	..	..	..	..
Other transformation	..	0	..	..	..	..	0	..
Energy industries own use	..	..	..	..	..	*-21	*-21	..
Losses	..	..	..	..	..	*-58	*-58	..
Final consumption	..	1910	..	..	0	*263	2173	0
Final energy consumption	..	1870	..	..	0	*263	2133	0
Manufacturing, const., mining	..	..	..	..	..	*22	*22	..
Transport	..	1778	..	..	..	..	1778	..
Road	..	*505	..	..	..	..	*505	..
Domestic aviation	..	..	..	..	..	..	..	..
Domestic navigation	..	1273	..	..	..	..	1273	..
Other transport	..	..	..	..	..	..	..	..
Other	..	*92	..	..	0	*241	*334	0
Agriculture, forestry, fishing	..	..	..	..	..	..	..	..
Commerce and public services	..	..	..	..	..	*158	*158	..
Households	..	*92	..	..	0	*83	*176	0
Other consumers	..	..	..	..	..	..	..	..
Non-energy use	..	*40	..	..	..	..	*40	..

Panama

Terajoules

	All Coal	All Oil	Natural Gas	Primary biofuels / Waste	Charcoal	Electricity	Total energy	of which: renewables
2017								
Primary production	..	..	..	13056	..	28452	41507	41507
Imports	2252	337012	..	..	..	24	339288	..
Exports	..	-19	..	..	..	-1143	-1162	..
International marine bunkers	..	-172670	..	..	..	..	-172670	..
International aviation bunkers	..	-30304	..	..	..	..	-30304	..
Stock changes	..	10856	..	..	..	..	10856	..
Total energy supply	2252	144875	..	13056	..	27332	187515	41507
Statistical Difference	0	10057	..	0	0	-149	9908	28452
Transfers	..	..	..	..	..	..	..	..
Transformation	-2252	-22401	..	-2886	34	11343	-16163	-2853
Electricity plants	-2252	-22401	..	-2843	..	11343	-16153	-2843
Charcoal plants	..	..	..	-44	34	..	-10	-10
Other transformation	0	0	..	0	..	..	0	0
Energy industries own use	..	..	..	..	..	-869	-869	..
Losses	..	..	..	..	..	-5211	-5211	..
Final consumption	..	112418	..	10169	34	32742	155364	10203
Final energy consumption	..	112418	..	10169	34	32742	155364	10203
Manufacturing, const., mining	..	29443	..	4504	..	2343	36289	4504
Transport	..	70090	..	..	..	148	70238	..
Road	..	68869	..	..	..	..	68869	..
Domestic aviation	..	1157	..	..	..	..	1157	..
Domestic navigation	..	..	..	..	..	..	..	..
Other transport	..	64	..	..	..	148	212	..
Other	..	12885	..	5666	34	30252	48836	5699
Agriculture, forestry, fishing	..	594	..	..	..	66	660	..
Commerce and public services	..	2439	..	..	13	19822	22275	13
Households	..	9852	..	5666	21	10364	25902	5686
Other consumers	..	..	..	..	..	..	..	..
Non-energy use	..	..	..	..	..	..	..	..
2018								
Primary production	..	..	..	12861	..	31242	44103	44103
Imports	5642	325978	9162	..	..	48	340830	..
Exports	..	-11	..	..	..	-1173	-1184	..
International marine bunkers	..	-166868	..	..	..	..	-166868	..
International aviation bunkers	..	-31948	..	..	..	..	-31948	..
Stock changes	..	1116	-3017	..	..	..	-1902	..
Total energy supply	5642	128266	6145	12861	..	30117	183031	44103
Statistical Difference	0	5333	0	-6	0	-617	4710	31236
Transfers	..	..	..	..	..	..	..	..
Transformation	-5642	-10631	-6145	-4451	33	9628	-17208	-4418
Electricity plants	-5642	-10631	-6145	-4409	..	9628	-17198	-4409
Charcoal plants	..	..	..	-42	33	..	-9	-9
Other transformation	0	0	0	0	..	..	0	0
Energy industries own use	..	..	..	..	..	-1772	-1772	..
Losses	..	..	..	..	..	-5124	-5124	..
Final consumption	..	112302	..	8417	33	33466	154218	8450
Final energy consumption	..	112302	..	8417	33	33466	154218	8450
Manufacturing, const., mining	..	29219	..	2772	..	2222	34213	2772
Transport	..	69304	..	..	..	146	69451	..
Road	..	68242	..	..	..	..	68242	..
Domestic aviation	..	999	..	..	..	..	999	..
Domestic navigation	..	..	..	..	..	..	..	..
Other transport	..	64	..	..	..	146	210	..
Other	..	13778	..	5645	33	31098	50554	5677
Agriculture, forestry, fishing	..	551	..	..	..	66	616	..
Commerce and public services	..	3047	..	..	13	20713	23773	13
Households	..	10181	..	5645	20	10319	26164	5664
Other consumers	..	..	..	..	..	..	..	..
Non-energy use	..	..	..	..	..	..	..	..

Papua New Guinea

Terajoules

2017	Primary coal and peat	Coal and peat products	Primary Oil	Oil Products	Natural Gas	Biofuels and waste	Nuclear	Electricity	Heat	Total energy	of which: renewables
Primary production	..	..	43907	..	113455	56687	..	3671	15120	232840	75478
Imports	..	..	59728	40170	..	..	..	..	..	99898	..
Exports	..	..	-43907	-19240	-96388	-7	..	..	..	-159542	-7
International marine bunkers	..	..	..	-367	..	..	..	..	..	-367	..
International aviation bunkers	..	..	..	-2557	..	..	..	..	..	-2557	..
Stock changes	..	..	-3426	-476	..	..	..	..	..	-3902	..
Total energy supply	..	..	56302	17530	17067	56680	..	3671	15120	166370	75471
Statistical difference	..	..	-3806	-44	-1472	0	..	0	0	-5323	5183
Transfers	..	..	..	-1943	..	..	..	..	..	-1943	..
Transformation	..	..	-60108	35464	-7838	*-497	..	12870	-15120	-35229	-14105
Electricity plants	..	..	..	-24374	-7838	..	..	12870	-15120	-34462	-13608
CHP plants	..	..	..	..	..	..	..	..	..	..	..
Heat plants	..	..	..	..	..	..	..	..	..	..	..
Coke ovens	..	..	..	..	..	..	..	..	..	..	..
Briquetting plants	..	..	..	..	..	..	..	..	..	..	..
Liquefaction plants	..	..	..	..	..	..	..	..	..	..	..
Gas works	..	..	..	..	..	..	..	..	..	..	..
Blast furnaces	..	..	..	..	..	..	..	..	..	..	..
NGL plants & gas blending	..	..	..	..	..	..	..	..	..	..	..
Oil refineries	..	..	-60108	59838	..	..	..	..	..	-270	..
Other transformation	..	..	..	..	..	*-497	..	..	..	*-497	*-497
Energy industries own use	..	..	..	..	-10701	..	..	-931	..	-11632	..
Losses	..	..	..	..	..	..	..	*-1217	..	*-1217	..
Final consumption	..	..	..	51095	..	*56183	..	*14393	..	121671	*56183
Final energy consumption	..	..	..	51095	..	*56183	..	*14393	..	121671	*56183
Manufacturing, const., mining	..	..	..	20490	..	*5818	..	*10566	..	36873	*5818
Iron and steel	..	..	..	..	..	..	..	..	..	..	..
Chemical and petrochemical	..	..	..	..	..	..	..	..	..	..	..
Non-ferrous metals	..	..	..	..	..	..	..	..	..	..	..
Non-metallic minerals	..	..	..	..	..	..	..	..	..	..	..
Transport equipment	..	..	..	..	..	..	..	..	..	..	..
Machinery	..	..	..	..	..	..	..	..	..	..	..
Mining and quarrying	..	..	..	..	..	..	..	..	..	..	..
Food and tobacco	..	..	..	..	..	*880	..	..	..	*880	*880
Paper, pulp and printing	..	..	..	..	..	..	..	..	..	..	..
Wood and wood products	..	..	..	..	..	..	..	..	..	..	..
Textile and leather	..	..	..	..	..	..	..	..	..	..	..
Construction	..	..	..	..	..	..	..	..	..	..	..
Industries n.e.s	..	..	..	20490	..	*4938	..	*10566	..	35993	*4938
Transport	..	..	..	24201	..	..	..	..	..	24201	..
Road	..	..	..	21076	..	..	..	..	..	21076	..
Rail	..	..	..	..	..	..	..	..	..	..	..
Domestic aviation	..	..	..	3126	..	..	..	..	..	3126	..
Domestic navigation	..	..	..	..	..	..	..	..	..	..	..
Pipeline transport	..	..	..	..	..	..	..	..	..	..	..
Transport, n.e.s	..	..	..	..	..	..	..	..	..	..	..
Other	..	..	..	6404	..	*50365	..	*3827	..	*60596	*50365
Agriculture, forestry, fishing	..	..	..	4279	..	..	..	*252	..	4531	..
Commerce, public services	..	..	..	893	..	..	..	*353	..	1246	..
Households	..	..	..	1232	..	*50365	..	*3222	..	*54819	*50365
Other consumers	..	..	..	..	..	..	..	..	..	..	..
Non-energy use	..	..	..	..	..	..	..	..	..	..	..

Papua New Guinea

Terajoules

2018	Primary coal and peat	Coal and peat products	Primary Oil	Oil Products	Natural Gas	Biofuels and waste	Nuclear	Electricity	Heat	Total energy	of which: renewables
Primary production	..	..	*44127	..	*114590	56739	..	3159	*15300	*233915	75198
Imports	..	..	*60028	*40328	..	..	..	..	..	*100356	..
Exports	..	..	*-44127	*-19340	*-97352	-7	..	..	..	*-160826	-7
International marine bunkers	..	..	..	*-369	..	..	..	..	..	*-369	..
International aviation bunkers	..	..	..	*-2570	..	..	..	..	..	*-2570	..
Stock changes	..	..	*-3443	*-477	..	..	..	..	..	*-3920	..
Total energy supply	..	..	*56585	*17571	*17238	56733	..	3159	*15300	*166585	75191
Statistical difference	..	..	*-3824	*-87	*-1433	0	..	0	0	*-5343	4689
Transfers	..	..	..	*-1953	..	..	..	..	..	*-1953	..
Transformation	..	..	*-60409	*35654	*-7916	*-502	..	*12978	*-15300	*-35495	*-14272
Electricity plants	..	..	..	*-24496	*-7916	..	..	*12978	*-15300	*-34734	*-13770
CHP plants	..	..	..	..	..	..	..	..	..	..	..
Heat plants	..	..	..	..	..	..	..	..	..	..	..
Coke ovens	..	..	..	..	..	..	..	..	..	..	..
Briquetting plants	..	..	..	..	..	..	..	..	..	..	..
Liquefaction plants	..	..	..	..	..	..	..	..	..	..	..
Gas works	..	..	..	..	..	..	..	..	..	..	..
Blast furnaces	..	..	..	..	..	..	..	..	..	..	..
NGL plants & gas blending	..	..	..	..	..	..	..	..	..	..	..
Oil refineries	..	..	*-60409	*60150	..	..	..	..	..	*-259	..
Other transformation	..	..	..	..	..	*-502	..	..	..	*-502	*-502
Energy industries own use	..	..	..	..	*-10754	..	..	*-688	..	*-11442	..
Losses	..	..	..	..	..	..	..	*-1224	..	*-1224	..
Final consumption	..	..	..	*51359	..	*56230	..	*14225	..	*121814	*56230
Final energy consumption	..	..	..	*51359	..	*56230	..	*14225	..	*121814	*56230
Manufacturing, const., mining	..	..	..	*20592	..	*5867	..	*10443	..	*36902	*5867
Iron and steel	..	..	..	..	..	..	..	..	..	..	..
Chemical and petrochemical	..	..	..	..	..	..	..	..	..	..	..
Non-ferrous metals	..	..	..	..	..	..	..	..	..	..	..
Non-metallic minerals	..	..	..	..	..	..	..	..	..	..	..
Transport equipment	..	..	..	..	..	..	..	..	..	..	..
Machinery	..	..	..	..	..	..	..	..	..	..	..
Mining and quarrying	..	..	..	..	..	..	..	..	..	..	..
Food and tobacco	..	..	..	..	..	*880	..	..	..	*880	*880
Paper, pulp and printing	..	..	..	..	..	..	..	..	..	..	..
Wood and wood products	..	..	..	..	..	..	..	..	..	..	..
Textile and leather	..	..	..	..	..	..	..	..	..	..	..
Construction	..	..	..	..	..	..	..	..	..	..	..
Industries n.e.s	..	..	..	*20592	..	*4987	..	*10443	..	*36022	*4987
Transport	..	..	..	*24322	..	..	..	..	..	*24322	..
Road	..	..	..	*21181	..	..	..	..	..	*21181	..
Rail	..	..	..	..	..	..	..	..	..	..	..
Domestic aviation	..	..	..	*3141	..	..	..	..	..	*3141	..
Domestic navigation	..	..	..	..	..	..	..	..	..	..	..
Pipeline transport	..	..	..	..	..	..	..	..	..	..	..
Transport, n.e.s	..	..	..	..	..	..	..	..	..	..	..
Other	..	..	..	*6445	..	*50363	..	*3782	..	*60590	*50363
Agriculture, forestry, fishing	..	..	..	*4300	..	..	..	*249	..	*4549	..
Commerce, public services	..	..	..	*902	..	..	..	*349	..	*1250	..
Households	..	..	..	*1244	..	*50363	..	*3184	..	*54791	*50363
Other consumers	..	..	..	..	..	..	..	..	..	..	..
Non-energy use	..	..	..	..	..	..	..	..	..	..	..

Paraguay

Terajoules

	All Coal	All Oil	Natural Gas	Primary biofuels / Waste	Charcoal	Electricity	Total energy	of which: renewables
2017								
Primary production	..	..	..	147583	..	214862	362445	362445
Imports	38	107891	..	..	..	..	107929	..
Exports	..	..	..	..	-3085	-157085	-160170	-3085
International marine bunkers	..	..	..	..	..	..	..	..
International aviation bunkers	..	-2655	..	..	..	..	-2655	..
Stock changes	..	5204	..	..	..	..	5204	..
Total energy supply	38	110440	..	147583	-3085	57777	312754	359360
Statistical Difference	0	-3896	..	0	0	0	-3896	214862
Transfers	..	..	..	..	..	..	..	..
Transformation	..	-20	..	-40104	13103	5	-27016	-27001
Electricity plants	..	-20	..	..	..	5	-15	..
Charcoal plants	..	..	..	-40104	13103	..	-27001	-27001
Other transformation	..	0	..	0	..	..	0	0
Energy industries own use	..	..	..	..	..	-1784	-1784	..
Losses	..	..	..	..	..	-14401	-14401	..
Final consumption	38	114316	..	107479	10018	41598	273449	117498
Final energy consumption	38	112173	..	107479	10018	41598	271306	117498
Manufacturing, const., mining	38	1874	..	56461	647	16027	75048	57108
Transport	..	106850	..	6439	..	..	113289	6439
Road	..	106697	..	6439	..	..	113136	6439
Domestic aviation	..	153	..	..	..	..	153	..
Domestic navigation	..	..	..	..	..	..	..	..
Other transport	..	..	..	..	..	..	..	..
Other	..	3449	..	44579	9372	25570	82969	53950
Agriculture, forestry, fishing	..	..	..	..	..	..	..	..
Commerce and public services	..	..	..	..	..	1788	1788	..
Households	..	14	..	44558	..	17713	62286	44558
Other consumers	..	3434	..	20	9372	6069	18895	9392
Non-energy use	..	2143	..	..	..	..	2143	..
2018								
Primary production	..	..	..	132578	..	213159	345737	345737
Imports	151	120585	..	..	..	..	120737	..
Exports	..	..	..	..	-3281	-151939	-155221	-3281
International marine bunkers	..	..	..	..	..	..	..	..
International aviation bunkers	..	-3159	..	..	..	..	-3159	..
Stock changes	..	-837	..	..	..	..	-837	..
Total energy supply	151	116589	..	132578	-3281	61220	307257	342456
Statistical Difference	0	-4262	..	0	0	0	-4262	213159
Transfers	..	..	..	..	..	..	..	..
Transformation	..	-21	..	-25480	12801	6	-12694	-12679
Electricity plants	..	-21	..	..	..	6	-15	..
Charcoal plants	..	..	..	-25480	12801	..	-12679	-12679
Other transformation	..	0	..	0	..	..	0	0
Energy industries own use	..	..	..	..	..	-1738	-1738	..
Losses	..	..	..	..	..	-14474	-14474	..
Final consumption	151	120830	..	107098	9519	45013	282612	116618
Final energy consumption	151	118525	..	107098	9519	45013	280307	116618
Manufacturing, const., mining	151	2112	..	57898	451	16903	77515	58349
Transport	..	112703	..	7030	..	..	119734	7030
Road	..	112570	..	7030	..	..	119600	7030
Domestic aviation	..	133	..	..	..	..	133	..
Domestic navigation	..	..	..	..	..	..	..	..
Other transport	..	..	..	..	..	..	..	..
Other	..	3710	..	42170	9068	28110	83058	51238
Agriculture, forestry, fishing	..	..	..	..	..	..	..	..
Commerce and public services	..	..	..	..	..	1809	1809	..
Households	..	14	..	42149	..	19356	61520	42149
Other consumers	..	3695	..	20	9068	6946	19730	9089
Non-energy use	..	2305	..	..	..	..	2305	..

Peru

Terajoules

2017	Primary coal and peat	Coal and peat products	Primary Oil	Oil Products	Natural Gas	Biofuels and waste	Nuclear	Electricity	Heat	Total energy	of which: renewables
Primary production	8142	..	232476	..	470939	88842	..	109721	1382	911502	199945
Imports	14366	1833	264805	240830	..	13348	..	60	..	535242	13348
Exports	-9549	0	-3308	-262265	-206427	..	..	0	..	-481548	..
International marine bunkers	..	..	..	..	..	..	..	..	..	..	..
International aviation bunkers	..	..	..	-29882	..	..	..	..	..	-29882	..
Stock changes	15851	395	-2706	24130	..	207	..	..	..	37877	207
Total energy supply	28810	2228	491267	-27187	264513	102397	..	109781	1382	973190	213500
Statistical difference	-710	0	-5542	6524	-2429	843	..	3	0	-1311	110564
Transfers	..	..	57448	-38388	..	..	..	..	..	19060	..
Transformation	-9026	..	-554256	519294	-149002	-20558	..	80154	..	-133395	-20558
Electricity plants	-9026	..	..	-21400	-149002	-18667	..	80154	..	-117941	-18667
CHP plants	..	..	..	..	..	..	..	..	..	..	..
Heat plants	..	..	..	..	..	..	..	..	..	..	..
Coke ovens	..	..	..	..	..	..	..	..	..	..	..
Briquetting plants	..	..	..	..	..	..	..	..	..	..	..
Liquefaction plants	..	..	..	..	..	..	..	..	..	..	..
Gas works	..	..	..	..	..	..	..	..	..	..	..
Blast furnaces	..	..	..	..	..	..	..	..	..	..	..
NGL plants & gas blending	..	..	-140412	141950	..	..	..	..	..	1538	..
Oil refineries	..	..	-413844	398745	..	..	..	..	..	-15100	..
Other transformation	..	..	..	..	..	-1892	..	..	..	-1892	-1892
Energy industries own use	..	..	..	-8083	-37344	..	..	-2708	..	-48135	..
Losses	..	..	..	..	..	..	..	-19953	..	-19953	..
Final consumption	20495	2228	..	439112	80596	80996	..	167270	1382	792079	82378
Final energy consumption	20495	2228	..	426570	80596	80996	..	167270	1382	779537	82378
Manufacturing, const., mining	20492	2228	..	41184	50257	13343	..	96178	3	223684	13346
Iron and steel	1264	2228	..	..	0	..	..	..	..	3492	..
Chemical and petrochemical	..	..	..	..	..	..	..	..	..	..	..
Non-ferrous metals	..	..	..	..	..	..	..	..	..	..	..
Non-metallic minerals	..	..	..	..	..	..	..	..	..	..	..
Transport equipment	..	..	..	..	..	..	..	..	..	..	..
Machinery	..	..	..	..	..	..	..	..	..	..	..
Mining and quarrying	..	..	..	17191	..	899	..	53806	1	71896	900
Food and tobacco	..	..	..	..	..	..	..	..	..	..	..
Paper, pulp and printing	..	..	..	..	..	..	..	..	..	..	..
Wood and wood products	..	..	..	..	..	..	..	..	..	..	..
Textile and leather	..	..	..	..	..	..	..	..	..	..	..
Construction	..	..	..	..	..	..	..	..	..	..	..
Industries n.e.s	19228	0	..	23993	50257	12444	..	42372	2	148296	12446
Transport	..	..	..	323909	25700	11026	..	191	..	360826	11026
Road	..	..	..	301782	..	11026	..	..	..	312809	11026
Rail	..	..	..	..	..	..	..	..	..	..	..
Domestic aviation	..	..	..	14685	..	..	..	..	..	14685	..
Domestic navigation	..	..	..	7442	..	..	..	..	..	7442	..
Pipeline transport	..	..	..	..	..	..	..	..	..	..	..
Transport, n.e.s	..	..	..	..	25700	..	..	191	..	25890	..
Other	3	..	..	61476	4640	56627	..	70902	1379	195027	58006
Agriculture, forestry, fishing	3	..	..	4475	73	258	..	4586	7	9402	264
Commerce, public services	..	..	..	17482	944	3727	..	31853	535	54542	4262
Households	..	..	..	39519	3623	52642	..	34463	837	131084	53479
Other consumers	..	..	..	..	..	..	..	..	..	..	..
Non-energy use	..	..	..	12542	..	..	..	..	..	12542	..

Peru

Terajoules

2018	Primary coal and peat	Coal and peat products	Primary Oil	Oil Products	Natural Gas	Biofuels and waste	Nuclear	Electricity	Heat	Total energy	of which: renewables
Primary production	5808	..	235481	..	462896	93046	..	118930	1437	917597	213412
Imports	9742	2228	238084	244825	..	11211	..	76	..	506166	11211
Exports	-17021	0	-13704	-201450	-189365	..	..	..	..	-421541	..
International marine bunkers	..	..	..	-20797	..	..	..	..	..	-20797	..
International aviation bunkers	..	..	..	-30257	..	..	..	..	..	-30257	..
Stock changes	26917	-28	9881	12967	..	240	..	..	..	49977	240
Total energy supply	25446	2200	469741	5288	273531	104496	..	119006	1437	1001144	224862
Statistical difference	-997	0	0	13128	2073	-654	..	-5	0	13546	118276
Transfers	..	..	65661	-36941	..	..	..	..	..	28720	..
Transformation	-4743	..	-535402	499535	-151408	-16474	..	79006	..	-129487	-16474
Electricity plants	-4743	..	..	-14061	-151408	-14220	..	79006	..	-105427	-14220
CHP plants	..	..	..	..	..	..	..	..	..	..	..
Heat plants	..	..	..	..	..	..	..	..	..	..	..
Coke ovens	..	..	..	..	..	..	..	..	..	..	..
Briquetting plants	..	..	..	..	..	..	..	..	..	..	..
Liquefaction plants	..	..	..	..	..	..	..	..	..	..	..
Gas works	..	..	..	..	..	..	..	..	..	..	..
Blast furnaces	..	..	..	..	..	..	..	..	..	..	..
NGL plants & gas blending	..	..	-132205	128421	..	..	..	..	..	-3783	..
Oil refineries	..	..	-403198	385175	..	..	..	..	..	-18023	..
Other transformation	..	..	..	..	..	-2254	..	..	..	-2254	-2254
Energy industries own use	..	..	..	-8676	-33414	..	..	-2675	..	-44765	..
Losses	..	..	..	..	..	..	..	-21487	..	-21487	..
Final consumption	21699	2200	..	446078	86636	88676	..	173855	1437	820580	90112
Final energy consumption	21699	2200	..	434139	86636	88676	..	173855	1437	808641	90112
Manufacturing, const., mining	21696	2200	..	46124	47006	16936	..	100195	3	234161	16940
Iron and steel	1259	2200	..	..	..	..	..	..	..	3459	..
Chemical and petrochemical	..	..	..	..	..	..	..	..	..	..	..
Non-ferrous metals	..	..	..	..	..	..	..	..	..	..	..
Non-metallic minerals	..	..	..	..	..	..	..	..	..	..	..
Transport equipment	..	..	..	..	..	..	..	..	..	..	..
Machinery	..	..	..	..	..	..	..	..	..	..	..
Mining and quarrying	..	..	..	17188	1712	586	..	57056	1	76543	587
Food and tobacco	..	..	..	..	..	..	..	..	..	..	..
Paper, pulp and printing	..	..	..	..	..	..	..	..	..	..	..
Wood and wood products	..	..	..	..	..	..	..	..	..	..	..
Textile and leather	..	..	..	..	..	..	..	..	..	..	..
Construction	..	..	..	..	..	..	..	..	..	..	..
Industries n.e.s	20437	0	..	28936	45294	16350	..	43139	2	154159	16353
Transport	..	..	..	330920	26980	13288	..	216	..	371404	13288
Road	..	..	..	314133	..	13288	..	..	..	327420	13288
Rail	..	..	..	..	..	..	..	..	..	..	..
Domestic aviation	..	..	..	15523	..	..	..	..	..	15523	..
Domestic navigation	..	..	..	1265	..	..	..	..	..	1265	..
Pipeline transport	..	..	..	..	..	..	..	..	..	..	..
Transport, n.e.s	..	..	..	..	26980	..	..	216	..	27196	..
Other	3	..	..	57095	12650	58452	..	73444	1433	203076	59885
Agriculture, forestry, fishing	3	..	..	3482	145	203	..	5627	7	9466	210
Commerce, public services	..	..	..	11748	7992	3705	..	32022	556	56023	4261
Households	..	..	..	41865	4513	54544	..	35795	870	137586	55414
Other consumers	..	..	..	..	..	..	..	..	..	..	..
Non-energy use	..	..	..	11939	..	..	..	..	..	11939	..

Philippines

Terajoules

2017	Primary coal and peat	Coal and peat products	Primary Oil	Oil Products	Natural Gas	Biofuels and waste	Nuclear	Electricity	Heat	Total energy	of which: renewables
Primary production	263680	..	25799	..	137729	258095	..	42921	369724	1097948	670476
Imports	490025	8291	447940	530723	..	10098	..	..	..	1487077	10098
Exports	-136398	..	-24775	-63446	..	..	..	..	..	-224618	..
International marine bunkers	..	..	..	-4089	..	..	..	..	..	-4089	..
International aviation bunkers	..	..	..	-70609	..	..	..	..	..	-70609	..
Stock changes	28548	..	10101	-7579	..	3971	..	..	..	35042	3971
Total energy supply	645856	8291	459065	385001	137729	272165	..	42921	369724	2320752	684546
Statistical difference	-1374	0	12995	-3359	0	0	..	133	0	8394	79894
Transfers	..	..	..	..	..	..	..	..	..	..	..
Transformation	-514939	-4978	-439074	381716	-131524	46140	..	301766	-369724	-730616	-286348
Electricity plants	*-514939	..	..	*-41687	*-131524	*-14659	..	301766	-369724	*-770766	-347147
CHP plants	..	..	..	..	..	..	..	..	..	..	..
Heat plants	..	..	..	..	..	..	..	..	..	..	..
Coke ovens	..	..	..	..	..	..	..	..	..	..	..
Briquetting plants	..	..	..	..	..	..	..	..	..	..	..
Liquefaction plants	..	..	..	..	..	..	..	..	..	..	..
Gas works	..	..	..	..	..	..	..	..	..	..	..
Blast furnaces	..	-4978	..	..	..	..	..	..	..	-4978	..
NGL plants & gas blending	..	..	..	..	..	..	..	..	..	..	..
Oil refineries	..	..	-439074	423403	..	..	..	..	..	-15671	..
Other transformation	..	..	..	..	..	60800	..	..	..	60800	60800
Energy industries own use	..	..	-6996	..	-3965	..	..	-34758	..	-45719	..
Losses	..	..	..	..	..	..	..	-29742	..	-29742	..
Final consumption	132291	3313	..	770076	2241	318305	..	280054	..	1506280	318305
Final energy consumption	125808	3313	..	708853	2241	318305	..	280054	..	1438573	318305
Manufacturing, const., mining	125808	3313	..	64412	2241	43964	..	92064	..	331802	43964
Iron and steel	8938	3313	..	5075	..	22	..	18769	..	36116	22
Chemical and petrochemical	596	..	..	9611	..	36	..	5591	..	15834	36
Non-ferrous metals	..	..	..	..	..	..	..	..	..	..	..
Non-metallic minerals	97770	..	..	9726	..	45	..	7011	..	114552	45
Transport equipment	..	..	..	..	..	..	..	..	..	..	..
Machinery	..	..	..	7443	..	76	..	23018	..	30537	76
Mining and quarrying	..	..	..	11225	..	153	..	2866	..	14244	153
Food and tobacco	13174	..	..	9332	..	43090	..	16830	..	82426	43090
Paper, pulp and printing	4190	..	..	185	..	1	..	5156	..	9531	1
Wood and wood products	..	..	..	592	..	4	..	2179	..	2776	4
Textile and leather	364	..	..	502	..	1	..	7135	..	8002	1
Construction	..	..	..	10107	..	164	..	865	..	11136	164
Industries n.e.s	775	0	..	616	2241	372	..	2645	..	6648	372
Transport	..	..	..	489373	0	27082	..	402	..	516857	27082
Road	..	..	..	426253	0	26843	..	..	..	453096	26843
Rail	..	..	..	95	..	2	..	402	..	498	2
Domestic aviation	..	..	..	22852	..	..	..	..	..	22852	..
Domestic navigation	..	..	..	40173	..	238	..	..	..	40411	238
Pipeline transport	..	..	..	..	..	..	..	..	..	..	..
Transport, n.e.s	..	..	..	..	..	..	..	..	..	..	..
Other	..	..	..	155068	..	247259	..	187588	..	589915	247259
Agriculture, forestry, fishing	..	..	..	12777	..	211	..	9208	..	22196	211
Commerce, public services	..	..	..	91245	..	16124	..	81965	..	189333	16124
Households	..	..	..	51047	..	230924	..	96415	..	378386	230924
Other consumers	..	..	..	..	..	..	..	..	..	..	..
Non-energy use	6483	..	..	61223	..	..	..	..	..	67707	..

Philippines

Terajoules

2018	Primary coal and peat	Coal and peat products	Primary Oil	Oil Products	Natural Gas	Biofuels and waste	Nuclear	Electricity	Heat	Total energy	of which: renewables
Primary production	259771	..	24561	..	153765	261636	..	42490	375671	1117894	679526
Imports	576880	8657	495003	528168	..	9490	..	..	..	1618198	9490
Exports	-111694	..	-23419	-72787	..	..	..	..	..	-207900	..
International marine bunkers	..	..	..	-3538	..	..	..	..	..	-3538	..
International aviation bunkers	..	..	..	-72611	..	..	..	..	..	-72611	..
Stock changes	-44748	..	-427	-17093	..	2873	..	..	..	-59396	2873
Total energy supply	680208	8657	495718	362140	153765	273999	..	42490	375671	2392647	691889
Statistical difference	-2798	0	-4454	22693	0	-3	..	-328	0	15111	80054
Transfers	..	..	..	..	..	..	..	..	..	..	..
Transformation	-575508	-5191	-496725	446970	-141933	47085	..	317954	-375671	-783019	-290748
Electricity plants	*-575508	..	..	*-31486	*-141933	*-15957	..	317954	-375671	*-822600	-353789
CHP plants	..	..	..	..	..	..	..	..	..	..	..
Heat plants	..	..	..	..	..	..	..	..	..	..	..
Coke ovens	..	..	..	..	..	..	..	..	..	..	..
Briquetting plants	..	..	..	..	..	..	..	..	..	..	..
Liquefaction plants	..	..	..	..	..	..	..	..	..	..	..
Gas works	..	..	..	..	..	..	..	..	..	..	..
Blast furnaces	..	-5191	..	..	..	..	..	..	..	-5191	..
NGL plants & gas blending	..	..	..	..	..	..	..	..	..	..	..
Oil refineries	..	..	-496725	478456	..	..	..	..	..	-18269	..
Other transformation	..	..	..	..	..	63042	..	..	..	63042	63042
Energy industries own use	..	..	-3447	..	-9296	..	..	-34880	..	-47624	..
Losses	..	..	..	..	..	..	..	-29308	..	-29308	..
Final consumption	107498	3466	..	786416	2536	321087	..	296583	..	1517586	321087
Final energy consumption	100722	3466	..	733607	2536	321087	..	296583	..	1458001	321087
Manufacturing, const., mining	100722	3466	..	63742	2536	44567	..	99642	..	314674	44567
Iron and steel	8793	3466	..	5527	..	13	..	21944	..	39743	13
Chemical and petrochemical	792	..	..	6324	..	29	..	6537	..	13681	29
Non-ferrous metals	..	..	..	..	..	..	..	..	..	..	..
Non-metallic minerals	62994	..	..	9559	..	39	..	8197	..	80788	39
Transport equipment	..	..	..	..	..	..	..	..	..	..	..
Machinery	..	..	..	6078	..	68	..	26911	..	33057	68
Mining and quarrying	..	..	..	9469	..	136	..	3351	..	12956	136
Food and tobacco	5828	..	..	13458	..	43743	..	19677	..	82705	43743
Paper, pulp and printing	20162	..	..	326	..	0	..	6028	..	26516	0
Wood and wood products	..	..	..	652	..	3	..	2548	..	3203	3
Textile and leather	359	..	..	200	..	0	..	347	..	906	0
Construction	..	..	..	10037	..	155	..	1012	..	11204	155
Industries n.e.s	1795	0	..	2113	2536	380	..	3092	..	9915	380
Transport	..	..	..	507629	..	27936	..	379	..	535944	27936
Road	..	..	..	443499	..	27713	..	..	..	471211	27713
Rail	..	..	..	73	..	0	..	379	..	452	0
Domestic aviation	..	..	..	26068	..	..	..	..	..	26068	..
Domestic navigation	..	..	..	37988	..	223	..	..	..	38212	223
Pipeline transport	..	..	..	..	..	..	..	..	..	..	..
Transport, n.e.s	..	..	..	..	..	..	..	..	..	..	..
Other	..	..	..	162236	..	248584	..	196563	..	607383	248584
Agriculture, forestry, fishing	..	..	..	9166	..	152	..	8365	..	17684	152
Commerce, public services	..	..	..	97795	..	16458	..	86459	..	200712	16458
Households	..	..	..	55275	..	231974	..	101739	..	388988	231974
Other consumers	..	..	..	..	..	..	..	..	..	..	..
Non-energy use	6776	..	..	52809	..	..	..	..	..	59585	..

Poland

Terajoules

2017	Primary coal and peat	Coal and peat products	Primary Oil	Oil Products	Natural Gas	Biofuels and waste	Nuclear	Electricity	Heat	Total energy	of which: renewables
Primary production	2085426	..	41952	..	147036	350288	..	63482	3885	2692069	385729
Imports	323198	6740	1049911	426118	545413	*31739	..	47776	..	2430895	*31739
Exports	-171481	-192068	-9258	-217091	-42509	-39129	..	-39542	..	-711078	-39129
International marine bunkers	..	..	..	-11214	..	..	..	..	..	-11214	..
International aviation bunkers	..	..	..	-36515	..	..	..	..	..	-36515	..
Stock changes	48397	2632	-11782	-13864	-3298	-117	..	..	..	21968	-117
Total energy supply	2285539	-182696	1070823	147435	646642	342781	..	71716	3885	4386125	378221
Statistical difference	-29941	83	80	-7871	2059	28	..	0	0	-35562	63509
Transfers	..	..	62147	-60423	..	..	..	..	..	1724	..
Transformation	-1883147	272355	-1132891	1126258	-108392	*-72249	..	548489	298364	-951212	*-68124
Electricity plants	-23018	..	..	-86	..	*-10442	..	14594	-738	-19690	*-10442
CHP plants	-1433981	-40512	..	-16543	-75274	*-58427	..	533898	196697	-894143	*-54702
Heat plants	-116110	-524	..	-1092	-8193	*-3380	..	-4	102405	-26897	*-2981
Coke ovens	-301159	348368	..	..	..	..	..	..	..	47209	..
Briquetting plants	-72	46	..	..	..	..	..	..	..	-26	..
Liquefaction plants	..	..	24820	..	..	..	..	..	..	24820	..
Gas works	..	..	..	..	..	..	..	..	..	..	..
Blast furnaces	-8806	-34184	..	..	..	..	..	..	..	-42990	..
NGL plants & gas blending	..	..	..	..	..	..	..	..	..	..	..
Oil refineries	..	..	-1157711	1144637	..	..	..	..	..	-13074	..
Other transformation	..	-839	..	-658	-24925	..	..	..	..	-26422	..
Energy industries own use	-3491	-44776	..	-32559	-59841	-56	..	-95382	-27277	-263382	-50
Losses	..	..	..	..	-525	..	..	-35986	-28195	-64705	..
Final consumption	428842	44801	..	1188582	475826	*270448	..	488837	246777	3144112	*246538
Final energy consumption	426075	44801	..	1026930	384576	*270448	..	488837	246777	2888444	*246538
Manufacturing, const., mining	116633	38968	..	31456	154265	100990	..	196351	30221	668884	74059
Iron and steel	1684	28849	..	241	23715	*1	..	24509	3905	82904	*1
Chemical and petrochemical	51416	2176	..	13150	13020	1598	..	31442	5379	118182	*104
Non-ferrous metals	96	2608	..	704	7555	..	..	8424	1252	20639	..
Non-metallic minerals	22379	4311	..	3347	44574	30743	..	19739	1011	126103	5706
Transport equipment	385	..	..	659	4529	*4	..	10541	1953	18071	*4
Machinery	1323	61	..	1333	9764	*93	..	17294	2652	32521	*87
Mining and quarrying	409	165	..	3106	1601	71	..	9947	2789	18088	*5
Food and tobacco	24277	728	..	3419	29943	*1494	..	24332	2969	87162	*1494
Paper, pulp and printing	9239		..	1748	8709	*34176	..	16794	3296	73963	*33881
Wood and wood products	1853		..	607	1876	*16451	..	8640	2963	*32389	*16451
Textile and leather	378		..	219	1726	*7	..	2182	523	5036	*7
Construction	1052	70	..	1936	1443	*8	..	3251	351	8111	*8
Industries n.e.s	2141	0	..	986	5810	16344	..	19256	1178	45717	16311
Transport	..	..	..	859532	16014	25164	..	11977	..	912687	25164
Road	..	..	..	854514	466	25164	..	97	..	880242	25164
Rail	..	..	..	3612	..	..	..	11034	..	14646	..
Domestic aviation	..	..	..	1147	..	..	..	..	..	1147	..
Domestic navigation	..	..	..	215	..	..	..	..	..	215	..
Pipeline transport	..	..	..	43	15548	..	..	846	..	16437	..
Transport, n.e.s	..	..	..	..	..	..	..	..	..	..	..
Other	309443	5833	..	135942	214297	*144293	..	280508	216556	1306873	*147315
Agriculture, forestry, fishing	36442	933	..	91733	1519	*21646	..	6188	900	159361	*21646
Commerce, public services	25008	700	..	18451	60806	*12922	..	169268	48911	336066	*13199
Households	247994	4200	..	25714	151972	*109725	..	105052	166745	811401	*112470
Other consumers	..	..	..	44	..	..	..	..	..	44	..
Non-energy use	2767	..	..	161652	91249	..	..	..	..	255668	..

Poland

Terajoules

2018	Primary coal and peat	Coal and peat products	Primary Oil	Oil Products	Natural Gas	Biofuels and waste	Nuclear	Electricity	Heat	Total energy	of which: renewables
Primary production	2013004	..	43206	..	145240	353546	..	54248	3831	2613076	374440
Imports	467803	7040	1144052	404722	547530	*37534	..	49738	..	2658419	*37534
Exports	-119594	-194753	-12580	-247782	-23650	-28062	..	-29236	..	-655657	-28062
International marine bunkers	..	..	..	-11278	..	..	..	..	..	-11278	..
International aviation bunkers	..	..	..	-43218	..	..	..	..	..	-43218	..
Stock changes	-80054	-4064	-23545	-5896	5964	-726	..	..	..	-108320	-726
Total energy supply	2281159	-191776	1151133	96548	675085	362292	..	74750	3831	4453022	383185
Statistical difference	2377	-5875	4630	-7933	20935	2	..	-7	-2	14127	54248
Transfers	..	..	54017	-51295	..	..	..	..	..	2722	..
Transformation	-1854764	272793	-1200520	1194451	-128031	*-77156	..	556384	292805	-944039	*-71643
Electricity plants	-21719	..	..	-43	..	*-12396	..	14306	-1411	-21263	*-12396
CHP plants	-1405760	-41124	..	-15600	-92478	*-60962	..	542081	193323	-880521	*-55696
Heat plants	-112670	-534	..	-842	-8529	*-3798	..	-4	100893	-25483	*-3551
Coke ovens	-306924	351618	..	..	..	..	..	..	..	44694	..
Briquetting plants	-407	325	..	..	..	..	..	..	..	-82	..
Liquefaction plants	..	..	27030	..	..	..	..	..	..	27030	..
Gas works	..	..	..	..	..	..	..	..	..	..	..
Blast furnaces	-7283	-36231	..	..	..	..	..	..	..	-43514	..
NGL plants & gas blending	..	..	..	..	..	..	..	..	..	..	..
Oil refineries	..	..	-1227550	1211557	..	..	..	..	..	-15993	..
Other transformation	..	-1261	..	-621	-27024	..	..	..	..	-28906	..
Energy industries own use	-3978	-45703	..	-34849	-51071	-77	..	-93427	-31134	-260239	*-65
Losses	..	..	..	..	-510	..	..	-32018	-27873	-60402	..
Final consumption	420040	41189	..	1212788	474537	*285056	..	505696	237631	3176937	*257229
Final energy consumption	417429	41189	..	1058688	390827	*285056	..	505696	237631	2936516	*257229
Manufacturing, const., mining	115604	35697	..	31359	163682	*105503	..	202504	34648	688997	*74482
Iron and steel	2132	25118	..	209	25022	1	..	24577	3835	80894	1
Chemical and petrochemical	51098	2501	..	12720	15171	890	..	31921	10217	124518	146
Non-ferrous metals	647	3098	..	462	7959	..	..	8600	940	21706	..
Non-metallic minerals	22683	3977	..	3866	43116	35180	..	20516	1207	130546	5369
Transport equipment	359	..	..	748	5603	4	..	11020	1886	19621	*2
Machinery	1198	59	..	1248	10028	*52	..	18454	2512	33551	*51
Mining and quarrying	503	118	..	3239	1574	77	..	10141	3103	18756	*8
Food and tobacco	24339	756	..	3411	36320	*1618	..	26489	2561	95493	*1618
Paper, pulp and printing	7378	..	..	1585	8513	*36594	..	16736	3310	74117	*36234
Wood and wood products	1725	..	..	1040	1705	*15991	..	9068	3180	32709	*15991
Textile and leather	441	..	..	260	1823	*15	..	2351	368	5257	*15
Construction	1080	70	..	1717	1267	*21	..	3546	317	8018	*21
Industries n.e.s	2021	0	..	854	5582	*15060	..	19084	1212	43812	*15026
Transport	..	..	..	885161	20443	37984	..	12488	..	956076	37984
Road	..	..	..	879320	3313	37984	..	101	..	920718	37984
Rail	..	..	..	4343	..	..	..	11524	..	15867	..
Domestic aviation	..	..	..	1412	..	..	..	..	..	1412	..
Domestic navigation	..	..	..	86	..	..	..	..	..	86	..
Pipeline transport	..	..	..	..	17130	..	..	864	..	17994	..
Transport, n.e.s	..	..	..	..	..	..	..	..	..	..	..
Other	301825	5492	..	142168	206702	*141569	..	290704	202983	1291443	*144763
Agriculture, forestry, fishing	35534	876	..	96261	1266	*21066	..	6674	800	162477	*21066
Commerce, public services	23452	977	..	18817	56325	*12488	..	178607	42311	332976	*12810
Households	242840	3640	..	27090	149111	*108015	..	105422	159872	795990	*110887
Other consumers	..	..	..	..	..	..	..	..	..	..	..
Non-energy use	2611	..	..	154100	83710	..	..	..	..	240421	..

Portugal

Terajoules

2017	Primary coal and peat	Coal and peat products	Primary Oil	Oil Products	Natural Gas	Biofuels and waste	Nuclear	Electricity	Heat	Total energy	of which: renewables
Primary production	..	..	..	..	..	137800	..	68890	11560	218250	211224
Imports	142320	370	613852	159016	227679	4676	..	19822	..	1167734	2790
Exports	..	..	..	-295590	..	-12324	..	-29484	..	-337398	-12324
International marine bunkers	..	..	..	-32819	..	..	..	..	..	-32819	..
International aviation bunkers	..	..	..	-54993	..	..	..	..	..	-54993	..
Stock changes	-7574	..	-3249	2278	-948	-488	..	..	..	-9981	-488
Total energy supply	134746	370	610602	-222107	226732	129664	..	59227	11560	950793	201201
Statistical difference	-847	31	0	-3790	-1220	89	..	-4	-1	-5742	69760
Transfers	..	..	51631	-51509	..	..	..	..	..	122	..
Transformation	-135518	..	-662234	652055	-150389	-39436	..	138827	11289	-185406	-41559
Electricity plants	-135518	..	..	-7282	-90948	-23197	..	113087	-7812	-151670	-25858
CHP plants	..	..	..	-3274	-49077	-15858	..	25740	19101	-23368	-15319
Heat plants	..	..	..	..	..	..	..	..	..	..	..
Coke ovens	..	..	..	..	..	..	..	..	..	..	..
Briquetting plants	..	..	..	..	..	..	..	..	..	..	..
Liquefaction plants	..	..	0	..	..	..	..	..	..	0	..
Gas works	..	..	..	..	..	..	..	..	..	..	..
Blast furnaces	..	..	..	..	..	..	..	..	..	..	..
NGL plants & gas blending	..	..	..	..	..	..	..	..	..	..	..
Oil refineries	..	..	-670754	663225	..	..	..	..	..	-7529	..
Other transformation	..	..	8520	-614	-10364	-382	..	..	..	-2840	-382
Energy industries own use	..	..	..	-32038	-4412	..	..	-11783	-10496	-58729	..
Losses	..	..	..	..	-264	..	..	-18364	..	-18627	..
Final consumption	75	339	..	350191	72887	90138	..	167911	12354	693894	89882
Final energy consumption	75	339	..	299061	72887	90138	..	167911	12354	642764	89882
Manufacturing, const., mining	75	339	..	26437	50834	46505	..	58115	7509	189813	42501
Iron and steel	75	123	..	86	1714	..	..	5598	..	7596	..
Chemical and petrochemical	..	..	..	302	7052	48	..	8550	749	16700	44
Non-ferrous metals	..	..	..	95	725	..	..	414	..	1233	..
Non-metallic minerals	..	216	..	13609	18673	7478	..	6912	361	47249	3494
Transport equipment	..	..	..	267	779	..	..	1890	..	2936	..
Machinery	..	..	..	789	1377	3	..	3906	44	6119	3
Mining and quarrying	..	..	..	1302	77	74	..	1537	25	3015	74
Food and tobacco	..	..	..	3028	6590	1243	..	7114	1125	19099	1243
Paper, pulp and printing	..	..	..	2118	6613	35769	..	11131	3354	58986	35769
Wood and wood products	..	..	..	260	422	1418	..	2527	..	4627	1418
Textile and leather	..	..	..	437	5740	276	..	4568	1409	12430	276
Construction	..	..	..	4009	645	151	..	2106	..	6911	151
Industries n.e.s	0	0	..	138	427	45	..	1861	442	2913	29
Transport	..	..	..	232155	615	10107	..	1746	..	244623	10107
Road	..	..	..	220387	615	10033	..	7	..	231042	10033
Rail	..	..	..	430	..	..	..	1717	..	2147	..
Domestic aviation	..	..	..	7233	..	..	..	..	..	7233	..
Domestic navigation	..	..	..	4106	..	74	..	..	..	4179	74
Pipeline transport	..	..	..	..	..	..	..	22	..	22	..
Transport, n.e.s	..	..	..	..	..	..	..	..	..	..	..
Other	..	..	..	40469	21438	33526	..	108050	4845	208329	37274
Agriculture, forestry, fishing	..	..	..	15117	244	134	..	3794	..	19288	134
Commerce, public services	..	..	..	5978	10697	1395	..	58932	2599	79600	2933
Households	..	..	..	18391	10498	31998	..	45324	2246	108457	34208
Other consumers	..	..	..	983	..	..	..	..	..	983	..
Non-energy use	..	..	..	51130	..	..	..	..	..	51130	..

Portugal

Terajoules

2018	Primary coal and peat	Coal and peat products	Primary Oil	Oil Products	Natural Gas	Biofuels and waste	Nuclear	Electricity	Heat	Total energy	of which: renewables
Primary production	..	..	..	..	..	139583	..	93658	12305	245545	238252
Imports	111366	277	547866	159429	212504	5801	..	20405	..	1057647	5008
Exports	..	..	..	-226515	..	-14917	..	-29970	..	-271402	-14917
International marine bunkers	..	..	..	-34211	..	..	..	..	..	-34211	..
International aviation bunkers	..	..	..	-58565	..	..	..	..	..	-58565	..
Stock changes	1239	..	-4703	-14674	-2222	368	..	..	..	-19993	368
Total energy supply	112604	277	543163	-174536	210281	130835	..	84092	12305	919021	228711
Statistical difference	99	-31	43	-1488	1016	-9	..	-7	1	-376	94477
Transfers	..	..	48990	-48899	..	..	..	..	..	91	..
Transformation	-112406	..	-592110	581001	-129826	-39137	..	116582	11900	-163996	-42265
Electricity plants	-112406	..	..	-7363	-69067	-23549	..	91105	-8280	-129560	-26940
CHP plants	..	..	..	-2565	-51498	-15207	..	25477	20180	-23612	-14943
Heat plants	..	..	..	..	..	..	..	..	..	..	..
Coke ovens	..	..	..	..	..	..	..	..	..	..	..
Briquetting plants	..	..	..	..	..	..	..	..	..	..	..
Liquefaction plants	..	..	0	..	..	..	..	..	..	0	..
Gas works	..	..	..	..	..	..	..	..	..	..	..
Blast furnaces	..	..	..	..	..	..	..	..	..	..	..
NGL plants & gas blending	..	..	..	..	..	..	..	..	..	..	..
Oil refineries	..	..	-599910	591512	..	..	..	..	..	-8397	..
Other transformation	..	..	7800	-584	-9261	-381	..	..	..	-2426	-381
Energy industries own use	..	..	..	-28735	-3962	..	..	-9810	-10541	-53048	..
Losses	..	..	..	..	-265	..	..	-18216	..	-18481	..
Final consumption	99	308	..	330320	75213	91707	..	172656	13663	683965	91970
Final energy consumption	99	308	..	299776	75213	91707	..	172656	13663	653422	91970
Manufacturing, const., mining	99	308	..	24642	51998	46967	..	59033	8551	191597	43205
Iron and steel	99	123	..	86	2006	..	..	6052	..	8366	..
Chemical and petrochemical	..	..	..	585	7559	175	..	8579	2183	19080	169
Non-ferrous metals	..	..	..	95	701	109	..	403	..	1308	..
Non-metallic minerals	..	185	..	12104	18669	6893	..	6948	370	45168	3263
Transport equipment	..	..	..	354	967	..	..	1984	..	3304	..
Machinery	..	..	..	748	1536	6	..	4187	47	6524	6
Mining and quarrying	..	..	..	1175	65	74	..	1584	26	2924	74
Food and tobacco	..	..	..	2944	6359	1492	..	7319	1067	19180	1492
Paper, pulp and printing	..	..	..	1873	6508	36400	..	10987	3232	59000	36400
Wood and wood products	..	..	..	303	554	1285	..	2606	..	4747	1285
Textile and leather	..	..	..	437	6058	367	..	4608	1392	12862	367
Construction	..	..	..	3802	568	151	..	1843	..	6364	151
Industries n.e.s	0	0	..	138	449	17	..	1933	234	2771	0
Transport	..	..	..	233866	671	10950	..	1764	..	247250	10950
Road	..	..	..	221527	671	10840	..	18	..	233055	10840
Rail	..	..	..	430	..	..	..	1724	..	2154	..
Domestic aviation	..	..	..	7674	..	..	..	..	..	7674	..
Domestic navigation	..	..	..	4236	..	110	..	..	..	4346	110
Pipeline transport	..	..	..	..	..	..	..	22	..	22	..
Transport, n.e.s	..	..	..	..	..	..	..	..	..	..	..
Other	..	..	..	41268	22545	33789	..	111859	5112	214574	37814
Agriculture, forestry, fishing	..	..	..	15150	162	96	..	3992	..	19401	96
Commerce, public services	..	..	..	6929	10949	1612	..	60300	2666	82456	3235
Households	..	..	..	18069	11434	32081	..	47567	2446	111596	34483
Other consumers	..	..	..	1121	..	..	..	..	..	1121	..
Non-energy use	..	..	..	30543	..	..	..	..	..	30543	..

Qatar

Terajoules

2017	Primary coal and peat	Coal and peat products	Primary Oil	Oil Products	Natural Gas	Biofuels and waste	Nuclear	Electricity	Heat	Total energy	of which: renewables
Primary production	..	..	3115651	..	6203790	47	..	..	..	9319487	47
Imports	..	..	..	4945	..	342	..	..	..	5287	342
Exports	..	..	-1975233	-944880	-4610552	-1	..	..	..	-7530666	-1
International marine bunkers	..	..	..	..	..	..	..	..	..	..	..
International aviation bunkers	..	..	..	-121143	..	..	..	..	..	-121143	..
Stock changes	..	..	..	15125	..	..	..	..	..	15125	..
Total energy supply	..	..	1140418	-1045952	1593238	388	..	..	..	1688091	388
Statistical difference	..	..	-42	19054	-155502	0	..	-4	..	-136494	0
Transfers	..	..	-155484	187500	..	..	..	..	..	32016	..
Transformation	..	..	-984976	1197507	-833362	*-20	..	163998	..	-456853	*-20
Electricity plants	..	..	..	..	-394979	..	..	163998	..	-230981	..
CHP plants	..	..	..	..	..	..	..	..	..	..	..
Heat plants	..	..	..	..	..	..	..	..	..	..	..
Coke ovens	..	..	..	..	..	..	..	..	..	..	..
Briquetting plants	..	..	..	..	..	..	..	..	..	..	..
Liquefaction plants	..	..	155484	..	-438383	..	..	..	..	-282899	..
Gas works	..	..	..	..	..	..	..	..	..	..	..
Blast furnaces	..	..	..	..	..	..	..	..	..	..	..
NGL plants & gas blending	..	..	-470376	502503	..	..	..	..	..	32126	..
Oil refineries	..	..	-670084	695004	..	..	..	..	..	24921	..
Other transformation	..	..	..	..	..	*-20	..	..	..	*-20	*-20
Energy industries own use	..	..	..	-6655	-541637	..	..	-10192	..	-558484	..
Losses	..	..	..	..	..	..	..	-9702	..	-9702	..
Final consumption	..	..	..	313345	373740	*368	..	144108	..	831561	*368
Final energy consumption	..	..	..	232522	259066	*368	..	144108	..	636064	*368
Manufacturing, const., mining	..	..	..	40964	259066	..	..	40543	..	340573	..
Iron and steel	..	..	..	..	22364	..	..	..	..	22364	..
Chemical and petrochemical	..	..	..	..	161788	..	..	..	..	161788	..
Non-ferrous metals	..	..	..	..	..	..	..	..	..	..	..
Non-metallic minerals	..	..	..	..	74914	..	..	..	..	74914	..
Transport equipment	..	..	..	..	..	..	..	..	..	..	..
Machinery	..	..	..	..	..	..	..	..	..	..	..
Mining and quarrying	..	..	..	..	..	..	..	..	..	..	..
Food and tobacco	..	..	..	..	..	..	..	..	..	..	..
Paper, pulp and printing	..	..	..	..	..	..	..	..	..	..	..
Wood and wood products	..	..	..	..	..	..	..	..	..	..	..
Textile and leather	..	..	..	..	..	..	..	..	..	..	..
Construction	..	..	..	..	..	..	..	..	..	..	..
Industries n.e.s	..	..	..	40964	0	..	..	40543	..	81507	..
Transport	..	..	..	185078	..	..	..	..	..	185078	..
Road	..	..	..	185078	..	..	..	..	..	185078	..
Rail	..	..	..	..	..	..	..	..	..	..	..
Domestic aviation	..	..	..	..	..	..	..	..	..	..	..
Domestic navigation	..	..	..	..	..	..	..	..	..	..	..
Pipeline transport	..	..	..	..	..	..	..	..	..	..	..
Transport, n.e.s	..	..	..	..	..	..	..	..	..	..	..
Other	..	..	..	6480	..	*368	..	103565	..	110413	*368
Agriculture, forestry, fishing	..	..	..	..	..	..	..	..	..	..	..
Commerce, public services	..	..	..	..	..	..	..	26482	..	26482	..
Households	..	..	..	6480	..	*368	..	64012	..	70860	*368
Other consumers	..	..	..	..	..	..	..	13072	..	13072	..
Non-energy use	..	..	..	80823	114674	..	..	..	..	195498	..

Qatar

Terajoules

2018	Primary coal and peat	Coal and peat products	Primary Oil	Oil Products	Natural Gas	Biofuels and waste	Nuclear	Electricity	Heat	Total energy	of which: renewables
Primary production	..	..	2968179	..	6170256	47	..	..	..	9138482	47
Imports	..	..	..	9737	..	223	..	..	..	9960	223
Exports	..	..	-1918823	-720486	-4560997	-1	..	..	..	-7200306	-1
International marine bunkers	..	..	..	..	..	..	..	..	..	..	..
International aviation bunkers	..	..	..	-126082	..	..	..	..	..	-126082	..
Stock changes	..	..	..	-12897	..	..	..	..	..	-12897	..
Total energy supply	..	..	1049357	-849728	1609259	269	..	..	..	1809157	269
Statistical difference	..	..	-44	-6564	-35115	0	..	0	..	-41723	0
Transfers	..	..	-114228	137780	..	..	..	..	..	23552	..
Transformation	..	..	-935173	1058312	-728927	*-20	..	172487	..	-433321	*-20
Electricity plants	..	..	..	..	-406850	..	..	172487	..	-234363	..
CHP plants	..	..	..	..	..	..	..	..	..	..	..
Heat plants	..	..	..	..	..	..	..	..	..	..	..
Coke ovens	..	..	..	..	..	..	..	..	..	..	..
Briquetting plants	..	..	..	..	..	..	..	..	..	..	..
Liquefaction plants	..	..	114228	..	-322078	..	..	..	..	-207850	..
Gas works	..	..	..	..	..	..	..	..	..	..	..
Blast furnaces	..	..	..	..	..	..	..	..	..	..	..
NGL plants & gas blending	..	..	-351302	375035	..	..	..	..	..	23733	..
Oil refineries	..	..	-698099	683277	..	..	..	..	..	-14822	..
Other transformation	..	..	..	..	..	*-20	..	..	..	*-20	*-20
Energy industries own use	..	..	..	-6844	-542196	..	..	-11732	..	-560773	..
Losses	..	..	..	..	..	..	..	-10030	..	-10030	..
Final consumption	..	..	..	346084	373252	*249	..	*150725	..	870309	*249
Final energy consumption	..	..	..	262133	255694	*249	..	*150725	..	668800	*249
Manufacturing, const., mining	..	..	..	93988	255694	..	..	43909	..	393590	..
Iron and steel	..	..	..	..	21781	..	..	..	..	21781	..
Chemical and petrochemical	..	..	..	..	165856	..	..	..	..	165856	..
Non-ferrous metals	..	..	..	..	..	..	..	..	..	..	..
Non-metallic minerals	..	..	..	..	68057	..	..	..	..	68057	..
Transport equipment	..	..	..	..	..	..	..	..	..	..	..
Machinery	..	..	..	..	..	..	..	..	..	..	..
Mining and quarrying	..	..	..	..	..	..	..	..	..	..	..
Food and tobacco	..	..	..	..	..	..	..	..	..	..	..
Paper, pulp and printing	..	..	..	..	..	..	..	..	..	..	..
Wood and wood products	..	..	..	..	..	..	..	..	..	..	..
Textile and leather	..	..	..	..	..	..	..	..	..	..	..
Construction	..	..	..	..	..	..	..	..	..	..	..
Industries n.e.s	..	..	..	93988	0	..	..	43909	..	137897	..
Transport	..	..	..	161571	..	..	..	..	..	161571	..
Road	..	..	..	161571	..	..	..	..	..	161571	..
Rail	..	..	..	..	..	..	..	..	..	..	..
Domestic aviation	..	..	..	..	..	..	..	..	..	..	..
Domestic navigation	..	..	..	..	..	..	..	..	..	..	..
Pipeline transport	..	..	..	..	..	..	..	..	..	..	..
Transport, n.e.s	..	..	..	..	..	..	..	..	..	..	..
Other	..	..	..	6575	..	*249	..	*106816	..	*113639	*249
Agriculture, forestry, fishing	..	..	..	..	..	..	..	..	..	..	..
Commerce, public services	..	..	..	..	..	..	..	30161	..	30161	..
Households	..	..	..	6575	..	*249	..	*61765	..	*68589	*249
Other consumers	..	..	..	..	..	..	..	14890	..	14890	..
Non-energy use	..	..	..	83951	117558	..	..	..	..	201509	..

Republic of Moldova

Terajoules

2017	Primary coal and peat	Coal and peat products	Primary Oil	Oil Products	Natural Gas	Biofuels and waste	Nuclear	Electricity	Heat	Total energy	of which: renewables
Primary production	..	..	212	..	4	31601	..	205	..	32021	31713
Imports	5041	..	0	40595	31505	85	..	12283	..	89510	85
Exports	..	..	..	-1468	..	-1	..	..	..	-1469	-1
International marine bunkers	..	..	..	..	..	..	..	..	..	..	..
International aviation bunkers	..	..	..	-2073	..	..	..	..	..	-2073	..
Stock changes	-581	..	-42	362	47	23	..	..	..	-192	23
Total energy supply	4460	..	169	37417	31556	31708	..	12488	..	117798	31820
Statistical difference	197	..	0	0	0	428	..	0	0	625	633
Transfers	..	..	458	-469	..	..	..	..	..	-11	..
Transformation	-48	..	-627	164	-13535	-707	..	3020	10251	-1482	-707
Electricity plants	..	..	..	0	..	-84	..	22	..	-62	-84
CHP plants	..	..	..	-404	-10360	-198	..	2999	6893	-1070	-198
Heat plants	-48	..	..	-40	-3175	-386	..	..	3358	-292	-386
Coke ovens	..	..	..	..	..	..	..	..	..	..	..
Briquetting plants	..	..	..	..	..	..	..	..	..	..	..
Liquefaction plants	..	..	..	..	..	..	..	..	..	..	..
Gas works	..	..	..	..	..	..	..	..	..	..	..
Blast furnaces	..	..	..	..	..	..	..	..	..	..	..
NGL plants & gas blending	..	..	..	..	..	..	..	..	..	..	..
Oil refineries	..	..	-627	608	..	..	..	..	..	-19	..
Other transformation	..	..	..	..	..	-39	..	..	..	-39	-39
Energy industries own use	..	..	..	..	-5	..	..	-630	-69	-704	..
Losses	-24	..	0	-90	-1852	-1	..	-1544	-1659	-5171	-1
Final consumption	4190	..	..	37022	16163	30572	..	13334	8523	109804	30479
Final energy consumption	4166	..	..	35527	16163	30572	..	13334	8523	108285	30479
Manufacturing, const., mining	1235	..	..	700	2235	38	..	2750	1958	8916	38
Iron and steel	..	..	..	..	0	..	..	7	..	7	..
Chemical and petrochemical	..	..	..	0	26	2	..	158	55	242	2
Non-ferrous metals	..	..	..	..	..	..	..	..	..	..	..
Non-metallic minerals	1187	..	..	488	1186	..	..	479	0	3339	..
Transport equipment	..	..	..	..	2	1	..	11	..	14	1
Machinery	..	..	..	..	9	0	..	169	4	182	0
Mining and quarrying	..	..	..	43	..	..	..	54	..	97	..
Food and tobacco	48	..	..	40	919	33	..	1436	1796	4273	33
Paper, pulp and printing	..	..	..	..	10	..	..	36	23	69	..
Wood and wood products	..	..	..	..	0	0	..	94	0	94	0
Textile and leather	..	..	..	..	14	1	..	187	74	276	1
Construction	..	..	..	129	22	..	..	32	1	184	..
Industries n.e.s	0	..	..	0	48	1	..	86	5	140	1
Transport	..	..	..	27870	947	..	..	295	..	29112	..
Road	..	..	..	27354	664	..	..	155	..	28173	..
Rail	..	..	..	430	..	..	..	..	..	430	..
Domestic aviation	..	..	..	..	..	..	..	..	..	..	..
Domestic navigation	..	..	..	43	..	..	..	..	..	43	..
Pipeline transport	..	..	..	..	283	..	..	140	..	423	..
Transport, n.e.s	..	..	..	43	..	..	..	..	..	43	..
Other	2931	..	..	6957	12982	30534	..	10289	6565	70257	30441
Agriculture, forestry, fishing	48	..	..	4171	79	52	..	176	1	4528	52
Commerce, public services	727	..	..	90	3474	520	..	4223	1742	10776	514
Households	2156	..	..	2696	9428	29962	..	5890	4822	54954	29875
Other consumers	0	..	..	0	..	0	..	..	..	0	0
Non-energy use	24	..	..	1494	0	..	..	..	..	1519	..

Republic of Moldova

Terajoules

2018	Primary coal and peat	Coal and peat products	Primary Oil	Oil Products	Natural Gas	Biofuels and waste	Nuclear	Electricity	Heat	Total energy	of which: renewables
Primary production	..	..	212	..	3	32946	..	238	22	33420	33205
Imports	3579	..	0	43644	34425	86	..	12600	..	94334	86
Exports	..	..	..	-1153	..	..	..	..	..	-1153	..
International marine bunkers	..	..	..	..	..	..	..	..	..	..	..
International aviation bunkers	..	..	..	-2381	..	..	..	..	..	-2381	..
Stock changes	-174	..	0	-15	-87	-114	..	..	..	-390	-114
Total energy supply	3405	..	212	40095	34341	32918	..	12838	22	123830	33177
Statistical difference	-25	..	0	47	279	554	..	0	0	855	799
Transfers	..	..	208	-207	..	..	..	..	..	1	..
Transformation	-50	..	-420	78	-14337	-917	..	3190	10636	-1820	-931
Electricity plants	..	..	..	0	..	-150	..	47	-22	-125	-164
CHP plants	..	..	..	-283	-11063	-163	..	3143	7106	-1260	-163
Heat plants	-50	..	..	-40	-3274	-558	..	..	3552	-370	-558
Coke ovens	..	..	..	..	..	..	..	..	..	..	..
Briquetting plants	..	..	..	..	..	..	..	..	..	..	..
Liquefaction plants	..	..	..	..	..	..	..	..	..	..	..
Gas works	..	..	..	..	..	..	..	..	..	..	..
Blast furnaces	..	..	..	..	..	..	..	..	..	..	..
NGL plants & gas blending	..	..	..	..	..	..	..	..	..	..	..
Oil refineries	..	..	-420	401	..	..	..	..	..	-19	..
Other transformation	..	..	..	..	..	-46	..	..	..	-46	-46
Energy industries own use	..	..	..	..	-2	..	..	-612	-70	-684	..
Losses	0	..	0	-135	-1675	-1	..	-1588	-1625	-5023	-1
Final consumption	3380	..	..	39784	18048	31446	..	13828	8963	115449	31446
Final energy consumption	3380	..	..	37018	18048	31446	..	13828	8963	112683	31446
Manufacturing, const., mining	1118	..	..	1650	2879	64	..	2776	1973	10460	64
Iron and steel	..	..	..	..	0	..	..	7	..	7	..
Chemical and petrochemical	..	..	..	129	27	3	..	151	53	363	3
Non-ferrous metals	..	..	..	..	..	..	..	..	..	..	..
Non-metallic minerals	1044	..	..	1073	1599	..	..	508	0	4223	..
Transport equipment	..	..	..	..	6	1	..	29	..	36	1
Machinery	..	..	..	..	23	0	..	176	11	210	0
Mining and quarrying	..	..	..	151	..	..	..	54	..	205	..
Food and tobacco	75	..	..	47	1067	49	..	1368	1810	4416	49
Paper, pulp and printing	..	..	..	..	46	4	..	47	21	118	4
Wood and wood products	..	..	..	..	0	5	..	32	0	37	5
Textile and leather	..	..	..	..	45	1	..	184	73	303	1
Construction	..	..	..	298	34	..	..	40	..	372	..
Industries n.e.s	0	..	..	-47	31	1	..	180	5	170	1
Transport	..	..	..	28436	934	..	..	259	..	29630	..
Road	..	..	..	28135	686	..	..	166	..	28987	..
Rail	..	..	..	241	..	..	..	..	..	241	..
Domestic aviation	..	..	..	..	..	..	..	..	..	..	..
Domestic navigation	..	..	..	17	..	..	..	..	..	17	..
Pipeline transport	..	..	..	..	248	..	..	94	..	342	..
Transport, n.e.s	..	..	..	43	..	..	..	..	..	43	..
Other	2262	..	..	6932	14235	31382	..	10793	6990	72594	31382
Agriculture, forestry, fishing	75	..	..	4214	110	46	..	234	1	4679	46
Commerce, public services	746	..	..	22	3322	518	..	4648	1867	11122	518
Households	1442	..	..	2696	10803	30818	..	5911	5122	56792	30818
Other consumers	0	..	..	0	..	0	..	..	..	0	0
Non-energy use	0	..	..	2766	..	..	..	..	..	2766	..

Romania

Terajoules

2017	Primary coal and peat	Coal and peat products	Primary Oil	Oil Products	Natural Gas	Biofuels and waste	Nuclear	Electricity	Heat	Total energy	of which: renewables
Primary production	187073	..	154561	..	356806	161359	124297	85518	1654	1071267	244582
Imports	21849	20068	333814	136562	39886	12243	..	17431	..	581853	12243
Exports	-15	..	-3436	-214105	-869	-3139	..	-27846	..	-249410	-3139
International marine bunkers	..	..	..	-1204	..	..	..	..	..	-1204	..
International aviation bunkers	..	..	..	-12877	..	..	..	..	..	-12877	..
Stock changes	-1562	-897	7892	-847	6562	-410	..	..	..	10739	-333
Total energy supply	207345	19171	492831	-92471	402386	170053	124297	75103	1654	1400368	253353
Statistical difference	1356	53	1027	11206	6944	-132	0	504	-1585	19372	85649
Transfers	..	..	31777	-31777	..	..	..	..	..	0	..
Transformation	-194761	-10554	-523273	525336	-127118	-8139	-124297	144655	74065	-244086	-8390
Electricity plants	-151898	-832	..	-81	-41712	-1225	-124297	110671	..	-209374	-1225
CHP plants	-42702	-192	..	-8309	-67802	-5716	..	33984	57493	-33244	-5716
Heat plants	-162	-215	..	-3687	-13537	-1167	..	..	16572	-2196	-1419
Coke ovens	..	..	..	..	..	..	..	..	..	..	..
Briquetting plants	..	..	..	..	..	..	..	..	..	..	..
Liquefaction plants	..	..	2664	..	..	..	..	..	..	2664	..
Gas works	..	..	..	..	..	..	..	..	..	..	..
Blast furnaces	..	-9315	..	..	..	..	..	..	..	-9315	..
NGL plants & gas blending	..	..	..	..	..	..	..	..	..	..	..
Oil refineries	..	..	-525937	537413	..	..	..	..	..	11476	..
Other transformation	..	..	..	0	-4066	*-31	..	..	..	-4097	*-31
Energy industries own use	-770	-583	..	-37365	-19625	-513	..	-33152	-11533	-103542	-513
Losses	0	-1296	-42	-182	-3232	0	..	-25178	-11732	-41663	0
Final consumption	10457	6686	265	352334	245467	161533	..	160924	54039	991705	158801
Final energy consumption	10457	6633	265	319449	231123	161533	..	160924	54039	944423	158801
Manufacturing, const., mining	8394	6633	265	38817	91318	15908	..	78210	11414	250959	12216
Iron and steel	5971	6290	..	206	20371	44	..	9148	46	42074	0
Chemical and petrochemical	1076	290	265	10689	24568	814	..	11149	6914	55765	205
Non-ferrous metals	..	..	..	..	..	..	..	12089	..	12089	..
Non-metallic minerals	1232	0	..	13436	11289	4717	..	9529	294	40496	2016
Transport equipment	..	..	..	..	3977	..	..	5152	486	9615	..
Machinery	..	..	..	669	6201	159	..	8842	583	16454	178
Mining and quarrying	..	..	..	645	31	94	..	950	3	1723	94
Food and tobacco	108	53	..	1934	12356	1712	..	6793	1047	24003	1439
Paper, pulp and printing	..	..	..	0	4057	236	..	2696	132	7122	153
Wood and wood products	..	..	..	608	1051	6906	..	3791	1462	13818	6907
Textile and leather	..	..	..	86	4071	31	..	2452	157	6796	32
Construction	8	..	..	10325	2644	167	..	1451	82	14677	165
Industries n.e.s	0	0	0	221	702	1028	..	4169	208	6327	1028
Transport	..	..	..	244183	9	12459	..	3920	..	260571	12459
Road	..	..	..	235664	..	12454	..	137	..	248254	12454
Rail	..	..	..	4902	..	..	..	3708	..	8610	..
Domestic aviation	..	..	..	1897	..	..	..	..	..	1897	..
Domestic navigation	..	..	..	1720	..	..	..	..	..	1720	..
Pipeline transport	..	..	..	..	9	..	..	76	..	85	..
Transport, n.e.s	..	..	..	..	..	5	..	..	..	5	5
Other	2063	..	..	36450	139796	133167	..	78793	42625	432894	134127
Agriculture, forestry, fishing	492	..	..	12562	4425	254	..	2671	417	20821	268
Commerce, public services	0	..	..	3774	33998	195	..	30773	8360	77100	994
Households	1571	..	..	11600	101372	127719	..	45349	33848	321459	127866
Other consumers	..	..	..	8514	..	4999	..	..	..	13513	4999
Non-energy use	..	53	..	32885	14344	..	..	..	..	47282	..

Romania

Terajoules

2018	Primary coal and peat	Coal and peat products	Primary Oil	Oil Products	Natural Gas	Biofuels and waste	Nuclear	Electricity	Heat	Total energy	of which: renewables
Primary production	168230	..	152410	..	354891	160276	122872	92725	1588	1052992	247293
Imports	18708	19013	355400	137371	50589	9374	..	13309	..	603763	9374
Exports	-43	..	-1637	-228116	-1029	-2662	..	-22468	..	-255955	-2662
International marine bunkers	..	..	..	-774	..	..	..	..	..	-774	..
International aviation bunkers	..	..	..	-5248	..	..	..	..	..	-5248	..
Stock changes	4995	686	-3964	7240	7654	-591	..	..	..	16019	-449
Total energy supply	191891	19698	502208	-89527	412105	166396	122872	83567	1588	1410798	253554
Statistical difference	-1916	-64	1722	15930	7442	-3244	0	835	-1231	19474	89727
Transfers	..	..	28423	-28423	..	..	..	..	..	0	..
Transformation	-182902	-10646	-528338	530498	-129840	-7595	-122872	139262	70978	-241455	-7832
Electricity plants	-146184	-1255	..	-124	-47095	-513	-122872	108781	..	-209261	-513
CHP plants	-36628	-170	..	-8606	-61944	-6175	..	30481	51447	-31596	-6175
Heat plants	-90	-134	..	-4068	-17174	-878	..	..	19531	-2812	-1115
Coke ovens	..	..	..	..	..	..	..	..	..	..	..
Briquetting plants	..	..	..	..	..	..	..	..	..	..	..
Liquefaction plants	..	..	2376	..	..	..	..	..	..	2376	..
Gas works	..	..	..	..	..	..	..	..	..	..	..
Blast furnaces	..	-9087	..	..	..	..	..	..	..	-9087	..
NGL plants & gas blending	..	..	..	..	..	..	..	..	..	..	..
Oil refineries	..	..	-530714	543345	..	..	..	..	..	12630	..
Other transformation	..	..	..	-50	-3627	*-29	..	..	..	-3705	*-29
Energy industries own use	..	-655	-85	-34753	-17789	-192	..	-32548	-9478	-95499	-192
Losses	..	-1737	..	-87	-3043	..	..	-25402	-11140	-41409	..
Final consumption	10905	6724	486	361778	253990	161854	..	164045	53179	1012961	155803
Final energy consumption	10905	6698	486	332090	238559	161854	..	164045	53179	967817	155803
Manufacturing, const., mining	8723	6698	486	40449	94569	17195	..	80014	12113	260246	10186
Iron and steel	5963	6197	..	33	13775	46	..	8690	26	34730	..
Chemical and petrochemical	1306	185	486	13215	24226	973	..	11664	7625	59680	171
Non-ferrous metals	..	..	..	..	7036	..	..	12546	..	19582	..
Non-metallic minerals	1446	264	..	13212	15329	5899	..	9079	114	45343	91
Transport equipment	..	..	..	271	5655	..	..	5969	502	12396	1
Machinery	..	..	..	483	6495	249	..	9932	679	17839	255
Mining and quarrying	..	..	..	559	60	86	..	893	4	1602	86
Food and tobacco	..	53	..	1390	11840	1443	..	6883	784	22394	1200
Paper, pulp and printing	..	..	..	..	2617	193	..	2736	307	5853	84
Wood and wood products	..	..	..	606	1458	6987	..	3730	1632	14413	6988
Textile and leather	..	..	..	133	3386	69	..	2387	202	6177	63
Construction	7	..	..	10325	2193	68	..	1397	62	14053	67
Industries n.e.s	0	0	0	221	498	1182	..	4108	176	6184	1182
Transport	..	..	..	250898	9	12429	..	3802	..	267137	12429
Road	..	..	..	243062	..	12427	..	140	..	255629	12427
Rail	..	..	..	3999	..	..	..	3593	..	7592	..
Domestic aviation	..	..	..	2117	..	..	..	..	..	2117	..
Domestic navigation	..	..	..	1720	..	..	..	..	..	1720	..
Pipeline transport	..	..	..	..	9	..	..	68	..	77	..
Transport, n.e.s	..	..	..	..	..	2	..	..	..	2	2
Other	2182	..	..	40744	143981	132230	..	80230	41066	440433	133189
Agriculture, forestry, fishing	632	..	..	15401	4676	218	..	2711	206	23843	226
Commerce, public services	30	..	..	4307	34057	4493	..	31511	7979	82377	5294
Households	1521	..	..	12049	105249	126630	..	46008	32881	324338	126780
Other consumers	..	..	..	8987	..	*889	..	..	..	9876	*889
Non-energy use	..	26	..	29687	15431	..	..	..	..	45144	..

Russian Federation

Terajoules

2017	Primary coal and peat	Coal and peat products	Primary Oil	Oil Products	Natural Gas	Biofuels and waste	Nuclear	Electricity	Heat	Total energy	of which: renewables
Primary production	9304591	..	23173173	..	24323368	322879	2208538	668559	15658	60016767	791830
Imports	*717967	3047	33353	49719	302162	207	..	23076	..	*1129530	207
Exports	-4863638	-84743	-10840588	*-5100420	-7852572	-1210	..	-61222	..	-28804393	-1210
International marine bunkers	..	..	..	-729104	..	..	..	..	..	-729104	..
International aviation bunkers	..	..	..	-238126	..	..	..	..	..	-238126	..
Stock changes	-227323	1799	68448	-4357	-514173	6453	..	..	..	-669152	6101
Total energy supply	4931598	-79898	12434387	*-6022288	16258786	328329	2208538	630413	15658	30705523	796928
Statistical difference	66013	24	1767	307730	450396	10	0	0	0	825940	670134
Transfers	..	..	*54504	..	..	..	..	..	..	*54504	..
Transformation	-4666655	433318	-12224166	11940971	-8459190	-180174	-2208538	3250108	5309534	-6804793	-40617
Electricity plants	..	..	..	-47460	-212436	..	-2193945	787703	-15658	-1681796	-14092
CHP plants	-2359184	-128171	-591	-68970	-6226705	-91964	-14593	2475552	2863590	-3551037	-1261
Heat plants	-459767	-16393	-20703	-135211	-1901424	-84583	..	-13147	2461602	-169627	-21636
Coke ovens	-1680789	1440474	..	..	..	..	..	..	..	-240315	..
Briquetting plants	-518	254	..	..	..	..	..	..	..	-264	..
Liquefaction plants	..	..	88128	..	..	..	..	..	..	88128	..
Gas works	..	..	..	..	..	..	..	..	..	..	..
Blast furnaces	-166396	-862858	..	..	..	..	..	..	..	-1029253	..
NGL plants & gas blending	..	..	..	..	..	..	..	..	..	..	..
Oil refineries	..	..	-12290999	12192612	..	..	..	..	..	-98387	..
Other transformation	..	..	..	..	-118625	-3627	..	..	..	-122253	-3627
Energy industries own use	-29103	-44237	-11565	-512055	-582804	-6237	..	-762397	-487478	-2435876	..
Losses	..	..	*-250289	..	-244863	..	..	-378939	-393764	-1267855	..
Final consumption	169827	309159	1104	5098898	6521532	141908	..	2739185	4443950	19425563	86177
Final energy consumption	164280	309159	1104	*3856359	4861169	141908	..	2739185	4443950	16517114	86177
Manufacturing, const., mining	49153	308993	588	667620	1192051	50986	..	1219626	1721578	5210595	2638
Iron and steel	..	300481	..	13667	513818	20465	..	220046	260168	1328646	12
Chemical and petrochemical	6250	1915	425	403520	284356	4320	..	169632	498772	1369190	381
Non-ferrous metals	..	..	..	..	..	..	..	331832	..	331832	..
Non-metallic minerals	35835	3085	4	5734	393877	1202	..	65663	95835	601234	18
Transport equipment	886	514	..	7735	23221	43	..	49258	84816	166471	25
Machinery	57	817	..	6111	54349	5	..	71429	291736	424504	2
Mining and quarrying	627	1886	..	60178	62971	1308	..	100436	31477	258883	458
Food and tobacco	4775	0	159	29247	54336	3038	..	63067	178580	333201	154
Paper, pulp and printing	10	..	..	3701	19110	2678	..	57387	166268	249153	300
Wood and wood products	0	..	..	6665	9593	17652	..	16496	46763	97168	1180
Textile and leather	0	0	..	664	2646	59	..	6872	40277	50518	6
Construction	609	273	0	27192	170396	121	..	45754	22076	266421	62
Industries n.e.s	104	23	0	103208	-396622	95	..	21754	4810	-266627	40
Transport	..	..	..	*2487251	1266961	..	..	279312	..	*4033524	..
Road	..	..	..	*2116270	9923	..	..	..	..	*2126193	..
Rail	..	..	..	83024	..	..	..	182931	..	265955	..
Domestic aviation	..	..	..	231968	..	..	..	..	..	231968	..
Domestic navigation	..	..	..	18169	..	..	..	..	..	18169	..
Pipeline transport	..	..	..	7773	1256406	..	..	77289	..	1341469	..
Transport, n.e.s	..	..	..	30046	632	..	..	19092	..	49770	..
Other	115127	166	516	701488	2402157	90922	..	1240247	2722372	7272995	83539
Agriculture, forestry, fishing	2328	..	465	148750	55613	4370	..	65416	113295	390237	2112
Commerce, public services	43575	..	..	105145	103664	48057	..	575529	773853	1649822	42932
Households	69224	166	..	447592	2242880	37340	..	599303	1835224	5231730	37340
Other consumers	..	..	51	..	..	1155	..	..	..	1205	1155
Non-energy use	5547	..	..	1242538	1660363	..	..	..	..	2908449	..

Russian Federation

Terajoules

2018	Primary coal and peat	Coal and peat products	Primary Oil	Oil Products	Natural Gas	Biofuels and waste	Nuclear	Electricity	Heat	Total energy	of which: renewables
Primary production	10587938	..	23559700	..	24979740	364080	2223358	691537	15348	62421701	825974
Imports	*703627	3482	26940	45520	322875	354	..	18637	..	*1121434	354
Exports	*-5890766	-79472	-11198997	*-5074335	-7589875	-1446	..	-64004	..	-29898894	-1446
International marine bunkers	..	..	..	*-496949	..	..	..	..	..	*-496949	..
International aviation bunkers	..	..	..	-245996	..	..	..	..	..	-245996	..
Stock changes	-195176	346	-98742	-13596	635694	-3780	..	..	..	324746	-2185
Total energy supply	5205622	-75644	12288901	*-5785357	18348434	359209	2223358	646170	15348	33226042	822698
Statistical difference	21519	3	1894	-44556	0	-5	0	0	0	-21144	693067
Transfers	..	..	*69120	..	..	..	..	..	..	*69120	..
Transformation	-4993254	421882	-12080631	12115555	-9718645	-186189	-2223358	3301945	5466727	-7895968	-38364
Electricity plants	..	..	..	-45143	-238790	..	-2209347	802795	-15348	-1705833	-13814
CHP plants	-2544129	-119456	-899	-75218	-6853957	-98688	-14011	2513215	3026488	-4166655	-1051
Heat plants	-548630	-21986	-19392	-137349	-1904438	-83875	..	-14066	2455587	-274149	-19874
Coke ovens	-1722283	1047741	..	..	..	..	..	..	..	-674542	..
Briquetting plants	-586	287	..	..	..	..	..	..	..	-299	..
Liquefaction plants	..	..	103896	..	..	..	..	..	..	103896	..
Gas works	..	..	..	..	..	..	..	..	..	..	..
Blast furnaces	-177626	-484705	..	..	..	..	..	..	..	-662331	..
NGL plants & gas blending	..	..	..	..	..	..	..	..	..	..	..
Oil refineries	..	..	-12164236	12373265	..	..	..	..	..	209029	..
Other transformation	..	..	..	..	-721461	-3625	..	..	..	-725086	-3625
Energy industries own use	-30289	-62506	-9143	*-531046	-588308	-6366	..	-842392	-565520	-2635570	..
Losses	..	..	-265638	..	-256903	..	..	-371229	-426804	-1320574	..
Final consumption	160560	283729	715	5843708	7784578	166659	..	2734494	4489752	21464195	91267
Final energy consumption	152256	283729	715	4143407	5954445	166659	..	2734494	4489752	17925457	91267
Manufacturing, const., mining	48999	283495	512	*714301	1602948	70303	..	1225064	1541850	5487471	2920
Iron and steel	..	275827	..	13728	508120	35311	..	225762	265845	1324593	5
Chemical and petrochemical	8508	1164	415	*397271	295332	3805	..	170036	*527420	*1403949	242
Non-ferrous metals	..	..	..	..	..	..	..	338643	..	338643	..
Non-metallic minerals	33717	3602	13	14137	356279	1484	..	59986	87629	556847	13
Transport equipment	373	609	..	7298	28375	61	..	48390	87362	172469	20
Machinery	106	585	..	4204	51187	8	..	71924	77951	205966	5
Mining and quarrying	650	1686	..	60370	72523	1097	..	98456	32669	267451	305
Food and tobacco	4612	0	85	27229	62913	2080	..	57929	173341	328189	136
Paper, pulp and printing	10	..	..	8576	22866	2486	..	65459	175015	274413	287
Wood and wood products	..	..	..	7030	10174	23355	..	17655	52870	111084	1732
Textile and leather	..	..	..	1249	2329	103	..	5527	41558	50766	6
Construction	816	0	..	63475	188633	89	..	45396	20190	318600	51
Industries n.e.s	205	23	0	*109733	4215	423	..	19902	0	134502	118
Transport	..	..	..	2607990	1351020	..	..	295234	..	4254244	..
Road	..	..	..	2199902	10406	..	..	..	..	2210308	..
Rail	..	..	..	111410	..	..	..	189885	..	301294	..
Domestic aviation	..	..	..	244711	..	..	..	..	..	244711	..
Domestic navigation	..	..	..	17499	..	..	..	..	..	17499	..
Pipeline transport	..	..	..	7965	1283109	..	..	81459	..	1372533	..
Transport, n.e.s	..	..	..	26502	57504	..	..	23891	..	107898	..
Other	103257	234	203	821116	3000477	96357	..	1214196	2947902	8183742	88347
Agriculture, forestry, fishing	2164	..	89	151898	57456	4119	..	67672	119209	402607	1742
Commerce, public services	24635	..	..	94339	100461	48946	..	547825	736954	1553159	43314
Households	76458	234	..	574880	2842560	42052	..	598699	2091739	6226622	42052
Other consumers	..	..	114	..	..	1239	..	..	..	1353	1239
Non-energy use	*8304	..	..	1700301	1830133	..	..	..	..	3538738	..

Rwanda

Terajoules

	All Coal	All Oil	Natural Gas	Primary biofuels / Waste	Charcoal	Electricity	Total energy	of which: renewables
2017								
Primary production	..	..	*678	*84309	..	1238	*86224	*85546
Imports	..	13832	..	..	..	310	14142	..
Exports	..	..	..	..	..	-15	-15	..
International marine bunkers	..	..	..	..	..	..	..	..
International aviation bunkers	..	*-1230	..	..	..	..	*-1230	..
Stock changes	..	*131	..	..	..	..	*131	..
Total energy supply	..	12733	*678	*84309	..	1533	*99252	*85546
Statistical Difference	..	0	0	0	0	33	*33	*1238
Transfers	..	..	..	..	..	..	..	..
Transformation	..	*-2967	*-678	*-34128	*18349	1273	*-18150	*-15779
Electricity plants	..	*-2967	*-678	*-36	..	1273	*-2408	*-36
Charcoal plants	..	..	..	*-34092	*18349	..	*-15743	*-15743
Other transformation	..	0	0	0	..	..	0	0
Energy industries own use	..	..	..	..	..	-90	-90	..
Losses	..	..	..	..	..	-537	-537	..
Final consumption	..	*9766	..	*50181	*18349	2145	*80441	*68530
Final energy consumption	..	*9405	..	*50181	*18349	2145	*80080	*68530
Manufacturing, const., mining	..	*391	..	*5693	..	538	*6622	*5693
Transport	..	*7410	..	..	..	..	*7410	..
Road	..	*6352	..	..	..	..	*6352	..
Domestic aviation	..	*1058	..	..	..	..	*1058	..
Domestic navigation	..	..	..	..	..	..	..	..
Other transport	..	..	..	..	..	..	..	..
Other	..	*1603	..	*44487	*18349	1607	*66047	*62836
Agriculture, forestry, fishing	..	..	..	..	..	..	..	..
Commerce and public services	..	..	..	..	..	400	400	..
Households	..	*750	..	*44487	*18349	1207	*64794	*62836
Other consumers	..	*853	..	..	..	..	*853	..
Non-energy use	..	*361	..	..	..	..	*361	..
2018								
Primary production	*72	..	*694	*84657	..	1326	*86748	*85982
Imports	..	15061	..	..	..	338	15399	..
Exports	..	..	..	..	..	-16	-16	..
International marine bunkers	..	..	..	..	..	..	..	..
International aviation bunkers	..	*-1323	..	..	..	..	*-1323	..
Stock changes	..	*131	..	..	..	..	*131	..
Total energy supply	*72	13870	*694	*84657	..	1647	*100940	*85982
Statistical Difference	0	0	0	0	0	33	*33	*1326
Transfers	..	..	..	..	..	..	..	..
Transformation	*-72	*-3010	*-694	*-34356	*18467	1303	*-18363	*-15889
Electricity plants	*-72	*-3010	*-694	*-36	..	1303	*-2509	*-36
Charcoal plants	..	..	..	*-34320	*18467	..	*-15853	*-15853
Other transformation	0	0	0	0	..	..	0	0
Energy industries own use	..	..	..	..	..	-8	-8	..
Losses	..	..	..	..	..	*-504	*-504	..
Final consumption	..	*10860	..	*50300	*18467	2405	*82032	*68767
Final energy consumption	..	*10498	..	*50300	*18467	2405	*81670	*68767
Manufacturing, const., mining	..	*530	..	*5740	..	657	*6926	*5740
Transport	..	*7854	..	..	..	..	*7854	..
Road	..	*6918	..	..	..	..	*6918	..
Domestic aviation	..	*935	..	..	..	..	*935	..
Domestic navigation	..	..	..	..	..	..	..	..
Other transport	..	..	..	..	..	..	..	..
Other	..	*2114	..	*44561	*18467	1749	*66890	*63028
Agriculture, forestry, fishing	..	..	..	..	..	..	..	..
Commerce and public services	..	..	..	..	..	423	423	..
Households	..	*1037	..	*44561	*18467	1325	*65390	*63028
Other consumers	..	*1077	..	..	..	..	*1077	..
Non-energy use	..	*362	..	..	..	..	*362	..

Samoa

Terajoules

	All Coal	All Oil	Natural Gas	Primary biofuels / Waste	Charcoal	Electricity	Total energy	of which: renewables
2017								
Primary production	..	..	..	*1466	..	171	*1637	*1634
Imports	..	4462	..	..	0	..	4462	0
Exports	..	*-29	..	..	..	..	*-29	..
International marine bunkers	..	..	..	..	..	..	..	..
International aviation bunkers	..	*-532	..	..	..	..	*-532	..
Stock changes	..	*-259	..	..	..	..	*-259	..
Total energy supply	..	3643	..	*1466	0	171	5280	*1634
Statistical Difference	..	*-2	..	0	0	2	0	*165
Transfers	..	..	..	..	..	..	..	..
Transformation	..	*-989	..	*-30	16	387	*-615	*-14
Electricity plants	..	*-989	..	..	..	387	*-602	..
Charcoal plants	..	..	..	*-30	16	..	*-14	*-14
Other transformation	..	0	..	0	..	..	0	0
Energy industries own use	..	..	..	..	..	-16	-16	..
Losses	..	..	..	..	..	-54	-54	..
Final consumption	..	*2656	..	*1437	*16	*487	*4595	*1456
Final energy consumption	..	*2535	..	*1437	*16	*487	*4475	*1456
Manufacturing, const., mining	..	*215	..	..	..	19	*234	..
Transport	..	*1966	..	..	..	..	*1966	..
Road	..	*1708	..	..	..	..	*1708	..
Domestic aviation	..	..	..	..	..	..	..	..
Domestic navigation	..	*258	..	..	..	..	*258	..
Other transport	..	..	..	..	..	..	..	..
Other	..	*354	..	*1437	*16	*467	*2275	*1456
Agriculture, forestry, fishing	..	*35	..	*5	..	..	*40	*5
Commerce and public services	..	*179	..	..	..	*320	*499	*3
Households	..	*140	..	*1432	*16	*148	*1736	*1448
Other consumers	..	..	..	..	..	..	..	..
Non-energy use	..	*121	..	..	..	..	*121	..
2018								
Primary production	..	..	..	*1466	..	234	*1699	*1696
Imports	..	4129	..	..	..	..	4129	..
Exports	..	*-29	..	..	..	..	*-29	..
International marine bunkers	..	..	..	..	..	..	..	..
International aviation bunkers	..	*-532	..	..	..	..	*-532	..
Stock changes	..	*-21	..	..	..	..	*-21	..
Total energy supply	..	3548	..	*1466	..	234	5247	*1696
Statistical Difference	..	*-4	..	0	0	0	*-4	*228
Transfers	..	..	..	..	..	..	..	..
Transformation	..	*-843	..	*-27	*15	322	*-533	*-13
Electricity plants	..	*-843	..	..	..	322	*-521	..
Charcoal plants	..	..	..	*-27	*15	..	*-13	*-13
Other transformation	..	0	..	0	..	..	0	0
Energy industries own use	..	..	..	..	..	-15	-15	..
Losses	..	..	..	..	..	-54	-54	..
Final consumption	..	*2708	..	*1438	*15	487	*4648	*1456
Final energy consumption	..	*2588	..	*1438	*15	487	*4528	*1456
Manufacturing, const., mining	..	*215	..	..	..	20	*235	..
Transport	..	*2014	..	..	..	..	*2014	..
Road	..	*1756	..	..	..	..	*1756	..
Domestic aviation	..	..	..	..	..	..	..	..
Domestic navigation	..	*258	..	..	..	..	*258	..
Other transport	..	..	..	..	..	..	..	..
Other	..	*358	..	*1438	*15	467	*2279	*1456
Agriculture, forestry, fishing	..	*35	..	*5	..	..	*40	*5
Commerce and public services	..	*178	..	..	..	327	505	*3
Households	..	*145	..	*1433	*15	140	*1733	*1448
Other consumers	..	..	..	..	..	..	..	..
Non-energy use	..	*121	..	..	..	..	*121	..

Sao Tome and Principe

Terajoules

	All Coal	All Oil	Natural Gas	Primary biofuels / Waste	Charcoal	Electricity	Total energy	of which: renewables
2017								
Primary production	..	..	..	1033	..	*27	1060	1060
Imports	..	*2342	..	..	..	..	*2342	..
Exports	..	..	..	..	..	..	..	..
International marine bunkers	..	..	..	..	..	..	..	..
International aviation bunkers	..	*-498	..	..	..	..	*-498	..
Stock changes	..	..	..	..	..	..	..	..
Total energy supply	..	*1844	..	1033	..	*27	*2904	1060
Statistical Difference	..	0	..	0	0	0	0	27
Transfers	..	..	..	..	..	..	..	..
Transformation	..	*-783	..	*-532	286	*300	*-728	*-246
Electricity plants	..	*-783	..	..	..	*300	*-482	..
Charcoal plants	..	..	..	*-532	286	..	*-246	*-246
Other transformation	..	0	..	0	..	..	0	0
Energy industries own use	..	..	..	..	..	*-23	*-23	..
Losses	..	..	..	..	..	*-43	*-43	..
Final consumption	..	*1061	..	*502	*286	*260	*2109	*788
Final energy consumption	..	*1057	..	*502	*286	*260	*2105	*788
Manufacturing, const., mining	..	*430	..	..	..	..	*430	..
Transport	..	*447	..	..	..	..	*447	..
Road	..	*399	..	..	..	..	*399	..
Domestic aviation	..	*49	..	..	..	..	*49	..
Domestic navigation	..	..	..	..	..	..	..	..
Other transport	..	..	..	..	..	..	..	..
Other	..	*180	..	*502	*286	*260	*1228	*788
Agriculture, forestry, fishing	..	..	..	..	..	..	..	..
Commerce and public services	..	..	..	..	..	*130	*130	..
Households	..	*180	..	*502	*286	*131	*1098	*788
Other consumers	..	..	..	..	..	..	..	..
Non-energy use	..	*4	..	..	..	..	*4	..
2018								
Primary production	..	..	..	1039	..	23	1061	1061
Imports	..	*2390	..	..	..	..	*2390	..
Exports	..	..	..	..	..	..	..	..
International marine bunkers	..	..	..	..	..	..	..	..
International aviation bunkers	..	*-507	..	..	..	..	*-507	..
Stock changes	..	..	..	..	..	..	..	..
Total energy supply	..	*1883	..	1039	..	23	*2944	1061
Statistical Difference	..	0	..	0	0	0	0	23
Transfers	..	..	..	..	..	..	..	..
Transformation	..	*-796	..	*-537	289	*306	*-738	*-248
Electricity plants	..	*-796	..	..	..	*306	*-490	..
Charcoal plants	..	..	..	*-537	289	..	*-248	*-248
Other transformation	..	0	..	0	..	..	0	0
Energy industries own use	..	..	..	..	..	-23	-23	..
Losses	..	..	..	..	..	*-42	*-42	..
Final consumption	..	*1088	..	*502	*289	*263	*2141	*791
Final energy consumption	..	*1084	..	*502	*289	*263	*2137	*791
Manufacturing, const., mining	..	*439	..	..	..	..	*439	..
Transport	..	*456	..	..	..	..	*456	..
Road	..	*408	..	..	..	..	*408	..
Domestic aviation	..	*49	..	..	..	..	*49	..
Domestic navigation	..	..	..	..	..	..	..	..
Other transport	..	..	..	..	..	..	..	..
Other	..	*189	..	*502	*289	*263	*1242	*791
Agriculture, forestry, fishing	..	..	..	..	..	..	..	..
Commerce and public services	..	..	..	..	..	*130	*130	..
Households	..	*189	..	*502	*289	*133	*1113	*791
Other consumers	..	..	..	..	..	..	..	..
Non-energy use	..	*4	..	..	..	..	*4	..

Saudi Arabia

Terajoules

2017	Primary coal and peat	Coal and peat products	Primary Oil	Oil Products	Natural Gas	Biofuels and waste	Nuclear	Electricity	Heat	Total energy	of which: renewables
Primary production	..	..	23572339	..	4530338	..	..	15	..	28102693	15
Imports	..	..	181010	1046510	..	300	..	11	..	1227831	300
Exports	..	..	-14697726	-4513663	..	..	..	-136	..	-19211525	..
International marine bunkers	..	..	..	-134330	..	..	..	..	..	-134330	..
International aviation bunkers	..	..	..	-135387	..	..	..	..	..	-135387	..
Stock changes	..	..	159545	26660	..	..	..	..	..	186205	..
Total energy supply	..	..	9215168	-3710209	4530338	300	..	-110	..	10035487	315
Statistical difference	..	..	-95226	-99284	-34064	0	..	95081	..	-133493	15
Transfers	..	..	..	*-2946	..	..	..	..	..	*-2946	..
Transformation	..	..	-9213823	7488898	-2191601	..	..	1278270	..	-2638256	..
Electricity plants	..	..	*-1029065	-649303	-2191601	..	..	1278270	..	-2591699	..
CHP plants	..	..	..	..	..	..	..	..	..	..	..
Heat plants	..	..	..	..	..	..	..	..	..	..	..
Coke ovens	..	..	..	..	..	..	..	..	..	..	..
Briquetting plants	..	..	..	..	..	..	..	..	..	..	..
Liquefaction plants	..	..	..	..	..	..	..	..	..	..	..
Gas works	..	..	..	..	..	..	..	..	..	..	..
Blast furnaces	..	..	..	..	..	..	..	..	..	..	..
NGL plants & gas blending	..	..	-1786078	1899035	..	..	..	..	..	112957	..
Oil refineries	..	..	-6398680	6239167	..	..	..	..	..	-159513	..
Other transformation	..	..	..	..	..	..	..	..	..	..	..
Energy industries own use	..	..	*-42	-349192	-656372	..	..	-83106	..	-1088712	..
Losses	..	..	..	..	..	..	..	-148324	..	-148324	..
Final consumption	..	..	*96529	3525836	1716429	300	..	951649	..	6290742	300
Final energy consumption	..	..	*96529	2461787	*1500936	300	..	951649	..	5011201	300
Manufacturing, const., mining	..	..	*96529	*650234	728359	..	..	120600	..	1595722	..
Iron and steel	..	..	..	..	..	..	..	13054	..	13054	..
Chemical and petrochemical	..	..	..	..	..	..	..	27709	..	27709	..
Non-ferrous metals	..	..	..	..	..	..	..	..	..	..	..
Non-metallic minerals	..	..	..	..	..	..	..	1422	..	1422	..
Transport equipment	..	..	..	..	..	..	..	..	..	..	..
Machinery	..	..	..	..	..	..	..	..	..	..	..
Mining and quarrying	..	..	..	..	..	..	..	842	..	842	..
Food and tobacco	..	..	..	..	..	..	..	..	..	..	..
Paper, pulp and printing	..	..	..	..	..	..	..	..	..	..	..
Wood and wood products	..	..	..	..	..	..	..	..	..	..	..
Textile and leather	..	..	..	..	..	..	..	..	..	..	..
Construction	..	..	..	..	..	..	..	..	..	..	..
Industries n.e.s	..	..	*96529	*650234	728359	..	..	77573	..	1552695	..
Transport	..	..	..	1736576	..	..	..	..	..	1736576	..
Road	..	..	..	1693314	..	..	..	..	..	1693314	..
Rail	..	..	..	..	..	..	..	..	..	..	..
Domestic aviation	..	..	..	43262	..	..	..	..	..	43262	..
Domestic navigation	..	..	..	..	..	..	..	..	..	..	..
Pipeline transport	..	..	..	..	..	..	..	..	..	..	..
Transport, n.e.s	..	..	..	..	..	..	..	..	..	..	..
Other	..	..	..	74976	*772577	300	..	831049	..	1678903	300
Agriculture, forestry, fishing	..	..	..	..	..	..	..	..	..	..	..
Commerce, public services	..	..	..	..	..	..	..	313254	..	313254	..
Households	..	..	..	74976	..	300	..	516503	..	591779	300
Other consumers	..	..	..	..	*772577	..	..	1292	..	*773870	..
Non-energy use	..	..	..	1064049	215492	..	..	..	..	1279542	..

Saudi Arabia

Terajoules

2018	Primary coal and peat	Coal and peat products	Primary Oil	Oil Products	Natural Gas	Biofuels and waste	Nuclear	Electricity	Heat	Total energy	of which: renewables
Primary production	..	..	23861263	..	4705933	..	..	*16	..	28567212	*16
Imports	..	..	191867	1781157	..	300	..	7	..	1973331	300
Exports	..	..	-15548203	-4957950	..	..	..	-130	..	-20506283	..
International marine bunkers	..	..	..	-142127	..	..	..	..	..	-142127	..
International aviation bunkers	..	..	..	-151969	..	..	..	..	..	-151969	..
Stock changes	..	..	*228928	-19213	..	..	..	..	..	*209714	..
Total energy supply	..	..	8733855	-3490102	4705933	300	..	-106	..	9949879	316
Statistical difference	..	..	-133020	-198854	1	0	..	0	..	-331873	16
Transfers	..	..	..	..	..	..	..	..	..	..	..
Transformation	..	..	-8836630	7391983	-2104203	..	..	1237583	..	-2311267	..
Electricity plants	..	..	*-749091	*-616175	-2104203	..	..	1237583	..	-2231885	..
CHP plants	..	..	..	..	..	..	..	..	..	..	..
Heat plants	..	..	..	..	..	..	..	..	..	..	..
Coke ovens	..	..	..	..	..	..	..	..	..	..	..
Briquetting plants	..	..	..	..	..	..	..	..	..	..	..
Liquefaction plants	..	..	..	..	..	..	..	..	..	..	..
Gas works	..	..	..	..	..	..	..	..	..	..	..
Blast furnaces	..	..	..	..	..	..	..	..	..	..	..
NGL plants & gas blending	..	..	*-1749480	1857476	..	..	..	..	..	107995	..
Oil refineries	..	..	-6338059	6150682	..	..	..	..	..	-187377	..
Other transformation	..	..	..	..	..	..	..	..	..	..	..
Energy industries own use	..	..	..	-361991	-687979	..	..	-161952	..	-1211922	..
Losses	..	..	..	..	..	..	..	-119178	..	-119178	..
Final consumption	..	..	*30244	3738743	1913750	300	..	956347	..	6639385	300
Final energy consumption	..	..	*30244	2488981	1691918	300	..	956347	..	5167791	300
Manufacturing, const., mining	..	..	*30244	*1003003	853578	..	..	160078	..	*2046903	..
Iron and steel	..	..	..	..	..	..	..	17262	..	17262	..
Chemical and petrochemical	..	..	..	..	..	..	..	36644	..	36644	..
Non-ferrous metals	..	..	..	..	..	..	..	..	..	..	..
Non-metallic minerals	..	..	..	..	..	..	..	1879	..	1879	..
Transport equipment	..	..	..	..	..	..	..	..	..	..	..
Machinery	..	..	..	..	..	..	..	..	..	..	..
Mining and quarrying	..	..	..	..	..	..	..	..	..	..	..
Food and tobacco	..	..	..	..	..	..	..	..	..	..	..
Paper, pulp and printing	..	..	..	..	..	..	..	..	..	..	..
Wood and wood products	..	..	..	..	..	..	..	..	..	..	..
Textile and leather	..	..	..	..	..	..	..	..	..	..	..
Construction	..	..	..	..	..	..	..	..	..	..	..
Industries n.e.s	..	..	*30244	*1003003	853578	..	..	104292	..	*1991117	..
Transport	..	..	..	1408751	..	..	..	..	..	1408751	..
Road	..	..	..	1373471	..	..	..	..	..	1373471	..
Rail	..	..	..	..	..	..	..	..	..	..	..
Domestic aviation	..	..	..	35280	..	..	..	..	..	35280	..
Domestic navigation	..	..	..	..	..	..	..	..	..	..	..
Pipeline transport	..	..	..	..	..	..	..	..	..	..	..
Transport, n.e.s	..	..	..	..	..	..	..	..	..	..	..
Other	..	..	..	77227	*838340	300	..	796270	..	1712137	300
Agriculture, forestry, fishing	..	..	..	..	..	..	..	..	..	..	..
Commerce, public services	..	..	..	..	..	..	..	326729	..	326729	..
Households	..	..	..	77227	..	300	..	469541	..	547068	300
Other consumers	..	..	..	..	*838340	..	..	..	..	*838340	..
Non-energy use	..	..	..	1249762	221832	..	..	..	..	1471594	..

Senegal

Terajoules

2017	Primary coal and peat	Coal and peat products	Primary Oil	Oil Products	Natural Gas	Biofuels and waste	Nuclear	Electricity	Heat	Total energy	of which: renewables
Primary production	..	..	..	..	662	67492	..	356	533	69044	67848
Imports	15887	..	50760	69493	..	..	..	1296	..	137436	..
Exports	..	..	..	-11348	..	..	..	..	..	-11348	..
International marine bunkers	..	..	..	-4980	..	..	..	..	..	-4980	..
International aviation bunkers	..	..	..	-9790	..	..	..	..	..	-9790	..
Stock changes	..	..	*5034	668	..	..	..	..	..	*5701	..
Total energy supply	15887	..	55794	44043	662	67492	..	1652	533	186063	67848
Statistical difference	0	..	0	5139	0	0	..	2088	0	7227	356
Transfers	..	..	..	-359	..	..	..	..	..	-359	..
Transformation	-4665	..	-55794	17402	-662	*-29788	..	15548	-533	-58492	*-29788
Electricity plants	-4665	..	..	-33964	-662	*-2127	..	15548	-533	-26403	*-2127
CHP plants	..	..	..	..	..	..	..	..	..	..	..
Heat plants	..	..	..	..	..	..	..	..	..	..	..
Coke ovens	..	..	..	..	..	..	..	..	..	..	..
Briquetting plants	..	..	..	..	..	..	..	..	..	..	..
Liquefaction plants	..	..	..	..	..	..	..	..	..	..	..
Gas works	..	..	..	..	..	..	..	..	..	..	..
Blast furnaces	..	..	..	..	..	..	..	..	..	..	..
NGL plants & gas blending	..	..	..	..	..	..	..	..	..	..	..
Oil refineries	..	..	-55794	51366	..	..	..	..	..	-4428	..
Other transformation	..	..	..	..	..	*-27661	..	..	..	*-27661	*-27661
Energy industries own use	..	..	..	-743	..	..	..	-194	0	-937	..
Losses	..	..	..	..	..	..	..	-2419	..	-2419	..
Final consumption	*11222	..	..	55204	..	37704	..	12499	..	116629	37704
Final energy consumption	*11222	..	..	55204	..	37704	..	12499	..	116629	37704
Manufacturing, const., mining	*11222	..	..	6636	..	*831	..	1606	..	*20294	*831
Iron and steel	..	..	..	..	..	..	..	..	..	..	..
Chemical and petrochemical	..	..	..	121	..	..	..	1217	..	1338	..
Non-ferrous metals	..	..	..	..	..	..	..	..	..	..	..
Non-metallic minerals	*11222	..	..	568	..	..	..	50	..	*11840	..
Transport equipment	..	..	..	..	..	..	..	..	..	..	..
Machinery	..	..	..	..	..	..	..	..	..	..	..
Mining and quarrying	..	..	..	..	..	..	..	..	..	..	..
Food and tobacco	..	..	..	..	..	..	..	148	..	148	..
Paper, pulp and printing	..	..	..	..	..	..	..	..	..	..	..
Wood and wood products	..	..	..	..	..	..	..	..	..	..	..
Textile and leather	..	..	..	..	..	..	..	86	..	86	..
Construction	..	..	..	..	..	..	..	29	..	29	..
Industries n.e.s	0	..	..	5946	..	*831	..	76	..	*6853	*831
Transport	..	..	..	42851	..	..	..	..	..	42851	..
Road	..	..	..	40725	..	..	..	..	..	40725	..
Rail	..	..	..	..	..	..	..	..	..	..	..
Domestic aviation	..	..	..	..	..	..	..	..	..	..	..
Domestic navigation	..	..	..	2126	..	..	..	..	..	2126	..
Pipeline transport	..	..	..	..	..	..	..	..	..	..	..
Transport, n.e.s	..	..	..	..	..	..	..	..	..	..	..
Other	..	..	..	5718	..	36873	..	10894	..	53484	36873
Agriculture, forestry, fishing	..	..	..	..	..	..	..	407	..	407	..
Commerce, public services	..	..	..	237	..	..	..	4464	..	4701	..
Households	..	..	..	5094	..	36873	..	4360	..	46327	36873
Other consumers	..	..	..	387	..	..	..	1663	..	2050	..
Non-energy use	..	..	..	..	..	..	..	..	..	..	..

Senegal

Terajoules

2018	Primary coal and peat	Coal and peat products	Primary Oil	Oil Products	Natural Gas	Biofuels and waste	Nuclear	Electricity	Heat	Total energy	of which: renewables
Primary production	..	..	..	..	415	67626	..	288	969	69298	67914
Imports	24957	..	43315	89745	..	..	..	1296	..	159313	..
Exports	..	..	..	*-18735	..	..	..	..	..	*-18735	..
International marine bunkers	..	..	..	*-5590	..	..	..	..	..	*-5590	..
International aviation bunkers	..	..	..	-8908	..	..	..	..	..	-8908	..
Stock changes	..	..	1100	*-5152	..	..	..	..	..	*-4052	..
Total energy supply	24957	..	44415	51360	415	67626	..	1584	969	191327	67914
Statistical difference	0	..	-42	-644	0	0	..	493	0	-194	288
Transfers	..	..	..	-357	..	..	..	..	..	-357	..
Transformation	-6764	..	-44457	1483	-415	*-29780	..	15919	-969	-64982	*-29780
Electricity plants	-6764	..	..	-40460	-415	*-3062	..	15919	-969	-35751	*-3062
CHP plants	..	..	..	..	..	..	..	..	..	..	..
Heat plants	..	..	..	..	..	..	..	..	..	..	..
Coke ovens	..	..	..	..	..	..	..	..	..	..	..
Briquetting plants	..	..	..	..	..	..	..	..	..	..	..
Liquefaction plants	..	..	..	..	..	..	..	..	..	..	..
Gas works	..	..	..	..	..	..	..	..	..	..	..
Blast furnaces	..	..	..	..	..	..	..	..	..	..	..
NGL plants & gas blending	..	..	..	..	..	..	..	..	..	..	..
Oil refineries	..	..	-44457	41943	..	..	..	..	..	-2514	..
Other transformation	..	..	..	..	..	*-26718	..	..	..	*-26718	*-26718
Energy industries own use	..	..	..	-644	..	..	..	-198	0	-842	..
Losses	..	..	..	..	..	..	..	-2419	..	-2419	..
Final consumption	*18193	..	..	52488	..	37847	..	14393	..	122920	37847
Final energy consumption	*18193	..	..	52488	..	37847	..	14393	..	122920	37847
Manufacturing, const., mining	*18193	..	..	1365	..	*726	..	3870	..	*24154	*726
Iron and steel	..	..	..	..	..	..	..	..	..	..	..
Chemical and petrochemical	..	..	..	81	..	..	..	3456	..	3537	..
Non-ferrous metals	..	..	..	..	..	..	..	..	..	..	..
Non-metallic minerals	*18193	..	..	953	..	..	..	54	..	*19200	..
Transport equipment	..	..	..	..	..	..	..	..	..	..	..
Machinery	..	..	..	..	..	..	..	..	..	..	..
Mining and quarrying	..	..	..	..	..	..	..	..	..	..	..
Food and tobacco	..	..	..	..	..	..	..	158	..	158	..
Paper, pulp and printing	..	..	..	..	..	..	..	..	..	..	..
Wood and wood products	..	..	..	..	..	..	..	..	..	..	..
Textile and leather	..	..	..	..	..	..	..	94	..	94	..
Construction	..	..	..	..	..	..	..	29	..	29	..
Industries n.e.s	0	..	..	331	..	*726	..	79	..	*1136	*726
Transport	..	..	..	35941	..	..	..	..	..	35941	..
Road	..	..	..	33682	..	..	..	..	..	33682	..
Rail	..	..	..	..	..	..	..	..	..	..	..
Domestic aviation	..	..	..	..	..	..	..	..	..	..	..
Domestic navigation	..	..	..	2259	..	..	..	..	..	2259	..
Pipeline transport	..	..	..	..	..	..	..	..	..	..	..
Transport, n.e.s	..	..	..	..	..	..	..	..	..	..	..
Other	..	..	..	15182	..	37121	..	10523	..	62826	37121
Agriculture, forestry, fishing	..	..	..	..	..	..	..	428	..	428	..
Commerce, public services	..	..	..	2649	..	..	..	4831	..	7480	..
Households	..	..	..	5567	..	37121	..	3758	..	46446	37121
Other consumers	..	..	..	*6966	..	..	..	1505	..	*8471	..
Non-energy use	..	..	..	..	..	..	..	..	..	..	..

Serbia

Terajoules

2017	Primary coal and peat	Coal and peat products	Primary Oil	Oil Products	Natural Gas	Biofuels and waste	Nuclear	Electricity	Heat	Total energy	of which: renewables
Primary production	302127	..	39546	..	16305	46244	..	33173	213	437608	79586
Imports	7815	20918	105508	45829	72764	1516	..	23577	..	277926	1516
Exports	-565	-96	-160	-36049	..	-2615	..	-20607	..	-60091	-2615
International marine bunkers	..	..	..	-616	..	..	..	..	..	-616	..
International aviation bunkers	..	..	..	-5649	..	..	..	..	..	-5649	..
Stock changes	-344	-137	-166	-1848	-427	401	..	..	..	-2520	401
Total energy supply	309033	20686	144728	1667	88642	45546	..	36144	213	646657	78888
Statistical difference	5	11	-925	-19	0	2	..	0	0	-926	33175
Transfers	..	..	8329	-8142	..	..	..	..	..	187	..
Transformation	-299003	-4265	-153982	150813	-31203	-1695	..	98034	37089	-204212	-1675
Electricity plants	-142839	..	..	..	..	..	..	50371	..	-92468	..
CHP plants	-143988	-4966	..	-59	-6730	-499	..	47663	10803	-97777	-479
Heat plants	-2958	-126	..	-4966	-20365	-95	..	..	26286	-2225	-95
Coke ovens	..	..	..	..	..	..	..	..	..	..	..
Briquetting plants	-7115	9035	..	..	..	..	..	..	..	1920	..
Liquefaction plants	..	..	0	..	..	..	..	..	..	0	..
Gas works	..	..	..	..	..	..	..	..	..	..	..
Blast furnaces	-2102	-8208	..	..	..	..	..	..	..	-10310	..
NGL plants & gas blending	..	..	..	..	..	..	..	..	..	..	..
Oil refineries	..	..	-156731	156071	..	..	..	..	..	-660	..
Other transformation	..	..	2749	-233	-4108	-1100	..	..	..	-2692	-1100
Energy industries own use	..	-3388	..	-8466	-6767	..	..	-15629	-2166	-36416	..
Losses	-7	-2556	..	..	-1204	-1	..	-17302	-3472	-24542	-1
Final consumption	10018	10466	..	135891	49469	43847	..	101247	31664	382601	44036
Final energy consumption	9921	10466	..	110323	39491	43847	..	101247	31664	346958	44036
Manufacturing, const., mining	5197	4666	..	13018	22742	7797	..	30247	8965	92632	7773
Iron and steel	526	2392	..	12	3650	..	..	3312	602	10493	..
Chemical and petrochemical	1107	798	..	2528	6620	263	..	4542	3617	19475	239
Non-ferrous metals	..	..	..	294	853	110	..	1602	420	3280	110
Non-metallic minerals	2606	163	..	5270	3132	264	..	2708	44	14187	264
Transport equipment	1	1	..	277	1103	19	..	923	24	2348	19
Machinery	236	2	..	1408	537	961	..	2365	46	5555	961
Mining and quarrying	..	..	..	620	11	8	..	1634	..	2274	8
Food and tobacco	216	318	..	1471	4739	2484	..	5851	2131	17211	2484
Paper, pulp and printing	47	641	..	92	1153	227	..	1814	772	4747	227
Wood and wood products	..	0	..	34	50	780	..	476	4	1344	780
Textile and leather	165	0	..	224	430	973	..	1353	60	3205	973
Construction	16	..	..	687	..	..	..	1224	..	1927	..
Industries n.e.s	278	350	..	99	464	1706	..	2444	1246	6587	1706
Transport	..	..	..	86911	177	..	..	1349	..	88437	..
Road	..	..	..	86197	99	..	..	..	..	86295	..
Rail	..	..	..	430	..	..	..	1349	..	1779	..
Domestic aviation	..	..	..	..	..	..	..	..	..	..	..
Domestic navigation	..	..	..	284	..	..	..	..	..	284	..
Pipeline transport	..	..	..	..	78	..	..	..	..	78	..
Transport, n.e.s	..	..	..	..	..	..	..	..	..	..	..
Other	4723	5800	..	10395	16572	36050	..	69650	22698	165888	36263
Agriculture, forestry, fishing	5	..	..	5619	752	255	..	1231	132	7994	387
Commerce, public services	1448	120	..	2781	7818	2155	..	18685	6034	39041	2236
Households	3271	5680	..	1994	8001	33641	..	49734	16532	118853	33641
Other consumers	..	..	..	..	..	..	..	..	..	..	..
Non-energy use	98	0	..	25568	9978	..	..	..	..	35643	..

Serbia

Terajoules

2018	Primary coal and peat	Coal and peat products	Primary Oil	Oil Products	Natural Gas	Biofuels and waste	Nuclear	Electricity	Heat	Total energy	of which: renewables
Primary production	276720	..	39080	..	14988	47943	..	38887	215	417833	86996
Imports	10147	22478	113856	41643	73288	596	..	23040	..	285047	596
Exports	-588	-36	-360	-38930	..	-2917	..	-22622	..	-65453	-2917
International marine bunkers	..	..	..	-731	..	..	..	..	..	-731	..
International aviation bunkers	..	..	..	-5954	..	..	..	..	..	-5954	..
Stock changes	4171	2123	-152	-2401	982	-180	..	..	..	4544	-180
Total energy supply	290450	24565	152425	-6372	89258	45442	..	39305	215	635286	84495
Statistical difference	-23	18	-381	134	0	-83	..	0	0	-335	38804
Transfers	..	..	10273	-9986	..	..	..	..	..	287	..
Transformation	-280064	-8739	-163078	157757	-31417	-1585	..	93132	36178	-197816	-1563
Electricity plants	-144808	..	..	..	..	..	..	51588	..	-93220	..
CHP plants	-124039	-5418	..	-2990	-7302	-758	..	41544	11178	-87784	-736
Heat plants	-2869	-142	..	-4410	-19457	-103	..	..	25000	-1981	-103
Coke ovens	..	..	..	..	..	..	..	..	..	..	..
Briquetting plants	-5731	7509	..	..	..	..	..	..	..	1778	..
Liquefaction plants	..	..	0	..	..	..	..	..	..	0	..
Gas works	..	..	..	..	..	..	..	..	..	..	..
Blast furnaces	-2616	-10687	..	..	..	..	..	..	..	-13303	..
NGL plants & gas blending	..	..	..	..	..	..	..	..	..	..	..
Oil refineries	..	..	-166437	165439	..	..	..	..	..	-999	..
Other transformation	..	..	3359	-283	-4658	-724	..	..	..	-2306	-724
Energy industries own use	..	-4176	..	-6470	-6579	..	..	-15145	-2157	-34528	..
Losses	..	-2546	..	..	-1224	..	..	-16315	-3104	-23189	..
Final consumption	10409	9087	..	134795	50037	43940	..	100976	31132	380376	44128
Final energy consumption	10292	9087	..	110592	43457	43940	..	100976	31132	349475	44128
Manufacturing, const., mining	7158	3058	..	13777	25756	7291	..	31446	8899	97384	7264
Iron and steel	716	2104	..	43	7242	..	..	4835	3156	18096	..
Chemical and petrochemical	780	53	..	2373	3956	258	..	4853	3660	15933	231
Non-ferrous metals	..	..	..	326	1165	59	..	1584	172	3305	59
Non-metallic minerals	4910	82	..	6355	3784	212	..	2657	22	18022	212
Transport equipment	..	..	..	43	590	15	..	767	33	1447	15
Machinery	272	..	..	291	832	1115	..	2358	10	4877	1115
Mining and quarrying	28	..	..	1247	23	85	..	1465	..	2848	85
Food and tobacco	74	160	..	1586	4701	3195	..	5749	876	16340	3195
Paper, pulp and printing	96	160	..	81	1826	137	..	1501	369	4170	137
Wood and wood products	..	..	..	43	75	292	..	382	..	791	292
Textile and leather	224	..	..	242	649	851	..	1235	50	3251	851
Construction	22	..	..	735	..	..	..	1220	..	1978	..
Industries n.e.s	37	498	..	412	914	1072	..	2840	551	6324	1072
Transport	..	..	..	87845	445	..	..	1350	..	89639	..
Road	..	..	..	87114	369	..	..	..	..	87483	..
Rail	..	..	..	473	..	..	..	1350	..	1823	..
Domestic aviation	..	..	..	..	..	..	..	..	..	..	..
Domestic navigation	..	..	..	258	..	..	..	..	..	258	..
Pipeline transport	..	..	..	..	76	..	..	..	..	76	..
Transport, n.e.s	..	..	..	..	..	..	..	..	..	..	..
Other	3134	6029	..	8971	17256	36649	..	68180	22233	162451	36864
Agriculture, forestry, fishing	..	..	..	4739	783	279	..	1228	132	7160	411
Commerce, public services	934	124	..	2671	8339	1161	..	18659	5168	37056	1244
Households	2200	5904	..	1561	8134	35209	..	48294	16933	118235	35209
Other consumers	..	..	..	..	..	..	..	..	..	..	..
Non-energy use	118	..	..	24203	6581	..	..	..	..	30901	..

Seychelles

Terajoules

	All Coal	All Oil	Natural Gas	Primary biofuels / Waste	Charcoal	Electricity	Total energy	of which: renewables
2017								
Primary production	..	..	..	29	..	35	63	63
Imports	..	17610	..	..	0	..	17610	0
Exports	..	..	..	..	0	..	0	0
International marine bunkers	..	-7197	..	..	..	..	-7197	..
International aviation bunkers	..	*-2306	..	..	..	..	*-2306	..
Stock changes	..	*-430	..	..	..	..	*-430	..
Total energy supply	..	7677	..	29	0	35	7740	64
Statistical Difference	..	-263	..	0	0	5	-258	35
Transfers	..	..	..	..	..	..	..	..
Transformation	..	-4668	..	..	..	1812	-2857	..
Electricity plants	..	-4668	..	..	..	1812	-2857	..
Charcoal plants	..	..	..	..	..	..	..	..
Other transformation	..	0	..	..	..	..	0	..
Energy industries own use	..	..	..	..	..	*-43	*-43	..
Losses	..	..	..	..	..	*-107	*-107	..
Final consumption	..	*3271	..	*29	0	*1692	*4992	*29
Final energy consumption	..	*3231	..	*29	0	*1692	*4952	*29
Manufacturing, const., mining	..	*125	..	..	..	*830	*955	..
Transport	..	*2184	..	..	..	..	*2184	..
Road	..	*1849	..	..	..	..	*1849	..
Domestic aviation	..	*335	..	..	..	..	*335	..
Domestic navigation	..	..	..	..	..	..	..	..
Other transport	..	..	..	..	..	..	..	..
Other	..	*922	..	*29	0	*862	*1813	*29
Agriculture, forestry, fishing	..	..	..	..	..	..	..	..
Commerce and public services	..	*68	..	..	..	*432	*500	..
Households	..	*209	..	*29	0	431	669	*29
Other consumers	..	*645	..	..	..	..	*645	..
Non-energy use	..	*40	..	..	..	..	*40	..
2018								
Primary production	..	..	..	29	..	39	68	68
Imports	..	15605	..	..	0	..	15605	0
Exports	..	..	..	..	0	..	0	0
International marine bunkers	..	*-6692	..	..	..	..	*-6692	..
International aviation bunkers	..	*-1220	..	..	..	..	*-1220	..
Stock changes	..	0	..	..	..	..	0	..
Total energy supply	..	7693	..	29	0	39	7761	68
Statistical Difference	..	*-253	..	0	0	0	*-253	39
Transfers	..	..	..	..	..	..	..	..
Transformation	..	*-4334	..	..	..	1825	*-2508	..
Electricity plants	..	*-4334	..	..	..	1825	*-2508	..
Charcoal plants	..	..	..	..	..	..	..	..
Other transformation	..	0	..	..	..	..	0	..
Energy industries own use	..	..	..	..	..	-44	-44	..
Losses	..	..	..	..	..	*-108	*-108	..
Final consumption	..	*3612	..	*29	0	*1713	*5354	*29
Final energy consumption	..	*3572	..	*29	0	*1713	*5314	*29
Manufacturing, const., mining	..	*117	..	..	..	*839	*956	..
Transport	..	*2664	..	..	..	..	*2664	..
Road	..	*2486	..	..	..	..	*2486	..
Domestic aviation	..	*178	..	..	..	..	*178	..
Domestic navigation	..	..	..	..	..	..	..	..
Other transport	..	..	..	..	..	..	..	..
Other	..	*791	..	*29	0	874	1694	*29
Agriculture, forestry, fishing	..	..	..	..	..	..	..	..
Commerce and public services	..	*49	..	..	..	*419	*468	..
Households	..	*161	..	*29	0	455	645	*29
Other consumers	..	*581	..	..	..	..	*581	..
Non-energy use	..	*40	..	..	..	..	*40	..

Sierra Leone

Terajoules

	All Coal	All Oil	Natural Gas	Primary biofuels / Waste	Charcoal	Electricity	Total energy	of which: renewables
2017								
Primary production	..	..	..	53996	..	*809	54804	54804
Imports	..	*13444	..	..	..	..	*13444	..
Exports	..	..	..	..	..	..	..	..
International marine bunkers	..	..	..	..	..	..	..	..
International aviation bunkers	..	*-450	..	..	..	..	*-450	..
Stock changes	..	..	..	..	..	..	..	..
Total energy supply	..	*12994	..	53996	..	*809	67798	54804
Statistical Difference	..	0	..	0	0	0	0	809
Transfers	..	..	..	..	..	..	..	..
Transformation	..	*-903	..	*-24846	13334	*302	*-12113	*-11512
Electricity plants	..	*-903	..	*-72	..	*302	*-673	*-72
Charcoal plants	..	..	..	*-24774	13334	..	*-11440	*-11440
Other transformation	..	0	..	0	..	..	0	0
Energy industries own use	..	..	..	..	..	*-31	*-31	..
Losses	..	..	..	..	..	*-324	*-324	..
Final consumption	..	*12091	..	*29150	*13334	*756	*55330	*42484
Final energy consumption	..	*11890	..	*29150	*13334	*756	*55129	*42484
Manufacturing, const., mining	..	*1414	..	*201	..	*281	*1896	*201
Transport	..	*6377	..	..	..	..	*6377	..
Road	..	*6377	..	..	..	..	*6377	..
Domestic aviation	..	..	..	..	..	..	..	..
Domestic navigation	..	..	..	..	..	..	..	..
Other transport	..	..	..	..	..	..	..	..
Other	..	*4099	..	*28949	*13334	*475	*46857	*42283
Agriculture, forestry, fishing	..	..	..	..	..	..	..	..
Commerce and public services	..	..	..	..	..	*245	*245	..
Households	..	*57	..	*28949	..	*230	*29236	*28949
Other consumers	..	*4042	..	..	*13334	..	*17376	*13334
Non-energy use	..	*201	..	..	..	..	*201	..
2018								
Primary production	..	..	..	54416	..	*303	54719	54719
Imports	..	*13875	..	..	..	..	*13875	..
Exports	..	..	..	..	..	..	..	..
International marine bunkers	..	..	..	..	..	..	..	..
International aviation bunkers	..	*-410	..	..	..	..	*-410	..
Stock changes	..	..	..	..	..	..	..	..
Total energy supply	..	*13464	..	54416	..	*303	68183	54719
Statistical Difference	..	*1648	..	0	0	0	*1648	303
Transfers	..	..	..	..	..	..	..	..
Transformation	..	*-817	..	*-25385	13629	*286	*-12287	*-11756
Electricity plants	..	*-817	..	*-72	..	*286	*-603	*-72
Charcoal plants	..	..	..	*-25313	13629	..	*-11684	*-11684
Other transformation	..	0	..	0	..	..	0	0
Energy industries own use	..	..	..	..	..	*-26	*-26	..
Losses	..	..	..	..	..	*-259	*-259	..
Final consumption	..	*10999	..	*29031	*13629	*303	*53963	*42660
Final energy consumption	..	*10818	..	*29031	*13629	*303	*53782	*42660
Manufacturing, const., mining	..	*1285	..	*201	..	*113	*1598	*201
Transport	..	*5800	..	..	..	..	*5800	..
Road	..	*5800	..	..	..	..	*5800	..
Domestic aviation	..	..	..	..	..	..	..	..
Domestic navigation	..	..	..	..	..	..	..	..
Other transport	..	..	..	..	..	..	..	..
Other	..	*3733	..	*28830	*13629	*191	*46383	*42459
Agriculture, forestry, fishing	..	..	..	..	..	..	..	..
Commerce and public services	..	..	..	..	..	*97	*97	..
Households	..	*53	..	*28830	..	*94	*28976	*28830
Other consumers	..	*3681	..	..	*13629	..	*17310	*13629
Non-energy use	..	*181	..	..	..	..	*181	..

Singapore

Terajoules

2017	Primary coal and peat	Coal and peat products	Primary Oil	Oil Products	Natural Gas	Biofuels and waste	Nuclear	Electricity	Heat	Total energy	of which: renewables
Primary production	..	..	..	..	..	27009	..	608	..	27617	14246
Imports	37623	..	2469472	5016769	371982	3041	..	..	..	7898887	3041
Exports	-17	..	-53513	-4295770	..	-172	..	..	..	-4349472	-172
International marine bunkers	..	..	..	-2050949	..	..	..	..	..	-2050949	..
International aviation bunkers	..	..	..	*-332393	..	..	..	..	..	*-332393	..
Stock changes	*-17544	..	..	-6563	-3238	..	..	..	..	*-27346	..
Total energy supply	20062	..	2415959	-1668906	368744	29878	..	608	..	1166344	17115
Statistical difference	70	..	406836	-543141	-2894	0	..	833	..	-138296	608
Transfers	..	..	313371	-312409	..	..	..	..	..	962	..
Transformation	-12464	..	-2322494	2316112	-316978	-29697	..	188011	..	-177510	-16326
Electricity plants	-12464	..	..	-7401	-316978	-29593	..	188011	..	-178426	-16222
CHP plants	..	..	..	..	..	..	..	..	..	..	..
Heat plants	..	..	..	..	..	..	..	..	..	..	..
Coke ovens	..	..	..	..	..	..	..	..	..	..	..
Briquetting plants	..	..	..	..	..	..	..	..	..	..	..
Liquefaction plants	..	..	..	..	..	..	..	..	..	..	..
Gas works	..	..	..	..	..	..	..	..	..	..	..
Blast furnaces	..	..	..	..	..	..	..	..	..	..	..
NGL plants & gas blending	..	..	..	..	..	..	..	..	..	..	..
Oil refineries	..	..	-2322494	2323514	..	..	..	..	..	1020	..
Other transformation	..	..	..	..	..	*-104	..	..	..	*-104	*-104
Energy industries own use	..	..	..	-93361	-455	..	..	-608	..	-94424	..
Losses	..	..	..	..	..	..	..	-8697	..	-8697	..
Final consumption	7528	..	..	784578	54204	*181	..	178481	..	1024972	*181
Final energy consumption	7528	..	..	256384	54204	*181	..	178481	..	496777	*181
Manufacturing, const., mining	7528	..	..	161863	48173	..	..	*77223	..	294786	..
Iron and steel	..	..	..	..	..	..	..	*5427	..	*5427	..
Chemical and petrochemical	..	..	..	128677	..	..	..	*3475	..	132152	..
Non-ferrous metals	..	..	..	..	..	..	..	..	..	..	..
Non-metallic minerals	..	..	..	..	..	..	..	..	..	..	..
Transport equipment	..	..	..	..	..	..	..	..	..	..	..
Machinery	..	..	..	..	..	..	..	..	..	..	..
Mining and quarrying	..	..	..	..	..	..	..	..	..	..	..
Food and tobacco	..	..	..	..	..	..	..	..	..	..	..
Paper, pulp and printing	..	..	..	..	..	..	..	..	..	..	..
Wood and wood products	..	..	..	..	..	..	..	..	..	..	..
Textile and leather	..	..	..	..	..	..	..	..	..	..	..
Construction	..	..	..	..	..	..	..	..	..	..	..
Industries n.e.s	7528	..	..	33187	48173	..	..	*68320	..	157207	..
Transport	..	..	..	90216	260	..	..	9903	..	100378	..
Road	..	..	..	87077	..	..	..	..	..	87077	..
Rail	..	..	..	..	..	..	..	..	..	..	..
Domestic aviation	..	..	..	..	..	..	..	..	..	..	..
Domestic navigation	..	..	..	3139	..	..	..	..	..	3139	..
Pipeline transport	..	..	..	..	..	..	..	..	..	..	..
Transport, n.e.s	..	..	..	..	260	..	..	9903	..	10162	..
Other	..	..	..	4304	5772	*181	..	91356	..	101612	*181
Agriculture, forestry, fishing	..	..	..	..	..	..	..	..	..	..	..
Commerce, public services	..	..	..	3169	3336	..	..	64095	..	70601	..
Households	..	..	..	1135	2344	..	..	26265	..	29744	..
Other consumers	..	..	..	..	92	*181	..	995	..	1268	*181
Non-energy use	..	..	..	528194	..	..	..	..	..	528194	..

Singapore

Terajoules

2018	Primary coal and peat	Coal and peat products	Primary Oil	Oil Products	Natural Gas	Biofuels and waste	Nuclear	Electricity	Heat	Total energy	of which: renewables
Primary production	..	..	..	..	..	25082	..	608	..	25690	13281
Imports	20308	..	2394229	4484003	375282	3621	..	..	..	7277443	3621
Exports	-21	..	-32952	-3855256	..	-180	..	..	..	-3888408	-180
International marine bunkers	..	..	..	-2017813	..	..	..	..	..	-2017813	..
International aviation bunkers	..	..	..	*-350413	..	..	..	..	..	*-350413	..
Stock changes	..	..	..	21763	1294	..	..	..	..	23057	..
Total energy supply	20287	..	2361277	-1717715	376576	28524	..	608	..	1069557	16722
Statistical difference	-103	..	369865	-550666	1465	0	..	550	..	-178888	608
Transfers	..	..	306624	-296388	..	..	..	..	..	10237	..
Transformation	-12347	..	-2298036	2136986	-319039	-28156	..	190457	..	-330135	-15746
Electricity plants	-12347	..	..	-5701	-319039	-28043	..	190457	..	-174673	-15634
CHP plants	..	..	..	..	..	..	..	..	..	..	..
Heat plants	..	..	..	..	..	..	..	..	..	..	..
Coke ovens	..	..	..	..	..	..	..	..	..	..	..
Briquetting plants	..	..	..	..	..	..	..	..	..	..	..
Liquefaction plants	..	..	..	..	..	..	..	..	..	..	..
Gas works	..	..	..	..	..	..	..	..	..	..	..
Blast furnaces	..	..	..	..	..	..	..	..	..	..	..
NGL plants & gas blending	..	..	..	..	..	..	..	..	..	..	..
Oil refineries	..	..	-2298036	2142687	..	..	..	..	..	-155350	..
Other transformation	..	..	..	..	..	*-113	..	..	..	*-113	*-113
Energy industries own use	..	..	..	-85291	-452	..	..	-608	..	-86351	..
Losses	..	..	..	..	..	..	..	-8291	..	-8291	..
Final consumption	8043	..	..	588259	55620	*368	..	181616	..	833906	*368
Final energy consumption	8043	..	..	268273	55620	*368	..	181616	..	513919	*368
Manufacturing, const., mining	8043	..	..	169402	49542	..	..	*77223	..	304209	..
Iron and steel	..	..	..	..	..	..	..	*5405	..	*5405	..
Chemical and petrochemical	..	..	..	136985	..	..	..	*3475	..	140460	..
Non-ferrous metals	..	..	..	..	..	..	..	..	..	..	..
Non-metallic minerals	..	..	..	..	..	..	..	..	..	..	..
Transport equipment	..	..	..	..	..	..	..	..	..	..	..
Machinery	..	..	..	..	..	..	..	..	..	..	..
Mining and quarrying	..	..	..	..	..	..	..	..	..	..	..
Food and tobacco	..	..	..	..	..	..	..	..	..	..	..
Paper, pulp and printing	..	..	..	..	..	..	..	..	..	..	..
Wood and wood products	..	..	..	..	..	..	..	..	..	..	..
Textile and leather	..	..	..	..	..	..	..	..	..	..	..
Construction	..	..	..	..	..	..	..	..	..	..	..
Industries n.e.s	8043	..	..	32416	49542	..	..	*68342	..	158344	..
Transport	..	..	..	94613	107	..	..	10597	..	105316	..
Road	..	..	..	91393	..	..	..	..	..	91393	..
Rail	..	..	..	..	..	..	..	..	..	..	..
Domestic aviation	..	..	..	..	..	..	..	..	..	..	..
Domestic navigation	..	..	..	3219	..	..	..	..	..	3219	..
Pipeline transport	..	..	..	..	..	..	..	..	..	..	..
Transport, n.e.s	..	..	..	..	107	..	..	10597	..	10704	..
Other	..	..	..	4258	5972	*368	..	93796	..	104394	*368
Agriculture, forestry, fishing	..	..	..	..	..	..	..	..	..	..	..
Commerce, public services	..	..	..	3201	3427	..	..	66825	..	73452	..
Households	..	..	..	1058	2401	..	..	25997	..	29456	..
Other consumers	..	..	..	..	144	*368	..	975	..	1486	*368
Non-energy use	..	..	..	319986	..	..	..	..	..	319986	..

Sint Maarten (Dutch part)

Terajoules

	All Coal	All Oil	Natural Gas	Primary biofuels / Waste	Charcoal	Electricity	Total energy	of which: renewables
2017								
Primary production	..	..	..	..	..	..	..	..
Imports	..	*21725	..	*1	*3	..	*21729	*4
Exports	..	..	..	..	..	..	..	..
International marine bunkers	..	*-7872	..	..	..	..	*-7872	..
International aviation bunkers	..	*-2161	..	..	..	..	*-2161	..
Stock changes	..	..	..	..	..	..	..	..
Total energy supply	..	*11693	..	*1	*3	..	*11696	*4
Statistical Difference	..	0	..	0	0	0	0	0
Transfers	..	..	..	..	..	..	..	..
Transformation	..	*-3297	..	..	..	*1196	*-2100	..
Electricity plants	..	*-3297	..	..	..	*1196	*-2100	..
Charcoal plants	..	..	..	..	..	..	..	..
Other transformation	..	0	..	..	..	..	0	..
Energy industries own use	..	..	..	..	..	0	0	..
Losses	..	..	..	..	..	*-182	*-182	..
Final consumption	..	*8396	..	*1	*3	*1014	*9414	*4
Final energy consumption	..	*6904	..	*1	*3	*1014	*7922	*4
Manufacturing, const., mining	..	*1963	..	..	..	*176	*2140	..
Transport	..	*4851	..	..	..	..	*4851	..
Road	..	*3475	..	..	..	..	*3475	..
Domestic aviation	..	..	..	..	..	..	..	..
Domestic navigation	..	*1376	..	..	..	..	*1376	..
Other transport	..	..	..	..	..	..	..	..
Other	..	*90	..	*1	*3	*838	*931	*4
Agriculture, forestry, fishing	..	..	..	..	..	..	..	..
Commerce and public services	..	..	..	..	..	*532	*532	..
Households	..	*90	..	*1	*3	*306	*400	*4
Other consumers	..	..	..	..	..	..	..	..
Non-energy use	..	*1491	..	..	..	..	*1491	..
2018								
Primary production	..	..	..	..	..	..	..	..
Imports	..	*20930	..	*1	*3	..	*20934	*4
Exports	..	..	..	..	..	..	..	..
International marine bunkers	..	*-7597	..	..	..	..	*-7597	..
International aviation bunkers	..	*-2108	..	..	..	..	*-2108	..
Stock changes	..	..	..	..	..	..	..	..
Total energy supply	..	*11225	..	*1	*3	..	*11229	*4
Statistical Difference	..	0	..	0	0	0	0	0
Transfers	..	..	..	..	..	..	..	..
Transformation	..	*-3066	..	..	..	*1049	*-2017	..
Electricity plants	..	*-3066	..	..	..	*1049	*-2017	..
Charcoal plants	..	..	..	..	..	..	..	..
Other transformation	..	0	..	..	..	..	0	..
Energy industries own use	..	..	..	..	..	0	0	..
Losses	..	..	..	..	..	*-200	*-200	..
Final consumption	..	*8158	..	*1	*3	*849	*9011	*4
Final energy consumption	..	*6703	..	*1	*3	*849	*7556	*4
Manufacturing, const., mining	..	*1879	..	..	..	*148	*2026	..
Transport	..	*4735	..	..	..	..	*4735	..
Road	..	*3389	..	..	..	..	*3389	..
Domestic aviation	..	..	..	..	..	..	..	..
Domestic navigation	..	*1346	..	..	..	..	*1346	..
Other transport	..	..	..	..	..	..	..	..
Other	..	*90	..	*1	*3	*701	*795	*4
Agriculture, forestry, fishing	..	..	..	..	..	..	..	..
Commerce and public services	..	..	..	..	..	*409	*409	..
Households	..	*90	..	*1	*3	*292	*386	*4
Other consumers	..	..	..	..	..	..	..	..
Non-energy use	..	*1455	..	..	..	..	*1455	..

Slovakia

Terajoules

	Primary coal and peat	Coal and peat products	Primary Oil	Oil Products	Natural Gas	Biofuels and waste	Nuclear	Electricity	Heat	Total energy	of which: renewables
2017											
Primary production	18688	..	344	..	4890	58247	164971	17410	632	265181	67898
Imports	118373	8010	234822	82993	182872	4880	..	56027	84	688060	4580
Exports	..	-1966	-2423	-166740	..	-5971	..	-45126	..	-222226	-5971
International marine bunkers	..	..	..	..	..	..	..	..	..	..	..
International aviation bunkers	..	..	..	-1720	..	..	..	..	..	-1720	..
Stock changes	-534	-899	865	2646	-14567	-268	..	..	..	-12756	-244
Total energy supply	136528	5145	233608	-82821	173195	56887	164971	28310	716	716540	66263
Statistical difference	40	-6	-54	-2022	0	0	0	0	0	-2042	17559
Transfers	..	..	9912	-9912	..	..	..	..	..	0	..
Transformation	-120733	35620	-243575	258346	-34586	*-24920	-164971	81288	37484	-176047	*-24285
Electricity plants	..	..	..	-43	-2275	-849	-45608	16801	..	-31974	-849
CHP plants	-41805	-3490	..	-9586	-16000	*-21212	-119362	64570	27696	-119191	*-20475
Heat plants	-67	-39	..	..	-9023	*-2727	..	-83	9788	-2151	*-2829
Coke ovens	-59494	59204	..	..	..	..	..	..	..	-290	..
Briquetting plants	..	..	..	..	..	..	..	..	..	..	..
Liquefaction plants	..	..	6059	..	..	..	..	..	..	6059	..
Gas works	..	..	..	..	..	..	..	..	..	..	..
Blast furnaces	-19367	-24809	..	..	..	..	..	..	..	-44176	..
NGL plants & gas blending	..	..	..	..	..	..	..	..	..	..	..
Oil refineries	..	..	-258664	268210	..	..	..	..	..	9546	..
Other transformation	..	4755	9030	-234	-7287	*-132	..	..	..	6131	*-132
Energy industries own use	-22	-16138	..	-24638	-3889	*-12	..	-12161	-5322	-62182	*-12
Losses	-11	-1183	..	..	-3472	..	..	-4547	-4518	-13731	..
Final consumption	15721	23450	..	142997	131248	*31955	..	92891	28360	466622	*24407
Final energy consumption	14822	22062	..	115403	115118	*31955	..	92891	28360	420611	*24407
Manufacturing, const., mining	10886	21353	..	7366	35792	*21621	..	44482	5607	147106	*14192
Iron and steel	9075	20276	..	..	6649	*146	..	9410	..	45557	*146
Chemical and petrochemical	..	..	..	4653	4600	1069	..	3989	2680	16991	..
Non-ferrous metals	..	142	..	133	1473	..	..	9414	..	11162	..
Non-metallic minerals	1331	821	..	2006	6737	6331	..	2182	168	19577	..
Transport equipment	67	..	..	0	2922	..	..	3488	135	6613	..
Machinery	..	..	..	47	4299	29	..	6095	..	10470	..
Mining and quarrying	22	..	..	176	100	..	..	148	..	446	..
Food and tobacco	390	113	..	43	3383	..	..	1717	199	5846	..
Paper, pulp and printing	..	..	..	40	1919	3	..	2869	2271	7102	3
Wood and wood products	..	..	..	..	235	..	..	688	76	999	..
Textile and leather	..	..	..	..	591	..	..	461	41	1093	..
Construction	..	..	..	267	647	..	..	263	37	1214	..
Industries n.e.s	0	0	..	0	2236	*14043	..	3758	0	20037	*14043
Transport	..	..	..	104761	6306	6087	..	2110	..	119263	6087
Road	..	..	..	103294	..	6087	..	90	..	109471	6087
Rail	..	..	..	..	..	..	..	1782	..	1782	..
Domestic aviation	..	..	..	..	..	..	..	..	..	..	..
Domestic navigation	..	..	..	..	..	..	..	..	..	..	..
Pipeline transport	..	..	..	..	6010	..	..	..	..	6010	..
Transport, n.e.s	..	..	..	1466	296	..	..	238	..	2000	..
Other	3937	709	..	3277	73020	4248	..	46300	22753	154242	4129
Agriculture, forestry, fishing	11	..	..	2627	945	1404	..	976	59	6022	1434
Commerce, public services	2594	544	..	271	23926	1397	..	27626	3529	59886	1003
Households	1332	166	..	378	48149	*1447	..	17698	19165	88334	*1692
Other consumers	..	..	..	..	..	..	..	..	..	..	..
Non-energy use	899	1388	..	27595	16130	..	..	..	..	46011	..

Slovakia

Terajoules

2018	Primary coal and peat	Coal and peat products	Primary Oil	Oil Products	Natural Gas	Biofuels and waste	Nuclear	Electricity	Heat	Total energy	of which: renewables
Primary production	15305	..	300	..	3248	59516	162221	15052	675	256318	67879
Imports	123037	9046	228480	81796	152871	4828	..	44741	76	644875	4418
Exports	..	-1654	-216	-151276	..	-6114	..	-31486	..	-190746	-6114
International marine bunkers	..	..	..	..	..	..	..	..	..	..	..
International aviation bunkers	..	..	..	-2029	..	..	..	..	..	-2029	..
Stock changes	-1652	-2484	-346	-1943	14579	-301	..	..	..	7853	-273
Total energy supply	136690	4908	228218	-73452	170699	57930	162221	28307	751	716271	65910
Statistical difference	50	-12	-26	-1964	0	3	0	0	0	-1948	15216
Transfers	..	..	9079	-9079	..	..	..	..	..	0	..
Transformation	-118833	36260	-237323	255959	-33541	-24169	-162221	80881	30995	-171992	-23715
Electricity plants	..	..	..	..	-3772	-1018	-44885	17294	..	-32380	-1018
CHP plants	-40492	-3499	..	-3386	-15276	*-20458	-117337	63709	22035	-114703	*-19914
Heat plants	-45	-33	..	..	-7998	*-2660	..	-122	8960	-1899	*-2750
Coke ovens	-60029	60171	..	..	..	..	..	..	..	142	..
Briquetting plants	..	..	..	..	..	..	..	..	..	..	..
Liquefaction plants	..	..	5437	..	..	..	..	..	..	5437	..
Gas works	..	..	..	..	..	..	..	..	..	..	..
Blast furnaces	-18266	-24861	..	..	..	..	..	..	..	-43128	..
NGL plants & gas blending	..	..	..	..	..	..	..	..	..	..	..
Oil refineries	..	..	-250236	259480	..	..	..	..	..	9245	..
Other transformation	..	4483	7476	-135	-6495	*-33	..	..	..	5295	*-33
Energy industries own use	-11	-16100	..	-21489	-4011	*-27	..	-11376	-4704	-57718	*-27
Losses	-11	-1779	..	..	-3383	..	..	-4446	-3207	-12826	..
Final consumption	17784	23301	..	153903	129763	*33731	..	93366	23835	475683	*26953
Final energy consumption	16599	22055	..	122528	110874	*33731	..	93366	23835	422988	*26953
Manufacturing, const., mining	12102	21423	..	15066	37159	*23379	..	46058	2634	157821	*16291
Iron and steel	10347	20319	..	..	6550	*306	..	9148	..	46670	*306
Chemical and petrochemical	..	..	..	12139	5630	1050	..	3460	477	22756	..
Non-ferrous metals	..	113	..	..	1379	..	..	9108	..	10600	..
Non-metallic minerals	1301	906	..	1888	4262	6002	..	2783	158	17299	..
Transport equipment	57	..	..	387	3614	..	..	4885	127	9070	..
Machinery	11	..	..	133	4748	38	..	6545	..	11476	2
Mining and quarrying	23	..	..	176	2019	..	..	259	..	2477	..
Food and tobacco	364	85	..	43	3531	..	..	1764	290	6076	..
Paper, pulp and printing	..	..	..	40	1891	2	..	2848	1318	6099	2
Wood and wood products	..	..	..	..	248	..	..	698	177	1124	..
Textile and leather	..	..	..	..	475	..	..	468	47	990	..
Construction	..	..	..	258	697	..	..	374	40	1369	..
Industries n.e.s	0	0	..	0	2117	*15981	..	3719	0	21816	*15981
Transport	..	..	..	104229	5574	6053	..	2117	..	117973	6053
Road	..	..	..	102716	..	6053	..	86	..	108855	6053
Rail	..	..	..	..	..	..	..	1789	..	1789	..
Domestic aviation	..	..	..	..	..	..	..	..	..	..	..
Domestic navigation	..	..	..	..	..	..	..	..	..	..	..
Pipeline transport	..	..	..	..	5314	..	..	..	..	5314	..
Transport, n.e.s	..	..	..	1514	260	..	..	241	..	2015	..
Other	4497	632	..	3234	68141	*4299	..	45191	21201	147194	*4609
Agriculture, forestry, fishing	11	..	..	2627	802	1239	..	864	66	5610	1268
Commerce, public services	3228	551	..	275	20494	*1404	..	25985	3417	55354	*1417
Households	1258	81	..	331	46845	*1656	..	18342	17718	86231	*1924
Other consumers	..	..	..	..	..	..	..	..	..	..	..
Non-energy use	1185	1246	..	31375	18889	..	..	..	..	52695	..

Slovenia

Terajoules

2017	Primary coal and peat	Coal and peat products	Primary Oil	Oil Products	Natural Gas	Biofuels and waste	Nuclear	Electricity	Heat	Total energy	of which: renewables
Primary production	39084	..	..	..	301	27985	67878	14969	2497	152713	43312
Imports	7366	903	..	201926	30753	1201	..	32879	..	275027	1201
Exports	..	..	..	-89197	-129	..	..	-34733	..	-124058	..
International marine bunkers	..	..	..	-6343	..	..	..	..	..	-6343	..
International aviation bunkers	..	..	..	-1103	..	..	..	..	..	-1103	..
Stock changes	163	..	..	-3461	..	-147	..	..	..	-3445	-147
Total energy supply	46613	903	..	101823	30925	29039	67878	13115	2497	292793	44366
Statistical difference	25	-30	..	-87	-1	0	0	7	0	-85	14987
Transfers	..	..	..	..	..	..	..	..	..	..	..
Transformation	-45916	..	..	-357	-5112	*-3953	-67878	42822	9417	-70976	*-3596
Electricity plants	..	..	..	-43	-125	-12	-67878	22676	..	-45382	-12
CHP plants	-45829	..	..	-90	-3744	-3419	..	20146	7571	-25366	-3044
Heat plants	-87	..	..	-224	-1243	*-522	..	..	1846	-229	*-540
Coke ovens	..	..	..	..	..	..	..	..	..	..	..
Briquetting plants	..	..	..	..	..	..	..	..	..	..	..
Liquefaction plants	..	..	..	..	..	..	..	..	..	..	..
Gas works	..	..	..	..	..	..	..	..	..	..	..
Blast furnaces	..	..	..	..	..	..	..	..	..	..	..
NGL plants & gas blending	..	..	..	..	..	..	..	..	..	..	..
Oil refineries	..	..	..	..	..	..	..	..	..	..	..
Other transformation	..	..	..	..	..	..	..	..	..	..	..
Energy industries own use	..	..	..	..	-53	..	..	-4010	-542	-4606	..
Losses	..	..	..	..	..	..	..	-3215	-1330	-4545	..
Final consumption	672	933	..	101553	25761	*25087	..	48704	10042	212751	*25784
Final energy consumption	562	752	..	96159	25534	*25087	..	48704	10042	206840	*25784
Manufacturing, const., mining	562	752	..	3904	18367	*4892	..	23202	2151	53831	*3128
Iron and steel	..	271	..	90	3265	0	..	2959	54	6640	0
Chemical and petrochemical	..	..	..	176	1958	*1003	..	2495	1237	6869	*950
Non-ferrous metals	55	..	..	284	1844	..	..	4864	30	7076	..
Non-metallic minerals	..	481	..	1286	3164	1750	..	1364	1	8047	*39
Transport equipment	..	..	..	90	542	*2	..	889	9	1532	*2
Machinery	..	..	..	447	1557	*72	..	3618	284	5978	*72
Mining and quarrying	..	..	..	86	156	..	..	529	..	771	..
Food and tobacco	..	..	..	357	1129	*47	..	1080	150	2763	*47
Paper, pulp and printing	508	..	..	43	3217	*495	..	2516	46	6825	*495
Wood and wood products	..	..	..	43	..	*1340	..	558	17	*1958	*1340
Textile and leather	..	..	..	47	349	*37	..	374	49	857	*37
Construction	..	..	..	864	202	*7	..	176	14	1263	*7
Industries n.e.s	0	0	..	90	985	*139	..	1778	260	3253	*139
Transport	..	..	..	79967	137	1017	..	839	..	81960	1017
Road	..	..	..	79562	137	1017	..	4	..	80720	1017
Rail	..	..	..	387	..	..	..	810	..	1197	..
Domestic aviation	..	..	..	18	..	..	..	..	..	18	..
Domestic navigation	..	..	..	..	..	..	..	..	..	..	..
Pipeline transport	..	..	..	..	..	..	..	..	..	..	..
Transport, n.e.s	..	..	..	..	..	..	..	25	..	25	..
Other	..	..	..	12287	7030	*19177	..	24664	7891	71049	*21638
Agriculture, forestry, fishing	..	..	..	2974	..	..	..	..	108	3082	108
Commerce, public services	..	..	..	2795	2046	34	..	12686	2591	20152	503
Households	..	..	..	5715	4984	*19143	..	11977	5192	47011	*21027
Other consumers	..	..	..	804	..	..	..	..	..	804	..
Non-energy use	110	181	..	5394	227	..	..	..	..	5911	..

Slovenia

Terajoules

2018	Primary coal and peat	Coal and peat products	Primary Oil	Oil Products	Natural Gas	Biofuels and waste	Nuclear	Electricity	Heat	Total energy	of which: renewables
Primary production	37742	..	49	..	571	26533	62381	17874	2524	147673	44401
Imports	8078	904	..	203162	30164	3175	..	32148	..	277631	3175
Exports	..	..	-49	-90578	-392	..	..	-33955	..	-124975	..
International marine bunkers	..	..	..	-9301	..	..	..	..	..	-9301	..
International aviation bunkers	..	..	..	-1499	..	..	..	..	..	-1499	..
Stock changes	626	..	..	830	..	-110	..	..	..	1346	-110
Total energy supply	46446	904	0	102614	30342	29598	62381	16067	2524	290874	47466
Statistical difference	-16	0	0	-607	-1	1	0	0	0	-623	17894
Transfers	..	..	..	..	..	..	..	..	..	..	..
Transformation	-45683	..	..	-357	-5050	-3785	-62381	40234	9265	-67756	-3395
Electricity plants	-37361	..	..	-86	-97	-16	-62381	35489	..	-64452	-16
CHP plants	-8284	..	..	-90	-3773	-3233	..	4745	7734	-2902	-2824
Heat plants	-38	..	..	-181	-1180	-536	..	..	1531	-403	-555
Coke ovens	..	..	..	..	..	..	..	..	..	..	..
Briquetting plants	..	..	..	..	..	..	..	..	..	..	..
Liquefaction plants	..	..	..	..	..	..	..	..	..	..	..
Gas works	..	..	..	..	..	..	..	..	..	..	..
Blast furnaces	..	..	..	..	..	..	..	..	..	..	..
NGL plants & gas blending	..	..	..	..	..	..	..	..	..	..	..
Oil refineries	..	..	..	..	..	..	..	..	..	..	..
Other transformation	..	..	..	..	..	..	..	..	..	..	..
Energy industries own use	..	..	..	-43	-35	..	..	-3751	-736	-4565	..
Losses	..	..	..	..	..	..	..	-3168	-1236	-4404	..
Final consumption	779	904	..	102820	25258	25812	..	49381	9817	214771	26177
Final energy consumption	670	723	..	96720	25019	25812	..	49381	9817	208143	26177
Manufacturing, const., mining	670	723	..	4959	19485	5213	..	24649	2097	57796	3092
Iron and steel	..	271	..	90	3150	0	..	2804	48	6364	0
Chemical and petrochemical	..	..	..	176	1895	804	..	2308	1203	6386	735
Non-ferrous metals	55	..	..	327	1787	2	..	4770	2	6942	2
Non-metallic minerals	..	452	..	1416	3173	2069	..	1436	1	8546	17
Transport equipment	..	..	..	90	481	3	..	864	11	1449	3
Machinery	..	..	..	765	2668	136	..	4842	372	8783	136
Mining and quarrying	..	..	..	215	156	..	..	583	..	954	..
Food and tobacco	..	..	..	443	1514	68	..	1177	144	3345	68
Paper, pulp and printing	615	..	..	133	3175	455	..	2671	38	7088	455
Wood and wood products	..	..	..	129	62	1326	..	623	14	2153	1326
Textile and leather	..	..	..	43	293	30	..	349	34	750	30
Construction	..	..	..	998	265	99	..	288	10	1659	99
Industries n.e.s	0	0	..	133	868	223	..	1933	220	3377	222
Transport	..	..	..	79681	140	2991	..	839	..	83650	2991
Road	..	..	..	79315	140	2991	..	4	..	82449	2991
Rail	..	..	..	344	..	..	..	810	..	1154	..
Domestic aviation	..	..	..	22	..	..	..	..	..	22	..
Domestic navigation	..	..	..	..	..	..	..	..	..	..	..
Pipeline transport	..	..	..	..	..	..	..	..	..	..	..
Transport, n.e.s	..	..	..	..	..	..	..	25	..	25	..
Other	..	..	..	12081	5395	17608	..	23893	7720	66697	20094
Agriculture, forestry, fishing	..	..	..	2974	..	..	..	..	112	3086	112
Commerce, public services	..	..	..	2752	750	45	..	11768	2545	17860	494
Households	..	..	..	5315	4645	17563	..	12125	5063	44711	19488
Other consumers	..	..	..	1041	..	..	..	..	..	1041	..
Non-energy use	109	181	..	6100	239	..	..	..	..	6628	..

Solomon Islands

Terajoules

	All Coal	All Oil	Natural Gas	Primary biofuels / Waste	Charcoal	Electricity	Total energy	of which: renewables
2017								
Primary production	..	..	..	*3305	..	15	*3320	*3320
Imports	..	*4535	..	..	0	..	*4535	0
Exports	..	..	..	0	0	..	0	0
International marine bunkers	..	*-233	..	..	..	..	*-233	..
International aviation bunkers	..	*-166	..	..	..	..	*-166	..
Stock changes	..	..	..	..	..	..	..	..
Total energy supply	..	*4136	..	*3305	0	15	*7456	*3320
Statistical Difference	..	0	..	0	0	0	0	*15
Transfers	..	..	..	..	..	..	..	..
Transformation	..	*-998	..	*-128	43	374	*-708	*-85
Electricity plants	..	*-998	..	*-48	..	374	*-671	*-48
Charcoal plants	..	..	..	*-80	43	..	*-37	*-37
Other transformation	..	0	..	0	..	..	0	0
Energy industries own use	..	..	..	..	..	*-18	*-18	..
Losses	..	..	..	..	..	*-47	*-47	..
Final consumption	..	*3138	..	*3176	*43	*325	*6683	*3220
Final energy consumption	..	*3077	..	*3176	*43	*325	*6622	*3220
Manufacturing, const., mining	..	*259	..	..	..	*134	*393	..
Transport	..	*2595	..	..	..	..	*2595	..
Road	..	*2212	..	..	..	..	*2212	..
Domestic aviation	..	*35	..	..	..	..	*35	..
Domestic navigation	..	*348	..	..	..	..	*348	..
Other transport	..	..	..	..	..	..	..	..
Other	..	*223	..	*3176	*43	191	*3634	*3220
Agriculture, forestry, fishing	..	*210	..	..	..	..	*210	..
Commerce and public services	..	..	..	..	..	*93	*93	..
Households	..	*13	..	*3176	*43	58	*3291	*3220
Other consumers	..	..	..	..	..	40	40	..
Non-energy use	..	*61	..	..	..	..	*61	..
2018								
Primary production	..	..	..	*3305	..	14	*3319	*3319
Imports	..	*4622	..	..	0	..	*4622	0
Exports	..	..	..	0	0	..	0	0
International marine bunkers	..	*-237	..	..	..	..	*-237	..
International aviation bunkers	..	*-168	..	..	..	..	*-168	..
Stock changes	..	..	..	..	..	..	..	..
Total energy supply	..	*4216	..	*3305	0	14	*7535	*3319
Statistical Difference	..	*2	..	0	0	0	*2	*14
Transfers	..	..	..	..	..	..	..	..
Transformation	..	*-1015	..	*-117	44	382	*-705	*-73
Electricity plants	..	*-1015	..	*-35	..	382	*-668	*-35
Charcoal plants	..	..	..	*-82	44	..	*-38	*-38
Other transformation	..	0	..	0	..	..	0	0
Energy industries own use	..	..	..	..	..	*-9	*-9	..
Losses	..	..	..	..	..	*-50	*-50	..
Final consumption	..	*3199	..	*3188	*44	*336	*6768	*3232
Final energy consumption	..	*3137	..	*3188	*44	*336	*6705	*3232
Manufacturing, const., mining	..	*264	..	..	..	*140	*404	..
Transport	..	*2645	..	..	..	..	*2645	..
Road	..	*2254	..	..	..	..	*2254	..
Domestic aviation	..	*36	..	..	..	..	*36	..
Domestic navigation	..	*355	..	..	..	..	*355	..
Other transport	..	..	..	..	..	..	..	..
Other	..	*228	..	*3188	*44	196	*3656	*3232
Agriculture, forestry, fishing	..	*214	..	..	..	..	*214	..
Commerce and public services	..	..	..	..	..	*97	*97	..
Households	..	*13	..	*3188	*44	60	*3306	*3232
Other consumers	..	..	..	..	..	38	38	..
Non-energy use	..	*62	..	..	..	..	*62	..

Somalia

Terajoules

	All Coal	All Oil	Natural Gas	Primary biofuels / Waste	Charcoal	Electricity	Total energy	of which: renewables
2017								
Primary production	..	..	..	139436	..	..	139436	139436
Imports	..	*12045	..	0	..	..	*12046	0
Exports	..	..	..	-7	0	..	-7	-7
International marine bunkers	..	*-1183	..	..	..	..	*-1183	..
International aviation bunkers	..	-1895	..	..	..	..	-1895	..
Stock changes	..	..	..	..	..	..	..	..
Total energy supply	..	*8967	..	139429	0	..	148396	139429
Statistical Difference	..	0	..	0	0	0	0	0
Transfers	..	..	..	..	..	..	..	..
Transformation	..	*-4300	..	*-69576	37447	*1260	*-35169	*-32129
Electricity plants	..	*-4300	..	..	..	*1260	*-3040	..
Charcoal plants	..	..	..	*-69576	37447	..	*-32129	*-32129
Other transformation	..	0	..	0	..	..	0	0
Energy industries own use	..	..	..	..	..	0	0	..
Losses	..	..	..	..	..	*-126	*-126	..
Final consumption	..	*4667	..	*69853	*37447	1134	*113101	*107300
Final energy consumption	..	*4667	..	*69853	*37447	1134	*113101	*107300
Manufacturing, const., mining	..	*1091	..	*527	..	..	*1617	*527
Transport	..	*1934	..	..	..	..	*1934	..
Road	..	*1934	..	..	..	..	*1934	..
Domestic aviation	..	..	..	..	..	..	..	..
Domestic navigation	..	..	..	..	..	..	..	..
Other transport	..	..	..	..	..	..	..	..
Other	..	1642	..	*69326	*37447	1134	*109550	*106774
Agriculture, forestry, fishing	..	..	..	..	..	..	..	..
Commerce and public services	..	..	..	..	..	..	..	..
Households	..	1642	..	*69326	..	..	*70968	*69326
Other consumers	..	..	..	..	*37447	1134	*38581	*37447
Non-energy use	..	..	..	..	..	..	..	..
2018								
Primary production	..	..	..	143069	..	..	143069	143069
Imports	..	*12047	..	..	..	..	*12047	..
Exports	..	..	..	..	..	..	..	..
International marine bunkers	..	*-1183	..	..	..	..	*-1183	..
International aviation bunkers	..	-1895	..	..	..	..	-1895	..
Stock changes	..	..	..	..	..	..	..	..
Total energy supply	..	*8969	..	143069	..	..	152038	143069
Statistical Difference	..	0	..	0	0	0	0	0
Transfers	..	..	..	..	..	..	..	..
Transformation	..	*-4300	..	*-72119	38816	*1260	*-36343	*-33303
Electricity plants	..	*-4300	..	..	..	*1260	*-3040	..
Charcoal plants	..	..	..	*-72119	38816	..	*-33303	*-33303
Other transformation	..	0	..	0	..	..	0	0
Energy industries own use	..	..	..	..	..	0	0	..
Losses	..	..	..	..	..	0	0	..
Final consumption	..	*4669	..	*70949	*38816	1260	*115695	*109766
Final energy consumption	..	*4669	..	*70949	*38816	1260	*115695	*109766
Manufacturing, const., mining	..	*1091	..	*530	..	..	*1621	*530
Transport	..	*1936	..	..	..	..	*1936	..
Road	..	*1936	..	..	..	..	*1936	..
Domestic aviation	..	..	..	..	..	..	..	..
Domestic navigation	..	..	..	..	..	..	..	..
Other transport	..	..	..	..	..	..	..	..
Other	..	1642	..	*70419	*38816	1260	*112138	*109236
Agriculture, forestry, fishing	..	..	..	..	..	..	..	..
Commerce and public services	..	..	..	..	..	..	..	..
Households	..	1642	..	*70419	..	..	*72061	*70419
Other consumers	..	..	..	..	*38816	1260	*40076	*38816
Non-energy use	..	..	..	..	..	..	..	..

South Africa

Terajoules

2017	Primary coal and peat	Coal and peat products	Primary Oil	Oil Products	Natural Gas	Biofuels and waste	Nuclear	Electricity	Heat	Total energy	of which: renewables
Primary production	5981538	..	4138	..	23014	339806	170024	32969	13984	6565473	386758
Imports	38000	..	723457	485292	111712	..	..	37998	..	1396458	..
Exports	-1660441	..	..	-155577	-449	-9145	..	-59576	..	-1885189	-9145
International marine bunkers	..	..	..	-32293	..	..	..	..	..	-32293	..
International aviation bunkers	..	..	..	-94990	..	..	..	..	..	-94990	..
Stock changes	..	..	..	..	..	..	..	..	..	..	..
Total energy supply	4359097	..	727595	202432	134276	330661	170024	11390	13984	5949459	377613
Statistical difference	-6593	-3541	0	5115	-32626	0	0	-37206	0	-74850	35442
Transfers	..	..	-126880	*201532	..	..	..	..	..	*74652	..
Transformation	-3282468	72942	-600715	784023	-79486	*-50973	-170024	878634	-7420	-2455488	*-55919
Electricity plants	-2916848	..	..	-381	..	-5181	-170024	878634	-7420	-2221220	-10127
CHP plants	..	..	..	..	..	-276	..	..	..	-276	-276
Heat plants	..	..	..	..	..	..	..	..	..	..	..
Coke ovens	-28251	60089	..	..	..	..	..	..	..	31839	..
Briquetting plants	..	..	..	..	..	..	..	..	..	..	..
Liquefaction plants	-268582	..	161280	..	-79486	..	..	..	..	-186788	..
Gas works	*-68788	21557	..	..	..	..	..	..	..	*-47231	..
Blast furnaces	..	-8704	..	..	..	..	..	..	..	-8704	..
NGL plants & gas blending	..	..	..	..	..	..	..	..	..	..	..
Oil refineries	..	..	-761995	784404	..	..	..	..	..	22409	..
Other transformation	..	..	..	..	..	*-45516	..	..	..	*-45516	*-45516
Energy industries own use	-701685	-1183	..	-35803	-10292	..	..	-121698	..	-870661	..
Losses	..	..	..	..	..	..	..	-75910	..	-75910	..
Final consumption	381536	75300	..	1147068	77124	*279688	..	729623	6564	2696903	*286252
Final energy consumption	338057	75300	..	1000042	77124	*279688	..	729623	6564	2506398	*286252
Manufacturing, const., mining	223774	75300	..	90696	75816	*112603	..	385585	..	963775	*112603
Iron and steel	66535	57435	..	374	8889	..	..	69210	..	202443	..
Chemical and petrochemical	..	5247	..	184	44996	..	..	31817	..	82244	..
Non-ferrous metals	3060	1747	..	20	455	..	..	54079	..	59361	..
Non-metallic minerals	38569	375	..	311	13611	..	..	8842	..	61707	..
Transport equipment	..	15	..	84	589	..	..	194	..	882	..
Machinery	..	358	..	1021	949	..	..	212	..	2540	..
Mining and quarrying	1233	1001	..	52977	..	..	..	110074	..	165285	..
Food and tobacco	..	3541	..	621	3443	..	..	2664	..	10269	..
Paper, pulp and printing	..	3541	..	123	562	..	..	4144	..	8369	..
Wood and wood products	..	..	..	45	..	..	..	1195	..	1240	..
Textile and leather	..	..	..	131	13	..	..	594	..	738	..
Construction	..	..	..	18766	..	..	..	655	..	19421	..
Industries n.e.s	114378	2040	..	16039	2310	*112603	..	101905	..	349275	*112603
Transport	47	..	..	666101	..	..	..	11984	..	678133	..
Road	..	..	..	624185	..	..	..	166	..	624351	..
Rail	..	..	..	7236	..	..	..	10699	..	17935	..
Domestic aviation	..	..	..	21385	..	..	..	..	..	21385	..
Domestic navigation	..	..	..	..	..	..	..	..	..	..	..
Pipeline transport	..	..	..	1915	..	..	..	284	..	2199	..
Transport, n.e.s	47	..	..	11380	..	..	..	835	..	12263	..
Other	114236	..	..	243245	1308	*167085	..	332053	6564	864490	*173649
Agriculture, forestry, fishing	1755	..	..	149102	..	..	..	21485	..	172342	..
Commerce, public services	14493	..	..	81573	1109	..	..	133200	..	230375	..
Households	14564	..	..	12370	199	*167085	..	174683	..	368901	*167085
Other consumers	83423	..	..	200	..	..	..	2686	6564	92873	6564
Non-energy use	43479	..	..	147026	..	..	..	..	..	190505	..

South Africa

Terajoules

2018	Primary coal and peat	Coal and peat products	Primary Oil	Oil Products	Natural Gas	Biofuels and waste	Nuclear	Electricity	Heat	Total energy	of which: renewables
Primary production	6061504	..	3884	..	35210	337304	125064	38819	16351	6618136	392474
Imports	19620	..	791264	446169	131650	..	..	34873	..	1423576	..
Exports	-1669989	..	..	-193313	..	-5989	..	-51790	..	-1921080	-5989
International marine bunkers	..	..	..	-110951	..	..	..	..	..	-110951	..
International aviation bunkers	..	..	..	-57904	..	..	..	..	..	-57904	..
Stock changes	..	..	-36209	..	..	..	..	..	..	-36209	..
Total energy supply	4411134	..	758939	84001	166860	331316	125064	21902	16351	5915568	386486
Statistical difference	-27328	-1	-43231	-80446	-1	-29	0	-43038	0	-194073	42494
Transfers	..	..	-174060	210960	..	..	..	..	..	36900	..
Transformation	-3148625	74667	-628110	810311	-86567	*-84590	-125064	866488	-11113	-2332605	*-91999
Electricity plants	-2756479	..	..	-1892	..	-5055	-125064	866268	-11113	-2033335	-12464
CHP plants	..	..	..	..	..	-441	..	220	..	-221	-441
Heat plants	..	..	..	..	..	..	..	..	..	..	..
Coke ovens	-90218	84933	..	..	..	..	..	..	..	-5285	..
Briquetting plants	..	..	..	..	..	..	..	..	..	..	..
Liquefaction plants	-235107	..	174060	..	-86567	..	..	..	..	-147614	..
Gas works	-66821	22724	..	..	..	..	..	..	..	-44097	..
Blast furnaces	..	-32990	..	..	..	..	..	..	..	-32990	..
NGL plants & gas blending	..	..	..	..	..	..	..	..	..	..	..
Oil refineries	..	..	-802170	812203	..	..	..	..	..	10033	..
Other transformation	..	..	..	..	..	*-79094	..	..	..	*-79094	*-79094
Energy industries own use	-670297	-1188	..	-37521	..	..	..	-110052	..	-819058	..
Losses	..	..	..	..	..	..	..	-81853	..	-81853	..
Final consumption	619540	73480	..	1148196	80294	*246755	..	739523	5238	2913026	*251993
Final energy consumption	576282	73480	..	996409	80294	*246755	..	739523	5238	2717981	*251993
Manufacturing, const., mining	260188	73480	..	80438	78925	*113715	..	390028	..	996774	*113715
Iron and steel	66489	58018	..	344	9254	..	..	70009	..	204113	..
Chemical and petrochemical	..	5268	..	175	46841	..	..	32184	..	84468	..
Non-ferrous metals	40292	1754	..	..	475	..	..	54702	..	97223	..
Non-metallic minerals	38370	377	..	259	14169	..	..	8946	..	62121	..
Transport equipment	..	15	..	87	613	..	..	198	..	913	..
Machinery	..	360	..	1013	988	..	..	212	..	2574	..
Mining and quarrying	1234	1006	..	51922	..	..	..	111341	..	165503	..
Food and tobacco	..	1079	..	559	3583	..	..	2693	..	7914	..
Paper, pulp and printing	..	3556	..	126	585	..	..	4194	..	8461	..
Wood and wood products	..	..	..	43	..	..	..	1210	..	1253	..
Textile and leather	..	..	..	135	14	..	..	601	..	750	..
Construction	..	..	..	20080	..	..	..	662	..	20742	..
Industries n.e.s	113804	2047	..	5695	2404	*113715	..	103075	..	340740	*113715
Transport	..	..	..	799823	7	..	..	11232	..	811062	..
Road	..	..	..	723734	7	..	..	169	..	723910	..
Rail	..	..	..	7921	..	..	..	10192	..	18113	..
Domestic aviation	..	..	..	56299	..	..	..	..	..	56299	..
Domestic navigation	..	..	..	11138	..	..	..	..	..	11138	..
Pipeline transport	..	..	..	731	..	..	..	292	..	1023	..
Transport, n.e.s	..	..	..	..	..	..	..	580	..	580	..
Other	316094	..	..	116148	1362	*133040	..	338263	5238	910145	*138278
Agriculture, forestry, fishing	19149	..	..	51082	..	..	..	21888	..	92119	..
Commerce, public services	96624	..	..	8404	1155	..	..	135691	..	241874	..
Households	195812	..	..	24854	207	*133040	..	177948	..	531861	*133040
Other consumers	4509	..	..	31808	..	..	..	2736	5238	44291	5238
Non-energy use	43258	..	..	151787	..	..	..	..	..	195045	..

South Sudan

Terajoules

	All Coal	All Oil	Natural Gas	Primary biofuels / Waste	Charcoal	Electricity	Total energy	of which: renewables
2017								
Primary production	..	258030	..	6890	..	11	264931	6901
Imports	..	20669	..	..	..	..	20669	..
Exports	..	-255027	..	..	..	..	-255027	..
International marine bunkers	..	..	..	..	..	..	..	..
International aviation bunkers	..	-3263	..	..	..	..	-3263	..
Stock changes	..	..	..	..	..	..	..	..
Total energy supply	..	20409	..	6890	..	11	27310	6901
Statistical Difference	..	-176	..	106	30	18	-22	146
Transfers	..	..	..	..	..	..	..	..
Transformation	..	-5636	..	-1504	266	1940	-4934	-1239
Electricity plants	..	-5636	..	..	..	1940	-3695	..
Charcoal plants	..	..	..	-1504	266	..	-1239	-1239
Other transformation	..	0	..	0	..	..	0	0
Energy industries own use	..	-2961	..	-10	..	-54	-3025	-10
Losses	..	-87	..	..	..	-86	-174	..
Final consumption	..	11901	..	5270	236	1793	19200	5506
Final energy consumption	..	11901	..	5270	236	1793	19200	5506
Manufacturing, const., mining	..	692	..	..	..	709	1402	..
Transport	..	9989	..	..	..	..	9989	..
Road	..	9813	..	..	..	..	9813	..
Domestic aviation	..	176	..	..	..	..	176	..
Domestic navigation	..	..	..	..	..	..	..	..
Other transport	..	..	..	..	..	..	..	..
Other	..	1219	..	5270	236	1084	7809	5506
Agriculture, forestry, fishing	..	904	..	14	..	238	1156	14
Commerce and public services	..	133	..	202	30	68	433	232
Households	..	182	..	5054	207	778	6220	5260
Other consumers	..	..	..	..	..	..	..	..
Non-energy use	..	..	..	..	..	..	..	..
2018								
Primary production	..	270720	..	6937	..	11	277668	6948
Imports	..	18235	..	..	..	..	18235	..
Exports	..	-267590	..	..	..	..	-267590	..
International marine bunkers	..	..	..	..	..	..	..	..
International aviation bunkers	..	-2602	..	..	..	..	-2602	..
Stock changes	..	..	..	..	..	..	..	..
Total energy supply	..	18763	..	6937	..	11	25711	6948
Statistical Difference	..	-44	..	107	30	382	474	147
Transfers	..	..	..	..	..	..	..	..
Transformation	..	-6066	..	-1513	266	2088	-5225	-1248
Electricity plants	..	-6066	..	..	..	2088	-3978	..
Charcoal plants	..	..	..	-1513	266	..	-1248	-1248
Other transformation	..	0	..	0	..	..	0	0
Energy industries own use	..	-3130	..	-10	..	-43	-3183	-10
Losses	..	-87	..	..	..	-68	-156	..
Final consumption	..	9525	..	5307	236	1606	16673	5543
Final energy consumption	..	9525	..	5307	236	1606	16673	5543
Manufacturing, const., mining	..	563	..	..	..	565	1129	..
Transport	..	7914	..	..	..	..	7914	..
Road	..	7782	..	..	..	..	7782	..
Domestic aviation	..	132	..	..	..	..	132	..
Domestic navigation	..	..	..	..	..	..	..	..
Other transport	..	..	..	..	..	..	..	..
Other	..	1047	..	5307	236	1040	7631	5543
Agriculture, forestry, fishing	..	732	..	15	..	187	935	15
Commerce and public services	..	133	..	204	30	68	435	234
Households	..	182	..	5088	207	785	6262	5295
Other consumers	..	..	..	..	..	..	..	..
Non-energy use	..	..	..	..	..	..	..	..

Spain

Terajoules

2017	Primary coal and peat	Coal and peat products	Primary Oil	Oil Products	Natural Gas	Biofuels and waste	Nuclear	Electricity	Heat	Total energy	of which: renewables
Primary production	47220	..	5076	..	997	335532	626821	275123	77236	1368006	677020
Imports	459778	7136	2790023	975139	1261304	36346	..	85543	..	5615270	36346
Exports	-5159	-3609	..	-1143606	-104960	-60785	..	-52535	..	-1370653	-60785
International marine bunkers	..	..	..	-279721	..	..	..	..	..	-279721	..
International aviation bunkers	..	..	..	-191791	..	..	..	..	..	-191791	..
Stock changes	25672	1367	-1692	54120	-15752	4309	..	..	..	68024	4309
Total energy supply	527511	4894	2793407	-585859	1141590	315402	626821	308131	77236	5209134	656889
Statistical difference	-23307	2105	0	23028	7982	-37	0	414	0	10186	296265
Transfers	..	..	33448	-27059	..	..	..	..	..	6389	..
Transformation	-535690	32613	-2826855	2664837	-415419	*-88003	-626821	709254	-63536	-1149621	*-119781
Electricity plants	-469099	-11941	..	-115016	-274579	*-71785	-626821	593845	-63536	-1038932	-105100
CHP plants	-1096	..	..	-20638	-141138	*-11474	..	115409	..	-58937	*-9937
Heat plants	..	..	..	..	..	..	..	..	..	..	..
Coke ovens	-47674	54166	..	..	..	..	..	..	..	6492	..
Briquetting plants	..	..	..	..	..	..	..	..	..	..	..
Liquefaction plants	..	..	..	..	..	..	..	..	..	..	..
Gas works	..	..	..	..	..	..	..	..	..	..	..
Blast furnaces	-17821	-9612	..	..	..	..	..	..	..	-27433	..
NGL plants & gas blending	..	..	..	..	298	-298	..	..	..	0	-298
Oil refineries	..	..	-2826855	2800641	..	..	..	..	..	-26214	..
Other transformation	..	..	..	-150	..	-4446	..	..	..	-4596	-4446
Energy industries own use	..	-7402	..	-206141	-130363	..	..	-70445	..	-414351	..
Losses	..	-1672	..	..	-4900	..	..	-85763	..	-92334	..
Final consumption	15129	26328	..	1822751	582926	227436	..	860764	13700	3549032	240844
Final energy consumption	15129	24704	..	1636473	564625	227436	..	860764	13700	3342830	240844
Manufacturing, const., mining	10960	21149	..	120634	316899	*60108	..	291668	120	821538	*60228
Iron and steel	5742	19837	..	3160	28994	1	..	51883	..	109616	1
Chemical and petrochemical	4527	219	..	4792	86481	208	..	34704	7	130938	215
Non-ferrous metals	..	547	..	2642	9484	..	..	36252	10	48935	10
Non-metallic minerals	357	..	..	58192	56327	131	..	22482	2	137492	133
Transport equipment	..	..	..	1279	7609	..	..	16196	10	25094	10
Machinery	..	..	..	4435	10051	..	..	17770	24	32280	24
Mining and quarrying	..	..	..	6901	6946	74	..	7139	1	21061	75
Food and tobacco	334	547	..	13637	49779	401	..	37948	42	102686	443
Paper, pulp and printing	..	..	..	3306	27948	1092	..	21514	1	53861	1093
Wood and wood products	..	..	..	930	7045	..	..	5735	..	13710	..
Textile and leather	..	..	..	1169	5898	..	..	6023	5	13094	5
Construction	..	..	..	18813	15259	626	..	8730	8	43435	634
Industries n.e.s	0	0	..	1380	5079	*57576	..	25294	10	89338	*57586
Transport	..	..	..	1264831	6862	52398	..	14353	..	1338443	52398
Road	..	..	..	1127200	4802	52177	..	209	..	1184388	52177
Rail	..	..	..	3311	..	..	..	13144	..	16455	..
Domestic aviation	..	..	..	90538	..	..	..	..	..	90538	..
Domestic navigation	..	..	..	40092	..	37	..	..	..	40129	37
Pipeline transport	..	..	..	..	2059	..	..	911	..	2970	..
Transport, n.e.s	..	..	..	3690	..	184	..	90	..	3964	184
Other	4169	3554	..	251009	240864	114931	..	554742	13580	1182849	128219
Agriculture, forestry, fishing	..	..	..	83647	3167	3133	..	21211	266	111424	3399
Commerce, public services	..	..	..	54078	120072	5693	..	271105	2304	453252	7705
Households	2978	..	..	111977	117611	106070	..	257015	10762	606413	116832
Other consumers	1191	3554	..	1307	14	35	..	5411	248	11761	283
Non-energy use	..	1624	..	186277	18301	..	..	..	..	206202	..

Spain

Terajoules

2018	Primary coal and peat	Coal and peat products	Primary Oil	Oil Products	Natural Gas	Biofuels and waste	Nuclear	Electricity	Heat	Total energy	of which: renewables
Primary production	36965	..	3680	..	3161	337459	602273	335185	66929	1385651	725961
Imports	378016	11265	2858888	874148	1268259	67443	..	86465	..	5544484	67443
Exports	-5408	-6699	..	-1059845	-118294	-84630	..	-46498	..	-1321373	-84630
International marine bunkers	..	..	..	-293117	..	..	..	..	..	-293117	..
International aviation bunkers	..	..	..	-199817	..	..	..	..	..	-199817	..
Stock changes	48922	246	9306	15020	-19252	12880	..	..	..	67122	12880
Total energy supply	458494	4812	2871874	-663612	1133874	333152	602273	375152	66929	5182948	721655
Statistical difference	-22361	3199	0	-2833	6512	27	0	1958	0	-13498	352733
Transfers	..	..	35020	-20862	..	..	..	..	..	14158	..
Transformation	-467191	31128	-2906894	2753729	-375614	*-87879	-602273	643954	-52564	-1063604	*-109488
Electricity plants	-402817	-12006	..	-104568	-227980	*-71267	-602273	525366	-52564	-948108	*-94417
CHP plants	-998	..	..	-20069	-147938	*-11862	..	118588	..	-62280	*-10320
Heat plants	..	..	..	..	..	..	..	..	..	..	..
Coke ovens	-43938	51122	..	..	..	..	..	..	..	7185	..
Briquetting plants	..	..	..	..	..	..	..	..	..	..	..
Liquefaction plants	..	..	..	..	..	..	..	..	..	..	..
Gas works	..	..	..	..	..	..	..	..	..	..	..
Blast furnaces	-19438	-7988	..	..	..	..	..	..	..	-27427	..
NGL plants & gas blending	..	..	..	..	304	-304	..	..	..	0	-304
Oil refineries	..	..	-2906894	2878514	..	..	..	..	..	-28380	..
Other transformation	..	..	..	-148	..	-4446	..	..	..	-4594	-4446
Energy industries own use	..	-8029	..	-204596	-129047	..	..	-67172	..	-408844	..
Losses	..	-2238	..	..	-5774	..	..	-91501	..	-99513	..
Final consumption	13664	22474	..	1867493	616928	245246	..	858474	14365	3638643	259434
Final energy consumption	13664	20906	..	1670168	597514	245246	..	858474	14365	3420336	259434
Manufacturing, const., mining	10028	15984	..	124820	348209	*61459	..	283172	120	843793	*61579
Iron and steel	3873	14535	..	3282	22918	1	..	54490	..	99098	1
Chemical and petrochemical	5370	301	..	5366	102692	208	..	32904	7	146848	215
Non-ferrous metals	..	465	..	2850	18195	..	..	32893	10	54413	10
Non-metallic minerals	356	..	..	60819	77828	131	..	22644	2	161781	133
Transport equipment	..	..	..	1182	8126	..	..	15606	10	24924	10
Machinery	..	..	..	4486	15457	..	..	18054	24	38021	24
Mining and quarrying	..	..	..	6381	5670	74	..	6822	1	18947	75
Food and tobacco	428	684	..	11904	40832	517	..	35978	42	90385	559
Paper, pulp and printing	..	..	..	3558	24294	1107	..	19940	1	48900	1108
Wood and wood products	..	..	..	975	3098	..	..	5090	..	9163	..
Textile and leather	..	..	..	1076	5680	..	..	5519	5	12280	5
Construction	..	..	..	21279	17321	920	..	10987	8	50516	928
Industries n.e.s	0	0	..	1663	6098	*58501	..	22244	10	88517	*58511
Transport	..	..	..	1282856	8504	68276	..	14566	..	1374202	68276
Road	..	..	..	1140527	6292	68018	..	410	..	1215247	68018
Rail	..	..	..	3397	..	..	..	13118	..	16515	..
Domestic aviation	..	..	..	94198	..	..	..	..	..	94198	..
Domestic navigation	..	..	..	41468	..	37	..	..	..	41505	37
Pipeline transport	..	..	..	..	2212	..	..	943	..	3155	..
Transport, n.e.s	..	..	..	3266	..	221	..	94	..	3581	221
Other	3636	4922	..	262491	240800	115511	..	560736	14245	1202341	129579
Agriculture, forestry, fishing	..	..	..	87436	6315	5064	..	18050	266	117132	5330
Commerce, public services	..	..	..	56590	118526	3978	..	268247	2322	449663	6123
Households	2566	..	..	116953	114731	106434	..	270022	11405	622111	117839
Other consumers	1069	4922	..	1512	1228	35	..	4417	252	13434	287
Non-energy use	..	1568	..	197325	19415	..	..	..	..	218308	..

Sri Lanka

Terajoules

	Primary coal and peat	Coal and peat products	Primary Oil	Oil Products	Natural Gas	Biofuels and waste	Nuclear	Electricity	Heat	Total energy	of which: renewables
2017											
Primary production	..	..	..	..	..	150277	..	16642	..	166919	166919
Imports	74061	..	63425	170869	..	..	..	..	..	308355	..
Exports	..	..	..	0	..	..	..	..	..	0	..
International marine bunkers	..	..	..	-22773	..	..	..	..	..	-22773	..
International aviation bunkers	..	..	..	-23805	..	..	..	..	..	-23805	..
Stock changes	*-10844	..	6201	36342	..	848	..	..	..	32547	848
Total energy supply	63217	..	69626	160633	..	151125	..	16642	..	461243	167767
Statistical difference	12	..	0	2519	..	-1	..	0	..	2529	16641
Transfers	..	..	..	..	..	..	..	..	..	..	..
Transformation	-61151	..	-69626	23388	..	-848	..	37373	..	-70864	-848
Electricity plants	-61151	..	..	-46569	..	-848	..	37373	..	-71195	-848
CHP plants	..	..	..	..	..	..	..	..	..	..	..
Heat plants	..	..	..	..	..	..	..	..	..	..	..
Coke ovens	..	..	..	..	..	..	..	..	..	..	..
Briquetting plants	..	..	..	..	..	..	..	..	..	..	..
Liquefaction plants	..	..	..	..	..	..	..	..	..	..	..
Gas works	..	..	..	..	..	..	..	..	..	..	..
Blast furnaces	..	..	..	..	..	..	..	..	..	..	..
NGL plants & gas blending	..	..	..	..	..	..	..	..	..	..	..
Oil refineries	..	..	-69626	69957	..	..	..	..	..	331	..
Other transformation	..	..	..	..	..	..	..	..	..	..	..
Energy industries own use	..	..	..	-644	..	..	..	-1211	..	-1854	..
Losses	..	..	..	..	..	..	..	-4245	..	-4245	..
Final consumption	2054	..	..	180859	..	150278	..	48559	..	381750	150278
Final energy consumption	2054	..	..	179982	..	150278	..	48559	..	380874	150278
Manufacturing, const., mining	2054	..	..	7378	..	60998	..	15737	..	86168	60998
Iron and steel	..	..	..	..	..	..	..	..	..	..	..
Chemical and petrochemical	..	..	..	..	..	..	..	..	..	..	..
Non-ferrous metals	..	..	..	..	..	..	..	..	..	..	..
Non-metallic minerals	..	..	..	..	..	..	..	..	..	..	..
Transport equipment	..	..	..	..	..	..	..	..	..	..	..
Machinery	..	..	..	..	..	..	..	..	..	..	..
Mining and quarrying	..	..	..	..	..	..	..	..	..	..	..
Food and tobacco	..	..	..	..	..	..	..	..	..	..	..
Paper, pulp and printing	..	..	..	..	..	..	..	..	..	..	..
Wood and wood products	..	..	..	..	..	..	..	..	..	..	..
Textile and leather	..	..	..	..	..	..	..	..	..	..	..
Construction	..	..	..	..	..	..	..	..	..	..	..
Industries n.e.s	2054	..	..	7378	..	60998	..	15737	..	86168	60998
Transport	..	..	..	149786	..	..	..	..	..	149786	..
Road	..	..	..	147697	..	..	..	..	..	147697	..
Rail	..	..	..	1647	..	..	..	..	..	1647	..
Domestic aviation	..	..	..	419	..	..	..	..	..	419	..
Domestic navigation	..	..	..	0	..	..	..	..	..	0	..
Pipeline transport	..	..	..	..	..	..	..	..	..	..	..
Transport, n.e.s	..	..	..	24	..	..	..	..	..	24	..
Other	..	..	..	22818	..	89280	..	32822	..	144920	89280
Agriculture, forestry, fishing	..	..	..	4	..	..	..	..	..	4	..
Commerce, public services	..	..	..	..	..	..	..	14274	..	14274	..
Households	..	..	..	22814	..	89280	..	18229	..	130323	89280
Other consumers	..	..	..	..	..	..	..	319	..	319	..
Non-energy use	..	..	..	*876	..	..	..	..	..	*876	..

Sri Lanka

Terajoules

2018	Primary coal and peat	Coal and peat products	Primary Oil	Oil Products	Natural Gas	Biofuels and waste	Nuclear	Electricity	Heat	Total energy	of which: renewables
Primary production	..	..	..	..	..	*150579	..	24888	..	*175467	*175467
Imports	63481	..	74575	179004	..	..	..	..	..	317060	..
Exports	..	..	..	-3943	..	..	..	..	..	-3943	..
International marine bunkers	..	..	..	-24920	..	..	..	..	..	-24920	..
International aviation bunkers	..	..	..	-22094	..	..	..	..	..	-22094	..
Stock changes	-2403	..	0	4192	..	*1119	..	..	..	2907	*1119
Total energy supply	61078	..	74575	132238	..	*151698	..	24888	..	444477	*176586
Statistical difference	0	..	3722	-5375	..	*1693	..	-548	..	-508	*26582
Transfers	..	..	..	..	..	..	..	..	..	..	..
Transformation	-58880	..	-70853	36258	..	*-1119	..	32660	..	-61934	*-1119
Electricity plants	-58880	..	..	-32629	..	*-1119	..	32660	..	-59968	*-1119
CHP plants	..	..	..	..	..	..	..	..	..	..	..
Heat plants	..	..	..	..	..	..	..	..	..	..	..
Coke ovens	..	..	..	..	..	..	..	..	..	..	..
Briquetting plants	..	..	..	..	..	..	..	..	..	..	..
Liquefaction plants	..	..	..	..	..	..	..	..	..	..	..
Gas works	..	..	..	..	..	..	..	..	..	..	..
Blast furnaces	..	..	..	..	..	..	..	..	..	..	..
NGL plants & gas blending	..	..	..	..	..	..	..	..	..	..	..
Oil refineries	..	..	-70853	68887	..	..	..	..	..	-1966	..
Other transformation	..	..	..	..	..	..	..	..	..	..	..
Energy industries own use	..	..	..	-644	..	..	..	-2203	..	-2846	..
Losses	..	..	..	..	..	..	..	-5065	..	-5065	..
Final consumption	2198	..	..	173227	..	*148885	..	50828	..	*375139	*148885
Final energy consumption	2198	..	..	170092	..	*148885	..	50828	..	*372003	*148885
Manufacturing, const., mining	2198	..	..	9116	..	*59560	..	16553	..	*87427	*59560
Iron and steel	..	..	..	..	..	..	..	..	..	..	..
Chemical and petrochemical	..	..	..	..	..	..	..	..	..	..	..
Non-ferrous metals	..	..	..	..	..	..	..	..	..	..	..
Non-metallic minerals	..	..	..	..	..	..	..	..	..	..	..
Transport equipment	..	..	..	..	..	..	..	..	..	..	..
Machinery	..	..	..	..	..	..	..	..	..	..	..
Mining and quarrying	..	..	..	..	..	..	..	..	..	..	..
Food and tobacco	..	..	..	..	..	..	..	..	..	..	..
Paper, pulp and printing	..	..	..	..	..	..	..	..	..	..	..
Wood and wood products	..	..	..	..	..	..	..	..	..	..	..
Textile and leather	..	..	..	..	..	..	..	..	..	..	..
Construction	..	..	..	..	..	..	..	..	..	..	..
Industries n.e.s	2198	..	..	9116	..	*59560	..	16553	..	*87427	*59560
Transport	..	..	..	134680	..	..	..	..	..	134680	..
Road	..	..	..	130036	..	..	..	..	..	130036	..
Rail	..	..	..	1419	..	..	..	..	..	1419	..
Domestic aviation	..	..	..	397	..	..	..	..	..	397	..
Domestic navigation	..	..	..	2828	..	..	..	..	..	2828	..
Pipeline transport	..	..	..	..	..	..	..	..	..	..	..
Transport, n.e.s	..	..	..	..	..	..	..	..	..	..	..
Other	..	..	..	*26296	..	*89325	..	34276	..	*149897	*89325
Agriculture, forestry, fishing	..	..	..	2	..	..	..	..	..	2	..
Commerce, public services	..	..	..	..	..	..	..	13604	..	13604	..
Households	..	..	..	*26294	..	*89325	..	20671	..	*136291	*89325
Other consumers	..	..	..	..	..	..	..	..	..	..	..
Non-energy use	..	..	..	3136	..	..	..	..	..	3136	..

St. Helena and Depend.

Terajoules

	All Coal	All Oil	Natural Gas	Primary biofuels / Waste	Charcoal	Electricity	Total energy	of which: renewables
2017								
Primary production	..	..	..	6	..	10	15	15
Imports	..	139	..	..	..	..	139	..
Exports	..	..	..	..	..	..	..	..
International marine bunkers	..	..	..	..	..	..	..	..
International aviation bunkers	..	..	..	..	..	..	..	..
Stock changes	..	..	..	..	..	..	..	..
Total energy supply	..	139	..	6	..	10	155	15
Statistical Difference	..	0	..	0	..	0	0	10
Transfers	..	..	..	..	..	..	..	..
Transformation	..	*-77	..	..	..	31	*-46	..
Electricity plants	..	*-77	..	..	..	31	*-46	..
Charcoal plants	..	..	..	..	..	..	..	..
Other transformation	..	0	..	..	..	..	0	..
Energy industries own use	..	..	..	..	..	0	0	..
Losses	..	..	..	..	..	*-7	*-7	..
Final consumption	..	*62	..	6	..	34	*102	6
Final energy consumption	..	*62	..	6	..	34	*102	6
Manufacturing, const., mining	..	..	..	..	..	..	..	..
Transport	..	*62	..	..	..	..	*62	..
Road	..	*62	..	..	..	..	*62	..
Domestic aviation	..	..	..	..	..	..	..	..
Domestic navigation	..	..	..	..	..	..	..	..
Other transport	..	..	..	..	..	..	..	..
Other	..	..	..	6	..	34	40	6
Agriculture, forestry, fishing	..	..	..	..	..	..	..	..
Commerce and public services	..	..	..	..	..	18	18	..
Households	..	..	..	6	..	16	21	6
Other consumers	..	..	..	..	..	..	..	..
Non-energy use	..	..	..	..	..	..	..	..
2018								
Primary production	..	..	..	5	..	15	20	20
Imports	..	171	..	..	..	..	171	..
Exports	..	..	..	..	..	..	..	..
International marine bunkers	..	..	..	..	..	..	..	..
International aviation bunkers	..	..	..	..	..	..	..	..
Stock changes	..	..	..	..	..	..	..	..
Total energy supply	..	171	..	5	..	15	191	20
Statistical Difference	..	0	..	0	..	0	0	15
Transfers	..	..	..	..	..	..	..	..
Transformation	..	*-69	..	..	..	28	*-41	..
Electricity plants	..	*-69	..	..	..	28	*-41	..
Charcoal plants	..	..	..	..	..	..	..	..
Other transformation	..	0	..	..	..	..	0	..
Energy industries own use	..	..	..	..	..	0	0	..
Losses	..	..	..	..	..	*-3	*-3	..
Final consumption	..	*102	..	5	..	40	*147	5
Final energy consumption	..	*102	..	5	..	40	*147	5
Manufacturing, const., mining	..	..	..	..	..	..	..	..
Transport	..	*102	..	..	..	..	*102	..
Road	..	*102	..	..	..	..	*102	..
Domestic aviation	..	..	..	..	..	..	..	..
Domestic navigation	..	..	..	..	..	..	..	..
Other transport	..	..	..	..	..	..	..	..
Other	..	..	..	5	..	40	45	5
Agriculture, forestry, fishing	..	..	..	..	..	..	..	..
Commerce and public services	..	..	..	..	..	23	23	..
Households	..	..	..	5	..	16	22	5
Other consumers	..	..	..	..	..	..	..	..
Non-energy use	..	..	..	..	..	..	..	..

St. Kitts-Nevis

Terajoules

	All Coal	All Oil	Natural Gas	Primary biofuels / Waste	Charcoal	Electricity	Total energy	of which: renewables
2017								
Primary production	..	..	..	0	..	40	40	40
Imports	..	*3662	..	..	..	..	*3662	..
Exports	..	..	..	..	..	..	..	..
International marine bunkers	..	..	..	..	..	..	..	..
International aviation bunkers	..	*-223	..	..	..	..	*-223	..
Stock changes	..	..	..	..	..	..	..	..
Total energy supply	..	*3438	..	0	..	40	*3478	40
Statistical Difference	..	*95	..	0	0	20	*114	40
Transfers	..	..	..	..	..	..	..	..
Transformation	..	*-2077	..	0	0	796	*-1281	0
Electricity plants	..	*-2077	..	..	..	796	*-1281	..
Charcoal plants	..	..	..	0	0	..	0	0
Other transformation	..	0	..	0	..	..	0	0
Energy industries own use	..	..	..	..	..	-18	-18	..
Losses	..	..	..	..	..	*-144	*-144	..
Final consumption	..	*1267	..	0	0	*653	*1920	0
Final energy consumption	..	*1245	..	0	0	*653	*1899	0
Manufacturing, const., mining	..	*58	..	..	..	*130	*188	..
Transport	..	*1044	..	..	..	..	*1044	..
Road	..	*1044	..	..	..	..	*1044	..
Domestic aviation	..	..	..	..	..	..	..	..
Domestic navigation	..	..	..	..	..	..	..	..
Other transport	..	..	..	..	..	..	..	..
Other	..	*143	..	0	0	*523	*666	0
Agriculture, forestry, fishing	..	*4	..	..	..	..	*4	..
Commerce and public services	..	*49	..	..	..	*339	*388	..
Households	..	*89	..	0	0	*185	*274	0
Other consumers	..	..	..	..	..	..	..	..
Non-energy use	..	*22	..	..	..	..	*22	..
2018								
Primary production	..	..	..	0	..	*40	*40	*40
Imports	..	*3710	..	..	..	..	*3710	..
Exports	..	..	..	..	..	..	..	..
International marine bunkers	..	..	..	..	..	..	..	..
International aviation bunkers	..	*-228	..	..	..	..	*-228	..
Stock changes	..	..	..	..	..	..	..	..
Total energy supply	..	*3482	..	0	..	*40	*3522	*40
Statistical Difference	..	*99	..	0	0	0	*99	*40
Transfers	..	..	..	..	..	..	..	..
Transformation	..	*-2090	..	0	0	*796	*-1294	0
Electricity plants	..	*-2090	..	..	..	*796	*-1294	..
Charcoal plants	..	..	..	0	0	..	0	0
Other transformation	..	0	..	0	..	..	0	0
Energy industries own use	..	..	..	..	..	*-18	*-18	..
Losses	..	..	..	..	..	*-144	*-144	..
Final consumption	..	*1294	..	0	0	*673	*1967	0
Final energy consumption	..	*1272	..	0	0	*673	*1945	0
Manufacturing, const., mining	..	*61	..	..	..	*133	*194	..
Transport	..	*1062	..	..	..	..	*1062	..
Road	..	*1062	..	..	..	..	*1062	..
Domestic aviation	..	..	..	..	..	..	..	..
Domestic navigation	..	..	..	..	..	..	..	..
Other transport	..	..	..	..	..	..	..	..
Other	..	*149	..	0	0	*540	*689	0
Agriculture, forestry, fishing	..	*4	..	..	..	..	*4	..
Commerce and public services	..	*51	..	..	..	*342	*393	..
Households	..	*94	..	0	0	*198	*292	0
Other consumers	..	..	..	..	..	..	..	..
Non-energy use	..	*22	..	..	..	..	*22	..

St. Lucia

Terajoules

	All Coal	All Oil	Natural Gas	Primary biofuels / Waste	Charcoal	Electricity	Total energy	of which: renewables
2017								
Primary production	..	..	..	*643	..	..	*643	*643
Imports	..	*8996	..	..	..	..	*8996	..
Exports	..	..	..	..	..	..	..	..
International marine bunkers	..	*-311	..	..	..	..	*-311	..
International aviation bunkers	..	-1350	..	..	..	..	-1350	..
Stock changes	..	..	..	..	..	..	..	..
Total energy supply	..	*7335	..	*643	..	..	*7978	*643
Statistical Difference	..	0	..	0	0	0	0	0
Transfers	..	..	..	..	..	..	..	..
Transformation	..	-3593	..	-194	115	1441	-2231	-79
Electricity plants	..	-3593	..	..	..	1441	-2152	..
Charcoal plants	..	..	..	-194	115	..	-79	-79
Other transformation	..	0	..	0	..	..	0	0
Energy industries own use	..	..	..	..	..	-48	-48	..
Losses	..	..	..	..	..	-99	-99	..
Final consumption	..	3742	..	449	115	1295	5601	564
Final energy consumption	..	3665	..	449	115	1295	5524	564
Manufacturing, const., mining	..	133	..	..	..	66	198	..
Transport	..	2983	..	..	..	..	2983	..
Road	..	2863	..	..	..	..	2863	..
Domestic aviation	..	71	..	..	..	..	71	..
Domestic navigation	..	49	..	..	..	..	49	..
Other transport	..	..	..	..	..	..	..	..
Other	..	549	..	449	115	1229	2343	564
Agriculture, forestry, fishing	..	84	..	..	..	..	84	..
Commerce and public services	..	92	..	..	..	39	131	..
Households	..	373	..	449	115	460	1398	564
Other consumers	..	..	..	..	..	730	730	..
Non-energy use	..	*77	..	..	..	..	*77	..
2018								
Primary production	..	..	..	*617	..	18	*635	*635
Imports	..	*8979	..	..	..	..	*8979	..
Exports	..	..	..	..	..	..	..	..
International marine bunkers	..	*-315	..	..	..	..	*-315	..
International aviation bunkers	..	-1347	..	..	..	..	-1347	..
Stock changes	..	..	..	..	..	..	..	..
Total energy supply	..	*7316	..	*617	..	18	*7952	*635
Statistical Difference	..	0	..	0	0	0	0	*18
Transfers	..	..	..	..	..	..	..	..
Transformation	..	-3593	..	-178	106	1437	-2228	-72
Electricity plants	..	-3593	..	..	..	1437	-2156	..
Charcoal plants	..	..	..	-178	106	..	-72	-72
Other transformation	..	0	..	0	..	..	0	0
Energy industries own use	..	..	..	..	..	-62	-62	..
Losses	..	..	..	..	..	-91	-91	..
Final consumption	..	3723	..	439	106	1302	5570	545
Final energy consumption	..	3644	..	439	106	1302	5491	545
Manufacturing, const., mining	..	140	..	..	..	63	203	..
Transport	..	2985	..	..	..	..	2985	..
Road	..	2866	..	..	..	..	2866	..
Domestic aviation	..	71	..	..	..	..	71	..
Domestic navigation	..	49	..	..	..	..	49	..
Other transport	..	..	..	..	..	..	..	..
Other	..	519	..	439	106	1239	2303	545
Agriculture, forestry, fishing	..	89	..	..	..	..	89	..
Commerce and public services	..	84	..	..	..	39	123	..
Households	..	346	..	439	106	457	1348	545
Other consumers	..	..	..	..	..	743	743	..
Non-energy use	..	*79	..	..	..	..	*79	..

St. Pierre-Miquelon

Terajoules

	All Coal	All Oil	Natural Gas	Primary biofuels / Waste	Charcoal	Electricity	Total energy	of which: renewables
2017								
Primary production	..	..	..	5	..	..	5	5
Imports	..	*1196	..	..	..	..	*1196	..
Exports	..	..	..	..	..	..	..	..
International marine bunkers	..	*-275	..	..	..	..	*-275	..
International aviation bunkers	..	..	..	..	..	..	..	..
Stock changes	..	..	..	..	..	..	..	..
Total energy supply	..	*921	..	5	..	..	*926	5
Statistical Difference	..	0	..	0	..	0	0	0
Transfers	..	..	..	..	..	..	..	..
Transformation	..	*-499	..	..	..	175	*-324	..
Electricity plants	..	*-499	..	..	..	175	*-324	..
Charcoal plants	..	..	..	..	..	..	..	..
Other transformation	..	0	..	..	..	..	0	..
Energy industries own use	..	..	..	..	..	-4	-4	..
Losses	..	..	..	..	..	*-6	*-6	..
Final consumption	..	*422	..	*5	..	*165	*593	*5
Final energy consumption	..	*422	..	*5	..	*165	*593	*5
Manufacturing, const., mining	..	..	..	..	..	..	..	..
Transport	..	*391	..	..	..	..	*391	..
Road	..	*142	..	..	..	..	*142	..
Domestic aviation	..	..	..	..	..	..	..	..
Domestic navigation	..	..	..	..	..	..	..	..
Other transport	..	*249	..	..	..	..	*249	..
Other	..	*31	..	*5	..	*165	*202	*5
Agriculture, forestry, fishing	..	..	..	..	..	..	..	..
Commerce and public services	..	..	..	..	..	*36	*36	..
Households	..	*31	..	*5	..	*129	*166	*5
Other consumers	..	..	..	..	..	..	..	..
Non-energy use	..	..	..	..	..	..	..	..
2018								
Primary production	..	..	..	5	..	..	5	5
Imports	..	*1058	..	..	..	..	*1058	..
Exports	..	..	..	..	..	..	..	..
International marine bunkers	..	*-211	..	..	..	..	*-211	..
International aviation bunkers	..	..	..	..	..	..	..	..
Stock changes	..	..	..	..	..	..	..	..
Total energy supply	..	*847	..	5	..	..	*853	5
Statistical Difference	..	0	..	0	..	0	0	0
Transfers	..	..	..	..	..	..	..	..
Transformation	..	*-507	..	..	..	183	*-324	..
Electricity plants	..	*-507	..	..	..	183	*-324	..
Charcoal plants	..	..	..	..	..	..	..	..
Other transformation	..	0	..	..	..	..	0	..
Energy industries own use	..	..	..	..	..	-5	-5	..
Losses	..	..	..	..	..	*-7	*-7	..
Final consumption	..	*340	..	*5	..	*171	*516	*5
Final energy consumption	..	*340	..	*5	..	*171	*516	*5
Manufacturing, const., mining	..	..	..	..	..	..	..	..
Transport	..	*318	..	..	..	..	*318	..
Road	..	*128	..	..	..	..	*128	..
Domestic aviation	..	..	..	..	..	..	..	..
Domestic navigation	..	..	..	..	..	..	..	..
Other transport	..	*189	..	..	..	..	*189	..
Other	..	*22	..	*5	..	*171	*199	*5
Agriculture, forestry, fishing	..	..	..	..	..	..	..	..
Commerce and public services	..	..	..	..	..	*37	*37	..
Households	..	*22	..	*5	..	*134	*161	*5
Other consumers	..	..	..	..	..	..	..	..
Non-energy use	..	..	..	..	..	..	..	..

St. Vincent-Grenadines

Terajoules

	All Coal	All Oil	Natural Gas	Primary biofuels / Waste	Charcoal	Electricity	Total energy	of which: renewables
2017								
Primary production	..	..	..	65	..	78	143	143
Imports	..	2622	..	..	0	..	2622	0
Exports	..	..	..	..	0	..	0	0
International marine bunkers	..	..	..	..	..	..	..	..
International aviation bunkers	..	*-3	..	..	..	..	*-3	..
Stock changes	..	*473	..	..	..	..	*473	..
Total energy supply	..	3092	..	65	0	78	3236	143
Statistical Difference	..	-23	..	0	0	0	-23	78
Transfers	..	..	..	..	..	..	..	..
Transformation	..	-1227	..	*-20	11	464	-773	*-9
Electricity plants	..	-1227	..	..	..	464	-763	..
Charcoal plants	..	..	..	*-20	11	..	*-9	*-9
Other transformation	..	0	..	0	..	..	0	0
Energy industries own use	..	..	..	..	..	-17	-17	..
Losses	..	..	..	..	..	-32	-32	..
Final consumption	..	*1888	..	*45	*11	493	*2437	*56
Final energy consumption	..	*1850	..	*45	*11	493	*2399	*56
Manufacturing, const., mining	..	..	..	..	..	26	26	..
Transport	..	*1495	..	..	..	..	*1495	..
Road	..	*1151	..	..	..	..	*1151	..
Domestic aviation	..	..	..	..	..	..	..	..
Domestic navigation	..	..	..	..	..	..	..	..
Other transport	..	*344	..	..	..	..	*344	..
Other	..	*355	..	*45	*11	467	877	*56
Agriculture, forestry, fishing	..	..	..	..	..	..	..	..
Commerce and public services	..	..	..	..	..	217	217	..
Households	..	*355	..	*45	*11	250	*661	*56
Other consumers	..	..	..	..	..	..	..	..
Non-energy use	..	*38	..	..	..	..	*38	..
2018								
Primary production	..	..	..	65	..	93	158	158
Imports	..	3722	..	..	0	..	3722	0
Exports	..	..	..	..	0	..	0	0
International marine bunkers	..	..	..	..	..	..	..	..
International aviation bunkers	..	*-3	..	..	..	..	*-3	..
Stock changes	..	*-215	..	..	..	..	*-215	..
Total energy supply	..	3504	..	65	0	93	3661	157
Statistical Difference	..	5	..	0	0	0	5	93
Transfers	..	..	..	..	..	..	..	..
Transformation	..	-1190	..	*-20	11	450	-749	*-9
Electricity plants	..	-1190	..	..	..	450	-740	..
Charcoal plants	..	..	..	*-20	11	..	*-9	*-9
Other transformation	..	0	..	0	..	..	0	0
Energy industries own use	..	..	..	..	..	-16	-16	..
Losses	..	..	..	..	..	-40	-40	..
Final consumption	..	*2309	..	*45	*11	486	*2851	*55
Final energy consumption	..	*2269	..	*45	*11	486	*2811	*55
Manufacturing, const., mining	..	..	..	..	..	25	25	..
Transport	..	*1881	..	..	..	..	*1881	..
Road	..	*1322	..	..	..	..	*1322	..
Domestic aviation	..	..	..	..	..	..	..	..
Domestic navigation	..	..	..	..	..	..	..	..
Other transport	..	*559	..	..	..	..	*559	..
Other	..	*388	..	*45	*11	461	905	*55
Agriculture, forestry, fishing	..	..	..	..	..	..	..	..
Commerce and public services	..	..	..	..	..	216	216	..
Households	..	*388	..	*45	*11	246	*689	*55
Other consumers	..	..	..	..	..	..	..	..
Non-energy use	..	*40	..	..	..	..	*40	..

State of Palestine

Terajoules

	All Coal	All Oil	Natural Gas	Primary biofuels / Waste	Charcoal	Electricity	Total energy	of which: renewables
2017								
Primary production	..	..	..	2552	..	5794	8347	8347
Imports	..	47887	..	31	..	20077	67995	31
Exports	..	-4	..	-5	..	..	-9	-5
International marine bunkers	..	..	..	..	..	..	..	..
International aviation bunkers	..	..	..	..	..	..	..	..
Stock changes	..	..	..	..	..	..	..	..
Total energy supply	..	47883	..	2579	..	25871	76333	8373
Statistical Difference	..	-4	..	1	..	0	-4	5795
Transfers	..	..	..	..	..	..	..	..
Transformation	..	-4949	..	..	..	1803	-3146	..
Electricity plants	..	-4949	..	..	..	1803	-3146	..
Charcoal plants	..	..	..	..	..	..	..	..
Other transformation	..	0	..	..	..	..	0	..
Energy industries own use	..	..	..	..	..	0	0	..
Losses	..	-153	..	..	..	-5461	-5614	..
Final consumption	..	42786	..	2578	..	22213	67577	2578
Final energy consumption	..	41777	..	2578	..	22213	66568	2578
Manufacturing, const., mining	..	1061	..	209	..	2333	3603	209
Transport	..	31670	..	..	..	..	31670	..
Road	..	31670	..	..	..	..	31670	..
Domestic aviation	..	..	..	..	..	..	..	..
Domestic navigation	..	..	..	..	..	..	..	..
Other transport	..	..	..	..	..	..	..	..
Other	..	9045	..	2369	..	19880	31294	2369
Agriculture, forestry, fishing	..	458	..	..	..	119	577	..
Commerce and public services	..	974	..	38	..	4973	5986	38
Households	..	7613	..	2330	..	14788	24732	2330
Other consumers	..	..	..	..	..	..	..	..
Non-energy use	..	1009	..	..	..	..	1009	..
2018								
Primary production	..	..	..	2420	..	5994	8414	8414
Imports	..	43956	..	34	..	21297	65287	34
Exports	..	-4	..	-5	..	..	-10	-5
International marine bunkers	..	..	..	..	..	..	..	..
International aviation bunkers	..	..	..	..	..	..	..	..
Stock changes	..	0	..	..	..	..	0	..
Total energy supply	..	43952	..	2448	..	27290	73691	8442
Statistical Difference	..	-4	..	0	..	0	-4	5994
Transfers	..	..	..	..	..	..	..	..
Transformation	..	-3275	..	..	..	1297	-1977	..
Electricity plants	..	-3275	..	..	..	1297	-1977	..
Charcoal plants	..	..	..	..	..	..	..	..
Other transformation	..	0	..	..	..	..	0	..
Energy industries own use	..	..	..	..	..	0	0	..
Losses	..	-140	..	..	..	-5626	-5766	..
Final consumption	..	40542	..	2448	..	22962	65952	2448
Final energy consumption	..	39022	..	2448	..	22962	64432	2448
Manufacturing, const., mining	..	1224	..	163	..	2573	3960	163
Transport	..	29899	..	..	..	..	29899	..
Road	..	29899	..	..	..	..	29899	..
Domestic aviation	..	..	..	..	..	..	..	..
Domestic navigation	..	..	..	..	..	..	..	..
Other transport	..	..	..	..	..	..	..	..
Other	..	7899	..	2285	..	20389	30573	2285
Agriculture, forestry, fishing	..	391	..	..	..	106	497	..
Commerce and public services	..	1072	..	54	..	5302	6428	54
Households	..	6436	..	2231	..	14981	23648	2231
Other consumers	..	..	..	..	..	..	..	..
Non-energy use	..	1520	..	..	..	..	1520	..

Sudan

Terajoules

2017	Primary coal and peat	Coal and peat products	Primary Oil	Oil Products	Natural Gas	Biofuels and waste	Nuclear	Electricity	Heat	Total energy	of which: renewables
Primary production	..	..	173223	..	..	204864	..	33649	..	411736	238513
Imports	..	..	31480	105007	..	..	..	3208	..	139694	..
Exports	..	..	-7056	-5387	..	..	..	..	..	-12443	..
International marine bunkers	..	..	..	-1161	..	..	..	..	..	-1161	..
International aviation bunkers	..	..	..	*-5901	..	..	..	..	..	*-5901	..
Stock changes	..	..	..	..	..	..	..	..	..	..	..
Total energy supply	..	..	197647	92559	..	204864	..	36857	..	531926	238513
Statistical difference	..	..	5224	1427	..	0	..	749	..	7399	33649
Transfers	..	..	..	..	..	..	..	..	..	..	..
Transformation	..	..	*-192423	116023	..	-48699	..	22722	..	*-102377	-48699
Electricity plants	..	..	*-31725	*-39345	..	..	..	22302	..	*-48768	..
CHP plants	..	..	..	..	..	*-2100	..	420	..	*-1681	*-2100
Heat plants	..	..	..	..	..	..	..	..	..	..	..
Coke ovens	..	..	..	..	..	..	..	..	..	..	..
Briquetting plants	..	..	..	..	..	..	..	..	..	..	..
Liquefaction plants	..	..	..	..	..	..	..	..	..	..	..
Gas works	..	..	..	..	..	..	..	..	..	..	..
Blast furnaces	..	..	..	..	..	..	..	..	..	..	..
NGL plants & gas blending	..	..	..	..	..	..	..	..	..	..	..
Oil refineries	..	..	*-160698	155368	..	..	..	..	..	*-5329	..
Other transformation	..	..	..	..	..	-46599	..	..	..	-46599	-46599
Energy industries own use	..	..	..	-990	..	..	..	-866	..	-1856	..
Losses	..	..	..	..	..	..	..	-11304	..	-11304	..
Final consumption	..	..	..	*206165	..	*156165	..	46660	..	*408989	*156165
Final energy consumption	..	..	..	*195459	..	*156165	..	46660	..	*398283	*156165
Manufacturing, const., mining	..	..	..	17529	..	*45714	..	7211	..	*70454	*45714
Iron and steel	..	..	..	..	..	..	..	..	..	..	..
Chemical and petrochemical	..	..	..	..	..	..	..	..	..	..	..
Non-ferrous metals	..	..	..	..	..	..	..	..	..	..	..
Non-metallic minerals	..	..	..	..	..	..	..	..	..	..	..
Transport equipment	..	..	..	..	..	..	..	..	..	..	..
Machinery	..	..	..	..	..	..	..	..	..	..	..
Mining and quarrying	..	..	..	..	..	..	..	..	..	..	..
Food and tobacco	..	..	..	..	..	*14610	..	..	..	*14610	*14610
Paper, pulp and printing	..	..	..	..	..	..	..	..	..	..	..
Wood and wood products	..	..	..	..	..	..	..	..	..	..	..
Textile and leather	..	..	..	..	..	..	..	..	..	..	..
Construction	..	..	..	..	..	..	..	..	..	..	..
Industries n.e.s	..	..	..	17529	..	*31104	..	7211	..	*55844	*31104
Transport	..	..	..	*132721	..	..	..	..	..	*132721	..
Road	..	..	..	*132721	..	..	..	..	..	*132721	..
Rail	..	..	..	..	..	..	..	..	..	..	..
Domestic aviation	..	..	..	..	..	..	..	..	..	..	..
Domestic navigation	..	..	..	..	..	..	..	..	..	..	..
Pipeline transport	..	..	..	..	..	..	..	..	..	..	..
Transport, n.e.s	..	..	..	..	..	..	..	..	..	..	..
Other	..	..	..	*45209	..	*110450	..	39449	..	*195108	*110450
Agriculture, forestry, fishing	..	..	..	..	..	..	..	..	..	..	..
Commerce, public services	..	..	..	*4635	..	*37854	..	5645	..	*48134	*37854
Households	..	..	..	*7042	..	*72596	..	26471	..	*106109	*72596
Other consumers	..	..	..	*33532	..	..	..	7333	..	*40865	..
Non-energy use	..	..	..	*10706	..	..	..	..	..	*10706	..

Sudan

Terajoules

2018	Primary coal and peat	Coal and peat products	Primary Oil	Oil Products	Natural Gas	Biofuels and waste	Nuclear	Electricity	Heat	Total energy	of which: renewables
Primary production	..	..	161506	..	..	207284	..	34765	..	403555	242049
Imports	..	..	*19035	113926	..	..	..	2909	..	135870	..
Exports	..	..	..	-4550	..	..	..	..	..	-4550	..
International marine bunkers	..	..	..	*-1204	..	..	..	..	..	*-1204	..
International aviation bunkers	..	..	..	*-5204	..	..	..	..	..	*-5204	..
Stock changes	..	..	..	..	..	..	..	..	..	..	..
Total energy supply	..	..	180541	102969	..	207284	..	37674	..	528467	242049
Statistical difference	..	..	*977	5182	..	0	..	0	..	6158	34765
Transfers	..	..	..	..	..	..	..	..	..	..	..
Transformation	..	..	*-179564	103291	..	-48730	..	24182	..	*-100821	-48730
Electricity plants	..	..	*-31725	*-39345	..	..	..	23756	..	*-47314	..
CHP plants	..	..	..	..	..	-2131	..	425	..	-1706	-2131
Heat plants	..	..	..	..	..	..	..	..	..	..	..
Coke ovens	..	..	..	..	..	..	..	..	..	..	..
Briquetting plants	..	..	..	..	..	..	..	..	..	..	..
Liquefaction plants	..	..	..	..	..	..	..	..	..	..	..
Gas works	..	..	..	..	..	..	..	..	..	..	..
Blast furnaces	..	..	..	..	..	..	..	..	..	..	..
NGL plants & gas blending	..	..	..	..	..	..	..	..	..	..	..
Oil refineries	..	..	*-147839	142636	..	..	..	..	..	*-5202	..
Other transformation	..	..	..	..	..	-46599	..	..	..	-46599	-46599
Energy industries own use	..	..	..	*-990	..	..	..	-1636	..	-2626	..
Losses	..	..	..	..	..	..	..	-10900	..	-10900	..
Final consumption	..	..	..	*200089	..	*158554	..	49320	..	*407963	*158554
Final energy consumption	..	..	..	*189124	..	*158554	..	49320	..	*396999	*158554
Manufacturing, const., mining	..	..	..	*18437	..	*47095	..	6462	..	*71995	*47095
Iron and steel	..	..	..	..	..	..	..	..	..	..	..
Chemical and petrochemical	..	..	..	..	..	..	..	..	..	..	..
Non-ferrous metals	..	..	..	..	..	..	..	..	..	..	..
Non-metallic minerals	..	..	..	..	..	..	..	..	..	..	..
Transport equipment	..	..	..	..	..	..	..	..	..	..	..
Machinery	..	..	..	..	..	..	..	..	..	..	..
Mining and quarrying	..	..	..	..	..	..	..	..	..	..	..
Food and tobacco	..	..	..	..	..	*14857	..	..	..	*14857	*14857
Paper, pulp and printing	..	..	..	..	..	..	..	..	..	..	..
Wood and wood products	..	..	..	..	..	..	..	..	..	..	..
Textile and leather	..	..	..	..	..	..	..	..	..	..	..
Construction	..	..	..	..	..	..	..	..	..	..	..
Industries n.e.s	..	..	..	*18437	..	*32238	..	6462	..	*57137	*32238
Transport	..	..	..	*135468	..	..	..	..	..	*135468	..
Road	..	..	..	*135468	..	..	..	..	..	*135468	..
Rail	..	..	..	..	..	..	..	..	..	..	..
Domestic aviation	..	..	..	..	..	..	..	..	..	..	..
Domestic navigation	..	..	..	..	..	..	..	..	..	..	..
Pipeline transport	..	..	..	..	..	..	..	..	..	..	..
Transport, n.e.s	..	..	..	..	..	..	..	..	..	..	..
Other	..	..	..	*35219	..	*111459	..	42858	..	*189536	*111459
Agriculture, forestry, fishing	..	..	..	..	..	..	..	..	..	..	..
Commerce, public services	..	..	..	*4290	..	*38114	..	4788	..	*47192	*38114
Households	..	..	..	*6781	..	*73345	..	28897	..	*109023	*73345
Other consumers	..	..	..	*24148	..	..	..	9173	..	*33321	..
Non-energy use	..	..	..	*10964	..	..	..	..	..	*10964	..

Suriname

Terajoules

2017	Primary coal and peat	Coal and peat products	Primary Oil	Oil Products	Natural Gas	Biofuels and waste	Nuclear	Electricity	Heat	Total energy	of which: renewables
Primary production	..	..	34150	..	123	1650	..	3348	..	39271	4999
Imports	..	..	599	19604	..	43	..	..	..	20246	43
Exports	..	..	..	-15826	..	..	..	..	..	-15826	..
International marine bunkers	..	..	..	-1758	..	..	..	..	..	-1758	..
International aviation bunkers	..	..	..	*-1786	..	..	..	..	..	*-1786	..
Stock changes	..	..	..	..	..	..	..	..	..	..	..
Total energy supply	..	..	34749	233	123	1694	..	3348	..	40146	5042
Statistical difference	..	..	-363	-3705	0	0	..	122	..	-3945	3349
Transfers	..	..	-5743	5485	..	..	..	..	..	-258	..
Transformation	..	..	-27722	13978	-123	..	..	4275	..	-9592	..
Electricity plants	..	..	..	-13371	-123	..	..	4275	..	-9219	..
CHP plants	..	..	..	..	..	..	..	..	..	..	..
Heat plants	..	..	..	..	..	..	..	..	..	..	..
Coke ovens	..	..	..	..	..	..	..	..	..	..	..
Briquetting plants	..	..	..	..	..	..	..	..	..	..	..
Liquefaction plants	..	..	..	..	..	..	..	..	..	..	..
Gas works	..	..	..	..	..	..	..	..	..	..	..
Blast furnaces	..	..	..	..	..	..	..	..	..	..	..
NGL plants & gas blending	..	..	..	..	..	..	..	..	..	..	..
Oil refineries	..	..	-27722	28207	..	..	..	..	..	486	..
Other transformation	..	..	..	-858	..	..	..	..	..	-858	..
Energy industries own use	..	..	-1647	-8434	..	..	..	-336	..	-10417	..
Losses	..	..	..	..	..	..	..	-781	..	-781	..
Final consumption	..	..	..	14966	..	1694	..	6384	..	23044	1694
Final energy consumption	..	..	..	14766	..	1694	..	6384	..	22844	1694
Manufacturing, const., mining	..	..	..	885	..	880	..	3066	..	4831	880
Iron and steel	..	..	..	..	..	..	..	..	..	..	..
Chemical and petrochemical	..	..	..	..	..	..	..	..	..	..	..
Non-ferrous metals	..	..	..	..	..	..	..	..	..	..	..
Non-metallic minerals	..	..	..	..	..	..	..	*845	..	*845	..
Transport equipment	..	..	..	..	..	..	..	..	..	..	..
Machinery	..	..	..	..	..	..	..	..	..	..	..
Mining and quarrying	..	..	..	..	..	..	..	*1029	..	*1029	..
Food and tobacco	..	..	..	..	..	..	..	..	..	..	..
Paper, pulp and printing	..	..	..	..	..	..	..	..	..	..	..
Wood and wood products	..	..	..	..	..	..	..	..	..	..	..
Textile and leather	..	..	..	..	..	..	..	..	..	..	..
Construction	..	..	..	371	..	..	..	..	..	371	..
Industries n.e.s	..	..	..	514	..	880	..	1193	..	2586	880
Transport	..	..	..	8769	..	..	..	..	..	8769	..
Road	..	..	..	3118	..	..	..	..	..	3118	..
Rail	..	..	..	..	..	..	..	..	..	..	..
Domestic aviation	..	..	..	*198	..	..	..	..	..	*198	..
Domestic navigation	..	..	..	..	..	..	..	..	..	..	..
Pipeline transport	..	..	..	..	..	..	..	..	..	..	..
Transport, n.e.s	..	..	..	5453	..	..	..	..	..	5453	..
Other	..	..	..	5112	..	814	..	3318	..	9244	814
Agriculture, forestry, fishing	..	..	..	4174	..	..	..	..	..	4174	..
Commerce, public services	..	..	..	345	..	17	..	1187	..	1549	17
Households	..	..	..	593	..	797	..	2131	..	3521	797
Other consumers	..	..	..	..	..	..	..	..	..	..	..
Non-energy use	..	..	..	*200	..	..	..	..	..	*200	..

Suriname

Terajoules

2018	Primary coal and peat	Coal and peat products	Primary Oil	Oil Products	Natural Gas	Biofuels and waste	Nuclear	Electricity	Heat	Total energy	of which: renewables
Primary production	..	..	34322	..	176	1652	..	3615	..	39764	5267
Imports	..	..	397	19328	..	43	..	..	..	19769	43
Exports	..	..	..	-15215	..	..	..	..	..	-15215	..
International marine bunkers	..	..	..	-1540	..	..	..	..	..	-1540	..
International aviation bunkers	..	..	..	*-1788	..	..	..	..	..	*-1788	..
Stock changes	..	..	..	..	..	..	..	..	..	..	..
Total energy supply	..	..	34719	785	176	1695	..	3615	..	40990	5310
Statistical difference	..	..	-201	-4144	0	0	..	0	..	-4345	3615
Transfers	..	..	-6054	5782	..	..	..	..	..	-272	..
Transformation	..	..	-27245	13716	-176	..	..	4621	..	-9084	..
Electricity plants	..	..	..	-13119	-176	..	..	4621	..	-8674	..
CHP plants	..	..	..	..	..	..	..	..	..	..	..
Heat plants	..	..	..	..	..	..	..	..	..	..	..
Coke ovens	..	..	..	..	..	..	..	..	..	..	..
Briquetting plants	..	..	..	..	..	..	..	..	..	..	..
Liquefaction plants	..	..	..	..	..	..	..	..	..	..	..
Gas works	..	..	..	..	..	..	..	..	..	..	..
Blast furnaces	..	..	..	..	..	..	..	..	..	..	..
NGL plants & gas blending	..	..	..	..	..	..	..	..	..	..	..
Oil refineries	..	..	-27245	27675	..	..	..	..	..	430	..
Other transformation	..	..	..	-840	..	..	..	..	..	-840	..
Energy industries own use	..	..	-1621	-9715	..	..	..	-281	..	-11616	..
Losses	..	..	..	-25	..	..	..	-1534	..	-1559	..
Final consumption	..	..	..	14688	..	1695	..	6420	..	22803	1695
Final energy consumption	..	..	..	14553	..	1695	..	6420	..	22668	1695
Manufacturing, const., mining	..	..	..	869	..	881	..	3083	..	4833	881
Iron and steel	..	..	..	..	..	..	..	..	..	..	..
Chemical and petrochemical	..	..	..	..	..	..	..	..	..	..	..
Non-ferrous metals	..	..	..	..	..	..	..	..	..	..	..
Non-metallic minerals	..	..	..	..	..	..	..	*907	..	*907	..
Transport equipment	..	..	..	..	..	..	..	..	..	..	..
Machinery	..	..	..	..	..	..	..	..	..	..	..
Mining and quarrying	..	..	..	..	..	..	..	897	..	897	..
Food and tobacco	..	..	..	..	..	..	..	..	..	..	..
Paper, pulp and printing	..	..	..	..	..	..	..	..	..	..	..
Wood and wood products	..	..	..	..	..	..	..	..	..	..	..
Textile and leather	..	..	..	..	..	..	..	..	..	..	..
Construction	..	..	..	363	..	..	..	..	..	363	..
Industries n.e.s	..	..	..	506	..	881	..	1280	..	2666	881
Transport	..	..	..	8684	..	..	..	..	..	8684	..
Road	..	..	..	3051	..	..	..	..	..	3051	..
Rail	..	..	..	..	..	..	..	..	..	..	..
Domestic aviation	..	..	..	*198	..	..	..	..	..	*198	..
Domestic navigation	..	..	..	..	..	..	..	..	..	..	..
Pipeline transport	..	..	..	..	..	..	..	..	..	..	..
Transport, n.e.s	..	..	..	5434	..	..	..	..	..	5434	..
Other	..	..	..	5000	..	814	..	3337	..	9151	814
Agriculture, forestry, fishing	..	..	..	4089	..	..	..	..	..	4089	..
Commerce, public services	..	..	..	341	..	17	..	1194	..	1552	17
Households	..	..	..	569	..	797	..	2143	..	3510	797
Other consumers	..	..	..	..	..	..	..	..	..	..	..
Non-energy use	..	..	..	*135	..	..	..	..	..	*135	..

Sweden

Terajoules

2017	Primary coal and peat	Coal and peat products	Primary Oil	Oil Products	Natural Gas	Biofuels and waste	Nuclear	Electricity	Heat	Total energy	of which: renewables
Primary production	4713	..	..	..	..	477628	709517	298735	464	1491057	744714
Imports	80121	2696	804190	436379	39483	66139	..	42826	..	1471834	62290
Exports	..	-842	..	-762750	-185	-11470	..	-111197	..	-886444	-11453
International marine bunkers	..	..	..	-97385	-797	..	..	..	..	-98183	..
International aviation bunkers	..	..	..	-38235	..	..	..	..	..	-38235	..
Stock changes	-3768	2920	16230	57843	..	13602	..	..	..	86826	13602
Total energy supply	81065	4774	820420	-404148	38501	545898	709517	230364	464	2026855	809153
Statistical difference	1305	1674	-2228	-7213	-1991	10862	0	0	0	2409	309598
Transfers	..	..	52650	-47151	..	..	..	..	..	5500	..
Transformation	-65568	18952	-875298	897562	-4762	*-251366	-709517	286916	189907	-513174	*-215421
Electricity plants	..	..	..	-170	..	..	-709517	236545	..	-473142	..
CHP plants	-11120	-9526	..	-2936	-4252	*-210328	..	55930	135248	-46984	*-177006
Heat plants	-880	-493	..	-1228	-229	*-41037	..	-5558	54659	5234	*-38415
Coke ovens	-43220	41322	..	..	..	..	..	..	..	-1897	..
Briquetting plants	..	..	..	..	..	..	..	..	..	..	..
Liquefaction plants	..	..	..	..	..	..	..	..	..	..	..
Gas works	..	..	..	..	-282	..	..	..	..	-282	..
Blast furnaces	-10348	-14657	..	..	..	..	..	..	..	-25005	..
NGL plants & gas blending	..	313	..	..	..	..	..	..	..	313	..
Oil refineries	..	..	-875298	901896	..	..	..	..	..	26598	..
Other transformation	..	1992	..	..	..	..	..	..	..	1992	..
Energy industries own use	..	-4479	..	-41796	-778	-756	..	-24984	0	-72792	-756
Losses	..	-1131	..	..	..	..	..	-34182	-6813	-42126	..
Final consumption	14193	16441	..	411680	34952	*282914	..	458114	183558	1401853	*283378
Final energy consumption	14193	15795	..	322874	20678	*282914	..	458114	183558	1298126	*283378
Manufacturing, const., mining	14193	15584	..	40813	15010	*177332	..	183380	21604	467916	*177332
Iron and steel	1971	14168	..	8871	3471	74	..	16423	..	44979	74
Chemical and petrochemical	126	..	..	1643	3153	*608	..	16758	..	22287	*608
Non-ferrous metals	1420	..	..	1502	286	..	..	10699	..	13908	..
Non-metallic minerals	6319	505	..	3850	2054	74	..	3712	..	16514	74
Transport equipment	..	309	..	915	359	74	..	7117	..	8774	74
Machinery	..	..	..	1362	662	74	..	11988	..	14086	74
Mining and quarrying	4203	399	..	4100	131	515	..	13417	..	22766	515
Food and tobacco	..	168	..	2106	3094	*1128	..	8629	..	15126	*1128
Paper, pulp and printing	154	..	..	7047	1409	*154474	..	72979	..	*236062	*154474
Wood and wood products	..	..	..	1011	4	*17219	..	6664	..	*24897	*17219
Textile and leather	..	..	..	138	82	..	..	731	..	950	..
Construction	..	..	..	6577	14	1840	..	4961	..	13392	1840
Industries n.e.s	0	34	..	1691	291	*1253	..	9302	21604	34175	*1253
Transport	..	..	..	248574	772	51517	..	8914	..	309777	51517
Road	..	..	..	233907	772	51517	..	..	..	286196	51517
Rail	..	..	..	559	..	..	..	8914	..	9473	..
Domestic aviation	..	..	..	8026	..	..	..	..	..	8026	..
Domestic navigation	..	..	..	6082	..	..	..	..	..	6082	..
Pipeline transport	..	..	..	..	..	..	..	..	..	..	..
Transport, n.e.s	..	..	..	..	..	..	..	..	..	..	..
Other	..	211	..	33487	4895	*54065	..	265820	161954	520433	*54529
Agriculture, forestry, fishing	..	..	..	14933	253	*9636	..	4118	300	29241	*9636
Commerce, public services	..	106	..	9568	3130	*4426	..	99227	51750	168207	*4426
Households	..	105	..	8986	1512	*40004	..	162475	109904	322986	*40468
Other consumers	..	..	..	..	..	..	..	..	..	..	..
Non-energy use	..	646	..	88806	14275	..	..	..	..	103727	..

Sweden

Terajoules

2018	Primary coal and peat	Coal and peat products	Primary Oil	Oil Products	Natural Gas	Biofuels and waste	Nuclear	Electricity	Heat	Total energy	of which: renewables
Primary production	6688	..	..	..	..	469313	740329	285264	457	1502051	725131
Imports	79365	6571	842113	397291	43385	75540	..	43927	..	1488191	71790
Exports	..	-253	..	-727296	-595	-14833	..	-105930	..	-848906	-14831
International marine bunkers	..	..	..	-75655	-896	..	..	..	..	-76551	..
International aviation bunkers	..	..	..	-40263	..	..	..	..	..	-40263	..
Stock changes	2242	-2555	5982	25856	..	-3971	..	..	..	27554	-3971
Total energy supply	88294	3763	848095	-420067	41894	526049	740329	223261	457	2052075	778119
Statistical difference	9023	640	-564	17870	-51	-1221	0	0	0	25697	284043
Transfers	..	..	82515	-81230	..	..	..	..	..	1285	..
Transformation	-65843	17368	-931174	922639	-6571	*-246119	-740329	298195	189709	-562125	*-212468
Electricity plants	..	..	..	-254	..	..	-740329	246856	..	-493728	..
CHP plants	-13993	-9649	..	-3622	-6092	*-205107	..	55976	136155	-46331	*-173929
Heat plants	-553	-270	..	-1388	-205	*-41012	..	-4637	53554	5489	*-38539
Coke ovens	-41526	38720	..	..	..	..	..	..	..	-2806	..
Briquetting plants	..	..	..	..	..	..	..	..	..	..	..
Liquefaction plants	..	..	..	..	..	..	..	..	..	..	..
Gas works	..	..	..	..	-274	..	..	..	..	-274	..
Blast furnaces	-9771	-13628	..	..	..	..	..	..	..	-23399	..
NGL plants & gas blending	..	304	..	..	..	..	..	..	..	304	..
Oil refineries	..	..	-931174	927904	..	..	..	..	..	-3270	..
Other transformation	..	1891	..	..	..	..	..	..	..	1891	..
Energy industries own use	..	-3994	..	-14415	-1421	-760	..	-24300	0	-44890	-760
Losses	..	-622	..	..	..	..	..	-37933	-5985	-44540	..
Final consumption	13428	15875	..	389057	33953	*280391	..	459223	184181	1376109	*280848
Final energy consumption	13428	15313	..	312780	19500	*280391	..	459223	184181	1284817	*280848
Manufacturing, const., mining	13428	15118	..	42620	14138	*177355	..	182588	21816	467063	*177355
Iron and steel	1897	13595	..	9568	3137	74	..	16564	..	44834	74
Chemical and petrochemical	126	..	..	1742	2782	*545	..	15800	..	20994	*545
Non-ferrous metals	1379	..	..	1492	290	..	..	10811	..	13972	..
Non-metallic minerals	6121	730	..	3717	2053	95	..	3672	..	16387	95
Transport equipment	..	337	..	1057	318	110	..	7164	..	8986	110
Machinery	..	..	..	1276	475	192	..	12236	..	14179	192
Mining and quarrying	3650	352	..	4775	181	626	..	13421	..	23004	626
Food and tobacco	..	56	..	1904	2934	*1121	..	8543	..	14558	*1121
Paper, pulp and printing	255	..	..	7322	1706	*154243	..	72108	..	*235634	*154243
Wood and wood products	..	..	..	1149	3	*16918	..	6570	..	*24640	*16918
Textile and leather	..	..	..	138	32	..	..	720	..	889	..
Construction	..	..	..	6718	3	2134	..	5339	..	14194	2134
Industries n.e.s	0	48	..	1763	226	*1297	..	9641	21816	34792	*1297
Transport	..	..	..	238344	478	55604	..	9263	..	303689	55604
Road	..	..	..	223363	478	55604	..	..	..	279445	55604
Rail	..	..	..	602	..	..	..	9263	..	9865	..
Domestic aviation	..	..	..	7585	..	..	..	..	..	7585	..
Domestic navigation	..	..	..	6793	..	..	..	..	..	6793	..
Pipeline transport	..	..	..	..	..	..	..	..	..	..	..
Transport, n.e.s	..	..	..	..	..	..	..	..	..	..	..
Other	..	195	..	31816	4884	*47433	..	267372	162365	514065	*47890
Agriculture, forestry, fishing	..	..	..	13608	249	*8848	..	4284	300	27289	*8848
Commerce, public services	..	103	..	10017	3266	*4805	..	100843	53795	172829	*4805
Households	..	92	..	8191	1369	*33780	..	162245	108270	313947	*34237
Other consumers	..	..	..	..	..	..	..	..	..	..	..
Non-energy use	..	562	..	76277	14453	..	..	..	..	91292	..

Switzerland

Terajoules

2017	Primary coal and peat	Coal and peat products	Primary Oil	Oil Products	Natural Gas	Biofuels and waste	Nuclear	Electricity	Heat	Total energy	of which: renewables
Primary production	..	..	..	..	..	106821	221381	129269	2526	459997	201941
Imports	4229	357	124301	334508	125994	7437	..	131386	..	728212	7437
Exports	..	..	..	-15682	..	-90	..	-111406	..	-127178	-90
International marine bunkers	..	..	..	-172	..	..	..	..	..	-172	..
International aviation bunkers	..	..	..	-75411	..	..	..	..	..	-75411	..
Stock changes	27	..	130	5739	..	-107	..	..	..	5789	-107
Total energy supply	4256	357	124431	248983	125994	114061	221381	149249	2526	991238	209181
Statistical difference	25	-26	0	-3968	2	39	0	7	-2	-3922	129307
Transfers	..	..	656	-656	..	..	..	..	..	0	..
Transformation	..	..	-125087	124302	-7497	-56220	-221381	87221	22391	-176270	-32592
Electricity plants	..	..	..	-129	..	-3	-220061	73404	..	-146789	-3
CHP plants	..	..	..	-176	-5012	-55117	-1320	13860	18988	-28777	-31489
Heat plants	..	..	..	-215	-3590	..	..	-43	3403	-445	..
Coke ovens	..	..	..	..	..	..	..	..	..	..	..
Briquetting plants	..	..	..	..	..	..	..	..	..	..	..
Liquefaction plants	..	..	..	..	..	..	..	..	..	..	..
Gas works	..	..	..	..	..	..	..	..	..	..	..
Blast furnaces	..	..	..	..	..	..	..	..	..	..	..
NGL plants & gas blending	..	..	..	..	1105	-1100	..	..	..	5	-1100
Oil refineries	..	..	-125087	124952	..	..	..	..	..	-135	..
Other transformation	..	..	..	-129	..	..	..	..	..	-129	..
Energy industries own use	..	..	..	-6192	-126	..	..	-9562	-2	-15881	..
Losses	..	..	..	..	-272	..	..	-16409	-1860	-18541	..
Final consumption	4231	383	..	370407	118097	57803	..	210492	23057	784468	47283
Final energy consumption	4231	383	..	351190	118097	57803	..	210492	23057	765252	47283
Manufacturing, const., mining	4129	383	..	12515	40643	21427	..	64426	7378	150900	10101
Iron and steel	306	102	..	129	3743	124	..	5173	..	9577	124
Chemical and petrochemical	..	..	..	860	13072	4450	..	10976	1295	30653	..
Non-ferrous metals	..	..	..	86	1553	..	..	1674	16	3329	..
Non-metallic minerals	3772	255	..	1463	3914	6128	..	3996	..	19528	..
Transport equipment	..	..	..	..	..	..	..	..	..	..	..
Machinery	..	..	..	3655	4371	183	..	15322	482	24013	166
Mining and quarrying	..	..	..	..	..	..	..	..	..	..	..
Food and tobacco	51	26	..	2107	8381	179	..	9659	358	20760	26
Paper, pulp and printing	..	..	..	301	2499	1872	..	6430	2577	13679	1331
Wood and wood products	..	..	..	..	..	..	..	..	..	..	..
Textile and leather	..	..	..	344	711	68	..	680	..	1803	68
Construction	..	..	..	1978	788	2881	..	1858	19	7523	2881
Industries n.e.s	0	0	..	1592	1612	5542	..	8658	2631	20035	5505
Transport	..	..	..	221740	1033	5398	..	11340	..	239511	5398
Road	..	..	..	217790	566	5398	..	..	..	223753	5398
Rail	..	..	..	387	..	..	..	11340	..	11727	..
Domestic aviation	..	..	..	2117	..	..	..	..	..	2117	..
Domestic navigation	..	..	..	1446	..	..	..	..	..	1446	..
Pipeline transport	..	..	..	..	467	..	..	..	..	467	..
Transport, n.e.s	..	..	..	..	..	..	..	..	..	..	..
Other	102	..	..	116935	76421	30978	..	134726	15679	374841	31784
Agriculture, forestry, fishing	..	..	..	..	..	801	..	3488	14	4303	815
Commerce, public services	..	..	..	33024	26282	11112	..	62017	5720	138155	9866
Households	102	..	..	76411	48173	19065	..	69221	9945	222916	21103
Other consumers	..	..	..	7500	1967	..	..	..	..	9467	..
Non-energy use	..	..	..	19217	..	..	..	..	..	19217	..

Switzerland

Terajoules

2018	Primary coal and peat	Coal and peat products	Primary Oil	Oil Products	Natural Gas	Biofuels and waste	Nuclear	Electricity	Heat	Total energy	of which: renewables
Primary production	..	..	..	..	..	105069	276890	133384	2582	517925	205789
Imports	2979	383	131528	299592	119512	9023	..	111672	..	674688	9023
Exports	..	..	..	-18026	..	-100	..	-117385	..	-135511	-100
International marine bunkers	..	..	..	-129	..	..	..	..	..	-129	..
International aviation bunkers	..	..	..	-79160	..	..	..	..	..	-79160	..
Stock changes	898	..	-214	18845	..	-314	..	..	..	19215	-314
Total energy supply	3877	383	131313	221123	119512	113678	276890	127670	2582	997028	214398
Statistical difference	25	0	0	-13502	2	-2	0	0	0	-13477	133383
Transfers	..	..	1355	-1355	..	..	..	..	..	0	..
Transformation	..	..	-132668	132885	-6175	-56401	-276890	105246	21794	-212210	-32462
Electricity plants	..	..	..	-86	..	-2	-275540	91886	..	-183742	-2
CHP plants	..	..	..	-86	-4434	-55229	-1350	13370	19102	-28627	-31290
Heat plants	..	..	..	-172	-2911	..	..	-11	2692	-401	..
Coke ovens	..	..	..	..	..	..	..	..	..	..	..
Briquetting plants	..	..	..	..	..	..	..	..	..	..	..
Liquefaction plants	..	..	..	..	..	..	..	..	..	..	..
Gas works	..	..	..	..	..	..	..	..	..	..	..
Blast furnaces	..	..	..	..	..	..	..	..	..	..	..
NGL plants & gas blending	..	..	..	..	1170	-1170	..	..	..	0	-1170
Oil refineries	..	..	-132668	133358	..	..	..	..	..	690	..
Other transformation	..	..	..	-129	..	..	..	..	..	-129	..
Energy industries own use	..	..	..	-6525	-120	..	..	-10177	0	-16822	..
Losses	..	..	..	..	-264	..	..	-15217	-1930	-17411	..
Final consumption	3851	383	..	359630	112952	57279	..	207522	22446	764062	48554
Final energy consumption	3851	383	..	340227	112952	57279	..	207522	22446	744659	48554
Manufacturing, const., mining	3749	383	..	12154	39464	19432	..	62320	7171	144673	9965
Iron and steel	281	77	..	129	3848	123	..	5080	..	9537	123
Chemical and petrochemical	..	..	..	817	12299	3688	..	11221	1359	29385	..
Non-ferrous metals	..	..	..	86	1669	..	..	1534	3	3291	..
Non-metallic minerals	3443	281	..	1747	3947	5127	..	3730	4	18278	..
Transport equipment	..	..	..	..	..	..	..	..	..	..	..
Machinery	..	..	..	3526	4342	179	..	14602	430	23078	164
Mining and quarrying	..	..	..	..	..	..	..	..	..	..	..
Food and tobacco	26	26	..	1892	8366	141	..	9256	376	20081	26
Paper, pulp and printing	..	..	..	258	1714	1824	..	5537	2619	11951	1318
Wood and wood products	..	..	..	..	..	..	..	..	..	..	..
Textile and leather	..	..	..	344	673	70	..	677	2	1766	68
Construction	..	..	..	1849	995	2855	..	1847	19	7565	2855
Industries n.e.s	0	0	..	1506	1612	5425	..	8838	2359	19740	5411
Transport	..	..	..	222843	1086	6810	..	11120	..	241859	6810
Road	..	..	..	218140	593	6773	..	..	..	225505	6773
Rail	..	..	..	387	..	..	..	11120	..	11507	..
Domestic aviation	..	..	..	2779	..	..	..	..	..	2779	..
Domestic navigation	..	..	..	1537	..	37	..	..	..	1574	37
Pipeline transport	..	..	..	..	493	..	..	..	..	493	..
Transport, n.e.s	..	..	..	..	..	..	..	..	..	..	..
Other	102	..	..	105230	72401	31037	..	134082	15275	358128	31779
Agriculture, forestry, fishing	..	..	..	..	..	950	..	3481	14	4445	964
Commerce, public services	..	..	..	29627	24728	11195	..	61891	5466	132907	9838
Households	102	..	..	68155	46346	18892	..	68710	9795	212000	20977
Other consumers	..	..	..	7448	1328	..	..	..	..	8776	..
Non-energy use	..	..	..	19403	..	..	..	..	..	19403	..

Syrian Arab Republic

Terajoules

2017	Primary coal and peat	Coal and peat products	Primary Oil	Oil Products	Natural Gas	Biofuels and waste	Nuclear	Electricity	Heat	Total energy	of which: renewables
Primary production	..	..	44009	..	125541	234	..	2714	..	172499	2949
Imports	..	28	291870	47212	..	..	..	..	..	339110	..
Exports	..	..	..	-34963	..	..	..	-1955	..	-36918	..
International marine bunkers	..	..	..	-15604	..	..	..	..	..	-15604	..
International aviation bunkers	..	..	..	-353	..	..	..	..	..	-353	..
Stock changes	..	..	..	..	..	..	..	..	..	..	..
Total energy supply	..	28	335880	-3708	125541	234	..	760	..	458735	2949
Statistical difference	..	0	0	31631	-42	0	..	-4	..	31585	2714
Transfers	..	..	..	..	..	..	..	..	..	..	..
Transformation	..	-25	-335880	249017	-102736	-25	..	63569	..	-126080	-25
Electricity plants	..	..	..	-82221	-102736	..	..	63569	..	-121388	..
CHP plants	..	..	..	..	..	..	..	..	..	..	..
Heat plants	..	..	..	..	..	..	..	..	..	..	..
Coke ovens	..	..	..	..	..	..	..	..	..	..	..
Briquetting plants	..	..	..	..	..	..	..	..	..	..	..
Liquefaction plants	..	..	..	..	..	..	..	..	..	..	..
Gas works	..	..	..	..	..	..	..	..	..	..	..
Blast furnaces	..	-25	..	..	..	..	..	..	..	-25	..
NGL plants & gas blending	..	..	-3359	3595	..	..	..	..	..	236	..
Oil refineries	..	..	-332520	327644	..	..	..	..	..	-4876	..
Other transformation	..	..	..	..	..	-25	..	..	..	-25	-25
Energy industries own use	..	..	..	-9718	-1879	..	..	-7574	..	-19172	..
Losses	..	..	..	..	..	..	..	-8694	..	-8694	..
Final consumption	..	3	..	203960	20968	*209	..	48064	..	273204	*209
Final energy consumption	..	3	..	187715	7401	*209	..	48064	..	243391	*209
Manufacturing, const., mining	..	3	..	34407	7401	..	..	16164	..	57975	..
Iron and steel	..	3	..	..	..	..	..	..	..	3	..
Chemical and petrochemical	..	..	..	..	7401	..	..	..	..	7401	..
Non-ferrous metals	..	..	..	..	..	..	..	..	..	..	..
Non-metallic minerals	..	..	..	..	..	..	..	..	..	..	..
Transport equipment	..	..	..	..	..	..	..	..	..	..	..
Machinery	..	..	..	..	..	..	..	..	..	..	..
Mining and quarrying	..	..	..	..	..	..	..	..	..	..	..
Food and tobacco	..	..	..	..	..	..	..	..	..	..	..
Paper, pulp and printing	..	..	..	..	..	..	..	..	..	..	..
Wood and wood products	..	..	..	..	..	..	..	..	..	..	..
Textile and leather	..	..	..	..	..	..	..	..	..	..	..
Construction	..	..	..	..	..	..	..	..	..	..	..
Industries n.e.s	..	0	..	34407	0	..	..	16164	..	50571	..
Transport	..	..	..	94724	..	..	..	..	..	94724	..
Road	..	..	..	91240	..	..	..	..	..	91240	..
Rail	..	..	..	..	..	..	..	..	..	..	..
Domestic aviation	..	..	..	3484	..	..	..	..	..	3484	..
Domestic navigation	..	..	..	..	..	..	..	..	..	..	..
Pipeline transport	..	..	..	..	..	..	..	..	..	..	..
Transport, n.e.s	..	..	..	..	..	..	..	..	..	..	..
Other	..	..	..	58584	..	*209	..	31900	..	90692	*209
Agriculture, forestry, fishing	..	..	..	10191	..	..	..	..	..	10191	..
Commerce, public services	..	..	..	7052	..	..	..	4997	..	12049	..
Households	..	..	..	37705	..	..	..	21985	..	59690	..
Other consumers	..	..	..	3636	..	*209	..	4918	..	8762	*209
Non-energy use	..	..	..	16245	13568	..	..	..	..	29813	..

Syrian Arab Republic

Terajoules

2018	Primary coal and peat	Coal and peat products	Primary Oil	Oil Products	Natural Gas	Biofuels and waste	Nuclear	Electricity	Heat	Total energy	of which: renewables
Primary production	..	..	41598	..	124862	217	..	2714	..	169392	2931
Imports	..	28	273089	44561	..	..	..	..	..	317678	..
Exports	..	..	..	-32785	..	..	..	-1955	..	-34740	..
International marine bunkers	..	..	..	-15174	..	..	..	..	..	-15174	..
International aviation bunkers	..	..	..	-353	..	..	..	..	..	-353	..
Stock changes	..	..	..	..	..	..	..	..	..	..	..
Total energy supply	..	28	314687	-3752	124862	217	..	760	..	436803	2931
Statistical difference	..	0	0	25214	-42	1	..	-4	..	25169	2715
Transfers	..	..	..	..	..	..	..	..	..	..	..
Transformation	..	-25	-314687	229044	-102181	-14	..	62842	..	-125021	-14
Electricity plants	..	..	..	-81404	-102181	..	..	62842	..	-120743	..
CHP plants	..	..	..	..	..	..	..	..	..	..	..
Heat plants	..	..	..	..	..	..	..	..	..	..	..
Coke ovens	..	..	..	..	..	..	..	..	..	..	..
Briquetting plants	..	..	..	..	..	..	..	..	..	..	..
Liquefaction plants	..	..	..	..	..	..	..	..	..	..	..
Gas works	..	..	..	..	..	..	..	..	..	..	..
Blast furnaces	..	-25	..	..	..	..	..	..	..	-25	..
NGL plants & gas blending	..	..	-3359	3595	..	..	..	..	..	236	..
Oil refineries	..	..	-311328	306854	..	..	..	..	..	-4475	..
Other transformation	..	..	..	..	..	-14	..	..	..	-14	-14
Energy industries own use	..	..	..	-9139	-1869	..	..	-7492	..	-18500	..
Losses	..	..	..	..	..	..	..	-8575	..	-8575	..
Final consumption	..	3	..	190940	20855	*203	..	47538	..	259538	*203
Final energy consumption	..	3	..	175660	7360	*203	..	47538	..	230763	*203
Manufacturing, const., mining	..	3	..	32171	7360	..	..	15988	..	55522	..
Iron and steel	..	3	..	..	..	..	..	..	..	3	..
Chemical and petrochemical	..	..	..	..	7360	..	..	..	..	7360	..
Non-ferrous metals	..	..	..	..	..	..	..	..	..	..	..
Non-metallic minerals	..	..	..	..	..	..	..	..	..	..	..
Transport equipment	..	..	..	..	..	..	..	..	..	..	..
Machinery	..	..	..	..	..	..	..	..	..	..	..
Mining and quarrying	..	..	..	..	..	..	..	..	..	..	..
Food and tobacco	..	..	..	..	..	..	..	..	..	..	..
Paper, pulp and printing	..	..	..	..	..	..	..	..	..	..	..
Wood and wood products	..	..	..	..	..	..	..	..	..	..	..
Textile and leather	..	..	..	..	..	..	..	..	..	..	..
Construction	..	..	..	..	..	..	..	..	..	..	..
Industries n.e.s	..	0	..	32171	0	..	..	15988	..	48158	..
Transport	..	..	..	88695	..	..	..	..	..	88695	..
Road	..	..	..	85476	..	..	..	..	..	85476	..
Rail	..	..	..	..	..	..	..	..	..	..	..
Domestic aviation	..	..	..	3219	..	..	..	..	..	3219	..
Domestic navigation	..	..	..	..	..	..	..	..	..	..	..
Pipeline transport	..	..	..	..	..	..	..	..	..	..	..
Transport, n.e.s	..	..	..	..	..	..	..	..	..	..	..
Other	..	..	..	54794	..	*203	..	31550	..	86547	*203
Agriculture, forestry, fishing	..	..	..	9546	..	..	..	..	..	9546	..
Commerce, public services	..	..	..	6579	..	..	..	4943	..	11522	..
Households	..	..	..	35275	..	..	..	21744	..	57019	..
Other consumers	..	..	..	3394	..	*203	..	4864	..	8460	*203
Non-energy use	..	..	..	15280	13495	..	..	..	..	28775	..

Tajikistan

Terajoules

2017	Primary coal and peat	Coal and peat products	Primary Oil	Oil Products	Natural Gas	Biofuels and waste	Nuclear	Electricity	Heat	Total energy	of which: renewables
Primary production	43688	..	994	..	73	*50225	..	61679	..	156659	111904
Imports	165	..	..	35331	..	*3	..	396	..	35895	*3
Exports	-118	..	..	..	..	..	..	-5116	..	-5233	..
International marine bunkers	..	..	..	..	..	..	..	..	..	..	..
International aviation bunkers	..	..	..	-772	..	..	..	..	..	-772	..
Stock changes	..	..	..	..	..	..	..	..	..	..	..
Total energy supply	43735	..	994	34559	73	*50228	..	56959	..	186548	111907
Statistical difference	3141	..	0	1	0	0	..	-400	0	2742	61679
Transfers	..	..	..	..	..	..	..	..	..	..	..
Transformation	-13851	..	-994	942	..	..	..	3640	1793	-8471	..
Electricity plants	..	..	..	..	..	..	..	..	..	..	..
CHP plants	-13851	..	..	..	..	..	..	3640	1793	-8418	..
Heat plants	..	..	..	..	..	..	..	..	..	..	..
Coke ovens	..	..	..	..	..	..	..	..	..	..	..
Briquetting plants	..	..	..	..	..	..	..	..	..	..	..
Liquefaction plants	..	..	..	..	..	..	..	..	..	..	..
Gas works	..	..	..	..	..	..	..	..	..	..	..
Blast furnaces	..	..	..	..	..	..	..	..	..	..	..
NGL plants & gas blending	..	..	..	..	..	..	..	..	..	..	..
Oil refineries	..	..	-994	942	..	..	..	..	..	-52	..
Other transformation	..	..	..	..	..	..	..	..	..	..	..
Energy industries own use	..	..	..	..	..	..	..	-1071	0	-1071	..
Losses	..	..	..	..	..	..	..	*-10342	..	*-10342	..
Final consumption	26743	..	..	35499	73	*50228	..	49586	1793	163923	*50228
Final energy consumption	26743	..	..	34828	73	*50228	..	49586	1793	163252	*50228
Manufacturing, const., mining	15365	..	..	..	..	..	..	15941	..	31306	..
Iron and steel	..	..	..	..	..	..	..	..	..	..	..
Chemical and petrochemical	..	..	..	..	..	..	..	364	..	364	..
Non-ferrous metals	1052	..	..	..	..	..	..	13968	..	15020	..
Non-metallic minerals	13762	..	..	..	..	..	..	..	..	13762	..
Transport equipment	..	..	..	..	..	..	..	..	..	..	..
Machinery	..	..	..	..	..	..	..	72	..	72	..
Mining and quarrying	125	..	..	..	..	..	..	..	..	125	..
Food and tobacco	251	..	..	..	..	..	..	238	..	488	..
Paper, pulp and printing	..	..	..	..	..	..	..	..	..	..	..
Wood and wood products	..	..	..	..	..	..	..	4	..	4	..
Textile and leather	175	..	..	..	..	..	..	479	..	654	..
Construction	..	..	..	..	..	..	..	817	..	817	..
Industries n.e.s	0	..	..	..	..	..	..	0	..	0	..
Transport	..	..	..	16149	..	..	..	108	..	16257	..
Road	..	..	..	16149	..	..	..	..	..	16149	..
Rail	..	..	..	..	..	..	..	68	..	68	..
Domestic aviation	..	..	..	..	..	..	..	..	..	..	..
Domestic navigation	..	..	..	..	..	..	..	..	..	..	..
Pipeline transport	..	..	..	..	..	..	..	..	..	..	..
Transport, n.e.s	..	..	..	..	..	..	..	40	..	40	..
Other	11378	..	..	18679	73	*50228	..	33538	1793	115689	*50228
Agriculture, forestry, fishing	..	..	..	..	..	..	..	7603	..	7603	..
Commerce, public services	31	..	..	..	..	..	..	6408	..	6439	..
Households	11347	..	..	..	..	*50228	..	19526	..	*81102	*50228
Other consumers	..	..	..	18679	73	..	..	..	1793	20545	..
Non-energy use	..	..	..	671	..	..	..	..	..	671	..

Tajikistan

Terajoules

	Primary coal and peat	Coal and peat products	Primary Oil	Oil Products	Natural Gas	Biofuels and waste	Nuclear	Electricity	Heat	Total energy	of which: renewables
2018											
Primary production	47154	..	986	..	22	*50225	..	66220	..	164607	116445
Imports	183	..	1912	40858	1966	*3	..	2012	..	46934	*3
Exports	-1084	..	..	..	..	..	..	-10602	..	-11686	..
International marine bunkers	..	..	..	..	..	..	..	..	..	..	..
International aviation bunkers	..	..	..	-1274	..	..	..	..	..	-1274	..
Stock changes	..	..	..	..	..	..	..	..	..	..	..
Total energy supply	46254	..	2898	39583	1987	*50228	..	57630	..	198581	116448
Statistical difference	37	..	986	0	0	0	..	1061	0	2083	66220
Transfers	..	..	..	..	..	..	..	..	..	..	..
Transformation	-21238	..	-1912	1922	..	..	..	4853	*3499	-12876	..
Electricity plants	..	..	..	..	..	..	..	..	..	..	..
CHP plants	-21238	..	..	..	..	..	..	4853	*3499	-12886	..
Heat plants	..	..	..	..	..	..	..	..	..	..	..
Coke ovens	..	..	..	..	..	..	..	..	..	..	..
Briquetting plants	..	..	..	..	..	..	..	..	..	..	..
Liquefaction plants	..	..	..	..	..	..	..	..	..	..	..
Gas works	..	..	..	..	..	..	..	..	..	..	..
Blast furnaces	..	..	..	..	..	..	..	..	..	..	..
NGL plants & gas blending	..	..	..	..	..	..	..	..	..	..	..
Oil refineries	..	..	-1912	1922	..	..	..	..	..	10	..
Other transformation	..	..	..	..	..	..	..	..	..	..	..
Energy industries own use	..	..	..	..	..	..	..	-736	0	-736	..
Losses	..	..	..	..	..	..	..	*-10683	..	*-10683	..
Final consumption	24979	..	..	41505	1987	*50228	..	50004	*3499	172203	*50228
Final energy consumption	24979	..	..	40709	1987	*50228	..	50004	*3499	171407	*50228
Manufacturing, const., mining	13845	..	..	..	1966	..	..	*12376	..	28187	..
Iron and steel	..	..	..	..	..	..	..	..	..	..	..
Chemical and petrochemical	..	..	..	..	..	..	..	..	..	..	..
Non-ferrous metals	275	..	..	..	1966	..	..	12376	..	14617	..
Non-metallic minerals	13385	..	..	..	..	..	..	..	..	13385	..
Transport equipment	..	..	..	..	..	..	..	..	..	..	..
Machinery	..	..	..	..	..	..	..	..	..	..	..
Mining and quarrying	185	..	..	..	..	..	..	..	..	185	..
Food and tobacco	..	..	..	..	..	..	..	..	..	..	..
Paper, pulp and printing	..	..	..	..	..	..	..	..	..	..	..
Wood and wood products	..	..	..	..	..	..	..	..	..	..	..
Textile and leather	..	..	..	..	..	..	..	..	..	..	..
Construction	..	..	..	..	..	..	..	..	..	..	..
Industries n.e.s	0	..	..	..	0	..	..	0	..	0	..
Transport	..	..	..	17177	..	..	..	25	..	17202	..
Road	..	..	..	17177	..	..	..	..	..	17177	..
Rail	..	..	..	..	..	..	..	..	..	..	..
Domestic aviation	..	..	..	..	..	..	..	..	..	..	..
Domestic navigation	..	..	..	..	..	..	..	..	..	..	..
Pipeline transport	..	..	..	..	..	..	..	..	..	..	..
Transport, n.e.s	..	..	..	..	..	..	..	25	..	25	..
Other	11134	..	..	23533	22	*50228	..	37602	*3499	126018	*50228
Agriculture, forestry, fishing	..	..	..	..	..	..	..	8068	..	8068	..
Commerce, public services	..	..	..	..	..	..	..	9450	..	9450	..
Households	11134	..	..	..	..	*50228	..	20084	..	*81447	*50228
Other consumers	..	..	..	23533	22	..	..	..	*3499	27053	..
Non-energy use	..	..	..	796	..	..	..	..	..	796	..

Thailand

Terajoules

2017	Primary coal and peat	Coal and peat products	Primary Oil	Oil Products	Natural Gas	Biofuels and waste	Nuclear	Electricity	Heat	Total energy	of which: renewables
Primary production	171874	..	833631	..	989068	1100627	..	37246	424	3132870	1136205
Imports	615925	2482	1957559	291338	518755	2921	..	88038	..	3477017	2921
Exports	-1187	..	-72100	-512880	..	-679	..	-3982	..	-590827	-679
International marine bunkers	..	..	..	-47066	..	..	..	..	..	-47066	..
International aviation bunkers	..	..	..	-182971	..	..	..	..	..	-182971	..
Stock changes	-102088	-846	266709	-155923	..	-1834	..	..	..	6017	-1834
Total energy supply	684525	1636	2985800	-607502	1507822	1101035	..	121302	424	5795040	1136613
Statistical difference	10	0	2341	35491	49489	-37	..	16996	0	104289	37212
Transfers	..	..	27979	-27219	..	..	..	..	..	760	..
Transformation	-375034	-929	-2979600	2933388	-920541	*-491222	..	616921	-36	-1217053	*-490494
Electricity plants	-375034	..	..	-2725	-920541	*-350090	..	616921	-36	-1031505	*-349362
CHP plants	..	..	..	..	..	..	..	..	..	..	..
Heat plants	..	..	..	..	..	..	..	..	..	..	..
Coke ovens	..	..	..	..	..	..	..	..	..	..	..
Briquetting plants	..	..	..	..	..	..	..	..	..	..	..
Liquefaction plants	..	..	..	..	..	..	..	..	..	..	..
Gas works	..	..	..	..	..	..	..	..	..	..	..
Blast furnaces	..	-929	..	..	..	..	..	..	..	-929	..
NGL plants & gas blending	..	..	-300825	319824	..	..	..	..	..	18999	..
Oil refineries	..	..	-2650391	2589069	..	..	..	..	..	-61322	..
Other transformation	..	..	-28383	27219	..	*-141132	..	..	..	*-142296	*-141132
Energy industries own use	..	..	..	-35213	-247516	..	..	-10980	..	-293709	..
Losses	..	..	-8545	..	..	..	..	-42912	..	-51457	..
Final consumption	309480	707	23293	2227962	290276	*609849	..	667336	388	4129292	*608906
Final energy consumption	309480	707	..	1380601	217060	*609849	..	667336	388	3185421	*608906
Manufacturing, const., mining	309480	707	..	167875	134809	*368032	..	315986	..	1296890	*366701
Iron and steel	..	707	..	14774	14844	..	..	32137	..	62461	..
Chemical and petrochemical	42	..	..	18687	44815	..	..	50339	..	113882	..
Non-ferrous metals	686	..	..	..	..	..	..	..	..	686	..
Non-metallic minerals	261541	..	..	11380	30823	..	..	32332	..	336076	..
Transport equipment	..	..	..	..	..	..	..	..	..	..	..
Machinery	..	..	..	12209	11501	..	..	75769	..	99479	..
Mining and quarrying	..	..	..	597	..	..	..	..	..	597	..
Food and tobacco	16222	..	..	37845	6837	*184582	..	63252	..	*308738	*184582
Paper, pulp and printing	349	..	..	5667	16379	..	..	11459	..	33854	..
Wood and wood products	..	..	..	4815	54	..	..	8276	..	13146	..
Textile and leather	42	..	..	5066	2723	..	..	32141	..	39972	..
Construction	..	..	..	4927	..	..	..	..	..	4927	..
Industries n.e.s	30597	0	..	51911	6833	*183450	..	10282	..	283073	*182119
Transport	..	..	..	998238	82153	74481	..	882	..	1155754	74481
Road	..	..	..	947191	82153	74481	..	..	..	1103824	74481
Rail	..	..	..	2924	..	..	..	882	..	3806	..
Domestic aviation	..	..	..	39911	..	..	..	..	..	39911	..
Domestic navigation	..	..	..	8213	..	..	..	..	..	8213	..
Pipeline transport	..	..	..	..	..	..	..	..	..	..	..
Transport, n.e.s	..	..	..	..	..	..	..	..	..	..	..
Other	..	..	..	214488	98	*167336	..	350467	388	732778	*167724
Agriculture, forestry, fishing	..	..	..	112841	..	..	..	1073	..	113913	..
Commerce, public services	..	..	..	32826	98	..	..	163073	388	196385	388
Households	..	..	..	68822	..	*167336	..	159746	..	395904	*167336
Other consumers	..	..	..	..	..	..	..	26575	..	26575	..
Non-energy use	..	..	23293	847361	73216	..	..	..	..	943871	..

Thailand

Terajoules

2018	Primary coal and peat	Coal and peat products	Primary Oil	Oil Products	Natural Gas	Biofuels and waste	Nuclear	Electricity	Heat	Total energy	of which: renewables
Primary production	157000	..	814112	..	957399	1073050	..	49475	459	3051496	1118969
Imports	681662	508	2069527	294259	529419	3629	..	95994	..	3674997	3629
Exports	-2216	..	-65557	-557715	..	-708	..	-3589	..	-629785	-708
International marine bunkers	..	..	..	-56196	..	..	..	..	..	-56196	..
International aviation bunkers	..	..	..	-197744	..	..	..	..	..	-197744	..
Stock changes	-175269	1213	173050	-163974	..	8	..	..	..	-164973	8
Total energy supply	661177	1720	2991133	-681371	1486818	1075978	..	141880	459	5677793	1121897
Statistical difference	16	0	2	-18729	-8824	0	..	15084	0	-12451	49479
Transfers	..	..	30189	-29369	..	..	..	..	..	820	..
Transformation	-379416	-877	-2990116	2990172	-904968	*-439244	..	606791	-36	-1117694	*-437861
Electricity plants	-379416	..	..	-2108	-904968	*-361166	..	606791	-36	-1040904	*-359783
CHP plants	..	..	..	..	..	..	..	..	..	..	..
Heat plants	..	..	..	..	..	..	..	..	..	..	..
Coke ovens	..	..	..	..	..	..	..	..	..	..	..
Briquetting plants	..	..	..	..	..	..	..	..	..	..	..
Liquefaction plants	..	..	..	..	..	..	..	..	..	..	..
Gas works	..	..	..	..	..	..	..	..	..	..	..
Blast furnaces	..	-877	..	..	..	..	..	..	..	-877	..
NGL plants & gas blending	..	..	-307323	326728	..	..	..	..	..	19405	..
Oil refineries	..	..	-2652125	2636184	..	..	..	..	..	-15941	..
Other transformation	..	..	-30667	29369	..	*-78077	..	..	..	*-79376	*-78077
Energy industries own use	..	..	..	-33040	-288997	..	..	-10159	..	-332196	..
Losses	..	..	-8883	..	..	..	..	-46454	..	-55337	..
Final consumption	281746	843	22321	2265122	301676	*636733	..	676973	423	4185837	*634557
Final energy consumption	281746	843	..	1356419	216966	*636733	..	676973	423	3170103	*634557
Manufacturing, const., mining	281746	843	..	120065	142651	*402728	..	316184	..	1264217	*400129
Iron and steel	..	843	..	11937	15077	..	..	32155	..	60011	..
Chemical and petrochemical	42	..	..	15897	51835	..	..	50371	..	118145	..
Non-ferrous metals	580	..	..	..	..	..	..	..	..	580	..
Non-metallic minerals	238164	..	..	8390	32029	..	..	32353	..	310936	..
Transport equipment	..	..	..	..	..	..	..	..	..	..	..
Machinery	..	..	..	8833	11917	..	..	75816	..	96565	..
Mining and quarrying	..	..	..	382	..	..	..	..	..	382	..
Food and tobacco	14745	..	..	24880	6987	*207837	..	63292	..	*317739	*207837
Paper, pulp and printing	371	..	..	3785	15484	..	..	11466	..	31106	..
Wood and wood products	..	..	..	2754	10	..	..	8284	..	11047	..
Textile and leather	42	..	..	3616	2413	..	..	32159	..	38230	..
Construction	..	..	..	4026	..	..	..	..	..	4026	..
Industries n.e.s	27801	0	..	35566	6900	*194891	..	10289	..	275448	*192292
Transport	..	..	..	1011920	74206	81368	..	778	..	1168272	81368
Road	..	..	..	963443	74206	81368	..	..	..	1119017	81368
Rail	..	..	..	3311	..	..	..	778	..	4089	..
Domestic aviation	..	..	..	36824	..	..	..	..	..	36824	..
Domestic navigation	..	..	..	8342	..	..	..	..	..	8342	..
Pipeline transport	..	..	..	..	..	..	..	..	..	..	..
Transport, n.e.s	..	..	..	..	..	..	..	..	..	..	..
Other	..	..	..	224434	109	*152637	..	360011	423	737614	*153060
Agriculture, forestry, fishing	..	..	..	122172	..	..	..	1314	..	123486	..
Commerce, public services	..	..	..	33015	109	..	..	169085	423	202632	423
Households	..	..	..	69247	..	*152637	..	162738	..	384622	*152637
Other consumers	..	..	..	..	..	..	..	26874	..	26874	..
Non-energy use	..	..	22321	908703	84711	..	..	..	..	1015734	..

Timor-Leste

Terajoules

	All Coal	All Oil	Natural Gas	Primary biofuels / Waste	Charcoal	Electricity	Total energy	of which: renewables
2017								
Primary production	..	85040	202987	813	..	9	288849	822
Imports	..	*7187	..	..	..	..	*7187	..
Exports	..	*-85040	-202987	..	..	..	-288027	..
International marine bunkers	..	..	..	..	..	..	..	..
International aviation bunkers	..	*-136	..	..	..	..	*-136	..
Stock changes	..	..	..	..	..	..	..	..
Total energy supply	..	*7051	0	813	..	9	7873	822
Statistical Difference	..	0	0	0	..	0	0	9
Transfers	..	..	..	..	..	..	..	..
Transformation	..	*-4812	..	..	..	1538	*-3274	..
Electricity plants	..	*-4812	..	..	..	1538	*-3274	..
Charcoal plants	..	..	..	..	..	..	..	..
Other transformation	..	0	..	..	..	..	0	..
Energy industries own use	..	..	..	..	..	-84	-84	..
Losses	..	..	..	..	..	*-306	*-306	..
Final consumption	..	*2239	..	*813	..	*1156	*4208	*813
Final energy consumption	..	*2239	..	*813	..	*1156	*4208	*813
Manufacturing, const., mining	..	..	..	..	..	..	..	..
Transport	..	*992	..	..	..	..	*992	..
Road	..	*992	..	..	..	..	*992	..
Domestic aviation	..	..	..	..	..	..	..	..
Domestic navigation	..	..	..	..	..	..	..	..
Other transport	..	..	..	..	..	..	..	..
Other	..	*1247	..	*813	..	*1156	*3216	*813
Agriculture, forestry, fishing	..	..	..	..	..	..	..	..
Commerce and public services	..	..	..	..	..	*303	*303	..
Households	..	..	..	*813	..	457	*1270	*813
Other consumers	..	*1247	..	..	..	*396	*1643	..
Non-energy use	..	..	..	..	..	..	..	..
2018								
Primary production	..	69406	*194910	776	..	9	*265101	785
Imports	..	*7285	..	..	..	..	*7285	..
Exports	..	*-69406	*-194910	..	..	..	*-264316	..
International marine bunkers	..	..	..	..	..	..	..	..
International aviation bunkers	..	*-139	..	..	..	..	*-139	..
Stock changes	..	..	..	..	..	..	..	..
Total energy supply	..	*7146	0	776	..	9	*7931	785
Statistical Difference	..	0	0	0	..	0	0	9
Transfers	..	..	..	..	..	..	..	..
Transformation	..	*-4872	..	..	..	1622	*-3250	..
Electricity plants	..	*-4872	..	..	..	1622	*-3250	..
Charcoal plants	..	..	..	..	..	..	..	..
Other transformation	..	0	..	..	..	..	0	..
Energy industries own use	..	..	..	..	..	-99	-99	..
Losses	..	..	..	..	..	*-324	*-324	..
Final consumption	..	*2274	..	*776	..	1208	*4258	*776
Final energy consumption	..	*2274	..	*776	..	1208	*4258	*776
Manufacturing, const., mining	..	..	..	..	..	..	..	..
Transport	..	*1010	..	..	..	..	*1010	..
Road	..	*1010	..	..	..	..	*1010	..
Domestic aviation	..	..	..	..	..	..	..	..
Domestic navigation	..	..	..	..	..	..	..	..
Other transport	..	..	..	..	..	..	..	..
Other	..	*1264	..	*776	..	1208	*3248	*776
Agriculture, forestry, fishing	..	..	..	..	..	..	..	..
Commerce and public services	..	..	..	..	..	239	239	..
Households	..	..	..	*776	..	451	*1228	*776
Other consumers	..	*1264	..	..	..	*517	*1781	..
Non-energy use	..	..	..	..	..	..	..	..

Togo

Terajoules

	Primary coal and peat	Coal and peat products	Primary Oil	Oil Products	Natural Gas	Biofuels and waste	Nuclear	Electricity	Heat	Total energy	of which: renewables
2017											
Primary production	..	..	..	..	..	106949	..	738	..	107687	107687
Imports	..	..	..	21735	0	..	..	2688	..	24423	..
Exports	..	..	..	..	..	..	..	..	..	..	..
International marine bunkers	..	..	..	-817	..	..	..	..	..	-817	..
International aviation bunkers	..	..	..	-2381	..	..	..	..	..	-2381	..
Stock changes	..	..	..	867	..	..	..	..	..	867	..
Total energy supply	..	..	..	19403	0	106949	..	3426	..	129778	107687
Statistical difference	..	..	..	15	0	0	..	-39	..	-24	738
Transfers	..	..	..	..	..	..	..	..	..	..	..
Transformation	..	..	..	-3879	0	-47010	..	1745	..	-49144	-47010
Electricity plants	..	..	..	-3879	0	..	..	1745	..	-2135	..
CHP plants	..	..	..	..	..	..	..	..	..	..	..
Heat plants	..	..	..	..	..	..	..	..	..	..	..
Coke ovens	..	..	..	..	..	..	..	..	..	..	..
Briquetting plants	..	..	..	..	..	..	..	..	..	..	..
Liquefaction plants	..	..	..	..	..	..	..	..	..	..	..
Gas works	..	..	..	..	..	..	..	..	..	..	..
Blast furnaces	..	..	..	..	..	..	..	..	..	..	..
NGL plants & gas blending	..	..	..	..	..	..	..	..	..	..	..
Oil refineries	..	..	..	..	..	..	..	..	..	..	..
Other transformation	..	..	..	..	..	-47010	..	..	..	-47010	-47010
Energy industries own use	..	..	..	..	..	..	..	-47	..	-47	..
Losses	..	..	..	..	..	..	..	-436	..	-436	..
Final consumption	..	..	..	15509	..	59939	..	4727	..	80176	59939
Final energy consumption	..	..	..	15509	..	59939	..	4727	..	80176	59939
Manufacturing, const., mining	..	..	..	2384	..	266	..	1570	..	4220	266
Iron and steel	..	..	..	..	..	..	..	..	..	..	..
Chemical and petrochemical	..	..	..	..	..	..	..	..	..	..	..
Non-ferrous metals	..	..	..	..	..	..	..	..	..	..	..
Non-metallic minerals	..	..	..	2384	..	..	..	734	..	3118	..
Transport equipment	..	..	..	..	..	..	..	..	..	..	..
Machinery	..	..	..	..	..	..	..	..	..	..	..
Mining and quarrying	..	..	..	..	..	..	..	515	..	515	..
Food and tobacco	..	..	..	..	..	..	..	14	..	14	..
Paper, pulp and printing	..	..	..	..	..	..	..	..	..	..	..
Wood and wood products	..	..	..	..	..	..	..	..	..	..	..
Textile and leather	..	..	..	..	..	..	..	..	..	..	..
Construction	..	..	..	..	..	..	..	122	..	122	..
Industries n.e.s	..	..	..	0	..	266	..	184	..	450	266
Transport	..	..	..	12208	..	..	..	..	..	12208	..
Road	..	..	..	12208	..	..	..	..	..	12208	..
Rail	..	..	..	..	..	..	..	..	..	..	..
Domestic aviation	..	..	..	..	..	..	..	..	..	..	..
Domestic navigation	..	..	..	..	..	..	..	..	..	..	..
Pipeline transport	..	..	..	..	..	..	..	..	..	..	..
Transport, n.e.s	..	..	..	..	..	..	..	..	..	..	..
Other	..	..	..	918	..	59673	..	3157	..	63748	59673
Agriculture, forestry, fishing	..	..	..	..	..	..	..	..	..	..	..
Commerce, public services	..	..	..	95	..	*7413	..	608	..	*8116	*7413
Households	..	..	..	823	..	52260	..	2264	..	55347	52260
Other consumers	..	..	..	..	..	..	..	284	..	284	..
Non-energy use	..	..	..	..	..	..	..	..	..	..	..

Togo

Terajoules

2018	Primary coal and peat	Coal and peat products	Primary Oil	Oil Products	Natural Gas	Biofuels and waste	Nuclear	Electricity	Heat	Total energy	of which: renewables
Primary production	..	..	..	..	..	113531	..	717	..	114248	114248
Imports	..	..	..	20836	1590	..	..	3175	..	25601	..
Exports	..	..	..	..	..	..	..	..	..	..	..
International marine bunkers	..	..	..	..	..	..	..	..	..	..	..
International aviation bunkers	..	..	..	-2734	..	..	..	..	..	-2734	..
Stock changes	..	..	..	742	..	..	..	..	..	742	..
Total energy supply	..	..	..	18844	1590	113531	..	3892	..	137857	114248
Statistical difference	..	..	..	355	0	0	..	76	..	430	717
Transfers	..	..	..	..	..	..	..	..	..	..	..
Transformation	..	..	..	-1488	-1590	-49771	..	1401	..	-51447	-49771
Electricity plants	..	..	..	-1488	-1590	..	..	1401	..	-1676	..
CHP plants	..	..	..	..	..	..	..	..	..	..	..
Heat plants	..	..	..	..	..	..	..	..	..	..	..
Coke ovens	..	..	..	..	..	..	..	..	..	..	..
Briquetting plants	..	..	..	..	..	..	..	..	..	..	..
Liquefaction plants	..	..	..	..	..	..	..	..	..	..	..
Gas works	..	..	..	..	..	..	..	..	..	..	..
Blast furnaces	..	..	..	..	..	..	..	..	..	..	..
NGL plants & gas blending	..	..	..	..	..	..	..	..	..	..	..
Oil refineries	..	..	..	..	..	..	..	..	..	..	..
Other transformation	..	..	..	..	..	-49771	..	..	..	-49771	-49771
Energy industries own use	..	..	..	..	..	..	..	-49	..	-49	..
Losses	..	..	..	..	..	..	..	-709	..	-709	..
Final consumption	..	..	..	17001	..	63760	..	4460	..	85222	63760
Final energy consumption	..	..	..	17001	..	63760	..	4460	..	85222	63760
Manufacturing, const., mining	..	..	..	1496	..	349	..	2174	..	4020	349
Iron and steel	..	..	..	172	..	..	..	..	..	172	..
Chemical and petrochemical	..	..	..	129	..	..	..	..	..	129	..
Non-ferrous metals	..	..	..	215	..	..	..	..	..	215	..
Non-metallic minerals	..	..	..	808	..	..	..	752	..	1560	..
Transport equipment	..	..	..	..	..	..	..	..	..	..	..
Machinery	..	..	..	..	..	..	..	..	..	..	..
Mining and quarrying	..	..	..	..	..	..	..	..	..	..	..
Food and tobacco	..	..	..	..	..	..	..	367	..	367	..
Paper, pulp and printing	..	..	..	..	..	..	..	..	..	..	..
Wood and wood products	..	..	..	..	..	..	..	..	..	..	..
Textile and leather	..	..	..	..	..	..	..	22	..	22	..
Construction	..	..	..	..	..	..	..	..	..	..	..
Industries n.e.s	..	..	..	172	..	349	..	1033	..	1555	349
Transport	..	..	..	13926	..	..	..	..	..	13926	..
Road	..	..	..	13926	..	..	..	..	..	13926	..
Rail	..	..	..	..	..	..	..	..	..	..	..
Domestic aviation	..	..	..	..	..	..	..	..	..	..	..
Domestic navigation	..	..	..	..	..	..	..	..	..	..	..
Pipeline transport	..	..	..	..	..	..	..	..	..	..	..
Transport, n.e.s	..	..	..	..	..	..	..	..	..	..	..
Other	..	..	..	1579	..	63411	..	2286	..	67275	63411
Agriculture, forestry, fishing	..	..	..	..	..	..	..	4	..	4	..
Commerce, public services	..	..	..	95	..	*8129	..	702	..	*8926	*8129
Households	..	..	..	1484	..	55282	..	1580	..	58346	55282
Other consumers	..	..	..	..	..	..	..	..	..	..	..
Non-energy use	..	..	..	..	..	..	..	..	..	..	..

Tonga

Terajoules

	All Coal	All Oil	Natural Gas	Primary biofuels / Waste	Charcoal	Electricity	Total energy	of which: renewables
2017								
Primary production	..	..	..	19	..	15	34	34
Imports	..	2337	..	0	1	..	2337	1
Exports	..	..	..	..	..	..	..	..
International marine bunkers	..	*-16	..	..	..	..	*-16	..
International aviation bunkers	..	*-206	..	..	..	..	*-206	..
Stock changes	..	0	..	..	..	..	0	..
Total energy supply	..	2114	..	19	1	15	2149	35
Statistical Difference	..	0	..	0	0	-2	-2	15
Transfers	..	..	..	..	..	..	..	..
Transformation	..	*-542	..	*-14	7	208	*-340	*-6
Electricity plants	..	*-542	..	..	..	208	*-334	..
Charcoal plants	..	..	..	*-14	7	..	*-6	*-6
Other transformation	..	0	..	0	..	..	0	0
Energy industries own use	..	..	..	..	..	-7	-7	..
Losses	..	..	..	..	..	-21	-21	..
Final consumption	..	*1572	..	*5	*8	*198	*1783	*13
Final energy consumption	..	*1571	..	*5	*8	*198	*1782	*13
Manufacturing, const., mining	..	..	..	..	..	..	..	..
Transport	..	*1474	..	..	..	..	*1474	..
Road	..	*747	..	..	..	..	*747	..
Domestic aviation	..	*4	..	..	..	..	*4	..
Domestic navigation	..	..	..	..	..	..	..	..
Other transport	..	*722	..	..	..	..	*722	..
Other	..	*97	..	*5	*8	*198	*309	*13
Agriculture, forestry, fishing	..	..	..	..	..	..	..	..
Commerce and public services	..	..	..	..	..	*65	*65	..
Households	..	*97	..	*5	*8	*72	*182	*13
Other consumers	..	..	..	..	..	*61	*61	..
Non-energy use	..	*1	..	..	..	..	*1	..
2018								
Primary production	..	..	..	19	..	15	34	34
Imports	..	2083	..	0	1	..	2083	1
Exports	..	..	..	..	..	..	..	..
International marine bunkers	..	*-16	..	..	..	..	*-16	..
International aviation bunkers	..	*-163	..	..	..	..	*-163	..
Stock changes	..	..	..	..	..	..	..	..
Total energy supply	..	1904	..	19	1	15	1938	34
Statistical Difference	..	0	..	0	0	6	6	15
Transfers	..	..	..	..	..	..	..	..
Transformation	..	*-594	..	*-14	7	229	*-372	*-6
Electricity plants	..	*-594	..	..	..	229	*-365	..
Charcoal plants	..	..	..	*-14	7	..	*-6	*-6
Other transformation	..	0	..	0	..	..	0	0
Energy industries own use	..	..	..	..	..	-7	-7	..
Losses	..	..	..	..	..	-21	-21	..
Final consumption	..	*1310	..	*5	*8	*210	*1533	*13
Final energy consumption	..	*1298	..	*5	*8	*210	*1521	*13
Manufacturing, const., mining	..	..	..	..	..	..	..	..
Transport	..	*1190	..	..	..	..	*1190	..
Road	..	*758	..	..	..	..	*758	..
Domestic aviation	..	*8	..	..	..	..	*8	..
Domestic navigation	..	..	..	..	..	..	..	..
Other transport	..	*424	..	..	..	..	*424	..
Other	..	*108	..	*5	*8	*210	*331	*13
Agriculture, forestry, fishing	..	..	..	..	..	..	..	..
Commerce and public services	..	..	..	..	..	*69	*69	..
Households	..	*108	..	*5	*8	*76	*197	*13
Other consumers	..	..	..	..	..	*65	*65	..
Non-energy use	..	*12	..	..	..	..	*12	..

Trinidad and Tobago

Terajoules

2017	Primary coal and peat	Coal and peat products	Primary Oil	Oil Products	Natural Gas	Biofuels and waste	Nuclear	Electricity	Heat	Total energy	of which: renewables
Primary production	..	..	197303	..	1169559	281	..	18	..	1367161	299
Imports	..	..	192634	89	..	..	..	..	..	192723	..
Exports	..	..	-59558	-219019	-536972	..	..	..	..	-815550	..
International marine bunkers	..	..	..	-21490	..	..	..	..	..	-21490	..
International aviation bunkers	..	..	..	-9878	..	..	..	..	..	-9878	..
Stock changes	..	..	..	-9549	..	..	..	..	..	-9549	..
Total energy supply	..	..	330379	-259848	632587	281	..	18	..	703417	299
Statistical difference	..	..	3154	-2023	6842	0	..	4	..	7977	18
Transfers	..	..	..	..	..	..	..	..	..	..	..
Transformation	..	..	-327225	314359	-91275	*-51	..	35741	..	-68451	*-51
Electricity plants	..	..	..	-462	-91275	..	..	35741	..	-55996	..
CHP plants	..	..	..	..	..	..	..	..	..	..	..
Heat plants	..	..	..	..	..	..	..	..	..	..	..
Coke ovens	..	..	..	..	..	..	..	..	..	..	..
Briquetting plants	..	..	..	..	..	..	..	..	..	..	..
Liquefaction plants	..	..	..	..	..	..	..	..	..	..	..
Gas works	..	..	..	..	..	..	..	..	..	..	..
Blast furnaces	..	..	..	..	..	..	..	..	..	..	..
NGL plants & gas blending	..	..	-42123	43859	..	..	..	..	..	1736	..
Oil refineries	..	..	-285102	270962	..	..	..	..	..	-14141	..
Other transformation	..	..	..	..	..	*-51	..	..	..	*-51	*-51
Energy industries own use	..	..	..	-3520	-120059	..	..	-1303	..	-124882	..
Losses	..	..	..	..	-3610	..	..	-907	..	-4517	..
Final consumption	..	..	..	53013	410801	*231	..	33545	..	497589	*231
Final energy consumption	..	..	..	52451	31215	*231	..	33545	..	117441	*231
Manufacturing, const., mining	..	..	..	6769	28317	..	..	20279	..	55364	..
Iron and steel	..	..	..	..	15936	..	..	..	..	15936	..
Chemical and petrochemical	..	..	..	..	..	..	..	..	..	..	..
Non-ferrous metals	..	..	..	..	..	..	..	..	..	..	..
Non-metallic minerals	..	..	..	..	3984	..	..	..	..	3984	..
Transport equipment	..	..	..	..	..	..	..	..	..	..	..
Machinery	..	..	..	..	..	..	..	..	..	..	..
Mining and quarrying	..	..	..	..	..	..	..	..	..	..	..
Food and tobacco	..	..	..	..	..	..	..	..	..	..	..
Paper, pulp and printing	..	..	..	..	..	..	..	..	..	..	..
Wood and wood products	..	..	..	..	..	..	..	..	..	..	..
Textile and leather	..	..	..	..	..	..	..	..	..	..	..
Construction	..	..	..	..	..	..	..	..	..	..	..
Industries n.e.s	..	..	..	6769	8396	..	..	20279	..	35444	..
Transport	..	..	..	42350	..	..	..	..	..	42350	..
Road	..	..	..	38027	..	..	..	..	..	38027	..
Rail	..	..	..	..	..	..	..	..	..	..	..
Domestic aviation	..	..	..	4322	..	..	..	..	..	4322	..
Domestic navigation	..	..	..	..	..	..	..	..	..	..	..
Pipeline transport	..	..	..	..	..	..	..	..	..	..	..
Transport, n.e.s	..	..	..	..	..	..	..	..	..	..	..
Other	..	..	..	3332	2898	*231	..	13266	..	19727	*231
Agriculture, forestry, fishing	..	..	..	..	..	..	..	..	..	..	..
Commerce, public services	..	..	..	301	..	..	..	3654	..	3955	..
Households	..	..	..	3031	2898	*231	..	9612	..	15772	*231
Other consumers	..	..	..	..	..	..	..	..	..	..	..
Non-energy use	..	..	..	563	379586	..	..	..	..	380149	..

Trinidad and Tobago

Terajoules

2018	Primary coal and peat	Coal and peat products	Primary Oil	Oil Products	Natural Gas	Biofuels and waste	Nuclear	Electricity	Heat	Total energy	of which: renewables
Primary production	..	..	174198	..	1260160	279	..	18	..	1434655	297
Imports	..	..	136756	..	..	..	..	..	..	136756	..
Exports	..	..	-48095	-170692	-605654	..	..	..	..	-824441	..
International marine bunkers	..	..	..	-17400	..	..	..	..	..	-17400	..
International aviation bunkers	..	..	..	-7982	..	..	..	..	..	-7982	..
Stock changes	..	..	..	-6226	..	..	..	..	..	-6226	..
Total energy supply	..	..	262859	-202300	654506	279	..	18	..	715362	297
Statistical difference	..	..	-1635	1925	5809	0	..	0	..	6099	18
Transfers	..	..	..	..	..	..	..	..	..	..	..
Transformation	..	..	-264494	252922	-87652	*-51	..	33192	..	-66083	*-51
Electricity plants	..	..	..	-301	-87652	..	..	33192	..	-54761	..
CHP plants	..	..	..	..	..	..	..	..	..	..	..
Heat plants	..	..	..	..	..	..	..	..	..	..	..
Coke ovens	..	..	..	..	..	..	..	..	..	..	..
Briquetting plants	..	..	..	..	..	..	..	..	..	..	..
Liquefaction plants	..	..	..	..	..	..	..	..	..	..	..
Gas works	..	..	..	..	..	..	..	..	..	..	..
Blast furnaces	..	..	..	..	..	..	..	..	..	..	..
NGL plants & gas blending	..	..	-37216	38663	..	..	..	..	..	1446	..
Oil refineries	..	..	-227278	214560	..	..	..	..	..	-12718	..
Other transformation	..	..	..	..	..	*-51	..	..	..	*-51	*-51
Energy industries own use	..	..	..	-5302	-126710	..	..	-1210	..	-133222	..
Losses	..	..	..	..	-18831	..	..	-1534	..	-20364	..
Final consumption	..	..	..	43395	415505	*228	..	30467	..	489595	*228
Final energy consumption	..	..	..	42953	31210	*228	..	30467	..	104858	*228
Manufacturing, const., mining	..	..	..	4884	28296	..	..	18418	..	51598	..
Iron and steel	..	..	..	..	15575	..	..	..	..	15575	..
Chemical and petrochemical	..	..	..	..	..	..	..	..	..	..	..
Non-ferrous metals	..	..	..	..	..	..	..	..	..	..	..
Non-metallic minerals	..	..	..	..	4346	..	..	..	..	4346	..
Transport equipment	..	..	..	..	..	..	..	..	..	..	..
Machinery	..	..	..	..	..	..	..	..	..	..	..
Mining and quarrying	..	..	..	..	..	..	..	..	..	..	..
Food and tobacco	..	..	..	..	..	..	..	..	..	..	..
Paper, pulp and printing	..	..	..	..	..	..	..	..	..	..	..
Wood and wood products	..	..	..	..	..	..	..	..	..	..	..
Textile and leather	..	..	..	..	..	..	..	..	..	..	..
Construction	..	..	..	..	..	..	..	..	..	..	..
Industries n.e.s	..	..	..	4884	8375	..	..	18418	..	31677	..
Transport	..	..	..	34773	..	..	..	..	..	34773	..
Road	..	..	..	31157	..	..	..	..	..	31157	..
Rail	..	..	..	..	..	..	..	..	..	..	..
Domestic aviation	..	..	..	3616	..	..	..	..	..	3616	..
Domestic navigation	..	..	..	..	..	..	..	..	..	..	..
Pipeline transport	..	..	..	..	..	..	..	..	..	..	..
Transport, n.e.s	..	..	..	..	..	..	..	..	..	..	..
Other	..	..	..	3296	2914	*228	..	12049	..	18487	*228
Agriculture, forestry, fishing	..	..	..	..	..	..	..	..	..	..	..
Commerce, public services	..	..	..	258	..	..	..	3319	..	3577	..
Households	..	..	..	3038	2914	*228	..	8730	..	14910	*228
Other consumers	..	..	..	..	..	..	..	..	..	..	..
Non-energy use	..	..	..	442	384295	..	..	..	..	384737	..

Tunisia

Terajoules

2017	Primary coal and peat	Coal and peat products	Primary Oil	Oil Products	Natural Gas	Biofuels and waste	Nuclear	Electricity	Heat	Total energy	of which: renewables
Primary production	..	..	87445	..	89567	45320	..	2156	5557	230045	49686
Imports	..	..	26861	173486	138009	..	..	1620	..	339975	..
Exports	..	..	-70307	-17811	..	..	..	-1739	..	-89856	..
International marine bunkers	..	..	..	-301	..	..	..	..	..	-301	..
International aviation bunkers	..	..	..	-11069	..	..	..	..	..	-11069	..
Stock changes	..	..	3342	1199	..	..	..	..	..	4540	..
Total energy supply	..	..	47340	145504	227576	45320	..	2038	5557	473334	49686
Statistical difference	..	..	2809	-3746	249	-365	..	284	0	-769	1791
Transfers	..	..	..	466	..	..	..	..	..	466	..
Transformation	..	..	-44014	43528	-156046	-9527	..	71965	-3347	-97440	-9527
Electricity plants	..	..	..	-764	-154742	..	..	70659	-3347	-88194	..
CHP plants	..	..	..	..	-1304	..	..	1305	..	1	..
Heat plants	..	..	..	..	..	..	..	..	..	..	..
Coke ovens	..	..	..	..	..	..	..	..	..	..	..
Briquetting plants	..	..	..	..	..	..	..	..	..	..	..
Liquefaction plants	..	..	..	..	..	..	..	..	..	..	..
Gas works	..	..	..	..	..	..	..	..	..	..	..
Blast furnaces	..	..	..	..	..	..	..	..	..	..	..
NGL plants & gas blending	..	..	-5437	5818	..	..	..	..	..	381	..
Oil refineries	..	..	-38578	38474	..	..	..	..	..	-104	..
Other transformation	..	..	..	..	..	-9527	..	..	..	-9527	-9527
Energy industries own use	..	..	-221	-1449	-6188	..	..	-3087	0	-10945	..
Losses	..	..	-296	..	-2336	..	..	-12625	..	-15258	..
Final consumption	..	..	..	191794	62756	36159	..	58007	2210	350925	38369
Final energy consumption	..	..	..	179258	62756	36159	..	58007	2210	338390	38369
Manufacturing, const., mining	..	..	..	35565	35851	..	..	19400	..	90816	..
Iron and steel	..	..	..	..	376	..	..	954	..	1330	..
Chemical and petrochemical	..	..	..	..	4684	..	..	2502	..	7186	..
Non-ferrous metals	..	..	..	..	..	..	..	..	..	..	..
Non-metallic minerals	..	..	..	23335	20464	..	..	5695	..	49494	..
Transport equipment	..	..	..	..	..	..	..	..	..	..	..
Machinery	..	..	..	..	..	..	..	..	..	..	..
Mining and quarrying	..	..	..	..	276	..	..	1159	..	1436	..
Food and tobacco	..	..	..	..	3361	..	..	2797	..	6158	..
Paper, pulp and printing	..	..	..	..	2597	..	..	724	..	3320	..
Wood and wood products	..	..	..	..	..	..	..	..	..	..	..
Textile and leather	..	..	..	..	2229	..	..	1624	..	3853	..
Construction	..	..	..	..	..	..	..	..	..	..	..
Industries n.e.s	..	..	..	12230	1864	..	..	3946	..	18040	..
Transport	..	..	..	97790	9383	..	..	338	..	107512	..
Road	..	..	..	96883	..	..	..	..	..	96883	..
Rail	..	..	..	731	..	..	..	266	..	997	..
Domestic aviation	..	..	..	176	..	..	..	..	..	176	..
Domestic navigation	..	..	..	..	..	..	..	..	..	..	..
Pipeline transport	..	..	..	..	9383	..	..	72	..	9455	..
Transport, n.e.s	..	..	..	..	..	..	..	..	..	..	..
Other	..	..	..	45903	17522	36159	..	38268	2210	140062	38369
Agriculture, forestry, fishing	..	..	..	16555	968	..	..	4165	..	21688	..
Commerce, public services	..	..	..	4304	7108	495	..	16247	91	28245	586
Households	..	..	..	25044	9446	35663	..	17856	2119	90129	37782
Other consumers	..	..	..	..	..	..	..	..	..	..	..
Non-energy use	..	..	..	12536	..	..	..	..	..	12536	..

Tunisia

Terajoules

2018	Primary coal and peat	Coal and peat products	Primary Oil	Oil Products	Natural Gas	Biofuels and waste	Nuclear	Electricity	Heat	Total energy	of which: renewables
Primary production	..	..	84504	..	85747	45636	..	2318	6567	224772	50396
Imports	..	..	21658	177358	144455	..	..	1375	..	344845	..
Exports	..	..	-58471	-22416	..	..	..	-1742	..	-82629	..
International marine bunkers	..	..	..	-432	..	..	..	..	..	-432	..
International aviation bunkers	..	..	..	-12524	..	..	..	..	..	-12524	..
Stock changes	..	..	2455	2525	..	..	..	..	..	4980	..
Total energy supply	..	..	50146	144511	230201	45636	..	1951	6567	479012	50396
Statistical difference	..	..	-169	3470	-383	0	..	-36	0	2882	2318
Transfers	..	..	..	482	..	..	..	..	..	482	..
Transformation	..	..	-50138	49616	-159143	-9489	..	73325	-4125	-99955	-9489
Electricity plants	..	..	..	-840	-157025	..	..	71204	-4125	-90786	..
CHP plants	..	..	..	..	-2119	..	..	2120	..	2	..
Heat plants	..	..	..	..	..	..	..	..	..	..	..
Coke ovens	..	..	..	..	..	..	..	..	..	..	..
Briquetting plants	..	..	..	..	..	..	..	..	..	..	..
Liquefaction plants	..	..	..	..	..	..	..	..	..	..	..
Gas works	..	..	..	..	..	..	..	..	..	..	..
Blast furnaces	..	..	..	..	..	..	..	..	..	..	..
NGL plants & gas blending	..	..	-5216	5581	..	..	..	..	..	366	..
Oil refineries	..	..	-44923	44875	..	..	..	..	..	-48	..
Other transformation	..	..	..	..	..	-9489	..	..	..	-9489	-9489
Energy industries own use	..	..	-177	-1507	-6219	..	..	-2995	0	-10898	..
Losses	..	..	..	..	..	..	..	-12902	..	-12902	..
Final consumption	..	..	..	189632	65222	36147	..	59414	2442	352857	38589
Final energy consumption	..	..	..	177379	65222	36147	..	59414	2442	340604	38589
Manufacturing, const., mining	..	..	..	32158	37936	..	..	20653	..	90747	..
Iron and steel	..	..	..	..	290	..	..	1138	..	1427	..
Chemical and petrochemical	..	..	..	..	4186	..	..	2675	..	6861	..
Non-ferrous metals	..	..	..	..	..	..	..	..	..	..	..
Non-metallic minerals	..	..	..	19565	22956	..	..	5828	..	48350	..
Transport equipment	..	..	..	..	..	..	..	..	..	..	..
Machinery	..	..	..	..	..	..	..	..	..	..	..
Mining and quarrying	..	..	..	..	339	..	..	1109	..	1448	..
Food and tobacco	..	..	..	..	3254	..	..	3046	..	6300	..
Paper, pulp and printing	..	..	..	..	2172	..	..	947	..	3119	..
Wood and wood products	..	..	..	..	..	..	..	..	..	..	..
Textile and leather	..	..	..	..	2553	..	..	1739	..	4292	..
Construction	..	..	..	..	..	..	..	..	..	..	..
Industries n.e.s	..	..	..	12593	2185	..	..	4172	..	18951	..
Transport	..	..	..	99388	7727	..	..	356	..	107472	..
Road	..	..	..	98550	..	..	..	..	..	98550	..
Rail	..	..	..	662	..	..	..	252	..	914	..
Domestic aviation	..	..	..	176	..	..	..	..	..	176	..
Domestic navigation	..	..	..	..	..	..	..	..	..	..	..
Pipeline transport	..	..	..	..	7727	..	..	104	..	7832	..
Transport, n.e.s	..	..	..	..	..	..	..	..	..	..	..
Other	..	..	..	45832	19559	36147	..	38405	2442	142385	38589
Agriculture, forestry, fishing	..	..	..	16648	1074	..	..	4201	3	21926	3
Commerce, public services	..	..	..	4266	7951	498	..	16193	101	29008	599
Households	..	..	..	24918	10535	35648	..	18011	2338	91450	37986
Other consumers	..	..	..	..	..	..	..	..	..	..	..
Non-energy use	..	..	..	12253	..	..	..	..	..	12253	..

Turkey

Terajoules

2017	Primary coal and peat	Coal and peat products	Primary Oil	Oil Products	Natural Gas	Biofuels and waste	Nuclear	Electricity	Heat	Total energy	of which: renewables
Primary production	656564	..	113021	..	12208	126778	..	284440	333742	1526753	742513
Imports	1020487	22519	1145008	1102912	1904469	0	..	9821	..	5205216	0
Exports	-2464	-3525	..	-286116	-21742	..	..	-11894	..	-325742	..
International marine bunkers	..	..	..	-35174	..	..	..	..	..	-35174	..
International aviation bunkers	..	..	..	-152321	..	..	..	..	..	-152321	..
Stock changes	-11805	-932	-10315	-13339	-43010	-27	..	..	..	-79427	-27
Total energy supply	1662782	18062	1247714	615962	1851925	126751	..	282366	333742	6139305	742487
Statistical difference	8283	-5319	16710	6499	-9001	1	..	0	0	17173	306498
Transfers	..	..	155044	-155259	..	..	..	..	..	-215	..
Transformation	-1255223	69279	-1386049	1352984	-742136	-23302	..	785758	-177270	-1375959	-219371
Electricity plants	-1059562	-34989	..	-5236	-646696	-14866	..	753124	-234729	-1242954	-213142
CHP plants	-9750	-1334	..	-4848	-78480	-8436	..	32634	43302	-26912	-6229
Heat plants	..	..	..	..	..	..	..	..	14157	14157	..
Coke ovens	-154270	153763	..	..	..	..	..	..	..	-507	..
Briquetting plants	..	..	..	..	..	..	..	..	..	..	..
Liquefaction plants	..	..	20599	..	..	..	..	..	..	20599	..
Gas works	..	..	..	..	..	..	..	..	..	..	..
Blast furnaces	-31642	-48161	..	..	..	..	..	..	..	-79803	..
NGL plants & gas blending	..	..	..	..	..	..	..	..	..	..	..
Oil refineries	..	..	-1406648	1368939	..	..	..	..	..	-37709	..
Other transformation	..	..	..	-5871	-16960	..	..	..	..	-22831	..
Energy industries own use	-9104	-36325	..	-112917	-65617	..	..	-58633	-1	-282597	..
Losses	..	..	..	..	-139	..	..	-124772	..	-124911	..
Final consumption	390173	56335	..	1694271	1053034	*103448	..	884718	156471	4338450	216618
Final energy consumption	390173	56335	..	1504832	1036031	*103448	..	884718	156471	4132007	216618
Manufacturing, const., mining	180960	56335	..	180821	431098	..	..	407574	55652	1312440	12351
Iron and steel	16978	51367	..	740	52453	..	..	91832	..	213370	..
Chemical and petrochemical	14739	405	..	219	69802	..	..	22072	..	107237	..
Non-ferrous metals	4036	1944	..	215	15406	..	..	13511	..	35112	..
Non-metallic minerals	98790	621	..	160067	74318	..	..	51818	..	385615	..
Transport equipment	120	..	..	590	6033	..	..	9486	..	16229	..
Machinery	447	81	..	318	9307	..	..	18958	..	29111	..
Mining and quarrying	1918	..	..	6635	4965	..	..	5047	..	18566	..
Food and tobacco	19485	1917	..	1239	42605	..	..	26939	..	92185	..
Paper, pulp and printing	7119	..	..	259	8496	..	..	12622	..	28495	..
Wood and wood products	316	..	..	172	6757	..	..	8374	..	15619	..
Textile and leather	17010	..	..	454	39124	..	..	61279	..	117868	..
Construction	0	..	..	3354	21059	..	..	13396	..	37809	..
Industries n.e.s	0	0	..	6558	80773	..	..	72241	55652	215224	12351
Transport	..	..	..	1149249	18249	4556	..	4493	..	1176547	4556
Road	..	..	..	1078670	2883	4556	..	..	..	1086109	4556
Rail	..	..	..	5074	..	..	..	3542	..	8616	..
Domestic aviation	..	..	..	52655	..	..	..	..	..	52655	..
Domestic navigation	..	..	..	12849	..	..	..	..	..	12849	..
Pipeline transport	..	..	..	..	15321	..	..	950	..	16271	..
Transport, n.e.s	..	..	..	..	46	..	..	..	..	46	..
Other	209213	0	..	174762	586683	*98892	..	472651	100819	1643021	199711
Agriculture, forestry, fishing	0	..	..	125517	4066	..	..	24473	25498	179554	25498
Commerce, public services	147691	0	..	38987	116757	..	..	252875	..	556310	..
Households	61522	..	..	10259	465860	*98892	..	195304	75321	907157	*174213
Other consumers	..	..	..	..	..	..	..	..	..	..	..
Non-energy use	..	..	..	189439	17004	..	..	..	..	206442	..

Turkey

Terajoules

2018	Primary coal and peat	Coal and peat products	Primary Oil	Oil Products	Natural Gas	Biofuels and waste	Nuclear	Electricity	Heat	Total energy	of which: renewables
Primary production	692756	..	126214	..	14709	135268	..	315673	386044	1670663	801227
Imports	1002917	21984	932519	1142062	1733370	..	..	8917	..	4841769	..
Exports	-2123	-3271	..	-210086	-23210	..	..	-11203	..	-249894	..
International marine bunkers	..	..	..	-38008	..	..	..	..	..	-38008	..
International aviation bunkers	..	..	..	-163082	..	..	..	..	..	-163082	..
Stock changes	2142	-829	3586	-28835	-7546	27	..	..	..	-31455	27
Total energy supply	1695691	17884	1062318	702051	1717323	135294	..	313387	386044	6029994	801254
Statistical difference	7964	2973	17460	-1124	3673	-2	..	0	0	30945	342424
Transfers	..	..	180110	-179904	..	..	..	..	..	206	..
Transformation	-1381634	75902	-1224968	1202204	-613692	-29224	..	781610	-225903	-1415705	-267643
Electricity plants	-1192408	-30510	..	-40	-517871	-17184	..	745531	-283416	-1295899	-257636
CHP plants	-7511	-1959	..	-2788	-78000	-12040	..	36079	41613	-24605	-10007
Heat plants	..	..	..	..	..	..	..	..	15900	15900	..
Coke ovens	-150802	157312	..	..	..	..	..	..	..	6510	..
Briquetting plants	..	..	..	..	..	..	..	..	..	..	..
Liquefaction plants	..	..	21646	..	..	..	..	..	..	21646	..
Gas works	..	..	..	..	..	..	..	..	..	..	..
Blast furnaces	-30913	-48941	..	..	..	..	..	..	..	-79854	..
NGL plants & gas blending	..	..	..	..	..	..	..	..	..	..	..
Oil refineries	..	..	-1246614	1210276	..	..	..	..	..	-36338	..
Other transformation	..	..	..	-5244	-17821	..	..	..	..	-23065	..
Energy industries own use	-9765	-39251	..	-61980	-55268	..	..	-63349	0	-229613	..
Losses	..	..	..	..	-103	..	..	-113886	..	-113989	..
Final consumption	296328	51562	..	1663495	1044588	*106072	..	917762	160141	4239949	191187
Final energy consumption	296328	51562	..	1503484	1007236	*106072	..	917762	160141	4042586	191187
Manufacturing, const., mining	176412	51562	..	179871	405011	34919	..	411887	54466	1314127	14359
Iron and steel	17717	48025	..	348	48913	..	..	91807	..	206810	..
Chemical and petrochemical	22479	27	..	224	56324	1172	..	24941	..	105166	..
Non-ferrous metals	4169	1755	..	172	10375	2680	..	12924	..	32075	..
Non-metallic minerals	86519	..	..	161715	71146	15659	..	51757	..	386796	..
Transport equipment	40	..	..	216	7583	..	..	9320	..	17160	..
Machinery	24	..	..	267	8962	*125	..	17795	..	27173	*83
Mining and quarrying	66	..	..	4839	5343	..	..	5735	..	15984	..
Food and tobacco	18989	1755	..	805	46224	7076	..	28098	..	102946	*461
Paper, pulp and printing	7962	..	..	184	7412	378	..	12380	..	28316	*41
Wood and wood products	484	..	..	301	2654	7578	..	8021	..	19038	*670
Textile and leather	13612	..	..	292	41984	*42	..	65077	..	121007	*42
Construction	1017	..	..	1598	22475	..	..	13669	..	38759	..
Industries n.e.s	3333	0	..	8911	75615	209	..	70362	54466	212897	13062
Transport	..	..	..	1157070	19377	6048	..	4522	..	1187017	6048
Road	..	..	..	1080718	3182	6048	..	..	..	1089948	6048
Rail	..	..	..	5332	..	..	..	3686	..	9018	..
Domestic aviation	..	..	..	54640	..	..	..	..	..	54640	..
Domestic navigation	..	..	..	16381	..	..	..	..	..	16381	..
Pipeline transport	..	..	..	..	16187	..	..	835	..	17023	..
Transport, n.e.s	..	..	..	..	7	..	..	..	..	7	..
Other	119917	..	..	166543	582848	*65105	..	501354	105675	1541442	170780
Agriculture, forestry, fishing	..	..	..	123883	7273	..	..	33401	26251	190808	26251
Commerce, public services	73718	..	..	33417	137742	..	..	271426	..	516303	..
Households	46198	..	..	9243	437833	*65105	..	196528	79424	834331	144529
Other consumers	..	..	..	..	..	..	..	..	..	..	..
Non-energy use	..	..	..	160011	37352	..	..	..	..	197363	..

Turkmenistan

Terajoules

2017	Primary coal and peat	Coal and peat products	Primary Oil	Oil Products	Natural Gas	Biofuels and waste	Nuclear	Electricity	Heat	Total energy	of which: renewables
Primary production	..	..	477371	..	2745059	121	..	..	..	3222550	121
Imports	..	..	..	..	..	295	..	..	..	295	295
Exports	..	..	-71910	-109285	-1851164	..	..	-11524	..	-2043883	..
International marine bunkers	..	..	..	..	..	..	..	..	..	..	..
International aviation bunkers	..	..	..	-20727	..	..	..	..	..	-20727	..
Stock changes	..	..	..	..	..	..	..	..	..	..	..
Total energy supply	..	..	405461	-130012	893894	416	..	-11524	..	1158235	416
Statistical difference	..	..	0	0	0	0	..	0	0	0	0
Transfers	..	..	..	..	..	..	..	..	..	..	..
Transformation	..	..	-405461	398734	-369677	..	..	81122	9846	-285435	..
Electricity plants	..	..	..	..	..	..	..	..	..	..	..
CHP plants	..	..	..	..	-369677	..	..	81122	9846	-278708	..
Heat plants	..	..	..	..	..	..	..	..	..	..	..
Coke ovens	..	..	..	..	..	..	..	..	..	..	..
Briquetting plants	..	..	..	..	..	..	..	..	..	..	..
Liquefaction plants	..	..	..	..	..	..	..	..	..	..	..
Gas works	..	..	..	..	..	..	..	..	..	..	..
Blast furnaces	..	..	..	..	..	..	..	..	..	..	..
NGL plants & gas blending	..	..	-28951	30981	..	..	..	..	..	2030	..
Oil refineries	..	..	-376510	367752	..	..	..	..	..	-8758	..
Other transformation	..	..	..	..	..	..	..	..	..	..	..
Energy industries own use	..	..	..	-5544	-86805	..	..	-14274	0	-106623	..
Losses	..	..	..	..	..	..	..	-10422	..	-10422	..
Final consumption	..	..	..	263177	437413	416	..	44903	9846	755754	416
Final energy consumption	..	..	..	263177	437413	416	..	44903	9846	755754	416
Manufacturing, const., mining	..	..	..	..	41913	..	..	16200	..	58113	..
Iron and steel	..	..	..	..	..	..	..	..	..	..	..
Chemical and petrochemical	..	..	..	..	..	..	..	5260	..	5260	..
Non-ferrous metals	..	..	..	..	..	..	..	..	..	..	..
Non-metallic minerals	..	..	..	..	..	..	..	..	..	..	..
Transport equipment	..	..	..	..	..	..	..	..	..	..	..
Machinery	..	..	..	..	..	..	..	..	..	..	..
Mining and quarrying	..	..	..	..	..	..	..	..	..	..	..
Food and tobacco	..	..	..	..	..	..	..	..	..	..	..
Paper, pulp and printing	..	..	..	..	..	..	..	..	..	..	..
Wood and wood products	..	..	..	..	..	..	..	..	..	..	..
Textile and leather	..	..	..	..	..	..	..	..	..	..	..
Construction	..	..	..	..	..	..	..	..	..	..	..
Industries n.e.s	..	..	..	..	41913	..	..	10940	..	52853	..
Transport	..	..	..	111392	69413	..	..	1166	..	181971	..
Road	..	..	..	111392	..	..		..	..	111392	..
Rail	..	..	..	..	..	..	..	1166	..	1166	..
Domestic aviation	..	..	..	..	..	..	..	..	..	..	..
Domestic navigation	..	..	..	..	..	..	..	..	..	..	..
Pipeline transport	..	..	..	..	69413	..	..	..	..	69413	..
Transport, n.e.s	..	..	..	..	..	..	..	..	..	..	..
Other	..	..	..	151786	326086	416	..	27536	9846	515670	416
Agriculture, forestry, fishing	..	..	..	..	..	..	..	14278	..	14278	..
Commerce, public services	..	..	..	..	300343	..	..	..	..	300343	..
Households	..	..	..	6570	..	416	..	9439	..	16425	416
Other consumers	..	..	..	145216	25744	..	..	3820	9846	184625	..
Non-energy use	..	..	..	..	..	..	..	..	..	..	..

Turkmenistan

Terajoules

2018	Primary coal and peat	Coal and peat products	Primary Oil	Oil Products	Natural Gas	Biofuels and waste	Nuclear	Electricity	Heat	Total energy	of which: renewables
Primary production	..	..	451909	..	2879412	121	..	..	..	3331442	121
Imports	..	..	..	..	..	295	..	..	..	295	295
Exports	..	..	-44415	-109285	-1985531	..	..	-11524	..	-2150754	..
International marine bunkers	..	..	..	..	..	..	..	..	..	..	..
International aviation bunkers	..	..	..	-20727	..	..	..	..	..	-20727	..
Stock changes	..	..	..	..	..	..	..	..	..	..	..
Total energy supply	..	..	407494	-130012	893882	416	..	-11524	..	1160256	416
Statistical difference	..	..	0	0	0	0	..	0	0	0	0
Transfers	..	..	..	..	..	..	..	..	..	..	..
Transformation	..	..	-407494	400896	-369671	..	..	81122	10876	-284270	..
Electricity plants	..	..	..	..	..	..	..	..	..	..	..
CHP plants	..	..	..	..	-369671	..	..	81122	10876	-277672	..
Heat plants	..	..	..	..	..	..	..	..	..	..	..
Coke ovens	..	..	..	..	..	..	..	..	..	..	..
Briquetting plants	..	..	..	..	..	..	..	..	..	..	..
Liquefaction plants	..	..	..	..	..	..	..	..	..	..	..
Gas works	..	..	..	..	..	..	..	..	..	..	..
Blast furnaces	..	..	..	..	..	..	..	..	..	..	..
NGL plants & gas blending	..	..	-31249	33441	..	..	..	..	..	2192	..
Oil refineries	..	..	-376244	367455	..	..	..	..	..	-8789	..
Other transformation	..	..	..	..	..	..	..	..	..	..	..
Energy industries own use	..	..	..	-5247	-86805	..	..	-14274	0	-106326	..
Losses	..	..	..	..	..	..	..	-10422	..	-10422	..
Final consumption	..	..	..	265637	437406	416	..	44903	10876	759238	416
Final energy consumption	..	..	..	265637	437406	416	..	44903	10876	759238	416
Manufacturing, const., mining	..	..	..	..	41911	..	..	16200	..	58111	..
Iron and steel	..	..	..	..	..	..	..	..	..	..	..
Chemical and petrochemical	..	..	..	..	..	..	..	5260	..	5260	..
Non-ferrous metals	..	..	..	..	..	..	..	..	..	..	..
Non-metallic minerals	..	..	..	..	..	..	..	..	..	..	..
Transport equipment	..	..	..	..	..	..	..	..	..	..	..
Machinery	..	..	..	..	..	..	..	..	..	..	..
Mining and quarrying	..	..	..	..	..	..	..	..	..	..	..
Food and tobacco	..	..	..	..	..	..	..	..	..	..	..
Paper, pulp and printing	..	..	..	..	..	..	..	..	..	..	..
Wood and wood products	..	..	..	..	..	..	..	..	..	..	..
Textile and leather	..	..	..	..	..	..	..	..	..	..	..
Construction	..	..	..	..	..	..	..	..	..	..	..
Industries n.e.s	..	..	..	..	41911	..	..	10940	..	52852	..
Transport	..	..	..	111392	69413	..	..	1166	..	181971	..
Road	..	..	..	111392	..	..	..	..	..	111392	..
Rail	..	..	..	..	..	..	..	1166	..	1166	..
Domestic aviation	..	..	..	..	..	..	..	..	..	..	..
Domestic navigation	..	..	..	..	..	..	..	..	..	..	..
Pipeline transport	..	..	..	..	69413	..	..	..	..	69413	..
Transport, n.e.s	..	..	..	..	..	..	..	..	..	..	..
Other	..	..	..	154246	326082	416	..	27536	10876	519155	416
Agriculture, forestry, fishing	..	..	..	..	..	..	..	14278	..	14278	..
Commerce, public services	..	..	..	..	300338	..	..	..	..	300338	..
Households	..	..	..	6570	..	416	..	9439	..	16425	416
Other consumers	..	..	..	147676	25744	..	..	3820	10876	188115	..
Non-energy use	..	..	..	..	..	..	..	..	..	..	..

Turks and Caicos Islands

Terajoules

	All Coal	All Oil	Natural Gas	Primary biofuels / Waste	Charcoal	Electricity	Total energy	of which: renewables
2017								
Primary production	..	..	..	11	..	..	11	11
Imports	..	*3225	..	..	..	..	*3225	..
Exports	..	..	..	..	..	..	..	..
International marine bunkers	..	..	..	..	..	..	..	..
International aviation bunkers	..	..	..	..	..	..	..	..
Stock changes	..	..	..	..	..	..	..	..
Total energy supply	..	*3225	..	11	..	..	*3236	11
Statistical Difference	..	0	..	0	0	0	0	0
Transfers	..	..	..	..	..	..	..	..
Transformation	..	*-2666	..	*-8	4	*866	*-1804	*-4
Electricity plants	..	*-2666	..	..	..	*866	*-1800	..
Charcoal plants	..	..	..	*-8	4	..	*-4	*-4
Other transformation	..	0	..	0	..	..	0	0
Energy industries own use	..	..	..	..	..	*-28	*-28	..
Losses	..	..	..	..	..	*-50	*-50	..
Final consumption	..	*559	..	*3	*4	787	1353	*7
Final energy consumption	..	*559	..	*3	*4	787	1353	*7
Manufacturing, const., mining	..	..	..	..	..	..	..	..
Transport	..	*559	..	..	..	..	*559	..
Road	..	*430	..	..	..	..	*430	..
Domestic aviation	..	..	..	..	..	..	..	..
Domestic navigation	..	*129	..	..	..	..	*129	..
Other transport	..	..	..	..	..	..	..	..
Other	..	..	..	*3	*4	787	794	*7
Agriculture, forestry, fishing	..	..	..	..	..	..	..	..
Commerce and public services	..	..	..	..	..	522	522	..
Households	..	..	..	*3	*4	*265	*272	*7
Other consumers	..	..	..	..	..	..	..	..
Non-energy use	..	..	..	..	..	..	..	..
2018								
Primary production	..	..	..	*11	..	..	*11	*11
Imports	..	*3290	..	..	..	..	*3290	..
Exports	..	..	..	..	..	..	..	..
International marine bunkers	..	..	..	..	..	..	..	..
International aviation bunkers	..	..	..	..	..	..	..	..
Stock changes	..	..	..	..	..	..	..	..
Total energy supply	..	*3290	..	*11	..	..	*3300	*11
Statistical Difference	..	0	..	0	0	0	0	0
Transfers	..	..	..	..	..	..	..	..
Transformation	..	*-2774	..	*-8	4	*925	*-1852	*-4
Electricity plants	..	*-2774	..	..	..	*925	*-1848	..
Charcoal plants	..	..	..	*-8	4	..	*-4	*-4
Other transformation	..	0	..	0	..	..	0	0
Energy industries own use	..	..	..	..	..	*-29	*-29	..
Losses	..	..	..	..	..	*-45	*-45	..
Final consumption	..	*516	..	*3	*4	*851	*1374	*7
Final energy consumption	..	*516	..	*3	*4	*851	*1374	*7
Manufacturing, const., mining	..	..	..	..	..	..	..	..
Transport	..	*516	..	..	..	..	*516	..
Road	..	*430	..	..	..	..	*430	..
Domestic aviation	..	..	..	..	..	..	..	..
Domestic navigation	..	*86	..	..	..	..	*86	..
Other transport	..	..	..	..	..	..	..	..
Other	..	..	..	*3	*4	*851	*858	*7
Agriculture, forestry, fishing	..	..	..	..	..	..	..	..
Commerce and public services	..	..	..	..	..	*564	*564	..
Households	..	..	..	*3	*4	*287	*294	*7
Other consumers	..	..	..	..	..	..	..	..
Non-energy use	..	..	..	..	..	..	..	..

Tuvalu

Terajoules

	All Coal	All Oil	Natural Gas	Primary biofuels / Waste	Charcoal	Electricity	Total energy	of which: renewables
2017								
Primary production	..	..	..	..	..	7	7	7
Imports	..	*129	..	..	..	..	*129	..
Exports	..	..	..	..	..	..	..	..
International marine bunkers	..	..	..	..	..	..	..	..
International aviation bunkers	..	*-8	..	..	..	..	*-8	..
Stock changes	..	..	..	..	..	..	..	..
Total energy supply	..	*121	..	..	..	7	*128	7
Statistical Difference	..	0	..	..	..	0	0	7
Transfers	..	..	..	..	..	..	..	..
Transformation	..	*-85	..	..	..	21	*-64	..
Electricity plants	..	*-85	..	..	..	21	*-64	..
Charcoal plants	..	..	..	..	..	..	..	..
Other transformation	..	0	..	..	..	..	0	..
Energy industries own use	..	..	..	..	..	-5	-5	..
Losses	..	..	..	..	..	..	..	..
Final consumption	..	*36	..	..	..	24	*60	..
Final energy consumption	..	*36	..	..	..	24	*60	..
Manufacturing, const., mining	..	..	..	..	..	..	..	..
Transport	..	*25	..	..	..	..	*25	..
Road	..	*17	..	..	..	..	*17	..
Domestic aviation	..	..	..	..	..	..	..	..
Domestic navigation	..	*8	..	..	..	..	*8	..
Other transport	..	..	..	..	..	..	..	..
Other	..	*11	..	..	..	24	35	..
Agriculture, forestry, fishing	..	*3	..	..	..	..	*3	..
Commerce and public services	..	..	..	..	..	13	13	..
Households	..	*8	..	..	..	10	18	..
Other consumers	..	..	..	..	..	..	..	..
Non-energy use	..	..	..	..	..	..	..	..
2018								
Primary production	..	..	..	..	..	7	7	7
Imports	..	*137	..	..	..	..	*137	..
Exports	..	..	..	..	..	..	..	..
International marine bunkers	..	..	..	..	..	..	..	..
International aviation bunkers	..	*-9	..	..	..	..	*-9	..
Stock changes	..	..	..	..	..	..	..	..
Total energy supply	..	*128	..	..	..	7	*136	7
Statistical Difference	..	0	..	..	..	0	0	7
Transfers	..	..	..	..	..	..	..	..
Transformation	..	*-92	..	..	..	*23	*-69	..
Electricity plants	..	*-92	..	..	..	*23	*-69	..
Charcoal plants	..	..	..	..	..	..	..	..
Other transformation	..	0	..	..	..	..	0	..
Energy industries own use	..	..	..	..	..	*-5	*-5	..
Losses	..	..	..	..	..	..	..	..
Final consumption	..	*36	..	..	..	*25	*61	..
Final energy consumption	..	*36	..	..	..	*25	*61	..
Manufacturing, const., mining	..	..	..	..	..	..	..	..
Transport	..	*25	..	..	..	..	*25	..
Road	..	*17	..	..	..	..	*17	..
Domestic aviation	..	..	..	..	..	..	..	..
Domestic navigation	..	*8	..	..	..	..	*8	..
Other transport	..	..	..	..	..	..	..	..
Other	..	*11	..	..	..	*25	*36	..
Agriculture, forestry, fishing	..	*4	..	..	..	..	*4	..
Commerce and public services	..	..	..	..	..	*14	*14	..
Households	..	*8	..	..	..	*11	*19	..
Other consumers	..	..	..	..	..	..	..	..
Non-energy use	..	..	..	..	..	..	..	..

Uganda

Terajoules

2017	Primary coal and peat	Coal and peat products	Primary Oil	Oil Products	Natural Gas	Biofuels and waste	Nuclear	Electricity	Heat	Total energy	of which: renewables
Primary production	..	..	..	..	..	789282	..	12502	..	801784	801784
Imports	*4	..	..	75620	..	1	..	235	..	75861	1
Exports	..	..	..	..	..	-1	..	-1140	..	-1141	-1
International marine bunkers	..	..	..	..	..	..	..	..	..	..	..
International aviation bunkers	..	..	..	-4498	..	..	..	..	..	-4498	..
Stock changes	..	..	..	..	..	..	..	..	..	..	..
Total energy supply	*4	..	..	71122	..	789283	..	11596	..	872006	801785
Statistical difference	0	..	..	1921	..	1	..	163	..	2085	12503
Transfers	..	..	..	..	..	..	..	..	..	..	..
Transformation	..	..	..	*-3515	..	-159450	..	1371	..	-161593	-159450
Electricity plants	..	..	..	*-3515	..	*-3050	..	1371	..	*-5194	*-3050
CHP plants	..	..	..	..	..	..	..	..	..	..	..
Heat plants	..	..	..	..	..	..	..	..	..	..	..
Coke ovens	..	..	..	..	..	..	..	..	..	..	..
Briquetting plants	..	..	..	..	..	..	..	..	..	..	..
Liquefaction plants	..	..	..	..	..	..	..	..	..	..	..
Gas works	..	..	..	..	..	..	..	..	..	..	..
Blast furnaces	..	..	..	..	..	..	..	..	..	..	..
NGL plants & gas blending	..	..	..	..	..	..	..	..	..	..	..
Oil refineries	..	..	..	..	..	..	..	..	..	..	..
Other transformation	..	..	..	..	..	-156400	..	..	..	-156400	-156400
Energy industries own use	..	..	..	..	..	..	..	0	..	0	..
Losses	..	..	..	..	..	..	..	-2719	..	-2719	..
Final consumption	*4	..	..	65686	..	629832	..	10086	..	705609	629832
Final energy consumption	*4	..	..	65259	..	629832	..	10086	..	705181	629832
Manufacturing, const., mining	*4	..	..	15108	..	54180	..	6498	..	75790	54180
Iron and steel	..	..	..	..	..	..	..	4918	..	4918	..
Chemical and petrochemical	..	..	..	..	..	..	..	..	..	..	..
Non-ferrous metals	..	..	..	..	..	..	..	..	..	..	..
Non-metallic minerals	..	..	..	..	..	..	..	..	..	..	..
Transport equipment	..	..	..	..	..	..	..	..	..	..	..
Machinery	..	..	..	..	..	..	..	..	..	..	..
Mining and quarrying	..	..	..	..	..	..	..	..	..	..	..
Food and tobacco	..	..	..	..	..	..	..	..	..	..	..
Paper, pulp and printing	..	..	..	..	..	..	..	..	..	..	..
Wood and wood products	..	..	..	..	..	..	..	..	..	..	..
Textile and leather	..	..	..	..	..	..	..	..	..	..	..
Construction	..	..	..	..	..	..	..	..	..	..	..
Industries n.e.s	*4	..	..	15108	..	54180	..	1580	..	70872	54180
Transport	..	..	..	43375	..	..	..	..	..	43375	..
Road	..	..	..	43375	..	..	..	..	..	43375	..
Rail	..	..	..	..	..	..	..	..	..	..	..
Domestic aviation	..	..	..	..	..	..	..	..	..	..	..
Domestic navigation	..	..	..	..	..	..	..	..	..	..	..
Pipeline transport	..	..	..	..	..	..	..	..	..	..	..
Transport, n.e.s	..	..	..	..	..	..	..	..	..	..	..
Other	..	..	..	6776	..	575652	..	3588	..	586016	575652
Agriculture, forestry, fishing	..	..	..	6280	..	..	..	..	..	6280	..
Commerce, public services	..	..	..	..	..	68175	..	1277	..	69451	68175
Households	..	..	..	*496	..	507478	..	2311	..	510285	507478
Other consumers	..	..	..	..	..	..	..	..	..	..	..
Non-energy use	..	..	..	*427	..	..	..	..	..	*427	..

Uganda

Terajoules

2018	Primary coal and peat	Coal and peat products	Primary Oil	Oil Products	Natural Gas	Biofuels and waste	Nuclear	Electricity	Heat	Total energy	of which: renewables
Primary production	..	..	..	..	..	829811	..	13083	..	842894	842894
Imports	*5	..	..	77877	..	0	..	303	..	78185	0
Exports	..	..	..	..	..	-1	..	-839	..	-840	-1
International marine bunkers	..	..	..	..	..	..	..	..	..	..	..
International aviation bunkers	..	..	..	-4768	..	..	..	..	..	-4768	..
Stock changes	..	..	..	..	..	..	..	..	..	..	..
Total energy supply	*5	..	..	73109	..	829810	..	12546	..	915471	842893
Statistical difference	0	..	..	-1231	..	-630	..	123	..	-1738	12453
Transfers	..	..	..	..	..	..	..	..	..	..	..
Transformation	..	..	..	-3015	..	-174470	..	1459	..	-176025	-174470
Electricity plants	..	..	..	-3015	..	*-4255	..	1459	..	-5810	*-4255
CHP plants	..	..	..	..	..	..	..	..	..	..	..
Heat plants	..	..	..	..	..	..	..	..	..	..	..
Coke ovens	..	..	..	..	..	..	..	..	..	..	..
Briquetting plants	..	..	..	..	..	..	..	..	..	..	..
Liquefaction plants	..	..	..	..	..	..	..	..	..	..	..
Gas works	..	..	..	..	..	..	..	..	..	..	..
Blast furnaces	..	..	..	..	..	..	..	..	..	..	..
NGL plants & gas blending	..	..	..	..	..	..	..	..	..	..	..
Oil refineries	..	..	..	..	..	..	..	..	..	..	..
Other transformation	..	..	..	..	..	-170215	..	..	..	-170215	-170215
Energy industries own use	..	..	..	..	..	..	..	0	..	0	..
Losses	..	..	..	..	..	..	..	-2841	..	-2841	..
Final consumption	*5	..	..	71326	..	655969	..	11042	..	738342	655969
Final energy consumption	*5	..	..	70766	..	655969	..	11042	..	737782	655969
Manufacturing, const., mining	*5	..	..	16083	..	65269	..	7243	..	88600	65269
Iron and steel	..	..	..	..	..	..	..	5497	..	5497	..
Chemical and petrochemical	..	..	..	..	..	..	..	..	..	..	..
Non-ferrous metals	..	..	..	..	..	..	..	..	..	..	..
Non-metallic minerals	..	..	..	..	..	..	..	..	..	..	..
Transport equipment	..	..	..	..	..	..	..	..	..	..	..
Machinery	..	..	..	..	..	..	..	..	..	..	..
Mining and quarrying	..	..	..	..	..	..	..	..	..	..	..
Food and tobacco	..	..	..	..	..	..	..	..	..	..	..
Paper, pulp and printing	..	..	..	..	..	..	..	..	..	..	..
Wood and wood products	..	..	..	..	..	..	..	..	..	..	..
Textile and leather	..	..	..	..	..	..	..	..	..	..	..
Construction	..	..	..	..	..	..	..	..	..	..	..
Industries n.e.s	*5	..	..	16083	..	65269	..	1746	..	83103	65269
Transport	..	..	..	47269	..	..	..	..	..	47269	..
Road	..	..	..	47269	..	..	..	..	..	47269	..
Rail	..	..	..	..	..	..	..	..	..	..	..
Domestic aviation	..	..	..	..	..	..	..	..	..	..	..
Domestic navigation	..	..	..	..	..	..	..	..	..	..	..
Pipeline transport	..	..	..	..	..	..	..	..	..	..	..
Transport, n.e.s	..	..	..	..	..	..	..	..	..	..	..
Other	..	..	..	7414	..	590701	..	3798	..	601914	590701
Agriculture, forestry, fishing	..	..	..	6824	..	..	..	..	..	6824	..
Commerce, public services	..	..	..	..	..	68493	..	1390	..	69883	68493
Households	..	..	..	590	..	522208	..	2408	..	525206	522208
Other consumers	..	..	..	..	..	..	..	..	..	..	..
Non-energy use	..	..	..	*560	..	..	..	..	..	*560	..

Ukraine

Terajoules

2017	Primary coal and peat	Coal and peat products	Primary Oil	Oil Products	Natural Gas	Biofuels and waste	Nuclear	Electricity	Heat	Total energy	of which: renewables
Primary production	570945	..	93955	..	647763	126532	930550	38408	22833	2430985	162433
Imports	505048	38938	43159	420246	471534	1447	..	180	..	1480552	1447
Exports	-15175	-5652	-3511	-13047	..	-17965	..	-18814	..	-74163	-17965
International marine bunkers	..	..	..	..	..	..	..	..	..	..	..
International aviation bunkers	..	..	..	*-5336	..	..	..	..	..	*-5336	..
Stock changes	-15250	-1532	-2074	13452	-91282	3316	..	..	..	-93368	3316
Total energy supply	1045568	31754	131529	415316	1028016	113330	930550	19775	22833	3738670	149231
Statistical difference	1201	0	0	68410	8135	91	0	0	0	77838	38500
Transfers	..	..	22720	-22776	..	..	..	..	..	-56	..
Transformation	-964215	155937	-153436	106303	-331878	-22489	-930550	517658	378792	-1243878	-22385
Electricity plants	-543555	-222	..	-2692	-5769	..	-924221	474286	*-3162	-1005335	..
CHP plants	-52779	-41108	..	-19920	-125622	-865	-6329	43373	143151	-60099	-865
Heat plants	-18795	-20506	..	-1938	-200487	-14369	..	..	238803	-17292	-14265
Coke ovens	-344817	342370	..	..	..	..	..	..	..	-2447	..
Briquetting plants	-4269	2743	..	..	..	..	..	..	..	-1527	..
Liquefaction plants	..	..	..	..	..	..	..	..	..	..	..
Gas works	..	-1482	..	..	..	..	..	..	..	-1482	..
Blast furnaces	..	-140324	..	..	..	..	..	..	..	-140324	..
NGL plants & gas blending	..	..	..	..	..	..	..	..	..	..	..
Oil refineries	..	..	-153436	130853	..	..	..	..	..	-22583	..
Other transformation	..	14467	..	..	..	-7255	..	..	..	7212	-7255
Energy industries own use	-3420	-19346	-260	-2204	-40164	..	..	-54482	-43211	-163088	..
Losses	-97	-19803	-296	-47	-21023	..	..	-60433	-30185	-131885	..
Final consumption	76634	148542	258	428180	626816	90749	..	422518	328229	2121926	88346
Final energy consumption	72078	132124	..	393929	577910	90749	..	422518	328229	2017537	88346
Manufacturing, const., mining	59918	130290	..	16105	109998	1579	..	180846	140464	639200	1544
Iron and steel	31214	130202	..	2667	58538	9	..	63367	50989	336986	9
Chemical and petrochemical	97	..	..	367	5905	9	..	10393	19026	35798	9
Non-ferrous metals	4191	..	..	232	6035	..	..	5472	10829	26759	..
Non-metallic minerals	22978	78	..	204	14152	90	..	8096	2969	48567	55
Transport equipment	..	..	..	706	871	18	..	2959	2002	6557	18
Machinery	97	..	..	172	5096	82	..	14324	3801	23573	82
Mining and quarrying	219	..	..	7046	11138	27	..	33934	3524	55888	27
Food and tobacco	1072	10	..	1127	6314	146	..	14688	34286	57642	146
Paper, pulp and printing	..	..	..	43	744	18	..	3571	5801	10178	18
Wood and wood products	..	..	..	219	117	1105	..	2491	4018	7951	1105
Textile and leather	..	..	..	83	249	9	..	1267	769	2378	9
Construction	49	..	..	2990	356	37	..	3211	1122	7765	37
Industries n.e.s	0	0	..	247	484	27	..	17071	1328	19158	27
Transport	219	..	..	320658	67497	1948	..	25358	..	415681	1948
Road	..	..	..	313457	1192	1903	..	..	..	316551	1903
Rail	171	..	..	5590	..	..	..	21694	..	27454	..
Domestic aviation	..	..	..	..	..	..	..	..	..	..	..
Domestic navigation	..	..	..	1396	..	..	..	..	..	1396	..
Pipeline transport	..	..	..	215	66220	..	..	2372	..	68808	..
Transport, n.e.s	49	..	..	..	86	46	..	1292	..	1472	46
Other	11940	1835	..	57167	400415	87222	..	216313	187765	962656	84854
Agriculture, forestry, fishing	317	10	..	48718	5504	923	..	13111	9114	77696	923
Commerce, public services	3899	361	..	6041	25214	3948	..	76957	67974	184394	1580
Households	7724	1464	..	2365	369694	82351	..	126155	110674	700427	82351
Other consumers	..	..	..	43	4	..	..	90	3	140	..
Non-energy use	4557	16418	258	34251	48906	..	..	..	..	104389	..

Ukraine

Terajoules

2018	Primary coal and peat	Coal and peat products	Primary Oil	Oil Products	Natural Gas	Biofuels and waste	Nuclear	Electricity	Heat	Total energy	of which: renewables
Primary production	609624	..	99435	..	690267	187780	917974	45803	22342	2573226	233583
Imports	556938	21102	32588	454944	354164	1560	..	115	..	1421411	1560
Exports	-1646	-653	..	-13820	..	-17856	..	-21956	..	-55932	-17856
International marine bunkers	..	..	..	..	..	..	..	..	..	..	..
International aviation bunkers	..	..	..	..	..	..	..	..	..	..	..
Stock changes	-3018	-1122	33	3143	29605	818	..	..	..	29458	818
Total energy supply	1161899	19327	132056	444266	1074036	172302	917974	23962	22342	3968163	218105
Statistical difference	9	-13579	0	49109	17683	-1	0	0	0	53221	45802
Transfers	..	..	35234	-26124	..	..	..	..	..	9110	..
Transformation	-1047473	174928	-166478	88412	-366281	-50942	-917974	523980	383598	-1378230	-50942
Electricity plants	-574225	0	..	-5550	-8895	..	-911498	468832	*-5427	-1036763	..
CHP plants	-59966	-44906	..	-6588	-151738	-5877	-6476	55148	135553	-84850	-5877
Heat plants	-23604	-7156	..	-1576	-205648	-38998	..	..	253472	-23510	-38998
Coke ovens	-380610	354200	..	..	..	..	..	..	..	-26410	..
Briquetting plants	-4754	4782	..	..	..	..	..	..	..	28	..
Liquefaction plants	..	..	..	..	..	..	..	..	..	..	..
Gas works	..	-1558	..	..	..	..	..	..	..	-1558	..
Blast furnaces	..	-141200	..	..	..	..	..	..	..	-141200	..
NGL plants & gas blending	..	..	..	..	..	..	..	..	..	..	..
Oil refineries	..	..	-166478	102126	..	..	..	..	..	-64352	..
Other transformation	-4313	14672	..	..	..	-6068	..	..	..	4291	-6068
Energy industries own use	-4733	-25004	-215	-2071	-39642	..	..	-59591	-46696	-177952	..
Losses	-132	-16961	-212	..	-24782	..	..	-61186	-44260	-147533	..
Final consumption	109552	165869	385	455374	625647	121361	..	427165	314984	2220336	121361
Final energy consumption	104258	149928	..	403511	588616	121361	..	427165	314984	2109823	121361
Manufacturing, const., mining	74939	147117	..	18627	122539	1480	..	186217	148285	699203	1480
Iron and steel	43400	142652	..	3268	60487	..	..	63608	52328	365744	..
Chemical and petrochemical	98	25	..	86	9053	27	..	11214	21399	41903	27
Non-ferrous metals	4681	..	..	1118	6293	..	..	5796	11497	29384	..
Non-metallic minerals	24874	557	..	1486	17987	73	..	9259	3070	57305	73
Transport equipment	..	..	..	259	929	38	..	3233	2206	6665	38
Machinery	98	100	..	452	6166	147	..	14706	4120	25789	147
Mining and quarrying	368	3753	..	6861	12440	52	..	33998	3754	61226	52
Food and tobacco	1323	29	..	841	7317	429	..	16330	36115	62385	429
Paper, pulp and printing	..	..	..	43	904	38	..	3668	6441	11094	38
Wood and wood products	..	..	..	434	57	411	..	2934	4138	7974	411
Textile and leather	0	..	..	164	268	55	..	1328	924	2740	55
Construction	74	..	..	3493	361	134	..	3470	661	8193	134
Industries n.e.s	25	0	..	122	278	74	..	16672	1632	18803	74
Transport	245	..	..	327267	60915	1501	..	25038	..	414965	1501
Road	..	..	..	319377	977	1501	..	..	..	321854	1501
Rail	221	..	..	5802	..	..	..	19321	..	25344	..
Domestic aviation	..	..	..	..	..	..	..	..	..	..	..
Domestic navigation	..	..	..	1872	..	..	..	..	..	1872	..
Pipeline transport	..	..	..	215	59925	..	..	2020	..	62159	..
Transport, n.e.s	25	..	..	..	14	..	..	3697	..	3735	..
Other	29074	2811	..	57617	405163	118380	..	215910	166699	995654	118380
Agriculture, forestry, fishing	294	10	..	49035	5118	1133	..	14018	62446	132054	1133
Commerce, public services	20179	185	..	5275	36248	2248	..	72482	9150	145769	2248
Households	8601	2616	..	3264	363796	114999	..	129409	95103	717788	114999
Other consumers	..	..	..	43	..	..	..	0	..	43	..
Non-energy use	5293	15941	385	51864	37031	..	..	..	..	110513	..

United Arab Emirates

Terajoules

2017	Primary coal and peat	Coal and peat products	Primary Oil	Oil Products	Natural Gas	Biofuels and waste	Nuclear	Electricity	Heat	Total energy	of which: renewables
Primary production	..	..	7885490	..	1899392	..	..	1926	2776	9789583	4702
Imports	89099	68	346926	741006	786257	1829	..	1850	..	1967036	1829
Exports	-39	-3	-5594779	-1994972	-490950	..	..	-2221	..	-8082963	..
International marine bunkers	..	..	..	-425254	..	..	..	..	..	-425254	..
International aviation bunkers	..	..	..	-325934	..	..	..	..	..	-325934	..
Stock changes	..	..	-17639	-56541	..	..	..	..	..	-74180	..
Total energy supply	89061	65	2619998	-2061696	2194699	1829	..	1555	2776	2848287	6531
Statistical difference	-3	0	-328106	-110174	0	0	..	0	0	-438282	2851
Transfers	..	..	..	..	..	..	..	..	..	..	..
Transformation	..	..	-2948103	2853364	-1244990	..	..	482465	-2776	-860041	-1850
Electricity plants	..	..	..	-24888	*-1244990	..	..	482465	-2776	*-790189	-1850
CHP plants	..	..	..	..	..	..	..	..	..	..	..
Heat plants	..	..	..	..	..	..	..	..	..	..	..
Coke ovens	..	..	..	..	..	..	..	..	..	..	..
Briquetting plants	..	..	..	..	..	..	..	..	..	..	..
Liquefaction plants	..	..	..	..	..	..	..	..	..	..	..
Gas works	..	..	..	..	..	..	..	..	..	..	..
Blast furnaces	..	..	..	..	..	..	..	..	..	..	..
NGL plants & gas blending	..	..	-659066	696420	..	..	..	..	..	37354	..
Oil refineries	..	..	-2289037	2181832	..	..	..	..	..	-107206	..
Other transformation	..	..	..	..	..	..	..	..	..	..	..
Energy industries own use	..	..	..	-22127	-24111	..	..	-26953	..	-73191	..
Losses	..	..	..	..	..	..	..	-42185	..	-42185	..
Final consumption	89063	65	..	879715	*925598	1829	..	414882	..	*2311153	1829
Final energy consumption	89063	65	..	612195	*913967	1829	..	414882	..	*2032002	1829
Manufacturing, const., mining	89063	65	..	*62979	*913967	..	..	54256	..	*1120330	..
Iron and steel	..	..	..	..	..	..	..	..	..	..	..
Chemical and petrochemical	..	..	..	*5369	7619	..	..	..	..	12987	..
Non-ferrous metals	..	..	..	..	..	..	..	..	..	..	..
Non-metallic minerals	87638	17	..	..	..	..	..	..	..	87656	..
Transport equipment	..	..	..	..	..	..	..	..	..	..	..
Machinery	..	..	..	..	..	..	..	..	..	..	..
Mining and quarrying	..	..	..	..	..	..	..	..	..	..	..
Food and tobacco	..	..	..	..	..	..	..	..	..	..	..
Paper, pulp and printing	..	..	..	..	..	..	..	..	..	..	..
Wood and wood products	..	..	..	..	..	..	..	..	..	..	..
Textile and leather	..	..	..	..	..	..	..	..	..	..	..
Construction	..	..	..	..	..	..	..	..	..	..	..
Industries n.e.s	1425	48	..	*57610	*906349	..	..	54256	..	*1019688	..
Transport	..	..	..	527600	..	..	..	..	..	527600	..
Road	..	..	..	512606	..	..	..	..	..	512606	..
Rail	..	..	..	..	..	..	..	..	..	..	..
Domestic aviation	..	..	..	14994	..	..	..	..	..	14994	..
Domestic navigation	..	..	..	..	..	..	..	..	..	..	..
Pipeline transport	..	..	..	..	..	..	..	..	..	..	..
Transport, n.e.s	..	..	..	..	..	..	..	..	..	..	..
Other	..	..	..	*21616	..	1829	..	360626	..	384072	1829
Agriculture, forestry, fishing	..	..	..	..	..	..	..	..	..	..	..
Commerce, public services	..	..	..	..	..	..	..	155408	..	155408	..
Households	..	..	..	*21616	..	..	..	158958	..	180574	..
Other consumers	..	..	..	..	..	1829	..	46260	..	48089	1829
Non-energy use	..	..	..	*267520	11631	..	..	..	..	*279150	..

United Arab Emirates

Terajoules

2018	Primary coal and peat	Coal and peat products	Primary Oil	Oil Products	Natural Gas	Biofuels and waste	Nuclear	Electricity	Heat	Total energy	of which: renewables
Primary production	..	..	7934726	..	1684575	..	..	3852	2517	9625671	6369
Imports	79647	763	333577	841338	784396	1770	..	1757	..	2043248	1770
Exports	-8	-3	-5777032	-2203750	-317874	..	..	-1861	..	-8300529	..
International marine bunkers	..	..	..	-357543	..	..	..	..	..	-357543	..
International aviation bunkers	..	..	..	-301088	..	..	..	..	..	-301088	..
Stock changes	..	..	-61927	*1528	..	..	..	..	..	-60400	..
Total energy supply	79639	760	2429343	-2019516	2151097	1770	..	3748	2517	2649359	8139
Statistical difference	-4	-3	-417768	-37092	0	0	..	-108	0	-454974	4691
Transfers	..	..	..	..	..	..	..	..	..	..	..
Transformation	..	..	-2847111	2891290	-1246314	..	..	485737	-2517	-718915	-1678
Electricity plants	..	..	..	-26575	*-1246314	..	..	485737	-2517	*-789670	-1678
CHP plants	..	..	..	..	..	..	..	..	..	..	..
Heat plants	..	..	..	..	..	..	..	..	..	..	..
Coke ovens	..	..	..	..	..	..	..	..	..	..	..
Briquetting plants	..	..	..	..	..	..	..	..	..	..	..
Liquefaction plants	..	..	..	..	..	..	..	..	..	..	..
Gas works	..	..	..	..	..	..	..	..	..	..	..
Blast furnaces	..	..	..	..	..	..	..	..	..	..	..
NGL plants & gas blending	..	..	-616723	651065	..	..	..	..	..	34342	..
Oil refineries	..	..	-2230388	2266800	..	..	..	..	..	36412	..
Other transformation	..	..	..	..	..	..	..	..	..	..	..
Energy industries own use	..	..	..	-21632	-25196	..	..	-17014	..	-63841	..
Losses	..	..	..	..	..	..	..	-30370	..	-30370	..
Final consumption	79643	763	..	887235	*879588	1770	..	442210	..	*2291207	1770
Final energy consumption	79643	763	..	612412	*868200	1770	..	442210	..	*2004997	1770
Manufacturing, const., mining	79643	763	..	*63504	*868200	..	..	49860	..	*1061969	..
Iron and steel	..	..	..	..	..	..	..	..	..	..	..
Chemical and petrochemical	..	..	..	*5004	7459	..	..	..	..	12464	..
Non-ferrous metals	..	..	..	..	..	..	..	..	..	..	..
Non-metallic minerals	78069	46	..	..	..	..	..	..	..	78116	..
Transport equipment	..	..	..	..	..	..	..	..	..	..	..
Machinery	..	..	..	..	..	..	..	..	..	..	..
Mining and quarrying	..	..	..	..	..	..	..	..	..	..	..
Food and tobacco	..	..	..	..	..	..	..	..	..	..	..
Paper, pulp and printing	..	..	..	..	..	..	..	..	..	..	..
Wood and wood products	..	..	..	..	..	..	..	..	..	..	..
Textile and leather	..	..	..	..	..	..	..	..	..	..	..
Construction	..	..	..	..	..	..	..	..	..	..	..
Industries n.e.s	1573	716	..	*58499	*860741	..	..	49860	..	*971390	..
Transport	..	..	..	528853	..	..	..	..	..	528853	..
Road	..	..	..	512977	..	..	..	..	..	512977	..
Rail	..	..	..	..	..	..	..	..	..	..	..
Domestic aviation	..	..	..	15876	..	..	..	..	..	15876	..
Domestic navigation	..	..	..	..	..	..	..	..	..	..	..
Pipeline transport	..	..	..	..	..	..	..	..	..	..	..
Transport, n.e.s	..	..	..	..	..	..	..	..	..	..	..
Other	..	..	..	*20055	..	1770	..	392350	..	414175	1770
Agriculture, forestry, fishing	..	..	..	..	..	..	..	..	..	..	..
Commerce, public services	..	..	..	..	..	..	..	142823	..	142823	..
Households	..	..	..	*20055	..	..	..	146081	..	166136	..
Other consumers	..	..	..	..	..	1770	..	103446	..	105216	1770
Non-energy use	..	..	..	*274823	11388	..	..	..	..	*286210	..

United Kingdom

Terajoules

2017	Primary coal and peat	Coal and peat products	Primary Oil	Oil Products	Natural Gas	Biofuels and waste	Nuclear	Electricity	Heat	Total energy	of which: renewables
Primary production	76232	..	2029084	..	1507847	406877	759629	241250	2213	5023132	603303
Imports	228212	29715	2028269	1770270	1675145	*125090	..	65401	..	5922103	*125090
Exports	-12409	-566	-1603802	-1057702	-403122	-16051	..	-12265	..	-3105916	-16051
International marine bunkers	..	..	..	-94709	..	..	..	..	..	-94709	..
International aviation bunkers	..	..	..	-500185	..	..	..	..	..	-500185	..
Stock changes	79190	-94	15908	-7078	38088	0	..	..	..	126014	0
Total energy supply	371225	29055	2469459	110597	2817959	515917	759629	294386	2213	7370440	712342
Statistical difference	-2770	135	-28	-33601	-2760	-85	0	-7	0	-39115	241165
Transfers	..	..	245500	-247057	..	..	..	..	..	-1556	..
Transformation	-315735	22602	-2714987	2676125	-1015923	-345768	-759629	967514	66565	-1419235	-302381
Electricity plants	-229611	-20972	..	-6040	-823721	*-299701	-759629	892174	..	-1247500	*-267155
CHP plants	-369	-734	..	-15790	-103021	-28828	..	75341	..	-73402	-18799
Heat plants	-158	-49	..	-2046	-97613	*-7336	..	..	66565	-40638	*-6524
Coke ovens	-49817	56088	..	..	-481	..	..	..	..	5791	..
Briquetting plants	-5462	5690	..	-2470	..	..	..	..	..	-2242	..
Liquefaction plants	..	..	..	..	..	..	..	..	..	..	..
Gas works	..	..	..	..	..	..	..	..	..	..	..
Blast furnaces	-30318	-17956	..	..	..	..	..	..	..	-48273	..
NGL plants & gas blending	..	..	-107804	111465	8913	-9903	..	..	..	2670	-9903
Oil refineries	..	..	-2607182	2593328	..	..	..	..	..	-13854	..
Other transformation	..	534	..	-2321	..	..	..	..	..	-1787	..
Energy industries own use	0	-19168	..	-187156	-183515	..	..	-86540	-13490	-489869	..
Losses	..	-4581	..	..	-17357	..	..	-96509	..	-118447	..
Final consumption	58260	27773	..	2386111	1603924	*170233	..	1078859	55288	5380449	*168796
Final energy consumption	58260	26261	..	2066193	1587868	*170233	..	1078859	55288	5042962	*168796
Manufacturing, const., mining	42745	19410	..	105607	334666	*45693	..	332431	28884	909436	*43254
Iron and steel	4881	19410	..	128	13815	..	..	9731	..	47965	..
Chemical and petrochemical	1794	..	..	4958	67926	1693	..	54842	11589	142803	942
Non-ferrous metals	844	..	..	301	10006	..	..	15502	..	26653	..
Non-metallic minerals	17573	..	..	7466	47871	*10176	..	22212	..	105298	*8510
Transport equipment	1425	..	..	7570	18366	..	..	17122	..	44483	..
Machinery	422	..	..	..	47644	44	..	44845	..	92956	22
Mining and quarrying	..	..	..	..	..	..	..	115	..	115	..
Food and tobacco	2032	..	..	4523	64100	*1733	..	39805	33	112226	*1733
Paper, pulp and printing	2929	..	..	1333	15039	*18306	..	38153	..	75760	*18306
Wood and wood products	..	..	..	1567	1827	*3468	..	..	..	*6862	*3468
Textile and leather	1662	..	..	1892	9588	..	..	9785	..	22927	..
Construction	132	..	..	8665	15141	..	..	5101	..	29039	..
Industries n.e.s	9050	0	..	67204	23343	*10273	..	75218	17262	202351	*10273
Transport	396	..	..	1711871	..	38842	..	17399	..	1768508	38842
Road	..	..	..	1611128	..	38842	..	662	..	1650633	38842
Rail	396	..	..	26230	..	..	..	16736	..	43362	..
Domestic aviation	..	..	..	37662	..	..	..	..	..	37662	..
Domestic navigation	..	..	..	36851	..	..	..	..	..	36851	..
Pipeline transport	..	..	..	..	..	..	..	..	..	..	..
Transport, n.e.s	..	..	..	..	..	..	..	..	..	..	..
Other	15119	6851	..	248715	1253202	*85698	..	729029	26404	2365018	*86700
Agriculture, forestry, fishing	..	..	..	39701	3306	*4096	..	15653	..	62755	*4096
Commerce, public services	818	..	..	93267	259839	*9878	..	334051	13304	711157	*8684
Households	14117	6851	..	97971	956048	*71724	..	379325	13100	1539135	*73920
Other consumers	185	..	..	17776	34010	..	..	..	..	51970	..
Non-energy use	..	1512	..	319918	16056	..	..	..	..	337486	..

United Kingdom

Terajoules

2018	Primary coal and peat	Coal and peat products	Primary Oil	Oil Products	Natural Gas	Biofuels and waste	Nuclear	Electricity	Heat	Total energy	of which: renewables
Primary production	64698	..	2212692	..	1458688	407249	702691	270940	2242	5119199	627673
Imports	267913	29840	1999562	1794063	1675341	*154513	..	76795	..	5998027	*154513
Exports	-15892	-340	-1855657	-1038786	-268561	*-12379	..	-8010	..	-3199626	*-12379
International marine bunkers	..	..	..	-102733	..	..	..	..	..	-102733	..
International aviation bunkers	..	..	..	-504198	..	..	..	..	..	-504198	..
Stock changes	-3961	-1998	12498	12275	-24755	-405	..	..	..	-6345	-405
Total energy supply	312758	27502	2369095	160621	2840713	548978	702691	339725	2242	7304325	769402
Statistical difference	280	366	1015	-24646	-2562	130	0	0	0	-25417	271069
Transfers	..	..	258982	-258682	..	..	..	..	..	300	..
Transformation	-253088	20308	-2627062	2591431	-971786	-372935	-702691	920394	66342	-1329087	-323905
Electricity plants	-173875	-19790	..	-5787	-776437	*-332268	-702691	843754	..	-1167095	*-294807
CHP plants	-419	-695	..	-11897	-109371	-27591	..	76640	..	-73332	-16685
Heat plants	-157	-49	..	-1904	-95957	*-7653	..	..	66342	-39379	*-6990
Coke ovens	-46271	52194	..	..	-596	..	..	..	..	5328	..
Briquetting plants	-5080	5577	..	-2340	..	..	..	..	..	-1843	..
Liquefaction plants	..	..	..	..	..	..	..	..	..	..	..
Gas works	..	..	..	..	..	..	..	..	..	..	..
Blast furnaces	-27286	-17591	..	..	..	..	..	..	..	-44877	..
NGL plants & gas blending	..	..	-88644	91564	10575	-11750	..	..	..	1744	-11750
Oil refineries	..	..	-2538418	2523974	..	..	..	..	..	-14444	..
Other transformation	..	662	..	-2178	..	..	..	..	..	-1516	..
Energy industries own use	..	-18689	..	-173942	-184632	..	..	-85226	-13459	-475948	..
Losses	..	-3787	..	..	-21344	..	..	-95756	..	-120887	..
Final consumption	59390	24968	..	2344074	1665514	*175913	..	1079136	55125	5404120	*174429
Final energy consumption	59390	23456	..	2028689	1649939	*175913	..	1079136	55125	5071648	*174429
Manufacturing, const., mining	44438	16662	..	88102	341525	*48708	..	335286	28353	903073	*45720
Iron and steel	3849	16662	..	209	13052	..	..	9216	..	42988	..
Chemical and petrochemical	1597	..	..	4958	70259	2676	..	54965	9870	144326	1377
Non-ferrous metals	786	..	..	301	10264	..	..	14717	..	26067	..
Non-metallic minerals	15947	..	..	7380	48081	*10045	..	22716	..	104169	*8379
Transport equipment	1283	..	..	6495	17258	..	..	17165	..	42201	..
Machinery	393	..	..	..	47716	40	..	45364	..	93513	20
Mining and quarrying	..	..	..	..	..	..	..	414	..	414	..
Food and tobacco	1938	..	..	4867	68064	*4001	..	42545	194	121609	*4001
Paper, pulp and printing	2671	..	..	1333	14997	*18036	..	37375	..	74412	*18036
Wood and wood products	..	..	..	1567	1805	*3100	..	..	..	6471	*3100
Textile and leather	1519	..	..	1849	9401	..	..	9796	..	22564	..
Construction	131	..	..	9181	15656	..	..	5026	..	29993	..
Industries n.e.s	14324	0	..	49961	24974	*10810	..	75989	18289	194347	*10807
Transport	393	..	..	1694289	..	53466	..	17939	..	1766087	53466
Road	..	..	..	1591991	..	53466	..	868	..	1646324	53466
Rail	393	..	..	26230	..	..	..	17071	..	43694	..
Domestic aviation	..	..	..	37970	..	..	..	..	..	37970	..
Domestic navigation	..	..	..	38098	..	..	..	..	..	38098	..
Pipeline transport	..	..	..	..	..	..	..	..	..	..	..
Transport, n.e.s	..	..	..	..	..	..	..	..	..	..	..
Other	14559	6794	..	246298	1308415	*73739	..	725911	26772	2402489	*75243
Agriculture, forestry, fishing	..	..	..	38340	3379	*5595	..	15552	..	62866	*5595
Commerce, public services	812	..	..	92811	268572	*7400	..	332125	13643	715363	*6679
Households	13564	6794	..	98413	1001712	*60744	..	378234	13129	1572590	*62969
Other consumers	183	..	..	16734	34753	..	..	..	..	51670	..
Non-energy use	..	1512	..	315385	15575	..	..	..	..	332472	..

United Rep. of Tanzania

Terajoules

	All Coal	All Oil	Natural Gas	Primary biofuels / Waste	Charcoal	Electricity	Total energy	of which: renewables
2017								
Primary production	14525	..	27169	701921	..	8600	752216	710521
Imports	..	105349	..	..	..	382	105731	..
Exports	..	..	..	..	..	..	..	..
International marine bunkers	..	-525	..	..	..	..	-525	..
International aviation bunkers	..	-5865	..	..	..	..	-5865	..
Stock changes	..	..	..	..	..	..	..	..
Total energy supply	14525	98959	27169	701921	..	8982	851556	710521
Statistical Difference	0	-3145	0	-1	0	425	-2721	8600
Transfers	..	..	..	..	..	..	..	..
Transformation	..	-16377	-21155	-143434	47643	17500	-115823	-95791
Electricity plants	..	-16377	-21155	-1297	..	17500	-21328	-1297
Charcoal plants	..	..	..	-142137	47643	..	-94495	-94495
Other transformation	..	0	0	0	..	..	0	0
Energy industries own use	..	..	..	..	..	-256	-256	..
Losses	..	..	..	..	..	-4442	-4442	..
Final consumption	14525	85727	6015	558488	47643	21359	733757	606131
Final energy consumption	14525	83516	6015	558488	47643	21359	731546	606131
Manufacturing, const., mining	14525	1737	6015	52218	..	5490	79985	52218
Transport	..	74147	..	..	..	..	74147	..
Road	..	71369	..	..	..	..	71369	..
Domestic aviation	..	2778	..	..	..	..	2778	..
Domestic navigation	..	..	..	..	..	..	..	..
Other transport	..	..	..	..	..	..	..	..
Other	..	7632	..	506270	47643	15869	577414	553913
Agriculture, forestry, fishing	..	989	..	36745	..	576	38310	36745
Commerce and public services	..	..	..	..	..	4356	4356	..
Households	..	6643	..	450610	47643	10433	515329	498253
Other consumers	..	..	..	18915	..	504	19419	18915
Non-energy use	..	2211	..	..	..	..	2211	..
2018								
Primary production	16202	..	26049	723120	..	8359	773731	731480
Imports	..	107317	..	..	..	425	107742	..
Exports	..	..	..	..	..	..	..	..
International marine bunkers	..	-202	..	..	..	..	-202	..
International aviation bunkers	..	-5777	..	..	..	..	-5777	..
Stock changes	..	..	..	..	..	..	..	..
Total energy supply	16202	101338	26049	723120	..	8784	875494	731480
Statistical Difference	0	-2513	-1	0	0	-1206	-3720	8359
Transfers	..	..	..	..	..	..	..	..
Transformation	..	-15892	-19963	-147735	49088	17669	-116832	-98647
Electricity plants	..	-15892	-19963	-1297	..	17669	-19482	-1297
Charcoal plants	..	..	..	-146438	49088	..	-97350	-97350
Other transformation	..	0	0	0	..	..	0	0
Energy industries own use	..	..	..	..	..	-317	-317	..
Losses	..	..	..	..	..	-4403	-4403	..
Final consumption	16202	87960	6087	575386	49088	22939	757662	624474
Final energy consumption	16202	85588	6087	575386	49088	22939	755290	624474
Manufacturing, const., mining	16202	687	6087	53798	..	6188	82962	53798
Transport	..	77464	..	..	..	..	77464	..
Road	..	74509	..	..	..	..	74509	..
Domestic aviation	..	2955	..	..	..	..	2955	..
Domestic navigation	..	..	..	..	..	..	..	..
Other transport	..	..	..	..	..	..	..	..
Other	..	7438	..	521588	49088	16751	594864	570676
Agriculture, forestry, fishing	..	989	..	37010	..	583	38582	37010
Commerce and public services	..	..	..	..	..	5875	5875	..
Households	..	6449	..	465091	49088	9781	530409	514179
Other consumers	..	..	..	19487	..	511	19998	19487
Non-energy use	..	2372	..	..	..	..	2372	..

United States

Terajoules

2017	Primary coal and peat	Coal and peat products	Primary Oil	Oil Products	Natural Gas	Biofuels and waste	Nuclear	Electricity	Heat	Total energy	of which: renewables
Primary production	15624436	..	24641100	..	26865788	4102804	9059699	2257214	801434	83352475	6974010
Imports	169131	1530	17170872	4431190	2947717	81524	..	236466	..	25038431	81524
Exports	-2313706	-31665	-2866694	-9202651	-3116459	-125703	..	-33736	..	-17690613	-125703
International marine bunkers	..	..	..	-978354	..	-8096	..	..	..	-986450	-8096
International aviation bunkers	..	..	..	-1026604	..	..	..	..	..	-1026604	..
Stock changes	461713	548	627088	181869	263183	4963	..	..	..	1539365	4963
Total energy supply	13941575	-29587	39572366	-6594549	26960229	4055493	9059699	2459945	801434	90226604	6926699
Statistical difference	-153632	0	-123813	-1103014	206941	-5779	0	0	-2	-1179299	2331763
Transfers	..	..	831924	-833671			..	..	..	-1747	..
Transformation	-13556342	256746	-40342657	39352254	-9829881	-847641	-9059699	13092001	-262548	-21197766	-1319782
Electricity plants	-12701486	-1808	..	-212431	-8089241	-631698	-9059699	11996611	-712876	-19412627	-1132394
CHP plants	-298970	-20270	..	-85726	-1604391	-58507	..	1095390	450328	-522146	-29952
Heat plants	..	..	..	..	..	..	..	..	..	..	..
Coke ovens	-430652	399111	..	..	..	..	..	..	..	-31541	..
Briquetting plants	..	..	..	..	..	..	..	..	..	..	..
Liquefaction plants	..	..	211922	..	..	..	..	..	..	211922	..
Gas works	-98436	58012	..	..	..	..	..	..	..	-40424	..
Blast furnaces	-26797	-120287	..	..	..	..	..	..	..	-147084	..
NGL plants & gas blending	..	-58012	-3683478	3724696	52211	..	..	..	..	35416	..
Oil refineries	..	..	-36967651	35925715	..	..	..	..	..	-1041936	..
Other transformation	..	..	96551	..	-188460	*-157436	..	..	..	-249345	*-157436
Energy industries own use	-1309	-48782	..	-1352418	-2423991	-4858	..	-1215922	-151029	-5198307	-4858
Losses	..	..	..	..	..	..	..	-878803	-53893	-932696	..
Final consumption	537557	178378	185445	31674631	14499417	*3208773	..	13457221	333966	64075387	*3270297
Final energy consumption	537557	178378	..	26876712	13492710	*3208773	..	13457221	333966	58085317	*3270297
Manufacturing, const., mining	517869	178378	..	779557	5218604	*1078344	..	2802370	193909	10768931	*1060619
Iron and steel	10448	149183	..	8969	352939	147	..	195865	7118	724669	147
Chemical and petrochemical	79378	..	..	78110	2203214	10451	..	521748	118825	3011726	2731
Non-ferrous metals	..	..	..	7441	127543	37	..	135526	3802	274348	37
Non-metallic minerals	208540	..	..	70615	256856	1019	..	79142	145	616318	919
Transport equipment	81	..	..	9744	156535	110	..	149526	4689	320686	110
Machinery	1624	..	..	27776	310138	405	..	336233	3515	679691	405
Mining and quarrying	..	..	..	120122	73553	3570	..	162526	..	359771	3570
Food and tobacco	124107	..	..	17846	718172	599	..	286099	21423	1168246	484
Paper, pulp and printing	55588	..	..	8335	383108	21770	..	291082	18021	777904	13721
Wood and wood products	..	..	..	18839	48729	515	..	62953	9862	140898	515
Textile and leather	2436	..	..	..	46861	..	..	51520	5668	106485	..
Construction	..	..	..	350187	12837	11482	..	180868	..	555373	11482
Industries n.e.s	35666	29195	..	61574	528019	*1028239	..	349283	841	2032818	*1026498
Transport	..	..	..	24421867	757679	1340938	..	39920	..	26560405	1340938
Road	..	..	..	21189860	47868	1319300	..	14209	..	22571237	1319300
Rail	..	..	..	481043	..	17112	..	25711	..	523866	17112
Domestic aviation	..	..	..	2415891	..	..	..	..	..	2415891	..
Domestic navigation	..	..	..	335074	..	4526	..	..	..	339600	4526
Pipeline transport	..	..	..	..	709811	..	..	..	..	709811	..
Transport, n.e.s	..	..	..	..	..	..	..	..	..	..	..
Other	19688	..	..	1675288	7516526	*789490	..	10614931	140057	20755980	*868739
Agriculture, forestry, fishing	..	..	..	588571	63091	12651	..	169675	..	833989	12651
Commerce, public services	19688	..	..	478133	3112742	34196	..	4862002	122062	8628822	95450
Households	..	..	..	608584	4340694	*574928	..	4945270	17995	10487471	*592923
Other consumers	..	..	..	..	..	*167714	..	637985	..	805699	*167714
Non-energy use	..	..	185445	4797919	1006707	..	..	..	..	5990071	..

United States

Terajoules

2018	Primary coal and peat	Coal and peat products	Primary Oil	Oil Products	Natural Gas	Biofuels and waste	Nuclear	Electricity	Heat	Total energy	of which: renewables
Primary production	15448805	..	28588643	..	30102763	4438575	9086353	2349284	866415	90880839	7464927
Imports	127740	3060	16755664	4504453	2791832	50719	..	209740	..	24443207	50719
Exports	-2787007	-30135	-4735654	-9684641	-3548891	-152360	..	-49694	..	-20988381	-152360
International marine bunkers	..	..	..	-916926	..	-5005	..	..	..	-921930	-5005
International aviation bunkers	..	..	..	-1042436	..	..	..	..	..	-1042436	..
Stock changes	706755	5340	-43597	49271	319023	-8141	..	..	..	1028651	-8141
Total energy supply	13496293	-21735	40565057	-7090278	29664726	4323789	9086353	2509330	866415	93399950	7350141
Statistical difference	-39385	0	-411119	-902148	-18614	2115	0	7	-1	-1369145	2433166
Transfers	..	..	766225	-767343	..	..	..	..	..	-1118	..
Transformation	-13028951	269639	-41503917	40662742	-11187009	-906755	-9086353	13612885	-241058	-21408777	-1380825
Electricity plants	-12128379	-1971	..	-309823	-9383456	-673189	-9086353	12495586	-718380	-19805965	-1174139
CHP plants	-322511	-22117	..	-93760	-1666011	-57220	..	1117300	477322	-566998	-30340
Heat plants	..	..	..	..	..	..	..	..	..	..	..
Coke ovens	-451357	426448	..	..	..	..	..	..	..	-24909	..
Briquetting plants	..	..	..	..	..	..	..	..	..	..	..
Liquefaction plants	..	..	211565	..	..	..	..	..	..	211565	..
Gas works	-100628	60567	..	..	..	..	..	..	..	-40061	..
Blast furnaces	-26075	-132721	..	..	..	..	..	..	..	-158796	..
NGL plants & gas blending	..	-60567	-4176388	4350251	54510	..	..	..	..	167806	..
Oil refineries	..	..	-37637045	36716074	..	..	..	..	..	-920972	..
Other transformation	..	..	97952	..	-192053	*-176346	..	..	..	-270447	*-176346
Energy industries own use	-1312	-52316	..	-1369008	-2561563	-4269	..	-1318968	-159833	-5467269	-4269
Losses	..	..	..	..	..	..	..	-760090	-57168	-817258	..
Final consumption	505416	195588	238484	32338260	15934768	*3410650	..	14043150	408357	67074673	*3531881
Final energy consumption	505416	195588	..	27442596	14921155	*3410650	..	14043150	408357	60926911	*3531881
Manufacturing, const., mining	487552	195588	..	894592	5586869	*1218679	..	2782177	205694	11371150	*1201026
Iron and steel	10446	164213	..	6452	395354	74	..	208062	7551	792151	74
Chemical and petrochemical	74013	..	..	100579	2338682	10667	..	438102	126046	3088089	2272
Non-ferrous metals	..	..	..	10096	143851	37	..	149008	4033	307024	37
Non-metallic minerals	200016	..	..	61233	365130	682	..	119304	154	746519	625
Transport equipment	54	..	..	10853	160043	37	..	142495	4974	318456	37
Machinery	1112	..	..	23893	336087	147	..	345571	3729	710539	147
Mining and quarrying	..	..	..	116510	82092	2834	..	170003	..	371438	2834
Food and tobacco	119526	..	..	14621	729175	480	..	288162	22725	1174688	376
Paper, pulp and printing	48721	..	..	7938	355225	26461	..	281534	19116	738995	18862
Wood and wood products	..	..	..	14765	52527	258	..	67950	10461	145961	258
Textile and leather	2062	..	..	..	47708	..	..	53039	6013	108822	..
Construction	..	..	..	467099	13699	11960	..	188762	..	681520	11960
Industries n.e.s	31601	31375	..	60554	567297	*1165043	..	330185	892	2186947	*1163545
Transport	..	..	..	24831384	898490	1319148	..	44219	..	27093240	1319148
Road	..	..	..	21435196	49599	1297068	..	18886	..	22800748	1297068
Rail	..	..	..	585620	..	17627	..	25333	..	628580	17627
Domestic aviation	..	..	..	2453596	..	..	..	..	..	2453596	..
Domestic navigation	..	..	..	356972	..	4453	..	..	..	361425	4453
Pipeline transport	..	..	..	..	848891	..	..	..	..	848891	..
Transport, n.e.s	..	..	..	..	..	..	..	..	..	..	..
Other	17864	..	..	1716620	8435796	*872824	..	11216754	202663	22462521	*1011708
Agriculture, forestry, fishing	..	..	..	604078	62510	10311	..	162162	..	839062	10311
Commerce, public services	17864	..	..	468874	3458111	30932	..	4940521	129226	9045528	96379
Households	..	..	..	643668	4915175	*639229	..	5262354	73437	11533864	*712666
Other consumers	..	..	..	..	..	*192351	..	851717	..	1044068	*192351
Non-energy use	..	..	238484	4895665	1013613	..	..	..	..	6147762	..

Uruguay

Terajoules

2017	Primary coal and peat	Coal and peat products	Primary Oil	Oil Products	Natural Gas	Biofuels and waste	Nuclear	Electricity	Heat	Total energy	of which: renewables
Primary production	..	..	..	..	..	94735	..	41619	..	136354	136354
Imports	43	0	22275	65041	2206	91	..	10	..	89667	91
Exports	..	..	..	-56	..	-58	..	-5262	..	-5377	-58
International marine bunkers	..	..	..	-4370	..	..	..	..	..	-4370	..
International aviation bunkers	..	..	..	-4300	..	..	..	..	..	-4300	..
Stock changes	..	..	2551	2328	..	174	..	..	..	5053	174
Total energy supply	43	0	24826	58643	2206	94942	..	36368	..	217027	136561
Statistical difference	0	0	0	-1243	-15	-6	..	-202	..	-1466	41613
Transfers	..	..	..	..	..	..	..	..	..	..	..
Transformation	..	..	-24758	21752	-328	-12792	..	10091	..	-6036	-12792
Electricity plants	..	..	..	-2204	-328	-12792	..	10091	..	-5233	-12792
CHP plants	..	..	..	..	..	..	..	..	..	..	..
Heat plants	..	..	..	..	..	..	..	..	..	..	..
Coke ovens	..	..	..	..	..	..	..	..	..	..	..
Briquetting plants	..	..	..	..	..	..	..	..	..	..	..
Liquefaction plants	..	..	..	..	..	..	..	..	..	..	..
Gas works	..	..	..	..	..	..	..	..	..	..	..
Blast furnaces	..	..	..	..	..	..	..	..	..	..	..
NGL plants & gas blending	..	..	..	..	..	..	..	..	..	..	..
Oil refineries	..	..	-24758	23955	..	..	..	..	..	-803	..
Other transformation	..	..	..	..	..	..	..	..	..	..	..
Energy industries own use	..	..	..	-1892	-106	..	..	-1419	..	-3417	..
Losses	..	..	-68	-570	-15	-110	..	-6098	..	-6861	-110
Final consumption	43	0	..	79175	1772	82047	..	39144	..	202180	82047
Final energy consumption	..	0	..	75157	1772	82047	..	39144	..	198120	82047
Manufacturing, const., mining	..	0	..	9453	603	62040	..	12211	..	84308	62040
Iron and steel	..	..	..	..	..	..	..	..	..	..	..
Chemical and petrochemical	..	..	..	..	..	..	..	..	..	..	..
Non-ferrous metals	..	..	..	..	..	..	..	..	..	..	..
Non-metallic minerals	..	..	..	..	..	..	..	..	..	..	..
Transport equipment	..	..	..	..	..	..	..	..	..	..	..
Machinery	..	..	..	..	..	..	..	..	..	..	..
Mining and quarrying	..	..	..	..	..	..	..	..	..	..	..
Food and tobacco	..	..	..	307	..	..	..	..	..	307	..
Paper, pulp and printing	..	..	..	118	..	43516	..	..	..	43635	43516
Wood and wood products	..	..	..	28	..	..	..	..	..	28	..
Textile and leather	..	..	..	0	..	..	..	..	..	0	..
Construction	..	..	..	..	..	..	..	..	..	..	..
Industries n.e.s	..	0	..	8999	603	18524	..	12211	..	40338	18524
Transport	..	..	..	52790	..	2810	..	1	..	55601	2810
Road	..	..	..	51911	..	2806	..	1	..	54719	2806
Rail	..	..	..	52	..	4	..	..	..	56	4
Domestic aviation	..	..	..	146	..	..	..	..	..	146	..
Domestic navigation	..	..	..	680	..	..	..	..	..	680	..
Pipeline transport	..	..	..	..	..	..	..	..	..	..	..
Transport, n.e.s	..	..	..	..	..	..	..	..	..	..	..
Other	..	..	..	12914	1169	17196	..	26932	..	58211	17196
Agriculture, forestry, fishing	..	..	..	6776	..	1995	..	1070	..	9841	1995
Commerce, public services	..	..	..	783	430	11	..	10549	..	11773	11
Households	..	..	..	5355	739	14122	..	15313	..	35529	14122
Other consumers	..	..	..	..	..	1068	..	..	..	1068	1068
Non-energy use	43	..	..	4017	..	..	..	..	..	4060	..

Uruguay

Terajoules

2018	Primary coal and peat	Coal and peat products	Primary Oil	Oil Products	Natural Gas	Biofuels and waste	Nuclear	Electricity	Heat	Total energy	of which: renewables
Primary production	..	..	..	..	..	94551	..	42128	..	136679	136679
Imports	43	..	90480	7830	2080	91	..	49	..	100574	91
Exports	..	..	..	-32	..	-13	..	-4302	..	-4348	-13
International marine bunkers	..	..	..	-6005	..	..	..	..	..	-6005	..
International aviation bunkers	..	..	..	-4608	..	..	..	..	..	-4608	..
Stock changes	..	..	1112	-133	..	-90	..	..	..	890	-90
Total energy supply	43	..	91592	-2949	2080	94539	..	37875	..	223180	136667
Statistical difference	0	..	0	-1231	-24	-50	..	-484	..	-1789	42079
Transfers	..	..	..	..	..	..	..	..	..	..	..
Transformation	..	..	-91571	85297	-102	-12974	..	10520	..	-8831	-12974
Electricity plants	..	..	..	-4160	-102	-12974	..	10520	..	-6716	-12974
CHP plants	..	..	..	..	..	..	..	..	..	..	..
Heat plants	..	..	..	..	..	..	..	..	..	..	..
Coke ovens	..	..	..	..	..	..	..	..	..	..	..
Briquetting plants	..	..	..	..	..	..	..	..	..	..	..
Liquefaction plants	..	..	..	..	..	..	..	..	..	..	..
Gas works	..	..	..	..	..	..	..	..	..	..	..
Blast furnaces	..	..	..	..	..	..	..	..	..	..	..
NGL plants & gas blending	..	..	..	..	..	..	..	..	..	..	..
Oil refineries	..	..	-91571	89457	..	..	..	..	..	-2115	..
Other transformation	..	..	..	..	..	..	..	..	..	..	..
Energy industries own use	..	..	..	-5783	-47	..	..	-1973	..	-7803	..
Losses	..	..	-21	-208	-40	-143	..	-5546	..	-5958	-143
Final consumption	43	..	..	77587	1916	81471	..	41360	..	202377	81471
Final energy consumption	..	..	..	72709	1916	81471	..	41360	..	197456	81471
Manufacturing, const., mining	..	..	..	10037	615	61660	..	13366	..	85678	61660
Iron and steel	..	..	..	..	..	..	..	..	..	..	..
Chemical and petrochemical	..	..	..	..	..	..	..	..	..	..	..
Non-ferrous metals	..	..	..	..	..	..	..	..	..	..	..
Non-metallic minerals	..	..	..	..	..	..	..	..	..	..	..
Transport equipment	..	..	..	..	..	..	..	..	..	..	..
Machinery	..	..	..	..	..	..	..	..	..	..	..
Mining and quarrying	..	..	..	..	..	..	..	..	..	..	..
Food and tobacco	..	..	..	*322	..	..	..	..	..	*322	..
Paper, pulp and printing	..	..	..	*118	..	41860	..	..	..	41978	41860
Wood and wood products	..	..	..	*28	..	..	..	..	..	*28	..
Textile and leather	..	..	..	..	..	..	..	..	..	..	..
Construction	..	..	..	..	..	..	..	..	..	..	..
Industries n.e.s	..	..	..	9569	615	19800	..	13366	..	43350	19800
Transport	..	..	..	48393	..	2650	..	3	..	51046	2650
Road	..	..	..	47594	..	2647	..	3	..	50243	2647
Rail	..	..	..	52	..	4	..	..	..	56	4
Domestic aviation	..	..	..	128	..	..	..	..	..	128	..
Domestic navigation	..	..	..	618	..	..	..	..	..	618	..
Pipeline transport	..	..	..	..	..	..	..	..	..	..	..
Transport, n.e.s	..	..	..	..	..	..	..	..	..	..	..
Other	..	..	..	14279	1301	17161	..	27991	..	60732	17161
Agriculture, forestry, fishing	..	..	..	6680	..	1958	..	1145	..	9783	1958
Commerce, public services	..	..	..	782	460	16	..	11130	..	12389	16
Households	..	..	..	5461	841	14119	..	15716	..	36137	14119
Other consumers	..	..	..	*1356	..	1068	..	..	..	*2423	1068
Non-energy use	43	..	..	4878	..	..	..	..	..	4921	..

Uzbekistan

Terajoules

2017	Primary coal and peat	Coal and peat products	Primary Oil	Oil Products	Natural Gas	Biofuels and waste	Nuclear	Electricity	Heat	Total energy	of which: renewables
Primary production	59667	..	125743	..	1925985	*924	..	28549	..	2140868	29472
Imports	13467	638	12132	*33506	55220	1143	..	25003	..	141110	1143
Exports	0	-2	..	*-1655	-398545	-1847	..	-27305	..	-429354	-1847
International marine bunkers	..	..	..	..	..	..	..	..	..	..	..
International aviation bunkers	..	..	..	*-3197	..	..	..	..	..	*-3197	..
Stock changes	-2544	..	..	-411	-11707	..	..	..	..	-14662	..
Total energy supply	70590	637	137875	*28243	1570953	219	..	26247	..	1834765	28768
Statistical difference	14	637	0	0	-1542	0	..	17964	0	17072	28549
Transfers	..	..	*33506	*-33506	..	..	..	..	..	0	..
Transformation	-49430	15610	-171381	155944	-489925	..	..	188614	121032	-229536	..
Electricity plants	..	..	..	-39	*-22353	..	..	4503	..	*-17888	..
CHP plants	-45679	..	..	-3681	*-413677	..	..	184110	*67415	*-211511	..
Heat plants	..	..	..	..	*-53896	..	..	..	*53617	*-278	..
Coke ovens	..	..	..	..	..	..	..	..	..	..	..
Briquetting plants	-3751	15610	..	..	..	..	..	..	..	11859	..
Liquefaction plants	..	..	..	..	..	..	..	..	..	..	..
Gas works	..	..	..	..	..	..	..	..	..	..	..
Blast furnaces	..	..	..	..	..	..	..	..	..	..	..
NGL plants & gas blending	..	..	..	..	..	..	..	..	..	..	..
Oil refineries	..	..	-171381	159663	..	..	..	..	..	-11718	..
Other transformation	..	..	..	..	..	..	..	..	..	..	..
Energy industries own use	-29	..	..	-5411	-280152	..	..	-2952	0	-288544	..
Losses	..	..	..	-137	-48513	..	..	*-12686	*-7199	-68536	..
Final consumption	21117	15610	..	145132	753905	*219	..	181259	*113834	1231077	*219
Final energy consumption	21117	15610	..	136067	753905	*219	..	181259	*113834	1222011	*219
Manufacturing, const., mining	1919	..	..	2353	*287761	..	..	81444	*19690	*393166	..
Iron and steel	..	..	..	..	*34016	..	..	..	*8944	*42960	..
Chemical and petrochemical	..	..	..	..	*88274	..	..	..	*1519	*89792	..
Non-ferrous metals	..	..	..	..	..	..	..	..	..	..	..
Non-metallic minerals	..	..	..	..	..	..	..	..	..	..	..
Transport equipment	..	..	..	..	..	..	..	..	..	..	..
Machinery	..	..	..	..	..	..	..	..	..	..	..
Mining and quarrying	..	..	..	..	..	..	..	..	..	..	..
Food and tobacco	..	..	..	..	..	..	..	..	..	..	..
Paper, pulp and printing	..	..	..	..	..	..	..	..	..	..	..
Wood and wood products	..	..	..	..	..	..	..	..	..	..	..
Textile and leather	..	..	..	92	..	..	..	..	..	92	..
Construction	..	..	..	1093	..	..	..	1170	..	2262	..
Industries n.e.s	1919	..	..	1168	*165471	..	..	80274	*9227	*258059	..
Transport	119	..	..	101323	107255	..	..	4400	..	213098	..
Road	..	..	..	93941	84755	..	..	..	..	178696	..
Rail	119	..	..	4141	..	..	..	2397	..	6657	..
Domestic aviation	..	..	..	*3197	..	..	..	..	..	*3197	..
Domestic navigation	..	..	..	..	..	..	..	..	..	..	..
Pipeline transport	..	..	..	..	*22500	..	..	2003	..	*24503	..
Transport, n.e.s	..	..	..	44	..	..	..	..	..	44	..
Other	19079	15610	..	32391	358889	*219	..	95416	*94144	615747	*219
Agriculture, forestry, fishing	4	..	..	..	968	..	..	34862	*2400	38234	..
Commerce, public services	..	..	..	..	..	..	..	14546	..	14546	..
Households	10348	..	..	10370	312338	..	..	46007	*47954	427017	..
Other consumers	8728	15610	..	22021	45582	*219	..	..	*43789	135950	*219
Non-energy use	..	..	..	*9066	..	..	..	..	..	*9066	..

Uzbekistan

Terajoules

2018	Primary coal and peat	Coal and peat products	Primary Oil	Oil Products	Natural Gas	Biofuels and waste	Nuclear	Electricity	Heat	Total energy	of which: renewables
Primary production	61882	..	131582	..	2094070	*926	..	21231	..	2309691	22157
Imports	21369	826	19272	*35037	0	2233	..	8039	..	86776	2233
Exports	0	-3	..	-13	-505642	-2627	..	-9456	..	-517742	-2627
International marine bunkers	..	..	..	..	..	..	..	..	..	..	..
International aviation bunkers	..	..	..	*-3954	..	..	..	..	..	*-3954	..
Stock changes	18992	..	..	-5056	55367	..	..	..	..	69302	..
Total energy supply	102243	823	150853	*26014	1643794	532	..	19814	..	1944074	21763
Statistical difference	12	823	0	17	-10541	313	..	14059	728	5410	21544
Transfers	..	..	*31106	*-31106	..	..	..	..	..	0	..
Transformation	-53853	14970	-181959	162620	-588848	..	..	203437	121507	-322127	..
Electricity plants	..	..	..	-39	-26866	..	..	3743	..	-23162	..
CHP plants	-48486	..	..	-5329	-497204	..	..	199694	*67679	-283646	..
Heat plants	..	..	..	-1769	-64778	..	..	..	*53828	-12720	..
Coke ovens	..	..	..	..	..	..	..	..	..	..	..
Briquetting plants	-5367	14970	..	..	..	..	..	..	..	9603	..
Liquefaction plants	..	..	..	..	..	..	..	..	..	..	..
Gas works	..	..	..	..	..	..	..	..	..	..	..
Blast furnaces	..	..	..	..	..	..	..	..	..	..	..
NGL plants & gas blending	..	..	..	..	..	..	..	..	..	..	..
Oil refineries	..	..	-181959	169757	..	..	..	..	..	-12202	..
Other transformation	..	..	..	..	..	..	..	..	..	..	..
Energy industries own use	-342	..	..	-7331	-286851	..	..	-3052	0	-297577	..
Losses	-14266	..	..	-274	-45268	..	..	*-13486	*-6780	-80074	..
Final consumption	33770	14970	..	149906	733368	*219	..	192654	113999	1238886	*219
Final energy consumption	33770	14970	..	137736	733368	*219	..	192654	113999	1226715	*219
Manufacturing, const., mining	3690	..	..	4322	189868	..	..	55519	18545	271944	..
Iron and steel	798	..	..	212	22444	..	..	26644	8424	58522	..
Chemical and petrochemical	..	..	..	119	58244	..	..	12787	1431	72580	..
Non-ferrous metals	..	..	..	679	..	..	..	..	..	679	..
Non-metallic minerals	2801	..	..	701	59847	..	..	3617	231	67198	..
Transport equipment	..	..	..	..	..	..	..	..	..	..	..
Machinery	5	..	..	50	1505	..	..	1162	397	3120	..
Mining and quarrying	..	..	..	218	14046	..	..	2637	2268	19169	..
Food and tobacco	5	..	..	14	4775	..	..	1798	3241	9832	..
Paper, pulp and printing	..	..	..	1	984	..	..	59	149	1192	..
Wood and wood products	..	..	..	..	..	..	..	..	..	..	..
Textile and leather	..	..	..	2	8979	..	..	3774	679	13433	..
Construction	..	..	..	..	..	..	..	1493	..	1493	..
Industries n.e.s	83	..	..	2325	19043	..	..	1548	1726	24725	..
Transport	141	..	..	109585	119615	..	..	5309	..	234649	..
Road	..	..	..	101773	97520	..	..	..	..	199293	..
Rail	141	..	..	3720	..	..	..	2973	..	6833	..
Domestic aviation	..	..	..	*3954	..	..	..	..	..	*3954	..
Domestic navigation	..	..	..	..	..	..	..	..	..	..	..
Pipeline transport	..	..	..	..	22095	..	..	2155	..	24250	..
Transport, n.e.s	..	..	..	138	..	..	..	181	..	319	..
Other	29939	14970	..	23829	423886	*219	..	131827	95453	720122	*219
Agriculture, forestry, fishing	2	..	..	133	1564	..	..	64994	2261	68954	..
Commerce, public services	..	..	..	..	..	..	..	17895	..	17895	..
Households	19739	..	..	19695	329717	..	..	48938	45167	463256	..
Other consumers	*10198	14970	..	4001	92604	*219	..	..	48025	170017	*219
Non-energy use	..	..	..	*12170	..	..	..	..	..	*12170	..

Vanuatu

Terajoules

	All Coal	All Oil	Natural Gas	Primary biofuels / Waste	Charcoal	Electricity	Total energy	of which: renewables
2017								
Primary production	..	..	..	859	..	59	918	918
Imports	..	2524	..	..	..	..	2524	..
Exports	..	..	..	0	..	..	0	0
International marine bunkers	..	*-202	..	..	..	..	*-202	..
International aviation bunkers	..	*-287	..	..	..	..	*-287	..
Stock changes	..	..	..	..	..	..	..	..
Total energy supply	..	2035	..	859	..	59	2954	918
Statistical Difference	..	0	..	0	0	4	4	59
Transfers	..	..	..	..	..	..	..	..
Transformation	..	-617	..	*-62	19	228	-433	*-43
Electricity plants	..	-617	..	*-27	..	228	-417	*-27
Charcoal plants	..	..	..	*-35	19	..	*-16	*-16
Other transformation	..	0	..	0	..	..	0	0
Energy industries own use	..	..	..	..	..	*-24	*-24	..
Losses	..	..	..	..	..	*-14	*-14	..
Final consumption	..	*1418	..	*797	*19	*245	*2478	*815
Final energy consumption	..	*1330	..	*797	*19	*245	*2390	*815
Manufacturing, const., mining	..	..	..	..	..	*83	*83	..
Transport	..	*1268	..	..	..	..	*1268	..
Road	..	*1149	..	..	..	..	*1149	..
Domestic aviation	..	..	..	..	..	..	..	..
Domestic navigation	..	*119	..	..	..	..	*119	..
Other transport	..	..	..	..	..	..	..	..
Other	..	*61	..	*797	*19	*162	*1039	*815
Agriculture, forestry, fishing	..	..	..	..	..	..	..	..
Commerce and public services	..	..	..	..	..	*75	*75	..
Households	..	*61	..	*797	*19	*83	*960	*815
Other consumers	..	..	..	..	..	*4	*4	..
Non-energy use	..	*88	..	..	..	..	*88	..
2018								
Primary production	..	..	..	859	..	62	920	920
Imports	..	3259	..	..	..	..	3259	..
Exports	..	..	..	0	..	..	0	0
International marine bunkers	..	*-259	..	..	..	..	*-259	..
International aviation bunkers	..	*-463	..	..	..	..	*-463	..
Stock changes	..	..	..	..	..	..	..	..
Total energy supply	..	2537	..	859	..	62	3458	920
Statistical Difference	..	0	..	0	0	0	0	62
Transfers	..	..	..	..	..	..	..	..
Transformation	..	-667	..	*-63	19	*225	-486	*-44
Electricity plants	..	-667	..	*-27	..	*225	-469	*-27
Charcoal plants	..	..	..	*-35	19	..	*-16	*-16
Other transformation	..	0	..	0	..	..	0	0
Energy industries own use	..	..	..	..	..	*-1	*-1	..
Losses	..	..	..	..	..	*-32	*-32	..
Final consumption	..	*1871	..	*796	*19	*253	*2939	*815
Final energy consumption	..	*1782	..	*796	*19	*253	*2850	*815
Manufacturing, const., mining	..	..	..	..	..	*87	*87	..
Transport	..	*1721	..	..	..	..	*1721	..
Road	..	*1562	..	..	..	..	*1562	..
Domestic aviation	..	..	..	..	..	..	..	..
Domestic navigation	..	*158	..	..	..	..	*158	..
Other transport	..	..	..	..	..	..	..	..
Other	..	*62	..	*796	*19	*166	*1043	*815
Agriculture, forestry, fishing	..	..	..	..	..	..	..	..
Commerce and public services	..	..	..	..	..	*83	*83	..
Households	..	*62	..	*796	*19	*80	*957	*815
Other consumers	..	..	..	..	..	*4	*4	..
Non-energy use	..	*88	..	..	..	..	*88	..

Venezuela (Bolivar. Rep.)

Terajoules

2017	Primary coal and peat	Coal and peat products	Primary Oil	Oil Products	Natural Gas	Biofuels and waste	Nuclear	Electricity	Heat	Total energy	of which: renewables
Primary production	15282	..	4802719	..	874967	32510	..	218459	..	5943937	250969
Imports	..	..	..	336261	0	..	..	0	..	336261	..
Exports	-11859	..	-3487127	-488269	..	..	..	-3830	..	-3991086	..
International marine bunkers	..	..	..	-6879	..	..	..	..	..	-6879	..
International aviation bunkers	..	..	..	-11598	..	..	..	..	..	-11598	..
Stock changes	..	..	..	0	..	..	..	..	..	0	..
Total energy supply	3423	..	1315591	-170486	874967	32510	..	214628	..	2270635	250969
Statistical difference	0	..	-82570	45549	43879	0	..	-2488	..	4370	218459
Transfers	..	..	*231469	-236866	..	..	..	..	..	-5397	..
Transformation	..	..	-1629630	1348288	-282427	*-221	..	155504	..	-408487	*-221
Electricity plants	..	..	..	-213257	-282427	..	..	155504	..	-340181	..
CHP plants	..	..	..	..	..	..	..	..	..	..	..
Heat plants	..	..	..	..	..	..	..	..	..	..	..
Coke ovens	..	..	..	..	..	..	..	..	..	..	..
Briquetting plants	..	..	..	..	..	..	..	..	..	..	..
Liquefaction plants	..	..	..	..	..	..	..	..	..	..	..
Gas works	..	..	..	..	..	..	..	..	..	..	..
Blast furnaces	..	..	..	..	..	..	..	..	..	..	..
NGL plants & gas blending	..	..	-100025	106719	..	..	..	..	..	6694	..
Oil refineries	..	..	-1529605	1454826	..	..	..	..	..	-74779	..
Other transformation	..	..	..	..	..	*-221	..	..	..	*-221	*-221
Energy industries own use	..	..	..	-202166	-294185	..	..	-8184	..	-504535	..
Losses	..	..	..	..	..	..	..	-116053	..	-116053	..
Final consumption	3423	..	..	693222	254477	*32289	..	248382	..	1231793	*32289
Final energy consumption	3423	..	..	616384	254477	*32289	..	248382	..	1154956	*32289
Manufacturing, const., mining	3423	..	..	69930	211771	*21152	..	79988	..	386265	*21152
Iron and steel	..	..	..	..	37984	..	..	2999	..	40982	..
Chemical and petrochemical	..	..	..	..	124617	..	..	9439	..	134056	..
Non-ferrous metals	..	..	..	..	5984	..	..	23792	..	29777	..
Non-metallic minerals	3423	..	..	1576	11707	..	..	..	..	16706	..
Transport equipment	..	..	..	..	..	..	..	..	..	..	..
Machinery	..	..	..	..	..	..	..	..	..	..	..
Mining and quarrying	..	..	..	..	..	..	..	..	..	..	..
Food and tobacco	..	..	..	..	..	*14123	..	..	..	*14123	*14123
Paper, pulp and printing	..	..	..	..	..	..	..	..	..	..	..
Wood and wood products	..	..	..	..	..	..	..	..	..	..	..
Textile and leather	..	..	..	..	..	..	..	..	..	..	..
Construction	..	..	..	..	..	..	..	..	..	..	..
Industries n.e.s	0	..	..	68355	31479	*7029	..	43758	..	150621	*7029
Transport	..	..	..	502335	780	..	..	0	..	503116	..
Road	..	..	..	494133	..	..	..	..	..	494133	..
Rail	..	..	..	..	..	..	..	0	..	0	..
Domestic aviation	..	..	..	8203	..	..	..	..	..	8203	..
Domestic navigation	..	..	..	..	..	..	..	..	..	..	..
Pipeline transport	..	..	..	..	..	..	..	..	..	..	..
Transport, n.e.s	..	..	..	..	780	..	..	..	..	780	..
Other	..	..	..	44119	41926	*11137	..	168394	..	265575	*11137
Agriculture, forestry, fishing	..	..	..	..	..	..	..	1685	..	1685	..
Commerce, public services	..	..	..	11769	10532	*2085	..	78404	..	102790	*2085
Households	..	..	..	32350	31394	*9052	..	88304	..	161100	*9052
Other consumers	..	..	..	..	..	..	..	..	..	..	..
Non-energy use	..	..	..	76838	..	..	..	..	..	76838	..

Venezuela (Bolivar. Rep.)

Terajoules

2018	Primary coal and peat	Coal and peat products	Primary Oil	Oil Products	Natural Gas	Biofuels and waste	Nuclear	Electricity	Heat	Total energy	of which: renewables
Primary production	6113	..	3601227	..	762981	28024	..	209617	..	4607963	237641
Imports	..	..	..	409119	..	..	..	..	..	409119	..
Exports	-4737	..	-2781056	-495718	..	..	..	-3683	..	-3285194	..
International marine bunkers	..	..	..	-5561	..	..	..	..	..	-5561	..
International aviation bunkers	..	..	..	-10099	..	..	..	..	..	-10099	..
Stock changes	..	..	..	..	..	..	..	..	..	..	..
Total energy supply	1375	..	820172	-102259	762981	28024	..	205934	..	1716228	237641
Statistical difference	0	..	-342926	2214	-3813	*-1	..	821	..	-343705	209616
Transfers	..	..	226180	-230328	..	..	..	..	..	-4148	..
Transformation	..	..	-1389278	1134636	-271427	*-180	..	149436	..	-376813	*-180
Electricity plants	..	..	..	-204927	-271427	..	..	149436	..	-326918	..
CHP plants	..	..	..	..	..	..	..	..	..	..	..
Heat plants	..	..	..	..	..	..	..	..	..	..	..
Coke ovens	..	..	..	..	..	..	..	..	..	..	..
Briquetting plants	..	..	..	..	..	..	..	..	..	..	..
Liquefaction plants	..	..	..	..	..	..	..	..	..	..	..
Gas works	..	..	..	..	..	..	..	..	..	..	..
Blast furnaces	..	..	..	..	..	..	..	..	..	..	..
NGL plants & gas blending	..	..	-106478	113679	..	..	..	..	..	7201	..
Oil refineries	..	..	-1282800	1225884	..	..	..	..	..	-56916	..
Other transformation	..	..	..	..	..	*-180	..	..	..	*-180	*-180
Energy industries own use	..	..	..	-171090	-256532	..	..	-6905	..	-434527	..
Losses	..	..	..	..	..	..	..	-111535	..	-111535	..
Final consumption	1375	..	..	628746	238835	*27845	..	236110	..	1132910	*27845
Final energy consumption	1375	..	..	561618	238835	*27845	..	236110	..	1065783	*27845
Manufacturing, const., mining	1375	..	..	76019	198799	*17840	..	74268	..	368301	*17840
Iron and steel	..	..	..	..	35657	..	..	871	..	36528	..
Chemical and petrochemical	..	..	..	..	116984	..	..	8903	..	125887	..
Non-ferrous metals	..	..	..	..	5617	..	..	22439	..	28056	..
Non-metallic minerals	1375	..	..	1252	10990	..	..	..	..	13618	..
Transport equipment	..	..	..	..	..	..	..	..	..	..	..
Machinery	..	..	..	..	..	..	..	..	..	..	..
Mining and quarrying	..	..	..	..	..	..	..	..	..	..	..
Food and tobacco	..	..	..	..	..	*11060	..	..	..	*11060	*11060
Paper, pulp and printing	..	..	..	..	..	..	..	..	..	..	..
Wood and wood products	..	..	..	..	..	..	..	..	..	..	..
Textile and leather	..	..	..	..	..	..	..	..	..	..	..
Construction	..	..	..	..	..	..	..	..	..	..	..
Industries n.e.s	0	..	..	74766	29552	*6780	..	42055	..	153153	*6780
Transport	..	..	..	443183	680	..	..	..	..	443864	..
Road	..	..	..	434231	..	..	..	..	..	434231	..
Rail	..	..	..	..	..	..	..	..	..	..	..
Domestic aviation	..	..	..	8952	..	..	..	..	..	8952	..
Domestic navigation	..	..	..	..	..	..	..	..	..	..	..
Pipeline transport	..	..	..	..	..	..	..	..	..	..	..
Transport, n.e.s	..	..	..	..	680	..	..	..	..	680	..
Other	..	..	..	42416	39355	*10005	..	161842	..	253618	*10005
Agriculture, forestry, fishing	..	..	..	..	..	..	..	1620	..	1620	..
Commerce, public services	..	..	..	11343	9184	*1870	..	75352	..	97749	*1870
Households	..	..	..	31073	30172	*8135	..	84870	..	154249	*8135
Other consumers	..	..	..	..	..	..	..	..	..	..	..
Non-energy use	..	..	..	67128	..	..	..	..	..	67128	..

Viet Nam

Terajoules

2017	Primary coal and peat	Coal and peat products	Primary Oil	Oil Products	Natural Gas	Biofuels and waste	Nuclear	Electricity	Heat	Total energy	of which: renewables
Primary production	900537	..	618413	..	327051	635160	..	320922	..	2802083	956082
Imports	2292	6091	49956	637046	..	..	..	8467	..	703853	..
Exports	-35661	-5499	-287894	-70463	..	..	..	-6570	..	-406087	..
International marine bunkers	..	..	..	-8646	..	..	..	..	..	-8646	..
International aviation bunkers	..	..	..	-37926	..	..	..	..	..	-37926	..
Stock changes	-9636	..	-77071	3914	..	..	..	..	..	-82793	..
Total energy supply	857532	592	303404	523926	327051	635160	..	322819	..	2970484	956082
Statistical difference	-21629	28	-21911	-3993	0	0	..	18382	..	-29123	320922
Transfers	..	..	..	..	..	..	..	..	..	..	..
Transformation	-561954	..	-304166	307016	-283363	-34875	..	393674	..	-483667	-34875
Electricity plants	*-561954	..	..	-7324	-283363	-1319	..	393674	..	-460285	-1319
CHP plants	..	..	..	..	..	..	..	..	..	..	..
Heat plants	..	..	..	..	..	..	..	..	..	..	..
Coke ovens	..	..	..	..	..	..	..	..	..	..	..
Briquetting plants	..	..	..	..	..	..	..	..	..	..	..
Liquefaction plants	..	..	..	..	..	..	..	..	..	..	..
Gas works	..	..	..	..	..	..	..	..	..	..	..
Blast furnaces	..	..	..	..	..	..	..	..	..	..	..
NGL plants & gas blending	..	..	-44951	46004	..	..	..	..	..	1053	..
Oil refineries	..	..	-259214	268336	..	..	..	..	..	9121	..
Other transformation	..	..	..	..	..	-33556	..	..	..	-33556	-33556
Energy industries own use	..	..	*-21150	..	..	..	..	-19426	..	*-40576	..
Losses	..	..	..	..	..	..	..	-49936	..	-49936	..
Final consumption	317207	564	..	834935	43688	600285	..	628751	..	2425429	600285
Final energy consumption	317207	564	..	813187	43688	600285	..	628751	..	2403681	600285
Manufacturing, const., mining	225064	564	..	163286	43512	420855	..	344848	..	1198128	420855
Iron and steel	..	..	..	9868	..	..	..	..	..	9868	..
Chemical and petrochemical	22672	..	..	8823	38826	..	..	..	..	70321	..
Non-ferrous metals	..	..	..	..	..	..	..	..	..	..	..
Non-metallic minerals	..	..	..	4989	4686	..	..	..	..	9676	..
Transport equipment	..	..	..	2223	..	..	..	..	..	2223	..
Machinery	..	..	..	5770	..	..	..	..	..	5770	..
Mining and quarrying	..	..	..	7773	..	..	..	..	..	7773	..
Food and tobacco	..	..	..	6184	..	..	..	..	..	6184	..
Paper, pulp and printing	..	..	..	1201	..	..	..	..	..	1201	..
Wood and wood products	..	..	..	4389	..	..	..	..	..	4389	..
Textile and leather	..	..	..	6712	..	..	..	..	..	6712	..
Construction	..	..	..	6576	..	..	..	..	..	6576	..
Industries n.e.s	202392	564	..	98778	0	420855	..	344848	..	1067436	420855
Transport	..	..	..	535720	176	..	..	..	..	535896	..
Road	..	..	..	502448	..	..	..	..	..	502448	..
Rail	..	..	..	..	..	..	..	..	..	..	..
Domestic aviation	..	..	..	31091	..	..	..	..	..	31091	..
Domestic navigation	..	..	..	2182	..	..	..	..	..	2182	..
Pipeline transport	..	..	..	..	..	..	..	..	..	..	..
Transport, n.e.s	..	..	..	..	176	..	..	..	..	176	..
Other	*92143	..	..	114181	..	179430	..	283903	..	669657	179430
Agriculture, forestry, fishing	*492	..	..	18435	..	13188	..	15689	..	47804	13188
Commerce, public services	*21148	..	..	50441	..	..	..	34470	..	106059	..
Households	*70502	..	..	45305	..	166242	..	207508	..	489557	166242
Other consumers	..	..	..	..	..	..	..	26237	..	26237	..
Non-energy use	..	..	..	21748	..	..	..	..	..	21748	..

Viet Nam

Terajoules

2018	Primary coal and peat	Coal and peat products	Primary Oil	Oil Products	Natural Gas	Biofuels and waste	Nuclear	Electricity	Heat	Total energy	of which: renewables
Primary production	985834	..	550407	..	339470	373099	..	304362	..	2553171	677461
Imports	66668	6514	29762	596698	..	..	..	6201	..	705843	..
Exports	-4459	-5894	-14898	-94283	..	..	..	-2638	..	-122172	..
International marine bunkers	..	..	..	-11554	..	..	..	..	..	-11554	..
International aviation bunkers	..	..	..	-48245	..	..	..	..	..	-48245	..
Stock changes	..	..	-85945	-16075	..	..	..	..	..	-102020	..
Total energy supply	1048042	620	479326	426541	339470	373099	..	307925	..	2975022	677461
Statistical difference	-58019	0	0	48939	40225	0	..	2216	..	33361	304362
Transfers	..	..	..	..	..	..	..	..	..	..	..
Transformation	-684450	..	*-479326	493732	-259435	-35375	..	462874	..	-501980	-35375
Electricity plants	*-684450	..	..	-2720	-259435	-2177	..	462874	..	-485908	-2177
CHP plants	..	..	..	..	..	..	..	..	..	..	..
Heat plants	..	..	..	..	..	..	..	..	..	..	..
Coke ovens	..	..	..	..	..	..	..	..	..	..	..
Briquetting plants	..	..	..	..	..	..	..	..	..	..	..
Liquefaction plants	..	..	..	..	..	..	..	..	..	..	..
Gas works	..	..	..	..	..	..	..	..	..	..	..
Blast furnaces	..	..	..	..	..	..	..	..	..	..	..
NGL plants & gas blending	..	..	-43272	44630	..	..	..	..	..	1358	..
Oil refineries	..	..	*-436054	451822	..	..	..	..	..	15768	..
Other transformation	..	..	..	..	..	-33198	..	..	..	-33198	-33198
Energy industries own use	..	..	0	..	..	..	..	-21838	..	-21838	..
Losses	..	..	..	..	..	..	..	-53022	..	-53022	..
Final consumption	421611	620	..	871333	39810	337724	..	693724	..	2364823	337724
Final energy consumption	421611	620	..	817023	39810	337724	..	693724	..	2310512	337724
Manufacturing, const., mining	331202	620	..	195856	36965	231979	..	382090	..	1178711	231979
Iron and steel	..	..	..	14880	..	..	..	..	..	14880	..
Chemical and petrochemical	30862	..	..	19617	32821	..	..	..	..	83299	..
Non-ferrous metals	..	..	..	..	..	..	..	..	..	..	..
Non-metallic minerals	..	..	..	4419	4145	..	..	..	..	8563	..
Transport equipment	..	..	..	3012	..	..	..	..	..	3012	..
Machinery	..	..	..	5897	..	..	..	..	..	5897	..
Mining and quarrying	..	..	..	7804	..	..	..	..	..	7804	..
Food and tobacco	..	..	..	2017	..	..	..	..	..	2017	..
Paper, pulp and printing	..	..	..	1337	..	..	..	..	..	1337	..
Wood and wood products	..	..	..	4256	..	..	..	..	..	4256	..
Textile and leather	..	..	..	5352	..	..	..	..	..	5352	..
Construction	..	..	..	7952	..	..	..	..	..	7952	..
Industries n.e.s	300340	620	..	119315	0	231979	..	382090	..	1034344	231979
Transport	..	..	..	510084	2845	..	..	..	..	512929	..
Road	..	..	..	472736	..	..	..	..	..	472736	..
Rail	..	..	..	1978	..	..	..	..	..	1978	..
Domestic aviation	..	..	..	32502	..	..	..	..	..	32502	..
Domestic navigation	..	..	..	2868	..	..	..	..	..	2868	..
Pipeline transport	..	..	..	..	..	..	..	..	..	..	..
Transport, n.e.s	..	..	..	..	2845	..	..	..	..	2845	..
Other	90410	..	..	111084	..	105745	..	311634	..	618872	105745
Agriculture, forestry, fishing	483	..	..	18547	..	13787	..	19584	..	52401	13787
Commerce, public services	26017	..	..	57173	..	..	..	38819	..	122009	..
Households	63909	..	..	35364	..	91958	..	224899	..	416130	91958
Other consumers	..	..	..	..	..	..	..	28332	..	28332	..
Non-energy use	..	..	..	54310	..	..	..	..	..	54310	..

Wallis and Futuna Is.

Terajoules

	All Coal	All Oil	Natural Gas	Primary biofuels / Waste	Charcoal	Electricity	Total energy	of which: renewables
2017								
Primary production	..	..	..	..	..	*2	*2	*2
Imports	..	393	..	..	..	..	393	..
Exports	..	..	..	..	..	..	..	..
International marine bunkers	..	..	..	..	..	..	..	..
International aviation bunkers	..	-46	..	..	..	..	-46	..
Stock changes	..	..	..	..	..	..	..	..
Total energy supply	..	348	..	..	..	*2	350	*2
Statistical Difference	..	0	..	..	..	0	0	*2
Transfers	..	..	..	..	..	..	..	..
Transformation	..	*-183	..	..	..	*69	*-114	..
Electricity plants	..	*-183	..	..	..	*69	*-114	..
Charcoal plants	..	..	..	..	..	..	..	..
Other transformation	..	0	..	..	..	..	0	..
Energy industries own use	..	..	..	..	..	*-9	*-9	..
Losses	..	..	..	..	..	*-1	*-1	..
Final consumption	..	*165	..	..	..	*61	*226	..
Final energy consumption	..	*165	..	..	..	*61	*226	..
Manufacturing, const., mining	..	..	..	..	..	..	..	..
Transport	..	*110	..	..	..	..	*110	..
Road	..	*110	..	..	..	..	*110	..
Domestic aviation	..	..	..	..	..	..	..	..
Domestic navigation	..	..	..	..	..	..	..	..
Other transport	..	..	..	..	..	..	..	..
Other	..	*55	..	..	..	*61	*115	..
Agriculture, forestry, fishing	..	..	..	..	..	..	..	..
Commerce and public services	..	..	..	..	..	..	..	..
Households	..	..	..	..	..	*35	*35	..
Other consumers	..	*55	..	..	..	*25	*80	..
Non-energy use	..	..	..	..	..	..	..	..
2018								
Primary production	..	..	..	..	..	*2	*2	*2
Imports	..	406	..	..	..	..	406	..
Exports	..	..	..	..	..	..	..	..
International marine bunkers	..	..	..	..	..	..	..	..
International aviation bunkers	..	-52	..	..	..	..	-52	..
Stock changes	..	..	..	..	..	..	..	..
Total energy supply	..	354	..	..	..	*2	356	*2
Statistical Difference	..	0	..	..	..	0	0	*2
Transfers	..	..	..	..	..	..	..	..
Transformation	..	*-188	..	..	..	*71	*-117	..
Electricity plants	..	*-188	..	..	..	*71	*-117	..
Charcoal plants	..	..	..	..	..	..	..	..
Other transformation	..	0	..	..	..	..	0	..
Energy industries own use	..	..	..	..	..	*-9	*-9	..
Losses	..	..	..	..	..	*-3	*-3	..
Final consumption	..	*167	..	..	..	*62	*228	..
Final energy consumption	..	*167	..	..	..	*62	*228	..
Manufacturing, const., mining	..	..	..	..	..	..	..	..
Transport	..	*111	..	..	..	..	*111	..
Road	..	*111	..	..	..	..	*111	..
Domestic aviation	..	..	..	..	..	..	..	..
Domestic navigation	..	..	..	..	..	..	..	..
Other transport	..	..	..	..	..	..	..	..
Other	..	*55	..	..	..	*62	*117	..
Agriculture, forestry, fishing	..	..	..	..	..	..	..	..
Commerce and public services	..	..	..	..	..	..	..	..
Households	..	..	..	..	..	*36	*36	..
Other consumers	..	*55	..	..	..	*26	*81	..
Non-energy use	..	..	..	..	..	..	..	..

Yemen

Terajoules

2017	Primary coal and peat	Coal and peat products	Primary Oil	Oil Products	Natural Gas	Biofuels and waste	Nuclear	Electricity	Heat	Total energy	of which: renewables
Primary production	..	..	47476	..	21648	5120	..	659	..	74902	5779
Imports	3277	..	..	76419	..	..	..	..	..	79695	..
Exports	..	..	..	*-10225	..	..	..	..	..	*-10225	..
International marine bunkers	..	..	..	-4415	..	..	..	..	..	-4415	..
International aviation bunkers	..	..	..	-265	..	..	..	..	..	-265	..
Stock changes	..	..	..	..	..	..	..	..	..	..	..
Total energy supply	3277	..	47476	61514	21648	5120	..	659	..	139693	5779
Statistical difference	0	..	0	-3	0	0	..	1314	..	1311	659
Transfers	..	..	..	..	..	..	..	..	..	..	..
Transformation	..	..	-46249	11384	-21648	-2672	..	14854	..	-44331	-2672
Electricity plants	..	..	..	-30845	-21648	..	..	14854	..	-37639	..
CHP plants	..	..	..	..	..	..	..	..	..	..	..
Heat plants	..	..	..	..	..	..	..	..	..	..	..
Coke ovens	..	..	..	..	..	..	..	..	..	..	..
Briquetting plants	..	..	..	..	..	..	..	..	..	..	..
Liquefaction plants	..	..	..	..	..	..	..	..	..	..	..
Gas works	..	..	..	..	..	..	..	..	..	..	..
Blast furnaces	..	..	..	..	..	..	..	..	..	..	..
NGL plants & gas blending	..	..	*-4287	*4588	..	..	..	..	..	*301	..
Oil refineries	..	..	-41962	37640	..	..	..	..	..	-4321	..
Other transformation	..	..	..	..	..	-2672	..	..	..	-2672	-2672
Energy industries own use	..	..	-1227	-689	..	..	..	-2257	..	-4173	..
Losses	..	..	..	..	..	..	..	-3686	..	-3686	..
Final consumption	3277	..	..	72211	..	2449	..	8255	..	86191	2449
Final energy consumption	3277	..	..	71929	..	2449	..	8255	..	85909	2449
Manufacturing, const., mining	3277	..	..	9354	..	..	..	310	..	12940	..
Iron and steel	..	..	..	..	..	..	..	..	..	..	..
Chemical and petrochemical	..	..	..	..	..	..	..	..	..	..	..
Non-ferrous metals	..	..	..	..	..	..	..	..	..	..	..
Non-metallic minerals	3277	..	..	..	..	..	..	..	..	3277	..
Transport equipment	..	..	..	..	..	..	..	..	..	..	..
Machinery	..	..	..	..	..	..	..	..	..	..	..
Mining and quarrying	..	..	..	..	..	..	..	..	..	..	..
Food and tobacco	..	..	..	..	..	..	..	..	..	..	..
Paper, pulp and printing	..	..	..	..	..	..	..	..	..	..	..
Wood and wood products	..	..	..	..	..	..	..	..	..	..	..
Textile and leather	..	..	..	..	..	..	..	..	..	..	..
Construction	..	..	..	..	..	..	..	..	..	..	..
Industries n.e.s	0	..	..	9354	..	..	..	310	..	9664	..
Transport	..	..	..	36375	..	..	..	..	..	36375	..
Road	..	..	..	36375	..	..	..	..	..	36375	..
Rail	..	..	..	..	..	..	..	..	..	..	..
Domestic aviation	..	..	..	..	..	..	..	..	..	..	..
Domestic navigation	..	..	..	..	..	..	..	..	..	..	..
Pipeline transport	..	..	..	..	..	..	..	..	..	..	..
Transport, n.e.s	..	..	..	..	..	..	..	..	..	..	..
Other	..	..	..	26200	..	2449	..	7945	..	36594	2449
Agriculture, forestry, fishing	..	..	..	1548	..	..	..	..	..	1548	..
Commerce, public services	..	..	..	2657	..	..	..	965	..	3622	..
Households	..	..	..	21995	..	..	..	6217	..	28212	..
Other consumers	..	..	..	..	..	2449	..	763	..	3212	2449
Non-energy use	..	..	..	281	..	..	..	..	..	281	..

Yemen

Terajoules

2018	Primary coal and peat	Coal and peat products	Primary Oil	Oil Products	Natural Gas	Biofuels and waste	Nuclear	Electricity	Heat	Total energy	of which: renewables
Primary production	..	..	63642	..	3608	5306	..	1649	..	74205	6955
Imports	3199	..	..	77405	..	..	..	..	..	80605	..
Exports	..	..	..	*-13780	..	..	..	..	..	*-13780	..
International marine bunkers	..	..	..	-4289	..	..	..	..	..	-4289	..
International aviation bunkers	..	..	..	-221	..	..	..	..	..	-221	..
Stock changes	..	..	..	44	..	..	..	..	..	44	..
Total energy supply	3199	..	63642	59160	3608	5306	..	1649	..	136564	6955
Statistical difference	0	..	0	0	0	0	..	648	..	648	1649
Transfers	..	..	..	..	..	..	..	..	..	..	..
Transformation	..	..	-61781	13649	-3608	-2769	..	11344	..	-43165	-2769
Electricity plants	..	..	..	-30127	-3608	..	..	11344	..	-22392	..
CHP plants	..	..	..	..	..	..	..	..	..	..	..
Heat plants	..	..	..	..	..	..	..	..	..	..	..
Coke ovens	..	..	..	..	..	..	..	..	..	..	..
Briquetting plants	..	..	..	..	..	..	..	..	..	..	..
Liquefaction plants	..	..	..	..	..	..	..	..	..	..	..
Gas works	..	..	..	..	..	..	..	..	..	..	..
Blast furnaces	..	..	..	..	..	..	..	..	..	..	..
NGL plants & gas blending	..	..	*-530	568	..	..	..	..	..	37	..
Oil refineries	..	..	-61250	43209	..	..	..	..	..	-18042	..
Other transformation	..	..	..	..	..	-2769	..	..	..	-2769	-2769
Energy industries own use	..	..	-1861	-1096	..	..	..	-1692	..	-4649	..
Losses	..	..	..	..	..	..	..	-2761	..	-2761	..
Final consumption	3199	..	..	71714	..	2537	..	7891	..	85341	2537
Final energy consumption	3199	..	..	71352	..	2537	..	7891	..	84979	2537
Manufacturing, const., mining	3199	..	..	10181	..	..	..	230	..	13611	..
Iron and steel	..	..	..	..	..	..	..	..	..	..	..
Chemical and petrochemical	..	..	..	..	..	..	..	..	..	..	..
Non-ferrous metals	..	..	..	..	..	..	..	..	..	..	..
Non-metallic minerals	3199	..	..	..	..	..	..	..	..	3199	..
Transport equipment	..	..	..	..	..	..	..	..	..	..	..
Machinery	..	..	..	..	..	..	..	..	..	..	..
Mining and quarrying	..	..	..	..	..	..	..	..	..	..	..
Food and tobacco	..	..	..	..	..	..	..	..	..	..	..
Paper, pulp and printing	..	..	..	..	..	..	..	..	..	..	..
Wood and wood products	..	..	..	..	..	..	..	..	..	..	..
Textile and leather	..	..	..	..	..	..	..	..	..	..	..
Construction	..	..	..	..	..	..	..	..	..	..	..
Industries n.e.s	0	..	..	10181	..	..	..	230	..	10412	..
Transport	..	..	..	36725	..	..	..	..	..	36725	..
Road	..	..	..	36725	..	..	..	..	..	36725	..
Rail	..	..	..	..	..	..	..	..	..	..	..
Domestic aviation	..	..	..	..	..	..	..	..	..	..	..
Domestic navigation	..	..	..	..	..	..	..	..	..	..	..
Pipeline transport	..	..	..	..	..	..	..	..	..	..	..
Transport, n.e.s	..	..	..	..	..	..	..	..	..	..	..
Other	..	..	..	24446	..	2537	..	7661	..	34643	2537
Agriculture, forestry, fishing	..	..	..	1935	..	..	..	..	..	1935	..
Commerce, public services	..	..	..	2632	..	..	..	720	..	3352	..
Households	..	..	..	19879	..	..	..	6368	..	26247	..
Other consumers	..	..	..	..	..	2537	..	572	..	3109	2537
Non-energy use	..	..	..	362	..	..	..	..	..	362	..

Zambia

Terajoules

2017	Primary coal and peat	Coal and peat products	Primary Oil	Oil Products	Natural Gas	Biofuels and waste	Nuclear	Electricity	Heat	Total energy	of which: renewables
Primary production	19691	..	..	..	..	382966	..	43913	..	446570	426879
Imports	..	*1466	22002	34977	..	..	..	2711	..	61156	..
Exports	..	*-56	..	-444	..	..	..	-3827	..	-4328	..
International marine bunkers	..	..	..	..	..	..	..	..	..	..	..
International aviation bunkers	..	..	..	-1150	..	..	..	..	..	-1150	..
Stock changes	..	..	..	..	..	..	..	..	..	..	..
Total energy supply	19691	*1410	22002	33383	..	382966	..	42797	..	502249	426879
Statistical difference	0	0	-4244	-4353	..	-9	..	0	..	-8605	43904
Transfers	..	..	..	..	..	..	..	..	..	..	..
Transformation	-15342	..	-26246	18712	..	-88727	..	7153	..	-104449	-88727
Electricity plants	-15342	..	..	-5324	..	*-1367	..	7153	..	-14880	*-1367
CHP plants	..	..	..	..	..	..	..	..	..	..	..
Heat plants	..	..	..	..	..	..	..	..	..	..	..
Coke ovens	..	..	..	..	..	..	..	..	..	..	..
Briquetting plants	..	..	..	..	..	..	..	..	..	..	..
Liquefaction plants	..	..	..	..	..	..	..	..	..	..	..
Gas works	..	..	..	..	..	..	..	..	..	..	..
Blast furnaces	..	..	..	..	..	..	..	..	..	..	..
NGL plants & gas blending	..	..	..	..	..	..	..	..	..	..	..
Oil refineries	..	..	-26246	24036	..	..	..	..	..	-2210	..
Other transformation	..	..	..	..	..	-87360	..	..	..	-87360	-87360
Energy industries own use	..	..	..	-495	..	..	..	-1238	..	-1733	..
Losses	..	..	..	..	..	..	..	-4820	..	-4820	..
Final consumption	4348	*1410	..	55953	..	294249	..	43891	..	399851	294249
Final energy consumption	4348	*1410	..	53139	..	294249	..	43891	..	397037	294249
Manufacturing, const., mining	4348	*1410	..	16258	..	73430	..	25291	..	120737	73430
Iron and steel	..	..	..	..	..	..	..	..	..	..	..
Chemical and petrochemical	..	..	..	..	..	..	..	..	..	..	..
Non-ferrous metals	..	..	..	1135	..	..	..	22327	..	23462	..
Non-metallic minerals	..	..	..	..	..	..	..	..	..	..	..
Transport equipment	..	..	..	..	..	..	..	..	..	..	..
Machinery	..	..	..	..	..	..	..	..	..	..	..
Mining and quarrying	..	..	..	12096	..	89	..	426	..	12610	89
Food and tobacco	..	..	..	..	..	..	..	..	..	..	..
Paper, pulp and printing	..	..	..	..	..	..	..	..	..	..	..
Wood and wood products	..	..	..	..	..	..	..	..	..	..	..
Textile and leather	..	..	..	..	..	2508	..	..	..	2508	2508
Construction	..	..	..	1419	..	..	..	35	..	1454	..
Industries n.e.s	4348	*1410	..	1608	..	70834	..	2503	..	80703	70834
Transport	..	..	..	29050	..	..	..	115	..	29165	..
Road	..	..	..	29050	..	..	..	..	..	29050	..
Rail	..	..	..	0	..	..	..	115	..	115	..
Domestic aviation	..	..	..	..	..	..	..	..	..	..	..
Domestic navigation	..	..	..	..	..	..	..	..	..	..	..
Pipeline transport	..	..	..	..	..	..	..	..	..	..	..
Transport, n.e.s	..	..	..	..	..	..	..	..	..	..	..
Other	..	..	..	7831	..	220819	..	18485	..	247135	220819
Agriculture, forestry, fishing	..	..	..	946	..	..	..	941	..	1887	..
Commerce, public services	..	..	..	1370	..	..	..	2304	..	3674	..
Households	..	..	..	*223	..	220819	..	14926	..	235968	220819
Other consumers	..	..	..	5292	..	..	..	314	..	5606	..
Non-energy use	..	..	..	2814	..	..	..	..	..	2814	..

Zambia

Terajoules

2018	Primary coal and peat	Coal and peat products	Primary Oil	Oil Products	Natural Gas	Biofuels and waste	Nuclear	Electricity	Heat	Total energy	of which: renewables
Primary production	29005	..	..	..	..	394757	..	45601	..	469363	440358
Imports	..	*1466	26159	27421	..	..	..	547	..	55594	..
Exports	..	*-56	..	-488	..	..	..	-4412	..	-4957	..
International marine bunkers	..	..	..	..	..	..	..	..	..	..	..
International aviation bunkers	..	..	..	-1279	..	..	..	..	..	-1279	..
Stock changes	..	..	..	..	..	..	..	..	..	..	..
Total energy supply	29005	*1410	26159	25653	..	394757	..	41736	..	518721	440358
Statistical difference	25	0	-1205	-11501	..	1	..	0	..	-12681	45602
Transfers	..	..	..	..	..	..	..	..	..	..	..
Transformation	-24484	..	-27364	13583	..	-91308	..	12686	..	-116887	-91308
Electricity plants	-24484	..	..	*-11907	..	*-1367	..	12686	..	-25071	*-1367
CHP plants	..	..	..	..	..	..	..	..	..	..	..
Heat plants	..	..	..	..	..	..	..	..	..	..	..
Coke ovens	..	..	..	..	..	..	..	..	..	..	..
Briquetting plants	..	..	..	..	..	..	..	..	..	..	..
Liquefaction plants	..	..	..	..	..	..	..	..	..	..	..
Gas works	..	..	..	..	..	..	..	..	..	..	..
Blast furnaces	..	..	..	..	..	..	..	..	..	..	..
NGL plants & gas blending	..	..	..	..	..	..	..	..	..	..	..
Oil refineries	..	..	-27364	25490	..	..	..	..	..	-1875	..
Other transformation	..	..	..	..	..	-89941	..	..	..	-89941	-89941
Energy industries own use	..	..	..	-594	..	..	..	-1469	..	-2063	..
Losses	..	..	..	..	..	..	..	-6521	..	-6521	..
Final consumption	4496	*1410	..	50143	..	303448	..	46432	..	405930	303448
Final energy consumption	4496	*1410	..	47209	..	303448	..	46432	..	402996	303448
Manufacturing, const., mining	4496	*1410	..	14523	..	76126	..	26217	..	122772	76126
Iron and steel	..	..	..	..	..	..	..	..	..	..	..
Chemical and petrochemical	..	..	..	..	..	..	..	..	..	..	..
Non-ferrous metals	..	..	..	1014	..	..	..	24055	..	25069	..
Non-metallic minerals	..	..	..	..	..	..	..	..	..	..	..
Transport equipment	..	..	..	..	..	..	..	..	..	..	..
Machinery	..	..	..	..	..	..	..	..	..	..	..
Mining and quarrying	..	..	..	10793	..	89	..	531	..	11413	89
Food and tobacco	..	..	..	..	..	..	..	..	..	..	..
Paper, pulp and printing	..	..	..	..	..	..	..	..	..	..	..
Wood and wood products	..	..	..	..	..	..	..	..	..	..	..
Textile and leather	..	..	..	..	..	2596	..	..	..	2596	2596
Construction	..	..	..	1419	..	..	..	39	..	1458	..
Industries n.e.s	4496	*1410	..	1297	..	73442	..	1592	..	82237	73442
Transport	..	..	..	28663	..	..	..	117	..	28780	..
Road	..	..	..	28663	..	..	..	..	..	28663	..
Rail	..	..	..	..	..	..	..	117	..	117	..
Domestic aviation	..	..	..	..	..	..	..	..	..	..	..
Domestic navigation	..	..	..	..	..	..	..	..	..	..	..
Pipeline transport	..	..	..	..	..	..	..	..	..	..	..
Transport, n.e.s	..	..	..	..	..	..	..	..	..	..	..
Other	..	..	..	*4023	..	227322	..	20098	..	251443	227322
Agriculture, forestry, fishing	..	..	..	1032	..	..	..	1069	..	2101	..
Commerce, public services	..	..	..	1574	..	..	..	2570	..	4144	..
Households	..	..	..	*331	..	227322	..	15613	..	243266	227322
Other consumers	..	..	..	*1085	..	..	..	846	..	*1932	..
Non-energy use	..	..	..	2935	..	..	..	..	..	2935	..

Zimbabwe

Terajoules

2017	Primary coal and peat	Coal and peat products	Primary Oil	Oil Products	Natural Gas	Biofuels and waste	Nuclear	Electricity	Heat	Total energy	of which: renewables
Primary production	79071	..	..	..	..	333442	..	14288	..	426802	347731
Imports	810	902	..	49376	..	..	..	9248	..	60337	..
Exports	-2646	-2010	..	..	..	..	..	-1264	..	-5919	..
International marine bunkers	..	..	..	..	..	..	..	..	..	..	..
International aviation bunkers	..	..	..	-2516	..	..	..	..	..	-2516	..
Stock changes	-13498	..	..	..	..	..	..	..	..	-13498	..
Total energy supply	63738	-1107	..	46861	..	333442	..	22273	..	465206	347731
Statistical difference	-5561	124	..	266	..	0	..	36	..	-5136	14288
Transfers	..	..	..	..	..	..	..	..	..	..	..
Transformation	-61929	5335	..	-559	..	-2943	..	12870	..	-47226	-2943
Electricity plants	-55288	..	..	-559	..	-2180	..	12870	..	-45156	-2180
CHP plants	..	..	..	..	..	..	..	..	..	..	..
Heat plants	..	..	..	..	..	..	..	..	..	..	..
Coke ovens	-6641	5335	..	..	..	..	..	..	..	-1306	..
Briquetting plants	..	..	..	..	..	..	..	..	..	..	..
Liquefaction plants	..	..	..	..	..	..	..	..	..	..	..
Gas works	..	..	..	..	..	..	..	..	..	..	..
Blast furnaces	..	..	..	..	..	..	..	..	..	..	..
NGL plants & gas blending	..	..	..	..	..	..	..	..	..	..	..
Oil refineries	..	..	..	..	..	..	..	..	..	..	..
Other transformation	..	..	..	..	..	-764	..	..	..	-764	-764
Energy industries own use	..	-779	..	-559	..	..	..	-515	..	-1853	..
Losses	..	..	..	..	..	..	..	-6224	..	-6224	..
Final consumption	7370	3325	..	45477	..	*330500	..	28368	..	*415040	*330500
Final energy consumption	7370	3325	..	44592	..	*330500	..	28368	..	*414155	*330500
Manufacturing, const., mining	6830	3325	..	2283	..	6117	..	12092	..	30647	6117
Iron and steel	27	2320	..	80	..	..	..	..	..	2428	..
Chemical and petrochemical	54	..	..	87	..	..	..	..	..	141	..
Non-ferrous metals	..	..	..	..	..	..	..	..	..	..	..
Non-metallic minerals	2322	..	..	259	..	..	..	..	..	2581	..
Transport equipment	27	..	..	..	..	..	..	..	..	27	..
Machinery	54	..	..	87	..	..	..	..	..	141	..
Mining and quarrying	54	..	..	775	..	..	..	5821	..	6650	..
Food and tobacco	2808	..	..	300	..	..	..	..	..	3107	..
Paper, pulp and printing	486	..	..	87	..	..	..	..	..	573	..
Wood and wood products	918	..	..	43	..	..	..	..	..	961	..
Textile and leather	81	..	..	43	..	..	..	..	..	124	..
Construction	..	..	..	214	..	..	..	..	..	214	..
Industries n.e.s	0	1005	..	307	..	6117	..	6271	..	13700	6117
Transport	297	..	..	30447	..	1045	..	..	..	31789	1045
Road	..	..	..	28942	..	1045	..	..	..	29987	1045
Rail	297	..	..	1505	..	..	..	..	..	1802	..
Domestic aviation	..	..	..	..	..	..	..	..	..	..	..
Domestic navigation	..	..	..	..	..	..	..	..	..	..	..
Pipeline transport	..	..	..	..	..	..	..	..	..	..	..
Transport, n.e.s	..	..	..	..	..	..	..	..	..	..	..
Other	243	..	..	11863	..	*323337	..	16276	..	*351719	*323337
Agriculture, forestry, fishing	162	..	..	4359	..	16821	..	1548	..	22890	16821
Commerce, public services	81	..	..	..	..	..	..	4817	..	4898	..
Households	..	..	..	3201	..	*306516	..	9698	..	*319416	*306516
Other consumers	..	..	..	4302	..	..	..	212	..	4515	..
Non-energy use	..	..	..	884	..	..	..	..	..	884	..

Zimbabwe

Terajoules

2018	Primary coal and peat	Coal and peat products	Primary Oil	Oil Products	Natural Gas	Biofuels and waste	Nuclear	Electricity	Heat	Total energy	of which: renewables
Primary production	90383	..	..	..	..	339251	..	18176	..	447810	357428
Imports	297	677	..	61548	..	..	..	4237	..	66759	..
Exports	-3105	-2613	..	..	..	..	..	-580	..	-6297	..
International marine bunkers	..	..	..	..	..	..	..	..	..	..	..
International aviation bunkers	..	..	..	-3045	..	..	..	..	..	-3045	..
Stock changes	-7208	..	..	..	..	..	..	..	..	-7208	..
Total energy supply	80367	-1936	..	58503	..	339251	..	21834	..	498020	357428
Statistical difference	-2970	32	..	700	..	0	..	18	..	-2220	18176
Transfers	..	..	..	..	..	..	..	..	..	..	..
Transformation	-75616	6456	..	-688	..	-3413	..	15728	..	-57532	-3413
Electricity plants	-67571	..	..	-688	..	-2687	..	15728	..	-55218	-2687
CHP plants	..	..	..	..	..	..	..	..	..	..	..
Heat plants	..	..	..	..	..	..	..	..	..	..	..
Coke ovens	-8045	6456	..	..	..	..	..	..	..	-1588	..
Briquetting plants	..	..	..	..	..	..	..	..	..	..	..
Liquefaction plants	..	..	..	..	..	..	..	..	..	..	..
Gas works	..	..	..	..	..	..	..	..	..	..	..
Blast furnaces	..	..	..	..	..	..	..	..	..	..	..
NGL plants & gas blending	..	..	..	..	..	..	..	..	..	..	..
Oil refineries	..	..	..	..	..	..	..	..	..	..	..
Other transformation	..	..	..	..	..	-726	..	..	..	-726	-726
Energy industries own use	..	-839	..	-688	..	..	..	-630	..	-2157	..
Losses	..	..	..	..	..	..	..	-6293	..	-6293	..
Final consumption	7721	3650	..	56428	..	*335839	..	30622	..	*434259	*335839
Final energy consumption	7721	3650	..	55503	..	*335839	..	30622	..	*433334	*335839
Manufacturing, const., mining	7208	3650	..	2413	..	6204	..	13331	..	32805	6204
Iron and steel	27	2582	..	80	..	..	..	..	..	2690	..
Chemical and petrochemical	54	..	..	87	..	..	..	..	..	141	..
Non-ferrous metals	..	..	..	..	..	..	..	..	..	..	..
Non-metallic minerals	2457	..	..	302	..	..	..	..	..	2759	..
Transport equipment	27	..	..	..	..	..	..	..	..	27	..
Machinery	54	..	..	87	..	..	..	..	..	141	..
Mining and quarrying	54	..	..	775	..	..	..	5227	..	6056	..
Food and tobacco	2970	..	..	343	..	..	..	..	..	3312	..
Paper, pulp and printing	513	..	..	87	..	..	..	..	..	600	..
Wood and wood products	972	..	..	43	..	..	..	..	..	1015	..
Textile and leather	81	..	..	43	..	..	..	..	..	124	..
Construction	..	..	..	214	..	..	..	..	..	214	..
Industries n.e.s	0	1068	..	351	..	6204	..	8104	..	15726	6204
Transport	351	..	..	39198	..	1662	..	..	..	41210	1662
Road	..	..	..	37349	..	1662	..	..	..	39010	1662
Rail	351	..	..	1849	..	..	..	..	..	2200	..
Domestic aviation	..	..	..	..	..	..	..	..	..	..	..
Domestic navigation	..	..	..	..	..	..	..	..	..	..	..
Pipeline transport	..	..	..	..	..	..	..	..	..	..	..
Transport, n.e.s	..	..	..	..	..	..	..	..	..	..	..
Other	162	..	..	13893	..	*327974	..	17291	..	*359319	*327974
Agriculture, forestry, fishing	108	..	..	5398	..	17060	..	1800	..	24366	17060
Commerce, public services	54	..	..	..	..	..	..	5065	..	5119	..
Households	..	..	..	3332	..	*310914	..	10202	..	*324449	*310914
Other consumers	..	..	..	5162	..	..	..	223	..	5386	..
Non-energy use	..	..	..	925	..	..	..	..	..	925	..